Brexit and Agriculture

Acknowledging the challenges and opportunities raised by Brexit for the agri-food supply chain and agricultural policies across the UK, this book provides the first in-depth analysis of agricultural policy developments across the UK's four nations rooted in strong theoretical and practical underpinnings.

Arguing that the four nations could be more ambitious in departing from the Common Agricultural Policy and extending beyond the 'public money for public goods' approach adopted across the UK, it critiques the core attributes of their policies with focuses including the debate over outcome-based schemes, governance mechanisms, impacts on farm diversity and path dependency on the Common Agricultural Policy and English approaches. It promotes a 'resilient agriculture' paradigm and utilises social-ecological services, net zero, agroecology and agri-food democracy as the main pathways to achieve this. In doing so, it scrutinises the evolving contextual, political and legal landscape within which devolved and UK agricultural policies are developing from a multilevel governance perspective, examining the implications of WTO law for the UK and its devolved administrations to determine environmental, food and animal welfare standards under the GATT, the SPS and TBT Agreements and financial support schemes under the Agreement on Agriculture.

The book assesses the significance of the Northern Ireland Protocol, the Trade and Cooperation Agreement with the EU and other free trade agreements for standards across the UK and access to markets. From a domestic perspective, challenges to devolution and the stability of the Union are highlighted. Elements of unilateral recentralisation are visible via financing mechanisms, the UK Internal Market Act and the Agriculture Act.

The book's interdisciplinary nature makes it of interest to lawyers, political scientists, economists, human geographers and scientists, as well as policy-makers, agricultural communities, civil society organisations and think tanks in the devolved administrations, the UK, the EU and beyond.

Legal Perspectives on Brexit

Series Editor: Richard Lang, University of Brighton, UK

'Legal Perspectives on Brexit' is a peer-reviewed series of books which goes beyond responding to public curiosity aroused by the triggering of Article 50 to recognize the ongoing legal and political disputes Brexit has prompted. Aimed at academics and professionals it provides expert commentary on and predictions about the possible legislative and judicial implications of Brexit for each of the different sectors of regulation which have for so long been dominated by EU Law, creating a valuable one stop resource which exposes, explores and perhaps even resolves legal problems stemming from the separation of UK and EU legal systems.

Brexit and Aviation Law
Jan Walulik

Brexit and Procurement Law
Catherine Maddox

Brexit and the Car Industry
Matthew Humphreys and Doug Munro

Brexit and Competition Law
Andreas Stephan and Barry Rodger

Brexit and Agriculture
Ludivine Petetin and Mary Dobbs

Forthcoming

Brexit and Intellectual Property Law
Janice Denoncourt

https://www.routledge.com/law/series/BREXIT

Brexit and Agriculture

Ludivine Petetin and Mary Dobbs

Routledge
Taylor & Francis Group
LONDON AND NEW YORK

First published 2022
by Routledge
2 Park Square, Milton Park, Abingdon, Oxon OX14 4RN

and by Routledge
605 Third Avenue, New York, NY 10158

Routledge is an imprint of the Taylor & Francis Group, an informa business

British Library Cataloguing-in-Publication Data
A catalogue record for this book is available from the British Library

Library of Congress Cataloging-in-Publication Data
Names: Petetin, Ludivine, author. | Dobbs, Mary, author.
Title: Brexit and agriculture/Ludivine Petetin and Mary Dobbs.
Description: Abingdon, Oxon; New York, NY: Routledge, 2022. |
Series: Legal perspectives on Brexit |
Includes bibliographical references and index.
Identifiers: LCCN 2021039105 (print) | LCCN 2021039106 (ebook) |
ISBN 9781138587823 (hardback) | ISBN 9781032190730 (paperback) |
ISBN 9780429503719 (ebook)
Subjects: LCSH: Agricultural laws and legislation–Great Britain. |
Agricultural industries–Law and legislation–Great Britain. | Foreign
trade regulation–Great Britain. | European Union–Great Britain.
Classification: LCC KD2241 .P48 2022 (print) | LCC KD2241 (ebook) |
DDC 343.4107/6–dc23
LC record available at https://lccn.loc.gov/2021039105
LC ebook record available at https://lccn.loc.gov/2021039106

ISBN: 978-1-138-58782-3 (hbk)
ISBN: 978-1-032-19073-0 (pbk)
ISBN: 978-0-429-50371-9 (ebk)

DOI: 10.4324/9780429503719

Typeset in Galliard
by Deanta Global Publishing Services, Chennai, India

Endorsements

'Food and farming stands out as one of the biggest complications in Brexit and the authors have done a hugely valuable deep dive into farm policy and in identifying the "wicked" problems and complications for food supply as a nation breaks away from its natural trading block. Complexity is at the heart of natural systems but also characterises the food chains and policies that ensure it reaches consumers safely, sustainably and fairly. That means we need deep analyses such as these to understand the problems including those we had even before Brexit – and in how we manage food supply whilst climate, nature and public health challenges loom large. From governance and trade to building resilience and genuinely sustainable agriculture systems for these future challenges, this book covers it all.'

Vicki Hird MSc FRES, Head of Sustainable Farming, Sustain: The Alliance for Better Food and Farming

'Emerging from the EU and the shadow of the CAP, this work offers valuable insights into the development of agricultural policies in each of four parts of the UK addressing their international, environmental and social dimensions. It is a "must-read" for all those interested in the creation of resilient and sustainable bespoke agricultural policies.'

Professor Joseph McMahon, UCD Sutherland School of Law, University College Dublin

'In *Brexit and Agriculture*, the authors shine a timely light on the task facing UK governments, with the implications for devolution, often left out of debates. They illuminate a pathway to more resilient, fair and sustainable policies, aligned to tackle the urgent crises in climate, nature and health.'

Sue Pritchard, Chief Executive, Food Farming and Countryside Commission

'The authors have provided a most welcome and timely analysis of the legal dimension of post-Brexit agricultural policy across the United Kingdom and, in particular, they reveal admirably how account will need to be taken of both WTO rules and the United Kingdom's constitutional settlement.'

Professor Michael Cardwell, School of Law, University of Leeds

'UK and EU agriculture policy must deliver for the dual nature and climate crisis – an intergenerational challenge like no other. *Brexit and Agriculture* succeeds in navigating the salient issues as the UK forges ahead with a domestic agriculture policy with one eye on international markets.'

John Martin, Head of Policy and Advocacy,
RSPB Northern Ireland

Contents

About the Authors

Dr Ludivine Petetin is a Senior Lecturer in Law at the School of Law and Politics of Cardiff University, UK. Her expertise lies in the areas of agri-environmental issues and international trade from multilevel and multidisciplinary perspectives. More specifically, her research focuses on the impact of Brexit and COVID-19 on these areas and, in particular, the challenges for agriculture, food and environmental law, policy and governance across the UK, especially for Wales. She is also one of the co-editors of the forthcoming edited collection entitled 'The Governance of Agriculture in Post-Brexit UK' (Routledge). She regularly engages with governments, legislatures and stakeholders (including civil society organisations) across the UK on these matters.

Ludivine is a member of the Wales Governance Centre of Cardiff University, an associate of the Brexit and Environment Network and a member of the Environmental Governance Stakeholder Group within Welsh Government. She has also held visiting positions at the University of Illinois at Urbana-Champaign (USA), the University of Georgia (USA) and the Sant'Anna School of Advanced Studies (Italy).

Dr Mary Dobbs is a Lecturer in the Department of Law in Maynooth University, Ireland. She is also a Visiting Fellow in the School of Law, Queen's University Belfast, UK; a member of the Brexit and Environment Network and a member of the Future Earth Ireland committee based in the Royal Irish Academy. She previously worked in Queen's University Belfast for eight years as a Lecturer and then Senior Lecturer.

Mary specialises in environmental law and governance and the overlapping areas of agriculture and food production. She has undertaken funded research (including from the British Academy and Jean Monnet programmes) on genetically modified crops, sustainability and the role of EU environmental soft law. Her current research encompasses issues raised by Brexit for agriculture and environmental governance across the UK and also in Ireland, including via several articles and chapters in edited collections. She has engaged extensively with politicians, the civil service, agri-business, environmental NGOs and the public – including via oral evidence to parliamentary committees.

Acknowledgements

This project has been a long time coming and challenging in various ways, in particular, due to the continuously shifting context and the broad uncertainties surrounding the processes of Brexit, the repatriation of powers to the UK and the devolved administrations, trade agreements and the formulation of agricultural policies. It has been the result of many engagement exercises in participating in oral and written evidence across the UK, briefing UK and devolved governments, Members of the Senedd Cymru, the Northern Ireland Assembly, the House of Commons, the House of Lords, their different Committees and their staff.

The quality has been enhanced by the opportunities over the years to engage with, and receive crucial feedback and insights from, farmers, trade union representatives and members (in particular NFU Cymru, FUW, UFU), the Agricultural Law Association, the UK Environmental Law Association, the European Council for Rural Law (CEDR), civil society organisations (especially the Soil Association, the RSPB including RSPB Cymru and NI, the Food Farming and Countryside Commission, NIEL, NI Matters, GWCT and Sustain) and civil servants (in particular those in DAERA and the Welsh Government). We anticipate the book will not simply contribute to academic debate, but also prove a key resource for stakeholders affected by these issues.

Our sincere thanks to: Professor Ben Pontin, Professor Fiona Smith, Professor Alan Matthews, Dr Brian Jack, Dr Caer Smyth; the Brexit and Environment Network, in particular Professor Charlie Burns, Professor Colin Reid, Dr Brendan Moore and Professor Andy Jordan; members of the Centre for European and Transnational Studies (CETS) in Queen's University Belfast, including Professor Dagmar Schiek and Dr Billy Melo Araujo; and participants at two workshops we hosted in Cardiff University (*Agricultural Sustainability*, 2018) and Queen's University Belfast (*Sustainable Food Production*, 2018). All provided feedback, engaged in hearty discussions or simply encouraged us in this endeavour – too many to name here, but greatly appreciated. We also would like to thank Dr Nerys Llewelyn Jones for writing the foreword.

This project would not have been possible without the support of our respective institutions: the School of Law and Politics and the Wales Governance Centre of Cardiff University, the Department of Law at Maynooth University and the School of Law at Queen's University Belfast. This includes the financial support received to run the two abovementioned workshops from the Centre of Law and Society at Cardiff and Faculty Research Initiative Fund, School of Law, and CETS in Queen's. Sincere thanks are also due to the staff at Routledge, especially Siobhán Poole.

We are especially indebted to Dr Viviane Gravey, Professor Michael Cardwell and Professor Joseph McMahon who have helped sharpen our thoughts, acted as sounding boards and provided detailed comments on draft content. We are exceedingly grateful for their support and guidance throughout this project and more generally.

Finally, this book would not have been completed without our friends and families. Merci beaucoup/go raibh míle maith agaibh/diolch yn fawr for your patience and support in this endeavour.

Foreword

It is a pleasure to write a few words of introduction to this interesting and thought-provoking book. Having had the benefit of experiencing the work of both Mary and Ludivine previously, it comes as no surprise that this book provides an in-depth analysis of agricultural policy in the context of Brexit and how this revolutionary event will impact relationships and governance not just at a domestic level within the UK but also on an international footing. The book is a substantial resource for those who seek to understand and appreciate the changes that Brexit brings and how this will impact not just from a legal point of view but also importantly the implications on a practical level in terms of implementation.

The book, despite being written in the context of the early post-Brexit days, is forward-looking and goes well beyond an analysis of the known factors to also deal with the unknown and the 'what ifs' that so many of us are questioning ourselves about. It covers and describes all the major factors in the UK's powers and obligations, its legal obligations and relationships at an international level and those that are at work internally within the UK in the context of devolution. It was refreshing to be able to have the position in each of the devolved nations within the UK set out in one volume and to be able to compare and contrast the approaches in each to the implementation of agricultural policy with ease. It is an important resource for agricultural practitioners, advisers, academics and policy makers and it will certainly be a volume that I have at hand to refer to especially during this transition period in agricultural policy.

The authors demand ambition from policymakers and explain that there is much more work to do to ensure that the agricultural policies that we have within each nation meet the needs and objectives of our agriculture and wider environmental and sustainability goals and ambitions. Brexit will lead to transformational change within our industry and this book recognises the need to build resilience within farming businesses and confirms that achieving this requires co-design and cooperation in policy creation, implementation and enforcement. For those of us that have studied change and recognise the stages identified by the Kubler-Ross Change Curve, we know that after the initial period of denial, there will be gradual acceptance of change before it is embraced. It is only then that the opportunities which that change enables to bring about improvements and maximise potential are recognised and this book takes us on that journey of change in terms of agricultural policy, setting out where we were, what changes must be accepted and importantly the opportunities that this presents to develop new strategies and re-design our future approach.

People are at the heart of all change, from the international relationships that need to be maintained and new ones to be created, citizens who must take responsibility and actively engage in agri-food democracy, to farmers who must participate in policy design, adapt and effect change in their approaches to respond to the market and wider public demands. This emphasis on people is evident throughout the book which means it is realistic and pragmatic.

The focus placed on solutions and a way forward in this book is commendable. It is a frank analysis of the position, which focuses not just on policy and law but also on the practical impact that they have. That is essential when at the end of the day we need these policies to be implemented and for the desired outcomes to be achieved in practice for them to achieve the desired effect. The last chapter highlights that resilience can only be achieved by a proper, complete, holistic and sustainable approach and summarises the challenges to the viability of agriculture within the UK if law and policy do not ensure that the new schemes and programmes are successful in the long term. Not only do the authors conclude but they recommend practical solutions to how we can achieve resilience in agriculture which I hope those working on policy implementation and enforcement within the UK but also internationally in the context of agriculture will consider. Overall, this book offers a concrete, useful, and in-depth look at agricultural policy at an international and UK level in a post-Brexit world.

Dr Nerys Llewelyn Jones FALA
Managing Partner
Agri Advisor

List of Abbreviations

AES	agri-environment scheme
AMR	antimicrobial resistance
AMS	aggregate measurement of support
APPG	All-Party Parliamentary Group
BCP	border control post
BEIS	Department for Business, Energy and Industrial Strategy
BPS	basic payment scheme
BTA	border tax adjustment
CAP	Common Agricultural Policy
CCC	UK Committee on Climate Change
CEPA	UK-Japan Comprehensive Economic Partnership Agreement 2020
CET	EU Common External Tariff
CETA	Comprehensive Economic and Trade Agreement between Canada, of the one Part, and the European Union and its Member States, of the other Part (2017)
CITES	Convention on International Trade in Endangered Species of Wild Fauna and Flora (1973)
CJEU	Court the Justice of the European Union
CPTPP	Comprehensive and Progressive Agreement for Trans-Pacific Partnership (2018)
DIT	Department of International Trade
DSU	Uruguay Round Understanding on Rules and Procedures Governing the Settlement of Disputes (1994)
EFA	ecological focus areas
ELMS	Environmental Land Management Scheme
ESA	environmentally sensitive area
EU	European Union
FTA	free trade agreement
GAEC	good agricultural and environmental condition
GATS	Uruguay Round General Agreement on Trade in Services (1994)
GATT	Uruguay Round General Agreement on Tariffs and Trade (1994)
GM	genetically modified
GMO	genetically modified organism

IDDRI	L'Institut du développement durable et des relations internationals/Institute for Sustainable Development and International Relations
IPAFFS	Import of products, animals, food and feed system
IPBES	Intergovernmental Science-Policy Platform on Biodiversity and Ecosystem Services
ISDS	investor-state dispute settlement
ISO	International Organization for Standardization
IUCN	International Union for Conservation of Nature
JMC	Joint Ministerial Committee
LAG	Local Action Group
LEADER	Liaison Entre Actions de Développement de l'Économie Rurale (links between the rural economy and development actions)
LEAF	Linking Environment and Farming
MFN	most favoured nation
PDO	protected designation of origin
PES	payment for ecosystem services
PGI	protected geographical indication
PPM	process and production method
RBAPS	results-based agri-environment payment scheme
rBST	recombinant bovine somatotropin
RDP	rural development programme
SCM	Uruguay Round Agreement on Subsidies and Countervailing Measures (1994)
SFI	Sustainable Farming Incentive
SMR	statutory management requirement
SPS	sanitary and phytosanitary
SPS Agreement	Uruguay Round Agreement on the Application of Sanitary and Phytosanitary Measures (1994)
SSSI	Site of Special Scientific Interest
TAC	Trade and Agriculture Commission
TBT	Technical barriers to trade
TBT Agreement	Uruguay Round Agreement on Technical Barriers to Trade (1994)
TCA	Trade and Cooperation Agreement between the European Union and the European Atomic Energy Community, of the One Part, and the United Kingdom of Great Britain and Northern Ireland, of the Other Part [2020] OJ L 444/14
TFEU	Consolidated Version of the Treaty on the Functioning of the European Union (TFEU) [2008] OJ C115/47
TRACES	Trade Control and Expert System
TRQ	tariff-rate quota
TTIP	Transatlantic Trade and Investment Partnership
UK	United Kingdom

UKGT United Kingdom Global Tariff
UNCTAD United Nations Conference on Trade and Development
UNEP United Nations Environment Programme
US United States of America
USMCA Agreement between the United States of America, the United Mexican States, and Canada (2020)
VAT value added tax
vCJD variant Creutzfeldt-Jakob disease
WTO World Trade Organization

Table of Cases

	Pages in book
United Kingdom	
R (on the application of Miller and another) v Secretary of State for Exiting the European Union [2017] UKSC 5	
Paragraphs 148–151	p. 63
R (on the application of the Counsel General for Wales) v the Secretary of State for Business, Energy and Industrial Strategy [2021] EWHC 950 (Admin)	p. 70
Paragraph 30	p. 252
Paragraph 32	p. 252
Paragraph 33	p. 252
Paragraph 38	p. 252
The UK Withdrawal from the European Union (Legal Continuity) (Scotland) Bill [2018] UKSC 64	p. 63
European Union	
C-1/96 *The Queen v Minister of Agriculture, Fisheries and Food, ex parte Compassion in World Farming* [1998] ECR I-1251	p. 8
International Court of Justice	
Certain Activities Carried Out by Nicaragua in the Border Area (Costa Rica v. Nicaragua) and Construction of a Road in Costa Rica along the San Juan River (Nicaragua v. Costa Rica), Judgment, ICJ Reports 2015	
Page 665, paragraph 107	p. 27
WTO and GATT	
Australia – Measures Affecting Importation of Salmon (Australia-Salmon), WT/DS18/AB/R, 20 October 1998	p. 229
Paragraph 124	p. 228
Paragraph 199	p. 230
Brazil – Measures Affecting Imports of Retreaded Tyres, WT/DS332/R, 12 June 2007	
Paragraph 7.46	p. 226
Canada – Certain Measures Concerning Periodicals, WT/DS31/AB/R, 30 June 1997	
Page 15	p. 216

Table of Legislation

	Pages in book
National	
United Kingdom and devolved administrations	
Agricultural Holdings Act 1986	pp. 159, 160
Section 19A	p. 161
Agricultural Tenancies Act 1995	pp. 159, 161
Section 8	p. 160
Agriculture Act 1947	p. 8
Agriculture Act 1957	p. 8
Agriculture Act 1986	pp. 10, 180
Agriculture Act 2020	pp. 22, 63, 64, 68, 73–82, 83, 90, 97, 98, 99, 108, 109, 125, 130, 131, 132, 133, 136, 140, 162, 175, 180, 210, 211, 238, 240, 243, 244, 257, 259, 260, 271, 272
Section 1	p. 130
Section 1(1)	pp. 74, 75, 77
Section 1(1)(d)	p. 136
Section 1(1)(e)	p. 136
Section 1(1)(j)	p.136
Section 1(2)	pp. 74, 78
Section 1(2)(a)	p. 78
Section 1(2)(b)	p. 78
Section 1(4)	pp. 80, 125
Section 1(5)	pp. 80, 131
Section 4	p. 73
Section 13	pp. 147, 260
Section 16	p. 82
Section 19	p. 81
Section 21	p. 102
Section 29	pp. 80, 125, 176
Sections 30–32	pp. 80, 176
Section 36	p. 161

Regulations

1 The challenge of Brexit

Agriculture is of considerable significance across the United Kingdom (UK). It makes up approximately 72% of land use (not including forestry), with nearly half a million directly employed in agriculture and contributing approximately £10 billion to the gross domestic product.[1] The UK agri-food sector is the biggest manufacturing sector, worth £113.2 billion to the UK economy and employing just under four million people.[2] Although the UK remains a net importer overall[3] (Northern Ireland being an exception[4]), domestic agriculture contributes significantly to the provision of food – something that is essential for food security and hopefully helping to address the urgent issue of food poverty in the UK.[5]

In light of the extent of its land use, agriculture clearly has a significant potential to positively or negatively impact the environment – its relationship with nature conservation, greenhouse gases and climate change, and water quality being particularly key. Positive land stewardship by farmers, for instance, through

1 DEFRA, DAERA, Welsh Government Knowledge and Analytical Services and the Scottish Government, Rural and Environment Science and Analytical Services, 'Agriculture in the United Kingdom 2019' (2020) https://assets.publishing.service.gov.uk/government/uploads/system/uploads/attachment_data/file/950618/AUK-2019-07jan21.pdf accessed 1 May 2021, 10.

2 N8 AgriFood, 'N8 AgriFood Academics Give Evidence to House of Commons International Trade Committee on COVID-19 and the Impacts on the Food System' (4 May 2020) www.n8agrifood.ac.uk/international-trade-committee-covid19-evidence/ accessed 1 May 2021.

3 On trade generally, see HMRC, 'UK Regional Trade in Goods Statistics – Quarter 2 2020' (17 September 2020) https://assets.publishing.service.gov.uk/government/uploads/system/uploads/attachment_data/file/917852/RTS_Q2_2020.pdf) accessed 1 May 2021; and on trade in agricultural goods see DEFRA et al. (n 1), 129–131, Figure 13.1 and Table 13.1a.

4 This is based on HMRC Regional Trade Statistics. See A. Stennett, 'Northern Ireland Trade in Goods, 2018' (Northern Ireland Assembly Research Matters 8 April 2019) www.assemblyresearchmatters.org/2019/04/08/northern-ireland-trade-in-goods-2018/ accessed 1 May 2021.

5 United Nations General Assembly, 'Visit to the United Kingdom of Great Britain and Northern Ireland, Report of the Special Rapporteur on Extreme Poverty and Human Rights' (April 2019) https://undocs.org/A/HRC/41/39/Add.1 accessed 1 May 2021. See also, House of Lords Food, Poverty, Health and the Environment Committee, 'Hungry for Change: Fixing the Failures in Food' (Report of Session 2019–20, HL Paper 85, July 2020).

DOI: 10.4324/9780429503719-1

crop diversification, crop rotation, seed saving, the use of nitrogen-fixing plants and the use of hedgerows – can help develop and maintain habitats;[6] foster genetic diversity and protection of unusual strains or species;[7] and improve soil nutrients and stability.[8] And, for some, agriculture simply holds a special place in their hearts due to the cultural, bucolic and historical connection with the land.[9]

In developed countries, including the UK, agriculture has benefited from sustained levels of financial support since WWII. However, the sector's increasing competitiveness and market orientation beg the question of why this agricultural exceptionalism continues. On the one hand, agriculture is like other economic sectors, as producers participate in the production of food, fibre and fuel for markets. On the other hand, it possesses particular attributes because of the potential for the delivery of environmental and social goods and wider ecosystem services (often called 'public goods' in the UK)[10] that are not and cannot be commodified in the same manner as marketed goods. For these reasons, it is often asserted that 'securing the provision of public goods provides a valid reason for public intervention in a market economy'.[11] Farming also delivers dietary needs for a healthy life. The 2019 EAT-Lancet Report calls for a holistic approach between agricultural and food policy to deliver a 'healthy reference diet' based on increased consumption of fresh fruit, vegetables, nuts and wholegrain food, with fewer fats and sugar and reduced but high quality and better-sourced meat and dairy, to be further in line with dietary recommendations.[12]

6 See L.E. Hanon and T.D. Sisk, 'Hedgerows in an Agri-Natural Landscape: Potential Habitat Value for Native Bees' (2009) 142(10) *Biological Conservation* 2140; S. Wehling and M. Diekmann, 'Importance of Hedgerows as Habitat Corridors for Forest Plants in Agricultural Landscapes' (2009) 142(11) *Biological Conservation* 2522.

7 See B.B. Lin, 'Resilience in Agriculture through Crop Diversification: Adaptive Management for Environmental Change' (2011) 61(3) *BioScience* 183; S. Ceccarelli et al., 'Plant Genetic Resources and Plant Improvement as Tools to Develop Sustainable Agriculture' (1992) 28(1) *Experimental Agriculture* 89; and R. Vellvé, *Saving the Seed: Genetic Diversity and European Agriculture* (Earthscan 1992).

8 R.T.T. Forman and J. Baudry, 'Hedgerows and Hedgerow Networks in Landscape Ecology' (1984) 8 Environmental Management 495; J.K. Ladha and M.B. Peoples (eds), *Management of Biological Nitrogen Fixation for the Development of More Productive and Sustainable Agricultural Systems* (Springer 1995).

9 See, for example, the popularity amongst UK viewers of the BBC television programme *Countryfile*.

10 See Chapters 3 and 4.

11 T. Cooper, K. Hart and D. Baldock, 'Provision of Public Goods through Agriculture in the European Union' (Institute for European Environmental Policy 2009) 162.

12 W. Willett et al., 'Food in the Anthropocene: The EAT–Lancet Commission on Healthy Diets from Sustainable Food Systems' (2019) 393(10170) *The Lancet* 447. See also IPCC, 'Climate Change and Land: An IPCC Special Report on Climate Change, Desertification, Land Degradation, Sustainable Land Management, Food Security, and Greenhouse Gas Fluxes in Terrestrial Ecosystems' (August 2019) 5.6.3.1; and *Royal Society of Arts*, 'Food Farming and Countryside Commission, Our Future in the Land' (July 2019) 21.

However, agriculture is also a highly complex and vulnerable area. It entails substantial investment in land, equipment, labour, livestock/plant materials, feed/fertiliser and much more, over seasons and even generations.[13] Agriculture is also highly dependent on external factors – in its production and then in its role as an economic activity. Thus, it is vulnerable to environmental changes (whether individual, short-term changes or more broadly due to climate change), pollution, diseases, changes in consumer tastes, fluctuations in the market, price volatility etc.[14] – changes that may occur abruptly or sometimes without sufficient time for agricultural producers or other actors in the supply chain to respond and adapt to or mitigate the impacts. It is also vulnerable to international markets and their volatility. Indeed, the economic activity of farmers often depends on external, international factors. Globalisation can also increase both resilience and vulnerabilities for agriculture. For instance, whilst seeds can be procured from an alternative source if the original source is diseased, new pests, diseases, or invasive species may be introduced into an environment. Longer supply chains may also be more easily disrupted, as exemplified by COVID-19.[15]

Whilst farming can beneficially contribute to the environment and human health, it can also lead to environmental degradation through deforestation, soil erosion, changing the nutrient or chemical balance of the environment, monocultures and depleting biodiversity and ecosystems.[16] Indeed, the relationship between agriculture and environmental protection could be considered 'bittersweet'. When one considers the objectives at play, the vulnerabilities of farming and the uncertainties that arise, for example, regarding the rate and impacts of climate change – it becomes clear that agriculture is a 'wicked problem'[17] that agricultural policy-makers find difficult to address including in the UK. This is only intensified when one considers that agricultural policy is not simply decided at the UK level, but is a devolved matter as well as an international one due to obligations via international trade agreements and World Trade Organization (WTO) law. Agriculture, therefore, permeates all levels of governance.

13 See FAO, 'The State of Food and Agriculture: Migration, Agriculture and Rural Development' (2018) www.fao.org/state-of-food-agriculture/2018/en/ accessed 1 May 2021.

14 FAO, 'Price Volatility in Agricultural Markets: Evidence, Impact on Food Security and Policy Responses' (December 2010) www.fao.org/economic/es-policybriefs/briefs-detail/en/?no_cache=1&uid=48900 accessed 1 May 2021.

15 See L. Petetin, 'The COVID-19 Crisis: An Opportunity to Integrate Food Democracy into Post-Pandemic Food Systems' (2020) 11(S2) *European Journal of Risk Regulation* 326.

16 See P.F. Donald, F.J. Sanderson, I.J. Burfield and F.P.J. van Bommel, 'Further Evidence of Continent-Wide Impacts of Agricultural Intensification on European Farmland Birds, 1990–2000' (2006) 116(3–4) *Agriculture, Ecosystems & Environment* 189; Royal Society for the Protection of Birds, 'State of Nature 2019' (2019). See also V. Gravey, 'Agricultural Policy' in C. Burns, A. Jordan and V. Gravey (eds), *The EU Referendum and the UK Environment: An Expert Review* (The UK in a Changing Europe 2016) 36.

17 H.W.J. Rittel and M.M. Webber, 'Dilemmas in a General Theory of Planning' (1973) 4 Policy Sciences 155; and B.G. Peters, 'What is So Wicked about Wicked Problems? A Conceptual Analysis and a Research Program' (2017) 36(3) *Policy and Society* 385.

1.1 A 21st-century UK agriculture – divided, yet united?

Farming varies considerably across the UK, both within the different nations but also between them. For instance, when comparing agricultural statistics across the UK[18] it can be seen that there are proportionally more large farms in England, followed by Scotland, Wales and lastly by Northern Ireland;[19] English farms are on average more profitable than elsewhere across the UK;[20] tenancies are a major factor across Great Britain (England, Scotland and Wales), whereas Northern Ireland has more owners farming and then a specific type of land interest called 'conacre'.[21] Farming in Northern Ireland, Wales, Scotland and some parts of Northern England includes more cattle and sheep farming,[22] as well as considerable swathes of land in less favoured areas.[23] Northern Ireland is the sole net exporter of food and live animals across the UK, with England being a substantial net importer.[24] The landscape, attitudes, environment, culture, infrastructure and role in the economy also all vary to different degrees. Think even of the attitudes

18 For the whole of the UK, see DEFRA et al. (n 1); for England: DEFRA, 'Farming Statistics: Land Use, Livestock Populations and Agricultural Workforce at 1 June 2019 – England' (2019) https://assets.publishing.service.gov.uk/government/uploads/system/uploads/attachment_data/file/868945/structure-jun19-eng-28feb20.pdf accessed 1 May 2021; for Wales, Welsh Government, 'Farming Facts and Figures, Wales 2019' (2019) https://gov.wales/sites/default/files/statistics-and-research/2019-07/farming-facts-and-figures-2019-492.pdf accessed 1 May 2021; for Scotland, RESAS (Scottish Government), 'Agricultural Facts and Figures: 2019' (2020) www.gov.scot/binaries/content/documents/govscot/publications/statistics/2019/06/agriculture-facts-figures-2019/documents/agriculture-facts-figures-2019/agriculture-facts-figures-2019/govscot%3Adocument/agriculture-facts-figures-2019.pdf accessed 1 May 2021, and more generally, Scottish Government, 'Scottish Agriculture: Economic Reports' (2021) www.gov.scot/collections/economic-report-on-scottish-agriculture/ accessed 1 May 2021; and for Northern Ireland, DAERA, 'Statistical Review of Northern Ireland Agriculture 2019' (2020), www.daera-ni.gov.uk/sites/default/files/publications/daera/Stats%20Review%202019%20final.pdf accessed 1 May 2021. For more on intra-UK trade, see A. Greig, M. Spowage and G. Roy, 'UK Interregional Trade Estimation: Estimates of Trade between Northern Ireland, Scotland, Wales and England' (Economic Statistics Centre of Excellence, Discussion Paper June 2020) www.escoe.ac.uk/publications/uk-interregional-trade-estimation-estimates-of-trade-between-northern-ireland-scotland-wales-and-england/ accessed 1 May 2021.

19 See DEFRA et al. (n 1). From calculations based on the figures on page seven of the report, 41% of English farms, 27% of Welsh farms, 27% of Scottish farms and 24% of Northern Irish farms have at least 50 hectares, with 24% of English farms, 14% of Welsh farms, 18% of Scottish farms and 8% of Northern Irish farms with 100 hectares or more. Comparisons can also be made based on the number of labourers required (Standard Labour Requirements) under which, for instance, Northern Ireland has 77% very small farms, see DAERA (n 18) 40.

20 DEFRA et al. (n1) Table 3.4.

21 DAERA (n18) 41. Conacre is a short-term interest akin to leasing for just under a year, typically in small patches.

22 Ibid 41 and 44; RESAS (n18) 4; and Welsh Government (n 18) 2.

23 DAERA (n18) 36, 39 and 44; RESAS (n18) 4; and Welsh Government (n18) 3.

24 See Stennett (n4) and the underpinning HMRC regional trade statistics mentioned above.

towards the cultivation of genetically modified organisms (GMOs) and similar technologies such as gene editing with CRISPR – Wales is part of the GMO-Free Regions Network and Scotland, Wales and Northern Ireland all availed of the EU opt-out mechanism, whereas the UK Government has typically been an advocate for such technologies.[25] A completely uniform approach to agriculture would simply not be appropriate. This is something which is reflected in the EU approach of shared competence (and governance) and minimum harmonisation regarding agriculture whereby the EU provides a framework and then the Member States are left to develop the details in implementing agricultural policy depending on their individual contexts, especially under Pillar 2 of the Common Agricultural Policy (CAP) (see further below).[26] Hence, why agriculture is also devolved and there is not one but four agricultural policies across Wales, Northern Ireland, Scotland and England.

However, the nature of UK farming and the agri-food industry has changed significantly over the decades. It exists in the context of a globalised world, where now one in six people in the world are fed with agricultural products that have been traded on the international markets.[27] In 2019, 64% of UK food consumption originated from national production, rising to 77% in the case of indigenous foods.[28] Imports are vital to ensuring adequate supplies, with £47.9 billion of food imported during the same period – 70% of these UK agri-food imports were from the EU.[29] The United States of America (US) is the main non-EU country to import its agri-food products to the UK for a value of £1.4 billion.[30] The UK also exports agri-food products, amounting to a value of £23.6 billion in 2019.[31] Again in 2019, 60% of UK agri-food exports were to the EU whilst the US is the main non-EU market for exports valued at £2.4 billion, followed by China with £0.7 billion.[32]

25 See M. Dobbs, 'Attaining Subsidiarity-Based Multilevel Governance of Genetically Modified Cultivation?' (2016) 28(2) *Journal of Environmental Law* 245; and L. Petetin, 'Managing Novel Food Technologies and Member States' Interests: Shifting More Powers towards the Member States?' in M. Varju (eds), *Between Compliance and Particularism: Member State Interests and European Union Law* (Springer 2019) 233. The 2021 DEFRA consultation on gene editing indicates such a preference in England. See DEFRA, 'Consultation: The Regulation of Genetic Technologies' (8 January 2021) https://consult.defra.gov.uk/agri-food-chain-directorate/the-regulation-of-genetic-technologies/ accessed 1 May 2021.

26 This indicates an application of the EU principle of subsidiarity. See Consolidated version of the Treaty on European Union [2008] OJ C115/13, Article 5.

27 WTO, 'Trade Dialogues on Food' Series, Webinar on 'International Trade and Food Security in the Era of COVID-19' (30 April 2020) www.youtube.com/watch?v=g0J9IfP0TGY accessed 1 May 2021. Comment by Doaa Abdel-Motaal, Senior Counsellor, WTO Agriculture and Commodities Division at 1 minute 45 seconds.

28 DEFRA et al. (n1) Table 14.1.

29 Ibid, 135.

30 Ibid, Figure 13.3.

31 Ibid, 129–130. It should be noted that whiskey is the highest contributor towards such exports (£5bn), which highlights a lower level of *food* exports.

32 Ibid, Figure 13.2.

The links with the EU are further highlighted by the role of EU workers in the UK agricultural industry, with heavy reliance on EU workers for two professions in particular (beyond logistics matters and the availability of hauliers): veterinarians and seasonal labourers (or agricultural workers). 95% of veterinarians working in abattoirs come from overseas, mostly the EU.[33] Further, of the 80,000 seasonal workforces in horticulture, 98% are migrants from the EU27.[34] The end of the free movement of persons in the UK directly impacts on the access to this skilled labour force. Consequently, trade relationships between the UK, the EU and other states are key factors in globalised supply chains and any changes to trading relationships and any future trade deals will have ramifications on this key UK economic sector, especially with the erection of non-tariff barriers.[35] Yet, one of the biggest changes of all is that the UK has now left the CAP.

1.2 EU Membership and coming out of the shadow of the CAP

The UK has both benefited from and been restricted by its membership of the EU – including in agricultural policy.[36] EU trade deals enable Member States to benefit from the negotiating powers of the world's largest trade bloc with, for instance, preferential access to markets. However, this was undertaken by limiting the UK's sovereignty in concluding external trade deals and thereby curtailing some policy choices that the UK may wish to make. These pros and cons are intensified when one looks internally within the EU. The UK was part of the EU's internal market and customs union, meaning that products commercialised in the UK faced no tariffs or non-tariff barriers when trading with the EU – for both imports and exports. The free movement of goods and persons, directly and indirectly, benefited UK agriculture. For instance, during membership there was

33 British Veterinary Association, 'New Immigration Rules Risk No Vets in Abattoirs, Warns BVA' (19 December 2018) www.bva.co.uk/news-and-blog/news-article/new-immigration-rules-risk-no-vets-in-abattoirs-warns-bva/ accessed 1 May 2021. See also L. Petetin, 'Cloud Nine or Down to Earth? The Implications of a No Deal Brexit on Agriculture' (The UK in a Changing Europe 15 August 2019) https://ukandeu.ac.uk/cloud-nine-or-down-to-earth-the-implications-of-a-no-deal-brexit-on-agriculture/ accessed 1 May 2021.

34 House of Lords, European Union Committee, 'Brexit: Agriculture' (20th Report of Session 2016–17, HL 169, May 2017) 68.

35 This is further explored in Chapter 5.

36 Ongoing and future CAP reforms may also provide useful insight into alternative approaches to agricultural policy and are considered further in Chapters 3 and 4. The term 'shadow of the CAP' was first coined in L. Petetin, V. Gravey and B. Moore, 'Setting the Bar for a Green Brexit in Food and Farming' (Soil Association 2019) www.soilassociation.org/green-brexit/ accessed 1 May 2021. See also V. Gravey, 'Finally Free to Green Agriculture Policy? UK Post-Brexit Policy Developments in the Shadow of the CAP and Devolution' 18(2) (2019) *EuroChoices* 11. For more on the relationship between the UK and the CAP, see V. Gravey, 'Brexit and the Common Agricultural Policy: There and Back Again' in I. Antonopoulos, M. Bell, A. Cavoski and L. Petetin (eds), *The Governance of Agriculture in Post-Brexit UK* (Routledge, forthcoming 2022).

no requirement for sanitary and phytosanitary (SPS) checks to be undertaken between EU Member States. This was of considerable value to UK agricultural actors, considering that the EU is the largest external market for UK agri-food products and the level of dependence on EU workers, especially farm labourers picking crops and veterinarian officers. It also enabled ease of access to input materials produced in or transported through other EU Member States. The Island of Ireland provides a prime example here, with substantial quantities of milk crossing the land border between Ireland and Northern Ireland on a regular basis and Ireland being the main market for live animal exports from Northern Ireland.[37] At the consumer end, it also enables access to a wide range of agri-food products at competitive prices – which are also typically high-quality due to EU membership. Additionally, EU membership meant that UK products were protected against exports from outside the EU due to the high EU Common External Tariffs on agri-food products.

In a post-Brexit UK, farmers in Great Britain, in particular, compete on a harsher and more competitive world scene and need to be more resilient and build management strategies for these risks.[38] Further, under the CAP, the principle of Community (EU) preference plays a central role to protect EU farmers from foreign competition.[39] The principle results in the setting of high import tariffs to provide the EU industry with a competitive advantage and deter non-EU imports. It restricts free access to the EU single market and protects EU farmers and their produce from world competition, prices and volatility. UK agri-food products and farmers are now outside this protective bubble, and subject to fierce international competition, especially from countries where it is cheaper to produce due to economies of scale and lower standards.

The EU also creates binding legal frameworks across a range of related regimes, including regarding the environment, food and human health. These are founded on objectives such as a high level of environmental and human health protection, ensuring high standards across the Member States – comprising the UK until the end of the transition period in 2020. These shared standards and governance mechanisms (including regulatory convergence) also help build trust across the Member States and the creation of level playing fields, which are necessary if there

37 See M. Allen, 'Northern Ireland's Agri-Food Sector – Background and Possible "Brexit" Considerations' (Northern Ireland Assembly, Research and Information Service 345-16 Paper 66/16, 22 September 2016) www.niassembly.gov.uk/assembly-business/committees/2016-2017/agriculture-environment-and-rural-affairs/research-papers-2016/northern-irelands-agri-food-sector--background-and-possible-brexit-considerations/ accessed 1 May 2021; and DAERA (n 18) 57.

38 The Northern Ireland Protocol provides a halfway house that enables protection for the Northern Irish industry. See Chapter 2, Section 2.3.

39 Consolidated Version of the Treaty on the Functioning of the European Union (TFEU) [2008] OJ C115/47, Article 39. EU agricultural MFN tariffs tend to be much higher mostly to reduce the amount of agricultural products and protect EU farming. See A. Matthews, 'The Protective Effect of EU Agricultural Tariffs' (CAP Reform 24 February 2020) http://capreform.eu/the-protective-effect-of-eu-agricultural-tariffs/ accessed 1 May 2021.

is to be an effective internal market and free movement of goods and persons. However, they limit the potential for unilateral approaches to varying degrees.[40]

UK agricultural policy, therefore, operated within a complex system with a myriad of rules, policies and structures. This was intensified when one turns to examine agricultural policy itself and the CAP. In doing so, it is important to recollect that this is an area of shared competence between the EU and the Member States (and their regions). Thus, the CAP is no longer a 'one-size-fits-all' policy (and has not been for many decades) but enables differentiation between and within Member States (including within the UK) in the design and implementation of agricultural policies. One example of such practices is social agriculture[41] and its governmental support across the various EU Member States and in particular Italy.[42] As shall be seen, the umbrella created by the CAP has created a shadow of the past and the present over UK agricultural policies and its support systems – and post-Brexit, it will still have long-lasting direct and indirect consequences on agricultural policies across the UK due to close trade relationships and geographical proximity – leading to a path dependency.[43]

1.2.1 Shadow of the past: an overhaul of the UK support system

Before joining the EU, the UK had its own agricultural policy and financial system to support farmers, which had to be amended to access the EU. After WWII, the 1947 and 1957 Agriculture Acts laid the foundation for post-war UK agricultural policy. Between 1947 and 1973, the UK supported its farming sector with

40 Member States may still take unilateral actions that hinder free movement of goods where specific criteria are met. This is easier where there is no or minimal harmonisation (with a directive) rather than where there is maximum harmonisation (with a regulation). See C-1/96 *The Queen v Minister of Agriculture, Fisheries and Food, ex parte Compassion in World Farming* [1998] ECR I-1251. In this case, the UK was at the forefront of animal welfare standards against the use of veal crates in live transport. This led to a 1997 EU directive, which banned such practices from 2007. See Council Directive 97/2/EC of 20 January 1997 Amending Directive 91/629/EEC Laying Down Minimum Standards for the Protection of Calves [1997] OJ L025/24, Article 3(3). More generally on harmonisation, see V. Gravey, 'Balancing Positive and Negative Integration in the EU's Internal Market' (Brexit and Environment Network 16 October 2020) www.brexitenvironment.co.uk/2020/10/16/internal-market-bill-why-negative-integration-is-causing-such-negative-feelings/ accessed 1 May 2021.

41 Social agriculture can be defined as an innovative, inclusive, participatory and generative model of agricultural practices that delivers recreational, educational and assistance services by including disadvantaged persons. See, L. Lopez Marco, 'Social Agriculture as Multiculturalism and Symbol of a Generative Welfare' (29 June 2018) www.simra-h2020.eu/index.php/2018/06/29/social-agriculture-as-multiculturalism-and-symbol-of-a-generative-welfare/ accessed 1 May 2021; and A. Sinibaldi, 'Sustainability, Biodiversity and Territory: The Social Agriculture Role' (Interreg Europe 2018) www.interregeurope.eu/fileadmin/user_upload/tx_tevprojects/library/Forum%20social%20Agriculture.pdf accessed 1 May 2021.

42 See Petetin, Gravey and Moore (n36) 23.

43 Ibid (whole report). These points are further explored in Chapters 2, 3 and 4.

deficiency payments whereby farmers received direct subsidies equal to the difference between the price obtained by farmers on the market on specific agricultural products and the price guaranteed to them by the UK Government.[44] When farm products were sold below the guaranteed price, the subsidies would make up the deficiency. These annual payments came from the Government Exchequer directly to farmers. This policy was considered both economically and socially justifiable since it guaranteed farmers' income and kept market prices (and therefore consumer prices) low whilst ensuring a steady supply of produce and food security.

Agriculture was a key obstacle to the UK joining the EU in the early 1970s because of this different system of support. At that point in time, EU agricultural integration was already a tenet of the common market. Ever since joining the EU, agriculture has been a stumbling point in UK politics and affairs. In 1984, Margaret Thatcher negotiated a permanent rebate for Britain on its budget contributions as the UK historically received fewer agricultural subsidies than other states, notably France.

When the UK joined the EU in 1973, it had to radically reform its agricultural policy and support system to fit under the overarching framework of the CAP.[45] At that time, the CAP primarily focused on price support to remove the threat of starvation in the EU[46] – the more farmers would produce, the more they would receive subsidies.[47] External inputs such as herbicides, pesticides, inorganic fertilisers and other nutrients were utilised to increase food production – although UK farming already followed a similar pattern. Under this productivist paradigm, intensive farming decisively shaped the farming landscape (in particular the practices of agricultural land consolidation – also called reparcelling) and led to environmental degradation.[48] It is worth noting that whilst there were differences in precise objectives and tools, both UK and EU approaches focused on increasing production and protecting farmers' livelihoods, including through relying on direct and indirect financial incentives that would guarantee farmers income.

1.2.2 Shadow of the present: a sustainability turn

Today, the CAP has greatly evolved. On paper, the objectives have remained constant and are laid out in Article 39 of the Treaty on the Functioning of the

44 See J.K. Bowers, 'British Agricultural Policy Since the Second World War' (1985) 33(1) *The Agricultural History Review* 66.
45 Prior to UK entry, the debate revolved around the effects of membership on food prices (they would likely increase for the consumer) and on the benefits to farmers (where it was anticipated that EU supported prices would be higher than the guaranteed prices).
46 Ensuring 'the availability of [agricultural] supplies' has been a central objective of the CAP since its creation. See TFEU, Article 39(1)(d).
47 For more on this aspect, see F.G. Snyder, *Law of the Common Agricultural Policy* (Sweet and Maxwell 1985).
48 See Donald et al. (n16).

European Union (TFEU), aiming to increase agricultural productivity; ensure a fair standard of living for farmers; stabilise markets; assure the availability of supplies; and ensure the reasonable prices of these supplies. However, it became clear in the 1970s that agriculture was having negative environmental impacts due to incentivising production.[49] Early signs of such awareness resulted in the UK becoming one of the first EU Member States to actively support environmentally sensitive areas (ESAs), which were the first national financial support schemes in agriculture to support ecologically vulnerable areas.[50] This was authorised by the Agriculture Act 1986 to protect habitats and ecosystems from intensive agricultural practices by reducing fertilisers, pesticides and herbicides.[51]

In 1986, the Single European Act introduced an Environmental Title within the Treaty and now CAP objectives are complemented by EU environmental objectives where sustainability and a high level of environmental protection are to be integrated across all EU policies.[52] But it is the 1992 CAP reform that triggered the 'greening of the CAP' and embraced a turn towards sustainability that has continued to date.[53] This turn has had long-term consequences on the UK and devolved agriculture in terms of design, objectives and implementation.

The successive CAP reforms introduced direct payments granted to farmers to support their incomes under Pillar 1 and to compensate them for their production of public goods and ecosystem services, such as sound management of soil and water, carbon sequestration and flood control under Pillar 2 (see further information on both pillars in the next paragraph).[54] The Article 39 objectives

49 See Declaration of the Council of the European Communities and of the Representatives of the Governments of the Member States Meeting in the Council of 22 November 1973 on the Programme of Action of the European Communities on the Environment (1973) OJ C112/1 ('First Environmental Action Plan' 1973–1977).

50 Council Regulation (EEC) 797/85 on Improving the Efficiency of Agricultural Structures [1985] OJ L93/1. It is only in 1987 that Regulation 1760/87 amended Regulation 797/85 and authorised the co-financing of the scheme for ESAs. See Council Regulation (EEC) 1760/87 amending Regulations (EEC) 797/85, (EEC) 270/79, (EEC) 1360/78 and (EEC) 355/77 as regards Agricultural Structures, the Adjustment of Agriculture to the New Market Situation and the Preservation of the Countryside [1987] OJ L167/1. ESAs were replaced under the 2003 CAP reform by various agri-environmental scheme (AES) programmes.

51 In the UK, the first schemes started as early as 1987.

52 Single European Act [1987] OJ L169, Title VII Environment. For more, D. Baldock, 'Twisted Together: European Agriculture, Environment and the Common Agricultural Policy' in J.A. McMahon and M.N. Cardwell (eds), ***Research Handbook on EU Agriculture Law*** (Research Handbook in European Law, Edward Elgar Publishing 2015) 125.

53 See M. Cardwell, *The European Model of Agriculture* (OUP 2004); B. Jack, *Agriculture and EU Environmental Law* (Ashgate Publishing 2009); and J.A. McMahon, *EU Agricultural Law and Policy* (Edward Elgar 2019).

54 The full list of the greening of the CAP reforms: the 1992 MacSharry reform; the Agenda 2000 Reform; the 2003 Mid-Term Review; the 2008 Health Check; and the 2013 Reform Package. See European Parliament, 'The Common Agricultural Policy – Instruments and Reforms' (Fact Sheets on the European Union November 2020) www.europarl.europa.eu/factsheets/en/sheet/107/the-common-agricultural-policy-instruments-and-reforms

remain, but are no longer the sole focus for the CAP. Today, European agriculture aims to deliver a sustainable agriculture that ensures the production of food, feed, fibre and fuel,[55] while trying to achieve a higher level of environmental protection and other social objectives with rural development programmes (RDPs). The current UK and devolved agricultural practices and policies have been directly informed by both the range of CAP (and environmental) objectives and the shifts in CAP reforms.

This sustainable turn of the CAP is currently visible through three main pathways present under both pillars of the CAP. First, the basic payment scheme (BPS) forms the greater part of Pillar 1 (representing 70% of direct payments) and is subject to respecting cross-compliance. Cross-compliance aims to ensure that the pressures on the environment and ecological networks are reduced and includes two components. The first are specific European legal requirements, known as statutory management requirements (SMRs), which relate to the environment, animal and plant health, public health and animal welfare and are based on existing EU directives and regulations. The second are standards set at national and sub-national levels that require farmers to keep their land in good agricultural and environmental conditions (GAEC) and are often based on or adapted from existing standards of 'good agricultural practices' (also called 'good farming practices').[56] GAEC standards include addressing the issues of soil erosion, soil organic matter and soil structure, as well as ensuring a minimum level of maintenance to avoid the deterioration of habitats and protection. GAECs are the only pathway for the CAP to deal with soil at a national level since Member States could not find agreement on the Proposal for a Soil Directive.[57]

---

accessed 1 May 2021. For more on direct payments, see M.N. Cardwell, 'The Direct Payments Regime: Delivering "A Fair Standard of Living for the Agricultural Community"?' in J.A. McMahon and M.N. Cardwell (eds), *Research Handbook on EU Agriculture Law* (Research Handbook in European Law, Edward Elgar Publishing 2015) 41.

55 The 'food versus fuel' debate highlights the dilemma in addressing the risks of using farmland and crops for the production of biofuels to the detriment of the food supply. Two reports link higher food prices to increased biofuel demands. See FAO, 'State of Food and Agriculture 2012' (2012) www.fao.org/docrep/017/i3028e/i3028e.pdf accessed 1 May 2021, 100; and OECD and FAO, 'The OECD-FAO Agricultural Outlook 2013–2022' (2013) www.oecd.org/site/oecd-faoagriculturaloutlook accessed 1 May 2021, 9.

56 OECD, 'Environmental Cross Compliance in Agriculture' (2010) www.oecd.org/agriculture/topics/agriculture-and-the-environment/documents/environmental-cross-compliance-in-agriculture.pdf accessed 1 May 2021, 18. Good agricultural practices are 'practices that address environmental, economic and social sustainability for on-farm processes, and result in safe and quality food and non-food agricultural products'. See FAO, 'Report of the Expert Consultation on a Good Agricultural Practices (GAP) Approach' (2003) www.fao.org/tempref/GI/Reserved/FTP_FaoRlc/old/foro/bpa/pdf/good.pdf accessed 1 May 2021.

57 Proposal for a Directive of the European Parliament and of the Council Establishing a Framework for the Protection of Soil and Amending Directive 2004/35/EC, COM/2006/0232 final. The UK was one of the key Member States that blocked the proposal. See Euractiv, 'EU Soil Protection Law Blocked by UK, France and Germany' (21 December 2007) www

Second, 30% of the Pillar 1 budget is allocated to rewarding farmers for specific 'greening' practices that are additional to BPS.[58] Three practices are required for farmers to receive such payments: crop diversification to discourage monocultures, permanent pasture to deter ploughing of permanent pasture and the development of ecological focus areas (EFAs) to encourage small spaces for nature on every farm.[59] With these payments, farmers provide basic levels of public goods. Overall, Pillar 1 payments make a substantial contribution to farm income across the EU[60] and thereby incentivise environmentally-friendly behaviour.[61]

Third, and under Pillar 2, RDPs aim to improve the social and environmental effects of agriculture by enhancing social cohesion, economic expansion and sustainability in rural areas, particularly through the development of agri-environment schemes (AESs).[62] It is important to bear in mind that Pillar 2 is broader than AESs and in the UK includes technical assistance, investments in physical assets, services and village renewal, local economic partnerships and the bottom-up, community-led LEADER approach,[63] which focuses on job creation and economic growth in rural areas as well as increasing social components.[64]

.euractiv.com/section/climate-environment/news/eu-soil-protection-law-blocked-by-uk-france-and-germany/ accessed 1 May 2021. There is, nonetheless, an EU Soil Thematic Strategy. See Communication from the Commission to the Council, the European Parliament, the European Economic and Social Committee and the Committee of the Regions – Thematic Strategy for Soil Protection, COM/2006/0231 final. In 2021, the EU Commission was consulting on a new EU Soil Strategy. European Commission, 'Commission Consults on New EU Soil Strategy' (2 February 2021) https://ec.europa.eu/environment/news/commission-consults-new-eu-soil-strategy-2021-02-02_en accessed 1 May 2021.

58 European Commission, 'CAP Reform – An Explanation of the Main Elements' (European Commission Memo 25 October 2013).

59 Regulation (EU) No 1307/2013 of the European Parliament and of the Council of 17 December 2013 Establishing Rules for Direct Payments to Farmers Under Support Schemes Within the Framework of the Common Agricultural Policy and Repealing Council Regulation (EC) No 637/2008 and Council Regulation (EC) No 73/2009 [2013] OJ L347/608, respectively Articles 44, 45 and 46.

60 See M. Thimont Jack, 'Common Agricultural Policy' (Institute for Government 17 March 2020) www.instituteforgovernment.org.uk/explainers/common-agricultural-policy accessed 1 May 2021.

61 However, the effectiveness of greening payments has been repeatedly questioned. See European Court of Auditors, 'Greening: A More Complex Income Support Scheme, Not Yet Environmentally Effective' (Special Rapport n. 21/2017); and A. Gocht et al., 'Economic and Environmental Impacts of CAP Greening: CAPRI Simulation Results' (Joint Research Centre, European Commission 2016) https://publications.jrc.ec.europa.eu/repository/bitstream/JRC102519/jrc%20report_cap%20greening-capri%20v12.pdf accessed 1 May 2021.

62 No double funding is allowed, which means that a measure under Pillar 1 (direct payments) cannot also be paid for under Pillar 2 (rural development).

63 LEADER originates from the phrase 'Liaison Entre Actions de Développement de l'Économie Rurale' or 'Links between the rural economy and development actions'.

64 For more on the rural development programmes across the UK, see European Commission, 'United Kingdom – Country Files' https://ec.europa.eu/info/food-farming-fisheries/key-policies/common-agricultural-policy/rural-development/country/uk_en accessed 1 May 2021.

AESs – the main component of Pillar 2 – acknowledge the interactions between agriculture, the environment and climate change. Member States have to spend at least 30% of their rural development funding on these measures,[65] which aim at 'preserving and promoting the changes indispensable in agricultural practices that make a positive impact on the environment and climate'.[66] The receipt of both direct payments and financial support under Pillar 2 is subject to cross-compliance requirements.[67] AESs establish another route through which to integrate environmental concerns into agricultural policy. Payments support the creation of wildlife habitats, the conservation of traditional animal breeds and investment in pollution reduction. AESs play a decisive role in offsetting the 'damaging environmental effects of input-linked and production-linked policies'.[68] Farmers can select specific activities from these programmes, including low-input or organic production methods, which go beyond legal requirements, for example, the regulatory baseline, and favour greater environmental protection to reverse the trend in favour of sustainability rather than intensification by requiring extra buy-in from farmers.[69]

Notwithstanding these reforms and perceived improvements, the CAP has not managed to reverse its overall negative impact on the environment. AESs have contributed to reducing the decline in environmentally-friendly practices linked to economic and competitive pressures. However, the CAP struggles to reverse the ongoing deterioration in soil, air and water quality, land clearing, loss of biodiversity and the degradation of marine, freshwater and terrestrial ecosystems.[70] In a 2009 report on public goods, the Institute for European Environmental Policy concluded that combining cross-compliance and AESs 'over and above a regulatory baseline is an appropriate one' by improving environmental methods on farms, preventing land abandonment and strengthening extensive and organic practices[71] – but these are no longer sufficient to reverse the severity of

65 See Regulation (EU) No 1305/2013 of the European Parliament and of the Council of 17 December 2013 on Support for Rural Development by the European Agricultural Fund for Rural Development (EAFRD) and Repealing Council Regulation (EC) No 1698/2005 [2013] OJ L347/487.

66 L. Petetin, 'The EU Common Agricultural Policy: Towards a More Sustainable Agriculture?' in R. Ako and D. Olawuyi (eds), *Food and Agricultural Law: Readings on Sustainable Agriculture and the Law in Nigeria* (Afe Babalola University Press 2015) 215.

67 Regulation (EU) No 1306/2013 of the European Parliament and of the Council of 17 December 2013 on the Financing, Management and Monitoring of the Common Agricultural Policy and Repealing Council Regulations (EEC) No 352/78, (EC) No 165/94, (EC) No 2799/98, (EC) No 814/2000, (EC) No 1290/2005 and (EC) No 485/2008 [2013] OJ L347/549, Article 91.

68 V. Vojtech, 'Policy Measures Addressing Agri-Environmental Issues' (OECD Food, Agriculture and Fisheries Papers, No. 24/2010) 9.

69 Petetin (n66) 214.

70 See European Environment Agency, 'The European Environment – State and Outlook 2020: Knowledge for Transition to a Sustainable Europe' (2019); and Gravey (n16) 36.

71 Cooper, Hart and Baldock (n11) 109.

biodiversity loss across the EU.[72] Further reforms to deliver a truly sustainable agriculture are in great need for European agriculture – as well as UK agriculture – to embrace ongoing challenges and goals, including net-zero ambitions, a circular economy and reversal of the biodiversity and climate crises.[73]

Through multiple CAP reforms, the EU shifted the focus more towards a holistic approach underpinned by environmental objectives and in doing so also decentralised the powers for agricultural policy-making. For example, implementation and enforcement have been left to the Member States and their subnational entities. With the strengthening of the principle of subsidiarity, flexibility was accommodated in the development of the CAP and there is now a wide diversity of agricultural policies across the EU Member States and their regions – this is even more visible in the direction of the current EU reforms.[74] This differentiation has occurred between countries as well as within them, including within the UK as noted.

1.2.3 The four nations and the CAP

As discussed above, the nature of farming and the context within which it operates varies considerably across the UK. Considering this and the flexibility provided by CAP, it is hardly surprising that prior to Brexit there was not one but four agricultural policies across Wales, Northern Ireland, Scotland and England.[75] Each policy implemented the CAP with different slants (see Table 1.1).[76] As such there is 'heterogeneity' within the farming policies, for example, different minimum and maximum caps, various emphases in financial support and rural development schemes.[77]

For instance, the minimum claim size for farms in Scotland and Northern Ireland (three hectares) was lower than in England or Wales (five hectares), reflecting the substantial proportion of very small farms in both nations and the desire to ensure their economic viability (reflecting their heavy dependence on farm payments also). At the other end, only England refrained from imposing upper limits on claims, enabling highly profitable farms to benefit further from the available financial support. Further, all four nations provided for AESs, but not only did their design vary but their availability and uptake differed considerably. This is reflected in the proportion of rural development funds focused on AESs across the four nations, but also, for example, in the decline of participation

72 See European Environment Agency (n70).
73 See also IPCC (n12).
74 See Chapter 4, Section 4.5.2.1.
75 Gravey (n36).
76 For a more detailed analysis, see C.P. Rodgers, *Agricultural Law* (Bloomsbury Professional Ltd 2016).
77 Petetin, Gravey and Moore (n36) 6.

Table 1.1 Different Policies in the UK within the 2014–2020 Common Agricultural Policy

Minimum claim size	England and Wales had a minimum claim size of 5 hectares, whilst Northern Ireland and Scotland chose 3 hectares.
Coupled support	Northern Ireland, Wales and England had no coupled payments while Scotland opted to keep these payments in some cases (for beef calves and hill sheep).
Capping payment size	Northern Ireland capped direct payments at €150,000 whilst the caps for Wales and Scotland were much higher (€300,000 and €500,000 respectively). There was no cap in England.
Main agri-environment-climate schemes	England with the Countryside Stewardship Scheme. Wales with Glastir. Northern Ireland with the Environmental Farming Scheme. Scotland with the Agri-Environment Climate Scheme.
Agri-environment-climate payments	Payments represented 16% of Scottish, 14% of Northern Irish and 28% of Welsh rural development funds compared to 65% in England.

Source: adapted from L. Petetin, V. Gravey and B. Moore, 'Setting the Bar for a Green Brexit in Food and Farming' (Soil Association 2019) www.soilassociation.org/green-brexit/.

in these schemes in Northern Ireland.[78] It is worth noting that none of Scotland, Wales and Northern Ireland met the criterion of 30% of Pillar 2 payments being for AESs, being balanced out by England – thereby leading to the UK as a whole complying with this EU obligation.[79]

78 P. McCann, 'Agri Environment Scheme Area Down by 30%' (*Irish Farmers Journal* 3 June 2020) www.farmersjournal.ie/agri-environment-scheme-area-down-by-30-548992 accessed 1 May 2021; and Nature Friendly Farming Network, 'NI Agri-Environment Scheme Update' www.nffn.org.uk/ni-agri-environment-scheme-update/ accessed 1 May 2021.

79 European Commission, 'Factsheet on 2014–2020 Rural Development Programme for Wales (United Kingdom)' (2020) https://ec.europa.eu/info/sites/info/files/food-farming-fisheries/key_policies/documents/rdp-factsheet-wales_en.pdf accessed 2021; European Commission, 'Factsheet on 2014–2020 Rural Development Programme for England (United Kingdom)' (2020) https://ec.europa.eu/info/sites/info/files/food-farming-fisheries/key_policies/documents/rdp-factsheet-england_en.pdf accessed 2021; European Commission, 'Factsheet on 2014–2020 Rural Development Programme for Northern Ireland (United Kingdom)' (2020) https://ec.europa.eu/info/sites/default/files/food-farming-fisheries/key_policies/documents/rdp-factsheet-northern-ireland_en.pdf accessed 2021; and European Commission, 'Factsheet on 2014–2020 Rural Development Programme for Scotland (United Kingdom)' (2020) https://ec.europa.eu/info/sites/info/files/food-farming-fisheries/key_policies/documents/rdp-factsheet-scotland_en.pdf accessed 2021.

Finally, whilst the CAP (and complementary EU regimes) provided an overarching framework for UK agriculture, the flexibility enabled variations across the UK[80] and indeed led to situations where individual nation's policies could approximate those in another Member State more closely than in the rest of the UK. Thus, Northern Ireland's approach to implementing the CAP arguably was closer to that of the Republic of Ireland[81] than that of the rest of the UK and especially England.

1.3 Brexit: a new context for developing agricultural policies?

The UK is no longer an EU Member State and instead is a third party – irrespective of political, economic or cultural linkages. Post-transition, it is no longer part of existing trade agreements that the EU ratified with other countries and has exited the EU internal market and customs union, with the free movements of goods, services, capital and persons no longer applicable. Similarly, EU standards and rules no longer are part of the UK, unless incorporated into domestic law and retained. Although the UK Government created the European Union (Withdrawal) Act 2018[82] as a 'patchwork' to convert existing EU law into domestic law ('retained EU law'), the entire EU acquis was not retained, with noticeable governance gaps including the omission of subsidiarity and environmental principles in the TFEU[83] – despite the proposed Environment Bill.[84] Such omissions increase the likelihood of policy and regulatory divergence over time, with potential knock-on effects, for instance, on trade between the EU and the UK.

80 Although, as discussed, such opportunities were not always embraced fully. See Petetin, Gravey and Moore (n36).

81 B. Jack, 'Implementing European Agricultural Law in Northern Ireland and the Republic of Ireland: A Common Policy?' (2003) 54(4) *Northern Ireland Legal Quarterly* 377.

82 It is worth noting that this was achieved through a considerable recentralisation of powers, including via 'Henry VIII' clauses, Section 8 of the Act enables amendments of legislation to address future 'deficiencies' that may materialise, without creating Acts of Parliament.

83 See C. Burns, B. Moore, V. Gravey and A. Jordan, 'Green Brexit: Rhetoric or Reality?' (2019) 10(2) *Political Insight* 37; V. Gravey, A. Jordan and C. Burns, 'Environmental Policy after Brexit: Mind the Governance Gap' (The UK in a Changing Europe 10 August 2016) www.brexitenvironment.co.uk/2016/08/10/environmental-policy-after-brexit-mind-the-governance-gap/ accessed 1 May 2021; and M. Lee, 'Brexit and Environmental Protection in the United Kingdom: Governance, Accountability and Law Making' (2018) 36(3) *Journal of Energy & Natural Resources Law* 351. More generally on Brexit and the environment, see B. Pontin, *The Environmental Case for Brexit: A Socio-legal Perspective* (Hart Publishing 2019); C. Abbot and M. Lee, *Environmental Groups and Legal Expertise: Shaping the Brexit Process* (UCL Press 2021); and C. Burns, 'Will Brexit Degrade UK Environmental Policy?' (2020) 119(815) *Current History* 101.

84 See Environment Bill 2019–2021. For some criticism of an earlier version of the Environment Bill, see M. Lee, 'The Environment Bill: A Framework for Progressive Environmental Law?' (Brexit and Environment Network 18 October 2019) www.brexitenvironment.co.uk/2019/10/18/framework-progressive-environmental-law/ accessed 1 May 2021.

Instead, international law underpins the UK's relationship with the EU, as with other countries. The crucial instruments central to this new relationship between the UK and the EU include the UK/EU Withdrawal Agreement[85] – in particular its Northern Ireland Protocol[86] – and now also the UK/EU Trade and Cooperation Agreement (TCA).[87] Further, considerable attention must be given to elements such as the WTO's Agreement on Agriculture[88] on trade in agricultural products and the General Agreement on Tariffs and Trade[89] (GATT) as well as the Sanitary and Phyto-Sanitary Agreement[90] (SPS Agreement) and the Technical Barriers to Trade Agreement[91] (TBT Agreement) for non-tariff barriers. All trade agreements, including the TCA, build upon the WTO framework[92] and determine elements such as tariff and non-tariff barriers, as well as, for instance, specific standards or other criteria that must be met. The spectrum of relationships possible is extensive with widely differentiating consequences. Agreements may be more or less detailed and more or less all-encompassing, but any agreement will involve compromises as demonstrated in the negotiations of the TCA. As will be observed in the remainder of the book, individually and cumulatively, these agreements have profound implications for UK agricultural policies, practices and legislation.

The UK/EU Withdrawal Agreement must be considered initially in light of its centrality to Brexit.[93] After considerable tumultuous drafts and redrafts, this international agreement came into force on 31 January 2020, binding both the EU and the UK, with a range of general provisions on issues such as compliance, good

85 Agreement on the Withdrawal of the United Kingdom of Great Britain and Northern Ireland from the European Union and the European Atomic Energy Community [2019] OJ C384I /1.

86 Protocol on Ireland/Northern Ireland to the Agreement on the Withdrawal of the United Kingdom of Great Britain and Northern Ireland from the European Union and the European Atomic Energy Community [2019] OJ C384I /1.

87 Trade and Cooperation Agreement between the European Union and the European Atomic Energy Community, of the One Part, and the United Kingdom of Great Britain and Northern Ireland, of the Other Part [2020] OJ L 444/14. The TCA was implemented into domestic law with the European Union (Future Relationship) Act 2020.

88 Uruguay Round Agreement on Agriculture (1994).

89 Uruguay Round General Agreement on Tariffs and Trade (1994).

90 Uruguay Round Agreement on the Application of Sanitary and Phytosanitary Measures (1994).

91 Uruguay Round Agreement on Technical Barriers to Trade (1994).

92 GATT, Article XXIV.

93 For a summary of the UK/EU Withdrawal Agreement, see J. Owen, 'Brexit Deal: The Withdrawal Agreement' (Institute for Government 2 July 2020) www.instituteforgovernment.org.uk/explainers/brexit-deal-withdrawal-agreement accessed 1 May 2021. The UK/EU Withdrawal Agreement was implemented into domestic law with the European Union (Withdrawal Agreement) Act 2020. For more on the Act itself, see M. Thimont Jack, 'Withdrawal Agreement Act' (Institute for Government 2 July 2020) www.instituteforgovernment.org.uk/explainers/withdrawal-agreement-act accessed 1 May 2021.

faith and dispute resolution.[94] It created a transition period until 31 December 2020, during which the UK was largely[95] treated as an EU Member State. During that time, the application of EU law in its entirety remained, with the same legal effects, but the UK was no longer part of the political institutions of the EU.[96] Thus, the internal market and free movement principles continued to apply across the UK, along with policies and financing including the CAP.[97] The intention was to provide for some stability and certainty whilst both the EU and the UK prepared for the impacts of Brexit, for instance, investing in necessary resources and infrastructure, and also whilst they negotiated the TCA.

Despite being primarily a stop-gap measure, the UK/EU Withdrawal Agreement addresses some limited aspects for the long-term, such as continued respect for geographical indications after the end of the transition period[98] and the challenges posed by Northern Ireland and its shared land border, history, economic linkages and general connections with the Republic of Ireland. This Irish border was a significant issue at the heart of the negotiations, reflected in the original draft 'backstop'[99] and now in the 'frontstop' that is the Northern Ireland Protocol. The Protocol remains in place in the post-transition period and aims to maintain a soft border between Ireland and Northern Ireland, uphold the Belfast Agreement/Good Friday Agreement 1998, guarantee free trade between Great Britain and Northern Ireland as well as within the Island of Ireland,[100] and broadly maintain peace and cooperation across the Island of Ireland.[101] Consequently, the Protocol provides for unique treatment for Northern Ireland, as outlined in Chapter 2, Section 2.3.

After 11 months of intensive negotiations and multiple stalemates along the way around sticking points such as regulatory alignment, level playing fields and state aid provisions (as well as fisheries), the UK and the EU agreed to the TCA on Christmas Eve 2020 – exactly four and a half years after the referendum vote. There are four main features identified for cooperation between the two blocs:[102] a free trade agreement; wide-ranging economic, social and environmental aspects as well as fisheries cooperation (including level playing field

94 UK/EU Withdrawal Agreement, respectively Articles 4, 5 and 167.
95 Exceptions include, for instance, the inability to vote on EU policies or authorisations or to act as lead competent authorities for risk assessments.
96 UK/EU Withdrawal Agreement, Article 4.
97 Although specific domestic legislation was required to do so – in particular, the Direct Payments to Farmers (Legislative Continuity) Act 2020.
98 UK/EU Withdrawal Agreement, Article 54.2.
99 For more on the Irish 'backstop' under Theresa May's Brexit deal, see Institute for Government, 'Irish Backstop' (24 February 2020) www.instituteforgovernment.org.uk/explainers/irish-backstop accessed 1 May 2021.
100 Northern Ireland Protocol, Articles 4 and 5.
101 Ibid Article 1.
102 European Commission, 'EU-UK Trade and Cooperation Agreement: A New Relationship with Big Changes' (December 2020) https://ec.europa.eu/info/sites/info/files/brexit_files/info_site/6_pager_final.pdf accessed 1 May 2021.

provisions); arrangements for citizens' security; and a governance or institutional framework.[103] In the end, both parties had to make compromises but the UK more so than the EU, since the UK had more to lose than the EU. It is important to highlight that in 2019, around 13% of EU trade in goods with third countries was with the UK, whilst UK trade in goods to the EU was around 50%.[104] However, the EU still had to make some concessions, especially in relation to state aid and the jurisdiction of the Court of Justice of the EU (CJEU), due to the economic weight the UK represents for EU trade.

The TCA is a considerable improvement on a 'no-deal' Brexit.[105] It positively enables tariff-free and quota-free trade between the UK and the EU for agricultural products, but non-tariff barriers remain in place (initially at least).[106] While regulatory divergence is possible under the Agreement, it could lead to losing access to the EU market and result in trade disputes. Furthermore, there are obligations to maintain a level playing field and non-regression in the field of environmental, social and labour standards to prevent unfair competition.[107] Such provisions aim to avoid environmental and social dumping by either of the parties. They also influence how competitive the UK and EU agri-food industries will be and indeed how viable it is, for instance, for the UK agri-food industries to export to the EU markets (and vice versa). The UK–EU relationship is to be reinvented.[108]

103 Many aspects of these remain to be ironed out. TCA aspects central to agriculture are addressed in Chapter 5, Section 5.1.2. However, a key question going beyond the scope of this book is who is going to sit on the panels and committees created by the TCA? This question of representation within the institutional architecture of the Agreement is crucial, especially for the devolved administrations.

104 European Commission, 'Questions & Answers: EU-UK Trade and Cooperation Agreement' (24 December 2020) https://ec.europa.eu/commission/presscorner/detail/en/qanda_20_2532 accessed 1 May 2021.

105 For a detailed explanation of the TCA, see Institute for Government, 'UK-EU Future Relationship: The Deal' (2020) www.instituteforgovernment.org.uk/publication/future-relationship-trade-deal accessed 1 May 2021.

106 This is dependent upon satisfying rules of origin under the Agreement, which are proving problematic to fulfil. See further, Chapter 5, Section 5.1.2. See also M. Dobbs and L. Petetin, 'Agriculture: Environmental, Food and Animal Health Standards' in H. Kassin, A. Jordan and S. Ennis (eds), *UK Regulation after Brexit* (The UK in a Changing Europe 25 February 2021) https://ukandeu.ac.uk/wp-content/uploads/2021/02/UK-regulation-after-Brexit.pdf accessed 1 May 2021, 51.

107 TCA, Articles 355, 387 and 391.

108 For example, in January 2021, UK goods exports to the EU fell by 40% whilst EU imports to the UK dropped by almost 30%. See Office for National Statistics, 'UK Trade: January 2021' (12 March 2021) www.ons.gov.uk/economy/nationalaccounts/balanceofpayments/bulletins/uktrade/january2021 accessed 1 May 2021. However, in February 2021, trade started to pick up again. Office for National Statistics, 'UK Trade: February 2021' (13 April 2021) www.ons.gov.uk/economy/nationalaccounts/balanceofpayments/bulletins/uktrade/february2021 accessed 1 May 2021. See also, N. Calcea, 'How Much Has Brexit Cost the UK?' (New Statesman, 18 March 2021) www.newstatesman.com/politics/economy/2021/03/how-much-has-brexit-cost-uk accessed 1 May 2021.

Whilst the TCA is indeed better than a 'no deal', it nonetheless brings considerable challenges of its own for agricultural policy through re-shaping the context. Its implications are examined in more detail in Chapter 5, Section 5.1.1., but the crucial point to note here is that there was no guarantee that this would be the outcome of the negotiations – a wide spectrum of outcomes was possible.[109] Consequently, the UK and the devolved administrations have had to design and introduce policies in a cloud of uncertainty – for instance, would farmers have tariff-free access to EU markets and, if so, would a trade agreement impose conditions regarding subsidies/state aid or agri-food standards? This uncertainty helped delay and shape the evolution of the policies, which will now need to be re-evaluated in light of the changes introduced by the Agreement. Furthermore, the UK now faces increased challenges within the international community due to changes to its weaker (and more isolated) economic position, its relationships with (future) trading partners and increased volatility in agricultural markets.

Consequently, the UK (encompassing the devolved administrations) is in unchartered waters and needs to consider its next steps very carefully. It is faced with a new and evolving context in which to develop agricultural policy – or indeed agricultural policies, in light of both devolution and the heterogeneity of the farming systems, ecosystems and resulting agricultural, social and environmental focus points.[110] However, it remains unclear what shape precisely this new context will take in the end. In addressing the wicked problem of designing agricultural policies, the UK and the devolved administrations must reflect on what is permissible, practically possible and desirable or appropriate. They need to do so in light of the new context and landscape – legal, political, economic.

However, whilst there is an understandable focus on addressing immediate concerns and, in particular, those posed by Brexit, it is also essential to develop suitable long-term approaches – especially considering the loss of the objectives in Article 39 TFEU and the importance of clarity and certainty for those in such a vulnerable industry. The difficulty is that farming is under considerable pressure and the context is perpetually changing. Shocks or crises such as COVID-19, Brexit, extreme weather events, or climate change all need to be addressed (through mitigation and adaptation), but they also signal broader challenges. They highlight a situation of turbulence, where the ground is shifting underfoot and the status quo may be challenged in new ways on a regular basis[111]

109 J. Davis, S. Feng, M. Patton and J. Binfield, 'Impacts of Alternative Post-Brexit Trade Agreements on UK Agriculture: Sector Analyses Using the FAPRI-UK Model' (FAPRI-UK Project, Agri-Food and Biosciences Institute, August 2017) https://content17.green17creative.com/media/99/files/FAPRI_UK_Brexit_Report.pdf accessed 1 May 2021.

110 Petetin, Gravey and Moore (n36) 6.

111 C.K. Ansell, E. Sørensen and J. Torfing, 'The COVID-19 Pandemic as a Game Changer for Public Administration and Leadership? The Need for Robust Governance Responses to Turbulent Problems' (2021) 23(7) *Public Management Review* 1.

– these may challenge agricultural policies and practices.[112] Consequently, there is a need to prepare for shocks – for the unexpected – through building resilience into the system, policies and practices by whatever means possible.[113] This raises key questions over what is meant by resilience, how it can be built into agriculture and what mechanisms might achieve it. As discussed in Chapter 4, applying socio-ecological resilience to agriculture enables a holistic approach that takes into account and addresses agriculture's multifaceted nature, the specific vulnerabilities it faces and the undesirable effects it creates. This, for instance, can encompass biodiversity, soil stability, healthy farmers, steady income and short and/or diverse supply chains.

1.4 Book focus and structure

Steps have been taken by both the UK Government and the devolved administrations to develop their own agricultural policies in preparation for Brexit and beyond. Whilst they include some interesting changes and innovations, they also have some significant weaknesses, and it is unclear as to how they might function in practice individually or in conjunction with each other. Furthermore, the UK's relationships with the EU and other key trading partners remain only partially drawn. Consequently, there is considerable confusion and uncertainty for all concerned. Nonetheless, useful insights can be drawn from developments to date and crucial evaluations undertaken.

This book outlines the proposed agricultural policies of England/the UK, Wales, Northern Ireland and Scotland (in this order), providing clarity where possible. It evaluates them in light of (i) the legal and political parameters that exist at devolved, national and international levels; (ii) the UK and devolved administrations' rhetoric and focus points; and (iii) alternative, future-looking ambitious goals for agriculture. It considers whether the policies are permissible, feasible and desirable/appropriate or whether (and, if so, how) more ambitious policies could be developed – especially based on the concept of resilience and identifies pathways to deliver a resilient agriculture. In doing so, it must consider key challenges posed for agriculture in light of its nature, as well as relevant UK internal relationships and, indeed, international relationships. In particular, changes to governance within and beyond the UK, both in terms of its framing (away from the EU and subsidiarity, towards the UK internal market and the increased role of international law) and its practicalities and consequences on the UK, are assessed.

112 V. Gravey, L. Petetin and M. Dobbs, 'Quitter le PAC, Comment et Pour Quoi Faire? La (Re)Construction des Politiques Agricoles Britanniques au Cœur des Turbulences du Brexit' (2021) 73(3) *Politique Europeenne* 150.

113 Ansell, Sørensen and Torfing (n111); and M. Dobbs, V. Gravey and L. Petetin, 'Driving the European Green Deal in Turbulent Times' (2021) 9(3) *Politics and Governance* 316.

To this end, the remainder of the book considers the following aspects: Chapter 2 focuses on the web of powers and obligations that exist and impact any potential UK agricultural policies and practices. This includes consideration of both existing international obligations and relationships, including under WTO law and the Northern Ireland Protocol, as well as the domestic, constitutional and political aspects of devolution, whether devolved, (imposed) centralised actions or more collaborative common frameworks are feasible and appropriate.[114] This complex web provides insight into the parameters within which any agricultural policies or indeed trade deals can be developed. It, however, postpones consideration of the TCA until later in the book,[115] as the purpose here is to focus on the existing parameters within which the UK and devolved administrations are operating.

Chapter 3 outlines the four main approaches being developed across the UK, based largely on 'public money for public goods' and productivity. It introduces the UK Agriculture Act, including its main focus on England, specific provisions on the UK as a whole and enabling Schedules for Wales and Northern Ireland. It also considers the key documents and discussions across Wales, Northern Ireland and Scotland, with the caveat that none have reached the same stage of development as England. The chapter builds on this outline to sketch out the core components of the policies from a practical perspective and how they compare with each other, before undertaking an initial evaluation of these policies in light of the parameters sketched out in Chapter 2 – specifically, the legality of such policies (including in relation to the Agreement on Agriculture). It also provides a springboard for the analysis in the remainder of the book.

Chapter 4 takes the analysis a step further by considering the over-arching focus of the policies, critiquing the current dominant themes of 'public money for public goods' and economics (including productivity), as well as the mechanics of the policies and their schemes. It proposes alternative, more ambitious frameworks for agricultural policies underpinned by the concept of resilience (and not 'only' sustainability). It puts forward four main, interconnected pathways to achieve a resilient agriculture through the provision of social-ecological services, net zero, agroecological systems and agri-food democracy to deliver a truly, forward-looking 21st-century agriculture. The chapter also analyses the existing policies in terms of their impact on the diversity of the farms and farmers, their approach to governance and how they address interconnectedness. Reflections on the existing proposals are provided in light of these ideas, with suggestions to build upon and improve the proposals.

Chapter 5 is the final substantive chapter and examines how significant ongoing and future changes within the UK and between the UK and its existing and potential trading partners could shape the governance setting and, thereby,

114 This also clearly raises issues regarding subsidiarity, which will be addressed therein.

115 Despite the TCA being an existing agreement, its importance is future-looking and as such will be dealt with in Chapter 5.

impact domestic agricultural policies and practices. It is within this chapter that the newly agreed TCA is considered, along with potential issues and how it might evolve in the future. For instance, the Agreement can either be enhanced or watered down every five years depending on the political will on either side of the Channel.[116] While Chapter 2 looked at the parameters created by the existing relationships and obligations, this chapter looks to the future and recognises that the context does not stand still. By examining these components last, it considers not only how these potential changes might impact domestic agricultural policies and the resilience of agriculture, but also how internal and external relationships and commitments might need to be developed to help deliver a resilient agriculture.

Chapter 6 draws the book's strands together and provides a synopsis of the preceding material. It highlights key elements from the four agricultural policies and their central strengths and weaknesses, before reiterating the significance of resilience and the core pathways to achieve it and outlining how the post-Brexit governance landscape for agriculture is evolving. Finally, the chapter concludes by highlighting some steps that could be taken to deliver an ambitious, resilient 21st-century agriculture.

116 TCA, Article 776.

2 'Taking back control'?

A web of powers and constraints

To understand Brexit's impact on agriculture across the United Kingdom (UK), it is necessary to consider the core components of the existing regimes and the context within which they operate. UK agricultural practices, policies and laws do not exist in isolation, but instead are interwoven with different areas or objectives and are affected by legal, political and trade relationships across various levels, not to mind the very nature of the land, climate and culture. Whilst an exhaustive investigation of the context is beyond the scope of this book, this chapter focuses primarily on the core powers and constraints currently acting upon policy-makers across the UK within a multilevel governance framework.

As observed in Chapter 1, the UK has developed strong links legally and economically with the European Union (EU). EU law and policy, including the complex umbrella of the Common Agricultural Policy (CAP), will continue to directly impact UK agriculture post-transition due to integrated markets, the competition between the two systems and the newly agreed Trade and Cooperation Agreement (TCA).[1] However, the EU is not the 'be all and end all' when it comes to understanding the web of powers and constraints at play. As noted in Chapter 1, UK agriculture is part of a globalised world with considerable imports and exports throughout the year. However, it also is of local importance and the context varies across the UK.

This chapter first outlines the nature of multilevel governance and the issue of subsidiarity. It then considers the UK's core legal and political relationships that exist both on the international level and on the domestic level – focusing on those that directly impact the design of agricultural policies. Consequently, aspects of the complex legal geometry, encompassing the Northern Ireland Protocol,[2] World Trade Organization (WTO) law and devolution, are examined in some detail. These relationships have proven particularly contentious and

1 Trade and Cooperation Agreement between the European Union and the European Atomic Energy Community, of the One Part, and the United Kingdom of Great Britain and Northern Ireland, of the Other Part [2020] OJ L 444/14.

2 Protocol on Ireland/Northern Ireland to the Agreement on the Withdrawal of the United Kingdom of Great Britain and Northern Ireland from the European Union and the European Atomic Energy Community [2019] OJ C384I /1.

DOI: 10.4324/9780429503719-2

seemingly surprising to some, perhaps because much has changed internationally and domestically since the UK became a Member of the EU. As noted previously, consideration of the TCA will predominately be left until Chapter 5. This chapter does not seek to provide a comprehensive treatment of multilateral environmental agreements such as the Paris Agreement[3] or the Convention on Biological Diversity.[4]

2.1 Allocation of powers and multilevel governance in agriculture

The slogan 'taking back control' has been a common refrain since early in the Brexit campaign, raising images of reclaiming sovereignty, power and autonomy.[5] The EU was cast as the nemesis, sapping powers away from the UK and constraining its actions, with little in compensation.[6] To an extent this is true – the world has seen a shift away from Westphalian sovereignty of the nation-state, with the UK seeing a decline in its individual powers over the decades. Further, by signing up to any supranational body (or indeed to any international agreement), a nation-state consents to cede some sovereignty at least temporarily – reflected clearly in the 1969 Vienna Convention on the Law of Treaties.[7] First, however, there have also been considerable benefits to the UK and other Member States via membership of the EU.[8] Second, it is exceedingly simplistic to claim that membership of the EU is the only limiter on a nation-state's sovereignty or ability to act. For instance, trade negotiations are multilevel – multilateral within the WTO (the Doha Round was launched in 2001 but has still not concluded and is currently in stalemate), regional (the EU, the Comprehensive and Progressive Agreement for Trans-Pacific Partnership [CPTPP][9]) or bilateral (partnerships

3 See United Nations Framework Convention on Climate Change – Adoption of the Paris Agreement (2015).
4 United Nations Convention on Biological Diversity (1992).
5 Vote Leave Campaign, 'Briefing – Taking Back Control from Brussels' (2016) www.voteleavetakecontrol.org/briefing_control.html accessed 1 May 2021.
6 See F. Zappettini, 'From Euroscepticism to Outright Populism: The Evolution of British Tabloids' (LSE Blog 4 January 2019) https://blogs.lse.ac.uk/brexit/2019/01/04/from-euroscepticism-to-outright-populism-the-evolution-of-british-tabloids/ accessed 1 May 2021. See also C. Ruzza and M. Pejovic, 'Populism at Work: The Language of the Brexiteers and the European Union' (2019) 16(4) *Critical Discourse Studies* 432; and M. Maccaferri, 'Splendid Isolation Again? Brexit and the Role of the Press and Online Media in Re-Narrating the European Discourse' (2019) 16(4) *Critical Discourse Studies* 389.
7 United Nations Vienna Convention on the Law of Treaties (1969).
8 Examples of such benefits include the single market, EU citizenship and resulting mobility, economic and social integration, non-discrimination, security, peace, democracy and the rule of law, and of course environmental protection. See European Parliament, 'Briefing – The Benefits of EU Membership Are Not Measured by Net Operating Balances' www.europarl.europa.eu/RegData/etudes/BRIE/2020/648145/IPOL_BRI(2020)648145_EN.pdf accessed 1 May 2021.
9 Comprehensive and Progressive Agreement for Trans-Pacific Partnership (2018).

with neighbouring countries and those further afield). The negotiated and resulting agreements often comprise agriculture-specific provisions, which significantly impact domestic agriculture (and the relevant partners' agriculture) in terms of environmental, health, safety and animal welfare standards.

Multilevel governance theories acknowledge the 'reallocation of authority upwards, downwards and sideways from central states'.[10] This dispersal or 'reallocation of authority' can vary across different issues or areas, from a relatively simple, hierarchical approach with, for instance, delegated powers to a complex or fragmented system where power *loci* are abundant and diffuse. Thus, situations may arise where there is 'functional interconnection between regulatory areas, and within the same regulatory area among different regulatory levels'.[11]

Conversely, a system of multilevel governance also leads to an intricate web that opens the potential for gaps, confusion and conflict between different power loci. It needs frameworks to ensure coherency,[12] and also clarity as to which powers lie where and how they interact – otherwise, there is considerable potential for chaos. This complex system of multilevel governance is exemplified by the area of agriculture, where powers relating to trade, financial support, environmental protection, consumer protection, sanitary and phytosanitary (SPS) (that is plant, human and animal health) risks and much more are spread across the levels. Accordingly, the policy and regulation of agriculture in the UK are an example of multilevel governance, where powers are spread in various directions – vertically and horizontally. As noted in Chapter 1, there were four concomitant agricultural policies during EU membership and there remain four agricultural policies with diverse emphases and focuses post-Brexit. Each of these policies must be cognisant of the others, but also the broader context and dispersal of powers – including internationally and domestically.

Multilevel governance also raises the question of where the powers *ought* to be allocated. One useful mechanism for determining whether powers ought to be centralised or not, and to what extent if so, is that of subsidiarity – not the EU tailored version, but the broader concept rooted in ideas of democracy, Catholicism and economics.[13] Simply put, it suggests that the powers ought to

10 L. Hooghe and G. Marks, 'Unraveling the Central State, But How? Types of Multi-Level Governance' (2003) 97(2) *American Political Science Review* 233, 233. See also N. Chowdhury and R. Wessel, 'Conceptualising Multilevel Regulation in the EU: A Legal Translation of Multilevel Governance?' (2012) 18 *European Law Journal* 335.

11 A. Estella, *The EU Principle of Subsidiarity and Its Critique* (OUP 2002) 114.

12 See OECD, 'Water Governance in OECD Countries: A Multi-Level Approach' (OECD Studies on Water 2011) 19; European Commission, 'European Governance – A White Paper', COM(2001)428, [2001] OJ C287/1, 7; and R. Brownsword, 'Regulatory Coherence-A European Challenge' in K. Purnhagen and P. Rott (eds), *Varieties of European Economic Law and Regulation* (Springer 2014) 235.

13 See M. Dobbs, 'Attaining Subsidiarity-Based Multilevel Governance of Genetically Modified Cultivation?' (2016) 28(2) *Journal of Environmental Law* 245; and R. Vischer, 'Subsidiarity as a Principle of Governance: Beyond Devolution' (2001–2002) 35 *Indiana Law Review* 103, 126.

rest at the lower levels unless there is good reason for shifting them upwards[14] and then they ought to only be centralised to the extent necessary to ensure effectiveness or minimise negative externalities. Subsidiarity can be applied broadly,[15] including regarding agriculture[16] – and will be especially relevant to Section 5 of this chapter, which details the debate over the allocation of powers between the devolved and centralised levels within the UK and the consideration of whether UK-wide frameworks are needed in the form of common frameworks or centrally imposed ones.

2.2 The international level, law-making and free trade agreements

Due to the inherently global, transboundary nature of agri-environmental matters, there is a need for action and cooperation on the international stage – especially in relation to trade issues. As there are multiple international law regimes spanning relevant issues that bind the UK, it is key to succinctly explore how international law is formed and note some key instruments, before scrutinising the Northern Ireland Protocol and the WTO system.

Within the international community, states have created two main methods to establish legally binding obligations: custom and treaties. Both methods respond to the need to not impose obligations on states who do not wish to be bound by them. No outside 'legislator', that is beyond an individual state, is tolerated since states can only be bound by agreeing, more specifically giving consent, to a specific international rule. Custom is generally defined as 'international custom as evidence of a general practice accepted as law'.[17] The result is the creation of a legally binding norm at the global (or possibly regional) level. An example of customary international law is the obligation for a state to prevent significant transboundary environmental harm.[18] The second and main method of creating international rules is of greater significance to agriculture – the conclusion of

14 Y. Blank, 'Federalism, Subsidiarity, and the Role of Local Governments in an Age of Global Multilevel Governance' (2009) 37 *Fordham Urban Law Journal* 509, 545; and Estella (n11) 91.

15 See M. Dobbs, 'National Governance of Public Health Responses in a Pandemic?' (2020) 11(2) *European Journal of Risk Regulation* 240.

16 See Dobbs (n13).

17 Statute of the International Court of Justice (1946) Article 38.1 (b). This is the most authoritative definition of the concept. Custom is constituted of two elements: first, the *usus* that is the general or state practice and, second, the *opinio juris* that is the conviction that such practice reflects the law or the *opinio necessitatis*, which is that such practice is required by social, economic or political demands.

18 See *Trail Smelter Arbitration* (United States v. Canada) (1938 and 1941) 3 RIAA 1905. See more recently *Certain Activities Carried Out by Nicaragua in the Border Area (Costa Rica v. Nicaragua) and Construction of a Road in Costa Rica along the San Juan River* (Nicaragua v. Costa Rica), Judgment, *ICJ Reports* 2015, page 665, paragraph 107.

international agreements.[19] An international agreement entails the combination of the wills of two (or more) states for the purpose of regulating their interests. Within international agreements, treaties only bind the contracting parties (states) that have agreed to be compelled by their provisions. States are free to enter into international agreements – or not. These agreements are the main method available at international level for states to work together on different global agri-environmental issues, e.g. the United Nations Framework Convention on Climate Change,[20] the Paris Agreement, the Convention on Biological Diversity and the United Nations International Treaty on Plant Genetic Resources for Food and Agriculture (2001)[21] – the UK is a party to all of these. Although consideration of the full range of international instruments or regimes applicable to agriculture is beyond the scope of this book,[22] it is worth noting that the UK has committed therefore to ideas such as sustainability and sustainable development, conservation and sustainable use of plant genetic resources, fair and equitable sharing of plant genetic resources, reducing carbon and other greenhouse gas emissions and building resilience to adapt to climate change.[23]

Free trade agreements (FTAs) are another example of international agreements, such as the EU-Canada Comprehensive Economic and Trade Agreement[24] (CETA) or the United States-Mexico-Canada Agreement[25] (USMCA). The new relationship between the UK and the EU is largely based on an FTA – initially on the TCA. FTAs contribute to greater trade liberalisation (and arguably economic growth) and enable parties to strengthen their economic partnerships and integration on specific sectors of the economy (goods, services, intellectual property, government procurement). Consequently, FTAs aim to reduce (and possibly eliminate) tariffs as well as non-tariff barriers that can hinder free trade. Parties to each treaty decide on its content (and therefore its exclusions), as well as how disputes are to be settled. Agreements are difficult to negotiate and often take multiple years to be agreed upon, since they often call for a certain regulatory alignment (especially regarding environmental, food, health and animal welfare standards) between all the parties – as proven by the UK/EU negotiations resulting in the

19 International agreements can also be called treaties, conventions, protocols, covenants or acts. The terminology varies.

20 United Nations Framework Convention on Climate Change (1992).

21 According to Article 1.1 of the Treaty, its objectives are 'the conservation and sustainable use of plant genetic resources for food and agriculture and the fair and equitable sharing of the benefits arising out of their use, in harmony with the Convention on Biological Diversity, for sustainable agriculture and food security'.

22 As noted above, justification for preferring WTO law and the Northern Ireland Protocol is explained by the fact that they have greatest resonance for policy- and law-making in the agricultural sector.

23 See Chapter 4.

24 Comprehensive Economic and Trade Agreement (CETA) between Canada, of the one Part, and the European Union and its Member States, of the other Part (2017).

25 Agreement between the United States of America, the United Mexican States, and Canada (2020).

TCA and the multiple stalemates along the way to its conclusion.[26] Typically underpinning FTAs, including ongoing and future trade UK relationships, are the WTO Agreements – covering aspects such as tariffs, SPS measures and other non-tariff barriers and subsidies for agricultural production. WTO law is, therefore, of utmost relevance to UK agriculture and hence these Agreements form the focus of Section 2.4. However, before turning to the WTO, it is necessary to consider the unique situation of Northern Ireland and the resulting Protocol within the UK/EU Withdrawal Agreement.

Northern Ireland raises particular challenges for a smooth Brexit. It shares a land border with the Republic of Ireland, but one that was largely invisible at the time of the referendum. Northern Ireland and the Republic of Ireland share numerous political, economic, social and cultural connections. However, the historical connections, including the serious conflict of the Troubles are equally pertinent – an open, easy border has not always been the case. The Belfast Agreement/Good Friday Agreement 1998 helped to bring an end to the Troubles and usher in a period of relative peace and reconciliation – with the disarmament of paramilitaries and an unusual power-sharing system established (between nationalist and unionist representatives).[27] Concerns arose that any form of Brexit might lead to a hard border on the Island of Ireland,[28] with serious consequences for day-to-day life (for example, cross-border workers or indeed cross-border farms/animals, as well as supply chains and logistics) and the potential for a recurrence of violence. A substantial focus of the negotiations and political debates surrounding Brexit therefore turned to the border[29] – it even developed its own Twitter account (@ BorderIrish) with a recurring image of it as the elephant in the room,[30] before publishing a book.[31] Such concerns led to first a draft 'backstop'[32] and then the

26 The TCA is further discussed in Chapter 5, Section 5.1.2.
27 For more on the peace process and the role of the EU, see G. Lagana, *The European Union and the Northern Ireland Peace Process* (Palgrave 2021).
28 See C. Barnard, 'Northern Ireland in the Negotiations and the Withdrawal Agreement' in A. Menon (eds), 'Brexit and the Island of Ireland' (The UK in a Changing Europe 2018) https://ukandeu.ac.uk/wp-content/uploads/2018/05/Brexit-and-Island-of-Ireland.pdf accessed 1 May 2021, 12.
29 See K. Hayward, 'When it Comes to the Irish Border, The Government's Reheated Customs Proposals Are Nothing Less Than Magical Thinking' (Prospect Magazine 14 May 2018) www.prospectmagazine.co.uk/politics/when-it-comes-to-the-irish-border-the-governments-reheated-customs-proposals-are-nothing-less-than-magical-thinking accessed 1 May 2021.
30 The Irish Border, Twitter post (8 February 2018) https://twitter.com/BorderIrish/status/961582201363148801 accessed 1 May 2021.
31 @BorderIrish, *I am the border, so I am* (HarperCollins 2019).
32 Protocol on Ireland/Northern Ireland in the Draft 'Agreement on the Withdrawal of the United Kingdom of Great Britain and Northern Ireland from the European Union and the European Atomic Energy Community, as Endorsed by Leaders at a Special Meeting of the European Council on 25 November 2018' (2018 Draft Agreement) (2018) https://assets.publishing.service.gov.uk/government/uploads/system/uploads/attachment_data/file/759019/25_November_Agreement_on_the_withdrawal_of_the_United_Kingdom

eventual 'frontstop' – both Protocols to avoid a hard border on the Island of Ireland and to uphold the Belfast Agreement/Good Friday Agreement. They were also central to major political ruptures within the UK Government and eventually to the political downfall of then Prime Minister May. Nonetheless, a Protocol was finally agreed upon between the UK Government and the EU –which is now discussed.

2.3 UK/EU relationships and the Northern Ireland Protocol

As noted in Chapter 1, there is significant interdependence between the UK and the rest of the EU and access to the EU market is extremely valuable for the UK agri-food industry, with the EU being the main export market for UK agri-food. The impacts of EU membership were widespread and profound, including free movement of goods and persons (without tariffs or non-tariff barriers); the existence of a level playing field across the EU, with common health, safety, welfare and labelling standards, and traceability requirements; protection against non-EU imports via the EU Commons External Tariff (CET), and membership of the CAP. Since the end of the transition period, the EU granted UK third-country status, confirming the UK meets the required animal health and biosecurity standards to keep exporting its agri-food products to the EU. However, for instance, British seed potatoes were not granted such status and exports from Great Britain to Northern Ireland and the EU are threatened, especially for the Scottish industry.[33] Brexit fundamentally changes the UK–EU relationship, but how precisely remains to be seen.

Despite how contested and long-drawn-out the negotiations were on the eventual UK/EU Withdrawal Agreement[34] (similar to the TCA), as noted in Chapter 1, it does little to resolve the future UK–EU relationship. It provided a transition period as a breathing space, with Article 184 noting that the parties must negotiate a future relationship in good faith,[35] and creates a frontstop to address issues posed by the Island of Ireland and the land border between Northern Ireland and the Republic of Ireland – the Northern Ireland Protocol. Whilst the TCA is addressed later in Chapter 5, it is important to consider the Protocol here

_of_Great_Britain_and_Northern_Ireland_from_the_European_Union_and_the_European _Atomic_Energy_Community.pdf accessed 1 May 2021.

33 J. Smail, 'Third Country Status for UK in Trade Deal with EU' (Food Manufacture 24 December 2020) www.foodmanufacture.co.uk/Article/2020/12/24/Brexit-third-country-status-for-UK-in-trade-deal-with-EU accessed 1 May 2021.

34 Agreement on the Withdrawal of the United Kingdom of Great Britain and Northern Ireland from the European Union and the European Atomic Energy Community [2019] OJ C384I /1.

35 The UK/EU Withdrawal Agreement is supplemented by the Political Declaration, intended to provide a basis for such negotiations. See Political Declaration Setting Out the Framework for the Future Relationship between the European Union and the United Kingdom [2019] OJ C384I /178.

as it was formed during the Brexit process and introduced new parameters that helped shape both the agricultural policies and related developments.

2.3.1 The functioning of the Northern Ireland Protocol

The Northern Ireland Protocol operates within the particular context of the general Brexit process, the UK/EU Withdrawal Agreement and the Belfast Agreement/ Good Friday Agreement. The Northern Ireland Protocol applies for four years after the transition period (unless it is superseded in part or entirely by a Future Relationship Agreement,[36] such as the TCA) and can continue to be extended where the Northern Ireland Assembly consents to this.[37] It aims at avoiding a hard border on the Island of Ireland, upholding the Belfast Agreement/Good Friday Agreement and broadly maintaining peace and cooperation across the Island.[38] To achieve this, it essentially provides for Northern Ireland to be treated like part of the EU on numerous fronts and, crucially, it would allow for goods (including agri-food products) to cross the border between Northern Ireland and the Republic of Ireland without inspections, checks, delays, quantitative restrictions or tariffs.[39] The one exception that the Protocol makes through omission is that EU Member States, including the Republic of Ireland, are not prevented from imposing *measures equivalent to* quantitative restrictions on goods coming from Northern Ireland – something that is prohibited between Member States under EU law.[40] To achieve this, it essentially provides for Northern Ireland to be treated like part of the EU on numerous fronts but crucially third party countries are not legally required to do the same, which raises concerns for onward trade, especially regarding 'rules of origin' requirements as discussed in Chapter 5.

However, it is not a free for all – Northern Ireland/the UK must comply with numerous conditions, including a swathe of EU law and especially many rules of the Single Market, in particular, the 2002 EU General Food Law[41] and

36 Northern Ireland Protocol, Article 13(8).
37 Ibid Article 17.
38 Ibid Article 1.
39 Ibid Article 5(5). This Article provides for Articles 30 and 110 of the Treaty on the Functioning of the European Union (TFEU) (regarding customs and taxes) to apply between the EU and Northern Ireland, and similarly prohibits quantitative restrictions. See Consolidated Version of the Treaty on the Functioning of the European Union (TFEU) [2008] OJ C115/47.
40 Whereas Article 7(1) of the Northern Ireland Protocol applies Articles 34 and 36 TFEU to goods imported from the EU and placed on the market in Northern Ireland, Article 5(5) only prohibits quantitative restrictions between the EU and Northern Ireland, without specifying also measures equivalent to quantitative restrictions or Article 34 TFEU. The difference in language and scope is significant.
41 Regulation (EC) No 178/2002 of the European Parliament and of the Council of 28 January 2002 Laying Down the General Principles and Requirements of Food Law, Establishing the European Food Safety Authority and Laying Down Procedures in Matters of Food Safety [2002] OJ L 31/1.

rules apply to aspects including pesticides, fertilisers and persistent organic pollutants.[42] In doing so, the responsibility for day-to-day implementation and application of the Protocol lies with the UK, whereas the EU is left with considerable powers regarding supervision and enforcement, including via the jurisdiction of the Court of Justice of the European Union (CJEU) to solve disputes under the Protocol.[43] The difficulty is that such division of roles is a blunt instrument that can lead to further conflict and even risk ruptures between the UK and the EU – especially in light of the political context of Brexit, the mantra of 'taking back control' and the UK's original 'red lines' including avoiding the jurisdiction of the CJEU. This is where the Joint Committee(s) created by the UK/EU Withdrawal Agreement are key.

The Joint Committee (including its specialised committees)[44] is comprised of representatives of both the EU and the UK.[45] It provides a mechanism for developing some specific aspects and also ironing out wrinkles at a political level.[46] This Committee is tasked with the smooth implementation and application of the UK/EU Withdrawal Agreement and its Protocols. This can be achieved, for instance, through agreeing to interpretations or amendments that are mutually acceptable to the EU and the UK. Consequently, the UK/EU Withdrawal Agreement could be concluded even though the Northern Ireland Protocol's fine details were yet to be determined – as, in principle, these details could be resolved by the dedicated Joint Committee on the Northern Ireland Protocol[47] during the transition period or later, as appropriate. It is important to note that there has been some significant progress made by the Joint Committee on the Protocol's implementation and that the TCA also indirectly impacts its implementation.[48]

2.3.2 *The Northern Ireland Protocol and agri-food products*

Three key aspects within the Protocol are directly relevant to agriculture,[49] being the potential challenges or restrictions on both (i) exports and imports between Northern Ireland and Great Britain; (ii) the focus of EU law that Northern Ireland must continue to abide by; and (iii) the control of state aid.[50] Before examin-

42 Northern Ireland Protocol, Annex 2.
43 Ibid Articles 12 and 13.
44 The Joint Committee can also sit in the form of specialised committees – in which case the European Commission and UK Government will designate appropriate co-chairs.
45 Typically co-chaired by a UK Government Minister and an EU Commissioner.
46 UK/EU Withdrawal Agreement, Article 164 and Northern Ireland Protocol, Article 15.
47 UK/EU Withdrawal Agreement, Article 165.
48 However, challenges still arise and the UK Government again threatened to breach the Protocol, leading to the EU commencing legal action against the UK. See J. Campbell, 'Brexit: EU to Begin Legal Action Over Alleged NI Protocol Breach' (BBC News 15 March 2021) https://www.bbc.com/news/uk-northern-ireland-56381046 accessed 1 May 2021. This is addressed in Chapter 5, Section 5.2.
49 A wide range of other aspects is also relevant but is beyond the scope of this book.
50 The Northern Ireland Protocol' Command Paper addresses some of these issues. See UK Government, 'The Northern Ireland Protocol' (Cm 346, December 2020) https://assets

ing the content and implications of the Protocol, it is worth noting again that the obligations under the UK/EU Withdrawal Agreement for the UK to ensure compliance and act in good faith[51] apply equally in relation to the Protocol.

2.3.2.1 Non-tariff barriers and tariffs

As has been stated numerous times,[52] by avoiding restrictions and extra procedures or requirements between Northern Ireland and the Republic of Ireland, whilst still leaving the EU, some restrictions come into play for the border between Northern Ireland and Great Britain (Wales, Scotland and England). The extent of these will depend largely on the UK/Northern Ireland's implementation of the Protocol and decisions by the Joint Committee, as well as the evolution of the TCA and any regulatory divergence between Great Britain and the EU.

Regarding exports from Northern Ireland to Great Britain (whether inputs or outputs in the agri-food supply chain), this is arguably the simplest and least arduous aspect, both for individual actors and for Northern Ireland and the UK to implement, reflecting the Protocol's statement that Northern Ireland should have unfettered access to the Great Britain and EU markets – which could positively impact Northern Irish businesses compared to a situation where no Protocol applied.[53] The EU only imposes restrictions on Northern Ireland necessary to comply with international law.[54] Under this, some limited requirements must be fulfilled, which include summary export declarations for the EU Customs Code and checks to ensure compliance with the Convention on International Trade on Endangered Species (CITES).[55] To what extent this requires physical infrastructure at ports or paper documentation is unclear, but some mechanism is required to facilitate this. It is possible for Great Britain/the UK to impose further checks and restrictions on Northern Irish goods entering Great Britain, but again Northern Ireland's 'integral place' within the UK is recognised in the

.publishing.service.gov.uk/government/uploads/system/uploads/attachment_data/file/950601/Northern_Ireland_Protocol_-_Command_Paper.pdf accessed 1 May 2021.

51 UK/EU Withdrawal Agreement, Articles 4 and 5 respectively.

52 See K. Hayward and T. Smith, 'Making the Irish Sea Border Work Will Require Partnership, Cross-Border Cooperation, and Preparation' (LSE Blog 15 May 2020) https://blogs.lse.ac.uk/brexit/2020/05/15/making-the-irish-sea-border-work-will-require-partnership-cross-border-cooperation-and-preparation/ accessed 1 May 2021; A. Stojanovic, 'Brexit Deal: The Northern Ireland Protocol' (Institute for Government 5 February 2020) www.instituteforgovernment.org.uk/explainers/brexit-deal-northern-ireland-protocol accessed 1 May 2021; T. Edgington and C. Morris, 'Brexit: What is the Northern Ireland Protocol and Why Are There Checks?' (BBC News 15 March 2021) www.bbc.com/news/explainers-53724381 accessed 1 May 2021; and J. Campbell, 'Brexit: What Are the Backstop Options?' (BBC News 16 October 2019) www.bbc.com/news/uk-northern-ireland-politics-44615404 accessed 1 May 2021.

53 Although this entails more restrictions than during EU membership.

54 Northern Ireland Protocol, Article 6(1).

55 Convention on International Trade in Endangered Species of Wild Fauna and Flora (1973).

Protocol and both the EU and the UK are to use 'their best endeavours' to facilitate such trade.[56] To this end, the UK has stated that it would take steps to facilitate Northern Irish 'qualifying goods', including agri-food products, continuing to have free access to markets in Great Britain, for example, with no export declarations, checks or controls.[57] The UK has also legislated to ensure that no tariffs are due on such goods going from Northern Ireland to Great Britain, irrespective of any potential tariffs between the EU and the UK.[58] However, it is worth noting that any UK restrictions on EU goods entering Great Britain (especially if re-routed through Northern Ireland)[59] are likely to at least cause delays for Northern Irish agri-food products – and at a minimum the UK is required to provide some checks to comply with international law obligations.

Imports from Great Britain to Northern Ireland: again, there is positive rhetoric in the Northern Ireland Protocol on this front, but the practicalities are very challenging. At the very least, from an EU perspective, those importing agricultural products from Great Britain into Northern Ireland need, for instance, plant or health certificates,[60] continued notification via the EU's TRACES online system[61] and to submit to SPS checks.[62] This last point, in particular, requires extra infrastructure and resources at ports in Northern Ireland to ensure adequate border control posts, with the alternative being even greater delays and risks of agri-food products such as milk perishing or animal health and welfare issues. Beyond SPS controls, there also needs to be some checks to ensure products comply with other EU rules/standards – the extent of such checks may depend on the level of regulatory divergence between the EU and Great Britain. The TCA's inclusion

56 Northern Ireland Protocol, Article 6(2).

57 UK Government (n50), especially pages 7–9. This is also reflected in Section 47 of the Internal Market Act.

58 Customs (Northern Ireland) (EU Exit) Regulations 2020. See more generally KPMG, 'VAT and Customs Changes – December 2020: The Key Changes for Businesses Operating on the Island of Ireland' (22 December 2020) https://home.kpmg/ie/en/home/insights/2020/12/brexit-vat-and-customs.html accessed 1 May 2021.

59 These are not to benefit from the same advantages as Northern Irish qualifying goods. This differential treatment is to be achieved by 'anti-avoidance provisions'. See UK Government (n50) 7. Anti-avoidance measures regarding customs are now reflected in provisions such as the Taxation (Post-transition Period) Act 2020, Section 2.

60 The Northern Ireland Retail Consortium has estimated a potential extra cost of £40,000 for every shipment of animal products from Great Britain into Northern Ireland, based simply on animal health certificates. See D. Hipwell and J. Mayes, 'Northern Ireland Faces Brexit Food Time Bomb on New Paperwork' (Bloomberg 4 August 2020) www.bloomberg.com/news/articles/2020-08-04/northern-ireland-faces-brexit-food-time-bomb-on-new-paperwork?sref=yMmXm5Iy accessed 1 May 2021.

61 European Commission, 'TRACES' https://ec.europa.eu/food/animals/traces_en accessed 1 May 2021.

62 M. Dobbs and L. Petetin, 'Agriculture: Environmental, Food and Animal Health Standards' in H. Kassin, A. Jordan and S. Ennis (eds), *UK Regulation after Brexit* (The UK in a Changing Europe 25 February 2021) https://ukandeu.ac.uk/wp-content/uploads/2021/02/UK-regulation-after-Brexit.pdf accessed 1 May 2021, 51.

of a non-regression principle helps maintain standards and may promote continued regulatory alignment (or rather dynamic alignment) but provides no such guarantee.[63] There are consequently considerable non-tariff barriers for imports from Great Britain into Northern Ireland, with impacts for regulators, officials, industry and consumers.[64]

Further, issues arise in the context of tariffs. Article 5 of the Protocol addresses the possibility of customs duties on goods travelling from outside of the EU, including Great Britain, into Northern Ireland, unless those goods are not deemed 'at risk' of subsequently entering the EU via Northern Ireland. However, such a good automatically '*shall be* considered to be at risk.... *unless* it is established that that good: (a) will not be subject to commercial processing in Northern Ireland; ***and*** fulfils the criteria established by the Joint Committee' (emphasis added).[65] It would seem on the face of the provision that it will be quite difficult for goods, including agri-food products, imported into Northern Ireland from Great Britain to *not* be considered 'at risk'. Furthermore, criteria aside momentarily, clearly if there were significant tariffs imposed on agri-food products going from Great Britain into the EU or if there were significant regulatory divergence between Great Britain and the EU, this would logically increase the risk of such products travelling on to the EU via Northern Ireland. However, the Joint Committee helped resolve this to a large extent late in the day in December 2020 by limiting what is deemed 'at risk' by excluding goods moved by 'authorised' traders (trusted trader scheme),[66] or where the EU tariff is zero or lower than the UK tariff (for non-UK, non-EU goods).[67] This has been eased further by the TCA excluding tariffs between the EU and the UK for the moment,[68] but this does not remain guaranteed for the future and consequently the Joint Committee decision is crucial for easing trade between Great Britain and Northern Ireland.

However, none of this amounts to continued EU membership and neither the Joint Committee decision nor the TCA remove the need for SPS checks, customs declarations or general administrative burdens,[69] which are having

63 TCA, Articles 387 and 391.
64 Dobbs and Petetin (n62) 51.
65 Northern Ireland Protocol, Article 5(2).
66 UK Government (n50) especially pages 9–12.
67 UK Government, 'Decision of the Withdrawal Agreement Joint Committee on the Determination of Goods Not at Risk' (17 December 2020) https://assets.publishing.service.gov.uk/government/uploads/system/uploads/attachment_data/file/949846/Decision_of_the_Withdrawal_Agreement_Joint_Committee_on_the_determination_of_goods_not_at_risk.pdf accessed 1 May 2021; and J. Curtis, 'Joint Committee Decisions on the Northern Ireland Protocol' (House of Commons Library, CBP-9102, 23 December 2020) https://researchbriefings.files.parliament.uk/documents/CBP-9102/CBP-9102.pdf accessed 1 May 2021.
68 TCA, Article 21.
69 A. Connolly, 'What the Brexit Deal Means for Northern Ireland' (The UK in a Changing Europe 31 December 2020) https://ukandeu.ac.uk/what-the-brexit-deal-means-for-northern-ireland/ accessed 1 May 2021; Dobbs and Petetin (n62) 51; and M. Dobbs,

considerable impacts on imports into Northern Ireland – including, early on in 2021, significant delays at ports and many suppliers ceasing to provide agri-food products to Northern Ireland due to the costs and/or complexities involved.[70] This is also despite the Joint Committee using non-binding 'unilateral declarations'[71] to provide grace periods for full-compliance with the EU's SPS regime by approved suppliers (three months – April 2021),[72] or regarding certain chilled meats such as sausages (six months – July 2021)[73] and some rules on human and veterinary medicines (one year – January 2022).[74] The system is close to breaking even with the Joint Committee's effort to smooth the implementation and the various grace periods. The challenges for industry are acknowledged by the UK's unilateral decision to extend some grace periods until October 2021 – however, such unilateral decisions are in breach of the Protocol,[75] increase the stresses

---

'Northern Ireland's Agricultural Quagmire: How to Develop a Sustainable Agricultural Policy?' in I. Antonopoulos, M. Bell, A. Cavoski and L. Petetin (eds), *The Governance of Agriculture in Post-Brexit UK* (Routledge, forthcoming 2022).

70 See S. McBride, 'System for Getting Supplies to Northern Ireland May Be Five Days from Collapse Due to Irish Sea Border, Hauliers Warn Michael Gove' (NewsLetter 9 January 2021) www.newsletter.co.uk/news/politics/system-getting-supplies-northern-ireland-may-be-five-days-collapse-due-irish-sea-border-hauliers-warn-michael-gove-3090602 accessed 1 May 2021. This resulted in empty food shelves across Northern Ireland. See C. Andrews, 'Brexit: Why Are the Shelves Empty in some Supermarkets?' (BBC News 7 January 2021) www.bbc.co.uk/news/uk-northern-ireland-55575988 accessed 1 May 2021.

71 Curtis (n67) 7.

72 UK Government, 'Unilateral Declarations by the United Kingdom of Great Britain and Northern Ireland and the European Union in the Withdrawal Agreement Joint Committee on Official Certifications' (17 December 2020) https://assets.publishing.service.gov.uk/government/uploads/system/uploads/attachment_data/file/946284/Unilateral_declarations_by_the_United_Kingdom_of_Great_Britain_and_Northern_Ireland_and_the_European_Union_in_the_Withdrawal_Agreement_Joint_Committee_on_official_certification.pdf accessed 1 May 2021.

73 UK Government, 'Unilateral Declarations by the United Kingdom of Great Britain and Northern Ireland and the European Union in the Withdrawal Agreement Joint Committee on Meat Products' (17 December 2020) https://assets.publishing.service.gov.uk/government/uploads/system/uploads/attachment_data/file/946283/Unilateral_declarations_by_the_United_Kingdom_of_Great_Britain_and_Northern_Ireland_and_the_European_Union_in_the_Withdrawal_Agreement_Joint_Committee_on_meat_products.pdf accessed 1 May 2021.

74 UK Government, 'Unilateral Declarations by the European Union and the United Kingdom of Great Britain and Northern Ireland in the Withdrawal Agreement Joint Committee on Human and Veterinary Medicines' (17 December 2020) https://assets.publishing.service.gov.uk/government/uploads/system/uploads/attachment_data/file/946659/Unilateral_declarations_by_the_European_Union_and_the_United_Kingdom_of_Great_Britain_and_Northern_Ireland_in_the_Withdrawal_Agreement_Joint_Committee_on_human_and_veterinary_medicines.pdf accessed 1 May 2021.

75 J. Campbell, 'Brexit: EU Says UK Grace Period Extension Breaches International Law' (BBC News 3 March 2021) www.bbc.com/news/uk-northern-ireland-56262527 accessed 1 May 2021.

on the Northern Ireland/UK/EU relationships[76] and thereby risk undermining further the operation of the Protocol and the precarious position of Northern Ireland at the intersection of the two unions (UK and EU). The UK also further delayed elements such as import controls on EU goods arriving into Great Britain (a matter for itself and not a breach of the Protocol) until January 2022.[77] More recently, the Permanent Secretary of DAERA stated that it would not be possible to have permanent facilities in place in Northern Ireland to undertake post-Brexit checks until 2023 – with a limited number currently being undertaken in temporary facilities and 'repurposed port buildings'.[78] Permanent facilities will be essential following the end of the grace periods, especially for SPS checks.

2.3.2.2 The Protocol and the application of EU law

The Protocol provides for vast swathes of EU law to continue to apply in Northern Ireland (and even in some instances across the UK), but with some noticeable gaps. In particular, Article 5(4) provides for the continued application of EU law listed in Annex 2 of the Protocol, including subsequent EU laws that amend or replace these laws.[79] Annex 2 is extensive and covers issues across the supply chain from farm to fork, including emissions from agricultural tractors, technical regulations, SPS, pesticides, biocides, fertilisers, feed, animal welfare, alien species and waste. It is clearly not just relevant to production, but later stages also as it includes aspects such as the General Food Law (encompassing the precautionary principle applied to human health), marketing framework, nutrition and health claims and organic food criteria. It also addresses some potentially controversial issues such as genetically modified organisms (GMOs). These laws apply largely unchanged to Northern Ireland, but with adjustments to address that Northern Ireland is no longer part of the EU.[80] For instance, EU laboratories and officials bear ultimate responsibility for ensuring procedures are followed and standards met and also determining authorisations or prohibitions of specific products, including for agri-food products. Crucially, the EU continues to play its supervision and enforcement roles here and CJEU judgments are applicable, including in light of the environmental principles found in the TFEU.[81] Overall,

76 Campbell (n48).
77 J. Partridge, 'Eight Major Government U-Turns on Post-Brexit Controls' (The Guardian 13 March 2021) www.theguardian.com/politics/2021/mar/13/eight-major-government-u-turns-on-post-brexit-controls accessed 1 May 2021.
78 D. Young, 'Permanent Facilities for Brexit Checks at NI Ports Will Not Be Ready "Until 2023"' (Irish Examiner 15 April 2021) www.irishexaminer.com/news/arid-40266926.html accessed 1 May 2021.
79 Northern Ireland Protocol, Article 13. It is worth noting that under Article 13(4), the Joint Committee can also decide that new EU laws that fall within the scope of the Protocol but do not technically amend or replace laws listed in the Annexes can be added to the Protocol.
80 See Northern Ireland Protocol, Article 7(2).
81 TFEU, Article 191.

this provides some legal certainty for Northern Ireland's agri-food industry and officials, as well as providing a relatively level playing field for regulation between Northern Ireland and the EU – thereby justifying the continued open border on the Island. Further, it should be highlighted that this does not prevent Northern Ireland from developing its own agricultural policy, but merely creates some parameters.

The issue of GMOs bears highlighting here. Annex 2 provides for the majority of the key EU GMO laws (with slight adjustments) to apply to Northern Ireland. This includes not merely laws on Genetically Modified (GM) food and feed,[82] but also on GM cultivation and overarching elements regarding coexistence of GM crops alongside non-GM crops[83] – crucial in the context of the shared land border with Ireland. This will mean that the EU will continue to determine which GMOs are authorised for sale, use, consumption and cultivation in Northern Ireland. Northern Ireland's role will remain as it currently stands – primarily on implementation and enforcement. Westminster will only be relevant when it comes to placing Northern Irish agri-food products on the Great British market.[84]

Considering the UK Government's welcoming attitude towards biotechnology and desire to develop advantageous traits,[85] it is very possible that there will be future divergence between the EU and the UK regarding approaches and authorisations.[86] As Northern Ireland remains bound by EU law here, this means that there will also be divergence between Northern Ireland and the rest of the UK.[87] Interestingly, EU law introduced an opt-out clause in 2016 that permitted Member States or parts thereof to impose restrictions on cultivation of GMOs – potentially even without justifications.[88] Northern Ireland availed of this option,

82 Regulation (EC) No 1829/2003 of the European Parliament and of the Council of 22 September 2003 on Genetically Modified Food and Feed [2003] OJ L268/1; and Regulation (EC) No 1830/2003 of the European Parliament and of the Council of 22 September 2003 Concerning the Traceability and Labelling of Genetically Modified Organisms and the Traceability of Food and Feed Products Produced from Genetically Modified Organisms and Amending Directive 2001/18/EC [2003] OJ L268/24.

83 Directive 2001/18/EC of the European Parliament and of the Council of 12 March 2001 on the Deliberate Release into the Environment of Genetically Modified Organisms and Repealing Council Directive 90/220/EEC [2001] OJ L106/1.

84 Such decisions could impact rules in Wales and Scotland due to the Internal Market Act or future trade deals discussed in Chapter 5, Section 5.2.3. Interestingly, GMOs are no longer to be subject of a common framework. See House of Lords, Common Frameworks Scrutiny Committee, 'Common Frameworks: Building a Cooperative Union' (1st Report of Session 2019–21, HL Paper 259, 31 March 2021) 16 and 60.

85 See Chapter 1, Section 1.1.

86 A. Engel and L. Petetin, 'International Obligations and Devolved Powers – Ploughing through Competences and GM Crops' (2018) 20(1) *Environmental Law Review* 16.

87 The Internal Market Act discussed in Chapter 5, Section 5.2.3 would indicate that only limited divergence across Great Britain may be possible, unless facilitated by a common framework.

88 L. Petetin, 'Managing Novel Food Technologies and Member States' Interests: Shifting More Powers towards the Member States?' in M. Varju (eds), *Between Compliance and Par-*

alongside Wales and Scotland. It would seem that Northern Ireland will continue to be able to avail of that clause – subject to the UK Government making the relevant request on behalf of Northern Ireland to the EU as and when needed. This could open a Pandora's box in the future if the UK Government determines that the use of the opt-out would be detrimental to the UK internal market or trade deals – would the UK Government be willing to facilitate Northern Ireland opting out from cultivation of specific GM crops if this might impact negatively on the UK internal market or trade?

However, returning to Annex 2 of the Protocol, there are noticeable gaps in the applicable EU law, in particular regarding environmental protection. For instance, what of nature, water or environmental governance? What of the Habitats Directive or Nitrates Directive[89] especially with the controls on storing and spreading slurry or hedge cutting? These are essential to environmental protection and are relevant to the level playing field yet are missing from the Protocol, creating substantive gaps in environmental protection and siloed approaches. Furthermore, environmental principles and rights that were laid out in the backstop in the previous draft UK/EU Withdrawal Agreement[90] are nowhere to be seen and the only statement regarding the level playing field has moved[91] to the non-binding Political Declaration (and to a certain extent the relevant provisions of the TCA). Consequently, for aspects such as nature protection that are not included in the Protocol, the responsibility lies foursquare on Northern Ireland – and without the support of EU environmental governance mechanisms. This could of course change either if Northern Ireland/the UK relies on Article 11 of the Protocol, enabling developing cooperation within the remit of the Belfast Agreement/Good Friday Agreement, or if the TCA or any subsequent EU-UK agreement addressed environmental issues. As shall be seen in Chapter 5 (and noted previously), the TCA does include a non-regression obligation and only

ticularism: Member State Interests and European Union Law (Springer 2019) 233; and M. Dobbs, 'Genetically Modified Crops, Agricultural Sustainability and National Opt-Outs – Enclosure as the Loophole?' (2017) 54(4) *Common Market Law Review* 1093.

89 Respectively, Council Directive 92/43/EEC of 21 May 1992 on the Conservation of Natural Habitats and of Wild Fauna and Flora [1992] OJ L206/7; and Council Directive 91/676/EEC of 12 December 1991 Concerning the Protection of Waters against Pollution Caused by Nitrates from Agricultural Sources [1991] OJ L375/1.

90 See Northern Ireland Protocol in the 2018 Draft Agreement (n32), Annex 4, Part Two, Articles 2 and 3. On this point, see B. Moore, 'Loosening the Constraints: The Environment in the Revised Brexit Deal' (Brexit and Environment Network 17 October 2019) www.brexitenvironment.co.uk/2019/10/17/revised-brexit-deal/ accessed 1 May 2021; and C. Burns, V. Gravey and M. Dobbs, 'Written Evidence on the UK Environment Bill for the Committee on Environment, Agriculture and Rural Affairs of the Northern Ireland Assembly' (March 2020) www.niassembly.gov.uk/globalassets/committee-blocks/agriculture-environment-and-rural-affairs/2017---2022/brexit-and-environment-group-briefing-paper.pdf accessed 1 May 2021.

91 References to the level playing field were found in Article 6 of the Northern Ireland Protocol in the 2018 Draft Agreement (n 32), supported by the provisions in Annex 4.

addresses some environmental issues.[92] This clearly does not mean that Northern Ireland is free to act entirely independently when it comes to the environment,[93] as it still operates in a system of multilevel governance where, for instance, the UK Government can sign up to or leave international environmental agreements that create obligations for Northern Ireland. However, EU environmental law tends to be far more specific and more onerous than international environmental laws, with strong governance mechanisms including the European Commission and CJEU to help with enforcement, and this loss will be strongly felt.[94]

2.3.2.3 State aid provisions

Article 10 provides for the continued application of EU state aid law (outlined in Annex 5) to Northern Ireland and indeed to the UK where this would affect trade in Northern Ireland. For example, if the UK were to grant state aid to a business in England that grows seed or produces fertiliser that is then sold cheaply in Northern Ireland, this may lead to Northern Irish producers gaining an economic advantage over EU producers who do not have similar access to seed or fertiliser at cheap prices. Crucially, Article 10(2) provides an exception to this regarding agricultural support where certain criteria are met regarding the overall maximum level of expenditure and a minimum level (83% initially)[95] spent in compliance with Annex 2 of the Agreement on Agriculture of the WTO (that is the Green Box provisions on financial support that do not or minimally distort trade and which can address environmental objectives). This is expanded upon by Annex 6 of the Protocol, which provides for these to link to both UK and EU expenditure and agricultural policies, but with the Joint Committee to make the final decision. If the Committee cannot agree set figures, then EU state aid law applies instead. The implications of Article 10 are profound – it is clearly very valuable for Northern Ireland to fall within the exception, provided that the Joint Committee can come to an agreement on the parameters involved, as has now been achieved for an initial unspecified period at least, with provision for regular review.[96] However, the provision also has the potential to extend EU state aid

92 See Chapter 5, Section 5.1.2.

93 V. Gravey and L. Whitten, 'The NI Protocol and the Environment: The Implications for Northern Ireland, Ireland and the UK' (2021) (Brexit and Environment, Environmental Governance Island of Ireland Network Policy Briefs 1/2021) www.brexitenvironment.co.uk/research-projects/egii/ accessed 1 May 2021.

94 C. Brennan, M. Dobbs, and V. Gravey, 'Out of the Frying Pan, Into the Fire? Environmental Governance Vulnerabilities in Post-Brexit Northern Ireland' (2019) 21(2) *Environmental Law Review* 84.

95 As agreed under Article 3 of UK Government, 'Decision of the Withdrawal Agreement Joint Committee on Agricultural Subsidies' (17 December 2020) https://assets.publishing.service.gov.uk/government/uploads/system/uploads/attachment_data/file/949845/Decision_of_the_Withdrawal_Agreement_Joint_Committee_on_agricultural_subsidies.pdf accessed 1 May 2021.

96 ibid.

law to much of UK subsidies in practice, thereby impacting upon broad policy approaches – once again, the non-binding unilateral declarations between the UK and the EU come to the fore here, with the EU declaring that it will not extend EU state aid law unless the measures are liable to have a relevant effect on trade, 'based on the real foreseeable effects of the measure'.[97]

2.3.2.4 Consequences for Northern Ireland

Northern Ireland is in a halfway house situation. It is no longer in the EU, but it is treated like it is to a significant extent – but with some gaps and variations as noted. It is part of the UK's customs territory and can be part of UK trade deals, but only so long as it does not conflict with the Protocol.[98] Northern Ireland remains in the UK and is to have unfettered access (in so much as possible). This halfway house clearly brings some important advantages relative to the rest of the UK – with largely unchanged access to the EU markets and preferential access to Great Britain markets compared to EU Member States. Likewise the Northern Irish market is open to the EU and supposedly to Great Britain (subject to the points discussed above). Northern Ireland can therefore become a more attractive trading partner for the EU (compared to Great Britain) and for Great Britain (relative to the EU) – reflected in the significant increase in trade between Northern Ireland and Ireland since January 2021 compared to the decrease in trade between Great Britain and the Republic of Ireland.[99]

There are also considerably downsides. Brexit has led to significant delays and supply chain interruptions across the two islands[100] – relative attractiveness may have increased, but trade overall is nonetheless more difficult and the implications remain unclear. Further, Northern Ireland is not treated identically to the rest of the UK and does not have completely free access to markets in Great Britain. How substantive those hindrances are to access markets in Great Britain will be dependent on three factors: the continued work of the Joint Committee; regulatory alignment/divergence; and the TCA and any further developments between the EU and the UK. It also will be impacted by any other trade agreements the UK concludes, due to their knock-on effects on these three factors. It begs the

97 UK Government, 'Unilateral Declarations by the European Union and the United Kingdom of Great Britain and Northern Ireland in the Withdrawal Agreement Joint Committee on Article 10(1) of the Protocol' (17 December 2020) https://assets.publishing.service.gov.uk/government/uploads/system/uploads/attachment_data/file/946286/Unilateral_declarations_by_the_European_Union_and_the_United_Kingdom_of_Great_Britain_and_Northern_Ireland_in_the_Withdrawal_Agreement_Joint_Committee_on_Article_10_1__of_the_Protocol.pdf accessed 1 May 2021.

98 Northern Ireland Protocol, Article 4.

99 J. Campbell, 'Cross-Border Trade in Ireland "Has Increased Dramatically" in 2021' (BBC 15 April 2021) www.bbc.com/news/uk-northern-ireland-56760634 accessed 1 May 2021.

100 See Hipwell and Mayes (n60); and G. Ní Aodha, 'How Has Trade between Ireland and Great Britain Been Affected in the First Two Weeks of Brexit?' (The Journal 17 January 2021) www.thejournal.ie/brexit-trade-changes-5324709-Jan2021/ accessed 1 May 2021.

question as to how much Northern Ireland's position and the Protocol may influence these issues also. Could protecting Northern Ireland's unique place in the UK and simultaneously (effectively) in the EU lead to regulatory alignment and a closer relationship under the TCA and beyond? Could it also thereby impact external trade agreements, if protecting Northern Ireland's position and upholding the Protocol are taken as conditions precedent to the conclusion of any future agreements and factored in at an early stage? If so, the corollary is that this could help cement trust within the Joint Committee and iron out wrinkles in the implementation of the Protocol. In the end, the work of the Joint Committee and the negotiation of the TCA have been mutually beneficial to Northern Ireland, the EU and Great Britain.

It has not been entirely smooth operating for the Protocol, with *faux pas* by both the EU and the UK, as further discussed in Chapter 5. For instance, in autumn 2020, the UK proposed the Internal Market Bill 2019–2021 that would breach the Protocol (and therefore international law), but supposedly only in a 'very limited and specific way'[101] in order to protect the UK's internal market – leading to the EU threatening to take legal action,[102] before the UK eventually amended the Bill to address these concerns (partially in light of the progress of the Joint Committee in implementing the Protocol). Then in January 2021, the EU Commission briefly indicated that it was going to use Article 16 to prevent the movement of Covid-19 vaccines into Northern Ireland and thereby into Great Britain, following disputes over shortfalls in vaccine supplies despite purchase agreements.[103] Article 16's safeguard procedure enables either the UK or the EU to take unilateral measures, but only where the Protocol's applications lead, for instance, to serious economic, social or environmental differences that are liable to persist or to diversion of trade. The EU's move to use Article 16 understandably caused significant consternation, including immediate calls for the UK to trigger Article 16 itself for other purposes, before the EU backtracked swiftly and declared it an 'oversight'.[104] However, this has raised the spectre of the liberal use of Article 16.[105] Separately, in March 2021 the UK once more

101 See comment made by the Secretary of State for Northern Ireland, Brandon Lewis in HC Deb 8 September 2020, vol 679, col 509.

102 European Commission, 'Withdrawal Agreement: European Commission Sends Letter of Formal Notice to the United Kingdom for Breach of Its Obligations' (1 October 2020) https://ec.europa.eu/commission/presscorner/detail/en/ip_20_1798 accessed 1 May 2021.

103 Y. Lowe, 'Explainer: What Is Article 16 of the Northern Ireland Protocol?' (The Guardian 29 January 2021) www.theguardian.com/uk-news/2021/jan/29/explainer-what-is-article-16-of-the-northern-ireland-protocol accessed 1 May 2021.

104 J. Curtis, 'Northern Ireland Protocol: Article 16 and EU Vaccine Export Controls' (House of Commons Library, Insight 2 February 2021) https://commonslibrary.parliament.uk/northern-ireland-protocol-article-16-and-eu-vaccine-export-controls/ accessed 1 May 2021.

105 J. Sargeant, 'The Article 16 Vaccine Row Is Over – But the Damage Has Been Done' (Institute for Government 30 January 2021) www.instituteforgovernment.org.uk/blog/article-16-vaccine-row accessed 1 May 2021.

threatened not to implement the Protocol fully, through the unilateral extensions of grace periods for goods travelling from Great Britain into Northern Ireland.[106] The EU has responded by again threatening legal action[107] and, even if eventually resolved amicably, the dispute demonstrates the challenges in implementation and the potential for further conflict in the future. Brexit without a very close union between the EU and the UK as a whole simply creates significant hurdles and administrative burdens in a highly time-pressured context, not merely for ordinary individuals and businesses, but also for the regulators and state.

Returning more generally to the UK, the Northern Ireland Protocol addresses elements regarding one specific issue – the border on the Island of Ireland. It is not concerned with the UK as a whole, other than recognising Northern Ireland's position within it. However, it has the potential to impact the rest of the UK, including internal UK relationships and via the UK's relationship with the EU. The UK/EU Withdrawal Agreement, as noted in Chapter 1, also does not resolve the broader EU-UK relationship for the long-run. It leaves numerous aspects to be addressed, including tariffs, general controls on goods between the EU and Great Britain, free movement of workers (other than members of the Common Travel Area), regulatory alignment or divergence and level playing fields. Beyond simply concerns over gaps, such disparity in treatment between Northern Ireland and the rest of the UK raises valid concerns regarding the UK internal market and an 'Irish sea border'. Both the unresolved relationship with the EU and the disparity in treatment between Northern Ireland and Great Britain have the potential to influence the development of policies across the UK, including those relevant to agriculture as shall be seen across the following chapters. However, whilst the recently concluded TCA does not supersede the Protocol or lead to Great Britain having the same relationship with the EU as Northern Ireland does, it builds significantly upon the UK/EU Withdrawal Agreement and its implementation and evolution will be a major factor in future developments, as discussed in Chapter 5.

2.4 The WTO Agreements and relevant disciplines

When focusing on agriculture and agri-food products, four WTO Agreements covering both tariffs and non-tariff barriers are key[108] – the General Agreement on Tariffs and Trade (GATT),[109] the Agreement on Agriculture,[110] the Sanitary

106 Campbell (n75).
107 Campbell (n48).
108 Other instruments such as the Uruguay Round Agreement on Trade-Related Intellectual Property Rights (1994) and the Convention for the Protection of New Varieties of Plants (1991) (and originally adopted in 1961) are also relevant to agriculture, including through incentivizing the development of plant genetic resources or through leading to their control and 'enclosure'. See Dobbs (n88). However, these are beyond the scope of the book.
109 Uruguay Round General Agreement on Tariffs and Trade (1994).
110 Uruguay Round Agreement on Agriculture (1994).

and Phyto-Sanitary (SPS) Agreement[111] and the Technical Barriers to Trade (TBT) Agreement.[112] These Agreements and their disciplines[113] are all distinct in their design, focus and coverage but are complementary and their provisions bind the UK.[114]

2.4.1 WTO – the fundamentals

At an international level, the role of the WTO (and its precursor, the GATT) is to liberalise trade by removing tariff barriers and non-tariff barriers to trade.[115] Historically under the GATT regime, emphasis was placed on trade in goods. Basic principles underlying the GATT include the principle of non-discrimination with the most-favoured nation (MFN) and national treatment principles (Articles I and III), reciprocity (Article I), transparency (Article X) and the use of tariffs (customs duties) rather than relying on quantitative measures (prohibition under Article XI) to protect national industries.[116] Nonetheless, a measure contrary to GATT provisions (such as Articles I or III) can potentially be justified by one of the general exceptions under Article XX if the measures are necessary to protect objectives such as the environment, human, animal or plant life or health, or public morality.[117]

The 1986–1993 Uruguay Round negotiations led to the establishment of the WTO in 1995, which is crucial for two reasons. First, the WTO is an organisation that operates within the boundaries of public international law when concluding further agreements and resolving disputes. Indeed, apart from its focus on trade liberalisation and reducing non-tariff barriers, one of the main reasons why states want to join the WTO is its dispute settlement system, with its Dispute

111 Uruguay Round Agreement on the Application of Sanitary and Phytosanitary Measures (1994).

112 Uruguay Round Agreement on Technical Barriers to Trade (1994).

113 'Disciplines' is used in the WTO context to encompass regimes and provisions.

114 The impact and consequences of these agreements on the UK is explored in detail in Chapters 3, 4 and 5.

115 Liberalised trade theory postulates that free trade is beneficial to world economies based on the economic theory of 'comparative advantage', developed by Ricardo. See D. Ricardo, *On the Principles of Political Economy and Taxation* (John Murray 1817). However, a number of disputed assumptions underlie the basic theory of comparative advantage, such as full employment or the immobility of capital and labour. As such, there are still 'reasons' for maintaining protectionist trade policies such as infant industry, unfair competition, employment or environmental protection. See R. Schumacher, 'Deconstructing the Theory of Comparative Advantage' (2013) 2 *World Economic Review* 83.

116 For a general overview of WTO law, see P. Van den Bossche and D. Prévost, *Essentials of WTO Law* (2nd edn, CUP 2021). For a more detailed account, see P. Van den Bossche and W. Zdouc, *The Law and Policy of the World Trade Organization Text, Cases, and Materials* (5th edn, CUP 2021).

117 The role of the exceptions under GATT Article XX is explored in Chapter 5, Section 5.1.4.2.

Settlement Body and Appellate Body. The WTO's strong procedural rules are attractive to Members, especially due to its speediness[118] as well as its multilateral character.[119] But most importantly, it is the automatic and compulsory character of the dispute settlement system[120] that is of particular interest and is the envy of other international institutions. This mechanism means that when a state joins the WTO, it consents to future WTO dispute resolution; Members do not need to consent to each dispute resolution procedure they are a party to.[121] Second, WTO law has moved from a system of rules simply prohibiting trade measures (such as quantitative restrictions) to include also a system of obligations requiring positive actions from Members (for example, with SPS and TBT measures) to diminish non-tariff barriers.

2.4.2 The intricacies of the Agreement on Agriculture

The GATT is mostly silent about agriculture. The lack of application of three GATT principles highlights the specific status that agriculture enjoyed for major agricultural traders in the 1940s and its exceptionalism. First, there was a limited application of tariff bindings[122] to agricultural products under GATT Article II, where bindings were often negotiated through request or on an offer basis and were not formula-based. Second, under Article XI, the elimination of quantitative restrictions on imports and other non-tariff barriers did not apply. Consequently, agricultural measures often took either the form of non-tariff barriers to trade, including quotas, licensing, minimum pricing or so-called 'grey area' measures, such as voluntary export restraints or variable levies (including the variable import levy employed by the European Economic Community) to limit imports of certain agricultural products. Third, the GATT principle related to export subsidies under Article XVI:3 also excluded agricultural products. Further, Contracting

118 Uruguay Round Understanding on Rules and Procedures Governing the Settlement of Disputes (1994) (DSU), Article 3.3. Following the provisions of the DSU, there are 12 months from consultations to adoption for regular panel procedures. An appeal will extend the length by three to four months with a maximum duration of 15 to 16 months. Recently, however, the system has been in 'crisis' due to the blocking of new appointments of Members of the Appellate Body. For more, see S. Charnovitz, 'The WTO Appellate Body Crisis: A Critique of the EU's Article 25 Proposal' (International Economic Law and Policy Blog 2 June 2019) https://ielp.worldtradelaw.net/2019/06/the-wto-appellate-body-crisis-a-critique-of-the-eus-article-25-proposal.html accessed 1 May 2021.

119 No unilateral actions are permitted. See GATT, Article XXIII:1.

120 DSU Article 23.1 states that there is an obligation to use the Dispute Settlement Body of the WTO.

121 This is different from other international tribunals such as the International Court of Justice, which requires consent of all parties.

122 Tariff bindings entail Members agreeing not to increase tariffs for the foreseeable future.

Parties (its Members) generally disregarded other GATT obligations.[123] In any case, domestic agricultural support was subject to limited disciplines.[124]

The difficulty in reaching an agreement between Members on agriculture was one of the main reasons it took so long to complete the 1986–1993 Uruguay Round negotiations.[125] The Uruguay Round introduced various regimes governing international trade in agricultural products by focusing on four central areas: market access, export subsidies, domestic support (all three are pillars of the Agreement on Agriculture) and human, animal and plant health legislation used as barriers to trade (the SPS Agreement). To a lesser extent, the TBT Agreement also impacts the trading of agricultural products by ensuring that technical regulations and standards, such as labelling, do not create unnecessary obstacles to international trade. These various agreements, which will be scrutinised in turn,[126] mean that agriculture comes closer to but still does not fully fall under the main provisions on trade in manufactured goods. The agriculture-specificity in trade disciplines remains, which can be explained by the relevance of economic factors (stable farm income, average consumer prices, political influence, culture, values, and other societal factors), as well as core state powers (ensuring adequate food supply and food security).[127]

2.4.2.1 The scope and raison d'être of the Agreement on Agriculture

In 1994, the Agreement on Agriculture was perceived as a novelty by restricting barriers linked to the production and trade in agricultural products based on three pillars – market access, domestic support and export subsidies.[128] The

123 J.A. McMahon and M.G. Desta, 'The Agreement on Agriculture: Setting the Scene' in J.A. McMahon and M.G. Desta (eds), *Research Handbook on the WTO Agriculture Agreement: New and Emerging Issues in International Agricultural Trade Law* (Research Handbooks on the WTO Series, Edward Elgar 2013) 1.

124 Due to word constraints, emphasis is on current WTO law as implemented under the Uruguay Round since it created a tighter regime for agriculture.

125 A determining and triggering factor was the 1988–1989 Uruguay Round Mid-term Review. See GATT Newsletter, 'Mid-Term Review: Final Agreement at Geneva' (Uruguay Round Special Issue May 1989) https://docs.wto.org/gattdocs/q/GG/GATTFOCUS/61.pdf accessed 1 May 2021.

126 Chapter 5, Section 5.1.4 discusses the possibilities of WTO challenges against the UK.

127 F. Delcros, 'The Legal Status of Agriculture in the World Trade Organization' (2002) 36 *Journal of World Trade* 219. For more on food security under the Agriculture Act 2020, see M. Alabrese, *Il Regime della Food Security nel Commercio Agricolo Internazionale. Dall'Havana Charter al Processo di Riforma dell'Accordo Agricolo WTO* (Giappichelli 2018).

128 From the outset, Articles 1(e) and 9 of the Agreement on Agriculture required members to reduce subsidised export quantities and the amount of funding spent on subsidising agricultural exports. Export subsidies (such as direct export payments, payments financed by government action and subsidies to reduce the cost of marketing exports) can distort market prices and competition for agricultural production. In December 2015 at the 10th Ministerial Conference in Nairobi, WTO members agreed to abolish export subsidies for

Agreement on Agriculture applies only to the agricultural products specified in the text of the Agreement – it is a closed list that can only be amended through multilateral trade negotiations. The term 'agricultural products' is defined in Article 2, together with Annex 1. The definition is based on the customs classification or Harmonized System Code of agricultural products.[129] Whilst many products such as live animals, cereals and sugars are included, forestry and fish are not. Crucially, other products in their raw state such as jute (often nicknamed the 'golden fibre of Bangladesh') or natural rubber are not included. Some commodities and other raw crops specific to developing countries and least developed countries fall outside the scope of the Agreement. These are important gaps in the scope of the application of the Agreement, which reflect old approaches to farming and a North/South divide in the drafting of the Agreement. These limitations should be borne in mind when drafting future UK agricultural schemes and programmes. Whether a product falls under the scope of the Agreement is important since such a product can benefit from two key advantages: the receipt of domestic agricultural support and a possible exemption from domestic support reduction commitments.[130]

Recently, the Agreement on Agriculture has been heavily criticised for no longer being fit for a 21st-century agriculture because it perpetuates the special status and treatment of agriculture, which results in rights for states to protect their agricultural economic sector.[131] The answer to this criticism is reflected in the Preamble to the Agreement which states that the agreement constitutes 'a basis for initiating a process for reform of trade in agriculture' and a process to 'establish a fair and market-oriented agricultural trading system'[132] – combining short- and long-term objectives. Indeed, the Agreement on Agriculture was ever only meant as a blueprint towards the solidification of the liberalisation

agricultural products. This is the final step in a long journey towards ending a key type of agricultural subsidies and further liberalising trade in agricultural products. See WTO, 'Export Competition Ministerial Decision' (WT/MIN(15)/45 – WT/L/980, 19 December 2015) paragraphs 6 and 7, www.wto.org/english/thewto_e/minist_e/mc10_e/l980_e.htm accessed 1 May 2021.

129 The Harmonized System of the World Customs Organization was last updated in 2017. An update nomenclature will come into effect in January 2022. See World Customs Organization, 'The New 2022 Edition of the Harmonized System Has Been Accepted' (8 January 2020) www.wcoomd.org/en/media/newsroom/2020/january/the-new-2022-edition-of-the-harmonized-system-has-been-accepted.aspx accessed 1 May 2021.

130 If a product, such as jute, falls outside the scope of the Agreement on Agriculture, the receipt of financial support falls under the Subsidies Agreement – the generic Agreement on subsidies. See Uruguay Round Agreement on Subsidies and Countervailing Measures (1994) (SCM Agreement).

131 See M.R. Grossman, 'The Uruguay Round Agreement on Agriculture and Domestic Support' in M.N. Cardwell, M.R. Grossman and C.P. Rodgers (eds), *Agriculture and International Trade: Law, Policy, and the WTO* (CABI Publishing 2003) 27; and McMahon and Desta (n123) 1.

132 Agreement on Agriculture, Preamble.

of agricultural products in future international agreements under the remit of the WTO.[133] However, the ongoing negotiations to reform the Agreement on Agriculture and the WTO more generally are in stalemate – heavily impacting trade in agricultural products.

It is also crucial to note that the provisions of the Agreement on Agriculture 'do not restrict, or even address, Members' policy objectives. Instead, they govern the instruments that Members use to achieve those policy objectives that affect trade'.[134] This is an important point: the provisions do not look at agricultural objectives of Members; what matters is the tools or mechanisms established to deliver such objectives. This implies that key agricultural policy objectives such as net zero or combatting climate change cannot be recognised as legitimate to justify production and trade distortions – again indicating the age of the Agreement. Nonetheless, specific non-trade concerns such as 'food security and the need to protect the environment' are included in the Preamble to the Agreement. However, such non-trade concerns find little expression in the operative provisions, as they permit only a restricted and tangential ability to address policy objectives. This contrasts with other WTO Agreements such as the TBT Agreement, which enable Members to follow specific policy objectives and provide legitimacy for new regimes. It is consequently essential to consider the controls introduced over Members' tools and mechanisms.

2.4.2.2 Market access and the tariffication process

To facilitate market access, the Agreement on Agriculture required conversion of non-tariff barriers into tariffs through a process called tariffication when it entered into force.[135] The underlying assumption of the Agreement is that Members will always seek to 'protect' their domestic farmers from cheaper imports unless they are specifically prevented from doing so by multilateral trade rules. Consequently, only the most transparent restrictions, for example, tariffs, can be imposed to create more open and predictable measures and trade. According to McMahon and Desta, tariffication is 'the most significant aspect of the entire Agreement, since it means that virtually all agricultural protection is now in the form of tariffs, which are more transparent and easier to negotiate than non-tariff measures'.[136] Further,

133 For more on reforming the Agreement on Agriculture, see M.N. Cardwell, M.R. Grossman and C.P. Rodgers (eds), *Agriculture and International Trade: Law, Policy, and the WTO* (CABI Publishing 2003); and J.A. McMahon and M.G. Desta (eds), *Research Handbook on the WTO Agriculture Agreement: New and Emerging Issues in International Agricultural Trade Law* (Research Handbooks on the WTO Series, Edward Elgar 2013).

134 Grossman (n131) 34.

135 Agreement on Agriculture, Article 4.2.

136 McMahon and Desta (n123) 3. See also *Chile – Price Band System and Safeguard Measures Relating to Certain Agricultural Products*, WT/DS207/AB/R, 23 September 2002.

Members undertook specific commitments on the bindings and reduction of tariffs – applied to both existing tariffs and converted ones.[137]

The conversion of quotas and other non-tariff barriers into tariffs was not without its limits. This process could have resulted in the reduction of market access in cases where existing large quotas would be converted into high tariffs. To reduce the impact of tariffication each Member 'was required to include minimum and current access commitments, through a tariff-rate quota (TRQ) system, for all tariffied products in its Schedules'.[138] TRQs provide third countries access to a national market on preferential terms, lowering tariffs on limited quantities of goods imported into a Member's territory. Under a TRQ, imports (often of sensitive agricultural products) up to a stipulated ceiling may enter at one tariff rate (and often no tariff at all), while additional imports beyond that ceiling are subject to a higher tariff rate. As such, import protection is limited to tariffs and TRQs under the Agreement.

An exception to the general tariffication requirement, called the Special Safeguard, is included in Article 5, provided two conditions are fulfilled:[139] first, special safeguard measures can be adopted for tariffied products only; and, second, the specific product must be identified by the Member with the symbol 'SSG', that is the special (agricultural) safeguard, in its Schedule. Thirty-nine Members (a low proportion of WTO membership), including the EU, indicated the possible use of this right in their Schedules.[140] Such an article could be utilised by the UK against situations where the *quantity* or *value* of agricultural imports suddenly exceeds a set level.[141] The issue here is that the EU tariffied the products on behalf of the UK in its Schedule and not the UK itself. It is, therefore, unclear whether the UK can rely on the provision in case of import surges now it is no longer an EU Member State. Consequently, the UK could lose this additional means of protection for tariffied products.[142]

Despite these changes, tariffs on agricultural products remain higher than those for non-agricultural products.[143] This tariffication process has had limited positive consequences due to the fact that reduction commitments were notified

137 Agreement on Agriculture, Article 4.1.
138 McMahon and Desta (n123) 3.
139 Committee on Agriculture of the WTO, 'Special Session: Special Agricultural Safeguard' (Background Paper by the Secretariat, G/AG/NG/S/9/Rev.1, 19 February 2002) 1. Article 5.8 of the Agreement on Agriculture prevents the use of GATT Article XIX and the SCM Agreement when products are subject to Article 5. For more on Article 5, see J.A. McMahon, *The WTO Agreement on Agriculture: A Commentary* (Oxford Commentaries in International Law, OUP 2007) 54.
140 Committee on Agriculture of the WTO (n139) 1.
141 Agreement on Agriculture, Article 5.4. For more, see *European Communities – Measures Affecting the Importation of Certain Poultry Products*, WT/DS69/AB/R, 13 July 1998.
142 McMahon and Desta (n123) 6.
143 WTO, 'Agriculture: Fairer Markets for Farmers' (2021) www.wto.org/english/thewto_e/whatis_e/tif_e/agrm3_e.htm accessed 1 May 2021.

as an average reduction in tariffs rather than a reduction in the average tariff.[144] Therefore, 'import protection remains a significant impediment to the long-term realization of the objectives of the Agreement, which may be achieved through extensive reduction commitments',[145] especially since these commitments operate from a high base.[146]

2.4.2.3 Domestic support

Early on, the key objective of the Agreement on Agriculture 'to provide for substantial progressive reductions in agricultural support'[147] was called 'innovative'.[148] The Agreement introduced '[d]omestic support commitments [that] closely resemble tariff bindings' and create a ceiling, cap or upper limit in relation to what Members are allowed to do within their domestic agricultural policies and programmes[149] – which are in part determined by the nature of the domestic support. To this effect, different disciplines apply to measures related to domestic support, which the UK must follow when designing future support schemes.[150] These disciplines are referred to as 'Boxes' that are given the colours of traffic lights: amber (to be reduced, i.e. those deemed trade-distortive and as a result subject to reduction commitments); blue (permitted if restricting production, i.e. those subject to production-limiting conditions and which are exempted from reduction commitments); and green (permitted, i.e. those considered to have no or minimal trade-distorting effect and subject to no discipline).[151] Each Box is now addressed in turn.

144 H. De Gorter, M. Ingco, L. Ignacio and J. Hranaiova, 'Market Access: Agricultural Policy Reform and Developing Countries' (The World Bank Group, Trade Note, 10 September 2003) documents1.worldbank.org/curated/en/544511468761421468/pdf/269240TradeNote06.pdf accessed 1 May 2021.
145 McMahon (n139) 60.
146 B. O'Connor, 'The Impact of the Doha Round on the European Union's Common Agricultural Policy' in J.A. McMahon and M.N. Cardwell (eds), *Research Handbook on EU Agriculture Law* (Research Handbook in European Law, Edward Elgar Publishing 2015) 387.
147 Agreement on Agriculture, Paragraph 3 of the Preamble.
148 M.G. Desta, *The Law of International Trade in Agricultural Products: From GATT 1947 to the WTO Agreement on Agriculture* (Kluwer Law International 2002) 393.
149 Ibid 395.
150 For more see M.N. Cardwell, 'Brexit and Agriculture: Implementing a New Legal Framework for Agricultural Support' (2017) 19 *The Cambridge Yearbook of European Legal Studies* 311.
151 There is no 'Red Box' in the text of the Agreement on Agriculture *per se*, although domestic support exceeding the reduction commitment levels in the Amber Box is prohibited. See *China – Domestic Support for Agricultural Producers*, WT/DS511/R, 28 February 2019.

2.4.2.3.1 THE AMBER BOX (OR TRADE-DISTORTING SUPPORT)

The Amber Box comprises all domestic support measures considered to distort production and trade. Such distorting support measures include 'coupled' income or product support, i.e. incentives linked directly to production through, for example, market-price supports, per-unit payments or input subsidies such as subsidies on electricity, seeds, fertilisers and irrigation.

Amber Box support and Members' commitments on domestic support are expressed and quantified in the aggregate measurement of support (AMS). The AMS provides the basis for calculating domestic support and measuring reduction commitments for domestic support. The AMS is defined as 'the annual level of support, expressed in monetary terms, provided for an agricultural product in favour of the producers of the basic agricultural product or non-product-specific support provided in favour of agricultural producers in general'.[152] Product-specific subsidy refers to the total level of support provided for each individual agricultural commodity; for example, barley AMS is the financial support given specifically to barley. Non-product specific subsidy refers to the total level of support given to the agricultural sector as a whole, i.e. subsidies on inputs.

Calculation of the AMS takes into account some exemptions from reduction commitments for the support provided under qualifying programmes under Article 6 (Blue Box) and Annex 2 (Green Box). There is also an exemption from the calculation of the AMS and reduction commitments for domestic support that is typically limited to what is considered to be *de minimis*. There are two forms of *de minimis* support: product-specific domestic support that does not exceed 5% of a country's total value of production of an agricultural product and non-product-specific domestic support that does not exceed 5% of a country's total agricultural production.[153] Matthews argues that the UK would not find '*de minimis* subsidy limits too constraining' due to the existing level of support (especially when comparing the level of existing support exempt from the disciplines of the Agreement on Agriculture and the capacity under *de minimis* non-exempt support).[154]

Various WTO Members have an historic entitlement (by reference to a 1986-1988 base period) to provide domestic support within their reduction commitments.[155] These Members are allowed to use Amber Box measures for as long as they do not exceed their reduction commitment levels. There has been a lot of

152 Agreement on Agriculture, Article 1(a). Annex 3 to the Agreement provides guidance on the calculation of the AMS.

153 Agreement on Agriculture, Article 6.4. For developing countries, the level of *de minimis* support is 10%.

154 A. Matthews, 'Establishing the UK's Non-Exempt Limit on Agricultural Support after Brexit' (CAP Reform 29 January 2017) http://capreform.eu/establishing-the-uks-non-exempt-limit-on-agricultural-support-after-brexit/ accessed 1 May 2021.

155 Currently, 32 WTO Members (including the EU) can benefit from bespoke, higher support than the *de minimis* level.

discussion[156] as to whether the UK is entitled to a share of the EU Total AMS. But this should be a non-issue. The EU Total AMS has increased on the accession of new EU Member States, so it should correspondingly be reduced on the withdrawal of the UK. There is therefore a strong argument for the UK to successfully negotiate the allocation of a portion of the EU Total AMS post-Brexit with EU Member States and the WTO. In any case, there is scope for the UK to support farmers utilising *de minimis* support without having recourse to a share of the EU Total AMS.

The disciplines of the Agreement on Agriculture on domestic support can be seen as 'relatively weak' because the level of domestic support 'has remained largely unchanged'.[157] This is due to (i) reduction commitments not applying to the total agricultural support (and only to the AMS), (ii) trade distortion created by Blue and Green Box measures and (iii) switching support from the Amber to the Green Box.[158] For example, since 1995, when the Agreement on Agriculture entered into force, EU Amber Box measures have largely reduced from €81 billion to €6.9 billion in 2016–2017 ensuring that the EU complies with its reduction commitments (€72.38 billion per year) under the AMS.[159] The EU currently uses only 10% of its AMS. However, in 2016–2017, Blue Box and Green Box measures respectively reached €4.6 billion and €61.6 billion[160] – indicating that a substantial amount of the Amber Box payments was simply transferred rather than actually overhauling EU schemes. For these reasons, commentators assert that Amber Box conditions do not provide sufficient limits or constraints on Members.[161]

In the UK, Scotland has put in place two voluntary coupled support schemes for beef and sheep. The Scottish Suckler Beef Support Scheme and the Scottish Upland Sheep Support Scheme. Beef producers on the mainland can claim around €100 per homebred calf and island beef producers are eligible for higher payments of €160 per calf (calves must be at least 75% beef bred), whilst sheep producers in the most fragile areas are eligible for additional payments of around

156 M.N. Cardwell, 'Evidence on Brexit and Agriculture' (House of Lords, European Union Committee, ABR0049, 2017) http://data.parliament.uk/writtenevidence/committeeevidence.svc/evidencedocument/eu-energy-and-environment-subcommittee/brexit-agriculture/written/48863.html accessed 1 May 2021.

157 McMahon (n139) 85.

158 Ibid 85.

159 F. Nègre, 'WTO Agreement on Agriculture, Fact Sheets on the European Union' (European Parliament 2020) www.europarl.europa.eu/factsheets/en/sheet/111/wto-agreement-on-agriculture accessed 1 May 2021.

160 WTO Notification, 'Domestic Support: European Union – Reporting Period: Marketing Year from 1 July 2016 to 30 June 2017' (G/AG/N/EU/55, 28 March 2019). See also Nègre (n159).

161 See A. Matthews, 'Recent Trends in EU WTO Domestic Support Notifications'(CAP Reform 5 October 2018) http://capreform.eu/recent-trends-in-eu-wto-domestic-support-notifications/ accessed 1 May 2021; and Desta (n148) 425.

€100 per homebred ewe hogg.[162] Such schemes are trade-distorting because they provide coupled support and Scotland is the only domestic nation to allow such support.[163] There is, nonetheless, uncertainty as to whether these schemes fall under the Amber or Blue Boxes since it depends on categorisation and there are doubts as to the criteria of the Blue Box.[164]

2.4.2.3.2 THE BLUE BOX (PRODUCTION-LIMITING SUPPORT)

As noted, Blue Box and Green Box measures are exempt from reduction commitments and they include no limits on spending. Any support that would normally be in the Amber Box is placed in the Blue Box if the support requires farmers to limit production. This is the 'Amber Box with conditions' to reduce distortion. Blue Box programmes create ceilings where payments are based on fixed area and yields (not prices) or made on 85% or less of the base level of production or for livestock payments made on a fixed number of heads.[165] Examples consist of compensatory payments for oilseeds, grains, and livestock. In the Blue Box, all payments must be 'direct', meaning that 'they should not be transferred to the agricultural producers through market manipulation devices and the like. They have to be paid from governmental budgets'.[166] It is important to note that this definition of direct payments, i.e. the one under the Agreement on Agriculture, is different from the commonly used one under the CAP. Further, payments need not be decoupled from production. Currently, the UK does not possess any such schemes, although (as noted above) there is ambiguity regarding the Scottish Suckler Beef and the Upland Sheep Support Schemes.

2.4.2.3.3 THE GREEN BOX (NO OR MINIMAL TRADE-DISTORTING SUPPORT)

In order to qualify, Green Box support must 'have no, or at most minimal, trade-distorting effects or effects on production'.[167] Despite this important proviso or 'fundamental requirement',[168] Desta asserts that it is 'too vague to translate into concrete and enforceable obligations'.[169] Indeed, so far only the *US – Cotton* case has centred on a Green Box measure under paragraph 6 of Annex 2 on

162 Scotland's Rural College, 'Voluntary Coupled Support' (2020) www.sruc.ac.uk/info/120560/cap_reform/1397/voluntary_coupled_support accessed 1 May 2021.
163 W. Kenyon, 'SPICe Briefing – The UK Agriculture Bill' (The Scottish Parliament, SB18-69, October 2018) https://sp-bpr-en-prod-cdnep.azureedge.net/published/2018/10/29/The-UK-Agriculture-Bill/SB18-69.pdf accessed 1 May 2021, 13.
164 There is no WTO case law relating to the Blue Box and its requirements.
165 Agreement on Agriculture, Article 6.5(a).
166 Desta (n148) 411.
167 Agreement on Agriculture, Annex 2, paragraph 1.
168 Ibid.
169 Desta (n148) 420.

decoupled income support.[170] Green Box support is allowed *without limits*, provided programmes comply with the basic and policy-specific criteria set out in Annex 2 of the Agreement on Agriculture; yet, the list of practices in Annex 2 is non-exhaustive. There is no actual definition of a Green Box payment.

The basic criteria require the programmes, first, to be government-funded (not by charging consumer's higher prices) due to their 'transparency';[171] and, second, they must not involve price support for producers (paragraph 1). Policy-specific criteria (paragraphs 2 to 13) include programmes that are not targeted at particular products such as direct income supports for farmers that are not related to (or are 'decoupled' from) current production levels or prices. Specific eligibility requirements are detailed within each of the relevant paragraphs (see Table 2.1).

As indicated in Table 2.1, there are two types of Green Box support. The first involves public services programmes under paragraphs 2 to 4, for example, for research and training services, marketing, promotion, infrastructure, domestic food aid or public food security stocks, and encompasses expenditures (or revenue foregone).[172] The second involves direct payments (again this is a wider interpretation than under the CAP) to producers in paragraphs 5 to 13, which are fully decoupled from production and can include income guarantee and security programmes.[173] Problematically, there is no definition of a 'producer' in the Agreement,[174] simply requiring that they produce agricultural products as defined under Annex 1 (and its exclusions). There is a timid indication in paragraph 9(a) of Annex 2, which states that in relation to retirement programmes, producers should be 'engaged in marketable agricultural production'. Again, such uncertainty as to who is entitled to financial support should be borne in mind when designing future UK schemes, for example, if payments are made to conservation organisations who do not engage in the act of agricultural production.

170 The case dealt with production flexibility contract payments and direct payments under paragraph 6(b) mostly. However, the Panel and Appellate Body steered away from considering the definition of the 'fundamental requirement' (or proviso). See *United States – Subsidies on Upland Cotton*, WT/DS267/AB/R, 3 March 2005; and F. Smith, 'Mind the Gap: "Greening" Direct Payments and the World Trade Organization' in J.A. McMahon and M.N. Cardwell (eds), *Research Handbook on EU Agriculture Law* (Research Handbook in European Law, Edward Elgar Publishing 2015) 412, 431.

171 Desta (n148) 414.

172 Agreement on Agriculture, Annex 2, paragraphs 2–4.

173 Ibid paragraphs 5–13.

174 N8 AgriFood, 'Key Challenges for Agrifood Supply Chains Post-Brexit' (2019). This requirement has problematically led the EU to require the farmer to be 'active' to receive any direct payments under Article 9(1) of Regulation (EU) No 1307/2013 of the European Parliament and of the Council of 17 December 2013 Establishing Rules for Direct Payments to Farmers Under Support Schemes Within the Framework of the Common Agricultural Policy and Repealing Council Regulation (EC) No 637/2008 and Council Regulation (EC) No 73/2009 [2013] OJ L347/608. See also Smith (n170) 429.

Table 2.1 Programmes Mentioned in Annex 2 of the Agreement on Agriculture

Type of programmes	*Paragraph No.*	*Examples of programmes*
Public service programmes (including non-direct payments)	2	General services: research programmes, pest and disease control, training, extensions and advisory services, inspection, marketing and infrastructure specifically including 'infrastructural works associated with environmental programmes'
	3	Stockpiling of food for food security
	4	Domestic food aid (including nutrition programmes)
Direct payments to producers (fully decoupled from production)	5	Direct payments to producers (provided they comply with paragraph 1 standards and with specific paragraph 6 (b) to (e) requirements)
	6	Decoupled income support
	7	Revenue/income insurance and income safety-net programmes
	8	Crop insurance and natural/disaster relief
	9	Producer retirement programmes
	10	Structural adjustment assistance through resources retirement including land or livestock
	11	Structural adjustment assistance through investment aids
	12	Payments under environmental or conservation programmes
	13	Payments under regional assistance programmes (assistance to producers in disadvantaged regions)

Direct payments categories included in paragraphs 5, 6, 12 and 13 are of particular interest since they provide great avenues to support UK farmers post-Brexit. Paragraph 5 is quite broad-ranging, but also complex. It sets general requirements for direct payments enabling Members to support farmers beyond the disciplines covered in paragraphs 6 to 13. It provides that 'where exemption from reduction is claimed for any existing or new type of direct payment other than those specified in paragraphs 6 through 13', such support must comply with paragraph 1 and with paragraphs 6(b) through to (e) which deal with (decoupled) income support payments.[175] Such payments should not be related to, or based

175 Agreement on Agriculture, Annex 2, paragraph 5.

on, the type or volume of production (b); the prices, domestic or international, of products (c); or the factors of production employed in any year after the base period (d); whilst (e) requires that such payments be decoupled from production (and are *not* restricted to 'extra costs or loss of income'). To this date, direct payments falling under paragraph 5 have not been challenged in front of the WTO.

Eligibility for decoupled income support under paragraph 6 mentions payments determined 'by clearly-defined criteria such as income, status as a producer or landowner, factor use or production level in a defined and fixed base period'. Crucially, this is the only paragraph of the Annex (as well as the rest of the Agreement itself) to mention the eligibility of landowners for domestic support. This wide application of paragraph 6 is confirmed in the fact that the amount of direct income support appears to be unlimited. The largest category of EU direct payments fall under this paragraph. Further, McMahon identifies one key concern in particular – the lack of definition of 'decoupled payments' and suggests that if such a definition were to be included it would prevent Members from

> frustrat[ing] the process of reform by transferring payments into the Green Box and thus maintaining the overall level of support for agriculture with reducing the trade-distorting effects of such payments[176]
>
> – as undertaken by the EU.

Paragraphs 12 and 13 are of particular relevance for future UK schemes. Both types of direct payments are designed to offset the 'extra costs or loss of income' incurred by a producer to comply with environmental or conservation programmes (paragraph 12) or due to the geographical position of a farm in a disadvantaged area (paragraph 13)[177] – what has been nicknamed in the UK as 'income foregone'. This means that programmes have to 'comply with the requirement that they may not be given in excess of the actual losses suffered or extra costs incurred to implement the government programme'.[178] However, 'extra costs or loss of income' is not defined in the WTO Agreements or its jurisprudence. As such, the baseline or counterfactual is unspecified and the range of costs and income that can be included in the payment calculations remains ambiguous. To ensure consistency with WTO commitments, payments under current EU (and, therefore, UK) agri-environment schemes have been established on a stricter approach based on the additional costs *and* income foregone (as a basis to fund farmers) resulting from the commitments made.[179] This means that cumulative

176 McMahon (n139) 88.

177 In line with the provisions of Article 8.2 of the SCM Agreement.

178 Desta (n148) 421.

179 Regulation (EU) No 1305/2013 of the European Parliament and of the Council of 17 December 2013 on Support for Rural Development by the European Agricultural Fund for Rural Development (EAFRD) and Repealing Council Regulation (EC) No 1698/2005 [2013] OJ L347/487, Article 28(6). This article goes on to state that payments 'may also cover transaction costs up to a value of 20% of the premium paid for the agri-environ-

criteria have to be met rather than alternatives. Thus, the limitations and constraints linked to income foregone under the CAP are not due to the EU institutions but to WTO obligations – albeit interpreted more strictly.

Under its successive CAP reforms, the EU has moved its support payments through box-shifting exercises away from the Amber and Blue Boxes towards the Green Box.[180] Under the CAP, direct payments in the form of the Basic Payment Scheme (BPS) and greening payments are qualified by the EU as exempt from domestic support reduction commitments because they are considered to be payments decoupled from production and therefore falling under paragraph 6 of the Agreement on Agriculture. Similarly for the EU, agri-environment schemes (AES) fall under the scope of paragraph 12 Annex 2. Through ingenious tweaking of its turn towards sustainable agriculture and wide (re)interpretation and widening of Annex 2, the EU programmes now mostly fall under the Green Box. The line between trade-distorting and non-distorting measures is indeed blurred.

As noted, the Agreement on Agriculture was meant to be the first step in the direction of bringing domestic support under multilateral trading rules. Further multilateral steps could and should have included (i) transferring some Blue and Green Box measures towards the Amber Box; (ii) agreeing reduction commitments over *all* domestic support, especially the Green Box to further restrict the exceptionalism of agriculture (especially in Western countries that can financially support their farmers whilst other countries found it difficult or simply do not do it); and (iii) enabling Members to design schemes that are designed to fulfil specific objectives such as net zero or agroecological principles. However, these gaps remain unaddressed and lead to an Agreement on Agriculture that does not fully enable an agriculture that reflects 21st-century interests and objectives. Uncertainties in the text of the Agreement on Agriculture could be a hindrance when the UK and the devolved administrations are designing future support schemes.[181]

---

ment-climate commitments'. For more on eco-schemes under the current CAP reform and compatibility with the Green Box, see N. Röder, 'Payments for the Environment – New Turmoil Around an Old Issue' (CAP Reform 2 March 2021) http://capreform.eu/payments-for-the-environment-new-turmoil-around-an-old-issue/ accessed 1 May 2021.

180 M.N. Cardwell and F. Smith, 'Renegotiation of the WTO Agreement on Agriculture: Accommodating the New Big Issues' (2013) *International and Comparative Law Quarterly* 865, 881. For a previous account, see A. Swinbank and R. Tranter, 'Decoupling EU Farm Support: Does the New Single Payment Scheme Fit within the Green Box?' (2005) 6(1) *Etsey Centre Journal of International Law and Trade Policy* 47.

181 Chapter 3, Section 3.2.2 considers the compatibility of UK domestic support under the Green Box (as well as other Boxes).

2.4.3 Non-tariff barriers in the SPS and TBT Agreements

Disciplines under the SPS and TBT Agreements directly impact the UK's ability to regulate and set standards when it comes to non-tariff barriers to trade. Both Agreements rely on standards set by other (non-WTO) international bodies as a basis for their harmonisation. As such they do not lay down minimum standards but the use of stricter standards by Members is allowed under certain conditions. They also prohibit WTO Members from adopting measures that would constitute arbitrary or unjustifiable discrimination or a disguised restriction on international trade.

The SPS Agreement establishes binding rules and disciplines to prevent Members from using SPS measures as creating arbitrary or unjustifiable discrimination or disguised barriers to trade.[182] SPS measures protect human, animal or plant life or health and are an elaboration of Article XX (b) GATT.[183] They apply in the case of food-borne risks and pest or disease-borne risks;[184] they consequently bear a close link to agriculture. For example, they ensure that consumers are supplied with food that is safe to eat by setting strict sanitary standards for slaughterhouses. The Agreement sets out fundamental rights and obligations for Members, which constitute a '*code de bonne conduit*', and attempts to balance conflicting interests between the protection of life and health against SPS risks and the liberalisation of trade. It favours international harmonisation of SPS norms in cooperation with other international institutions such as the World Organisation for Animal Health or the Codex Alimentarius Commission of the Food and Agriculture Organization.

Unlike the GATT, which is based squarely on non-discrimination, the SPS Agreement also places science, scientific evidence and risk assessment at its centre.[185] According to Scott, a 'turn to science' has occurred in the SPS Agreement.[186] Any deviation from standards must be justified based on science and a risk assessment under Article 5 or the qualified exemption under Article 5.7 based on the precautionary principle (for provisional measures only)[187] and not purely grounded in discrimination as a basis for adjudication.[188] The establishment of the SPS Agreement has been a milestone in the emergence of the WTO

182 SPS Agreement, Articles 1.1 and 2.3.

183 Ibid Preamble.

184 Ibid Annex A(1). For more see *Japan – Measures Affecting the Importation of Apples*, WT/DS245/AB/R, 26 November 2003.

185 SPS Agreement, Article 5. See *European Communities – Measures Concerning Meat and Meat Products (EC-Hormones)*, WT/DS26/AB/R, 16 January 1998, paragraphs 177, 184–186 and 201.

186 J. Scott, *Commentary on the Sanitary and Phytosanitary Measures Agreement* (OUP 2007).

187 See *Japan – Measures Affecting Agricultural Products (Japan – Agricultural Products II)*, WT/DS76/AB/R, 22 February 1999, paragraphs 80 and 89; and *European Communities – Measures Affecting the Approval and Marketing of Biotech Products (EC-Biotech)*, WT/DS291/R, WT/DS292/R and WT/DS293/R, 29 September 2006, paragraphs 7.2529-7.3261.

188 Scott (n186) 3.

as a binding authority able to adjudicate science-based disputes. Crucially, as the SPS Agreement is a *lex specialis*, it is applied before the GATT.

One of the difficulties of the SPS Agreement is to identify protectionist and ill-founded SPS measures through scientific justification, consistency and least-trade restrictive requirements while Members are, in principle, perfectly entitled to protect their population by SPS regulations and to choose their own level of protection.[189] Even though the standards adopted must be based on scientific evidence and should be solely applied to the extent necessary to protect human, animal or plant life or health (including food safety), the tendency to rely on limited scientific evidence has given rise to controversy.[190] Over the years, WTO case-law has developed and it may be noted that it is difficult for Members to justify measures aiming at heightening standards of SPS measures, in particular due to a restricted interpretation of the precautionary principle developed by the Dispute Settlement Body.[191] Accordingly, there are those who believe that the SPS Agreement limits greatly Members' sovereign right to protect the health and food safety of their citizens,[192] especially where a measure is based on disputed or uncertain science and risks – rather than, for instance, where one country decides simply to have a higher level of protection based on undisputed scientific evidence.

Technical regulations and standards can create non-tariff barriers to trade, as exported goods comply with the technical regulations or standards of the importing state, which often vary from country to country. Such regulations or standards relate to specific characteristics of a product such as its size, shape, design, labelling, packaging and safety to protect animal life and health and the environment; they also apply to agricultural products.[193] The TBT Agreement aims to minimise the impact of both binding technical regulations and non-binding voluntary technical standards on international trade and to ensure that these are genuinely useful,

189 C. Button, *The Power to Protect: Trade, Health and Uncertainty in the WTO* (Hart 2004) 91.
190 S. Subedi, 'The Challenge of Managing the "Second Agricultural Revolution" Through International Law: Liberalization of Trade in Agriculture and Sustainable Development' in N.J. Schrijver and F. Weiss (eds), *International Law and Sustainable Development: Principles and Practice* (Martinus Nijhoff 2004) 161, 177. The interpretation of the precautionary principle under WTO law is narrower than under EU law. See A. Szajkowska, *Regulating Food Law* (Wageningen Academic Publishers 2012). Further, the claimant Member bears the initial burden of demonstrating a *prima facie* case of inconsistency of a measure with the SPS Agreement. Once this has been established, the burden of proof shifts to the defendant party (i.e. the one imposing the measure) to counter, or refute, the claim of inconsistency made by the complainant. See *Japan – Agricultural Products II*, paragraph 129.
191 See also *EC-Biotech* and *EC-Hormones*.
192 See M.A. Echols, *Food Safety and the WTO: The Interplay of Culture, Science and Technology* (Kluwer Law International 2001) 148.
193 TBT Agreement, Article 1.3. The TBT Agreement also covers conformity assessments and their procedures. See Articles 5 to 8 and 10.

as opposed to arbitrary or an excuse for protectionism.[194] Voluntary international standards include those from the International Organization for Standardization and their popular ISO standards that deal safety, reliability and good quality. When international standards exist, WTO Members should use those standards as the basis for their technical regulations.[195] Further, the TBT Agreement does not apply to measures governed by the SPS Agreement – they are mutually exclusive.[196] The TBT Agreement also centres on non-discrimination.[197]

The TBT Agreement allows technical regulations that are not more trade-restrictive than necessary and are designed to meet legitimate national objectives under Article 2.2 including avoiding consumer deception, protection of human health or safety together with animal health or the environment.[198] Consequently, technical requirements can be introduced for health or safety purposes, while others can be introduced to standardise products, ensure quality or avoid consumer deception. The adequate use of labels for agri-food products to signal quality attributes has been one of the most contentious issues in the implementation of the TBT Agreement.[199] More importantly, the list of legitimate objectives in Article 2.2 is not exhaustive as indicated by the words '*inter alia*'.[200] The Appellate Body reasoned that 'objectives expressly listed provide a reference point for which other objectives may be considered to be legitimate in the sense of Article 2.2'.[201] The extent of legitimate objectives has been broadly interpreted. Additional social priorities may be included[202] and could include animal welfare.[203]

194 TBT Agreement, Annex 1.1 and 1.2 respectively. For more on the technical regulations and standards, see A. Davies, 'Technical Regulations and Standards under the WTO Agreement on Technical Barriers to Trade' (2014) 41(1) *Legal Issues of Economic Integration* 37.

195 TBT Agreement, Article 2.4.

196 Ibid Article 1.5. For more on the relationship between the TBT Agreement, the SPS Agreement and the GATT, see G. Marceau and J.P. Trachtman, 'A Map of the World Trade Organization Law of Domestic Regulation of Goods: The Technical Barriers to Trade Agreement, the Sanitary and Phytosanitary Measures Agreement, and the General Agreement on Tariffs and Trade' (2014) 48(2) *Journal of World Trade* 351; and G. Marín Durán, 'Measures with Multiple Competing Purposes after *EC – Seal Products*: Avoiding a Conflict between GATT Article XX-Chapeau and Article 2.1 TBT Agreement' (2016) 19(2) *Journal of International Economic Law* 467.

197 The TBT Agreement contains a tight prohibition on non-discrimination in Article 2.1, which combines both national treatment and the most-favoured nation principles.

198 For more on the role of Articles 2.1. and 2.2, see S. Lester and W. Stemberg, 'The GATT Origins of TBT Agreement Articles 2.1 and 2.2' (2014) 17(1) *Journal of International Economic Law* 215.

199 A. Swinbank, 'Like Products, Animal Welfare and the World Trade Organization' (2006) 40 *Journal of World Trade* 687, 703.

200 *United States – Measures Concerning the Importation, Marketing and Sale of Tuna and Tuna Products (US – Tuna II (Mexico))*, WT/DS381/AB/R, 16 May 2012, paragraph 313.

201 Ibid paragraph 313.

202 Button (n189) 86.

203 This point is explored at length in Chapter 5, Section 5.1.4.4. It is essential here to note that the burden of proof is on the complainant to prove that a set objective is *not* legitimate

International law and more specifically WTO law create a binding framework for UK agricultural policies. As these agreements focus on trade liberalisation and the elimination of trade distortions between Members, they can directly impact the formulation of such policies and regulations internally. They create legal parameters within which states can operate, whether this is to do with tariffs, financial support, SPS standards, labelling criteria or wider non-tariff barriers. It is these Agreements that enable Members such as the UK or the EU to maintain SPS controls and checks at the border. Flexibility still exists, but such parameters shape domestic agricultural policies and must be borne in mind – including within the UK. However, international relations and obligations are not the only consideration for decision-making in a multilevel governance system and it is essential to consider the internal perspectives on the UK now.

2.5 Devolution and internal relationships/powers

A key question that has arisen within the UK since the Brexit vote is where do the powers (including over agricultural policy) held by the EU return? In particular, do they revert to the nation-state/Westminster or the devolved administrations, since agricultural policy is a devolved matter?[204] This raises primarily constitutional questions related to devolution, but also political and practical questions as to whether essentially, despite powers legally resting at a specific level, they should or could be utilised at another level.

2.5.1 Legal limits on legislation?

The Devolution Settlements provide for powers in specific policy areas to be devolved to the parliaments and governments in Scotland, Northern Ireland and Wales – enabling a degree of self-government.[205] These areas and powers vary for each of the devolved administrations, but both agriculture and environmental

within the scope of Article 2.2 TBT Agreement. See *United States – Certain Country of Origin Labelling (COOL) Requirements*, WT/DS384/AB/R, 29 June 2012, paragraph 449.

204 House of Lords, European Union Committee, 'Brexit: Devolution' (4th Report of Session 2017–19, HL 9, July 2017). It is insufficient to look where powers were allocated prior to EU membership, as devolution and the broader context have evolved.

205 The Scotland Act 1998, the Government of Wales Acts 1998 and 2006, and the Northern Ireland Act 1998. These are supplemented by the Memorandums of Understanding between the UK and devolved governments: The original Memorandum of Understanding and Supplementary Agreements between the United Kingdom Government, Scottish Ministers and the Cabinet of the National Assembly for Wales (Cm 4444, 1 October 1999), which has been revised numerous times. The latest was in 2013. See Memorandum of Understanding and Supplementary Agreements between the United Kingdom Government, the Scottish Ministers, the Welsh Ministers and the Northern Ireland Executive Committee (October 2013). See more generally, R. Hazell and R. Rawlings (eds), *Devolution, Law Making and the Constitution* (Inprint Academic 2005).

issues are devolved for these three parts of the UK. Agriculture and environment are also policy areas that have been Europeanised and belong to an area of UK 'shared governance'.[206] Consequently, on first instance, it would appear that the key relevant powers would revert to Scotland, Northern Ireland and Wales, as well as then to Westminster on behalf of England after the end of the transition period. This is reflected in the Joint Ministerial Committee (EU Negotiations) (JMC) mapping exercise evaluating the devolved competences returning from the EU,[207] with a wide range of areas listed relating to agriculture. However, key caveats need to be highlighted here.

First, whilst agriculture, environmental matters and economic development are devolved, related areas of fiscal matters (mainly centralised) and transport are concurrent with the UK, i.e. both the devolved and central administrations share relevant powers. In other areas the UK retains reserved, that is exclusive powers,[208] including crucially the ability to negotiate externally and conclude international agreements such as trade agreements.[209] Clearly, use of such powers may impact agricultural policy in the devolved administrations. This can arise most obviously in two scenarios. The first is where the UK determines the nature and level of taxes that impact (dis)incentives or the economic viability of specific activities. The second is where they sign international agreements that impact issues such as agricultural processes, food standards and associated regulations, environmental standards, and agricultural support and tariffs. Even if such agreements did not directly impact upon the powers of the devolved administrations, by changing the situation for England and what produce is allowed to be imported, this would impact the UK internal market and the competitiveness of produce created in the devolved nations. Thus, the devolved administrations may technically have the legal powers to design agricultural policy, but these may be curtailed in practice through the UK's use of their own powers.[210]

Second, despite any devolution agreements, the fundamental underpinnings of the UK legal system include parliamentary sovereignty, i.e. the sovereignty

206 J. Hunt, 'Devolution' in M. Dougan (eds), *The UK after Brexit: Legal and Policy Challenges* (Intersentia 2017) 35. See also L. Petetin, 'La Dimension Agricole du Brexit' in S. Abis and M. Brun (eds), *Le Déméter 2020* (Iris éditions 2020) 119.

207 UK Government, 'Frameworks Analysis' (2018) www.gov.uk/government/uploads/system/uploads/attachment_data/file/686991/20180307_FINAL__Frameworks_analysis_for_publication_on_9_March_2018.pdf accessed 1 May 2021. For the latest update, see UK Government, 'Frameworks Analysis 2020: Breakdown of Areas of EU Law that Intersect with Devolved Competence in Scotland, Wales and Northern Ireland' (2020) https://assets.publishing.service.gov.uk/government/uploads/system/uploads/attachment_data/file/919729/Frameworks-Analysis-2020.pdf accessed 1 May 2021.

208 D. Torrance, 'Reserved Matters in the United Kingdom' (House of Commons Library, CBP-8544, 5 April 2019) https://researchbriefings.files.parliament.uk/documents/CBP-8544/CBP-8544.pdf accessed 1 May 2021.

209 See 2013 Memorandum of Understanding (n205) 8.

210 A. Scott, 'The Role of Concordats in the New Governance of Britain: Taking Subsidiarity Seriously?' (2001) 5(1) *Edinburgh Law Review* 21.

of the Westminster Parliament.[211] Consequently, irrespective of any legal agreement to devolve powers to Northern Ireland, Scotland or Wales, the Westminster Parliament can in principle overrule this decentralisation of powers – including by amending the very Devolution Settlements.[212] The Sewel Convention initially appears to impose a limiter on parliamentary sovereignty. Introduced in 1999 in order to address the interface between parliamentary sovereignty and devolved powers, it states that the Westminster Parliament 'will not normally legislate with regard to devolved matters without the consent' of the devolved legislatures.[213] This includes not merely changes to the law, but also changes to legislative or executive competences of the devolved administrations.[214] The use of the resulting legislative consent motions before the devolved parliaments has been significant in addressing Brexit matters (these are currently components within Environment Bill 2019–2021) as well as previously with the European Union (Withdrawal) Act 2018, the European Union (Withdrawal Agreement) Act 2020 and the Agriculture Act 2020.[215]

However, it is essential to note that the Sewel Convention is not a blanket ban on unilateral UK action, but only that the UK Parliament is 'not normally' to legislate without consent – notably, 'not normally' is left undefined and without any criteria. Furthermore, this is a UK constitutional convention, not an international convention/treaty or a domestic piece of legislation – although uncertain until recently, the Supreme Court has determined, in its seminal *Miller* decision, that it consequently is not justiciable.[216] Thus, the Westminster Parliament can still legislate without the consent of one or more of the devolved administrations. It can even, as highlighted by the European Union (Withdrawal) Act and the Supreme Court *Scottish Continuity Bill* case, legislate without consent to limit the devolved competences.[217] Since then, Westminster has pushed through the European

211 M. Elliott and R. Thomas, *Public Law* (OUP 2011) 46.

212 G. Anthony, 'Devolution Issues, Legislative Power, and Legal Sovereignty' in A. Antoine (eds), *Le Droit Public Britannique: État des Lieux et Perspectives* (Société de Législation Comparée, 2015), 95, 98.

213 HL Deb 21 July 1998, vol 592, col 791. It was initially introduced by Lord Sewel in the context of Scotland. Such a legislative consent convention is now applicable to all of the devolved administrations. On the role of legislative consent conventions in the UK generally see G. Cowie, 'Brexit: Devolution and Legislative Consent' (House of Commons Library, BP-8274, 29 March 2018) https://researchbriefings.files.parliament.uk/documents/CBP-8274/CBP-8274.pdf accessed 1 May 2021.

214 This is reflected in the European Union (Withdrawal) Act, which contains 'protected' provisions that devolved administrations cannot repeal or legislate against – thereby limiting the devolved competences in practice.

215 A. Paun, J. Sargeant and E. Nicholson, 'Sewel Convention' (Institute for Government 8 December 2020) www.instituteforgovernment.or8g.uk/explainers/sewel-convention accessed 1 May 2021.

216 *R (on the application of Miller and another) v Secretary of State for Exiting the European Union* [2017] UKSC 5, 148–151; and Engel and Petetin (n86) 26.

217 *The UK Withdrawal from the European Union (Legal Continuity) (Scotland) Bill* [2018] UKSC 64. Scotland had sought to prepare for Brexit through legislating for the continu-

Union (Withdrawal Agreement) Act, despite consent being refused by each of the devolved legislatures, raising concerns that the Sewel Convention is 'broken' and devolution effectively undermined.[218] Consequently, devolution does not guarantee the devolved administrations autonomy or absolute power within the UK. Parliamentary sovereignty only applies to the *Westminster* Parliament, not the devolved ones.[219] Indeed, Westminster can legislate in reserved matters, in devolved matters with consent, or, if they really want, even in devolved matters without consent.

2.5.2 Devolution to centralisation: options and mechanisms?

Any decision to seek, grant, refuse or bypass legislative consent is a sensitive matter, due in particular to the political ramifications if consent is refused. Hence, usually there will be preliminary discussions between Westminster and the devolved administrations to iron out any issues in advance and ensure that consent will be granted[220] – with the European Union (Withdrawal) Act being the first time Westminster legislated where the devolved administrations withheld consent. The political consequences are amply highlighted by Scotland going on a 'Sewel strike'[221] since Westminster ignored their withholding of consent – they have consistently refused legislative consent regarding Brexit legislation as a matter of protest.[222]

---

ation of EU law in devolved matters. However, the UK Government was challenging this, especially in light of the European Union (Withdrawal) Act. Crucially, the Supreme Court ruled that as the European Union (Withdrawal) Act 2018 (which the Scottish Government did not give consent to) made itself a 'protected' enactment, Scotland could no longer legislate in conflict with provisions of the Act – even though technically it might be a devolved matter.

218 J. Sargeant, 'The Sewel Convention Has Been Broken by Brexit – Reform is Now Urgent' (Institute for Government 21 January 2020) www.instituteforgovernment.org.uk/blog/sewel-convention-has-been-broken-brexit-reform-now-urgent accessed 1 May 2021.

219 There is a reconfiguration of powers with the new acts created by withdrawal including the European Union (Withdrawal) Act 2018, the United Kingdom Internal Market Act 2020 and the Agriculture Act 2020, where devolved powers are being 're-reserved' or recentralised. With these acts, various powers are given to the executive rather than the legislative. For example, the Agriculture Act 2020, as an enabling Act, gives powers to the UK, the Welsh and the Northern Irish Governments possibility to the detriment of the legislatures. Further, 'Henry VIII' clauses in the European Union (Withdrawal) Act reinforces the powers of the central executive. There is also an increased reliance on statutory instruments being passed with the lack of transparency attached to this type of instrument. See ClientEarth, 'Environmental Groups Launch Brexit Regulation Court Challenge Over Wildlife Risk' (21 June 2019) www.clientearth.org/latest/latest-updates/news/environmental-groups-launch-brexit-regulation-court-challenge-over-wildlife-risk/ accessed 1 May 2021.

220 This also can lead to enhanced stakeholder engagement, with inquiries by devolved legislatures to seek expert comment.

221 Sargeant (n218).

222 This is reflected in Scottish Government, 'Legislative Consent Memorandum: Agriculture Bill' (October 2018) https://archive2021.parliament.scot/S5ChamberOffice/SPLCM

However, even without legislating, much can be undertaken informally instead. This is indicated by the Supplementary Agreements within the Devolution Settlements, which created a JMC[223] and outlines the importance of cooperation and coordination across the four nations. The Committee comprises senior representatives of each government and is perhaps the most significant political mechanism for the devolved and central governments to engage, discuss and plan policy – including the potential for shared legislative or political approaches. It can exist in various formats, having a range of sub-committees that address a wide array of issues. This includes a sub-committee on Europe generally and another (noted above) on EU negotiations, that is Brexit. However, a range of other informal mechanisms exist, whether this simply involves one minister picking up the phone to another minister or indeed through parliamentary committee members meeting in the relatively new Interparliamentary Forum on Brexit (created in 2017).[224] Whatever the final outcome of such discussions, the mechanisms and discussions will be essential post-Brexit if devolution is to be respected in any meaningful way and if there is to be any policy coherency across the UK.[225] However, this still leaves open the question of whether there is good cause for a devolved, UK-wide or perhaps Great Britain-wide approach regarding individual policy areas and, in light of the purpose of this book, for agriculture? There is not a simple answer.[226]

2.5.3 Practical push and pull factors?

It is useful to reflect here on the concept of subsidiarity noted above and considerations of democracy, effectiveness and efficiency. As noted in Chapter 1, agricultural conditions, policies and practices vary considerably across the UK in particular with the nature of the land, environment, climate, infrastructure, farming type and economic and societal significance. Therefore, a uniform approach to UK agriculture would not be suitable and hence why agriculture and the related issues of environmental and food policy are devolved. However, this is not to say that there are not also reasons for supporting some level of harmonisation within the UK, whether in order to ensure minimum food, environmental or animal welfare standards, facilitate cooperation on transboundary issues such as food and livestock traceability or water quality, protect the UK internal market and avoid internal competitive disadvantages, or indeed to facilitate trade

-S05-19.pdf accessed 1 May 2021, paragraphs 23–26 and 28. An exception is seen in the Direct Payments to Farmers (Legislative Continuity) Act 2020.

223 See 2013 Memorandum of Understanding (n205).

224 For examples of their reports, see Scottish Parliament, 'Interparliamentary Forum on Brexit' www.parliament.scot/parliamentarybusiness/CurrentCommittees/106398.aspx accessed 1 May 2021.

225 J. Sheldon and H. Phylip, 'Devolution Arrangements within the UK during the Next Phase of Brexit' (The UK in a Changing Europe 30 March 2020) https://ukandeu.ac.uk/brexit-and-intergovernmental-coordination-within-the-uk/ accessed 1 May 2021.

226 This is further explored in Chapters 4 and 5.

agreements. Clearly, neither a fully decentralised nor fully centralised approach is appropriate – yet what balance should be struck and how should it be achieved?

The JMC has been specifically examining the highly contentious issue[227] of whether UK common frameworks are desirable or necessary, following the return of devolved powers from the EU post-Brexit – which is particularly significant considering that there are existing EU-level common frameworks for these areas. It also has considered how such frameworks should be developed and what should be their nature. After considerable debate, the JMC specified that such common frameworks could be in the form of 'common goals, minimum or maximum standards, harmonisation, limits on action, or mutual recognition', whether in political or legally binding agreements on a UK-wide or Great Britain-wide basis.[228] They also agreed three 'principles', including recognition of the 'economic and social linkages between Northern Ireland and Ireland' and respect of the Belfast Agreement/Good Friday Agreement; respect of 'the devolution settlements and the democratic accountability of the devolved legislatures'; and some general criteria to help determine whether and what type of a common framework would be necessary. These criteria include enabling 'the functioning of the UK internal market' and 'management of common resources', as well as ensuring 'compliance with international obligations' and the UK's ability to negotiate 'trade agreements and international treaties'.[229] The JMC's principles and criteria largely reflect the concept of subsidiarity – democracy, effectiveness and efficiency are all embedded within them. Even the goal of internalising negative externalities is implicitly present within the ideas of common resources and the UK internal market.

Yet, despite these principles and criteria and the current existence of EU-level frameworks (determined proportionate under the EU version of subsidiarity), of 154 areas of devolved competences returning from the EU, the JMC (in an updated 2020 analysis) deemed that only 18 would require legislative frameworks, 22 would require non-legislative, political frameworks and 115 would require no frameworks.[230] This marks a substantial change even from the 2019 analysis,[231]

227 A. Paun, 'SPICe Briefing – Common UK Frameworks after Brexit' (SB18-09 February 2019) https://sp-bpr-en-prod-cdnep.azureedge.net/published/2018/2/2/Common-UK-Frameworks-after-Brexit/SB%2018-09.pdf accessed 1 May 2021; and V. Gravey and C. Reid, 'Taking Back and Sharing Control? Brexit and the Common Environmental Frameworks' (Brexit and Environment Network 12 March 2018) www.brexitenvironment.co.uk/2018/03/12/common-environmental-frameworks accessed 1 May 2021.

228 Joint Ministerial Committee (EU Negotiations), 'Communique – Common Frameworks: Definition and Principles' (16 October 2017) www.gov.uk/government/uploads/system/uploads/attachment_data/file/652285/Joint_Ministerial_Committee_communique.pdf accessed 1 May 2021, 2.

229 Ibid.

230 UK Government 2020 (n207) 7.

231 UK Government, 'Revised Frameworks Analysis: Breakdown of Areas of EU Law that Intersect with Devolved Competence in Scotland, Wales and Northern Ireland' (2019) https://assets.publishing.service.gov.uk/government/uploads/system/uploads/attachment_data/file/792738/20190404-FrameworksAnalysis.pdf accessed 1 May 2021.

which considered that of 160 areas (some were later merged), 21 would require legislative frameworks, 78 non-legislative frameworks and 63 would require none.[232] It should be noted that this is a significant shift towards decentralisation relative to under the EU[233] and raises questions over whether the principles and criteria were applied effectively or whether further frameworks would be appropriate. Whilst the 2020 analysis notes that the latest reviews and reclassifications were discussed and jointly agreed by the frameworks policy teams in the four administrations, considered the impact on the JMC's common frameworks principles and cooperation would continue to be monitored,[234] the JMC has neither provided explanations as to its thinking on individual areas nor engaged with stakeholders in these fields.[235] There has been a considerable lack of transparency on this front, undermining accountability and quite possibly effectiveness also. This has been exacerbated more recently by the subsequent decision that a further seven areas (previously deemed to need some common framework) no longer need any – this has not been updated within the JMC documents, but was clarified in evidence provided to the House of Lords' Scrutiny Committee as stated in their report in March 2021.[236] However, once more, no justifications or explanations have been provided for most changes – with a statement made to the Committee that some information would be provided in the JMC's September 2021 analysis.[237]

Furthermore, the JMC did not provide any guidance as to how common frameworks should be developed.[238] Whilst the principles include respect for devolution and the process was generally hoped to be collaborative with substantive involvement by the devolved administrations in designing the frameworks (and this has been reflected in practice to a large extent),[239] there were significant concerns – in particular by Scotland – over power-grabbing, disrespect of

232 UK Government 2020 (n207) 8 and 10–11. It states that the decrease in numbers requiring a non-legislative framework from the 2019 to 2020 analysis is 'largely due to collaborative work between the UK Government and devolved administrations leading to the shared understanding that no further action is required'.

233 Although, this may be countered in part in practice by the application of the Internal Market Act discussed in Chapter 5, Section 5.2.3.

234 UK Government 2020 (n207) 10–13.

235 House of Lords, Common Frameworks Scrutiny Committee (n84) 16–21.

236 Ibid 16–18 and 60.

237 Ibid 17–18.

238 Brennan, Dobbs and Gravey (n94) 98. See Welsh proposals, for instance, for a cooperative, intergovernmental approach through a 'UK Council of Ministers', rather than simply risking the UK Government imposing frameworks unilaterally on the devolved administrations. See Welsh Government, 'Securing Wales' Future: Transition from the European Union to a New Relationship with Europe' (2017) https://gov.wales/sites/default/files/2017-01/30683%20Securing%20Wales%C2%B9%20Future_ENGLISH_WEB.pdf accessed 1 May 2021.

239 House of Lords, Common Frameworks Scrutiny Committee (n84). In contrast, the Report (pages 18–23) notes that there has been very limited engagement with stakeholders.

devolution and imposition of English approaches for the UK as a whole.[240] This can lead to kickback and unwillingness to engage in the process. However, this risks a counterproductive outcome for the devolved administrations, as shall be seen across this book: if the UK Government deems that there is a need for shared frameworks or a degree of harmonisation but the common framework approach is being too slow or unwieldy, the UK Government may resort to a centralised approach determined at the UK-level instead.[241] This may be swifter and seemingly more effective, but risks running roughshod over devolution, creating unsuitable, blunt and encompassing instruments and also creating political fallout across the UK. The risk of such unilaterally imposed UK frameworks (with their knock-on effects) is an additional incentive for all concerned to focus on the more collaborative common frameworks and develop these instead where a framework of some sort is required. More is needed from the common framework approach than rhetoric or a mapping exercise – any appropriate frameworks need to be developed and implemented.[242] They must also facilitate engagement by all stakeholders if the frameworks are to be effective or legitimate.[243]

Finally, it is essential to note that even if the devolved administrations hold and seek to utilise the relevant powers, there is a very practical constraint upon them in the form of financial resources. Agriculture has received considerable funding under the CAP[244] and indeed much of agriculture is heavily dependent on financial support to simply survive,[245] but CAP funding is no longer available and

240 See D. Torrance, 'EU Powers after Brexit: "Power Grab" or "Power Surge"?' (House of Commons Library, Insight 29 July 2020) https://commonslibrary.parliament.uk/eu-powers-after-brexit-power-grab-or-power-surge/ accessed 1 May 2021; M. Russell MSP, 'Keynote Speech – Scotland, Brexit and Devolution' (Institute for Government 25 March 2019) www.instituteforgovernment.org.uk/events/keynote-speech-michael-russell-msp-scotland-brexit-and-devolution accessed 1 May 2021; and S. Morris and S. Carrell, 'Tories Using Brexit to Grab Back Devolved Powers, Say Ministers' (The Guardian 26 February 2018) www.theguardian.com/politics/2018/feb/26/tories-using-brexit-to-grab-back-devolved-powers-say-ministers accessed 1 May 2021. Similar comments regarding power-grabbing were made in relation to the European Union (Withdrawal) Bill 2017–2019. See The Scottish Government, 'Joint Statement on the EU (Withdrawal) Bill' (13 July 2017) https://news.gov.scot/news/eu-withdrawal-bill accessed 1 May 2021.

241 Arguably this has occurred with both the Agriculture and Internal Market Acts, as discussed in Chapter 5, Section 5.2.

242 A common framework (where possible) would more accurately reflect subsidiarity, in light of considerations of democracy and proportionality.

243 House of Lords, Common Frameworks Scrutiny Committee (n84) 18–23. The progress with the common frameworks is further discussed in Chapter 5, Section 5.2.2.

244 See DEFRA, 'Total Income from Farming in the United Kingdom, First Estimate for 2019' (7 May 2020) https://assets.publishing.service.gov.uk/government/uploads/system/uploads/attachment_data/file/884101/agricaccounts-tiffstatsnotice-07may20i.pdf accessed 1 May 2021.

245 Regarding Northern Ireland, see J. Tonge, 'The Impact of Withdrawal from the European Union upon Northern Ireland' (2016) 87(3) *Political Quarterly* 338. For data on agricultural funding levels across the four nations, see DEFRA, DAERA, Welsh Government Knowledge and Analytical Services and the Scottish Government, Rural and Environ-

the devolved administrations must consider whether and how to fund agriculture. The devolved administrations are highly dependent on the funding received from Westminster – via a block grant currently determined by the Barnett formula, which applies a *pro rata* approach based on population linked to how much England spends on the same area.[246] If applied to agriculture in future, once the current period of guaranteed funding has passed, this would lead to a significant decline in the funding received relative to that provided under the CAP and undermine the ability to support agriculture or land use in the devolved administrations. This would only be exacerbated if England were to reduce the funds it spends on agriculture, as there would be a corresponding *pro rata* decrease in the block grant for the devolved administrations. Further, the devolved administrations can spend the block grants as they wish and there would no longer be ring-fencing of the funding for agriculture – leading to agriculture needing to compete with other objectives (such as education or health) to obtain part of the (smaller) pot.[247]

However, this needs not be the only way. For instance, Westminster does provide some funding to the devolved administrations outside of the block grant, where the devolved administrations and UK negotiate the approach to be taken – this tends to be more limited and may even be a once-off payment, but nonetheless the option exists.[248] Further, even within the block grant, whilst the Barnett formula is the now conventional way for the quantum to be determined, it is not binding on Westminster, it can be bypassed and variations exist in its application.[249] Indeed, the then Secretary of State for Environment, Food and Rural Affairs, Michael Gove, guaranteed in October 2018 that the Barnett formula would not be used regarding agriculture post-Brexit[250] – but without providing detail as to the likely alternative. Various suggestions have been made since

ment Science and Analytical Services, 'Agriculture in the United Kingdom 2019' (2020) https://assets.publishing.service.gov.uk/government/uploads/system/uploads/attachment_data/file/950618/AUK-2019-07jan21.pdf accessed 1 May 2021.

246 M. Keep, 'The Barnett Formula' (House of Commons Library, CBP 7386, 23 January 2020) http://researchbriefings.files.parliament.uk/documents/CBP-7386/CBP-7386.pdf accessed 1 May 2021, section 1.2. The Barnett formula is used to determine the annual changes in the block grants, rather than being the basis for determining the block grants from scratch.

247 Financing is discussed further across Chapter 3, Section 3.2.3, Chapter 4, Section 4.5.2.2 and Chapter 5, Section 5.2.1.

248 Keep (n246) 4–5 and 9–10. As Keep notes at 9–10, the cash settlement for Northern Ireland as part of the Confidence and Supply Agreement between the Conservative and Unionist Party and the Democratic Unionist Party is a prime example of 'formula bypass'.

249 Keep (n246) 7–10. For instance, whilst the Barnett formula applies to Wales, the UK Government has agreed that a baseline applies determined by Wales' needs in the relevant area, i.e. if the formula would indicate £5,000,000 for a specific issue but Wales needs £10,000,000, then Wales will receive the latter. See Keep (n246), Section 1.4.

250 FarmingUK Team, 'Gove Guarantees Agri Funding Will Not Be "Barnettised" Post-Brexit' (Farming UK 12 October 2018) www.farminguk.com/news/gove-guarantees-agri-funding-will-not-be-barnettised-post-brexit_50455.html accessed 1 May 2021.

then,[251] but no definite approach has been decided yet. Either way, devolved policies can be facilitated or curtailed by either how much England spends on agriculture (under the Barnett formula) or by the determination of a new funding approach – both of which are reliant upon the UK Parliament/Government.

Overall, the political discourse, the legal actions before the Supreme Court and the very limited agreements on establishing common frameworks all highlight the complexity of where the legal, practical and political issues surrounding devolution intersect.[252] Devolution grants legal powers to the devolved administrations, but they are by no means sacrosanct. The UK retains essential powers and will play key roles in shaping agricultural policy, directly and indirectly.

2.6 Conclusion

The broader context and landscape highlight that neither the UK's devolved nor centralised legislatures or governments can develop their own agricultural policies unilaterally without considering their surroundings and other frameworks. A complex system of multilevel governance exists that reflects the very nature of agriculture in a globalised world. Significant legal, political and trade relationships exist internationally and domestically, with issues, constraints and powers intertwining across the levels.

To engage internationally regarding agriculture, the UK must consider its international legal obligations. Central to this are the Northern Ireland Protocol and WTO law. Specific standards must be met in Northern Ireland; checks and controls must be imposed on imports from Great Britain into Northern Ireland, with the possibility also of customs; minimal export procedures on Northern Irish products going to Great Britain are required; and EU state aid rules (or their exemptions) must be complied with. These obligations must be borne in mind and complied with – both generally and also when developing policies in Great Britain or negotiating FTAs. At the same time, the Agreements under WTO law impose more general obligations on the UK – including regarding tariffs, financial support, and non-tariff barriers including SPS and TBT measures such as labelling. These underpinning frameworks are in place currently and create parameters within which any future agricultural policies must operate. What future international agreements might ensue and how they might relate to internal agricultural policies remains to be seen in Chapter 5.

Yet the international aspects are not the only major considerations. The internal dynamics are highly relevant and similarly complex. It cannot be simply averred that solely one level or another is responsible for and capable of developing and

251 As discussed in Chapter 5, Section 5.2.1.

252 For example, the Counsel General for Wales sought permission for a judicial review of the Internal Market Act 2020 but this was rejected. See *R (On the Application of the Counsel General for Wales) v the Secretary of State for Business, Energy and Industrial Strategy* [2021] EWHC 950 (Admin). This is further explored in Chapter 5, Section 5.2.3.

implementing UK agricultural policy/policies. Devolution exists and must be respected, but it has legal, political and practical limits. The common framework approach might be a useful mechanism to help address this, along with other informal mechanisms, but it is questionable whether it is effective in the time-pressured and uncertain context of Brexit (and indeed COVID-19) and, therefore, also whether it will have a chance to succeed.

Consequently, there are both internal and external parameters for UK agricultural policies – even if they remain somewhat fuzzy at times. Chapter 3 scrutinises the current proposals for agricultural policies and consider them in light of these dynamics and parameters – looking to how the policies have been influenced to date, whether they respect the parameters and what scope there is for further development of forward-looking agricultural policies. This lays the foundation for Chapter 4 to evaluate the policies more deeply in light of key themes, assessing both grabbed and missed opportunities to deliver a 21st-century agriculture.

3 The essence of UK and devolved agricultural policies

Chapter 1 highlighted the existence of variations in agricultural policies and laws across the four nations – as well as reflecting the variations in conditions and practices. However, these policies and laws were designed and operated within the context of the European Union's (EU) Common Agricultural Policy (CAP). Brexit introduces many challenges and opportunities, not least of which is the prospect to design agricultural policies afresh, away from EU constraints – facilitating policies that are adapted to the needs and desires of each of the four nations across the United Kingdom (UK).

In framing such policies, the parameters identified in Chapter 2 must be abided by, including obligations under international agreements, such as the World Trade Organization's (WTO) Agreement on Agriculture. The policies also need to react to the practical impacts of Brexit to provide clarity, coherency and certainty for industry actors in the short-term, as well as looking forward to the future. The UK and devolved administrations took up the gauntlet early on, working with stakeholders to develop domestic agricultural policies. These have been progressed to varying stages and will continue to evolve and be adapted over time.

The development and introduction of new policies raise multiple questions, with the most fundamental being what do they entail? And do they comply with the legal parameters outlined in Chapter 2? Consequently, this chapter undertakes a preliminary, analysis of the agricultural policies proposed by the four nations as they stand at the time of writing. It outlines the main aspects of the four agricultural policies, before providing an initial evaluation of their fit with the parameters identified in Chapter 2.[1] This provides a springboard for the deeper analysis undertaken in Chapter 4, especially considering the concept of resilience and its application to agriculture.

1 The analysis of proposals across the UK is not meant to be exhaustive. It focuses on key aspects to enable comparisons between the policies and draws out common themes and gaps.

DOI: 10.4324/9780429503719-3

3.1 Core characteristics of the four UK agricultural policies

Analysing the four proposed policies across the UK enables one to compare and contrast the differences in emphasis between the four nations starting with the path set by DEFRA and England, followed by the reactions from Wales, Northern Ireland and Scotland.[2]

3.1.1 England: the Agriculture Act 2020 and beyond

DEFRA has been proactive in pursuing its Green Brexit drive for agriculture and has published various policy documents specifically targeting farming, including the *Health and Harmony Paper*,[3] the *Environmental Land Management Scheme (ELMS) Discussion Paper*[4] and the *Path to Sustainable Farming Transition Plan*.[5] Other policy documents, especially the *25 Year Environment Plan*[6] and the *Ten Point Plan for a Green Industrial Revolution*,[7] multiple acts, including the European Union (EU) Withdrawal Act 2018 and the Trade Act 2021, and bills, comprising the Environment Bill 2019–2021, also impact the future of agriculture.

At the heart of the future of English farming (and, for reserved matters, for the whole of the UK) sits the Agriculture Act 2020. In comparison to previous drafts, the Act paves the way for a multi-annual financial assistance plan originally for a period of seven years (2021–2027) and a minimum period of five years thereafter.[8] This approach replicates the Multiannual Financial Framework of the EU and the CAP, thereby allowing for some certainty for farmers and the ability to plan ahead. Regarding the allocated budget, the UK Government has indicated that the fund will be guaranteed until the end of this Parliament.

2 For an outline of policy developments across the UK at earlier stages, see E. Downing and S. Coe, 'Brexit: Future UK Agriculture Policy' (House of Commons Library, CBP-8218, 11 September 2018) https://researchbriefings.files.parliament.uk/documents/CBP-8218/CBP-8218.pdf accessed 1 May 2021.

3 DEFRA, 'Health and Harmony: The Future for Food, Farming and the Environment in a Green Brexit' (Cm 9577, February 2018).

4 DEFRA, 'Environmental Land Management: Policy Discussion Document' (February 2020) https://consult.defra.gov.uk/elm/elmpolicyconsultation/supporting_documents/ELM%20Policy%20Discussion%20Document%20230620.pdf accessed 1 May 2021.

5 DEFRA, 'The Path to Sustainable Farming: An Agricultural Transition Plan 2021 to 2024' (November 2020) https://assets.publishing.service.gov.uk/government/uploads/system/uploads/attachment_data/file/954283/agricultural-transition-plan.pdf accessed 1 May 2021.

6 DEFRA, 'A Green Future: Our 25 Year Plant to Improve the Environment' (2018) https://assets.publishing.service.gov.uk/government/uploads/system/uploads/attachment_data/file/693158/25-year-environment-plan.pdf accessed 1 May 2021.

7 HM Government, 'The Ten Point Plan for a Green Industrial Revolution' (2020) www.gov.uk/government/publications/the-ten-point-plan-for-a-green-industrial-revolution accessed 1 May 2021.

8 Agriculture Act 2020, Section 4.

However, by scrutinising the details of this announcement, the UK Government only committed to spend 2019 levels in England (£2.4 billion per annum) for the period 2021–2022 to 2024–2025.[9] Despite creating certainty over the next few years, this practice entails a cut to the farming budget in real terms. In Wales, the President of the Farmers' Union of Wales asserted that this allocation results in a £137 million cut, that is 35% less than previously, from 2022.[10]

The Act puts in place a gradual end to direct, land- or area-based CAP payments following an agricultural transition period of seven years (ending at the end of 2027). During this agricultural transition period, the level of direct payments given to farmers diminishes to fund new schemes mainly based on 'public money for public goods'. This transition is intended to give time to farmers to adapt to the emerging mechanisms and structures in place to receive financial support in the future and/or adapt to become self-sufficient without the need for further support. This could ultimately put a worrying end to agricultural exceptionalism over the long term.

Beyond the progressive reduction of direct payments, the Agriculture Act establishes the existence of two pathways for farmers to be financially supported: public money for public goods (Section 1(1)) and increased productivity (Section 1(2)). Indeed, 'paying for environmental and animal welfare outcomes' and 'improving farm prosperity' are the only two main mechanisms confirmed by DEFRA in its *Path to Sustainable Farming Transition Plan*. Around 9% of the funds allocated to farming are to be spent on the second prong between 2021 and 2025,[11] whilst the main shift in funds occurs between direct payments (from 68% in 2021 to 34% in 2025) towards public money for public goods payments (from 23% in 2021 to 57% in 2025).[12]

3.1.1.1 The first prong: public money for public goods

Under this first prong (that is Section 1(1) of the Agriculture Act), the Secretary of State 'may give financial assistance' to farmers when delivering 'any one or more' of the list of public goods. The first point to note is that there is no obligation on the Secretary of State to financially support farmers – it is only an *enabling* power. The Act presses on with the move towards supporting farmers to deliver

9 *Path to Sustainable Farming Transition Plan* (n5) 25.

10 Farmers' Union of Wales, 'FUW Stresses Need for Clarity on Funding for Wales at Roundtable Meeting with Secretary of State for Environment, Food and Rural Affairs' (19 March 2021) https://fuw.org.uk/en/news/14441-fuw-stresses-need-for-clarity-on-funding-for-wales-at-roundtable-meeting-with-secretary-of-state-for-environment-food-and-rural-affairs accessed 1 May 2021.

11 *Path to Sustainable Farming Transition Plan* (n5) 26.

12 Ibid 26. Allocation beyond 2024/2025 is not yet known since the amount of funding available to farming is only guaranteed until the end of this Parliament (i.e. December 2024).

an *exhaustive* list of ten public goods.[13] These public goods can be described as setting 'purposes'[14] for future schemes or programmes developed by DEFRA and are broadly linked to the environment, climate change, livestock and plant biodiversity as well as the natural and cultural heritage. The Act positively widens the definition of public goods to now contain native breeds, the improvement of the genetic diversity of livestock and plants as well as the protection and improvement of soil quality – in contrast with the Agriculture Bill 2017–2019.[15] Crucially, this list is a closed one, which means that future schemes can only reward farmers to deliver these public goods; potentially generating gaps between those farmers who fall under the scope of the funding and those who do not. Such gaps could lead to further inequalities in the system. Furthermore, with the different pressures placed on farming and the agri-food supply chain, not leaving the door open as time progresses for other grounds to fund farmers appears overly restrictive.

The main tool for the implementation of this prong is the Environmental Land Management Scheme (ELMS) and its three tiers (as well as pilots where relevant).[16] Initially, access to ELMS does not appear to be restricted especially

13 Agriculture Act 2010, Section 1(1) provides that 'The Secretary of State may give financial assistance for or in connection with any one or more of the following purposes—

(a) managing land or water in a way that protects or improves the environment;
(b) supporting public access to and enjoyment of the countryside, farmland or woodland and better understanding of the environment;
(c) managing land or water in a way that maintains, restores or enhances cultural or natural heritage;
(d) managing land, water or livestock in a way that mitigates or adapts to climate change;
(e) managing land or water in a way that prevents, reduces or protects from environmental hazards;
(f) protecting or improving the health or welfare of livestock;
(g) conserving native livestock, native equines or genetic resources relating to any such animal;
(h) protecting or improving the health of plants;
(i) conserving plants grown or used in carrying on an agricultural, horticultural or forestry activity, their wild relatives or genetic resources relating to any such plant;
(j) protecting or improving the quality of soil'.

14 Ibid. The public money for public goods approach for DEFRA was clearly present in 2005 when the UK Government was already trying to reform the CAP. See HM Treasury and DEFRA, 'A Vision for the Common Agricultural Policy' (December 2005).

15 For a brief comparison of the Agriculture Bill 2019–2021 and the Agriculture Bill 2017–2019, see L. Petetin and V. Gravey, 'The Agriculture Bill: 8 Key Provisions and Recommendations' (Brexit and Environment Network 24 January 2020) www.brexitenvironment.co.uk/2020/01/24/agriculture-bill-8-key-provisions/ accessed 1 May 2021. For more on the Agriculture Bill 2017–2019, and S. Coe and E. Downing, 'The Agriculture Bill (2017–19)' (House of Commons Library, CBP-8405, 25 October 2018) https://researchbriefings.files.parliament.uk/documents/CBP-8405/CBP-8405.pdf accessed 1 May 2021.

16 For a general overview of ELMS, see generally *Environmental Land Management Scheme Discussion Paper* (n4). Other programmes for financial support include tree health pilots, farming in protected landscapes projects and Countryside Stewardship agreements and capi-

for the lower tiers.[17] A certain flexibility seems to be built into the different tiers to adapt to each farm or group of farms. Tier 1, the entry scheme or the Sustainable Farming Incentive (SFI), seeks to 'encourage the adoption of some *simple actions* that achieve more important environmental outcomes' (emphasis added).[18] Such actions consist of cover crops, nutrient, pest or livestock management or wildflower margins.[19] Similarly to Tier 1, Tier 2, or Local Nature Recovery, enables collaboration between farmers for '*actions* that support local nature recovery and delivers local environmental priorities'[20] (emphasis added) linked to environmental outcomes such as tree, shrub and/or hedge planting, habitat creation, restoration, management and interventions to mitigate flooding.[21] The delivery of landscape and ecosystems recovery over the long term is to be supported with the Landscape Recovery scheme in Tier 3, by targeting land use change projects through large-scale tree planting, peatland, bog, or wetland restoration as well as facilitating collaboration between farmers.[22] Test and trials are ongoing for Tier 3.[23] Crucially and in contrast to the previous two tiers, this third tier is *solely* supported according to the *environmental outcomes* delivered rather than paying for *actions*.

Within ELMS, Tier 1, i.e. the SFI, is the most developed scheme. The aim of the SFI is to support farmers for the '*actions* they take (going beyond regulatory requirements) to manage their land in an environmentally sustainable way' (emphasis added).[24] The other aim is to simplify the scheme (especially its running and its enforcement and compliance aspects) so that it becomes 'attractive and straightforward' in line with the simplification rhetoric adopted by the UK Government since the referendum campaign. The SFI offers three lev-

---

tal grants. Another key transition scheme creates a dedicated animal health and welfare pathway that builds on the existing regulatory baseline and enhances consumer transparency. At the core of this scheme is a five-year National Action Plan on Antimicrobial Resistance to improve UK biosecurity – strengthening the close link between farming and public health. See *Path to Sustainable Farming Transition Plan* (n5) 47. DEFRA undertook early ELMS tests and trials since 2018, see DEFRA, 'Environmental Land Management Tests and Trials: 23 Burns Farmer Group' (14 October 2020) www.gov.uk/government/case-studies/environmental-land-management-tests-and-trials-23-burns-farmer-group accessed 1 May 2021.

17 Ibid 31.

18 Ibid 40.

19 *Environmental Land Management Scheme Discussion Paper* (n4) 14.

20 *Path to Sustainable Farming Transition Plan* (n5) 32.

21 DEFRA, 'Sustainable Farming Incentive: Defra's Plans for Piloting and Launching the Scheme' (*SFI Paper*) (16 March 2021) www.gov.uk/government/publications/sustainable-farming-incentive-scheme-pilot-launch-overview/sustainable-farming-incentive-defras-plans-for-piloting-and-launching-the-scheme accessed 1 May 2021; and *Environmental Land Management Scheme Discussion Paper* (n4) 22.

22 *Path to Sustainable Farming Transition Plan* (n5) 32.

23 The Team, 'Shaping the New Landscape Recovery Scheme' (DEFRA Blog 1 April 2021) https://defrafarming.blog.gov.uk/2021/04/01/shaping-the-new-landscape-recovery-scheme/ accessed 1 May 2021.

24 *SFI Paper* (n 21).

els – introductory, intermediate and advanced – to choose from. Positively and encouragingly, each level contains progressively stricter requirements that aim to create greater environmental outcomes. The piloting of this scheme (starting in late 2021) will be the first to implement Section 1 of the Agriculture Act 2020. However, DEFRA has supported similar schemes initiated by the CAP, in particular with results-based agri-environment payment scheme (RBAPS) since 2016.[25]

In its inception, the scheme will support farmers to deliver actions based on a set of eight standards that is likely to expand over time.[26] Most strikingly and in contrast to what the *SFI Paper* suggests, i.e. that farmers will only be supported beyond the regulatory baseline, some of the SFI standards are rather similar to those in existing environmental laws and requirements. This is especially the case for the introductory level:[27] in particular the arable and horticultural land standard imitates water pollution requirements,[28] whilst the arable and horticultural soil standard replicates good agricultural and environmental condition (GAEC) 4 on providing minimum soil cover.[29]

The issue of double funding, i.e the funding of one action being counted for two different standards is, however, not mentioned in the *SFI Paper*. This appears as a gap since some actions could fall under multiple standards. Most importantly, the framing of the SFI around the fact that farmers will pursue not actions, but *standards* is rather interesting – potentially to move away from CAP jargon but more crucially to make it look like DEFRA will fund *outcomes*. However, the emphasis for support is, in the end, on *actions*.[30]

25 Such schemes took place in North Yorkshire, Norfolk and Suffolk. For more see, S. Chaplin et al., 'Pilot Results-Based Payment Approaches for Agri-Environment Schemes in Arable and Upland Grassland Systems in England: Final Report' (Natural England and Yorkshire Dales National Park Authority 2019). It is important to note that these were EU pilot projects. See European Commission, 'Farming for Biodiversity: The Results-Based Agri-Environment Schemes' https://ec.europa.eu/environment/nature/rbaps/index_en.htm accessed 1 May 2021.

26 The initial eight standards in the pilot are: arable and horticultural land; arable and horticultural soils; improved grassland; improved grassland soils; low and no input grassland; hedgerow; on-farm woodland; and waterbody buffering. Two standards specifically focus on soil which is a welcome emphasis.

27 T. Lancaster, Twitter post (10 March 2021) https://twitter.com/tommlancaster/status/1369705217789472768 accessed 1 May 2021.

28 DEFRA and Environment Agency, 'Reduce Pollution Risks When You Use Manure or Fertiliser' (2 April 2018) www.gov.uk/guidance/rules-for-farmers-and-land-managers-to-prevent-water-pollution#reduce-pollution-risks-when-you-use-manure-or-fertiliser accessed 1 May 2021.

29 Rural Payments Agency, 'Guide to Cross Compliance in England: 2016' (6 January 2016) www.gov.uk/guidance/guide-to-cross-compliance-in-england-2016/gaec-4-providing-minimum-soil-cover accessed 1 May 2021.

30 For more regarding concerns on the SFI, see Sustain, 'Defra Launch the New Farm Support Scheme Pilot and Invite Farmers to Get Involved' (10 March 2021) www.sustainweb.org/news/mar21-details-sustainable-farm-incentive-pilot/ accessed 1 May 2021.

Problematically, the SFI is only open to the 88,000 recipients of the basic payment scheme (BPS). As observed in Chapter 1, England/DEFRA has made the deliberate choice of setting its minimum claim size for BPS to five hectares. The scheme will not be fully expanded until late 2024. Yet, in England in 2019, there were 16,325 holdings under five hectares that farmed 28,394 hectares and represented just over 15% of all commercial agricultural holdings.[31] The minimum claim size means that these small holders are locked out of this new scheme; they will not be able to participate in its co-design, pilot schemes or the launch of the actual scheme in mid-2022. This creates inequalities in the support system. Here, DEFRA is replicating the approach it adopted under the CAP to restrict access to financial support by small, family farms and rather prefers to fund bigger, more profitable (?) farms. However, small holdings are often more biodiversity- and environmentally-friendly as well as more business-minded since they often are profitable without receiving BPS.[32]

Further, DEFRA expects the need for advice to be minimal for the SFI. However, it seems that it is the private sector, rather than the public sector, who will be the main providers for advice thereby placing the costs on the farmers themselves to be able to join the schemes – either on their own or via their agents.[33]

3.1.1.2 The second prong: enhanced productivity

The second prong for financial support under Section 1(2) of the Act gives discretionary power to the Secretary of State (again) to support a profitable, business type of agriculture – consistent with a sustainable intensification, productivist

31 DEFRA, 'Structure of the Agricultural Industry in England and the UK at June' (Farm Type Breakdown for Commercial Holdings) (26 April 2021) www.gov.uk/government/statistical-data-sets/structure-of-the-agricultural-industry-in-england-and-the-uk-at-june accessed 1 May 2021. See also B. Driessen, 'Why Small Farms Must Be Included in New Land Use Schemes' (Food Research Collaboration 18 March 2021) https://foodresearch.org.uk/foodvoices/small-farmers-must-be-included-in-new-land-use-schemes/ accessed 1 May 2021.

32 For more on the importance of small farms, see Food Farming & Countryside Commission, 'Growing a Mandate for Change' (RSA 2017) www.thersa.org/globalassets/pdfs/reports/rsa-ffc-commission-prospectus.pdf accessed 1 May 2021; The Landworkers' Alliance, 'Feeding the Future' (November 2014) www.campaignforrealfarming.org/wp-content/uploads/2014/11/Feeding-the-Future-Landworkers-Alliance-A4-low-res.pdf accessed 1 May 2021; R. Laughton, 'A Matter of Scale: A Study of the Productivity, Financial Viability and Multifunctional Benefits of Small Farms (20 Ha and Less)' (The Landworkers' Alliance and the Centre for Agroecology, Water and Resilience 2017) www.scholacampesina.org/wp-content/uploads/2018/10/A-Matter-of-Scale-Report-LWA-2017.pdf accessed 1 May 2021; Ecological Land Cooperative, 'Small Farm Profits' (2018) https://ecologicalland.coop/small-farm-profits accessed 1 May 2021.

33 Support for advice under the SFI is available under the Future Farming Resilience Fund as will be observed in the following sub-section.

paradigm.[34] Indeed, support under Section 1(2)(a) aims to improve the productivity of the holding.[35] As noted, this is now called 'Improving Farm Prosperity' to enhance farm businesses.[36] Dedicated schemes comprise the 'Farming Investment Fund', 'Future Farming Resilience Fund', 'Research and Development and Innovation projects', 'Slurry Investment Scheme' and 'New Entrants Support Scheme',[37] with the first two having progressed the most.

The Farming Investment Fund comprises of two schemes.[38] First, the Farming Equipment and Technology Fund provides smaller grants to improve business performance by purchasing items from a list of equipment, technology and small infrastructure investments. Second, the Farming Transformation Fund supports larger or more complicated investments. Awarded grants could support on-farm water storage infrastructure, precision agriculture equipment, robotic or automated technology as well as equipment and technology for storing, sorting or processing products. Both schemes are similar to the Countryside Productivity Grants schemes that were available under the CAP.

The Future Farming Resilience Fund aims to provide nine million pounds for organisations that advise farmers during the agricultural transition on the impact of reductions to direct payments on their business, the adaptation of their business models, business planning, performance recording and succession planning.[39] However, this fund is limited to those farmers who are 'in receipt of Basic Payment Scheme (BPS) payments'.[40] So once again, small holders are excluded from crucial funds to transition towards the new regimes and the uncertainties they raise and from receiving crucial advice.

Section 1(2)(b) is complementary and enables financial support for ancillary activities 'carried on, by or for a producer', where 'ancillary activities' are defined as 'selling, marketing, preparing, packaging, processing or distributing products deriving from an agricultural, horticultural or forestry activity' in Section 1(5).

34 L. Petetin, 'Setting the Path for UK and Devolved Agriculture' in I. Antonopoulos, M. Bell, A. Cavoski and L. Petetin (eds) *The Governance of Agriculture in Post-Brexit UK* (Routledge forthcoming 2022). For more on sustainable intensification, see T. Garnett and C. Godfray, 'Sustainable Intensification in Agriculture: Navigating a Course through Competing Food System Priorities' (Food Climate Research Network, Oxford Martin Programme on the Future of Food 2012); and OECD, 'Policy Instruments to Support Green Growth in Agriculture' (OECD Green Growth Studies 2012).

35 Agriculture Act, Section 1(5).

36 *Path to Sustainable Farming Transition Plan* (n5) 12.

37 Ibid 24–25.

38 G. James, 'The Farming Investment Fund: An Overview' (DEFRA Blog 30 March 2021) https://defrafarming.blog.gov.uk/2021/03/30/the-farming-investment-fund-an-overview/ accessed 1 May 2021.

39 A. Powley, 'The Future Farming Resilience Fund: Supporting Farmers through Transition' (DEFRA Blog 25 March 2021) https://defrafarming.blog.gov.uk/2021/03/25/the-future-farming-resilience-fund-supporting-farmers-through-transition/ accessed 1 May 2021.

40 Ibid.

The introduced changes could act as an incentive, especially for owners of smaller farming holdings, to take up processing and packaging on a small scale, helping them to diversify, improve their business model and be more economically resilient. More general provisions on producer organisations could also facilitate such resilience in the agri-food supply chain.[41] Finally, when carefully scrutinising the Act and its two prongs, the similarities with the support under the CAP are rather striking. This sharply contrasts with earlier calls for an abrupt departure from the CAP.

3.1.1.3 Other key components

The Agriculture Act places greater emphasis on the relationship between agricultural production and the rest of agri-food supply than the Agriculture Bill 2017–2019, for example, with the provisions on fair dealing.[42] Originally, the Agriculture Bill 2017–2019 only focused on the contract between the primary producer and the first purchaser.[43] Now a linear approach to the agri-food supply chain under Section 29 acknowledges more holistically the asymmetries in bargaining power between the actors along the agri-food supply chain who are parties to a contract and the lack of transparency in price formation. A future system could receive some inspiration from the Spanish mixed model/approach based on voluntary initiatives and regulatory/statutory instruments of unfair trading practices to rebalance the agri-food supply chain in favour of the weak link, i.e. the primary producer,[44] as well as considering the 2019 EU Unfair Trading Practices Directive.[45]

Regarding food production, whilst improving the quality of agricultural products (not limited to food products) can be supported under Section 1(5) of the Act, it does not mention the production of healthy and nutritious food.[46] However, promoting healthy and high-quality food production should be two sides of the same coin.[47] Further, Section 1(4) requires that regard must be had to 'the need to encourage the production of food by producers in England and its production by them in an environmentally sustainable way' – indicating another link between financial support and food production and how these

41 Agriculture Act, Sections 30 to 32.

42 Agriculture Act, Section 29.

43 House of Commons, Environment, Food and Rural Affairs Committee, 'Scrutiny of the Agriculture Bill, Tenth Report of Session 2017–19' (HC 1591, 27 November 2018) 19.

44 L. Petetin, V. Gravey and B. Moore, 'Setting the Bar for a Green Brexit in Food and Farming' (Soil Association 2019) www.soilassociation.org/causes-campaigns/green-brexit/ accessed 1 May 2021, 20.

45 Directive (EU) 2019/633 of the European Parliament and the Council on Unfair Trading Practices in Business-to-Business Relationships in the Agricultural and Food Supply Chain [2019] OJ L111/59.

46 Although the production of healthy food is mentioned in passing in the *Path to Sustainable Farming Transition Plan* (n5) 7.

47 Petetin and Gravey (n15).

two aspects are not necessarily mutually exclusive or unrelated. When applying for assistance, farmers do not need to meet these overall objectives, rather the schemes themselves should achieve them – this should be particularly borne in mind when designing schemes under the second, productivity prong. Strikingly, this Section is the only time the word sustainability/sustainable is mentioned in the Act. Further, food security plays a much bigger role in the Act than in the original version of the Bill. Section 19 stipulates that the Secretary of State is under the obligation to report to Parliament on UK food security at least every five years, thereby aiming to guarantee the availability of supplies for UK citizens and replicating one of the pillars of the CAP whilst promoting environmental sustainability and resilience to ensure long-term food security. However, there is no obligation for the Secretary of State to act upon the report.[48] Finally, England is developing its own food strategy.[49]

Other main aspects covered by the Act include amendments to agricultural tenancies,[50] intervention in agricultural markets (public market intervention and private storage aid), transparency and fairness in agri-food supply chain to include the collection and sharing of data as well as fertilisers, identification and traceability of animals, red meat levy, marketing standards, organic products and carcass classification.[51] By regulating on these aspects which clearly impact the devolved administrations, DEFRA adopts a centralised approach. Indeed, the Act amends existing laws to facilitate (English?) approaches post-Brexit.[52]

The Act provides Wales[53] (temporarily)[54] and Northern Ireland[55] with enabling powers to financially support farmers. In these two nations, comparable approaches to England can be adopted to reduce and, in the long-term, eradicate direct payments. There is no schedule for Scotland in the Act as it has continu-

48 See in contrast the obligations under the Climate Change Act 2008, Section 9.
49 See National Food Strategy, 'Read Part One' www.nationalfoodstrategy.org/partone/ accessed 1 May 2021.
50 This aspect is discussed in Chapter 4, Section 4.4.4.
51 Whilst it is necessary and positive to have some progress on these matters, this chapter focuses on the fundamental underpinnings of agricultural policy and related changes.
52 L. Petetin, M. Dobbs, J. Hunt, B. Pontin and H. Pritchard, 'Written Evidence on the LCM in Relation to the UK Agriculture Bill' (Climate Change, Environment and Rural Affairs Committee of the Senedd Cymru, CCERA(5) AB09, 2021) https://business.senedd.wales/documents/s99656/Paper%20-%20Dr%20Ludivine%20Petetin%20Dr%20Mary%20Dobbs%20Prof%20Jo%20Hunt%20Prof%20Ben%20Pontin%20and%20Dr%20Huw%20Pritchard.html?CT=2 accessed 1 May 2021.
53 See Agriculture Act, Schedule 5 with certain provisions expiring at the end of 2024, especially Sections 46 and 47.
54 Agriculture Act, Section 47 establishes a 'sunset' clause regarding provisions relating to Wales, including Schedule 5 – generally providing for these to expire at the end of 2024.
55 See Agriculture Act, Schedule 6. No such sunset clause applies to Northern Ireland, despite this having been flagged as a concern in Northern Ireland Assembly debates and the Committee on Agriculture, Environment and Rural Affairs requesting such a clause. See Northern Ireland Assembly, 'Agriculture Bill: Legislative Consent Motion' (Debates 31 March 2020) www.theyworkforyou.com/ni/?id=2020-03-31.5.4&p=13867 accessed 1 May 2021.

ally rejected engagement in its formulation.[56] Nonetheless, as with Wales and Northern Ireland, the Act directly affects Scottish agricultural policy in reserved areas and indirectly when drafting future policies.[57] Crucially, there is limited content on rural development in the Act. Section 16 does not give powers to the Ministers in England, Wales or Northern Ireland to introduce new rural development schemes under retained EU legislation – these can only be modified.

3.1.2 Wales: sustainable land management

A key focus of the Welsh Government since the 2016 referendum has been to draft a dedicated future agricultural policy. This was undertaken via three key Consultations – the 2020 *Agriculture (Wales) White Paper*[58] which builds upon the 2019 *Sustainable Farming and our Land* Consultation[59] and the 2018 *Brexit and our Land* Consultation.[60] They provide a framework for the future of agricultural policy in Wales based on enabling powers. Emphasis is placed on the objective of sustainable land management and the future establishment of one support scheme – the Sustainable Farming Scheme – to enable a 'holistic assessment of the economic, environmental and social opportunities on farms'[61] in line with the Well-being of Future Generations (Wales) Act 2015 and the Environment (Wales) Act 2016,[62] whilst phasing out direct payments – similarly to the Agriculture Act. It is proposed that the new Scheme will start in 2025 after the enabling powers under the Agriculture Act expire at the end of 2024.

A farmer can join the proposed Sustainable Farming Scheme after going through a 'Farm Sustainability Review' (tailored to each farm), which itself results in a 'Farm Sustainability Plan'.[63] Advisory services are to be provided to farmers entering the Sustainable Farming Scheme at both stages of application to ensure dedicated, appropriate advice as to the specific piece of land they farm. However,

56 This was discussed in the Scottish Parliament in January 2019, but preference was given for an independent, Scottish approach. See, Scottish Parliament, 'Future Rural Policy and Support' (Debates 10 January 2019) https://archive2021.parliament.scot/parliamentarybusiness/report.aspx?r=11875&mode=html accessed 1 May 2021, 15.03.
57 See Chapter 4, Section 4.5.2.
58 Welsh Government, 'Consultation Document: Agriculture (Wales) White Paper (*White Paper*)' (16 December 2020). To see a response from Wales Environment Link on the 2020 consultation, see K. Whitfield, 'Agriculture (Wales) White Paper' (Wales Environment Link 21 April 2021) https://waleslink.org/agriculture-wales-white-paper/ accessed 1 May 2021.
59 Welsh Government, 'Consultation Document: Sustainable Farming and Our Land' (2019).
60 Welsh Government, 'Consultation Document: Brexit and Our Land – Securing the Future of Welsh Farming' (2018).
61 *Sustainable Farming and Our Land* (n59) paragraph 6.6.
62 It also supports the three pillars of sustainable development. For more on these acts and the concept of 'sustainable management of resources', see V. Jenkins, 'Sustainable Management of Natural Resources: Lessons from Wales' (2018) 30(3) *Journal of Environmental Law* 399; and V. Jenkins, 'Welsh Devolution and the Protection of the Environment: The Story So Far and the Future Challenges' (2016) 96 *E-law (now Murdoch University Law Review)* 23.
63 *Sustainable Farming and Our Land* (n59) paragraph 1.23.

such technical hurdles could result in increased costs for the farmers to join the scheme if these reviews and plans are costly to set up if they have to pay for advice themselves. Further, access to the scheme is meant to be universal (all farmers can apply) but not automatic (so not all applicants will be successful).

After joining the scheme, farmers have access to two complementary forms of farm support: the Sustainable Farming Payment and Business Support – imitating the two prongs in the Agriculture Act (and the CAP).[64] The Sustainable Farming Payment supports the delivery of environmental outcomes.[65] It possesses four main components to facilitate the provision of public goods (as such, it represents the majority of the budget):[66] a stable income to farmers;[67] payments for environmental outcomes; the reward of new and existing practices (i.e. for both maintenance and creation – the former being essential to reward farmers already undertaking best environmental practices); and a flexible application to all types of farms – replicating much of the content of the Agriculture Act apart from the stable income element. The Business Support payment, i.e. the second prong, provides both financial and practical support such as advice (i.e. business capacity), capital investment, knowledge transfer and skills development, whilst building upon the experience and expertise of Farming Connect[68] to generate economic outcomes.[69]

Similarly to the Agriculture Act, one of the biggest changes between the Consultations is the increased emphasis on sustainable food production as the responses to the *Brexit and our Land* Consultation indicated the 'importance of not separating food production from environmental work on a farm'[70]

64 A third pathway has been proposed to support the wider industry and supply chain (rather than just farmers) – including promoting a Welsh Brand – with sustainable land management still as the overarching umbrella. See *Sustainable Farming and Our Land* (n59) 66.

65 Such 'non-market goods' include improved soils, clean air, clean water, improved biodiversity, actions to reduce global warming. See *White Paper* (n58) 28. For more on the state of the environment in Wales, see Royal Society for the Protection of Birds Cymru, 'Wales' Annual Report 2019–2020' (2020). For more on local projects, see CLA Cymru, FWAG Cymru and GWCT Cymru, 'Final Report of the Berwyn, Migneint, Black Mountains & Radnor Upland Recovery Project' www.gwct.org.uk/wales/research/berwyn,-migneint,-black-mountains-radnor-upland-recovery-project/ accessed 1 May 2021. For more on the food system in Wales, see A. Sanderson Bellamy and T. Marsden, 'A Welsh Food System Fit for Future Generations' (WWF Cymru 2020).

66 *Sustainable Farming and Our Land* (n59) 46.

67 In order to provide farmers with a guaranteed income and paying for environmental outcomes rather than being compensated for costs/inputs. See *White Paper* (n58) paragraph 2.63.

68 For more on Farming Connect, see the following dedicated webpage https://businesswales.gov.wales/farmingconnect/ accessed 1 May 2021.

69 *Sustainable Farming and Our Land* (n59) 9.

70 Ibid paragraph 1.20. A specific consultation on food took place in 2019, see Welsh Government, 'Consultation Document: Our Ambition to Further Develop Wales' Food and Drink Sector' (2019) to follow Welsh Government, 'Food for Wales, Food from Wales 2010/2020 – Food strategy for Wales' (2010).

– including high-quality agri-food products.[71] Here stakeholders asked for a more holistic approach to the agri-food supply chain, albeit more in line with the current mechanisms for support under the CAP. This was reflected in the change of the name of the scheme. The 2018 *Brexit and our Land* Consultation simply referred to 'land management' whilst now the objective of 'sustainable land management' indicates a greater emphasis on sustainability and a more obvious link between land used for production and the delivery of public goods – unfortunately reproducing the sustainable intensification, productivist paradigm in the Agriculture Act; however, this link may be essential now in the aftermath of COVID-19 and the threat of global food shortages. However, the *White Paper*[72] disappointingly takes a step back when it comes to cooperation and collaboration at scale to deliver public money for public goods (even though it was one of the main components of *Brexit and our Land*[73] and to a lesser extent in the *Sustainable Farming and our Land*[74]) – possibly hindering a holistic approach to the countryside. These comments are largely echoed by the National Farmers' Union Cymru[75] and the Farmers' Union of Wales.[76]

Beyond the delivery of environmental outcomes, the Sustainable Farming Payment only *indirectly* contributes to the provision of economic and social outcomes.[77] There is some emphasis on public health, rural communities and the promotion and perennity of the Welsh language but they could have been strengthened.[78] As such it is assumed that most social outcomes are to be produced through economic and environmental outcomes rather than targeting social outcomes *per se*. Some exceptions are noted such as reducing antimicrobial resistance.[79] However, targeting social outcomes separately and of their own standing is necessary so that social outcomes do not feel like by-products.

One proposed type of payments within the *White Paper* (alongside the Sustainable Farming Scheme) could support the wider industry and supply chain

71 *White Paper* (n58) 29. There is, however, no content specifically related to diet.

72 There is only reference to collaboration in the *White Paper* (n58) 32.

73 *Brexit and our Land* (n60) 47.

74 *Sustainable Farming and Our Land* (n59) 55–56.

75 National Farmers' Union Cymru, 'White Paper Policy Proposals Do Not Match Industry's Ambition, Says NFU Cymru' (28 March 2021) www.nfu-cymru.org.uk/news/latest-news/white-paper-policy-proposals-do-not-match-industry/ accessed 1 May 2021; and National Farmers' Union Cymru, 'NFU Cymru Response: Welsh Government Consultation Agriculture (Wales) White Paper' (28 March 2021) www.nfu-cymru.org.uk/nfu-cymru/documents/consultation-response-white-paper-final/ accessed 1 May 2021.

76 Farmers' Union of Wales, 'FUW Reacts to Agriculture (Wales) White Paper' (16 December 2020) https://fuw.org.uk/en/news/14273-fuw-reacts-to-agriculture-wales-white-paper accessed 1 May 2021; and Farmers' Union of Wales, 'Farmers' Union of Wales Response to the Welsh Government's Agriculture (Wales) White Paper' (25 March 2021) www.fuw.org.uk/images/Consultation_Responses/Agriculture_Wales_White_Paper_FUW_Response-FINAL.pdf accessed 1 May 2021.

77 *White Paper* (n58) 29; *Sustainable Farming and Our Land* (n59) 27.

78 Ibid 8.

79 Ibid 28.

(beyond the farm gate), as in England.[80] This support would aim, for example, to[81] improve the promotional offer for farmers' produce, to encourage greater market alignment between production and consumption (that is, helping farmers understand what consumers and the agri-food supply chain want to purchase), to increase the amount and value of Welsh products used in the supply chain and to shorten supply chains to strengthen 'localism'.[82]

This scheme makes various connections between this proposed fund and rural development funds. How it does so is rather disconcerting since it seems to equate rural development with the rest of the agri-food supply chain – indicating the misunderstanding in Wales (but also throughout the rest of the UK) around what rural development is actually about. Funds do not seem to be available to cover broader ranging elements and objectives that are currently included in rural development programmes (RDPs) such as the pursuit of a balanced territorial development of rural economies and communities as well as the promotion of social cohesion and inclusion, or poverty reduction.[83] Another key component of current RDPs is LEADER.[84] The LEADER bottom-up approach supports local actors (farmers, rural businesses, local organisations, public authorities and individuals) to collaborate across different sectors to create local action groups (LAGs).[85] These groups aim to foster partnerships as well as to design and ensure the implementation of local development strategies.[86] In contrast, the proposed support for the wider industry and supply chain would only partially contribute to the development of rural economies and communities. Such a modification

80 *White Paper* (n58) 35.
81 Ibid 36.
82 Ibid 14.
83 Regulation (EU) No 1305/2013 of the European Parliament and of the Council of 17 December 2013 on Support for Rural Development by the European Agricultural Fund for Rural Development (EAFRD) and Repealing Council Regulation (EC) No 1698/2005 [2013] OJ L347/487, respectively Articles 4(c) and 5(6).
84 As noted in Chapter 1, LEADER originates from the phrase 'Liaison Entre Actions de Développement de l'Économie Rurale' or 'Links between the rural economy and development actions'.
85 European Commission, 'LEADER' https://ec.europa.eu/info/food-farming-fisheries/key-policies/common-agricultural-policy/rural-development_en#leader accessed 1 May 2021. See also European Network for Rural Development, 'LAG Database' https://enrd.ec.europa.eu/leader-clld/lag-database_en accessed 1 May 2021.
86 For more on RDPs, see K. Kis, J. Gal and A. Veha, 'Effectiveness, Efficiency and Sustainability in Local Rural Development Partnerships' (2015) 6(3–4) *Applied Studies in Agribusiness and Commerce* 31; J. Michalek, P. Ciaian and F. Di Marcantonio, 'Regional Impacts of the EU Rural Development Programme: Poland's Food Processing Sector' (2020) 54(10) *Regional Studies* 1389; I. Râmniceanu and R. Ackrill, 'EU Rural Development Policy in the New Member States: Promoting Multifunctionality?' (2007) 23(4) *Journal of Rural Studies* 416; A. Lopolito, G. Nardone and R. Sisto, 'Towards a Comprehensive Evaluation of Local Action Groups in LEADER Programmes' (2011) 10(1) *Mediterranean Journal of Economics, Agriculture and Environment* 43; and A. Andersson, S. Höjgård and E. Rabinowicz, 'Evaluation of Results and Adaptation of EU Rural Development Programmes' (2017) 67 *Land Use Policy* 298.

to the approach towards the countryside could negatively impact rural vitality – especially if RDPs are not continued in parallel. Problematically, the replacement of EU structural funds with the Levelling Up Fund and ultimately the UK Shared Prosperity Fund may not be adequate considering the uncertainty around the allocation system and the amount of funds available under this prospective fund.[87]

Other proposed schemes cover forestry and woodland management, animal health and welfare and monitoring through the effective use of data and remote technology. Further, notwithstanding a clear emphasis on health (including public health by focusing on air and water quality[88] and animal health and antimicrobial resistance[89]), there is no obvious link made between public health and the production of healthy, nutritious food for a good diet – as in England.

From a regulatory baseline perspective, the Welsh Consultations all indicate a great impetus for a reform of the regulatory framework for farming. It emphasises maintaining current standards with the creation of National Minimum Standards that would enter into force at the same time as the Sustainable Farming Scheme. National Minimum Standards aim to consolidate the regulatory framework directed at agriculture and agricultural production spread across various legislative instruments, especially those which support cross-compliance.[90] This could positively increase farmer's awareness of these legal requirements and ultimately facilitate and maintain compliance.[91]

Finally, and despite the objective of supporting farmers to deliver environmental *outcomes*, paragraph 1.31 of *Sustainable Farming and Our Land* states that '[i]f a farmer consistently implements the appropriate actions but the outcome does not arise for a reason beyond the farmer's control, it would be unfair for the farmer not to be paid. We propose the Welsh Government should bear the risk if agreed actions do not lead to outcomes'. Practically this means that both the Farm Sustainable Review and Plan allow payments for *actions* towards outcomes rather than outcomes *per se*.[92] This indicates, yet again, the difficulties of putting

87 For more on the Levelling Up Fund, see HM Treasury, Ministry to House, Communities and Local Government and Development for Transport, 'Levelling Up Fund: Prospectus' (March 2021) https://assets.publishing.service.gov.uk/government/uploads/system/uploads/attachment_data/file/966138/Levelling_Up_prospectus.pdf accessed 1 May 2021. For more on the UK Shared Prosperity Fund, see P. Brien, 'The UK Shared Prosperity Fund' (House of Commons Library, CBP-8527, 29 January 2021) https://commonslibrary.parliament.uk/research-briefings/cbp-8527/ accessed 1 May 2021. For more on these points, see Chapter 5, Section 4.5.2.2.

88 *White Paper* (n58) 9. See also Welsh Government, 'Antimicrobial Resistance in Animals and the Environment: Implementation Plan' (15 July 2019) https://gov.wales/antimicrobial-resistance-animals-and-environment-implementation-plan accessed 1 May 2021.

89 *White Paper* (n58) 9. See also Welsh Government, 'Animal Health and Welfare Framework: Implementation Plan 2019 to 2020' (19 July 2019) https://gov.wales/animal-health-and-welfare-framework-implementation-plan-2019-2020 accessed 1 May 2021.

90 *White Paper* (n58) 15.

91 Ibid.

92 *Sustainable Farming and Our Land* (n59) 15.

in place a support system based purely on the provision of public goods, especially when such provision does not materialise (and is beyond the farmer's control).[93] It also suggests that the Welsh Government could be acting as an underwriter where actions have not been delivered.[94]

Whilst it may be 'fair' to provide financial (and other) support for actions, agreed milestones and specific tasks completed and to guarantee an income to farmers, this system departs from a pure 'public money for public goods' model and reverses back towards the familiar system of payments for actions (rather than payments by outcomes) present under the current agri-environment schemes and again in line with some of the tiers in ELMS in England. This system enables the easing of farmers towards new financial systems but at the same time it waters down the public money for public goods turn and the provision of poorer environmental and social results could ensue. The path set by DEFRA is visibly affecting the formulation of Welsh agricultural policy.

3.1.3 Northern Ireland and its Strategy

As noted, Northern Ireland did not have a functioning Assembly or Executive from January 2017 until January 2020. In that political vacuum, the civil servants sought to keep things ticking over and also make inroads into developing the groundwork for future policies in the hope that their work would be of use when eventually the government was restored. A key element here was the creation of stakeholder groups by the previous Executive, including one on agriculture. Working with the agriculture stakeholder group, DAERA created a *Draft Agricultural Strategy* that it published in August 2018 in a public 'engagement' exercise – an informal consultation, since a Minister was needed to sign-off on an official consultation.[95]

The first point to note is that the *Draft Agricultural Strategy* distinguishes between a transitional period and a post-transitional period. The transitional

93 Arguably, this might constitute a means to encourage risk-averse farmers to participate in the schemes.

94 M. Cardwell, 'Results-Based Agri-Environmental Scheme Design: Regulatory Implications' – draft paper (2021). This approach was supported by the majority of the respondents to the Consultation. See Welsh Government, 'Summary of Responses Prepared by Wavehill Ltd: Sustainable Farming and Our Land' (2020) https://gov.wales/sites/default/files/consultations/2020-05/sustainable-farms-summary-of-responses_1.pdf accessed 1 May 2021, paragraph 3.5.

95 DAERA, 'Northern Ireland Future Agricultural Policy Framework: Stakeholder Engagement' (Draft Agricultural Strategy) (1 August 2018) www.daera-ni.gov.uk/sites/default/files/consultations/daera/NI%20Future%20Agricultural%20Policy%20Framework%20-%20Stakeholder%20Engagement%20-%20FINAL_0.pdf accessed 1 May 2021. For more on agricultural policy in Northern Ireland, please see M. Dobbs, 'Northern Ireland's Agricultural Quagmire: How to Develop a Sustainable Agricultural Policy?' in I. Antonopoulos, M. Bell, A. Cavoski and L. Petetin (eds) *The Governance of Agriculture in Post-Brexit UK* (Routledge forthcoming 2022).

period is intended to provide some short-term security and certainty for stakeholders who currently receive funding under CAP, by providing, for example, for the continuation of direct payments as they currently exist. It refers to a two-year period for 2020-2021[96] where the existing approach would largely remain (with some simplification), with an evolution then towards a future (but as yet, undetermined), well-signposted agricultural policy.[97] This is a very short time in the context of agricultural policies – especially considering the broader surrounding turbulence posed by Brexit, COVID-19 and climate change, but as it is linked to the UK Government's guarantee of funding, this should be taken as now being potentially extended until 2024 – since the current Government has guaranteed funding. Even so, this remains quite limited, and a new Northern Ireland agricultural policy would need to be designed, approved and communicated immediately – which brings us to the remainder of the *Strategy* and its broader points.

The *Draft Agricultural Strategy* lays out four central objectives: increased productivity, improved resilience, environmental sustainability and 'an integrated, efficient, sustainable, competitive and responsive supply chain'.[98] These largely mirror those identified by the previous DAERA Minister in a letter in March 2017.[99] The detail in the *Draft Agricultural Strategy* reflects a weighting in these objectives towards economic considerations and to an extent a certain fluffiness and occasional naivety. Agriculture in Northern Ireland is to aim somehow to 'at the very least, keep pace with the productivity growth of its competitors and indeed outperform them' – including America and France, according to the *Strategy*.[100] Despite noting that 'a healthy and sustainable environment [...] underpins resilience',[101] Section 5 clarifies that resilience focuses on economic resilience.[102] Further, no other aspects such as rural development, public health

96 *Draft Agricultural Strategy* (n95) 7.

97 Ibid 19.

98 Ibid 7 and 19.

99 Cited in the following DAERA, 'Letter from the Permanent Secretary for Northern Ireland to the Northern Ireland Affairs Committee' (20 June 2018) www.parliament.uk/globalassets/documents/commons-committees/northern-ireland-affairs/2017-19/Correspondence-2017-19/Correspondence-from-DAERA-relating-Brexit-and-Northern-Ireland-Agriculture-20-June-18.pdf accessed 1 May 2021, 2. Also see *Draft Agricultural Strategy* (n95) 7; and House of Commons, Northern Ireland Affairs Committee, 'Brexit and Agriculture in Northern Ireland' (5th Report of Session 2017–19, HC Paper 939, October 2018) https://publications.parliament.uk/pa/cm201719/cmselect/cmniaf/939/939.pdf accessed 1 May 2021, 16.

100 *Draft Agricultural Strategy* (n95) 21.

101 Ibid 20.

102 In contrast, Nature Matters NI (Northern Ireland Environment Link) in its response to the *Draft Agricultural Strategy* highlights the importance of 'a wider concept of resilience', flagging the links between environmental enhancement, financial stability and society to build resilience. See Nature Matters NI, 'Northern Ireland Future Agricultural Framework: A Response from Nature Matters Northern Ireland' (October 2018) https://www.nienvironmentlink.org/cmsfiles/Northern-Ireland-Future-Agricultural-Framework---Nature-Matters-NI-response.pdf accessed 1 May 2021.

or food quality are included. The *Strategy* does however hint at the possibility of expanding the objectives in the future if there is political will, as, although food security is not included as a 'primary objective'[103] (since the initial mandate provided by the Minister did not include it), nonetheless it is noted as very important.[104]

To achieve these objectives, a range of mechanisms is identified. Crucial to note in contrast with the developments in England is that the *Strategy* envisages the maintenance of some version of direct payments post-transition – even if reduced – which would be essential in Northern Ireland considering the nature of farming and heavy reliance on financial support. The intent is to provide some underlying and predictable payments, but in an evolved format, with possibly amended eligibility criteria and maximum caps.[105] However, this is then complemented by other mechanisms to achieve the objectives. The *Strategy* outlines the need to be 'synergistic', using science (the role of science and innovation is particularly emphasised as beneficial), education, incentivisation, regulation and investment.[106] Investment can be in a range of forms and needs to be carefully designed to avoid the creation of perverse incentives – the objectives as a whole need to be considered and not undermined. On the environmental front, Section 6 emphasises that *outcomes* will be rewarded – through paying for the delivery of public goods 'under a sustainable agricultural objective'.[107] Various aspects are discussed with differing levels of approbation, including proposals to dismiss greening requirements,[108] a need for proportionate and effective regulation as a backstop with the potential also to link this to payments[109] (*de facto* cross-compliance).[110] Yet, for instance, there is no discussion of what environmental regulation might be necessary or how to achieve this and the environmental 'principles' referred to in Section 6[111] are broad ideas and values rather than actual legal principles. The removal of greening requirements without a strong regulatory system would be particularly concerning. Interestingly, the *Strategy* also notes the issue of conacre – a form of landownership peculiar to the Island

103 *Draft Agricultural Strategy* (n95) 20.
104 Nature Matters NI raised multiple aspects of food in their response to the *Draft Agricultural Strategy*, including Scotland's proposal to introduce a Good Food Nation Bill. See Nature Matters NI (n102).
105 It should be noted that the need for maximum caps on payments is less important for Northern Ireland due to the nature of farms. Eligibility criteria could include that the farm is actively managed (reasonable and effective), but also potentially a minimum size of farms – this latter could be counterproductive and lead to land abandonment.
106 *Draft Agricultural Strategy* (n95) 20.
107 Ibid 36–37.
108 Ibid 17.
109 Ibid 37.
110 The attitude towards cross-compliance seems relatively open, but the *Draft Agricultural Strategy* is unclear and somewhat contradictory across the document.
111 *Draft Agricultural Strategy* (n95) 36–37.

of Ireland, which involves a variation on short-term leasing typically in small patches[112] – and the potential to re-think how this operates.[113]

However, noticeably, the *Draft Agricultural Strategy* remains quite vague and light on detail across the board – overarching ideas are outlined but need significant development.[114] This links to the absence of the politicians at the time and also the focus on co-design in the document and even the 'engagement' questions, but still poses challenges. Will this be an individualised or landscape or ecosystem approach? What would the balance between the four objectives be? Will only outcomes be rewarded, or would also some steps or milestones justify payments? How could supply chains be improved and how would Northern Ireland support this? How does the supply chain objective link to transboundary issues considering Northern Ireland is a net exporter? If cross-compliance is retained, what would this entail? What role will there be for private corporations and public bodies in considering the role of innovation in agricultural production and what considerations and protections will be in place? Fundamental questions remain that need to be reflected upon, carefully but swiftly in light of time pressures.

Following the restoration of the Assembly and Executive in January 2020, it was hoped that they would swiftly address the challenges posed by Brexit – including the implementation of the Northern Ireland Protocol[115] and the development of a range of policies and complementary regulatory regimes. However, a range of issues has added to the challenges, including the political upheavals in Westminster; the faltering developments in the Agriculture Act 2020; COVID-19; the progress with UK-EU negotiations (or lack thereof); and the Internal Market Act 2020. Furthermore, the agricultural portfolio changed hands – now resting with the Agriculture, Environment and Rural Affairs Minister, Edwin Poots from the Democratic Unionist Party, who has proven highly reluctant to

112 DAERA and NISRA, 'Statistical Review of Northern Ireland Agriculture 2019' (2020) www.daera-ni.gov.uk/sites/default/files/publications/daera/Stats%20Review%202019%20final.pdf accessed 1 May 2021, 41.

113 *Draft Agricultural Strategy* (n95) 27. This was also flagged in Expert Working Group on Sustainable Land Management, 'Delivering Our Future, Valuing Our Soils: A Sustainable Agricultural Land Management Strategy for Northern Ireland' (21 October 2016) www.daera-ni.gov.uk/sites/default/files/publications/daera/16.17.079%20Sustainable%20Land%20Management%20Strategy%20final%20amended.PDF accessed 1 May 2021, 3, 7, 22, 70, 84 and 93. The group advocated for incentivising a shift away from conacre to longer term leasing.

114 For more on agri-environment schemes in Northern Ireland, see P. McCann, 'Agri Environment Scheme Area Down by 30%' (Irish Farmers Journal 3 June 2020) www.farmersjournal.ie/agri-environment-scheme-area-down-by-30-548992 accessed 1 May 2021; Nature Friendly Farming Network, 'NI Agri-Environment Scheme Update' www.nffn.org.uk/ni-agri-environment-scheme-update/ accessed 1 May 2021; and Agri-Food and Biosciences Institute, 'Agri-Environment Scheme Monitoring' www.afbini.gov.uk/articles/agri-environment-scheme-monitoring accessed 1 May 2021.

115 Protocol on Ireland/Northern Ireland to the Agreement on the Withdrawal of the United Kingdom of Great Britain and Northern Ireland from the European Union and the European Atomic Energy Community [2019] OJ C384I /1.

implement the Northern Ireland Protocol and appeared reticent to take the *Draft Agricultural Strategy* any further.[116] Instead, Northern Ireland has now granted legislative consent to the Agriculture Act – including Schedule 6 pertaining to Northern Ireland (enabling the continuation of payments and generally providing a breathing space for Northern Ireland's agricultural policy and industry) without any sunset clause;[117] has similarly granted consent to the Direct Payments to Farmers (Legislative Continuity) Act 2020; and generally was putting decisions on agricultural policy on the long finger until late 2020.

The then Agriculture, Environment and Rural Affairs Minister, Edwin Poots, in November 2020 spoke to the Northern Ireland Assembly, outlining some of his thoughts on the future of Northern Ireland's agriculture.[118] The Minister stated that he would be launching a new agricultural policy framework in 'early 2021' (although still awaited). It is to be underpinned by the *Strategy*'s four objectives (and linked also to 'green growth principles' and natural capital), with the Minister noting that they are 'broadly supported by stakeholders' and that DAERA has undertaken work since 'to collate evidence, identify gaps and develop policies' to help deliver the objectives.[119] Interestingly, besides highlighting the 'inseparable twin goals' of better economic performance and better environmental performance, the Minister expressly states that 'no farmer should be left behind'. Whilst the new policy is not fully developed or outlined within the Assembly statement, hints are given regarding reducing direct payments to the level of a 'safety net' and using the remainder to incentivise increased productivity and better environmental outcomes. A somewhat startling and worrying facet highlighted in the Minister's statement is the proposal for re-introducing *coupled* support payments – although the Minister simultaneously says that 'this would not be a return to the coupled payments of the past' as they need to promote productivity and also environmental sustainability. Finally, the Minister notes that whilst the greening requirements are already being removed, the ban on plough-

116 For instance, Minister Poots temporarily halted work on infrastructure needed to undertake checks, including SPS checks under the Protocol. See S. McBride, 'DUP Minister Edwin Poots Halted Work on Irish Sea Border Posts after Party Meeting' (NewsLetter 15 September 2020) www.newsletter.co.uk/news/politics/dup-minister-edwin-poots-halted-work-irish-sea-border-posts-after-party-meeting-2971287 accessed 1 May 2021. This attitude was similarly reflected by Poots' temporary replacement, Democratic Unionist Party Minister Gordon Lyons, who also halted infrastructure work, as well as the recruitment of necessary inspection staff. See F. McClements, 'DUP Minister Orders Halt to Construction of Inspection Facilities for Post-Brexit Checks' (Irish Times 26 February 2021) www.irishtimes.com/news/politics/dup-minister-orders-halt-to-construction-of-inspection-facilities-for-post-brexit-checks-1.4496277 accessed 1 May 2021.

117 Northern Ireland Assembly Debates March 2020 (n55).

118 Northern Ireland Assembly 'Basic Payment Scheme Simplifications and the Direction of Travel for Future Agricultural Policy in Northern Ireland, Including Support Payments' (Debates 17 November 2020) www.theyworkforyou.com/ni/?id=2020-11-17.1.90 accessed 1 May 2021.

119 Ibid.

ing of environmentally sensitive permanent grassland is being retained. Seemingly cross-compliance is also retained for the time-being, but under review and to be proportionate, which quite likely will lead to the reduction of penalties.[120]

Yet, no policy has been launched and time is slipping by and much work needs to be achieved if a new policy and pilots are to be sufficiently developed in the time constraints. Advantage can be taken of considerable earlier or ongoing work, including on a land management strategy[121] and on ammonia emissions.[122] Furthermore, in February 2021, Minister for the Economy, Diane Dodds, indicated that DAERA will commission an 'independent strategic review' examining the future of Northern Ireland's agri-food sector.[123] Key focus points include 'productivity; enhancing economic and environmental sustainability; improving our carbon footprint; changing market demands for food products; and recovery from the pandemic'. The last point crucially reflects the newest challenge for agriculture in Northern Ireland, rather than merely focusing on historical issues – with the importance of flexibility and adaptability being emphasised. However, interestingly the term used is simply 'recovery', rather than 'green recovery', even though Minister Poots had mentioned 'green growth' in his earlier statement on agricultural policy to the Assembly.[124] Further, notably three of the points remain on productivity or monetary issues, and none consider, for instance, rural communities, rural development, public health, food quality or broader societal concerns.[125]

Overall, the *Draft Agricultural Strategy* remains the main official document for considering future Northern Ireland's agricultural policy as it was endorsed by Minister Poots[126] and was created by the civil servants working in conjunction with stakeholders, providing insight into key concerns and helping secure some buy-in to its operation. However, it is worth noting that since the *Draft Agricultural Strategy* 'engagement' exercise, the Food, Farming and Countryside Commission also published a report on Northern Ireland agriculture.[127] This is

120 Ibid.

121 For example, see Expert Working Group on Sustainable Land Management (n113).

122 For instance, see a series of articles from Agri-Food & Biosciences Institute and funded by DAERA, starting with J. McIlroy, 'Tackling Agricultural Ammonia Emissions in Northern Ireland' (Agri-Food and Biosciences Institute 4 February 2021) www.afbini.gov.uk/news/tackling-agricultural-ammonia-emissions-northern-ireland-first-article-series-seven-being accessed 1 May 2021.

123 R. Martin, 'Independent Strategic Review' to Examine Future of NI's Agri-Food Sector' (Agriland 9 February 2021) www.agriland.co.uk/farming-news/independent-strategic-review-to-examine-future-of-nis-agri-food-sector/ accessed 1 May 2021.

124 Northern Ireland Assembly Debates November 2020 (n118).

125 See DAERA, 'Independent Strategic Review of NI Agri-Food' (2021) www.daera-ni.gov.uk/articles/independent-strategic-review-ni-agri-food accessed 1 May 2021.

126 Ibid.

127 Food Farming & Countryside Commission, 'Lay of the Land: Report of the Northern Ireland Inquiry' (RSA 19 September 2019) www.thersa.org/globalassets/pdfs/reports/rsa-ffcc-northern-ireland---lay-of-the-land-final_september19.pdf accessed 1 May 2021.

a valuable alternative proposal that takes a more holistic approach, for instance, including 'food systems, health and rural communities' and a decent living for farmers.[128] However, it is perhaps focused more on overarching aims and relationships between stakeholders rather than on mechanisms to achieve the aims. It, nonetheless, provides a useful comparator with which to critique and challenge the official *Strategy*, especially as it is tailored for Northern Ireland.

3.1.4 Scotland: stability and simplicity

Scotland was relatively quick off the starting blocks when it came to considering future agricultural policies, indicating that it was keen to make use of devolved powers. Central to Scottish thinking initially was the work of the Agriculture Champions, with an interim discussion document and then a final report in 2018.[129] Two key goals surfaced: a transition period that would provide stability for industry and breathing space for policy-makers; and a carefully designed policy for the future, tailored for Scottish farming. However, there has been mixed progress in achieving these goals, with much more work still needed on the latter, in particular.[130]

Regarding the initial transition period, the Scottish Government conducted stakeholder meetings and subsequently published a Consultation document *Stability and Simplicity*[131] in mid-2018. The focus was largely on the short-term future of Scottish agriculture, entailing 'proposals for a rural funding transition period'. Within the document, four key principles were identified (stability, simplicity, sustainability and security)[132] – to underpin the transition period, but also clearly potentially of great significance for the long-term future agricultural policies.

128 V. Gravey, 'Northern Ireland Agriculture after Brexit: Policy Development in the Absence of Government' (Sustainable Food Trust 11 October 2019) https://sustainablefoodtrust.org/articles/northern-ireland-agriculture-after-brexit-policy-development-in-the-absence-of-government/ accessed 1 May 2021.

129 Scottish Government, 'A Future Strategy for Scottish Agriculture, Final Report by the Scottish Government's Agriculture Champions' (May 2018) www.gov.scot/binaries/content/documents/govscot/publications/progress-report/2018/05/future-strategy-scottish-agriculture-final-report-scottish-governments-agriculture-champions/documents/00536005-pdf/00536005-pdf/govscot%3Adocument/00536005.pdf accessed 1 May 2021.

130 T. Forshaw, 'The Devolved Nations and Agricultural Policy: Scotland' (Agriculture and Horticultural Development Board 4 December 2020) https://ahdb.org.uk/news/the-devolved-nations-and-agricultural-policy-scotland accessed 1 May 2021.

131 Scottish Government, 'Stability and Simplicity: Proposals for a Rural Funding Transition Period' (June 2018) www.gov.scot/publications/stability-simplicity-proposals-rural-funding-transition-period/ accessed 1 May 2021.

132 Ibid 7.

Elements of the Consultation document hint at the multifunctionality of agriculture;[133] at the variations in the nature of farms and farming, generally and across Scotland;[134] at building in flexibility within the system and reducing administrative burdens;[135] and a broad openness to considering how to revise approaches to agricultural policy and governance. It also seeks general opinions on the CAP and how it operates currently in Scotland. However, the document remains largely a continuation of the existing policy approaches under the CAP and does little to address existing issues to indicate pathways to adapt to the changes brought by Brexit or indeed to forge a truly innovative approach for Scotland – it is essentially a 'patchwork', noting the need for a future policy but without taking significant steps in that direction.[136] At best it asks for suggestions from the public and notes the possibility of undertaking pilot projects during the transition period, subject to funding availability, and seeks opinions as to the general desirability of this – without providing insight as to what these pilot projects might entail. Scotland has since created the Agriculture (Retained EU Law and Data) (Scotland) Act 2020, which legislates for the aspects covered within *Stability and Simplicity* – in particular providing for the continuation of the approaches under the CAP for the time being (including direct payments and rural development funding) and revisions to that in order to make them run more efficiently and smoothly.

However, the key issue remains Scotland's limited progress in developing a future agricultural policy. The Agriculture Champions highlight six strategic themes, with five of these being still relevant beyond the transition period: transformational change; enhancing natural capital; improving productive efficiency; identifying career opportunities in the rural sector; and improving supply chain integration.[137] They further state that future policy priorities 'must cover purely public goods', but could also encompass ones with 'public-private benefits – such as reducing waste and improving soil', that benefit business, the environment

133 For example, see the references to food production, environmental outcomes and benefits for rural communities, but these largely remain minimal and understated, with other issues such as public health or food quality left unaddressed other than, for instance, reference to being a 'Good Food Nation'. See *Stability and Simplicity* (n131) 25. However, the Good Food Nation Bill is still awaited, so the two policies are being created concurrently – facilitating a holistic approach but also leading to uncertainty currently as to what might be included in the parallel policy.

134 Ibid.

135 Ibid.

136 L. Petetin, 'Written Evidence on Support for Agriculture and the Rural Economy – Post Brexit Transition' (Scottish Government 14 August 2018) https://consult.gov.scot/agriculture-and-rural-communities/economy-post-brexit-transition/consultation/view_respondent?sort=submitted&order=descending&uuId=46918591 accessed 1 May 2021.

137 Scottish Government, 'An Interim Discussion Document from the Scottish Government's Agriculture Champions' (17 November 2017) www.gov.scot/publications/interim-discussion-document-scottish-governments-agriculture-champions/ accessed 1 May 2021.

and society.[138] Following both the work of the Agriculture Champions and the conclusion of the *Stability and Simplicity* Consultation, one might have hoped for the swift design and development of a longer-term policy that would take advantage of the transition period. Some initial steps have been made, including parliamentary debates leading to the identification of six key underpinning principles (sustainability; simplicity; profitability; innovation; inclusion; and productivity) and the establishment of a stakeholder group (Farming and Food Production – Future Policy Group) in January 2019 'to inform and recommend a new bespoke policy on farming and food production for Scotland'.[139] In doing so, Scottish specific aspects such as crofts[140] have been placed as a central matter to be addressed – indeed, in the parliamentary debates agreeing on the establishment of a stakeholder group, the Scottish Parliament used the word 'bespoke' 21 times in under two hours.[141] The Agriculture (Retained EU Law and Data) (Scotland) Act 2020 adds further impetus here, as it mandates the Scottish Ministers to lay a report on progress towards a new agricultural policy based on these six key principles before the Scottish Parliament – although only by 31 December 2024, which is very late in the day.[142]

The parliamentary debates in March 2019 provide some further insight, as the Scottish Parliament agreed that any future agricultural policy must also address rural activity, 'promote environmental stewardship',[143] promote 'those most in need' and 'tackle rural and food poverty'.[144] The stakeholder group has since undertaken considerable work and is seemingly close to releasing its report with

138 *A Future Strategy for Scottish Agriculture* (n129) 6.

139 Scottish Parliament Debates January 2019 (n56) from 15.03.

140 Noted by Sutherland et al. to be historically defined as: 'small-scale, tenanted properties, tied to employment on estates'. See L. Sutherland et al., 'Adaptation, Resilience and CAP Reform: A Comparison of Crofts and Livestock Farms in Scotland' (2017) 133(3–4) *Scottish Geographical Journal* 192, 192. Shucksmith and Rønningen describe crofts as 'small strips of land rented or owned by a family unit, and generally worked alongside shares in common grazings. They have their own distinct code of law and are specific to the Highlands of Scotland – the so-called "crofting counties", most of which are mountains and islands, classified as "severely disadvantaged areas" by the EU'. See M. Shucksmith and K. Rønningen, 'The Uplands after Neoliberalism? The Role of the Small Farm in Rural Sustainability' (2011) 27(3) *Journal of Rural Studies* 275, 278. Whilst they were originally 'created deliberately too small for crofters to subsist', now they have been heavily legislated for and have greater legal rights. They are also the focus of specific funding in Scotland under the CAP, for example, the Crofting Agricultural Grant Scheme.

141 Scottish Parliament Debates January 2019 (n56).

142 Agriculture (Retained EU Law and Data) (Scotland) Act 2020, Section 22.

143 This was also a key recommendation from the Agriculture Champions in *A Future Strategy for Scottish Agriculture* (n129) paragraph 9.

144 Scottish Parliament, 'Meeting of the Parliament: Session 5' (Debates 6 March 2019) www.parliament.scot/api/sitecore/CustomMedia/OfficialReport?meetingId=11979 accessed 1 May 2021, Motion on 'Supporting Scottish Agriculture' 93-94.

recommendations for the Scottish Government,[145] which will presumably provide the basis for the eventual Government report. Key questions that will arise include the balance or weighing between these principles and aims or objectives; to what extent and how the policy will interact with other policies or documents such as the 'Agricultural Transformation Programme',[146] 'A Healthier Future: Scotland's Diet and Healthy Weight Delivery Plan'[147] or the eventual Good Food Nation Bill (which has for its basis the Good Food Nation policy[148]) or those created by groups such as the National Council of Rural Advisers;[149] and how innovative or conservative the policy will be. And that is before one even considers the questions of how the policy will be designed, implemented and enforced, for example, through relationships with regulatory frameworks, the potential for landscape approaches or how compliance will be monitored and ensured. Will they, for instance, take on board the Agriculture Champions' recommendations

145 Farming and Food Production – Future Policy Group, 'Minutes from 27 October 2020' (27 October 2020) www.gov.scot/binaries/content/documents/govscot/publications/minutes/2020/11/farming-and-food-production-future-policy-group-update-october-2020/documents/farming-and-food-production-future-policy-group-update-october-2020/farming-and-food-production-future-policy-group-update-october-2020/govscot%3Adocument/FFP-FPG%2B-%2B27%2BOctober%2B2020%2B-%2BSummary%2BMinutes.pdf accessed 1 May 2021.

146 Scottish Government, 'Moving to Low Carbon Farming' (7 February 2020) www.gov.scot/news/moving-to-low-carbon-farming/ accessed 1 May 2021. Introduced in the Scottish Government's programme for government (2019–2020) and focused on climate change and lowering carbon emissions, it is interesting to note that this programme is based on the same six principles as intended for the future agricultural policy. See Scottish Government, 'Protecting Scotland's Future: The Government's Programme for Scotland 2019–2020' (3 September 2019) www.gov.scot/binaries/content/documents/govscot/publications/strategy-plan/2019/09/protecting-scotlands-future-governments-programme-scotland-2019-20/documents/governments-programme-scotland-2019-20/governments-programme-scotland-2019-20/govscot%3Adocument/governments-programme-scotland-2019-20.pdf accessed 1 May 2021, 36.

147 Scottish Government, 'A Healthier Future: Scotland's Diet and Healthy Weight Delivery Plan' (July 2018) www.gov.scot/binaries/content/documents/govscot/publications/strategy-plan/2018/07/healthier-future-scotlands-diet-healthy-weight-delivery-plan/documents/00537708-pdf/00537708-pdf/govscot%3Adocument/00537708.pdf accessed 1 May 2021.

148 Scottish Government, 'Recipe for Success: Scotland's National Food and Drink Policy' (2009) www.gov.scot/binaries/content/documents/govscot/publications/strategy-plan/2009/06/recipe-success-scotlands-national-food-drink-policy/documents/0083283-pdf/0083283-pdf/govscot%3Adocument/0083283.pdf?forceDownload=true accessed 1 May 2021. It became a Good Food Nation Policy in 2014. See Scottish Government, 'Food and Drink' www.gov.scot/policies/food-and-drink/good-food-nation/ accessed 1 May 2021.

149 See National Council of Rural Advisers, 'A New Blueprint for Scotland's Rural Economy: Recommendations to Scottish Ministers' (September 2018) www.gov.scot/binaries/content/documents/govscot/publications/research-and-analysis/2018/09/new-blueprint-scotlands-rural-economy-recommendations-scottish-ministers/documents/00540988-pdf/00540988-pdf/govscot%3Adocument/00540988.pdf accessed 1 May 2021.

regarding stakeholder engagement? Interestingly, the stakeholder group minutes from October 2020 indicate focus points that include the need for 'urgent radical change'; the value of systems approaches; the potential environmental and social contributions of farming; the importance of undertaking pilot schemes; the significance of all stages of the supply chain and the potential for private actors to improve the chain.[150]

Overall, Scotland is avoiding rushing the adoption of a future agricultural policy, all too aware of the dangers of flawed policies or indeed of multiple overhauls. A careful and collaborative design could lead to a well-designed, tailored, futuristic policy that will stand to Scotland's credit. However, the clear and obvious danger for Scotland is that by leaving the design and adoption of a future agricultural policy so late in the day (especially in light of the 31 December 2024 deadline for simply a report), there is little time for testing and revising of the policy, for pilot schemes,[151] or indeed for the industry to prepare and adapt – despite the Agriculture Champions expressly recommending the swift development of a new policy and testing of pilot schemes during the transition period to ensure effective transformational change.[152] The transition period may need to be extended to facilitate the effective implementation of any new policy, and that may or may not be feasible in light of Westminster's control over purse strings. Further, whilst the stakeholder group is preparing their report in light of the principles agreed previously by the Scottish Government, there is no guarantee that the Scottish Government will approve all or most of the eventual report – further time is likely to be needed to develop and test the eventual policy as well as establishing pilot schemes.

3.2 Initial thoughts on the four policies

The four policies across the UK are at different stages, having played leapfrog since 2018. The Agriculture Act, with its main provisions focusing on England is clearly the policy at the most advanced stage, addressing the immediate future and the years after – with the *Path to Sustainable Farming Transition Plan* providing some necessary detail, but obviously, it will benefit from further development and clarity over time. The Scottish and Welsh proposals contrast, however, with the Act. Both started out relatively early and with ambitious rhetoric. The Scottish proposal covers the period until 2024 and is focused on providing a breathing space to develop a future policy – or indeed 'stability and simplicity', including through largely a continuity of the existing systems. However, whilst work is being undertaken on a future policy, that has yet to be published and time is of the essence – especially if it is to be developed, tested and potentially revised by the end of 2024. The Welsh proposal evolved in quite a detailed manner through

150 Farming and Food Production - Future Policy Group (n145).
151 Described as a 'missed opportunity' in Petetin (n136).
152 *A Future Strategy for Scottish Agriculture* (n129).

three key renditions, but then the brakes were put on – the Welsh Government opted out of having detailed enabling provisions included within the Agriculture Act, noting that they wanted to delay deciding on future policy until they had ironed out issues until it was fully developed and now an Agriculture Bill for Wales will not be proposed until summer 2022.[153] Northern Ireland was late to the party and whilst it eventually created its *Draft Agricultural Strategy*, this remains quite sparse in detail, does not provide for a lengthy transition period and has not been developed since the Northern Ireland's Executive was back in situ. Minister Poots has indicated that this will be taken forward and built upon,[154] but again this is very late in the day, it risks being rushed and temporary patches may be needed until it is approved in its eventual form.

3.2.1 Comparisons across the four nations

Much remains unclear or uncertain regarding the proposed policies, in particular, regarding Northern Ireland and Scotland for after the transitional period. However, even at this stage some general comments can be made. There are broad similarities across the policies, for instance, with focus points on seeking to develop economic resilience, productivity and environmental objectives – especially through the notion of public money for public goods; or through seeking to provide transition periods to enable farmers to adapt to the new schemes; or indeed through the gradual (but not absolute) shift away from direct payments and the broader range of objectives under the CAP. Nonetheless, there are key differences across the policies, including in the objectives and how these are to be achieved (see Table 3.1).[155]

It is worthwhile highlighting some of the core components that actors and stakeholders would need to be aware of in seeking to rely on the policies after the initial transitional periods in each of the four nations. These components will be developed and examined in more detail in Chapter 4.

The proposals across the four nations all have core aims of promoting environmental objectives (labelled as public money for public goods or similar) and productivity – largely reflecting the two-pronged approach in the Agriculture Act. Further focus points within the policies, such as natural capital, economic resilience and supply chains, still fit within the two core prongs. Aspects such as food security, food quality or public health, which might have reasonably been expected to be included as core aims alongside environmental objectives and productivity, do not yet play this role for the main part. Wales bears highlighting as a partial exception to this point, as its focus on sustainable land management

153 *White Paper* (n58) 4.
154 Northern Ireland Assembly Debates November 2020 (n118).
155 These aspects are further developed in Chapter 4. The table emphasises policy and legislation adopted after the referendum vote.

Table 3.1 Outlook of Agricultural Policies Across the UK

	England	Wales	Northern Ireland	Scotland
Main policies and legislation	*Health and Harmony* (2018) Agriculture Bill (2017–2019) Agriculture Act 2020	*Brexit and our Land* (2018) *Sustainable Farming and our Land* (2019) *Agriculture (Wales) White Paper* (2020)	*Northern Ireland Future Agricultural Policy Framework* (2018)	*Stability and Simplicity* (2018) *Strategy Document from Agriculture Champions* (2018) Agriculture (Retained EU Law and Data) (Scotland) Act 2020
Related policy documents	*25 Year Environmental Plan* *Ten Point Plan for a Green Industrial Revolution* *The National Food Strategy – Part One*	Environmental Governance Stakeholder Task Group Report (2020) *Consultation Paper: Our Ambition to Further Develop Wales' Food and Drink Sector* (2019)	*Environmental Plans, Principles and Governance in Northern Ireland – Public Discussion Document* (2020) *Discussion Document on a Northern Ireland Climate Change Bill* (2020)	*Consultation on Environmental Principles and Governance in Scotland* (2019) *A Healthier Future: Scotland's Diet and Healthy Weight Delivery Plan* (2018)
Key themes	Public money for public goods Productivity	Sustainable Land Management	Productivity (Economic) resilience Environmentally sustainable agriculture Supply chains	Transformational change Natural capital Productive efficiency Career opportunities in the rural sector Supply chain integration Maintain standards (as per EU Continuity Act 2021)

(*Continued*)

Table 3.1 Continued

	England	*Wales*	*Northern Ireland*	*Scotland*
Key schemes	Environmental Land Management: • Sustainable Farming Incentive • Local Recovery Nature • Landscape Recovery	Sustainable Farming Scheme: • Sustainable farming payment • Business support	To be determined	Not yet determined for post transitional period
Main changes to policy and legal instruments	Lack of emphasis on rural development Progressive end to direct payments Regulatory baseline? Standards continue independently/ Cross-compliance?	Lack of emphasis on rural development Progressive end to direct payments National Minimum Standards	Lack of emphasis on rural development Direct payments maintained (but likely reduced) Separate environmental regulations to act as a baseline (amended version of cross-compliance likely)	Not yet determined for post transitional period, but likely: • Some support for rural development • Maintained, but reduced, direct payments • Amended version of cross-compliance

encompasses 'well-being' and within that 'public health'.[156] However, as noted above, the emphasis is on the environmental and economic aspects, with most well-being elements to be furthered by the two prongs[157] and the link with healthy food or food security not adequately addressed. Whether England in future revisions of their policy[158] or Wales, Scotland[159] or Northern Ireland[160] in finalising their policies stretch themselves by including such additional aims or an overarching objective such as resilience as discussed in Chapter 4, remains to be seen. Linked to this, direct payments will be largely eradicated after the transitional period, since they are focused simply on farmer support and considered not to promote specific environmental objectives or productivity – although with some level likely to be retained in Northern Ireland and Scotland.[161]

These objectives are to be facilitated by financial support schemes that are in the process of being developed – with the greatest detail available for the English schemes, in particular ELMS. Although most of these schemes will appear universally available,[162] some eligibility criteria will typically apply, e.g. being a farmer. In England, for the SFI fund, farms must be at least five hectares in size at least for the initial period. Northern Ireland has similarly indicated that they might impose a minimum threshold (and a maximum cap) for a proposed basic payment scheme. In contrast, whilst the future remains unclear for Scotland, its declared intention to help support crofts (very small farms) would indicate that such a threshold is unlikely to be applied across the board. Such exclusions could impact severely on small farms, especially without other sources of financial support equivalent to the previous level of support from direct payments or complementary funding from the EU.[163] One as yet unanswered question is whether farmers could come together to merge their farms for the purpose of meeting the eligibility criteria.

156 See *Sustainable Farming and Our Land* (n59) especially at 25. Both Wales and England also note the significance of antimicrobial resistance.

157 See *Sustainable Farming and Our Land* (n59) 28.

158 As noted, England includes an obligation on reporting on food security, but it is not a main aim or objective within the agricultural policy.

159 Food poverty was highlighted as an important issue to be addressed in Scottish Parliament Debates March 2019 (n144) 93–94.

160 The issues of food security was highlighted as important in *Draft Agricultural Strategy* (n95) 20.

161 See M. Cardwell, 'Farming Policy' in H. Kassin, A. Jordan and S. Ennis (eds), 'UK Regulation after Brexit' (The UK in a Changing Europe 25 February 2021) https://ukandeu.ac.uk/wp-content/uploads/2021/02/UK-regulation-after-Brexit.pdf accessed 1 May 2021, 48, 49; and A. Kay, 'Scottish Direct Payments Will Not Distort UK Market after Brexit, Says Eustice' (Farmers Guardian 23 November 2020) www.fginsight.com/news/news/scottish-direct-payments-will-not-distort-uk-market-after-brexit-says-eustice-114714 accessed 20201.

162 Some exceptions may be expected, for example, where they are targeted at young farmers or specific areas or types of farms.

163 See the EU Structural Funds discussed in Chapter 5, at Section 5.2.1.

Farmers will need to examine the array of schemes within their jurisdiction and identify which ones are suitable and open to their needs. This is a highly challenging exercise – despite the possibility of relying on agents to help with the process or seeking advice (potentially expensive in its own right). Beyond eligibility criteria, the nature of the scheme will be of interest. For instance regarding water or improving productivity, and what tier, i.e. how ambitious are the aims of the scheme and how much would the farmers need to undertake and achieve.[164] Interestingly, despite considerable rhetoric about outcomes, the Welsh and English schemes (more developed than those in Northern Ireland or Scotland) indicate the availability of payments also for process, i.e. for taking relevant actions.[165] Upon successful applications to the schemes, individual agreements will then be made with the farmers outlining the terms and conditions – including specific criteria and what will merit payments.

Four further brief points will be of interest to the farmers and other stakeholders: first, there may be the potential to build on the previous consultations regarding the policies and engage in the co-design of the schemes.[166] Second, there is a slim possibility to amend agricultural tenancies in England to facilitate meeting the aims of the schemes – this may yet occur elsewhere across the UK.[167] Third, beyond the specific support schemes, there have been discussions of emergency funds, insurance policies and similar measures to help withstand economic shocks. For instance, Section 21 of the Agriculture Act 2020 provides for the Secretary of State to provide financial assistance to farmers where there are exceptional market conditions. It remains to be seen how this will evolve elsewhere across the UK. Finally, all farmers, irrespective of any criteria for any scheme they sign up to or not, will need to continue to comply with current and future regulatory requirements, including food, health and environmental requirements.[168]

164 There are numerous variations within England, as highlighted by the *Environmental Land Management Scheme Discussion Paper* (n4); and *Path to Sustainable Farming Transition Plan* (n5). In the Welsh proposals, there would simply be one scheme, but with different payments available within it. The aim is that farmers would be involved in the production of a 'farm sustainability review' and 'farm sustainability plan' that would provide the basis for entry into the scheme and therefore inform the eventual contract. See *Sustainable Farming and Our Land* (n59), 7 and 15–16.

165 With Wales agreeing to underwrite the agreements 'if agreed actions do not lead to outcomes'. See *Sustainable Farming and Our Land* (n59) 8.

166 See Chapter 4, Section 6.2.1.

167 Northern Ireland and Wales (*Sustainable Farming and Our Land* (n59) 55) have flagged this as a possibility. Wales has held a consultation on agricultural tenancies. See Welsh Government, 'Consultation Document: Agricultural Tenancy Reform' (9 April 2019) https://gov.wales/sites/default/files/consultations/2019-04/agricultural-tenancy-reform-consultation-document.pdf accessed 1 May 2021. See Chapter 4, Section 4.4.4.

168 As highlighted in Wales *Sustainable Farming and Our Land* (n59) Section 7.

In some instances this may also affect whether they obtain funding under the financial schemes, for instance, via cross-compliance.[169]

What has occurred under the proposals is a change in emphasis in comparison to what existed under the CAP. Under the current proposals, 'Pillar 1' focuses on the delivery of environmental benefits and 'Pillar 2' focuses on productivity. The pillars are reversed, also switching the emphasis. However, this may differ in practice; the removal or residual direct payments combined with the move back towards paying for actions rather than outcomes tend to put the stability of farmers' income at the heart of the policies and therefore places greater weight back again on Pillar 1 as designed under the CAP.

On the face of the policies, they appear to comply with the legal parameters identified in Chapter 2. The very existence of four individual policies reflects the broad flexibility of the parameters under both international law and UK constitutional law; agricultural, environmental and, to a limited extent, social aspects are present within each policy – all devolved powers. In contrast, the policies largely avoid expressly addressing international obligations (a reserved matter), such as under the UK/EU Withdrawal Agreement[170] and the Northern Ireland Protocol – taking the approach of 'the less said, the better'. However, the Agriculture Act's provisions addressing the obligations arising from the World Trade Organization's (WTO) Agreement on Agriculture merit further consideration – as a distinct attempt by the UK Government to ensure that the UK, as a whole, complies with its obligations.

3.2.2 Consistency with the requirements of the WTO Agreement on Agriculture

The UK Government is now responsible for providing the WTO with a list of all UK support on an annual basis[171] and must ensure that support across all the devolved administrations fits within its WTO commitments as seen in the Agriculture Act.[172] These provisions, and those in the Agriculture Bill 2017–2019, have raised eyebrows in the devolved administrations.

Under the Agriculture Bill 2017–2019, Petetin and Dobbs expressed concern to the Climate Change, Environment and Rural Affairs Committee of the Welsh Parliament as to the recentralisation of powers related to financial support for

169 As noted above, this is a possibility for Northern Ireland. It is also proposed to be retained in Wales, linked to the eventual National Minimum Standards. See *Sustainable Farming and Our Land* (n59) 76.

170 Agreement on the Withdrawal of the United Kingdom of Great Britain and Northern Ireland from the European Union and the European Atomic Energy Community [2019] OJ C384I /1.

171 Uruguay Round Agreement on Agriculture (1994), Article 18.2.

172 Agriculture Act, Sections 43 to 45.

farmers and the design of support schemes across the UK.[173] To address these issues, the UK and Welsh Governments concluded a Bilateral Agreement on WTO provisions.[174] However concerns remained[175] and some of the concerns were further alleviated in the updated WTO provisions of the Agriculture Act.

Section 44 of the Act places a ceiling on the financial support under the Amber Box only (rather than the Amber, Green and Blue Boxes in the Agriculture Bill 2017–2019). Positively, the devolved administrations can set their own limits for support falling under the Green and Blue Boxes, without limitations decided by central government. However, a limit can be set centrally for payments falling under the Amber Box and these payments could be lower than the overall amount allowed for the UK under the Aggregate Measure of Support (AMS).[176] The Secretary of State can also set different limits on Amber Box support across the four nations.[177] In relation to the classification of financial support, Section 45 gives powers to the Secretary of State across the UK to set the rules for classification and for dispute resolution regarding classification. Whilst devolved administrations may be involved in the initial classification, the Section indicates that the Secretary of State can act as the 'final arbiter' and worryingly be the judge in their own court.

Whilst they provide improvements on the Agriculture Bill 2017–2019, the WTO Sections of the Agriculture Act maintain some problematic considerations (i) the Secretary of State can still decisively determine the classification of financial support across the UK; (ii) the Secretary of State now possesses powers that previously belonged to the devolved administrations; and (iii) the devolved administrations cannot input into the Amber Box ceilings set by central government. Overall, powers under these Sections still raise concerns, first, in relation to level playing fields across the four nations and potentially giving a competitive advantage to farmers in one nation over others and, second, because they maintain the recentralisation of powers already present in the Agriculture Bill 2017–2019.

173 L. Petetin and M. Dobbs, 'Written Evidence on the UK Agriculture Bill' (Climate Change, Environment and Rural Affairs Committee of the Senedd Cymru, November 2018) www.senedd.assembly.wales/documents/s80616/Paper%20-%20Dr%20Petetin%20and%20Dr%20Dobbs.pdf accessed 1 May 2021.

174 DEFRA and Welsh Government, 'UK and Welsh Government Bilateral Agreement on WTO Provisions within the Agriculture Bill' www.gov.uk/government/publications/agriculture-bill-progress-with-devolved-administrations/uk-and-welsh-government-bilateral-agreement-on-wto-provisions-within-the-agriculture-bill accessed 1 May 2021.

175 Climate Change, Environment and Rural Affairs (CCERA) Committee of the Senedd Cymru, 'Report on the Supplementary Legislative Consent Memorandum for the Agriculture Bill' (June 2019) https://senedd.wales/laid%20documents/cr-ld12551/cr-ld12551-e.pdf accessed 1 May 2021.

176 Agriculture Act, Section 44(3)(a).

177 Agriculture Act, Section 44(3)(b).

Future schemes, including public money for public goods payments to farmers could fall under the three Boxes of the Agreement on Agriculture.[178] In the UK, one of the key components of agricultural policies is to enhance farm productivity – as demonstrated in the policies across the four nations – and generally ensure food security. Consequently, it is unlikely that much support will fall under the Blue Box since this Box aims to reduce production – unless future ceilings can be adjusted above current levels to allow for expansion for as long as these ceilings remain below the requirements for coupled support under Blue Box programmes as noted in Chapter 2, Section 2.4.2.3.[179]

The Amber Box remains as a strong option for a robust level of support in the short to medium term.[180] There is even scope under the '*de minimis*' threshold for the UK to support its agriculture (whether or not the UK obtains a share of the EU's Support AMS).[181] More specifically, public money for public goods programmes could fall under the scope of non-product-specific domestic support (unless targeting a specific crop).[182] Agricultural support notified by the UK under this Box will be more difficult for WTO Members to challenge since Amber Box schemes are, by nature, trade-distorting. As such, the UK would not be open to legal challenges by other WTO Members for as long as UK support remains within the *de minimis* threshold (or, if available, its share of the EU's AMS). This is a crucial point to bear in mind when notifying support to the WTO.

Moving all 'public money for public goods' support under Annex 2 of the Agreement on Agriculture – that is the Green Box – is possible since the number of payments that can be given to farmers is unlimited.[183] Crucially, to obtain an exemption, the Agreement's obligations under one of its headings, such as environmental and regional development programmes, must be fulfilled as noted in Chapter 2, Section 2.4.2.3.3. Programmes providing advice to farmers, such as

178 As noted in Chapter 2, Section 2.4.2.3. See more generally, L. Brink and D. Orden, 'Taking Stock and Looking Forward on Domestic Support under the WTO Agreement on Agriculture' (*International Agricultural Trade Research Consortium Commissioned Paper No. 23*, 2020).

179 As observed, such payment ceilings are based on fixed area and yields (not prices) or made on 85 per cent or less of the base level of production or for livestock payments made on a fixed number of head. See Agreement on Agriculture, Article 6.5(a).

180 For more on this point, see L. Brink, 'UK Brexit and WTO Farm Support Limits' (CAP Reform 13 July 2016) http://capreform.eu/uk-brexit-and-wto-farm-support-limits/ accessed 1 May 2021; and K.P. Hasund and M. Johansson, 'Paying for Environmental Results is WTO Compliant' (2016) 15 *EuroChoices* 33.

181 A. Matthews, 'Establishing the UK's Non-Exempt Limit on Agricultural Support after Brexit' (CAP Reform 29 January 2017) http://capreform.eu/establishing-the-uks-non-exempt-limit-on-agricultural-support-after-brexit/ accessed 1 May 2021.

182 Cardwell (n94). See also J. McMahon, 'Brexit, Trade and Agriculture: Waiting for Answers' (2018) 17(1/2) *Journal of International Trade Law and Policy* 19.

183 For more on the Green Box, see R. Meléndez-Ortiz, C. Bellmann and J. Hepburn (eds), *Agricultural Subsidies in the WTO Green Box: Ensuring Coherence with Sustainable Development Goals* (CUP 2009).

the Future Farming Resilience Fund, are likely to fall under paragraph 2 if clearly linked to the delivery of public money for public goods programmes.

Public money for public goods programmes could fall under paragraph 12 and be considered as environmental programmes. For example, facilitating beekeeping to favour pollination would be an example of an environmental scheme. Paragraph 13 could be used by the devolved administrations to provide assistance to farmers, as Wales, Scotland and Northern Ireland could be considered as a 'disadvantaged region'. Wales has historically been considered as one of the most deprived regions in the EU (as well as some areas in England).[184] This provision could allow for upland and hill farmers in these regions, for instance, to receive further support and could pay for dedicated rural development programmes as is the case currently under Pillar 2 of the CAP and less favoured areas.

The level of payments under environmental and regional programmes is fixed and restricted to 'the extra costs *or* loss of income involved in undertaking agricultural production' (emphasis added) (often dubbed as 'income foregone'). Possible lower levels of support could encourage the profitability of farm businesses. However, the main issue is that farmers may not be fully rewarded for their public goods, especially if they are unable to recuperate the income generated by the sale of their products (since there may be no agri-food products for them to sell).[185]

It can be argued that the provisions on income foregone are sufficiently vague to accommodate adequate levels of 'public money for public goods'. Annex 2 does not specify any technical parameters for the definition of the 'extra costs' *or* 'loss of income'. What costs should be calculated? What loss of income? Loss of land? Hypothetical? Does income foregone focus on financial and economic incomes or environmental outcomes? The baseline or counterfactual is unspecified and the range of costs and income that can be included in the payment calculations remains unclear. There have been no formal rulings or WTO guidance on interpreting these criteria, so there is no reason to assume that higher levels of payments could be inadequate.[186] Provided payments are developed in an objective, transparent and non-discriminatory manner, these provisions may prove not to be overly restrictive; for as long as they comply with the fundamental requirement/proviso in Annex 2, paragraph 1.

Beyond the caps on financial support and the classification of support, it is essential to bear in mind that domestic programmes as designed to fit under any Box, *including* the Green Box, can affect production and trade despite the 'fundamental requirement' (or proviso) that such support under this Box must

184 P. Inman, 'Number of Europe's Poorest Regions in UK "More than Doubles"' (The Guardian 10 December 2019) www.theguardian.com/business/2019/dec/10/number-of-europes-poorest-regions-in-uk-more-than-doubles accessed 1 May 2021.

185 Such a loss could be categorised as 'income foregone' as will be observed next.

186 This issue was not addressed in the *US–Cotton* case. See *United States – Subsidies on Upland Cotton*, WT/DS267/AB/R, 3 March 2005.

'have no, or at most minimal, trade-distorting effects or effects on production'.[187] According to Grossman, even decoupled support under the Green Box schemes can affect and distort production in two ways:[188] first, increased available cash flow can improve competitiveness, for example, the preference for planting specific crops over others to feed wading birds over winter; second, a stable farm income can lead to farmers investing surplus funds in new technologies. These are consequences to consider when devising governmental programmes under all Boxes, but especially under the Green Box, across the four nations.

Further, since the aim with new schemes is to affect change – not merely to have inertia, supporting farmers beyond 'income foregone' would mean that either the payments could fall under paragraph 5 (on general requirements for direct payments) or paragraph 6 (on decoupled support)[189] of Annex 2 of the Agreement on Agriculture or under the Amber Box. Most importantly, payments under these two paragraphs are not limited to 'income foregone'. The financial incentive to sign up for a contract to deliver public goods must be high enough, otherwise, the uptake of the schemes would not be sufficient and the environment would suffer. Consequently, these paragraphs could offer great opportunities for UK schemes to fall under the Green Box. Crucially, collaboration at scale due to its decoupled benefits to the environment and the synergies created between farmers could involve extra costs that should be compensated effectively, which again would be undertaken under these two paragraphs.[190]

Any notification inconsistent with WTO rules would cause difficulties. Specifically, other WTO Members could seize the opportunity to challenge the new schemes to set a precedent against the (ab?)use by powerful WTO Members of the Green Box.[191] Maintaining post-Brexit UK support under the Amber Box for a transition period only, whilst moving away from area/land-based payments towards public money for public goods payments would enable the new schemes to be tested and framed so as to be compatible with Green Box conditions in the long term and such a choice might also be more politically

187 Agreement on Agriculture, Annex 2, paragraph 1.

188 M.R. Grossman, 'The Uruguay Round Agreement on Agriculture and Domestic Support' in M.N. Cardwell, M.R. Grossman and C.P. Rodgers (eds), *Agriculture and International Trade: Law, Policy, and the WTO* (CABI Publishing 2003) 27, 38.

189 As noted in Chapter 2, Section 2.4.2.3, paragraph 6 of the Annex has a broad scope and the amount of direct income support appears to be unlimited. Therefore, the UK could use this paragraph to justify providing its public money for public goods schemes with unlimited support. The EU utilises this paragraph to finance most its direct payments to farmers. See Chapter 2, Section 2.4.2.3.3.

190 For example, the CAP provides higher levels of payment for collaborative projects within agri-environment schemes. See Regulation (EU) 1305/2013, Article 28(6).

191 L. Petetin, 'Post-Brexit Agricultural Support and the WTO: Using Both the Amber and Green Boxes?' (Brexit and Environment Network 21 June 2018) www.brexitenvironment.co.uk/2018/06/21/post-brexit-agricultural-support-wto-using-amber-green-boxes/ accessed 1 May 2021.

satisfactory to WTO Members who do not benefit from the AMS.[192] The Green Box provides the best pathway to secure WTO compatibility for UK domestic support post-Brexit over the long term to the extent that 'income foregone' is not interpreted stringently.

Such uncertainty regarding Green Box conditions indicates the age of the Agreement on Agriculture and only reinforces calls for reform of the Agreement on Agriculture more generally.[193] Ingenuity will be needed when designing future schemes (public money for public goods ones and others) to spread their various elements amongst the three Boxes to ensure compliance with the Agreement on Agriculture. However, there is clearly potential to ensure each of the current four policy proposals complies with the Agreement and indeed there is scope to evolve them further in the future.

3.2.3 Devolution matters and their intricacies

Despite tentatively complying with the legal parameters, it is questionable whether the policies respect and reflect the complexities of devolution and the relationships between the devolved administrations and Westminster. First, the UK-wide and Great Britain-wide aspects within the Agriculture Act, such as regarding the Agreement on Agriculture, fertilisers and organic criteria, were largely developed by England but will apply across at least Great Britain and in part in Northern Ireland. Whilst Northern Ireland and Wales granted legislative consent to the relevant provisions, Scotland did not. Further, a more collaborative approach in the initial development would have been appropriate considering that these relate to devolved matters. These obligations are not collaborative common frameworks, but instead are centrally designed and imposed measures.[194] In contrast, it would also be highly valuable from a centralised/ UK Government's perspective to foster the devolved administrations' goodwill and encourage compliance.

Second, and from a devolved perspective, the devolved policies unsurprisingly entail financial support schemes that will depend on having sufficient public funds available – yet, the devolved administrations rely upon financing from

192 Ibid.

193 See Chapter 2, Section 2.4.2. See also M. Cardwell and F. Smith, 'Renegotiation of the WTO Agreement on Agriculture: Accommodating the New Big Issues' (2013) *International and Comparative Law Quarterly* 865; J.A. McMahon, *The WTO Agreement on Agriculture: A Commentary* (Oxford Commentaries in International Law, OUP 2007) Chapter 7; and F. Smith, *Agriculture and the WTO: Towards a New Theory of International Agricultural Trade Regulation* (Edward Elgar 2009).

194 See, for example, the discussion of the Agriculture Bill 2017–2019 in T. Mullen and J. Hunt, 'Review of Implications of Brexit-Related UK Legislation for Devolved Competence' (27 August 2019) https://archive2021.parliament.scot/S5_Finance/General%20Documents/201908_Paper_by_Prof_Tom_Mullen_and_Prof_Jo_Hunt.pdf accessed 1 May 2021, 5 and 13. See also, S. Douglas-Scott, 'The Future of the United Kingdom' (2019) SI *European Journal of Legal Studies* 245.

Westminster. Uncertainty persists as to what the future funding will be from Westminster following this current government. It is also possible that future UK level policies or international agreements decided by the UK Government, as well as the consequences of the Internal Market Act, might significantly impact the viability of devolved agricultural policies. The policies are all silent on these issues and the potential is that, despite supposed compliance with both international commitments and domestic laws currently, the policies may not comply if the policy, regulatory and contextual landscape progressively transforms.

3.3 Conclusion

The policies across the four nations (including Scotland's initial policy for the transition period) are largely based on a two-pronged approach, public money for public goods and productivity, which broadly replicates the two pillars of the CAP (with caveats). Despite a great impetus initially with public money for public goods, they revert partway back to old approaches, for example, by frequently paying for actions rather than outcomes or keeping some direct payments. Concerns can be raised about whether the goals of public goods or environmental outcomes will be achieved when the implementation of the approach relies mostly on actions rather than outcomes – a more balanced approach is needed as discussed in Chapter 4. Further, the documents to date across the four nations (including Scotland's initial suggestions for after their transition period) all envisage supporting farmers for enhanced productivity or economic resilience or performance. The public goods approach has been eroded in the development of the policies and schemes – indicating the lack of a clear overarching objective. Finally, the governmental approaches to simplify existing schemes appear to be greatly reduced in practice. Current proposals indicate a multiplicity of schemes offered to farmers, which could mean having to keep abreast of the various evolving requirements for each scheme and the numerous deadlines to meet; thereby ultimately complexifying the system for farmers to receive financial support.

The preliminary evaluation undertaken in this chapter identifies a range of other central elements, including the role of co-design in the initial policy and the financial schemes; the general lack of integration within the agricultural policies of other policy areas and corresponding documents; the variations in governance of the schemes, including eligibility criteria, monitoring and enforcement; the general lack of integration of regulatory baselines and seeming shift away from cross-compliance; and a degree of path dependency by the devolved administrations in mirroring the two-pronged English approach. All of this merits further investigation, which is undertaken in Chapter 4.

Overall, the four policies to date appear to fall easily within the parameters delineated in Chapter 2 – there is nothing that needs to be amended as a result. Whilst the Agriculture Act indicates a recentralisation of powers not only with its provisions on the Agreement on Agriculture and financing, but also on fertilisers and organics, this is legally possible even if politically sensitive. Indeed, there remains considerable scope for developing agricultural policies further within the parameters of Chapter 2, especially under the Agreement on Agriculture. The question arises as to whether the policies ought to be developed further, or whether the content suffices in light of the challenges facing agriculture in the 21st century. It is this question that will be addressed in Chapter 4, through engaging in a more in-depth examination of key aspects of the four policies.

4 Tailoring ambitious policies across the UK

Striving for resilience in agriculture

Brexit poses the challenge and the opportunity to rethink and overhaul agricultural policies across the United Kingdom (UK). The four nations were presented with the opportunity to address long-standing issues and make fundamental changes that go to the roots of the regimes. Chapter 3 outlined the agricultural policies developed (to varying degrees) by each of the four nations that – on the face of it – comply with the legal parameters identified in Chapter 2. However, although essential, the legal validity of agricultural policies cannot be their sole focus or criterion to evaluate their worth or success. This is not a paper exercise, but the development of policies that are to determine agricultural practices across the UK for the foreseeable future – impacting farmers, the environment, the economy, society and even the constitutional relationships within the UK. The design, implementation and enforcement of these policies must strive for something greater and worthwhile that recognises the nature of, and challenges for, agriculture in the 21st century.

Consequently, this chapter investigates whether the policies outlined in Chapter 3 truly are ambitious and forward-thinking – in their objectives and/or how they seek to achieve them – and whether they could strive for more. The chapter identifies five key themes that merit detailed examination: (i) the overarching ambition for agriculture; (ii) pathways to achieve this ambition; (iii) diversity of farms/farmers (and tailored approaches); (iv) governance approaches and mechanisms and (v) the recognition of interconnectedness. The four policies are analysed in light of these themes, to evaluate how they can be improved while still within the legal parameters identified in Chapter 2.[1] Due to the varied progress, focus at times is primarily on the Welsh and, in particular, English policies.

The first section is central to this investigation. It argues that resilience (rather than only sustainability) can provide the overarching ambition for a forward-looking agriculture, thereby also acting as a lens to evaluate the policies and the

1 As in Chapter 3, the analysis of the UK and devolved documents is not meant to be exhaustive.

DOI: 10.4324/9780429503719-4

remaining four themes. As discussed therein, resilience is a multifaceted, complex concept that seeks to develop a system's adaptive capacity to withstand shocks and survive in the long-term. Applied to agriculture, it considers the connection between all of the facets – including the farmers, land, society, environment and economy – and how to improve their resilience, via adaptive governance and management. In light of the policies' significance, governance structures and relationships between policy-makers must also be resilient – not simply agriculture or the policy content.

4.1 Overarching ambition: a resilient agriculture?

The European Union (Withdrawal) Act 2018 did not retain the objectives of the Common Agricultural Policy (CAP) outlined in Article 39 of the Treaty on the Functioning of the European Union (TFEU).[2] Consequently, an immediate need and opportunity arose for the four nations to identify and establish suitably ambitious objectives for their policies. This is the most fundamental ask for any of the policies and, if they get this right, then they could act as valuable exemplars beyond the UK. This section considers resilience as the overarching ambition for agriculture – arguing that it provides a suitably holistic, forward-looking framework that can help address the evolving challenges faced by agriculture in the 21st century.

Clearly, agriculture must be productive whereby agricultural producers participate in the production of food, fibre and fuel for markets. The fundamental purpose is to produce food for the population; food that is nutritious, of a sufficiently high quality and accessible. It raises important questions about food security,[3] food sovereignty,[4] right to food[5] and much more. It also is an economic activity intended to provide a sufficient income to those engaged in food production.[6] However, it is insufficient to leave the matter there, as this does not recognise the

2 Consolidated Version of the Treaty on the Functioning of the European Union (TFEU) [2008] OJ C115/47.

3 S.L. Hendriks (eds), *Food Security Policy, Evaluation and Impact Assessment* (Routledge 2019); and M.K. Blake, 'More than Just Food: Food Insecurity and Resilient Place Making through Community Self-Organising' (2019) 11(10) *Sustainability* 2942. For more on the relationship between food security and the right to food, see K. Mechlem, 'Food Security and the Right to Food in the Discourse' (2004) 10 *European Law Journal* 63.

4 A. Shattuck, C. Schiavoni and Z. VanGelder (eds), *The Politics of Food Sovereignty: Concept, Practice and Social Movements* (Routledge 2017). For comparisons between food sovereignty and food security, see L. Jarosz, 'Comparing Food Security and Food Sovereignty Discourses' (2014) 4(2) *Dialogues in Human Geography* 168.

5 O. De Schutter and K.Y. Cordes (eds), *Accounting for Hunger: The Right to Food in the Era of Globalisation* (Hart Publishing 2011). About the role of the Special Rapporteur on the right to food, see United Nations, Human Rights, Office of the High Commissioner, 'Special Rapporteur on the Right to Food' www.ohchr.org/en/issues/food/pages/foodindex.aspx accessed 1 May 2021.

6 Food production, access to food and a reasonable income for farmers are all reflected in Article 39 TFEU that applied in the UK under the CAP, pre-Brexit.

multifunctionality,[7] vulnerability or potential negative impacts of agriculture. As mentioned in Chapter 1, agriculture contributes positively to society in a multifaceted manner and is susceptible to shocks (economic, environmental, societal), but can also damage the environment and human health via pollution, disease and damage to the soil. Policy objectives must also address these aspects, and not simply productivity.

Sustainability has long been present in the context of farming. Its centrality in agriculture is reflected in the CAP reforms since the 1990s.[8] Originally, sustainable agriculture was understood to be underpinned by 'alternative' values inclusive of decentralisation, independence, community and harmony with nature, as well as social values such as equity (including the consideration of future generations), extensive agricultural systems, preservation of agrarian culture and preference for small, family farms[9] – truly reflecting the three (environmental, social and economic) elements of sustainable development. At that time, multiple methods of agriculture were explored such as organic, agroecology, permaculture, low-input, biodynamic and regenerative agriculture more generally.[10] More recently, it has become more mainstream and also been applied to large-scale and intensive farming. Today it is a core characteristic and focus of agriculture and agricultural policies.[11]

Nonetheless, sustainability no longer provides a sufficient driver for innovation. Whilst it can be a balanced, holistic concept that drives environmentally-friendly behaviour, it does not necessarily do so – it has lost some of its core significance, is ambiguous at times and has come to mean different things for different people. When implementing sustainability, the focus frequently appears to be on sustainable *development* or sustainable *intensification* instead, with the

7 The multifunctionality of agriculture provides goods and services valued by societal demand, alongside the production of food, fuel and fibre. For more, see M. Cardwell, *The European Model of Agriculture* (OUP 2004); and G. Van Huylenbroeck, V. Vandermeulen, E. Mettepenningen and A. Verspecht, 'Multifunctionality of Agriculture: A Review of Definitions, Evidence and Instruments' (2007) 1 *Living Reviews in Landscape Research* 3.

8 Chapter 1.

9 J.W. Hansen, 'Is Agricultural Sustainability a Useful Concept' (1996) 50 *Agricultural Systems* 117, 122.

10 R.J. MacRae, S.B. Hill, J. Henning and G.R. Mehuys, 'Agricultural Science and Sustainable Agriculture, A Review of the Existing Scientific Barriers to Sustainable Food Production and Potential Solutions' (1989) 6(3) *Biological Agriculture and Horticulture* 173; O.W. Bidwell, 'Where Do We Stand on Sustainable Agriculture?' (1986) 41 *Journal of Soil and Water Conservation* 317; H.O. Carter, 'Agricultural Sustainability: An Overview and Research Assessment' (1989) 43(3) *California Agriculture* 16 and 37; and R.J. MacRae, S.B. Hill, G.R. Mehuys and J. Henning, 'Farm-Scale Agronomic and Economic Conversion from Conventional to Sustainable Agriculture' (1990) 43 *Advances in Agronomy* 155.

11 See the close link between agriculture and the United Nations' Sustainable Development Goals, United Nations, Department of Economic and Social Affairs, 'The 17 Goals' https://sdgs.un.org/goals accessed 1 May 2021.

emphasis on the economic side rather than sustainability more holistically[12] – despite the existence of the three pillars in principle and the array of United Nations' Sustainable Development Goals. It often proves difficult to find the right balance between both aspects but in the end the emphasis should be on sustainability.[13] The presumption is in favour of development, with concessions in favour of the environment. Consider the CAP, where despite the reforms with greening requirements, cross-compliance and agri-environmental schemes, agriculture still remains a major source of pollution, biodiversity is declining in the wild and on farms, the age of farmers is increasing, mental health in the industry is in a poor state and many farms remain dependent on financial support. Add to this that sustainability is largely about day-to-day survival and maintaining the status quo – including meeting our needs whilst not compromising the needs of future generations. Consequently, the meaning of sustainable agriculture has become 'static' and is based on an assumption of slow, manageable changes, rather than addressing existing problems or adapting to deal with shocks and turbulence. Fine-tuning conventional agriculture to become more sustainable is no longer sufficient to mitigate the undesirable effects of conventional agriculture or address the vulnerabilities it faces.

4.1.1 The concept of resilience and its application to agriculture

Resilience has numerous definitions and understandings that vary according to discipline and even within a discipline.[14] The focus here will be on definitions relevant to social-ecological resilience,[15] rather than, for instance, engineering.[16]

Even within social-ecological resilience, numerous definitions are provided. Holling notes that resilience implies the capacity for a system to absorb change,

12 T. Garnett and C. Godfray, 'Sustainable Intensification in Agriculture: Navigating a Course through Competing Food System Priorities' (Food Climate Research Network, Oxford Martin Programme on the Future of Food 2012); J. Pretty, 'The Sustainable Intensification of Agriculture' (1997) 21 *Natural Resources Forum* 249; and OECD, 'Policy Instruments to Support Green Growth in Agriculture' (OECD Green Growth Studies 2012).

13 L. Petetin, 'The EU Common Agricultural Policy: Towards a More Sustainable Agriculture?' in R. Ako and D. Olawuyi (eds), *Food and Agricultural Law: Readings on Sustainable Agriculture and the Law in Nigeria* (Afe Babalola University Press 2015) 201.

14 A.S. Garmestani and C.R. Allen (eds), *Social-Ecological Resilience and Law* (Columbia University Press 2014).

15 C.S. Holling, 'Resilience and Stability of Ecological Systems' (1973) 4(1) *Annual Review of Ecology and Systematics* 1; Garmestani and Allen (n14) 1, 5–6; C.S. Holling and L.H. Gunderson, 'Resilience and Adaptive Cycles' in C.S. Holling and L.H. Gunderson (eds), *Panarchy: Understanding Transformations in Human and Natural Systems* (Island Press 2002) 25; and B. Bohman, *Legal Design for Social-Ecological Resilience* (CUP 2021).

16 For a discussion on the difference between these concepts, see J.B. Ruhl, 'General Design Principles for Resilience and Adaptive Capacity in Legal Systems – With Applications to Climate Change Adaptation' (2011) 89(5) *North Carolina Law Review* 1373, 1375–1378. Engineering resilience is focused more on stability or bouncing back, whereas social-ecological resilience is focused more on adaptability or bouncing forward.

that is to respond to crises and adjust to change whilst preserving its operations,[17] with Walker et al. providing a slight variation on this: '[t]he capacity of a system to experience shocks while retaining essentially the same function, structure, feedbacks, and therefore identity'.[18] It focuses on the ability to adjust and survive major shocks or turbulence[19] over the short to long term, without rupturing or having system failure, through being dynamic and forward-looking. 'The more resilient a system, the larger the disturbance it can absorb without shifting into an alternate regime'[20] or state. This is especially relevant today, where shocks and turbulence seem to be of increasing prevalence through Brexit, COVID-19, migration and climate change.[21]

For social-ecological resilience, in particular, this is not simply a matter of resistance – of identifying and knocking back shocks and changes.[22] Instead, it looks to adaptability, enabling systems and actors to respond to changes, uncertainties and shocks as they arise – not merely learning to survive but also to thrive in such contexts. In other words, adaptive capacity.[23] Kerner and Thomas group attributes of resilience into three categories: stability, adaptability and readiness.[24] Thus, rather than being perpetually in a state of flux or adaptation, the context will determine what actions or approaches should be taken:[25] maintenance/persistence (where the status quo is desirable and resilient), adaptation (where the status quo is generally desirable, but some adjustments or changes are required)

17 Holling (n15).
18 B.H. Walker et al., 'A Handful of Heuristics and Some Propositions for Understanding Resilience in Social-Ecological Systems' (2006) 11(1) *Ecology and Society*, Article 13. For an online version, see www.ecologyandsociety.org/vol11/iss1/art13/ accessed 1 May 2021.
19 C.K. Ansell and J. Trondal, 'Governing Turbulence: An Organizational-Institutional Agenda' (2018) 1(1) *Perspectives on Public Management and Governance* 43; C.K. Ansell, J. Trondal and M. Øgård, 'Turbulent Governance' in C.K. Ansell, J. Trondal and M. Øgård (eds), *Governance in Turbulent Times* (OUP 2016) 1; and V. Gravey, L. Petetin and M. Dobbs, 'Quitter la PAC, Comment et Pour Quoi Faire ? La (Re)Construction des Politiques Agricoles Britanniques au Coeur des Turbulences du Brexit' (2021) 73(3) *Politique Européenne* 150.
20 Walker et al. (n18). Sometimes it may be preferable to have a rupture leading to a new regime and then develop the new regime's resilience instead, for example, if the existing environment is heavily polluted or if there is continuous warfare.
21 Regarding the turbulence faced by the EU in the context of the European Green Deal and the need for developing holistic, resilient approaches, see M. Dobbs, V. Gravey and L. Petetin, 'Driving the European Green Deal in Turbulent Times' (2021) 9(3) *Politics and Governance* 316.
22 Ruhl (n16).
23 L. Gunderson, 'Ecological Resilience – In Theory and Application' (2000) 31 *Annual Review of Ecological Systems* 425; and G.C. Gallopín, 'Linkages between Vulnerability, Resilience, and Adaptive Capacity' (2006) 16(3) *Global Environmental Change* 293.
24 D.A. Kerner and J.S. Thomas, 'Resilience Attributes of Social-Ecological Systems: Framing Metrics for Management' (2014) 3 *Resources* 672.
25 E. Bennett et al., 'Toward a More Resilient Agriculture' (2014) 5 *The Solutions Journal* 65; and H.R. Howe and M. Ross, 'Brexit's Shades of Green – (Missing) the Opportunity to Transform Farming in England?' (2019) 31(3) *Journal of Environmental Law* 413.

and/or preparation (to adapt).[26] Further, whilst resilient systems should not typically entail ruptures, wholesale revolution or entirely upending the existing systems, as the general systems should survive in some recognisable manner, transformation may be required on occasion especially where they become stuck in undesirable situations. Designing resilience may itself require an initial rupture and radical transformation.[27]

To establish adaptive capacity, social-ecological resilience must also be multifaceted in nature – recognising the interconnectedness of different regimes or functions, society, the environment governance, law and, indeed, any aspect that might be relevant. For there to be overall resilience of a regime, policy area and ecosystem, then each component or aspect must be resilient – if one element fails, this may undermine the resilience of other elements.[28] From a governance or legal perspective, this means that the policy instruments, legal system and political, administrative or other relationships helping to deliver a resilient regime must also be resilient.

Resilience is highly pertinent to agriculture,[29] which tends to be vulnerable to shocks. Thus, the long-term viability of the land, agriculture, farms and farmers are dependent on the shared resilience of each other. For instance, all are dependent on the resilience of the soil, on long-term biodiversity, avoiding land abandonment, ensuring generational renewal and the maintaining of communities. None of these can be left at the tipping point where they are just about ticking along. Crucially, resilience must be built into the systems to help protect and insulate all from shocks – not merely ordinary challenges, but unexpected and unusually large shocks. The alternative is that any of these aspects can collapse where they encounter (increasingly common) shocks, with knock-on effects on the other aspects.[30]

Consequently, resilience bears some resemblance to the broad concept of sustainability, but remains distinct.[31] Two key points bear highlighting. First, the function or purpose of resilience extends beyond that of sustainability. Resilience encompasses the objective of maintaining functioning, but is more open to change

26 Kerner and Thomas (n24).

27 Bennett et al. (n25); and B. Walker, C.S. Holling, S.R. Carpenter and A.P. Kinzig, 'Resilience, Adaptability and Transformability in Social-Ecological Systems' (2004) 9(2) *Ecology and Society* 5.

28 C.A. Arnold and L.H. Gunderson, 'Adaptive Law' in A.S. Garmestani and C.R. Allen (eds), *Social-Ecological Resilience and Law* (Columbia University Press 2014) 317, 321. They refer to the need for 'poly-resilience'. See also Garmestani and Allen (n14); and E. Ostrom, M.A. Janssen and J.M. Anderies, 'Going beyond Panaceas' (2007) 104(39) *Proceedings of the National Academy of Sciences* 15176.

29 L. Sutherland et al., 'Adaptation, Resilience and CAP Reform: A Comparison of Crofts and Livestock Farms in Scotland' (2017) 133(3–4) *Scottish Geographical Journal* 192.

30 Bennett et al. (n25).

31 For discussion of the relationship between these concepts, see D. Marchese et al., 'Resilience and Sustainability: Similarities and Differences in Environmental Management Applications' (2018) 613 *Science of the Total Environment* 1275.

and also indicates that a system can preserve its capacity in a context of variability, disturbances and change. Second, the scope of resilience must necessarily be more expansive. It encompasses all aspects that are required in order to ensure the continued survival and viability of the farms, the farmers and the land more broadly. It, thereby, includes the three pillars of sustainability (social, economic and environmental), but, for instance, when applied to farming also the health of the farmers and the public, and the policies, legal systems, relationships and tools supporting the social-ecological system.

4.1.2 Operationalising resilience within law and governance structures

However, these two differences with sustainability highlight the complexity of resilience in practice. How does one operationalise it? First, resilience takes into account the interconnectedness of the subject matter at hand, bringing a holistic perspective, whereas frequently governance takes a siloed approach that is easier to manage (even if less effective). Second, resilience addresses the uncertain, unpredictable and turbulent context within which it operates. In contrast, society traditionally focuses on striving for scientific certainty, stability and legislating for the 'normal' situation and not the exception or unexpected. Resilience requires society to think outside the box and take innovative steps. These two aspects make operationalising resilience and achieving adaptive capacity highly challenging, including in developing agricultural policies.

Adaptive law, governance and management are central to implement resilience,[32] including for agriculture. For our purposes here, governance is more strategic and focuses on the overarching policy goals, mechanisms and accountability frameworks whereas management is about ensuring the day-to-day functioning of the regime or 'the activity of translating visions or strategies into reality';[33] therefore, adaptive governance would be required for the agricultural policies and adaptive management for overseeing the implementation of the schemes and individual agreements. Not only does the content of the policy need to focus on and facilitate resilience, but the policy documents and laws themselves need to be resilient and adaptive.[34]

Various proposals exist in the literature as to how to achieve this. The work of Bohman, Ruhl, and Arnold and Gunderson is especially useful here. Bohman proposes four groups of 'resilience features' for 'resilience governance': adaptivity, flexibility and transformability; multidimensional and polycentric structures; stakeholders and structures for participation; and operationalization, monitoring,

32 A.S. Garmestani, C.R. Allen, J.B. Ruhl and C.S. Holling, 'The Integration of Social-Ecological Resilience and Law' in A.S. Garmestani and C.R. Allen (eds), *Social-Ecological Resilience and Law* (Columbia University Press 2014) 368, 370–373 and 379.

33 Bohman (n15) 49–50 and 62.

34 Ruhl (n16); and Arnold and Gunderson (n28) 317–318, especially.

compliance and trust building.[35] As Bohman notes, some of these will be more challenging to integrate with law than others, as good governance principles and principles of law will need to be balanced with the resilience features.[36] Ruhl asserts that adaptive management 'rel[ies] on iterative cycles of goal determination, model building, performance standard setting, outcome monitoring, and standard recalibration'.[37] Arnold and Gunderson focus on the goals, structure, methods and processes of law, outlining descriptors for these features for adaptive law, for example, goals of resilience and adaptive capacity of social-ecological systems; polycentric structures with loose integration; multiple methods including adaptation and flexible or discretionary decision-making, as well as consideration of context and uncertainties; and processes that are iterative, avail of stakeholder engagement and reflect the interconnectedness of the social-ecological systems.[38] The following suggestions draw broadly on this work. In considering these suggestions, it is important to recognise the significance of information and of context and that resilience solutions may look differently in different locations or situations.[39] Consequently, approaches should be tailored. Linked to this, considerations of scale must be taken into account and may entail actions at all levels.[40] In that case, some degree of coordination or loose integration will be valuable so as to avoid conflicts and incoherency.[41]

An initial step might be to evaluate the multifaceted nature of agriculture and interconnectedness of issues that are required to facilitate adaptive capacity and thereby resilience, such as those relating to biodiversity, soil structure and nutrients, addressing climate change, a decent income above subsistence level, improved mental health, cultural identity, diversity of supply chains and quality produce. Upon identifying these, it then would be necessary to identify thresholds[42] for day-to-day survival and also to provide a buffer in the case of shocks – something that reflects adaptive capacity. To achieve this, it is essential to identify and address existing threats or weaknesses, and to identify a range of potential future shocks and vulnerabilities. Information is central. All will not be predict-

35 Bohman (n15) 63, in particular.

36 Ibid 205–206 and 212–213.

37 Ruhl (n16) 1391. He then identifies eight key steps for adaptive management: '(1) definition of the problem, (2) determination of goals and objectives for management of ecosystems, (3) determination of the ecosystem baseline, (4) development of conceptual models, (5) selection of future restoration actions, (6) implementation and management actions, (7) monitoring and ecosystem response, and (8) evaluation of restoration efforts and proposals for remedial actions'.

38 Arnold and Gunderson (n28) 319, including Table 11.1.

39 Bennett et al. (n25).

40 Garmestani, Allen, Ruhl and Holling (n32) 375–378. This reflects the nature of social-ecological systems and may call for local approaches or collaborations at scale.

41 For more, see N. Chowdhury and R.A. Wessel, 'Conceptualising Multilevel Regulation in the EU: A Legal Translation of Multilevel Governance?' (2012) 18(3) *European Law Journal* 335.

42 Garmestani, Allen, Ruhl and Holling (n32) 373–374.

able but, as with general insurance and contingency planning, insights may be gathered from experiences locally and elsewhere, regarding agriculture and other activities, including historically.

Policies and implementing measures (including schemes and individual agreements) should then adopt multiple methods in developing adaptive capacity.[43] These could derive from command-control or self-regulation. They could also include diverse approaches that encompass traditional tools, such as standard setting, (dis)incentives, monitoring and enforcement. However, innovative approaches and spaces for learning are also required.[44] Diversification throughout agriculture – in the farms, farmers, supply chains and crops – all can assist in resilience,[45] including through risk diversification and functional redundancy. It is also worth noting that great care should be taken to identify countervailing risks, including that measures to develop resilience and adaptability may actually lead to a lack of resilience for specific shocks or eventualities (especially in light of their unpredictable and uncertain nature).[46]

Adaptive law, as well as governance and management, also requires consideration of structures and processes. This can be achieved by various mechanisms,[47] including via polycentrism[48] and active roles for stakeholders[49] (with co-production and agri-food democracy). It is worth highlighting that the role for different stakeholders is of significance at all stages of policy design, implementation, enforcement and review.[50] As actors in the context of agriculture include varyingly farmers, suppliers, downstream business and consumers – all of whom may decide to participate in and support (or not) the official policy. As such, there is considerable value in their engagement and improving buy-in. This form of 'decentred' knowledge helps reflect the multilevel and 'multiple temporal' nature of social-ecological systems, including agriculture.[51] Without the active engagement by and support of actors, any policy might become swiftly redundant. They also have the ability to support and contribute to the policy outside the formal or official fora. However, engagement is not simply about instrumentalism, but also for

43 Arnold and Gunderson (n28) 337–345.
44 Bennett et al. (n25); and Howe and Ross (n25) 419–420.
45 Bennett et al. (n25); and Howe and Ross (n25) 419.
46 Walker et al. (n18) 8–9 (Proposition 11).
47 Arnold and Gunderson (n28) 319, including Table 11.1.
48 Ibid 328–336. This could relate, for instance, to policy or decision-making at different loci. If a polycentric approach is taken, then some integration or coordination is necessary to avoid conflicts, incoherency and gaps. See also Bohman (n15) 66–68.
49 Arnold and Gunderson (n28) 334; Bohman (n15) 68–69 and 115–168; and M. Pieraccini, 'Towards Just Resilience: Representing and Including New Constituencies in Adaptive Governance and Law' (2019) 31(2) *Journal of Environmental Law* 213.
50 Ibid.
51 Ibid 231.

instance regarding procedural justice.[52] As Pieraccini notes, it is therefore important to determine which interests are to be represented, by whom and why.[53]

One consideration is that those who might be affected by the decision-making should be included in the process and have the ability to influence the outcome (and not simply have a tokenistic engagement). In the context of agriculture, this could include groups that represent nature, future generations and vulnerable communities such as specific categories of farmers with poor mental health or those suffering from food poverty. Of course, as with all engagement mechanisms, care needs to be taken to avoid regulatory capture – but this risk can be offset to a large extent through widespread engagement of individuals or groups with competing interests, rather than having only limited voices heard.[54] This could be further supported through the engagement of actors from the devolved administrations. Positive relations will be necessary to ensure continued engagement.

Finally, the potential for regular reviews and facilitating reforms where needed is essential.[55] Monitoring and review are significant aspects of an adaptive approach – thresholds, focus points, methods and even the policy or schemes as a whole may need to be adapted (or indeed transformed). Especially in light of the ever-changing context of agriculture and the potential for unpredictable changes, it is essential to develop resilience as an iterative process. In contrast, if the policies are pre-determined or too constrained in their initial creation, implementation and development or reform, then they risk not being tailored appropriately or able to adapt accordingly in future.[56] This does not necessitate a complete overhaul of approaches to governance, but could build on existing systems and approaches – too severe an overhaul may lead to backlash or unintended consequences.[57]

4.1.3 Resilient ambitions across the UK?

Without an overarching ambition, the policies risk being rudderless and simply treading water – being dragged along by the prevailing current rather than steering in a purposeful manner. This is a clear instance of Brexit posing both an opportunity and a clear necessity for action. Resilience can provide the suitable ambition for all four nations, complemented by other secondary objectives including sustainability. Further, when aiming to achieve a resilient agriculture, the resilience of agri-food systems is a key component but supporting laws, policies and governance mechanisms also ought to be resilient.

52 Ibid.
53 Ibid 221.
54 R. Baldwin and J. Black, 'Really Responsive Regulation' (LSE Law, Society and Economy Working Papers 15/2007) www.lse.ac.uk/law/working-paper-series/2007-08/WPS15-2007BlackandBaldwin.pdf accessed 1 May 2021; and I. Ayres and J. Braithwaite, *Responsive Regulation* (OUP 1992).
55 Arnold and Gunderson (n28) 319, 341 and 345.
56 Ibid 318–319.
57 Ibid 326–327.

The four policies largely lack any express overarching ambition – much less a forward-looking, holistic one such as resilience. There are elements regarding environmental aims (linked to the public goods discussed below), sustainability, economic resilience and productivity (with a focus on profitability) in particular in Wales' sustainable land management (see further below) and England's *Path to Sustainable Farming Transition Plan*.[58] These still remain limited. Contrast instead the multiplicity of the CAP's objectives in Article 39 TFEU and via integrating the EU's other aims such as a high level of protection of the environment and human health. It is key to both recognise the multifunctionality of agriculture and to directly address the vulnerability of the sector. The Scottish stakeholder group (Farming and Food Production – Future Policy Group) has hinted at possibly broader considerations including the potential environmental and social contribution of farming.[59] If their eventual report reflects these broader considerations and the Scottish Government subsequently adopts them, it would be possible for a holistic approach to underpin Scottish agriculture policy that might implicitly support resilience.

The picture is more positive if one considers Wales's *White Paper* in conjunction with its Well-being of Future Generations (Wales) Act 2015 and the Environment (Wales) Act 2016. First, the *White Paper* proposes 'sustainable land management' as the 'overarching principle'.[60] As with sustainability generally, this is intended to address environmental, social and economic elements – but the weighting within the *Paper* is largely on the environmental and economic components. Further, although not the overarching objective, the *White Paper* mentions resilience 26 times (mostly economic references, some environmental references and only a social emphasis three times). Nonetheless, the foundations are present. Additionally, the objective of sustainable management of resources[61] within the Environment (Wales) Act 2016 is to 'maintain and enhance the resilience of ecosystems and the benefits they provide'[62] and two of the sustainable

58 Respectively Welsh Government, 'Consultation Document: Agriculture (Wales) White Paper' (*White Paper*) (16 December 2020); and DEFRA, 'The Path to Sustainable Farming: An Agricultural Transition Plan 2021 to 2024' (*Path to Sustainable Farming*) (November 2020) https://assets.publishing.service.gov.uk/government/uploads/system/uploads/attachment_data/file/954283/agricultural-transition-plan.pdf accessed 1 May 2021.

59 Farming and Food Production – Future Policy Group, 'Minutes from 27 October 2020' (27 October 2020) www.gov.scot/binaries/content/documents/govscot/publications/minutes/2020/11/farming-and-food-production-future-policy-group-update-october-2020/documents/farming-and-food-production-future-policy-group-update-october-2020/farming-and-food-production-future-policy-group-update-october-2020/govscot%3Adocument/FFP-FPG%2B-%2B27%2BOctober%2B2020%2B-%2BSummary%2BMinutes.pdf accessed 1 May 2021.

60 *White Paper* (n58) foreword and 27–33.

61 Referred to in the *White Paper* (n58) (page 35) in the context of support for rural development.

62 Environment (Wales) Act 2016, Section 3. For more on ecosystems resilience, see V. Jenkins, 'Sustainable Management of Natural Resources: Lessons from Wales' (2018) 30(3) *Journal of Environmental Law* 399.

management of resources principles refer to adaptive management and ecosystem resilience.[63] Finally, one of the well-being goals of the Well-being of Future Generations (Wales) Act 2015 is a resilient Wales, which is described therein as having 'healthy functioning ecosystems that support social, economic and ecological resilience and the capacity to change'[64] – thereby confirming a holistic approach. Consequently, Wales has the legal underpinnings and seemingly the motivation to deliver this overarching ambition of a resilient agriculture, if they were to link and adapt their agricultural proposals accordingly.

Irrespective, rhetoric must also be substantiated. It is insufficient for policies to proclaim themselves as resilient or as aiming to achieve resilience, if they do not then follow through with this. On the other hand, it is still possible for the policies to promote resilience even if they do not expressly delineate objectives such as resilience. Indeed, the very existence of devolution and the four policies already indicates some recognition of the multilevel considerations and the need to tailor approaches.[65] In examining the four policies across the remainder of the chapter, the content is analysed in light of what the policies are striving to do and general ideas such as effectiveness or democracy, as well as what they may lack in light of resilience and the development of adaptive capacity and management. Thus, the following section examines the role of objectives and potential pathways towards resilience. This is followed by sections on diversity (and tailored approaches), governance and wider considerations linked to agriculture's interconnectedness.

4.2 Pathways towards a resilient agriculture

This section considers potential pathways to further a resilient agriculture. It commences by investigating whether core approaches proposed in the UK policies (specifically, the public goods and productivity approaches) to date could facilitate resilience, before turning to a range of alternative pathways that may be more suitable – including due to their more holistic nature.

4.2.1 Public goods and productivity: new financial support schemes and their economic focus

According to economic theory discourse, public goods can be measured along two axes relating to the consumption of the good or service: rivalry and excludability.[66] Public goods possess low non-excludability (if the good is provided to one person, others cannot be excluded from the benefits it confers) and low non-rivalry (if the good is consumed by one person, it does not diminish the amount

63 Environment (Wales) Act 2016, Section 4.
64 Well-Being of Future Generations (Wales) Act 2015, Section 4, Table 1.
65 This mirrors ideas of subsidiarity discussed in Chapter 2.
66 P.A. Samuelson, 'The Pure Theory of Public Expenditure' (1954) 36 *The Review of Economics and Statistics* 387, 387.

available to others). It is important to note that public goods are not restricted to goods but can include services, described around characteristics of 'publicness'.[67] As such a public good can be defined as 'a good or service in which the benefit received by any one party does not diminish the availability of the benefits to others, and where access to the good cannot be restricted'.[68] This understanding of public goods is reflected to an extent within the policies.

The application of the theory of public goods theory to the agricultural sector provides a source of legitimacy for public intervention, due to recognising the environmental and social benefits that farmers can create.[69] Some (limited) public goods may be supplied 'incidentally, as a side-effect of economically viable activities, or as a result of farmer altruism or self-interest',[70] but the supply may not meet demand. To achieve a desirable level of provision, policy interventions and mechanisms are needed to incentivise farmers to go above and beyond legislative baselines and to pursue alternative farming practices. For instance, assisting farm conversions to organic agriculture or helping farms to diversify their businesses constitute market-based mechanisms that could be used to encourage related public goods.[71]

Payments for ecosystem services or payments-by-results schemes provide mechanisms to translate the non-market values of public goods into financial incentives for local actors to deliver these services.[72] They link farm payments to the provision of (typically environmental) outcomes (or gains) by placing monetary values on different assets or services. This payment can be defined as 'a transfer of resources between actors, which aims to create incentives, subject to clear conditions, to align individual and/or collective resource use decisions with the

67 T. Cooper, K. Hart and D. Baldock, 'Provision of Public Goods through Agriculture in the European Union' (Institute for European Environmental Policy, Report Prepared for DG Agriculture and Rural Development, Contract No 30-CE-0233091/00-28, 2009) vi.

68 R. Watson et al., 'UK National Ecosystem Assessment: Understanding Nature's Value to Society' (UNEP-WCMC 2011) 1455.

69 For more, see M. Lefebvre et al., 'Agricultural Landscapes as Multi-Scale Public Good and the Role of the Common Agricultural Policy' (2015) 58(12) *Journal of Environmental Planning and Management* 2088; and I. Hodge, 'Agri-Environment Policy in an Era of Lower Government Expenditure: CAP Reform and Conservation Payments' (2013) 56(2) *Journal of Environmental Planning and Management* 254.

70 Cooper, Hart and Baldock (n67) vi. See also HM Treasury and DEFRA, 'A Vision for the Common Agricultural Policy' (December 2005). More generally see J.M. Harris and B. Roach, *Environmental and Natural Resource Economics: A Contemporary Approach* (Routledge 2017).

71 National Trust, 'Public Money for Public Benefit: The Basis for a Post-Brexit Farm System' (19 June 2017) https://ntplanning.files.wordpress.com/2017/06/paper-2-national-trust-post-cap-series-public-benefits-june-20171.pdf accessed 1 May 2021, 8.

72 J. Dwyer et al., 'Public Goods and Ecosystem Services from Agriculture and Forestry – A Conceptual Approach (Institute for European Environmental Policy, Project Report Pegasus, 2015) 12.

social interest in the management of natural resources'.[73] Ecosystem services providers (for example, landholders, farmers or communities) voluntarily participate in schemes where they receive payments from public or private buyers (including a government, utility or private organisation) administered by intermediary actors (a semi-autonomous body or non-governmental organisation).[74] As noted in Chapter 3, Section 3.1.1, DEFRA is piloting payments for outcomes.[75]

However, assigning market value to non-market goods is difficult because of 'the complexity of ecological systems and the services they generate'.[76] A solution is to base valuation on natural capital. For DEFRA, promoting natural capital could result in due recognition of the environment and the way natural resources underpin economic activities.[77] References to natural capital have been present at some stage in all four policies. For example, the ***Sustainable Farming Incentive Paper*** mentions natural asset(s) four times, thereby indicating a natural capital rhetoric in the document's framing and the scheme itself.[78]

Natural capital assets such as land, referred to as 'stocks', produce goods and services, called 'flows' or 'benefits', that are necessary to economic production, i.e. ecosystem services.[79] Focusing on both stocks and flows/benefits is crucial: the former cannot be neglected, as otherwise it results in reduced flows (both qualitatively and quantitatively). The UK Natural Capital Committee defined natural capital as 'elements of nature that directly or indirectly produce value to people, including ecosystems, species, freshwater, land, minerals, the air and

73 H. Ishihara, U. Pascual and I. Hodge, 'Dancing with Storks: The Role of Power Relations in Payments for Ecosystem Services' (2017) 139 *Ecological Economics* 45, 45.

74 C.P. Rodgers, 'Legal Models for Implementing Agri-Environment Policy after Brexit' in I. Antonopoulos, M. Bell, A. Cavoski and L. Petetin (eds), *The Governance of Agriculture in Post-Brexit UK* (Routledge forthcoming 2022).

75 Similar schemes were piloted in England in the late 2010s, see S. Chaplin et al., 'Pilot Results-Based Payment Approaches for Agri-Environment Schemes in Arable and Upland Grassland Systems in England: Final Report' (Natural England and Yorkshire Dales National Park Authority 2019).

76 B. Fisher, R.K. Turner and P. Morling, 'Defining and Classifying Ecosystem Services for Decision Making' (2009) 68 *Ecological Economics* 643, 649. See also I.J. Bateman and B. Balmford, 'Public Funding for Public Goods: A Post-Brexit Perspective on Principles for Agricultural Policy' (2018) 79 *Land Use Policy* 293, 296.

77 DEFRA, 'A Green Future: Our 25 Year Plant to Improve the Environment' (2018) https://assets.publishing.service.gov.uk/government/uploads/system/uploads/attachment_data/file/693158/25-year-environment-plan.pdf accessed 1 May 2021 – throughout.

78 DEFRA, 'Sustainable Farming Incentive: Defra's Plans for Piloting and Launching the Scheme' (*SFI Paper*) (16 March 2021) www.gov.uk/government/publications/sustainable-farming-incentive-scheme-pilot-launch-overview/sustainable-farming-incentive-defras-plans-for-piloting-and-launching-the-scheme accessed 1 May 2021; and Welsh Government, 'Consultation Document: Brexit and Our Land – Securing the Future of Welsh Farming' (2018) 7.

79 H.E. Daly and J.B. Cobb jr, *For the Common Good: Redirecting the Economy towards Community, the Environment and a Sustainable Future* (Beacon Press 1994) 72–73; R.W. England, 'Natural Capital and the Theory of Economic Growth' (2000) 34 *Ecological Economics* 425, 426.

oceans'.[80] For instance, woodland can be considered as a natural capital asset, from which flows valuable benefits or ecosystem services such as flood risk reduction and carbon capture. Valuing natural capital enables the benefits derived from natural assets by managing and mitigating environmental risks to be incorporated into the decision-making process. Arguably, this could lead to better management of natural assets. The Wildlife and Countryside Link and the National Trust support natural capital restoration.[81] However, such an approach creates a marketisation of nature and the wider environment. It emphasises a purely economic approach to nature and, combined with the narrow definition of public goods in the Agriculture Act 2020,[82] does not allow for a true recognition of what natural assets (and consequently payments-by-results) encompass. Such an approach could also result in skewed economic valuations of payments-by-results schemes.[83]

The four policies also adopt a second prong of financial support where a productivist paradigm prevails. For instance, DEFRA has put clear emphasis on prosperity and productivity[84] and Wales, Northern Ireland and seemingly Scotland also are heading in the same direction. The clear aim is for farms to be self-sufficient, with them primarily receiving financial support under this prong to introduce money-saving/making changes through capital investment – including to enable farmers to operate in future without direct payments. Innovative approaches can modify farm operations to maximize use of resource-conserving technologies,[85] with examples of precision-farming or investing in renewable energy. However, despite the express reference in Section 1(4) of the Agriculture Act to design schemes in an 'environmentally sustainable way' when producing food, the focus is clearly on productivity rather than resource efficiency or preferably resource conservation, and with this comes the threat of reverting back to a sustainable intensification approach focusing on intensification rather than sustainability as

> farmers are engaged in competition to expand and to over-equip their farms, in an approach in which every agricultural advance consumes more and more

80 Natural Capital Committee, 'The State of Natural Capital: Restoring our Natural Assets' (2nd report to the Economic Affairs Committee March 2014).
81 Wildlife and Countryside Link, 'A Future Sustainable Farming and Land Management Policy for England' (discussion paper September 2017) 3; and National Trust (n71) 7.
82 Definitions in the devolved administrations have not yet been agreed.
83 This is reflected in the emphasis on farm business income, farm performance and agricultural productivity in DEFRA and Government Statistical Service, 'The Future Farming and Environment Evidence Compendium' (September 2019) https://assets.publishing.service.gov.uk/government/uploads/system/uploads/attachment_data/file/834432/evidence-compendium-26sep19.pdf accessed 1 May 2021.
84 *Path to Sustainable Farming* (n58).
85 D.R. Keeney, 'Toward a Sustainable Agriculture: Need for Clarification of Concepts and Terminology' (1989) 4(3–4) *American Journal of Alternative Agriculture* 101, 102. The use of GMOs or gene editing also springs to mind here.

> energy and imported nutrients, and in a continuous race between pesticides and pests. Maintaining agricultural potential has a high financial and environmental cost and, more worryingly, seems to have no end.[86]

This is not to say that economic considerations should not be a focus of agricultural policy – it is a fundamental issue, central to sustainability and also resilience. However, the question should not be whether farms can make more money, but instead whether farming (in an appropriate manner) is something desirable and suitable for public support. If so, then economic viability of farms should become the focus – including through enhancing their self-sufficiency. Where they cannot be independently economically viable, then the public/state should support them also in the long term to the degree considered appropriate to ensure resilience.

A reasonable income is needed for farmers, which could entail producing more or being more efficient, but numerous other mechanisms exist. For example, Wales' Sustainable Farming Scheme aims to provide a guaranteed income to farmers.[87] This could be achieved through ensuring market access, adapting supply chains, adopting cooperative approaches to farming (for example, sharing equipment or labour), developing cooperatives to strengthen bargaining powers to achieve fair prices,[88] adapting land-ownership rights and obligations to protect and incentivise long-term investments in the land.[89] Measures need to be tailored in light of specific contexts, e.g. changes to individual small farms in less favoured areas may not prove sufficient to enable them to become economically viable without continued support. Thus, economic viability (whether under sustainability or resilience) goes far beyond this productivity paradigm.

As a consequence, the proposals seem overly reductive with their economic, productive tone. Pushing the argument a step further, developing schemes underpinned by a paradigm of 'strength through exhaustion' of biodiversity, soil, water and air quality, must be avoided. Establishing a dichotomy between economic prosperity and environmental ambition is an old rhetoric. Yet, this is achieved here with potential conflicts between the two prongs and the overly narrow, restrictive approaches to both prongs. However, implemented in different ways and through different mechanisms, they would be key components to deliver a resilient agriculture.

A better balance between the two could improve the respective emphasis of these prongs. Establishing schemes centred also on environmental and social values, beyond simply economic aspects, could help farmers diversify and make them more resilient. Public goods (whether as understood in the policies currently

86 X. Poux and P.M. Aubert, 'An Agroecological Europe in 2050: Multifunctional Agriculture for Healthy Eating – Findings from the Ten Years for Agroecology (TYFA) Modelling Exercise' (IDDRI 2018) 4.

87 *White Paper* (n58) paragraph 2.63.

88 Section 29 of the Agriculture Act 2020 aims to help ameliorate such an issue.

89 Wales and England seek to address this in part. See Section 4.4.4 below.

or more broadly) and even productivity could form individual mechanisms, but they ought not be the only or even main focus points or objectives to achieve a more holistic and coherent approach to agriculture.[90] Consequently, the objection (from a resilience perspective or otherwise) is not to a public goods approach or consideration of economics or even productivity, but to limiting the policies to these relatively narrow focus points. At a minimum, they need to be complemented by other, wider mechanisms or pathways.

4.2.2 Alternative pathways? Addressing the holistic nature of resilience

If to achieve resilience, then several pathways may be of use. Fundamentally, these reflect the holistic nature of resilience and the multifunctional, interconnected, vulnerable nature of agriculture, as well as the importance of nature-based solutions to enhance ecosystem functioning, improve biodiversity and nurture the health of communities.[91] Agriculture is interdependent with the environment, society and the economy – all broadly understood. However, it is also functioning today in a society that does not always recognise its value, where urban migration and expansion exist, rural communities are frequently deprived or with poor infrastructure, and where the environment has often been already degraded. It is not operating in an optimal situation and is currently susceptible to the increasing shocks prevalent globally, in the form of pandemics, mass migration, war,

90 For more on this holistic view, see A. Buckwell et al., 'Towards a Common Agricultural and Rural Policy for Europe' (European Economy, Reports and Studies, No. 5, European Commission Directorate General for Economic and Financial Affairs 1997).

91 The International Union for Conservation of Nature (IUCN) defines nature-based solutions as 'actions to protect, sustainably manage, and restore natural or modified ecosystems, that address societal challenges effectively and adaptively, simultaneously providing human well-being and biodiversity benefits' and has developed eight key principles to support such an ecosystem approach. See Commission on Ecosystem Management, 'Nature-Based Solutions' (IUCN 2020) www.iucn.org/commissions/commission-ecosystem-management/our-work/nature-based-solutions accessed 1 May 2021. For more on nature-based solutions, see WWF and RSPB, 'Nature-Based Solutions' (2020) https://www.rspb.org.uk/globalassets/downloads/Nature_Based_Solutions_NDC_ReportV2.pdf accessed 1 May 2021; A. Barnett, 'Nature-Based Solutions in the Green Recovery' (RSPB 2020) www.rspb.org.uk/globalassets/downloads/policy-briefings/policy-briefing_nature-based-solutions-in-the-green-recovery_the-rspb.pdf accessed 1 May 2021; E. Gerritsen et al., 'Using Nature-Based Solutions to Foster Synergies between Biodiversity and Climate: Missed Chances and New Opportunities for a Sustainable Future' (Institute for European Environmental Policy and Ecologic Institute 2020) https://think2030.eu/wp-content/uploads/2021/04/Using-nature-based-solutions-to-foster-synergies-between-biodiversity-and-climate-23.04.21.pdf accessed 1 May 2021; and R. Stafford et al., 'Nature-Based Solutions for Climate Change in the UK: A Report by the British Ecological Society' (British Ecological Society 2021) www.britishecologicalsociety.org/nature-basedsolutions accessed 1 May 2021.

biodiversity decline and climate change.[92] In an ideal situation, ensuring resilience might simply entail avoiding pressing the red button. Here, the pathways to resilience are challenging and must address the vulnerabilities of agriculture; such pathways include social-ecological services, net zero, agroecology and agri-food democracy.

4.2.2.1 Social-ecological services

Enhanced definitions of public goods could reflect wider ecosystem services or social-ecological services approaches and justify corresponding payments. Indeed, ecosystem services can be an easier concept to grasp than public goods. The term 'public good' is often used inter-changeably with ecosystem services, but it is not accurate.[93] Ecosystems services might overlap with public goods, but only partially depending on the non-rivalry and non-excludability spectrum mentioned above. Like public goods, ecosystem services are a complex category of resources that can be both private and public in provision and demand.[94] Ecosystem services accommodate a wider, integrated 'ecosystem approach'[95] reflecting human dependence on ecological systems that involves citizens and values the environment beyond the economic/monetary valuation under the natural capital approach.

A more appropriate term may be social-ecological services to highlight the relationship between human and social interactions and ecosystems. Social-ecological services can be defined as the 'non-material benefits obtained from ecosystems through spiritual enrichment, cognitive development, reflection, aesthetic experience and include things like social relations, aesthetic values and human well-being'.[96] Put simply, social-ecological services entail the provision of environmental and social outcomes; it enables a holistic approach towards the countryside that furthers the balance and robustness of biological, physical and socio-economic factors in line with sustainable development goals and resilience. Bohman has described the ecosystem approach as 'the most concrete regulatory tool that is open to the inclusion of a social-ecological resilience perspective

92 For more, see IPCC, 'Climate Change and Land: An IPCC Special Report on Climate Change, Desertification, Land Degradation, Sustainable Land Management, Food security, and Greenhouse Gas Fluxes in Terrestrial Ecosystems' (August 2019).

93 A. Hejnowicz and S. Hartley, 'New Directions: A Public Goods Approach to Agricultural Policy Post-Brexit' (Brexit and Environment Network 2018) 10.

94 Rodgers (n74).

95 K. Waylen et al., 'The Need to Disentangle Key Concepts from Ecosystem-Approach Jargon' (2014) 28(5) *Conservation Biology* 1215; and S. Díaz et al., 'Summary for Policymakers of the Global Assessment Report on Biodiversity and Ecosystem Services' (IPBES Secretariat 2019).

96 Dwyer (n72) 11. See also T. Plieninger and C. Bieling (eds), *Resilience and the Cultural Landscape: Understanding and Managing Change in Human-Shaped Environments* (CUP 2012).

within the legal system' and 'offers [a]... stepping-stone for the study of law and social-ecological resilience'.[97]

Social-ecological systems enable a 'fuller understanding of the functional and institutional factors influencing supply and demand' of public goods and ecosystem services.[98] Following this train of thought, the frame of social-ecological services is also underpinned by the idea of supplying services in the public interest. In political science, the 'public good' refers to actions undertaken for the common good or in the public interest. Some economists argue that the public characteristic of a good results from collective and institutional choices about what is considered in the public interest.[99] In this sense, a 'public good' or 'common good' revolves around societal wellbeing or the good of the society. The public utility derived from a particular good or service may call for public intervention and/or governance, or some sort of collective action[100] and can legitimate resulting policies.[101] Numerous insights are available in the literature as to how to protect and promote these goods or services.

For instance, Hardin outlines the 'tragedy of the commons' whereby individuals acting in their own (immediate) self-interest would inevitably deplete or pollute a shared resource, exacerbated by the growing populations.[102] Hardin's solutions to this involve alternatively privatisation (incentivising owners to improve their management of the resource) or government regulation. However, neither approach is necessarily effective or appropriate.[103] Instead, Ostrom considers that (in particular, local) individuals and communities could themselves effectively manage these shared resources – or common pool resources – preventing their exhaustion or degradation. She provides a range of design principles on governing the commons, including regarding collective action and the incentivising thereof.[104]

Environmental and social goods and services are territorially and socially anchored. They are not static phenomena but are rather heterogeneous.[105] Their delivery is dependent on nature, geography, history, culture, available (monitoring) techniques, the scarcity of natural resources or extreme climate events (e.g.

97 Bohman (n15) 39.
98 Dwyer (n72) 14.
99 J. Ballet, 'Propriété, Biens Publics Mondiaux, Bien(s) Commun(s) : Une Lecture des Concepts Economiques' (2008) Développement Durable et Territoires (Dossier 10: Biens Communs et Propriété). Also available online http://developpementdurable.revues.org/5553 accessed 1 May 2021.
100 E. Ostrom, *Governing the Commons: The Evolution of Institutions for Collective Action* (CUP 1990).
101 Dwyer (n72).
102 G. Hardin, 'The Tragedy of the Commons' (1968) 162 *Science* 1243.
103 J.B. Millard and H. Bosse-Platière, 'Les Biens Communs en Agriculture, Tragédie ou Apologie ?' (AFDR, Agridées and LexisNexis 2020).
104 Ostrom (n100); and E. Ostrom, 'A General Framework for Analyzing Sustainability of Social-Ecological Systems' (2009) 325(5939) *Science* 419.
105 Fisher et al. (n76) 648.

drought or fire). Their distribution is not uniform across all types of land, farms or agricultural activities, nor is their provision constant over time.[106] Any policy based on social-ecological services should give a deciding role to farmers, civil society organisations and the public to choose which goods and services would be best suited on their land.

Dedicated financial support for the delivery of social-ecological services can result in the provision of strong, secondary outcomes that can stimulate the economic activities of rural areas, thereby improving rural vitality and the quality of life in rural communities.[107] For instance, the Welsh proposals focus on the Welsh culture and language – although the approach could be widened substantially. This 'second order' of social benefits indicates how the agricultural sector can improve society beyond the environment and its intrinsic value.[108] Further, more regenerative agricultural practices, such as agroecology, agroforestry and social agriculture,[109] that consider natural ecosystems and local knowledge could become key instruments of social-ecological services policies. This contrasts with the argument that a financially viable and prosperous farm (often via increased productivity) improves environmental benefits and rural vitality and favours local rural communities; this is an excessively restrictive reading of the relationship and, unfortunately, this is the reasoning adopted in the Agriculture Act where wider social-ecological services are portrayed only as by-products.[110]

Hejnowicz and Hartley argue that the social-ecological services frame should underpin the 'public money for public goods' model developed across the four nations to move away from economic characteristics towards the 'social-cultural co-production of these goods'.[111] Crucially, a social-ecological services frame does not aim to place humans at the centre and is not ethnocentric. This newer model of 'payment by results' could be an effective mode of land management, if payments are to be based on environmental *and* social outcomes rather than simply specific management practices (or actions), and thereby act as the main tool to deliver social-ecological services. However, the narrow definition of public goods adopted currently – at least in the Agriculture Act (although Section 1 extends to animal welfare and climate action) and Northern Ireland's *Draft Agricultural Strategy* – combined with a natural capital emphasis does not provide the required

106 Cooper, Hart and Baldock (n67) 166.
107 Ibid 122.
108 Ibid 111. See also Dwyer (n72) 8.
109 For more on these practices, see L. Petetin, V. Gravey and B. Moore, 'Setting the Bar for a Green Brexit in Food and Farming' (Soil Association 2019) www.soilassociation.org/green-brexit/ accessed 1 May 2021.
110 Emphasis on the environment (and productivity) alone is insufficient and leads to policies and strategies that are not integrated.
111 Hejnowicz and Hartley (n93) 32. See N. Stoeckl et al., 'The Crowding Out of Complex Social Goods' (2018) 144 *Ecological Economics* 65. More generally on co-production, see S. Jasanoff (ed.), *States of Knowledge: The Co-production of Science and Social Order* (Routledge 2004).

radical change in approach and could excessively restrict the delivery of social-ecological services.

With payment by results,[112] more responsibilities, autonomy and flexibility are given to farmers to innovate and design schemes that are appropriate for their land whilst enabling greater effort on climate and biodiversity provisions. Further, there is greater focus on the social aspects with training and increased expertise,[113] overall improving social capital.[114] However, payment by results-based schemes can be quite technical and intricate to negotiate[115] and entail high set-up costs (both for the farmer and responsible agencies). When designing such schemes, care should be taken to find the right balance between these different, sometimes contrasting aspects.

Rural communities across the UK will be affected negatively by the loss of Pillar 2 of the CAP and structural funds, when they already are struggling, including with mental health.[116] Social networks between rural families and communities also merit support to enhance rural vitality. Helm argues that the rural development fund addressed this public good,[117] whilst Bateman and Balford note the integral role farming plays in rural communities, not only by providing livelihoods but also by encouraging community cohesion.[118] These communities are likewise fundamental to farming. Yet, rural development does not appear to be a key component of the four proposals and is only perceived as a by-product, whilst it could help ameliorate a rather tense situation for farmers and build resilience across rural communities and agriculture.

Objectives such as those relating to public health (including obesity and alcohol consumption) remain generally absent from all proposals – apart from the focus on antimicrobial resistance. Whilst food quality is mentioned sparingly in the Agriculture Act[119] and multiple times in Wales' *White Paper*,[120] the complementary issue of healthy diets is barely mentioned.[121] However, whilst there is

112 See Section 4.4.2 below.
113 Hejnowicz and Hartley (n93) 27.
114 Dwyer (n72) 27. The *White Paper* in Wales mentions social capital for rural communities, see *White Paper* (n58) 8.
115 I. Herzon et al., 'Time to Look for Evidence: Results-Based Approach to Biodiversity Conservation on Farmland in Europe' (2018) 71 *Land Use Policy* 347. This explains why the policies are backtracking and mostly focusing on actions.
116 For more on the mental health of farmers, see Farm Safety Foundation, https://www.yellowwellies.org/ accessed 1 May 2021; and Farming Community Network, https://fcn.org.uk/ accessed 1 May 2021.
117 D. Helm, 'Agriculture after Brexit' (2017) 33 Suppl 1 *Oxford Review of Economic Policy* S124, S128.
118 Bateman and Balmford (n76) 295.
119 Agriculture Act, Section 1(5).
120 *White Paper* (n58) 7, 11 and 29.
121 L. Petetin and V. Gravey, 'The Agriculture Bill: 8 Key Provisions and Recommendations' (Brexit and Environment Network 24 January 2020) www.brexitenvironment.co.uk/2020/01/24/agriculture-bill-8-key-provisions/ accessed 1 May 2021.

some debate as to whether food security is a public good, food production is an ecosystem service.[122] Consequently, the production of healthy and nutritious food could also be worthy of support and drive positive social (and economic) consequences when considering that around two-thirds of adults across the UK are overweight or obese, with huge costs borne by the National Health Service.[123] The corollary is that financially supporting the production, for example, of apple, hop, barley, corn, rye or wheat – when the utilisation of the commodity results in alcohol production – is questionable (morally and on public health grounds).

The fact that the Agriculture Act was enacted before the *National Food Strategy* in England[124] was fully developed reflects the lack of holistic approaches to the agri-food supply chain. Similar approaches are reflected across the devolved administrations where few connections are being made between proposed policies and strategies.[125] They all fail to address the 'Food in the Anthropocene' agenda where the 2019 EAT-Lancet Report calls for an integrated agenda/approach between agricultural and environmental policies on the one side and food and human health policies on the other to ensure healthy diets.[126] Consequently, it is important to think about food consumption but also the diversity of types of food that is produced. In relation to food consumption, reducing/cutting food loss/waste[127] and managing issues and redistribution of food surplus[128] are crucial aspects to consider. As to the diversity of food, it is important to balance plant-based foods with better-sourced animal products,[129] bearing in mind their

122 T.C. Brown, J.C. Bergstrom and J.B. Loomis, 'Defining, Valuing, and Providing Ecosystem Goods and Services' (2007) 47(2) *Natural Resources Journal* 329, 333.

123 C. Baker, 'Obesity Statistics' (House of Commons Library, CBP 3336, 21 January 2021) 4.

124 National Food Strategy, 'Read Part One' www.nationalfoodstrategy.org/partone/ accessed 1 May 2021.

125 In Wales, see Welsh Government, 'Consultation Document: Our Ambition to Further Develop Wales' Food and Drink Sector (2019) to follow Welsh Government, 'Food for Wales, Food from Wales 2010/2020 – Food Strategy for Wales (2010). In Scotland, see Scottish Government, 'Recipe for Success: Scotland's National Food and Drink Policy' (2009) www.gov.scot/binaries/content/documents/govscot/publications/strategy-plan/2009/06/recipe-success-scotlands-national-food-drink-policy/documents/0083283-pdf/0083283-pdf/govscot%3Adocument/0083283.pdf?forceDownload=true accessed 1 May 2021. It became a Good Food Nation Policy in 2014. See Scottish Government, 'Food and Drink' www.gov.scot/policies/food-and-drink/good-food-nation/ accessed 1 May 2021.

126 W. Willett et al., 'Food in the Anthropocene: The EAT-Lancet Commission on Healthy Diets from Sustainable Food Systems' (2019) 393(10170) *The Lancet* 447.

127 For more, see C. Bradshaw, 'Waste Law and the Value of Food' (2018) 30(2) *Journal of Environmental Law* 311; and C. Bradshaw, 'England's Fresh Approach to Food Waste: Problem Frames in the Resources and Waste Strategy' (2020) 40(2) *Legal Studies* 321.

128 M.K. Blake, 'The Multiple Ontologies of Surplus Food' (2019) 27 *Europe Now* – available online www.europenowjournal.org/2019/05/06/the-multiple-ontologies-of-surplus-food/ accessed 1 May 2021.

129 See Willett et al. (n126); and J. Lewis, 'To Meat or Not to Meat' (Soil Association 2019) www.soilassociation.org/blogs/2019/november/25/eating-meat-good-or-bad-for-the-environment/ accessed 1 May 2021.

impacts on the climate[130] and the UK Government's net-zero ambitions and goal of reducing greenhouse gas emissions by 78% by 2035,[131] whilst acting more generally within planetary boundaries.[132]

Changing diets and land use approaches are intertwined. Modelling suggests that the UK only produces 16% of its fruit and 57% of its vegetables, whilst it needs to produce 63% of both from a nutritional perspective and to meet climate change ambitions.[133] Increasing the proportion of cropland and, in particular, horticulture, which represents just under 1% of the agricultural land in the UK,[134] is part of the solution. Therefore, agroecological practices (discussed below) can also play a crucial role here.

A lack of synergy and coherency between the agricultural policies and other policies regarding the countryside can also be seen, e.g. between the English environmental and conservation regimes and the Agriculture Act. For instance, neither the Agriculture Act nor the Environment Bill address the overlapping goals and commitments that will arise, despite them being formulated at the same time. The Environment Bill commitments include Local Nature Recovery Strategies (Clauses 97 to 101), biodiversity net gain (Clauses 92 to 94 and Schedule 14) and Conservation Covenants (Part 7). These would operate in parallel to the public goods schemes under the Agriculture Act, including the Local Nature Recovery Scheme and the Landscape Recovery Scheme – the latter which is expressly intended to support the UK Government's '30by30' target,

130 For contrasting views on the relationship between livestock farming and greenhouse gas emissions and soil carbon sequestration, see T. Garnett et al., 'Grazed and Confused' (Food Climate Research Network, Oxford Martin Programme on the Future of Food, Environmental Change Institute, University of Oxford 2017) www.oxfordmartin.ox.ac.uk/publications/grazed-and-confused/ accessed 1 May 2021; and Sustainable Food Trust, 'Grazed and Confused – An Initial Response from the Sustainable Food Trust' (3 October 2017) https://sustainablefoodtrust.org/articles/grazed-and-confused-an-initial-response-from-the-sustainable-food-trust/ accessed 1 May 2021.

131 HM Government, 'UK Enshrines New Target in Law to Slash Emissions by 78% by 2035' (20 April 2021) www.gov.uk/government/news/uk-enshrines-new-target-in-law-to-slash-emissions-by-78-by-2035 accessed 1 May 2021.

132 J. Rockström et al., 'Planetary Boundaries: Exploring the Safe Operating Space for Humanity' (2009) 14(2) *Ecology and Society* 32. Also available online www.ecologyandsociety.org/vol14/iss2/art32/ accessed 1 May 2021; W. Steffen et al., 'Planetary Boundaries: Guiding Human Development on a Changing Planet' (2015) 347(6223) *Science* 1259855.

133 T. Greenham, D. McCann and L. Macfarlane, 'Farming Smarter: Investing in Our Future' (Food Farming & Countryside Commission March 2021) https://ffcc.co.uk/assets/downloads/FINAL-Farming-Smarter-Investing-in-our-Future-1.pdf accessed 1 May 2021; and Sustain, 'Delivering Synergies and Multiple Public Goods: Why Whole Farm Systems Must Be Central to Environmental Land Management and the Agricultural Transition Plan' (February 2021) www.sustainweb.org/publications/delivering-synergies-and-multiple-public-goods/ accessed 1 May 2021.

134 DEFRA, 'Farming Statistics: Final Crop Areas, Yields, Livestock Populations and Agricultural Workforce at June 2019 – United Kingdom' (19 December 2019) www.gov.uk/government/statistics/farming-statistics-final-crop-areas-yields-livestock-populations-and-agricultural-workforce-at-1-june-2019-uk accessed 1 May 2021, 9.

i.e. to protect 30% of England's land by 2030 and the establishment of a Nature Recovery Network.[135] Yet, no clarity is provided as to how the policies interrelate or will operate in parallel or conjunction with each other. Similarly, joined-up thinking is not evident between the new schemes and existing nature conservation regimes, for example, via management agreements for the protection of sites of special scientific interests (SSSIs) under the Wildlife and Countryside Act 1981 and the Countryside and Rights of Way Act 2000.

Further, there is an ongoing move away from a command-and-control approach towards a voluntary approach or principle to joining the schemes and to choosing levels of environmental commitments via different available options (as in the Sustainable Farming Incentive (SFI)). This recalls the voluntary principle, for instance, used under the Wildlife and Countryside Act 1981 to ensure that landowners would participate in nature conservation measures via management agreements.[136] This was done to facilitate buy-in from landowners as well as to minimise the restriction of their property rights.[137] For Pontin, this voluntary principle is a key example of the 'British way' to approach nature conservation and possibly more generally environmental protection post-Brexit.[138] There may be here an indication to a return to the voluntary principle when delivering public goods.

From a resilience perspective, a social-ecological services approach supporting a healthy workforce, society and market, as well as coherent connections between strategies, are key pieces of the jigsaw – reflecting agriculture and resilience's multifaceted nature discussed above and stronger win-win situations for all.[139]

4.2.2.2 Net zero

Another pathway is to move agriculture towards net-zero emissions (comprising carbon neutrality) by 2050, as advocated by the UK Committee on Climate Change (CCC)[140] and in line with the 2015 Paris Agreement.[141] Considering that resilience focuses on the ability to respond to shocks – to adapt and, if needed,

135 *Path to Sustainable Farming* (n58) 16.
136 Wildlife and Countryside Act 1981, Section 28.
137 This was later amended by the Countryside and Rights of Way Act 2000. For more, see C.P. Rodgers, *The Law of Nature Conservation* (OUP 2013) Chapter 1.
138 B. Pontin, *The Environmental Case for Brexit: A Socio-Legal Perspective* (Hart Publishing 2019) Chapter 6.
139 But this rests on the practice and implementation.
140 Committee on Climate Change, 'Net Zero – The UK's Contribution to Stopping Global Warming' (May 2019). Net zero is also closely linked to achieving a circular economy.
141 The United Nations Framework Convention on Climate Change – Adoption of the Paris Agreement (2015) was adopted during COP21 (Conference of the Parties). The Intergovernmental Panel on Climate Change (IPCC) and Intergovernmental Science-Policy Platform on Biodiversity and Ecosystem Services (IPBES) call for immediate action. See Intergovernmental Panel on Climate Change, 'Special Report: Global Warming of 1.5°C' (2019); and Intergovernmental Science-Policy Platform on Biodiversity and Ecosystem Services, 'Global Assessment Report on Biodiversity and Ecosystem Services' (2019).

transform – it might be considered redundant to aim for net zero. Surely the aim should be adaptation, not mitigation? However, first, there is a moral obligation on farmers (and frequently now a legal obligation on states via international agreements) to reduce greenhouse gas emissions, as these cumulatively have global detrimental effects and, in particular, on the most vulnerable in society. Second, the impacts of climate change are increasing, evolving and erratic – it is not a matter of one simple adaptation and then continuing on as normal. It may be very difficult to predict the impacts or adapt in preparation for them. It is eminently logical to seek to minimise climate change and thereby the future impacts. Where possible, reducing emissions is a logical and worthy step.

Undertaking such a U-turn presents one of the most critical and transformational challenges faced by the agri-food sector.[142] Agriculture is a major contributor to climate change and accounts for around 10% of UK greenhouse gas emissions[143] – with agriculture being the largest source of nitrous oxide and methane emissions in the UK, contributing respectively around 70% and 53% of the UK's annual emissions of these gasses.[144] The sources of these emissions raise fundamental questions about farming, as they mostly derive from livestock, agricultural soils, stationary combustion sources and off-road machinery. By way of illustration, methane is the predominant greenhouse gas of the sector, making up 56% of the total.[145] The main source of methane emissions is 'enteric fermentation' from livestock (especially cattle): the gas is belched out by cattle and other ruminant animals as they digest grass as well as via urine and manure. Fermentation in the hindgut (i.e. intestines) contributes about 10% of the methane produced by livestock.[146] Nitrous oxide emissions are produced in agricultural soil from the breakdown of synthetic (nitrogen) fertilisers and animal manure to increase crop and pasture productivity and account for 33% of the sector's emissions.[147]

Thus, on the one hand, the CCC argues that it may prove 'difficult to reduce agriculture emissions to near-zero given the inherent biological processes and chemical reactions arising from crops, soils and livestock'.[148] Indeed, despite a

142 A. Lóránt and B. Allen, 'Net-Zero Agriculture in 2050: How to Get There?' (Institute for European Environmental Policy 2019) 8.

143 See BEIS, '2017 UK Greenhouse Gas Emissions' (2017) https://assets.publishing.service.gov.uk/government/uploads/system/uploads/attachment_data/file/776083/2017_Final_emissions_statistics_one_page_summary.pdf accessed 1 May 2021; and FAO, 'Livestock's Long Shadow? Environmental Issues and Options' (2006) www.fao.org/3/a0701e/a0701e00.htm accessed 1 May 2021.

144 BEIS, '2015 UK Greenhouse Gas Emissions, Final Figures. Statistical Release: National Statistics' (7 February 2017) https://assets.publishing.service.gov.uk/government/uploads/system/uploads/attachment_data/file/604350/2015_Final_Emissions_statistics.pdf accessed 1 May 2021, 19. In contrast, agriculture produces only 1% of annual carbon dioxide emissions.

145 Ibid 28.

146 Garnett et al. (n130) 8.

147 BEIS 2015 (n144) 28.

148 Committee on Climate Change (n140) 147.

general downward trend in emissions since the late 1990s, driven by a fall in animal numbers and a drop in synthetic fertiliser use,[149] there has been no further decrease in UK agriculture emissions from 2011 to 2017.[150] Furthermore, between 2018 and 2019 there was a 1% *increase* in emissions linked to carbon dioxide emissions from liming[151] – used to de-acidify soil. Further emission reductions may be difficult to achieve within current agricultural practices and levels. On the other hand, agriculture is uniquely placed to reduce its own emissions and increase carbon removals from the atmosphere, for instance, through reducing dairy or cattle farming in favour of horticulture. Alternate land use can absorb more greenhouse gases than it produces. Agriculture and forestry (including agroforestry) can take these gases from the atmosphere by capturing and extracting them from the environment and storing them using negative emissions practices such as afforestation, reforestation, carbon capture and carbon storage, soil carbon sequestration or habitat restoration. These may offer new commercial opportunities to farmers and landowners.

Consequently, having net zero as a key driver for change is both feasible and an essential component of the patchwork of mechanisms needed towards a resilient agriculture. To achieve these ambitions, targets should be put in place to achieve net zero.[152] Such approaches are positively indicated in the English *Path to Sustainable Farming Transition Plan* and the *SFI Paper*[153] and the Welsh *White Paper,* but not in the other proposals. At best, the idea is implicit in the Agriculture Act – for instance, when referring to mitigation of and adaptation to climate change,[154] managing land to prevent environmental hazards[155] or improving soil quality.[156] More decisively, the NFU has adopted the aim of net zero in the UK by 2040 – rather than 2050.[157] However, to achieve these ambitions, it is crucial to utilise mechanisms such as those noted above and including alternate land use, investments in agricultural research and development, financing extension services and support and advice to farmers.

149 BEIS, '2019 UK Greenhouse Gas Emissions, Final Figures. Statistical Release: National Statistics' (2 February 2021) https://assets.publishing.service.gov.uk/government/uploads/system/uploads/attachment_data/file/957887/2019_Final_greenhouse_gas_emissions_statistical_release.pdf accessed 1 May 2021, 19.

150 Ibid 19.

151 Ibid 18.

152 Lóránt and Allen (n142) 36.

153 *SFI Paper* (n78).

154 Agriculture Act, Section 1(1)(d).

155 Ibid Section 1(1)(e).

156 Ibid Section 1(1)(j).

157 National Farmers' Union, 'Achieving Net Zero: Farming's 2040 Goal' (2019). These pillars are similar to the Institute for European Environmental Policy modelling. See Lóránt and Allen (n142).

4.2.2.3 Agroecology

As apparent by now, resilient agriculture could be promoted by rewarding agroecology, which is a regenerative practice, i.e. a nature-based solution to climate change that provides increased conservation benefits.[158] Agroecology embraces the interconnections in nature, the landscape, biota and biome from multiscale and multifunctional perspectives: the field scale to the landscape level. Indeed, it is defined by the Food and Agriculture Organization (FAO) as 'an integrated approach that simultaneously applies ecological and social concepts and principles to the design and management of food and agricultural systems'.[159] Agroecological practices strengthen the resilience of farmers and rural communities by fostering the diversification of agroecosystems through, for instance, agroforestry systems, mixed crop-livestock, organic or grass/pasture-fed systems. They are also closely linked to healthy food,[160] wellbeing of communities,[161] sustainability and the right to food.[162]

Agroecological practices go beyond simply tweaking the practices of conventional agriculture (as has been undertaken with sustainable agriculture) to 'transform food and agricultural systems [by] addressing the root causes of problems in an integrated way and providing holistic and long-term solutions',[163] whilst acknowledging local conditions. The aim is to maximise 'available renewable

158 See M.A. Altieri, C.I. Nicholls, A. Henao and M.A. Lana, 'Agroecology and the Design of Climate Change-Resilient Farming Systems' (2015) 35 *Agronomy for Sustainable Development* 869; and FAO, 'The 10 Elements of Agroecology: Guiding the Transition to Sustainable Food and Agricultural Systems' (2018). There is an ongoing debate whether agroecology is a nature-based solution. See APPG Agroecology, 'Inquiry – Agroecology as a Nature Based Solution' (2021) https://agroecology-appg.org/inquiry-agroecology-as-a-nature-based-solution/ accessed 1 May 2021. However, the ten elements of agroecology identified by the FAO appear to fulfil the criteria for nature-based solutions developed by the United Nations Environment Programme. For example, see UNEP, 'The UN Environment Programme and Nature-Based Solutions' (2021) www.unep.org/unga/our-position/unep-and-nature-based-solutions accessed 1 May 2021.

159 FAO (n158) 1.

160 More specifically, the EU Biodiversity Strategy for 2030 states that '[a]groecology can provide healthy food while maintaining productivity, increase soil fertility and biodiversity, and reduce the footprint of food production'. See European Commission, 'EU Biodiversity Strategy for 2030: Bringing Nature Back into Our Lives' COM(2020) 380 final, 8. More generally, see O. de Schutter et al., 'Towards a Common Food Policy for the European Union: The Policy Reform and Realignment that is Required to Build Sustainable Food Systems in Europe' (IPES Food 2019); and C. Francis et al., 'Agroecology: The Ecology of Food Systems' (2003) 22 *Journal of Sustainable Agriculture* 99.

161 See S.R. Gliessman, *Agroecology: The Ecology of Sustainable Food Systems* (CRC Press 2015).

162 FAO (n158); Office of the United Nations High Commissioner for Human Rights, 'Agroecology and the Right to Food – Report Submitted by the Special Rapporteur on the Right to Food, Olivier De Schutter' (2010) A/HRC/16/49.

163 FAO (n158) 2.

inputs, ecological and structural features of the agricultural field, fallows, and surrounding vegetation'.[164]

Further, the application of agroecology does not simply rest at farm level. It provides social and health benefits by diversifying farming systems and diets, thus improving nutrition.[165] Local and regional markets can amplify agroecological initiatives by supplying local food, thereby creating local jobs and improving the economic viability of local farmers and food systems. Crucially, in its 'Ten Years for Agroecology' foresight model, the Institut du Développement Durable et des Relations Internationales (IDDRI) indicates how agroecological practices could be turned into effective policies whilst maintaining food security across Europe.[166] So agroecological practices do not necessarily result in less production[167] and they can deliver environmental and social benefits within the UK and beyond. Agroecology's holistic outlook to food systems therefore furthers social-ecological approaches and a resilient agriculture.

However, apart from the ambiguous reference to agroecology in the Agriculture Act – regenerative agriculture and agroecology are left out of the proposals.[168] This is disappointing since the climate change and biodiversity emergencies call for an overhaul of farming practices and agroecology could play an essential part of that answer.[169] Calls have been made by various organisations, especially Sustain and the Food, Farming & Countryside Commission, to financially support agroecological farm systems.[170] Such an emphasis on what used to be considered 'fringe' agricultural practices is now becoming a central tenet of farming across the globe,[171] but is lacking prominence in the four policies.

164 S.B. Hecht, 'The Evolution of Agroecological Thought' in M.A. Altieri (ed.), *Agroecology – The Science of Sustainable Agriculture* (2nd edn, CRC Press 2018) 1.

165 See F.A.J. DeClerck et al., 'Ecological Approaches to Human Nutrition' (2011) 32 Supp 1 Food and Nutrition Bulletin 41S; and Office of the United Nations High Commissioner for Human Rights, 'Final Report: The Transformative Potential of the Right to Food – Report of the Special Rapporteur on the Right to Food, Olivier De Schutter' (2014) A/HRC/25/57, 8.

166 Poux and Aubert, (n86).

167 Although this is debated, see H. Tuomisti et al., 'Does Organic Farming Reduce Environmental Impacts? – A Meta-Analysis of European Research' (2012) 112 *Journal of Environmental Management* 309.

168 Agriculture Act, Section 1(5).

169 For more on the relationship between agroecology and law, see M. Geelhoed, 'Agroecology, GMOs and Post-Brexit Regulations' in I. Antonopoulos, M. Bell, A. Cavoski and L. Petetin (eds), *The Governance of Agriculture in Post-Brexit UK* (Routledge forthcoming 2022); and M. Monteduro, P. Buongiorno, S. Di Benedetto and A. Isoni (eds), *Law and Agroecology – A Transdisciplinary Dialogue* (Springer 2015).

170 Greenham, McCann and Macfarlane (n134); and Sustain (n134).

171 France is an example of where agroecology and agroforestry are now placed at the heart of agricultural policies. For more, see Petetin, Gravey and Moore (n109) 26–29.

4.2.2.4 Agri-food democracy

Shocks such as Brexit and COVID-19 offer the opportunity to reshape and transform agri-food systems to foster enhanced resilience with a greater focus on farmers and citizens. Agri-food democracy[172] enables stakeholders to have their voice heard and contribute to this reshaping and transformation across the levels, facilitating tailored, just policies with greater buy-in – an essential component of resilient agriculture.

Often farmers and citizens feel powerless to influence agri-food production systems due to the choices and controls emanating from the international supply chains. For them, the power in agri-food systems is concentrated with a small number of large manufacturing and retail corporations that reflect a heavily industrialised system, often nicknamed 'Big Food',[173] despite farmers growing or rearing the much-needed raw agricultural commodities that result in the final products. However, during the height of COVID-19, deliveries of essential products, including meat, flour, fruit and vegetables by local farmers, growers and millers became a lifeline for the public; they kept the population food secure. This trend towards short supply chains has been maintained and demonstrates the rise of domestic agri-food systems by putting at its heart agricultural producers and citizens. Indeed, farmer-focused supply chains could provide part of the solution to rebalancing power along the agri-food supply chain.[174]

Agri-food democracy possesses four main characteristics that would alleviate such tensions and strengthen the role of farmers and citizens in the agri-food supply chain[175] to enhance food access, equity and fairness whilst including the health, cultural and ecological aspects of food. First, the information, choice and access offered to citizens should reflect calls for increased information regarding the process according to which foods are produced – for example, carbon-neutral labelling, GM-free or high animal welfare standards – and reduce inequalities in terms of food access by all sectors of the population. Second, upstream engagement and bottom-up approaches in the decision-making process would enable

172 L. Petetin, 'The COVID-19 Crisis: An Opportunity to Integrate Food Democracy into Post-Pandemic Food Systems' (2020) 11(S2) *European Journal of Risk Regulation* 326. Agri-food democracy can be also called 'food citizenship' but this latter concept focuses purely on food rather than examining agri-food systems more broadly. However, it contrasts with 'food sovereignty' and its ideas of self-sufficiency and nationalism by stopping exporting local products abroad. In the UK, the Food Ethics Council has greatly worked on food citizenship. For more on their work, see Food Ethics Council, 'Food Citizenship' www.foodethicscouncil.org/programme/food-citizenship/ accessed 1 May 2021.

173 N.D. Hamilton, 'Moving toward Food Democracy: Better Food, New Farmers, and the Myth of Feeding the World' (2011) 16 Drake Journal of Agricultural Law 117; and L. Petetin, 'Food Democracy in Food Systems' in P.B. Thompson and D.M. Kaplan (eds), *Encyclopedia of Food and Agricultural Ethics* (2nd edn, Springer 2016) 1.

174 V. Hird, 'Farmers Need Power and Money; It's Time for Ambitious Thinking on Trading Systems and Investment' (18 February 2021) www.sustainweb.org/blogs/feb21-farmers-need-power-money/ accessed 1 May 2021.

175 Petetin (n172).

greater participation by key actors.[176] Experiences and preferences of farmers and citizens could feed into developed frameworks. Further, greater connections between local areas and councils and higher levels of governance are required.[177] Third, the improvement of the livelihood, opportunities and rights of farmers and agricultural workers and their working conditions can no longer be postponed. The poor living conditions of these labourers were all over the media during 2020 and this issue should not be forgotten. Enhancing their skills, know-how and knowledge is also crucial. Fourth, faith and trust in the domestic agri-food system have been improved by the role of local farmers, with the preference for smaller supply chains being central. Agri-food democracy can provide a great catalyst for change towards a green recovery.[178] If the four points above are balanced with each other accordingly, they would lead to a democratic agri-food system that promotes decency, social justice and access to food. Of particular value here is high quality, local food production and short supply chains. However, some long food supply chains (both imports and exports) may be necessary also, to ensure diversity, access to markets and supply to populations in need of food supplies. Together, these will help enhance the resilience of agriculture.

Overall, social-ecological services, net zero, agroecology and agri-food democracy all provide different pathways that can be combined, with different emphasis placed on them (especially interconnectedness, coherence, climate change, ecosystem approaches, democracy and justice), to accommodate the multifaceted nature of agriculture. Not only is a holistic approach facilitated, but these pathways also address both existing challenges and vulnerabilities. Further, agri-food democracy, in particular, would facilitate stakeholder buy-in, fairness and justice in the agri-food supply chain and also policy reviews and an iterative process. Consequently, the pathways would help develop adaptive capacity and management and consequently a resilient agriculture.

However, the financial support schemes and their goals developed across the UK remain rather limited. The key focus is on filling the short-term gaps created by Brexit rather than considering and evaluating the long-term aspirations for farming and the countryside, what they are and what they should look like. Specifically, public goods as interpreted in the Agriculture Act and in other proposals to date do not fully reflect social-ecological services or a resilient paradigm that could underpin a 21st-century forward-looking agriculture. They rather establish an economic frame based on a narrow definition of public goods themselves founded in natural capital – indicating half-executed ideas that prevent

176 L. Petetin, 'Frankenburgers, Risks and Approval' (2014) 5(2) *European Journal of Risk Regulation* 168.

177 L. Petetin, 'Building Democratic Food Systems Following COVID-19' (Food Manifesto Wales 1 June 2020) https://foodmanifesto.wales/2020/06/01/building-democratic-food-systems-following-covid-19/ accessed 1 May 2021.

178 L. Petetin, 'A Road to a Green Recovery' (Green Recovery Wales Festival, RSPB Cymru 21 July 2020) https://community.rspb.org.uk/getinvolved/wales/b/wales-blog/posts/a-road-to-a-green-recovery accessed 1 May 2021.

the realisation of ambitious policies. However, while the Welsh policy remains largely embedded in the narrow understanding of public goods and productivity, it may still be developed in a more holistic manner in light of its mentions of resilience and sustainable land management. Similarly Scotland's transitional approach breaks little ground, but it may take a more expansive approach in light of the stakeholder group's early comments and the balance of power in the Scottish Parliament.

4.3 Continued diversity of farms: tailoring policy design

Maintaining the diversity of farmers and farms (as with crop and animal diversity) is essential, as each plays key roles within the system; they need to be individually resilient to ensure broader resilience of agriculture and agri-food systems. To this end, policies and schemes need to be tailored according to their context (including land and agricultural types, society and the environment) or they risk being ineffective, counterproductive or even creating countervailing risks.

4.3.1 Which farmers?

Proposed policies and their schemes appear to embrace any type of land manager,[179] including farmers, foresters and even processors (depending on the scheme), and therefore to be wider in scope than the current CAP. While farmers and land managers play an important role in conserving and enhancing the rural landscape,[180] Helm notes that actors like the National Trust are not eligible for Pillar 2/rural development payments unless they engage in farming.[181] However, actors like these could be eligible under the new 'public money for public goods' system. This nonetheless raises two key concerns. First, the voices and interests of farmers could be lost in this wider focus on land managers. Each type of land manager should receive dedicated support due to the different characteristics, mechanisms and supply chains that are affected and implicated. A one-size-fits-all approach simply will not do as farmers may receive unsuitable support, including insufficient or unnecessary support. For instance, the age of farmers also plays an important role when thinking of signing up to a scheme. However, the proposals include little content on young farmers. Second, as observed in Chapters 2 and 3, schemes must align with the requirements under the Agreement on Agriculture,

179 The issue of tenancies is discussed below in Section 4.4.4.

180 Helm (n117) and National Trust National Trust (n71) 7.

181 Helm (n117). Currently under the CAP, 'farmers, groups of farmers or groups of farmers and other land-managers' can apply for agri-environment schemes. Regulation (EU) No 1305/2013 of the European Parliament and the Council of 17 December 2013 on Support for Rural Development by the European Agricultural Fund for Rural Development (EAFRD) and Repealing Council Regulation (EC) No 1698/2005 [2013] OJ L347/487, Article 28.

especially that to be Green Box compliant direct payments can only be made to agricultural producers.[182]

4.3.2 Which farms?

The universalism of access to the new schemes proposed in Wales and in the Environmental Law Management Schemes (ELMS) in England could be a fundamental turning point in adopting an inclusive approach within the schemes – potentially encompassing different types of farming such as small-holdings, agroecology, organic and urban farms whilst differentiating their needs, make-up and being outside the CAP. However, this is not obvious in the proposals. Indeed, in contrast with the approach to land managers, it is arguable that in practice the schemes may be unnecessarily restrictive when it comes to the farm. Two complementary aspects deserve attention here: the geographical situation (urban, peri-urban, highland etc) of the farm and the type of holding.

In relation to financial support, Bateman and Balmford argue that targeting based on the use of new technologies could ensure the 'best value for money' and the 'efficiency' of the public goods that can be delivered.[183] However, the consequences of drafting policies based on spatial targeting that apply an economic approach based on natural capital, rather than a holistic social-ecological services paradigm, should be carefully considered. Balance ought to be found between focusing on the most rewarding sites and those that are in geographical settings that ought to be protected for the intrinsic value of their particular situation both in terms of the environmental and social components. Otherwise, the development of financial support deserts, i.e. areas where farmers would not receive support, would become a threat. Arguably, in Wales the proposed guaranteed income to farmers under the Sustainable Farming Scheme could lessen such an issue.[184] Similarly in England, this is why the SFI has been introduced as, in principle, it makes available some degree of funding to all farms. However, and as noted in Chapter 3, until late 2024 smallholders will be excluded thereby going back on claims of universalism.[185] Further, synergies across the UK could increase positive environmental and social externalities, through the adoption of common frameworks focused on agri-environmental matters, with many social-ecological services having strong cross-border/transboundary elements or being matters of UK common interest.

Differentiating between farm types is crucial if the policies and support measures are to be effective. The size of the farm and other influences such as quality of the soil, geology or topography – i.e. the geographical situation of a farm – matter. For instance, changes to financing regimes or agricultural policies have a

182 Chapter 2, Section 2.4 and Chapter 3, Section 3.2.2.
183 Bateman and Balmford (n76) 296.
184 *White Paper* (n58) paragraph 2.63.
185 *SFI Paper* (n78). See Chapter 3, Section 3.1.1.

greater short- and medium-term impact upon small farms and risk making them (increasingly) inefficient or unsustainable and go out of business. Further, dairy farming requires considerable (relatively flat) space and investment, as well as regular milking; arable farming calls for flat (and often consolidated) land parcels, big and expensive machinery and infrastructure; and sheep farming might take advantage of rugged landscapes and needs less day-to-day monitoring.[186] The challenges and opportunities vary considerably.

For instance, small, family and hill farms are the glue of rural communities.[187] Such farms provide space for nature, buffer zones, steppingstone habitats and the coherent patchwork to build ecological, natural and landscape connections as part of a resilient UK network with green corridors[188] – in line with the Lawton principles.[189] These farms, where run well, are essential to the 'development and maintenance of biodiversity – such as genetic diversity of crops and livestock – and thereby to agri-sustainability, environmental sustainability and food security on a national and global level'.[190] Not only do they contribute to the economy via the consumption of good quality local produce and tourism, which can facilitate the establishment and flourishing of businesses activities in the local area (including the retention of traditional practices and skills, such as stone masonry), but they also contribute widely to the language, society, environment and wider cultural services. They are indeed tied to the resilience of agriculture – yet the policies do not adequately address such farms. In contrast with the CAP, the policies largely[191] adopt a one-size-fits-all approach, without addressing expressly the diversity of farms.

186 It is worth noting that most very small farms in Northern Ireland farm a mix of cattle (not dairy) and sheep, with the majority of those again in 'less favoured areas'. DAERA and NISRA, 'Statistical Review of Northern Ireland Agriculture 2019' (2020) www.daera-ni.gov.uk/sites/default/files/publications/daera/Stats%20Review%202019%20final.pdf accessed 1 May 2021, table 4.6.

187 Chapter 3. See also M. Shucksmith and K. Rønningen, 'The Uplands after Neoliberalism? The Role of the Small Farm in Rural Sustainability' (2011) 27(3) *Journal of Rural Studies* 275.

188 Petetin (n13) 215.

189 J. Lawton et al., 'Making Space for Nature: A Review of England's Wildlife Sites and Ecological Network' (DEFRA 2010) https://webarchive.nationalarchives.gov.uk/20130402170324/http:/archive.defra.gov.uk/environment/biodiversity/documents/201009space-for-nature.pdf accessed 1 May 2021.

190 M. Dobbs, L. Petetin and V. Gravey, 'Written Evidence on the Scrutiny of Agriculture Bill' (House of Commons, EFRA Committee, SAB0044, October 2018) http://data.parliament.uk/writtenevidence/committeeevidence.svc/evidencedocument/environment-food-and-rural-affairs-committee/scrutiny-of-the-agriculturebill/written/91290.html accessed 1 May 2021.

191 The focus here is on England and Wales. As mentioned in Chapter 3, the Northern Irish and Scottish documents to date do highlight the special nature of conacre and crofts respectively and indicate some influence over policy content, but there is too little detail yet to know how this will be developed in future.

Nonetheless, a few significant variations exist. Northern Ireland and Scotland's policies could impact less drastically on small, less economically viable farms as they maintain elements of direct payments.[192] Further, productivity or economic resilience payments may facilitate or hinder such diversity, depending on how the schemes are operated and implemented. For example, Northern Ireland's *Draft Agricultural Strategy* could potentially place caps on 'basic farm resilience' payments for large farms, but also, more worryingly, require eligibility thresholds at the lower end for smaller farms that are 'non-commercial'[193] – similarly to the situation in England. An enhanced interpretation of public goods reflecting social-ecological services could provide a mechanism to fund smaller farms through linking into their contributions within rural communities and the wider environment building towards a resilient agriculture.

4.3.3 *What consequences for farming?*

The new policies and schemes will have long-lasting impacts on the make-up of farms, farmers and the wider countryside, which are likely to shake farming activities to their core. They are likely to affect current and future generations and lead to a major restructuring of the industry towards land consolidation, amalgamation and potentially abandonment, putting at risk the resilience of agriculture.

4.3.3.1 The likely disappearance of farms and restructure of the industry

The removal of direct payments in Wales and England with a gradual transition towards public money for public goods constitutes a tremendous departure from the CAP, although England's SFI and Wales' payment for actions mitigate such changes. Scotland and Northern Ireland will keep some direct payments, but their amount and longevity remain uncertain. The agricultural transition period is crucial if farmers are to have any real chance to adapt to the new schemes and become more productive and resilient, but, irrespective, many will find any change or reduction in support challenging.

192 M. Cardwell, 'Farming Policy' in H. Kassin, A. Jordan and S. Ennis (eds), 'UK Regulation after Brexit' (The UK in a Changing Europe 25 February 2021) https://ukandeu.ac.uk/wp-content/uploads/2021/02/UK-regulation-after-Brexit.pdf accessed 1 May 2021, 48, 49; and A. Kay, 'Scottish Direct Payments Will not Distort UK Market after Brexit, Says Eustice' (Farmers Guardian 23 November 2020) www.fginsight.com/news/news/scottish-direct-payments-will-not-distort-uk-market-after-brexit-says-eustice-114714 accessed 1 May 2021.

193 DAERA, 'Northern Ireland Future Agricultural Policy Framework: Stakeholder Engagement' (*Draft Agricultural Strategy*) (1 August 2018) www.daera-ni.gov.uk/sites/default/files/consultations/daera/NI%20Future%20Agricultural%20Policy%20Framework%20-%20Stakeholder%20Engagement%20-%20FINAL_0.pdf accessed 1 May 2021, 30. This would thereby exclude such farms from receiving relevant support.

Struggling farms will find the change in the support system particularly difficult. Many farms are currently profitable solely because of CAP direct payments. A good rule of thumb in England is that direct payments pay the rent. In 2019, out of 6,179,000 hectares of land owned in England, around 20% were let on farm business tenancies and around 17% were seasonally rented or let out.[194] So, many holdings would be negatively impacted. They also have restricted ability to adapt and become more profitable due to their limited finances available for investment, as well as the size and nature of the farms. Changes to the mechanisms for financial support, the limited amount of funding available combined with the narrow interpretation of public goods could result in economic and financial hardship for farmers. It is likely that the top, most profitable, 25% of English farmers will hardly feel the change in policy since they are already productive and resilient, whilst the 50% of farmers in the middle are likely to succeed in moving away from direct payments to environmental payments as they become more business-minded and profitable. It is, however, possible that the bottom 25% of farms that currently struggle or only survive because of the receipt of direct payments could disappear – even with a long transition period.[195] Such statistics vary across the devolved administrations and the situation will probably be worse beyond England. Northern Ireland, in particular, could be affected by a reduction in direct payments due to the combination of high dependence on subsidies,[196] the proportion of small farms and the proportion of farms in less-favoured areas.[197] Similarly, without basic payment support, on average 59% of Welsh farms surveyed by the Welsh Government would have made a loss or broken even at best in 2017/18 and this increases to 74% for sheep farms in severely disadvantaged areas.[198] The implications are likely to be amplified by the knock-on effects of both COVID-19 and restricted market access to the EU. A massive

194 DEFRA, 'Farming Statistics: Land Use, Livestock Populations and Agricultural Workforce at 1 June 2019 – England' (2019) https://assets.publishing.service.gov.uk/government/uploads/system/uploads/attachment_data/file/868945/structure-jun19-eng-28feb20.pdf accessed 1 May 2021, Table 2.

195 See comments made by Ludivine Petetin at the Game and Wildlife Conservation Trust All-Party Parliamentary Group in March 2018, Game and Wildlife Conservation Trust, 'March 2018: Balancing Environmental Payments and Trade' (March 2018) www.gwct.org.uk/policy/appg/march-2018/ accessed 1 May 2021. See also A. Kay, 'Defra Makes Decision to Let Quarter of UK Farms 'Disappear' (Farmers Guardian 29 March 2018) https://www.fginsight.com/news/news/defra-makes-decision-to-let-quarter-of-uk-farms-disappear-57116 accessed 1 May 2021; and T. Colson, 'Why 25% of English Farms Could Go Bankrupt after Brexit' (UK Business Insider 16 April 2018) www.businessinsider.com/quarter-english-farms-bankrupt-after-brexit-2018-4?r=US&IR=T accessed 1 May 2021. More generally, see O.M. Ojo et al., 'Brexit: Potential Impacts on the Economic Welfare of UK Farm Households' (2021) 55(9) *Regional Studies* 1583.

196 DAERA and NISRA (n186) 11–15; and Welsh Government, 'Agriculture in Wales' (2019) https://gov.wales/sites/default/files/publications/2019-06/agriculture-in-wales-evidence.pdf accessed 1 May 2021, 48–50.

197 Chapter 1.

198 Welsh Government (n196) 50.

restructuring of the farming industry is on its way, unless steps are taken. Small, family, hill farms are to be protected to avoid amalgamation into large, uniform and possibly intensive farms.[199] Although some larger farms could be environmentally sustainable and reward economies of scale, generally the consolidation and amalgamation of small holdings into larger units is a threat to rural communities[200] and could lead to a consolidation of the agri-food supply chain.

Suitable financial support is required from Westminster for the short- to long-term continuation of direct payments (where they are maintained) and the injection of capital for more tailored public goods financial support schemes, if farmers are to be kept on the land and to avoid land abandonment by local communities.[201] This is especially important for the small, family, hill farms that typically are the least economically viable. However, whether support will remain in the long term is difficult to assess, since it seems the UK Government wants to end agricultural exceptionalism across the UK.

4.3.3.2 Generational renewal

Two interrelated concerns arise here: the impacts on existing farmers and on new entrants. Many farms are barely financially viable and in 2016 the median age of UK farmers was 60 years old.[202] Consequently, existing farmers may struggle, but will also need to be replaced over time. From the perspective of a resilient agriculture, individual farmers are part of the broader community, playing a significant role within the social-ecological system. The concern is here double: land abandonment and/or local farmers, for example, speaking the Welsh language, being replaced by bigger, commercial farms such as Dyson farms.[203] It is also crucial to consider whether it is worthwhile (economically, environmentally, socially, culturally and morally) to retain farmers on the land even where they are

199 Bateman and Balmford (n76) 296.

200 N. Foote, 'Expert: UK Risks Farm Consolidation, Fragmentation Post-Brexit' (Euractiv 29 April 2021) www.euractiv.com/section/agriculture-food/news/expert-uk-risks-farm-consolidation-fragmentation-post-brexit/ accessed 1 May 2021.

201 L. Petetin, M. Dobbs and V. Gravey, 'Written Evidence Brexit and Our Land Consultation – Welsh Government' http://orca.cf.ac.uk/117590/ accessed 1 May 2021.

202 DEFRA, DAERA, Welsh Government Knowledge and Analytical Services and the Scottish Government, Rural and Environment Science and Analytical Services, 'Agriculture in the United Kingdom 2019' (2020) https://assets.publishing.service.gov.uk/government/uploads/system/uploads/attachment_data/file/950618/AUK-2019-07jan21.pdf accessed 1 May 2021, 23. In Wales, it was 61.2 years old in 2016. Welsh Government, 'Welsh Agricultural Statistics: 2016' (2016) https://gov.wales/welsh-agricultural-statistics-2016 accessed 1 May 2021, Table 3.3. Although such statistics only reflect the age of the lead figure of the holding, without acknowledging fully the involvement of other, younger persons.

203 A. Meredith, 'Dyson Farming Empire Now Worth More than £500m' (Farmers Weekly 2 October 2019) www.fwi.co.uk/business/dyson-farming-empire-now-worth-more-than-500m accessed 1 May 2021.

not economically viable without sustained financial support beyond the provision of public goods (widely defined), especially if the alternative is they are starving, homeless or depressed and ultimately sell their land.[204] Retaining farmers on the land should be considered a key public good, including both through supporting existing farmers and through safeguarding generational change where appropriate.

Consequently, generation renewal is central to ensuring the perennity and resilience of UK farming. Adequate support and suitable incentives are needed to ensure younger generations enter and stay in farming if farming is to be maintained on a community basis. Helm notes that the EU provides funds for young farmers, recognising the barriers to entry for young farmers.[205] Family farms could also be supported in this context. Yet, the proposals indicate little appetite to address adequately such challenges.[206]

In the Agriculture Act, a lump sum payment can be given to farmers to exit in place of direct payments.[207] Incentivising new entrants is now incorporated in the *Path to Sustainable Farming Transition Plan* for England, but strangely the scheme might only last for a couple of years between 2022 and 2024;[208] possibly confirming that DEFRA does not yet perceive generational renewal to be an issue which is problematic in and of itself. In Northern Ireland, the *Draft Agricultural Strategy* proposes to continue the Young Farmer Payments (and payments for new entrants) for the duration of the transitional period within the *Strategy* (with payments for up to five years after application approval), but it is not raised as a focus afterwards;[209] it positively aims to address generational renewal. Alternative mechanisms to encourage younger generations to engage may involve incentivising and rewarding education and skills but also improving resources in rural communities and the standard of rural life, including the protection of the mental health of farmers (as well as longer-term leases as discussed below). Overall, facilitating generational change should be one of the priorities of future policies and schemes to ensure rural proofing.[210] The loss of livelihood and employment across rural communities would undermine the objectives of the proposals and also have repercussions on the economy and society.

204 Petetin, Dobbs and Gravey (n201).
205 Helm (n117) 128.
206 Across the UK, there has generally been a lack of appetite for payments to young farmers.
207 Agriculture Act, Section 13. See also DEFRA, 'Consultation: Direct Payments to Farmers: Lump Sum Exit Scheme and Delinked Payments in England' (May 2021) https://consult.defra.gov.uk/agricultural-policy/lump-sum-and-delinked-payments-england/supporting_documents/lumpsumexitschemedelinkedpaymentsconsultation.pdf accessed 31 May 2021.
208 *Path to Sustainable Farming* (n58) 25.
209 *Draft Agricultural Strategy* (n193) 15 and 26.
210 The progressive loss of council farms is part of this threat. See T.L. Raphael, 'County Farms: Public Land for Public Good' (*Farming the Future* 26 June 2020) www.farmingthefuture.uk/post/county-farms-public-land-for-public-good accessed 1 May 2021.

Overall, the policies take varied approaches regarding encompassing different actors and farms, with profound consequences on the farming landscape. Despite references to (mostly economic) resilience in some policies, the policies are insufficiently tailored or supportive. Further, notwithstanding a possible broadening of access to schemes by referring to land managers (i.e., which participants?), there is a potential narrowing in relation to the land involved (restrictive eligibility criteria for the farms). On a day-to-day basis, many holdings are likely to be detrimentally affected due to the lack of renewal in the industry or its concentration. And if any severe shocks were to occur, it is likely that there would be no sufficient buffer or adaptive capacity developed for the individual, vulnerable farms and farmers. This lack of capacity and adaptability will have significant knock-on effects on the other aspects of agriculture, especially via land amalgamation, leading to the decline of the rural community and threatening the resilience of the countryside as a whole.

4.4 Patchy governance (with moments of vision!)

The next theme to be addressed relates to governance approaches. The first aspect within governance is that of the substantive focus points of the policies, which is discussed above and crucially lacks a holistic, ambitious approach across all four nations – the closest exception being Wales' sustainable land management and references to resilience. However, a crucial issue is then how to achieve these objectives: what mechanisms are availed of? And could they be improved? Issues arise regarding the initial process of policy design; what behaviour is incentivised and rewarded, or indeed disincentivised and penalised; and how this is achieved. The main focus here is on the first prong of the policies – the exception being when considering the enforcement of regulatory baselines. At times, there are moments of vision that could inspire innovative, flexible and potentially more tailored, effective policies. However, the four proposals also highlight numerous challenges in seeking to *ensure* effectiveness and legitimacy.

4.4.1 Policy design: a role for stakeholders

A significant element reflected across the policies is the role of stakeholders in the original design and evolution of the proposals (and resulting schemes). Engaging these voices in partnerships is essential. Farming policy calls for cooperation and collaboration both across levels (i.e. local, regional, national and beyond where relevant) and within individual levels (between farmers and other farmers/other stakeholders within rural communities and other actors in the agri-food supply chain) in both its design and implementation – purely centralised, top-down approaches are inappropriate and ineffective.[211] The process of policy design in Northern Ireland and Scotland has been particularly impressive to date, with central roles for stakeholders that have worked in a highly collaborative and productive manner.

In the context of no functioning Assembly or Executive in Northern Ireland and therefore without the presence of accountable politicians, the role of the grassroots increased in importance.[212] The agricultural stakeholder group became central in designing the *Draft Agricultural Strategy*.[213] DAERA expanded the original agricultural group[214] to include individuals from other stakeholder groups (rural development and the environment) and also academia. This thereby extended the available pool of expertise (including local knowledge and experiences), encompassed a broader range of interests and potentially facilitated greater buy-in across the community of any eventual *Strategy*.[215] The combined influence of these factors can be seen in the focus and balance of objectives, the approaches to payments generally and the level of nuance and details (or lack thereof) on various aspects.[216] Whilst very valuable, the key stumbling block was that without a Minister in place the potential for an official consultation was delayed and the *Strategy* remained undeveloped. It was only in November 2020 that the then Minister for Agriculture, Environment and Rural Affairs Edwin Poots indicated that DAERA would build on the *Strategy* to develop a future agricultural policy for Northern Ireland.[217]

211 L. Petetin and M. Dobbs, 'Collaborating for Agricultural Sustainability' (Centre for Environmental Justice 13 June 2018) https://blogs.cardiff.ac.uk/environmental-justice-research-unit/2018/06/13/collaborating-agricultural-sustainability/ accessed 1 May 2021; and Bohman (n15) 68.

212 M. Dobbs, 'Northern Ireland's Agricultural Quagmire: How to Develop a Sustainable Agricultural Policy?' in I. Antonopoulos, M. Bell, A. Cavoski and L. Petetin (eds), *The Governance of Agriculture in Post-Brexit UK* (Routledge forthcoming 2022).

213 *Draft Agricultural Strategy* (n193).

214 For more, see Chapter 3, Section 3.1.3.

215 Unsurprisingly, criticisms of the eventual policy still remain. See Nature Matters NI, 'Northern Ireland Future Agricultural Framework: A Response from Nature Matters Northern Ireland' (October 2018) www.nienvironmentlink.org/cmsfiles/Northern-Ireland-Future-Agricultural-Framework---Nature-Matters-NI-response.pdf accessed 1 May 2021; and M. Dobbs, V. Gravey, and L. Petetin, 'Written Evidence on the NI Future Agricultural Policy Framework' (October 2018) https://pureadmin.qub.ac.uk/ws/portalfiles/portal/159763464/DAERA_Engagement_on_NI_Future_Agricultural_Policy_Framework_Dobbs_Gravey_Petetin.pdf accessed 1 May 2021.

216 Dobbs (n212).

217 Northern Ireland Assembly, 'Basic Payment Scheme Simplifications and the Direction of Travel for Future Agricultural Policy in Northern Ireland, including Support Payments' (Debates 17 November 2020) www.theyworkforyou.com/ni/?id=2020-11-17.1.90 accessed 1 May 2021.

As noted in Chapter 3, following on from the Scottish Agricultural Champions, the Scottish Parliament similarly established a stakeholder group comprising of agricultural, environmental and consumer representatives to help design their future agricultural policy.[218] Thus, the approach to the design and formulation of the policy proposals has benefited considerably from wide stakeholder participation. It remains to be seen how the policy will develop, but the initial commentary from the stakeholder group is cognisant of the multifunctionality of agriculture, the need for change and the role of different actors.[219]

However, this early and substantive engagement has not been as apparent in the development of either the Welsh policy or the Agriculture Act – with also concerns by the devolved administrations that their voices were only heard to a limited extent in the development of the Agriculture Act, despite content impacting directly on devolved matters.[220] Nonetheless, all stakeholders and the public have had the opportunity to engage in the formulation of policies in the context of consultations or inquiries across the four nations, including through written and oral evidence to parliamentary committees.[221] But, this tends to lead to amendments to improve existing proposals rather than to broad-sweeping changes or overhauls in the proposed approaches.

Nonetheless, there has been strong support for stakeholders to be involved closely in the next stages of policy implementation, through helping co-design

218 Scottish Parliament, 'Future Rural Policy and Support' (Debates 10 January 2019) https://archive2021.parliament.scot/parliamentarybusiness/report.aspx?r=11875&mode=html accessed 1 May 2021, 15.03. See also Chapter 3, Section 3.1.4.

219 Farming and Food Production – Future Policy Group (n59).

220 L. Petetin, 'Setting the Path for UK and Devolved Agriculture' in I. Antonopoulos, M. Bell, A. Cavoski and L. Petetin (eds), *The Governance of Agriculture in Post-Brexit UK* (Routledge forthcoming 2022).

221 Examples include for England and/or the UK: DEFRA, 'Health and Harmony: The Future for Food, Farming and the Environment in a Green Brexit' (Cm 9577, February 2018); and House of Commons, Environment, Food and Rural Affairs Committee, 'Scrutiny of the Agriculture Bill, Tenth Report of Session 2017–19' (HC 1591, 27 November 2018). For Northern Ireland, *Draft Agricultural Strategy* (n193); and House of Commons, Northern Ireland Affairs Committee, 'Brexit and Agriculture in Northern Ireland' (5th Report of Session 2017–29, HC 939, October 2018) https://publications.parliament.uk/pa/cm201719/cmselect/cmniaf/939/939.pdf accessed 1 May 2021. For Scotland, Scottish Government, 'A Future Strategy for Scottish Agriculture, Final Report by the Scottish Government's Agriculture Champions' (May 2018) www.gov.scot/binaries/content/documents/govscot/publications/progress-report/2018/05/future-strategy-scottish-agriculture-final-report-scottish-governments-agriculture-champions/documents/00536005-pdf/00536005-pdf/govscot%3Adocument/00536005.pdf accessed 1 May 2021; and Scottish Government, 'Stability and Simplicity: Proposals for a Rural Funding Transition Period' (June 2018) www.gov.scot/publications/stability-simplicity-proposals-rural-funding-transition-period/ accessed 1 May 2021. For Wales, Welsh Government, 'Consultation Document: Sustainable Farming and Our Land' (*Sustainable Farming and Our Land*) (2019); and *White Paper* (n58).

the schemes[222] (including via pilot studies)[223] and feeding into other complementary aspects of the policies.[224] This will be an essential process across the four nations, promoting legitimacy, effectiveness, justice, buy-in and broadly helping the eventual resilience of the policies.[225] Key to this will be ensuring a broad range of stakeholders[226] who are affected are involved and that this occurs in a meaningful manner – thereby providing an array of interests and expertise, limiting the chances of regulatory capture[227] and avoiding tokenism.[228]

222 Co-design has now become a guiding principle for DEFRA. See J. Hughes, 'What We Mean by "Co-Design"' (DEFRA Blog 11 December 2020) https://defrafarming.blog.gov.uk/2020/12/11/what-we-mean-by-co-design/ accessed 1 May 2021. See also *Path to Sustainable Farming* (n58) 7 and throughout the document; DEFRA, 'Environmental Land Management: Policy Discussion Document' (*Environmental Land Management Document*) (February 2020) https://consult.defra.gov.uk/elm/elmpolicyconsultation/supporting_documents/ELM%20Policy%20Discussion%20Document%20230620.pdf accessed 1 May 2021; Northern Ireland: *Draft Agricultural Strategy* (n193) 38; Northern Ireland Assembly (n217); *White Paper* (n58) 37 (although not specifying 'co-design', the *White Paper* indicates that future schemes will '[m]ake full use of stakeholder input into the policy development and design stages, whilst also bringing in adequate external challenge and scrutiny on proposals'. It is presumed Scotland will do similarly, especially in light of their strong engagement with stakeholders to date.

223 *Path to Sustainable Farming* (n58) 40, referring to the opportunity within the Sustainable Farming Incentive pilot. For more on co-design in the UK after Brexit, see J. Lyon et al., 'Inclusive Design of Post-Brexit Agri-Environmental Policy: Identifying and Engaging the "Harder to Reach" Stakeholders. A Quick Scoping Review' (Universities of Sheffield and Reading 2020) https://figshare.shef.ac.uk/articles/report/Inclusive_design_of_post-Brexit_Agri-Environmental_Policy_Identifying_and_engaging_the_Harder_to_Reach_stakeholders_A_Quick_Scoping_Review/12506582 accessed 1 May 2021; P. Hurley et al., 'Co-Designing the Environmental Land Management Scheme in England: The Why, Who, and How of Engaging "Harder to Reach" Stakeholders' (University of Sheffield 2020) https://osf.io/preprints/socarxiv/k2ahd/ accessed 1 May 2021; and J. Tsouvalis-Gerber and R. Little, 'Co-Design, Co-production and Participatory Policy Making – Insights from the Social Sciences' (University of Sheffield 2020) https://figshare.shef.ac.uk/articles/report/Co-Design_Co-production_and_Participatory_Policy_Making_-_Insights_From_the_Social_Sciences/11569620/2 accessed 1 May 2021.

224 Welsh Government, 'Consultation Document: Agricultural Tenancy Reform' (9 April 2019) https://gov.wales/sites/default/files/consultations/2019-04/agricultural-tenancy-reform-consultation-document.pdf accessed 1 May 2021.

225 See Section 4.1 above; and Pieraccini (n49).

226 For example, DEFRA refers to varying groups, but with farmers repeatedly emphasised. *Path to Sustainable Farming* (n58) 7 noting co-design with 'farmers'; at page 11 with 'farmers, land managers and other partners'; and page 54 with certain 'other landowners and stakeholders'. It is unclear whether the different terminology is intentional (linked potentially to different schemes) and meant to be exclusive, but irrespective of intent there is a need for wide engagement with all stakeholder groups. In Northern Ireland, Minister Poots referred to 'farmers, land managers and environmental stakeholders', but this can still be extended further. Northern Ireland Assembly (n217).

227 Baldwin and Black (n54); Ayres and Braithwaite (n54).

228 M. Dobbs, V. Gravey and L. Petetin, 'Written Evidence on the NI Future Agricultural Policy Framework' (October 2018) https://pureadmin.qub.ac.uk/ws/portalfiles/por-

4.4.2 Outcomes versus actions?

A significant debate surrounds the issue of what payments should be for – in particular actions or outcomes.[229] In relation to financial support, agri-environment schemes (AES) under the CAP have followed a traditional command-and-control or action-based approach with mandatory or prohibitive elements included on positive and negative lists. As such, farmers are paid to act or not to act, to undertake prescriptive actions for which farmers get paid a flat rate.[230] This has been criticised regularly on the basis that the reward, and therefore incentive, is for actions and not for achieving the desired outcome. For instance, a farmer might be rewarded for planting hedgerow, but the plants might die and therefore a goal of extra habitats or enhanced biodiversity might flounder. Consequently, there has been a gradual shift within the EU towards outcome-focused, or 'results-based' AES more recently[231] – including in the most recent CAP reforms.[232] Indeed, and as noted in Chapter 3, the English pilot scheme on 'results-based payments' between 2016 and 2018 was funded by the EU.[233]

The move across the UK towards public money for public goods was intended as a more abrupt overhaul. The policies of the four nations aim to minimise negative externalities, such as water pollution or soil erosion, and to maximise

tal/159763464/DAERA_Engagement_on_NI_Future_Agricultural_Policy_Framework_Dobbs_Gravey_Petetin.pdf accessed 1 May 2021.

229 *Environmental Land Management Document* (n222) 20.

230 There is also some evidence of a shift towards results-based schemes in the EU. See European Commission, 'The Future of Food and Farming' COM(2017) 713, 18; and Proposal for a Regulation of the European Parliament and the Council Establishing Rules on Support for Strategic Plans to be Drawn Up by Member States under the Common Agricultural Policy (CAP Strategic Plans) and financed by the European Agricultural Guarantee Fund (EAGF) and by the European Agricultural Fund for Rural Development (EAFRD) and Repealing Regulation (EU) No 1305/2013 of the European Parliament and the Council and Regulation (EU) No 1307/2013 of the European Parliament and the Council – COM/2018/392 final, 129.

231 A. Saba, 'Results-Based Agri-Environmental Schemes for Delivering Ecosystem Services in the EU: Established and Emerging Trends' in M. Alabrese, M. Brunori, S. Rolandi and A. Saba (eds), *Agricultural Law* (Springer 2017) 83, for examples, within the Member States, see B. Matzdorf and J. Lorenz, 'How Cost-Effective Are Result-Oriented Agri-Environmental Measures? – An Empirical Analysis in Germany' (2010) 27(2) *Land Use Policy* 535; and D. Russi, H. Margue, R. Oppermann and C. Keenleyside, 'Result-Based Agri-Environment Measures: Market-Based Instruments, Incentives or Rewards? The Case of Baden-Württemberg' (2016) 54 *Land Use Policy* 69.

232 European Commission, 'The Future of Food and Farming' COM(2017) 713, 18; and Proposal for a Regulation of the European Parliament and the Council Establishing Rules on Support for Strategic Plans (n230) 129.

233 Chaplin et al. (n75). Further research funded by the EU includes C. Keenleyside et al., 'Results-Based Payments for Biodiversity Guidance Handbook: Designing and Implementing Results-Based Agri-Environment Schemes 2014–20' (Report prepared for the European Commission, Institute for European Environmental Policy, 2014) https://ec.europa.eu/environment/nature/rbaps/handbook/docs/rbaps-handbook.pdf accessed 1 May 2021. See also Chapter 3, Section 3.1.1.1.

positive externalities, here public goods, including peatland restoration or better flood management. This originally was, and on the face of the policies largely still is, to be achieved by rewarding outcomes (beyond regulatory baselines)[234] to be determined within schemes rather than actions or steps taken. Thus, England refers to public money to 'deliver environmental and animal welfare outcomes' and one of the principles for transition is to 'focus on achieving outcomes'.[235] This is reflected in the development of ELMS, in particular for Tiers 2 and 3.[236] Northern Ireland similarly states that the 'payments or incentives should recognise and reward the public goods *provided* by farmers and land managers who *achieve* a verified level of environmental performance through the *delivery* of identified *outcomes*' (emphasis added).[237] Wales talks repeatedly about outcomes, including how the Sustainable Farming Scheme 'is intended to reward farmers for the delivery of outcomes'. Consequently, the rhetoric across the policies to-date[238] is focused on outcomes rather than steps, actions or processes.

This seems perfectly logical – if the outcome is what is desired, that should be what is rewarded and incentivised.[239] However, several challenges arise,[240] including increased risks for the farmers[241] (with knock-on effects). For instance, farmers and other actors could invest their resources to fulfil the aims of the scheme but not achieve the end result, for example, due to negative actions by someone else or severe weather events. They would thereby lose out on their investments and with no reward, through no fault of their own.. This is amplified when one considers the time to achieve outcomes in land use and that much of agricultural land is rented (see Section 4.4.4 below on agricultural ownership). This could lead to the situation where these individuals become destitute or simply avoid risk-taking and therefore do not participate in the relevant schemes. Further challenges include, for instance, valuing outcomes and evaluating successes.[242]

234 *Path to Sustainable Farming* (n58) 15 stating '[w]e want a clear distinction, and coherent relationship, between the basic requirements farmers are obliged to meet by law, and scheme standards where they are paid to go beyond this minimum'. Also mentioned on page 33.

235 Ibid 7 and 8. See also the focus for schemes of 'paying for environmental and animal welfare outcomes' on page 11 and Annex B.

236 *Environmental Land Management Document* (n222) 12.

237 *Draft Agricultural Strategy* (n193) 36–37.

238 Developments in Scotland are awaited.

239 R.J.F. Burton and G. Schwarz, 'Result-Oriented Agri-Environment Schemes in Europe and Their Potential for Promoting Behavioural Change' (2013) 30(1) *Land Use Policy* 628; Keenleyside et al. (n233) 4; and M.S. Reed et al., 'Improving the Link between Payments and the Provision of Ecosystem Services in Agri-Environment Schemes' (2014) 9 *Ecosystem Services* 44.

240 A. Moxey and B. White, 'Result-Oriented Agri-Environment Schemes in Europe: A Comment' (2014) 39 *Land Use Policy* 397; and Reed et al. (n239).

241 Burton and Schwarz (n239); and Matzdorf and Lorenz (n231).

242 Burton and Schwarz (n239).

However, this outcomes-only focus has not been how the policies have developed in practice so far.

Alongside the rhetoric on outcomes, there are indications of a return to payment for actions in practice – in part or possibly even entirely. Thus, Wales guarantees to underwrite the schemes and pay farmers if they fail to deliver on their promised outcomes[243] – interestingly, without specifying conditions such as best efforts or due diligence, although this might manifest at a later stage. England's ELMS, in particular Tier 1 (and to a lesser extent Tier 2) also accept payments for actions.[244] This is similarly reflected in Northern Ireland's *Draft Agricultural Strategy*.[245] Consequently, there appears to be a more incremental approach in practice, although the precise balance remains unclear so far. In some instances, this appears to be due to the challenges in operationalising an outcomes-based approach, leading to a swing by default back towards paying for actions.

Despite the declared intention of the four nations, a full swing towards outcomes might not be desirable as outlined above. Instead, an arguably more effective approach than either purely outcomes/results-based or actions-based payments would be to combine them.[246] For instance, each scheme and support agreement could identify and reward suitable final outcomes, milestones and corresponding actions, with some flexibility built-in.[247] The rewards can be staggered over time and weighted in favour of the eventual outcomes, incentivising continued commitments and also helping address the time delay in outcomes manifesting (or not). It would also be possible to only reward final outcomes and milestones, if there were, for instance, quasi-defences of acts of nature and *novus actus interveniens* – equating to paying for best efforts or due diligence. Moxey and White also note the advantage of having a portfolio of options, including adapting to pay in some instances for outcomes and at other times for actions, as well as the value of non-monetary supports such as advice and information.[248] Crucially, payment for actions might also be suitable where the environment has previously been improved to a high level and therefore the desired action is to maintain it at such a level.[249]

243 *Sustainable Farming and Our Land* (n221) 8.
244 *Environmental Land Management Document* (n222) respectively 11–13 and 22.
245 *Draft Agricultural Strategy* (n193) 38–39.
246 Moxey and White (n240).
247 Dobbs, Gravey and Petetin (n229). For example, in the Proposed CAP Strategic Plan Regulation, *performance* of the Member States will be measured against a harmonised set of indicators (including environmental and climate ones), which include 'output, result and impact'. Proposal for a Regulation of the European Parliament and of the Council Establishing Rules on Support for Strategic Plans (n230) Annex I.
248 Moxey and White (n240); and *Environmental Land Management Document* (n222) 9 and 11–13.
249 Burton and Schwarz (n239). See also *Environmental Land Management Document* (n222) 9 and 11–13.

Irrespective of the precise balance between final outcomes and milestones or actions, the design of the schemes and their implementation is key.[250] There remain key questions regarding how to give effect to the schemes including: whether they should relate to individual farm(er)s or take a more landscape-based focus; how to address concerns posed by agricultural tenancies; and how to measure achievements (or failures). These issues are addressed in the discussion that follows, but also the pilot schemes that are being and will be undertaken[251] are crucial to developing and revising the policies and schemes. Practical insights are crucial and the design must be an iterative process if to be effective and promote resilience.

4.4.3 Farm focus or collaboration at scale?

Collaboration at scale is highly advantageous to actors in agriculture. This is reflected in considerations of the supply chain discussed below, but it is equally, if not more, important for farmers and their delivery of outputs – whether public goods or otherwise. This can be simply due to the increased efficiencies of scale, through, for instance, farmers coming together to co-purchase expensive equipment or strengthen their negotiating positions. Yet, farmers across the UK tend to be reluctant to collaborate and share practices and resources with one another.[252] Consequently, extra incentives (financial or otherwise) are needed to encourage collaborative approaches, if these are desired.

Considering the emphasis on delivering environmental public goods across the policies, Bateman and Balmford raise an important question of whether UK agriculture policy should focus on farm-related (farm-by-farm) or land-related (habitat, landscape or catchment area) public goods.[253] Three inter-related reasons support some degree of land-related approach and therefore collaboration at scale. First, such collaborations are essential to achieve overall goals and ensuring holistic approaches – as even if individual farms were aiming to achieve environmental objectives, these could be self-defeating or simply impractical on smaller scales, e.g. insufficient space for habitats or two adjoining farms seeking to maintain or drain wetlands. Similarly, aims regarding crop and livestock

250 Matzdorf and Lorenz (n231); Keenleyside et al. (n233) especially 20–25; and K. Prager, M. Reed and A. Scott, 'Encouraging Collaboration for the Provision of Ecosystem Services at a Landscape Scale – Rethinking Agri-Environmental Payments' (2012) 29(1) *Land Use Policy* 244.

251 The 2016–2018 scheme mentioned above (Chaplin et al. (n75)) was extended by England and paid for by DEFRA following the conclusion of the EU aspect. England intends to test ELMS potentially up until 2028, including via a National Pilot. *Environmental Land Management Document* (n222) 15–18.

252 K.L. Blackstock, K. Brown, B. Davies and P. Shannon, 'Individualism, Cooperation and Conservation in Scottish Farming Communities' in L. Cheshire, V. Higgins and G. Lawrence (eds), *Rural Governance* (Routledge 2007) 191. See also *Draft Agricultural Strategy* (n193) 43 – noting the low level of cooperation and collaboration in supply chains.

253 Bateman and Balmford (n76) 294.

diversity, general biodiversity or habitats all need to be developed in context, including what is happening – or will happen – in the adjoining farms. If every farm started growing a specific traditional crop variety (desirable to protect), this would not help enhance the overall diversity. Second, the process of collaboration can be highly beneficial, including through providing opportunities to identify and develop necessary innovative solutions.[254] It could encourage learning, sharing practices and communication and building trust between farmers, stakeholders and regulatory agencies,[255] which in itself could increase the uptake of collaborative payment-by-results schemes and foster co-production.[256] Finally, collaboration at landscape and catchment scale for payment-by-results schemes could facilitate coordination of practices and policies at the appropriate level to provide public goods more effectively and more efficiently.[257] This would combine a bottom-up approach with some over-arching coordination. A multilevel and multi-actor approach towards payment-by-results schemes could also combine national programmes with local and regional schemes and include private and public funding.[258] Collaboration at scale simply is essential for the delivery of social-ecological services and therefore a resilient agriculture.[259] This is of course not to say that it is not highly challenging or indeed costly to undertake – proper collaboration is more complex and costly than simply coordination at higher levels, but also more effective.[260]

Collaboration at scale has been taken to heart to varying degrees in the development of the policies.[261] Obvious examples including England's Landscape Recovery scheme, where the landscape-scale approach is reflected in its very name.[262] However, it is by no means singular. The policies generally focus initially on individual farmers or land users, but then provide for landscape or ecosystem approaches and collaboration between farmers within the schemes and their subsequent implementation. Thus, in England, ELMS contains the Local Nature Recovery (Tier 2) scheme alongside the Landscape Recovery (Tier 3) scheme – aimed at 'farmers who want to go even further to achieve outcomes in a local

254 On the need for space to develop innovative solutions to promote resilience, see Bennett et al. (n25); and Howe and Ross (n25) 419–420.
255 K.M.A. Chan, 'Payments for Ecosystem Services: Rife with Problems and Potential – For Transformation towards Sustainability' (2017) 140 *Ecological Economics* 110.
256 M.S. Reed et al., 'A Place-Based Approach to Payments for Ecosystem Services' (2017) 43 *Global Environmental Change* 92.
257 K. Prager, 'Agri-Environmental Collaboratives for Landscape Management in Europe' (2015) 12 *Current Opinion in Environmental Sustainability* 59.
258 Hejnowicz and Hartley (n93) 22. See also Wildlife and Countryside Link (n81); and Rodgers (n74).
259 Prager, Reed and Scott (n250); and Keenleyside et al. (n233) 18–19.
260 Prager (n257).
261 J.R. Franks, 'An Assessment of the Landscape-Scale Dimensions of Land Based Environmental Management Schemes Offered to Farmers in England' (2019) 83(2) *Land Use Policy* 147.
262 *Path to Sustainable Farming* (n58) 32.

area or at landscape and whole ecosystem scale'.[263] For both schemes, collaboration is noted as a valuable tool.[264] There may, however, be reliance on large-scale farms to achieve a landscape approach quickly for Landscape Recovery,[265] which would be excessively restrictive. Northern Ireland similarly has indicated support for landscape approaches and promoting cooperation and collaboration between farmers,[266] but it is understandably at a less developed stage and therefore lacking in detail. Finally, as noted in Chapter 3, Section 3.1.2, Wales has reduced its support for landscape-based approaches or collaboration at scale. Whilst collaboration formed a key element of the earlier *Brexit and Our Land*[267] and (to a lesser extent) the *Sustainable Farming and our Land*[268] consultations, generally and also regarding common land, it has since dipped off the radar somewhat and now plays only a minor role in the *White Paper*.[269] This begs the question of to what extent the earlier support for collaborations at scale remains applicable and whether such approaches will be suitably funded, facilitated and managed. Considering the significance of collaborations at scale and landscape approaches to Wales' focus on sustainable land management, one would expect reliance on such approaches within the Sustainable Farming Scheme.

However, this raises the question as to how this might be achieved.[270] First, is the landscape or ecosystem element simply addressed by those managing the schemes and the farmers continue largely as per normal (but possibly micro-managed to ensure cohesion and effectiveness)? Or could farmers perhaps come together within a landscape or catchment and propose group applications? Second, how are the incentives determined? In particular, individually or also on a group basis? For instance, there could be weighted incentives where farmers (and potentially other actors) in the relevant locality collaborate effectively

263 Ibid 32.

264 *Environmental Land Management Document* (n222) 12. Whilst this is expressly linked to Local Nature Recovery and not Landscape Recovery in the *Path to Sustainable Farming* (n58) (page 32), DEFRA's Test and Trial call clarifies that collaboration is also a facet of Landscape Recovery schemes. DEFRA, 'Test and Trials – Phase 3 "Landscape Recovery"' www.contractsfinder.service.gov.uk/Notice/cf1dcfa5-34af-4cee-819c-dd327e8cf2d5 accessed 1 May 2021.

265 *Path to Sustainable Farming* (n58) 32 also notes that '[e]ligibility for Landscape Recovery is likely to be … limited to land … at the right scale to deliver transformational landscape recovery'.

266 *Draft Agricultural Strategy* (n193) 38.

267 *Brexit and our Land* (n78) 47.

268 *Sustainable Farming and Our Land* (n221) 55–56.

269 The sole reference in the *White Paper* (n58) (page 32) to collaborative action amongst farmers is regarding 'the development of long-term farm business and primary supply chain resilience … including support for collaborative action between farmers and between farmers and others'. Similarly, landscape-scale changes and habitat resilience are only mentioned once in the summary to Chapter 1 (Introduction) of the *White Paper* (n58) (page 14).

270 Useful considerations can be found in the work of Elinor Ostrom, Nobel Prize winner for Economics. See E. Ostrom, 'Collective Action and the Evolution of Social Norms' (2000) 14(3) *Journal of Economic Perspectives* 137; Ostrom (n100); and Ostrom (n104).

together to achieve the relevant outcomes, i.e. beyond payments for individual actions/outcomes, there could be bonus payments[271] where there is positive group behaviour/achievements or landscape-wide improvements. For example, where all farmers demonstrate improved behaviour/standards regarding water pollution or quality within a catchment zone – this is particularly appropriate here due to the substantial difficulties in identifying and addressing sources of diffuse water pollution. Finally, how does the system address issues of bad behaviour by individuals within a landscape or catchment area, or simply 'free-riders'? Wales in particular proposes some options,[272] but detailed and tailored investigations will be needed.

Co-design discussed above will be of significance here also, especially due to the complexities of planning and implementing collaboration[273] – amplified when used in conjunction with outcomes-based payments.[274] Similarly, consideration of pilot studies or other examples of collaborative approaches will be helpful here – in the development of schemes and their implementation. A key example within the UK is the Welsh Glastir agri-environment scheme that combined five elements, including 'targeted' (pin-pointed, within farms) and 'common land' (collaborative) elements that could operate in conjunction with each other and rely on spatial targeting based on the land/nature.[275]

Whilst the discussion has so far focused on landscape or catchment-based approaches, this is due to the policies' emphasis on environmental goods. To promote resilience more generally, collaboration at scale would remain fundamental to effective policy, but the 'catchment' might look and behave differently depending on the aspect being targeted. For instance, if regarding social elements, then the catchment might look to communities and social groupings – although noting that collaboration of any sort could still help promote social cohesion[276] and enhance rural vitality. If regarding food quality or economic aspects, different types of farms might be grouped together collectively.

A final thought on collaborations at scale bears noting. The logic that applies to the benefits of collaboration between individual farms or farmers, and with and between other actors in agriculture, also extends beyond jurisdictional boundaries.[277] Just as nature does not recognise ownership boundaries, nor does it recognise jurisdictional or administrative boundaries. What of the situation where Farm A in England and Farm B in Wales are within the same landscape/river basin/ecosystem? The policies do not provide for either both farmers to apply to the same scheme or for the scheme administrators to facilitate cooperation and collaboration across borders – even if this might occur eventually in practice. This

271 Referred to also as agglomeration bonuses, see Reed et al. (n239).
272 *Sustainable Farming and Our Land* (n221) 55–56.
273 Prager, Reed and Scott (n250).
274 Moxey and White (n240).
275 Reed et al. (n239).
276 Prager (n257).
277 Reed et al. (n239).

undermines the effectiveness of the objectives and efforts on both sides of the borders. Overall, a combination of farm and landscape/catchment approaches or collaboration at scale is essential.

4.4.4 Agricultural land ownership

A major challenge regarding agriculture entails the length of time needed for outcomes to manifest, whether in the form of cultivating crops, building herds, developing environmental (and social) goods, installing infrastructure or otherwise – with related capital investments that are largely linked to the land itself. The intended outcomes across the four proposals, whether focused on environmental, social or economic aims, are dependent on incentivising farmers to invest resources in their farms. However, this is far less effective if their ownership claims over 'their' farms are limited in time and/or nature, e.g. where the farms are leased on a short-term basis or where there are restrictions on the activities permitted.[278] This is significant, as a considerable portion of farmland is rented across the UK,[279] including on a short-term basis in the form of crofts,[280] conacre[281] and farm business tenancies[282] and on a long-term basis in the form of agricultural holdings.[283]

Farm tenure insecurity can impact in several ways.[284] First, farmers may be automatically excluded from the schemes, as is the case under the ELMS pilot scheme – whereby farmers must have a tenancy that extends beyond the duration of the pilot.[285] Second, the farmer might sign up to the relevant scheme and invest accordingly, but then their lease ends or is terminated.[286] Third, farmers

278 Burton and Schwarz (n239).
279 DEFRA (n194).
280 Prevalent in Scotland, these are discussed briefly in Section 3.1.4. See also Shucksmith and Rønningen (n187).
281 Chapter 1. For further on conacre, see DAERA and NISRA (n186) 41; M. Patton, P. Kostov, S. McErlean and J. Moss, 'Assessing the Influence of Direct Payments on the Rental Value of Agricultural Land' (2008) 33(5) *Food Policy* 397; and BMcNeill, 'Is the Grass Always Greener? Understanding Grazing and Cropping Rights in Northern Ireland' (2021, forthcoming) 11 *Modern Studies in Property Law* 3.
282 Agricultural Tenancies Act 1995.
283 Agricultural Holdings Act 1986.
284 For more on agricultural tenancies, see C.P. Rodgers, 'Delivering a Better Natural Environment? The Agriculture Bill and Future Agri-Environment Policy' (2019) 21(1) *Environment Law Review* 31, 45–46; and M. Cardwell, 'Results-Based Agri-Environmental Scheme Design: Regulatory Implications' – draft paper (2021).
285 T. Graham, 'ELMS – The UK's Environmental Land Management Scheme' (Stephens Scown 6 April 2021) www.stephens-scown.co.uk/specialist-sectors/rural/elms-the-uks-environmental-land-management-scheme/ accessed 1 May 2021.
286 In England and Wales, the Agricultural Tenancies Act 1995 introduced 'farm business tenancies'. The Act creates minimal conditions, e.g. that all or part of the land be farmed for the purpose of a farming business (broadly understood). Otherwise, the tenancies are primarily based on contract, with limited security for the tenants, e.g. the requirement of

may be concerned that there may be little-to-no return for their investments. Thus, although the Agricultural Tenancies Act 1995 (applicable in England and Wales) was intended to provide flexibility and encourage diversification of activities, it was considered based on empirical research that the 'short duration of most' farm business tenancies under the Act led to 'a reluctance on the part of the farmer to invest in the absence of longer-term security'.[287] Fourth, it may also deter farmers from collaborating (including in the landscape approaches discussed above), where some are only renting on a short-term basis.[288] Overall, tenancies pose numerous challenges[289] – potentially effectively excluding tenants from financial support schemes and thereby undermining the policy objectives.[290]

Different mechanisms could be used to address these challenges, including ensuring that the incentives are at least delivered to the farmer who invests rather than the landlord or, perhaps, that the landlord must sign up to the scheme too and also contribute an appropriate portion of the investment, with an entitlement then to a proportionate amount of the funding.[291] The Agricultural Tenancies Act 1995 (likewise applicable in England and Wales) sought to encourage investment by farm business tenants including by providing for tenants to (i) remove fixtures they installed, with some exceptions[292] and (ii) recoup investments/claim compensation for efforts that have improved the property, subject to the landlord having consented in writing to the improvement. However, the investment and improvements may be challenging to determine and evaluate, even if consent has been given. Further, with multiple actors involved for each farm and the limitations on the funding schemes/incentives, it is questionable whether this will act as a sufficient incentive on each actor simultaneously – for instance, if the tenants only recoup their investments and no more, or if the landlords have to pass on most or all financial benefits.

Tenure insecurity is not the sole issue. Long-term tenancies, e.g. life-long holdings falling within the scope of the Agricultural Holdings Act 1986, can lead to inflexibility.[293] Farmers may be restricted in their activities due to agreements

12 months' written notice to terminate where the lease is for more than two years, or the potential for compensation for investment as noted in the core text.

287 D. Maye, B. Ilbery and D. Watts, 'Farm Diversification, Tenancy and CAP Reform: Results from a Survey of Tenant Farmers in England' (2009) 25 *Journal of Rural Studies* 333, 336 and 341.

288 *Environmental Land Management Document* (n222); and Cardwell (n284).

289 Payments for actions might be less affected by farm tenure insecurity than payments for outcomes, but would not be entirely insulated.

290 *Environmental Land Management Document* (n222); and Cardwell (n284).

291 Lessons could be drawn from issues surrounding dual use payments, for instance, under the Countryside Stewardship payments. See FarmingUK Team, 'Farmers "Will Be Frustrated" Over Defra Dual Use Announcement' (FarmingUK 22 September 2015) www.farminguk.com/news/farmers-will-be-frustrated-over-defra-dual-use-announcement_37134.html accessed 1 May 2021.

292 Agricultural Tenancies Act, Section 8.

293 Rodgers (n284).

created several decades (or even generations) ago and consequently when current agricultural policies were not even contemplated. The Agriculture Act attempted to address this issue of inflexibility with Schedule 3 via Section 36. Section 7 of the Schedule inserts a new Section 19A into the Agricultural Holdings Act 1986, which enables both England and Wales to make relevant regulations that effectively provide for agricultural holdings to be amended to facilitate the achievement of the objectives underpinning financial schemes in England (the public goods outlined earlier in the Act) and Wales (as determined by Wales, for the duration of the enabling powers under Schedule 5). However, Wales decided not to 'take forward [this] power' via the Agriculture Act, but instead determined to do so itself later via its own Bill.[294]

Whilst amendments by agreement are preferred, Section 19A of the Agriculture Holdings Act 1986 provides for the possibility of arbitration or 'third party determination' where there is a dispute regarding a request for landlord's consent (where required for a matter under the tenancy terms) or a variation of the tenancy terms.[295] Such requests must either relate to compliance with a statutory duty or to the financial assistance schemes within the Agriculture Act. The subsequent enabling regulations provide the arbitrator or third party with considerable flexibility in the orders they may make, including, for instance, facilitating conditions relating to the making of a successful application' for 'relevant financial assistance' or compensation.[296] Dispute mechanisms also exist in the Agricultural Tenancies Act 1995 regarding party rights and obligations, but Section 19A is significant as it enables amendments to life-long holdings where related to the financial assistance schemes – thereby facilitating the requisite flexibility.

The procedures might, nonetheless, prove more challenging, as the approach could become cumbersome. Tenants may also be reluctant to initiate a dispute against their landlords – even if it is arbitration. This might assist in individual instances, but there could be inertia towards the status quo and, therefore, to not adjusting the tenancy terms. An alternative option might be to provide further and more tailored incentives to amend tenancy agreements/create supplementary contracts[297] and engage with the schemes (and/or disincentives for lack of engagement with the schemes) – focusing simultaneously on the farmer and the landlord and thereby minimising the potential for conflict between the different parties. Furthermore, the Agriculture Act does not address the issue of tenure insecurity.

Whilst land law varies considerably across the UK, especially in Scotland and Northern Ireland, and the level and nature of farm ownership similarly varies, the

294 *White Paper* (n58) 50. As noted, the Bill is not expected until summer 2022.

295 For example, the Agricultural Law Association has set up a Dispute Resolution Panel in line with Schedule 3 of the Agriculture Act. For more, see ALA Dispute Resolution, https://aladisputeresolution.co.uk/ accessed 1 May 2021.

296 The Agricultural Holdings (Requests for Landlord's Consent or Variation of Terms and the Suitability Test) (England) Regulations 2021, Regulation 4.

297 Rodgers (n284).

potential to amend ownership relationships is something valuable to consider.[298] Such a possibility was highlighted in the Northern Ireland's *Draft Agricultural Strategy* regarding conacre, but without further discussion or development.[299] It was also flagged in the Welsh proposals[300] and a consultation was held on Agricultural Tenancies.[301] In part, the Welsh Government was investigating whether changes could 'ensure tenancy law does not stand in the way of tenants' and landlords' ability to adapt to change, access new schemes, improve productivity and enable structural change'.[302] As noted, the Welsh Government did not avail of the relevant powers in the Agriculture Act, but stated in the *White Paper* that, in light of the strong support in the consultation responses, they would take on similar powers via their own eventual Act.[303]

Land ownership is emotionally and culturally charged and unilaterally amending ownership relationships directly impacts private and property rights, but having a fall-back of the potential to amend this to further public goods is at least worthy of debate if the policies are to be effective.[304] Consideration should be given to going beyond the amendments within the Agriculture Act and those proposed by Wales. While farmers are open to diversification and investing in the land/farming in order to achieve worthwhile objectives, agriculture remains a long-term economic endeavour and farmers need both the requisite security and flexibility to make the necessary changes.[305] Alternative proposals of having short-term outcomes have been mooted,[306] but they risk undermining the overall objectives of the agricultural policies if not operating in conjunction with long-term outcomes (in light of the nature of agriculture and the environment) and a careful balance would need to be ensured.[307]

298 McNeill (n281); and Rodgers (n284).

299 *Draft Agricultural Strategy* (n193) 27. See also Expert Working Group on Sustainable Land Management, 'Delivering Our Future, Valuing Our Soils: A Sustainable Agricultural Land Management Strategy for Northern Ireland' (21 October 2016) www.daera-ni.gov.uk/sites/default/files/publications/daera/16.17.079%20Sustainable%20Land%20Management%20Strategy%20final%20amended.PDF accessed 1 May 2021, 3, 7, 22, 70, 84 and 93.

300 *Sustainable Farming and Our Land* (n221) 55.

301 Welsh Government (n224).

302 Ibid 2.

303 *White Paper* (n58) 50–51.

304 N. Ravenscroft, '"Post-Feudalism" and the Changing Structure of Agricultural Leasing' (1999) 16 *Land Use Policy* 247, 255 states that 'strong government intervention in the land market and the land-owner/tenant relation, [is] likely to achieve greatest long-term stability'.

305 Maye, Ilbery and Watts (n287).

306 *Environmental Land Management Document* (n222) 30; and *Sustainable Farming and Our Land* (n221) 55.

307 Ibid. See also above regarding outcomes and/or actions.

4.4.5 Upholding Baselines

Clearly, aiming to achieve a high level of protection of issues such as human health, the environment and consumer protection would be desirable. However, at the other end, regulatory baselines are essential to help ensure a minimum level of protection regarding these key objectives and therefore to overall resilience. Without minimum standards, and in light also of the potential for siloed public goods, a farmer, for instance, could be paid for one environmental outcome whilst simultaneously causing other or even greater environmental degradation. Consideration is given here to the incorporation of minimum standards and their enforcement, as related to agricultural policies.

4.4.5.1 Incorporation of minimum standards

The proposals to date generally do not establish minimum standards or regulatory baselines directly within the policies themselves. The Agriculture Act comes close through, for instance, Section 37 providing for regulations on marketing standards to be developed. A core component of the Welsh proposals is the establishment of National Minimum Standards for agricultural production. However, to be clear, this is largely an amalgamation and clarification exercise of existing obligations for farmers[308] – although the *White Paper* does note the possibility of building upon these and adding other areas.[309] Whilst valuable and greater clarity should help with compliance, a broader scope for minimum standards would help further resilience through reflecting the multifunctional nature of agriculture.[310] The potential to recognise social standards and link in with the development of 'Sustainable Brand Values' is noted in *Sustainable Farming and Our Land*.[311]

However, just because the policies do not establish minimum standards or regulatory baselines does not mean that they do not exist. As discussed in Chapter 1, while in the EU, UK farmers fell under the umbrella of the CAP and needed to comply with both domestic and EU law. Post-Brexit, not that much has changed at first glance. There are clearly regulatory baselines across the UK for issues such as environmental protection, human health and consumer protection, even if they

308 L. Griffiths, 'Written Statement – Publication of the Agriculture (Wales) White Paper' (Welsh Government 16 December 2020) https://gov.wales/written-statement-publication-agriculture-wales-white-paper accessed 1 May 2021. It is worth nothing that whilst all 'statutory management requirements' (SMRs) applicable under the CAP are part of the domestic regulatory framework, not all 'good agricultural and environmental conditions' (GAECs) are and, therefore, the latter are not automatically retained. The *White Paper* (n58) (page 16) discusses incorporating some GAECs within the National Minimum Standards, but some changes will likely occur across the UK on this front.

309 Ibid 17.

310 This would also help further reflect the obligations of integrating sustainable development under the Well-Being of Future Generations (Wales) Act 2015 and the Environment (Wales) Act 2016.

311 *White Paper* (n58) 76.

would benefit from being raised at times. Many of these rules derive from EU law and were retained via the European Union (Withdrawal) Act 2018. Although some elements have been weakened, especially through the loss of EU objectives and principles, as well as EU governance mechanisms,[312] nonetheless, most of the regulatory requirements remain much the same.

It should not be thought that the four nations seek to do away with the regulatory frameworks and the minimum standards therein. The policies recognise their value, as exemplified by Wales' proposed National Minimum Standards. Further, Northern Ireland's *Draft Agricultural Strategy*, albeit very briefly, notes the importance of environmental regulation, stating that '[a]ny future agricultural policy framework will need to recognise and be underpinned as appropriate, by proportionate, effective environmental regulation ...[that] should form a backstop' to prevent environmental harms. It also highlights the possibility of linking financial support with upholding 'minimum environmental standards as set out in regulations'.[313] Also, the UK Withdrawal from the European Union (Continuity) (Scotland) Act 2021 provides powers for the Scottish Ministers to maintain and advance on EU standards in specific devolved matters including on animal health and welfare, plant health and environmental protection.[314] This enables continued alignment with EU law, as well as increasing the current regulatory baseline.[315] Even England in declaring its intention to make major reforms to the regulatory regime, is nonetheless acknowledging its significance,[316] and states its intention to 'strengthe[n] the regulatory baseline' in areas such as animal health and welfare.[317]

However, two concerns arise. First, without integrating minimum standards or guarantees within the agricultural policies, changes across the regulatory landscape may lead to a watering down of standards, agricultural practices and ambitions.[318] Second, these minimum standards may be undermined or bypassed in practice. As with the main objectives of the policies, they depend also on their implementation and enforcement. Enforcement can be achieved outside or via agricultural policies.

312 From the environmental perspective, see A. Jordan, C. Burns, and V. Gravey, 'Three Brexit Governance Gaps No One is Talking About' (*Green Alliance Blog* 6 December 2017) https://greenallianceblog.org.uk/2017/12/06/three-brexit-governance-gaps-no-one-is-talking-about/ accessed 1 May 2021; M. Lee, 'Accountability for Environmental Standards after Brexit' (2017) 19(2) *Environmental Law Review* 89; and M. Lee, 'Brexit and Environmental Protection in the United Kingdom: Governance, Accountability and Law Making' (2018) 36(3) *Journal of Energy & Natural Resources Law* 351.

313 *Draft Agricultural Strategy* (n193) 37.

314 UK Withdrawal from the European Union (Continuity) (Scotland) Act 2021, Sections 1 and 2.

315 The Internal Market Act may, however, curtail Scotland when setting higher standards. See Chapter 5, Section 5.2.3.

316 *Path to Sustainable Farming* (n58) 15.

317 Ibid 46.

318 Such an outcome is possible, as discussed in Chapter 5.

4.4.5.2 Enforcement of baselines

Where individuals breach regulatory obligations, they may be liable for financial penalties or criminal sanctions or simply prohibited from selling their produce (e.g. where products do not comply with health and safety or marketing standards). However, these can be challenging mechanisms to apply in practice. For instance, environmental enforcement actions[319] are habitually lengthy, expensive and would create further strains on public resources. The breaches can be difficult to prove and, even if successful, the penalties are frequently minimal[320] – environmental offences are frequently not viewed as serious offences or crimes. Consequently, there could be insufficient deterrence and farmers (as with other individuals) could decide to internalise any potential fines as operational costs. This could be exacerbated if the farmers could still reap rewards via the financial support schemes within the policies even where they breach the regulatory baseline intentionally, for example, if they farm in a manner that allows them to claim under a support scheme and also sell their produce, with only a minimal fine at most for breaching regulations. On the other hand, arguably criminal penalties can be excessively harsh and a broader range of penalties may be desirable.

The CAP offered a complementary enforcement mechanism with the tool of cross-compliance,[321] which still continues to apply to varying extents across the UK. Cross-compliance avails of financial support schemes under the CAP to support regulatory baselines. As discussed in Chapter 1, the CAP obliges farmers to comply with statutory management requirements (SMRs) and also good agricultural and environmental condition of land (GAECs).[322] Where they do not do so, penalties can be imposed[323] – in particular via a reduction in support payments, typically the direct payments. Although cross-compliance can be criticised for its complexity, opaqueness, being disproportionate,[324] and arguably effectively

319 For detailed discussion of enforcement of environmental standards in the UK, see R. Macrory, *Regulation, Enforcement and Governance in Environmental Law* (2nd edn, Hart Publishing 2014).

320 *Sustainable Farming and Our Land* (n221) 78.

321 The EU has adapted to an approach based on conditionality more recently, as discussed below. Under the CAP, 1% of farmers receiving direct payments are to be inspected each year with 20 to 25% selected randomly whilst the rest is based on risk criteria. In cases of breaches, penalties are applied and deducted at source. This means that direct payments are not fully paid to the farmer who is in breach.

322 OECD, 'Environmental Cross Compliance in Agriculture' (2010) www.oecd.org/agriculture/topics/agriculture-and-the-environment/documents/environmental-cross-compliance-in-agriculture.pdf accessed 1 May 2021. See also Chapter 1, Section 1.2.

323 Regulation (EU) No 1306/2013 of the European Parliament and of the Council of 17 December 2013 on the Financing, Management and Monitoring of the Common Agricultural Policy and Repealing Council Regulations (EEC) No 352/78, (EC) No 165/94, (EC) No 2799/98, (EC) No 814/2000, (EC) No 1290/2005 and (EC) No 485/2008 [2013] OJ L347/549.

324 Dame Glenys Stacey, 'Farm Inspection and Regulation Review' (December 2018) https://assets.publishing.service.gov.uk/government/uploads/system/uploads/attachment_data

paying farmers not to break the law or take harmful actions (turning cross-compliance on its head), it does at least in principle help ensure a minimum level of protection by providing an effective deterrent.

Cross-compliance is given different treatment across the four policies. For example, cross-compliance is mentioned with varying degrees of approbation in Northern Ireland's *Draft Agricultural Strategy* and no clarity as to what role it might play in future.[325] Minister Poots has commenced a review of the system within Northern Ireland, with an aim to make the penalties more proportionate.[326] However, it does appear that some version will remain. In contrast, both the English and Welsh schemes are to be built on the application of the polluter pays principle.[327] England is therefore abandoning cross-compliance in its entirety following the transitional period, along with the end of direct payments[328] – instead, relying on the general regulatory regime, with the intent to revise it 'in partnership with industry' and make it more proportionate and 'fair, clear and effective' in future.[329] Theoretically, this constitutes a positive shift because farmers are no longer supported to fulfil cross-compliance requirements but to deliver additionality, that is to go beyond the regulatory baseline. However, in practice, it may undermine the enforcement of the regulatory regime.

Wales remains more of a halfway house. The *White Paper* proposes a fundamental overhaul of the system. First, Wales seeks to move away from the approach under the CAP where monitoring varied depending on whether farms were signed up to support schemes.[330] It intends to undertake 'risk based inspections to more effectively monitor those at highest risk of non-compliance. This would be balanced against the need to monitor compliance across a proportionate sample of farms in Wales'[331] – thereby reducing the burden on farmers and improving the effectiveness of inspections. In this regard, the possibility of gaining 'earned

/file/764286/farm-inspection-regulatio-review-final-report-2018.pdf accessed 1 May 2021. The review proposed a 'more supportive, flexible and incentives-led approach' to the regulatory framework for agriculture. See DEFRA, 'Dame Glenys Stacey Review Proposes Farm Regulation Shake-Up' (13 December 2018) www.gov.uk/government/news/dame-glenys-stacey-review-proposes-farm-regulation-shake-up accessed 1 May 2021.

325 *Draft Agricultural Strategy* (n193) 16. A similar approach is seen regarding greening requirements, with most being removed under the current proposals where they are addressed at all.

326 Northern Ireland Assembly (n217).

327 *Path to Sustainable Farming* (n58) 33, in respect of the Sustainable Farming Incentive. For more on the application of the polluter pays principle to farming, see M.N. Cardwell, 'The Polluter Pays Principle in European Community Law and Its Impact on UK Farmers' (2006) 59 *Oklahoma Law Review* 89; and M.R. Grossman (eds), *Agriculture and the Polluter Pays Principle* (British Institute of International and Comparative Law 2009).

328 *Path to Sustainable Farming* (n58) 10 and 14; and DEFRA (n207).

329 *Path to Sustainable Farming* (n58) 65–66. This will build also on Dame Glenys Stacey's review of the framework (n324).

330 *White Paper* (n58) 38–39.

331 Ibid 43.

recognition for regulatory compliance' is also mentioned.[332] The intention would be to seek more data initially that would facilitate remote monitoring[333] 'to better target farm visits'.[334]

Second, Wales expressly rejects the existing cross-compliance penalties as disproportionate (even though recognising their effectiveness as a deterrent) and too rigid. Consequently, the *White Paper* proposed introducing a range of new enforcement mechanisms (alongside the move away from the Basic Payment Scheme) to help support the National Minimum Standards. These include a range of civil sanctions such as compliance notices, restoration notices, stop notices, fixed monetary penalties, variable monetary penalties and enforcement undertaking (as an alternative to monetary or criminal sanctions), which would depend on severity and recurrence.[335] This would also help address Wales' earlier intention that 'in the interests of fairness' the standards should apply to all farmers and not simply those who receive funding.[336] Consequently, it would seem like cross-compliance is done away with, despite earlier indications that it would continue.[337] However, alongside the introduction of these new enforcement mechanisms, the *White Paper* then states that compliance with the National Minimum Standards may be a condition for entry into the Sustainable Farming Scheme and that failure to comply might lead to penalties under that also[338] – which is simply cross-compliance by another name. How this manifests in practice remains to be seen, but there is the potential for the standards to be either strengthened or undermined by these changes and similarly for the burdens to be increased or decreased on farmers.

The four nations respect the regulatory frameworks, but take different approaches to how these baselines are maintained and will evolve in future. However, England is disentangling these baselines from the support schemes – providing for a siloed approach to environmental protection of public goods on the one hand (based on voluntarism[339] and additionality) and regulatory frameworks on the other (based largely on command-control). Wales is building a more complex picture where cross-compliance appears to continue by another name, whereas with Scotland and Northern Ireland the precise role of cross-compliance remains unclear. This is especially the case as the gradual removal of direct payments or an equivalent payment available to all farmers undermines the potential effectiveness of cross-compliance as a tool to uphold regulatory standards. If the

332 Ibid.
333 Ibid 38–39.
334 Ibid 13.
335 Ibid 22.
336 *Sustainable Farming and Our Land* (n221) 10.
337 Ibid 19.
338 *White Paper* (n58) 31.
339 Previously reflected in management agreements regarding nature conservation. See Rodgers (n137) Chapter 1. This could play a significant role post-Brexit, see Pontin (n138) Chapter 6.

penalty for breaching cross-compliance is linked to a scheme that farmers have to opt-in to and also may not be universally available, then the reach of cross-compliance is automatically limited. Consequently, in England cross-compliance, in particular, would be undermined even if retained, whereas it would be more effective in Scotland, Wales or Northern Ireland – but not necessarily as effective as under the CAP. The main remaining alternative is prosecution (either civil or criminal) with corresponding impacts on overburdened courts, costs to the public purse and therefore taxpayers, and ultimately the environment due to harms that might continue in the meantime.

4.4.6 Measuring achievements and enforcement

A final core consideration for the policies and their schemes relates to measuring achievements and the determination and award of payments (or not). This raises a number of interrelated elements, including the need for suitable steps or indicators,[340] monitoring and evaluation (to determine whether criteria are fulfilled) and the application of corresponding rewards or 'sanctions'. These become more complex and potentially more costly in the context of outcomes-focused approaches, mixed approaches and collaborative approaches.[341] As with policy design, there is also the possibility for substantial roles for stakeholders at all stages here – but with varying added value and concerns depending on the element involved. Whilst much of this will be determined within the schemes as they are developed and individual agreements, insights can nonetheless be gained from the policies as they stand. The main focus below is on the SFI, as the most developed scheme.

4.4.6.1 Targets and corresponding payments

The first step is to determine what are appropriate outcomes (and/or actions) and what payments should be assigned to these. This includes both final outcomes/actions and milestones or steps en route, depending on the policy/scheme's approach. Once this is achieved on a general level, then specific indicators can be determined. They must be both objectively desirable (sufficiently so as to merit payment) and also tailored for the individual farm(er)s and localities – they must be feasible, taking into account existing practical constraints and the proposed support. The payments ought to be sufficient to at least offset any costs and preferably incentivise the desired actions/outcomes – although depending on the mechanisms, this could raise issues related to the Agreement on Agriculture of the World Trade Organization (WTO). This is an iterative process, as if the payments required are not possible, then the corresponding outcomes are pointless

340 Burton and Schwarz (n239).
341 Prager (n257).

as part of a financial support scheme – likewise, if the outcomes are not possible, then the proposed schemes are fictional.

Generally, the schemes seek to reward outcomes that are above the regulatory baseline and frequently above the status quo.[342] For example, in both the English and Welsh schemes farmers are (in principle) not supported to fulfil environmental cross-compliance requirements but to deliver additionality, i.e. outcomes over and above regulatory compliance – breaking away from past CAP practice. For instance, Wales' Sustainable Farming Payments are likely to be conditional on the 'delivery of outcomes above and beyond the requirements of regulation'[343] – that is above National Minimum Standards acting as the regulatory baseline.[344] Similarly in England, *The Path to Sustainable Farming* stated that '[w]e want a clear distinction, and coherent relationship, between the basic requirements farmers are obliged to meet by law, and scheme standards where they are paid to go beyond this minimum'.[345] Yet, this distinction remains unclear in England. It also is questionable how feasible this will be for farmers without the continuation of direct payments.

The SFI provides a useful example of the initial step. Each SFI agreement between the farmer and the public body will be different. However, to reduce bureaucracy and set-up costs, certain mechanisms have been established. At the heart of the SFI is a 'land management plan' which 'empowers' farmers to 'map and record the starting (baseline) condition of their land and plan their future land management activities. These plans are intended to be a flexible tool owned by farmers – something that can adjusted and updated to meet their individual needs and circumstances'.[346] Farmers can use 'self-declared information' to support their applications and agreements, which are based on trust. The basis for the SFI appears to be self-regulation where it appears to be assumed farmers, i.e. the regulatees, are trustworthy. This, therefore, raises three issues: first, the starting condition of their land is one that arises where famers have previously been supported via the CAP. To what extent will farmers be able to maintain that baseline without financial support? The required finance may go beyond the difference between the current condition and the desired outcome. Second, the role of farmers in providing key information and helping to determine indicators

342 The situation is still unfolding and remains unclear in Northern Ireland, which refers to future support potentially for not breaking environmental standards, but then also outlines sample target outcomes that are clearly beyond the regulatory baselines. See *Draft Agricultural Strategy* (n193) 37 and 39 respectively. This remains unknown in Scotland, but it would be expected that at least a majority of the payments would be for going above regulatory baselines.

343 *Sustainable Farming and Our Land* (n221) 47.

344 *White Paper* (n58) 13. Existing regulations spread across numerous legislative instruments would be consolidated in National Minimum Standards to increase farmers' awareness of these legal requirements, ultimately facilitating and maintaining compliance. *White Paper* (n58) 15.

345 *Path to Sustainable Farming* (n58) 15. See also at 33.

346 *SFI Paper* (n78).

and co-design individual agreements helps ensure suitably tailored agreements, as well as once more promoting buy-in and effectiveness. However, third, the corollary is that relying on the farmers without independent checks allows for the system to be potentially abused and agreements to be built on inaccurate information – some objective checks are required.

So what then of the objectives and indicators? The SFI has outlined an initial eight standards for farmers to choose from (e.g. arable and horticultural soils; arable and horticultural land; hedgerow; or waterbody buffering).[347] Within these, farmers choose also the level that they wish to aim for. This flexibility has been highlighted as a significant factor for farmers balancing risks and incentives in applying for schemes.[348] Detailed indicators or metrics for these standards within the SFI remain as 'an initial, high-level, summary', with detailed guidance to be published in summer 2021.[349] Some work has been undertaken already on indicators domestically via the pilot studies, with the identification of positive and negative indicators for specific objectives.[350] However, these need to be developed to a much larger extent and integrated within the schemes and individual agreements. Further guidance can be found in the literature and also in work undertaken in the EU.[351]

Payments under the SFI are then to be attributed to actions required to fulfil those goals, with potential for additional payments for set additional actions. There are fixed sums under the pilot scheme for each action and, whilst some changes will occur for the final scheme, the same approach can be expected.[352] Farmers will be able to choose from an *à la carte* menu of outcomes (and corresponding payments) in light of their own preferences. However, a farmer might dismiss some standards or levels if the payment is insufficient to facilitate or perhaps incentivise the actions.[353] What might be sufficient for one, might not be sufficient for another, e.g. depending on the current state of the land or on how profitable the farm is. It also raises the question as to what the payments are actually for and how they were calculated.

347 Ibid.
348 Chaplin et al. (n75) 120. The examples therein had numerous levels or tiers. The extra levels could be adopted more generally, enhancing the flexibility and ability to tailor agreements for those more or less ambitious.
349 *SFI Paper* (n78).
350 Chaplin et al. (n75); and Keenleyside et al. (n233).
351 Ibid 9–14; and E. Underwood, 'Result Indicators Used in Europe: Results-Based Payments for Biodiversity – Supplement to Guidance Handbook' (Supplement to the Report Prepared for the European Commission, Institute for European Environmental Policy 2014) https://ec.europa.eu/environment/nature/rbaps/handbook/docs/result-indicators.pdf accessed 1 May 2021.
352 *Path to Sustainable Farming* (n58) page 34 notes that the pilot schemes are being used to test aspects regarding calculating payments and that any payments must 'provide a fair return to participants'.
353 Although there are still further capital funds available if needed for the initial investment. See *SFI Paper* (n78).

In contrast, Northern Ireland has made little progress here, but has stated 'that strict adherence to the principle of 'income forgone/cost incurred' in setting environmental payments may be insufficient' and 'an additional incentive element may be necessary', potentially through innovative approaches.[354] Similarly, Wales has stated that their new Sustainable Farming Scheme 'is intended to reward farmers for the delivery of their outcomes rather than compensate them for the costs of their inputs' – protected from 'market volatility' and 'moving away from traditional agri-environment schemes which paid farmers on the basis of compensation for income foregone and additional costs incurred'.[355] Whilst this clearly could provide a greater incentive to participate, it does however raise questions regarding compliance with the Agreement on Agriculture.[356] Northern Ireland also noted that further support might be provided via other funds or indeed that 'market-led initiatives' could play a role.[357]

4.4.6.2 Monitoring

There must be suitable monitoring to facilitate the determination of whether the actions are undertaken, or indicators are met.[358] Choices will need to be made over who gathers the information (e.g. the farmers, other stakeholders or regulators), how often (e.g. every few months, setting times when indicators are meant to be met or when certain warning signs are present) and how (e.g. human eye, drones, satellite or equipment left *in situ*). Numerous mechanisms exist and there may be considerable scope for innovation here as well as for mixing methods. Overall, there appears to be a shift towards reducing the extent of monitoring, pushing more towards self-regulation and also the use of technology to assist. The main considerations seem to be cutting costs for all concerned and giving the benefit of doubt to farmers in the first instance.

The Welsh Government intends to avail of information from a combination of sources including farmers, on-site visits and remote technology, as well as through sharing existing and new data from various bodies.[359] It has emphasised the importance of the collection and processing of data on farms (and the environment), including through using new technologies such as satellite data and on-farm sensors,[360] and seeks to streamline the process of data collection

354 *Draft Agricultural Strategy* (n193) 38–39.
355 *White Paper* (n58) 30.
356 As discussed in Chapter 3, Section 3.2.2.
357 *Draft Agricultural Strategy* (n193) 39.
358 Monitoring also provides a crucial role in helping determine whether the agreements, indicators or schemes need to be revised, see Keenleyside et al. (n233) 25. See also *White Paper* (n58) page 39 stating that a primary purpose of data collection is to 'monitor and evaluate financial assistance schemes'.
359 *White Paper* (n58) 38–44.
360 Ibid 41.

and sharing for the purposes of financial support schemes.[361] The goal is that through improved data comparison and sharing between regulators and managers, the monitoring burden could be reduced, with knock-on effects on costs, value for money and effective compliance.[362] Further, new technologies could be used to reduce the reliance on farmers providing information and on-farm visits by scheme managers (or regulatory agents).[363] Some final checks would still be required, but the precise balance and frequency of monitoring or visits remains unknown currently.

The approach adopted by DEFRA regarding the SFI similarly creates a 'fundamental reset' to the compliance and monitoring agreements where the focus is on 'outcomes and improvement, rather than penalising shortcomings' – affecting approaches to both monitoring and enforcement.[364] Central to this is the aim that 'compliance checks ... be implemented simply and effectively, adding value by *supporting* long-term success' (emphasis added). Thus, farmers are to 'demonstrate success (or, failing that, demonstrate compliance)', without mentioning non-compliance.[365] The main role in monitoring is for the farmer, with targeted compliance checks (e.g. via random selection or risk-based selection). As with Wales, new ways of monitoring based on technology, including 'geospatial data' and 'remote sensing', as well as virtual checks are to be used – reducing the dependence on-farm checks.

The use of self-regulation, market forces and self-monitoring can help reduce burdens on the state (including financial burdens and human resources), further incentivise positive actions, and improve efficiency – especially where compliance with regulatory baselines is no longer a focus. However, the controls that are an inherent part of a state regulatory system are, therefore, lacking and could lead to regulatory capture.[366] The objective, independent actors (and potentially requirements) are not present, and the values and effectiveness of the policies may be undermined in practice. The proposals in Wales and England to increase the role of self-monitoring and reduce on-farm visits, therefore, increase the importance of the use of technology – potentially facilitating oversight by the regulators and scheme managers.

4.4.6.3 Rewarding and enforcing

The third aspect relates to the determination of consequences for desired and undesired behaviour and outcomes. Is this simply the (partial or full) non-payment of funds provided under the schemes? And what occurs if other facts are

361 Ibid 39.
362 Ibid 41.
363 Ibid.
364 *SFI Paper* (n78).
365 Ibid.
366 Baldwin and Black (n54); Ayres and Braithwaite (n54).

identified, via monitoring, that do not relate to the individual agreement indicators? For example, the farmer improved or destroyed a habitat in one part of their land, whereas the agreement related to hedgerows at the other end of their farm. The starting point will clearly be that where the actions are undertaken or the outcomes delivered, agreed payments will be made. This reflects the significance of having a combination of actions, milestones and final outcomes – otherwise, it would be an all-or-nothing system that would risk putting farmers off applying.[367]

Generally, the policies demonstrate an effort to reduce the penalties and provide opportunities to farmers to remedy whatever the issues might be. This is reflected in the new Countryside Stewardship Agreements where England has removed the application of certain additional penalties, extended the period for *force majeure* applications and crucially developed a system of warnings (along with signposting to relevant advice and guidance).[368] Similarly, for ELMS, England proposes 'a fairer, more supportive and effective approach to compliance'.[369] The use of multiple levels of targets could help facilitate this, through again enabling a graduated system of payments and avoiding an all-or-nothing approach.[370] Essentially, even when it comes to enforcement, farmers are to be supported for their activities and rewarded for what they do, rather than penalised 'for what they have not done well' or on 'shortcomings'[371] – with some caveats.

As a last resort, the SFI guidance indicates that 'future schemes will need to have safeguards against the possibility of serious and deliberate non-compliance', noting that such measures should be proportionate.[372] Consequently, penalties are only to be applied where there are important failures and even then the tone is one of leniency.[373] Similarly in Northern Ireland, in light of Minister Poots' mentions of proportionality above regarding cross-compliance, one would expect a relatively lenient approach. The Welsh *White Paper* does not yet detail how it will address the failure to take the necessary actions or deliver the relevant outcomes. However, when discussing the relationship with the regulatory framework (and the proposed National Minimum Standards), Wales notes the potential for payments under the Sustainable Farming Scheme to be affected (alongside other enforcement mechanisms and penalties). This element is to be developed and consulted upon at a later stage.[374]

One final point worth noting regarding measuring achievements is the potential costs of undertaking these steps. It may be labour intensive and costly for farmers and/or bodies managing the schemes, e.g. through monitoring and evaluating progress. This will need to be taken into consideration in determining

367 Chaplin et al. (n75) 9.
368 *Path to Sustainable Farming* (n58) 28.
369 Ibid 31.
370 Chaplin et al. (n75) 45.
371 *SFI Paper* (n78).
372 Ibid.
373 Ibid.
374 *White Paper* (n58) 31.

what funding the farmers require and also the feasibility and desirability of the schemes or individual agreements. Practicalities may impact the approaches taken to some of the more costly components and revisions may be seen in future. However, for an effective system, independent, objective monitoring is required (rather than a box-ticking exercise) and there must be suitable rewards and penalties to (dis)incentivise behaviour.

4.4.7 Concluding remarks on patchy governance

Overall, the policies are a mixed, and evolving, bag when it comes to governance. There are varying levels of stakeholder engagement in policy design, with Northern Ireland and Scotland leading the way here – although with caveats over delays and effectiveness. How this will reflect in the design of schemes and the reviews of both schemes and policies remains to be seen, but meaningful engagement (including co-design) with a wide range of stakeholders is central to furthering the effectiveness, legitimacy and resilience of the policies and their schemes.

While the shift towards outcomes has been watered down somewhat and swung partially back towards actions, with mixed approaches visible across the board so far, this is actually positive from a practical viewpoint. Mixed approaches are easier to implement (than a pure outcomes-based approach), enable varied payments and flexibility, and can increase incentives for farmers. However, they can also be complex to design, monitor and manage – especially when amplified by collaborations at scale. The value of this last point is undeniable and recognised across the policies to date, yet the discourse is unclear as to how this will be achieved in implementing the schemes.

Indeed, much remains to be developed still within the policies and schemes and this is especially true when it comes to the development of indicators and determining precisely how to implement and enforce individual agreements. Pilot studies are being developed and they will prove essential to the continued development across the four nations. On this front, Northern Ireland and Scotland bear special mention – with the latter barely discussed within this section for obvious reasons. Considering how far behind Northern Ireland and Scotland currently are, even if for good reason, the two nations will need to turn outward for as many insights as possible – even if the policies, landscape, practices and cultures vary across the four nations. Nonetheless, the experiences within the pilot studies, in particular, may help in identifying what approaches may or may not be viable and, for instance, feed into the initial determination of indicators.

The inclusion of regulatory baselines within the policies (directly or incorporated by reference) is valuable – especially if there are real-world consequences for breaking them and they are neither a form of green-washing nor abused to undermine the policy objectives. However, even if this is achieved via primary legislation and/or the finalised policies, this does not guarantee that the baselines will be maintained in the future. In particular, there is the potential for trade agreements or competition to impact baselines, as discussed in Chapter 5.

Finally, the policies demonstrate an iterative process. Even the Agriculture Act, which is inherently more fixed in nature, provides the basis for a regime that remains in flux – with schemes still being developed, piloted and revised, as highlighted by the SFI. Wales' *White Paper* similarly indicates that it will use monitoring not merely to evaluate compliance by farmers and facilitate comparisons, but also to evaluate the effectiveness of the policy, schemes and the regulatory framework[375] – with the potential to revise them in light of this. This brings some advantages, through enabling the policies and their schemes to be adapted as needed, but also leaves the situation uncertain, fragmented and also open to regulatory capture or simply being impacted excessively by external influence. Whilst some flexibility must be retained and an iterative process helps develop the resilience of the policies and thus agriculture, the establishment of the policies with sufficient detail and guidance is essential for stakeholders.

4.5 Acknowledging interconnectedness

Agriculture and its social-ecological systems are highly complex and necessitate consideration and management of issues across the levels, including where they intersect. This is highlighted in Chapters 1 to 3, when considering aspects such as globalisation, multifunctionality of agriculture, environmental impacts, or simply the legal and political relationships across the levels. Consequently, issues arise including supply chains, the nature of activities playing out at landscape or ecosystem levels, community considerations, the nature of borders and level playing fields and competition. This is reflected in resilience literature, where authors acknowledge the significance of multiscalar, multilevel, polycentric or similar approaches.[376]

The following sub-sections examine agriculture's interconnectedness from two perspectives. First, it considers if and how the policies acknowledge and seek to address the issues around strengthening integrated supply chains. Second, two areas of path dependency are examined – specifically the CAP and financial support schemes – where external actions and policy have heavily influenced the four nations in the design of their agricultural policies and will continue to do so. What can be seen across the policies is a quasi-blinkered approach to these external factors, even though these important considerations are fundamental to a resilient agriculture and at times are impacting indirectly the policies' design through path dependency.

4.5.1 Integrated supply chains

Supply chains are fundamental to agriculture and, especially in the globalised world, are inherently multilevel in nature – not merely looking downstream from

375 *White Paper* (n58) 43.
376 Arnold and Gunderson (n28) 328–336.

hayfork to the table fork, but also further upstream to the suppliers of machinery, equipment, seeds, feed, animals, chemicals and veterinary medicines. Once borders are involved, this also engages with access to markets, external standards and controls, tariff and non-tariff barriers. All of this has been highlighted by COVID-19, along with the related issue of access to workers.

COVID-19 has entailed the disruption of the international supply of agricultural inputs and products, imposition of protective measures by states, and obstacles posed for migrant labourers – demonstrating the lack of flexibility and resilience in the agri-food supply chain to resist shocks (but where local producers played an essential role in keeping the local population food secure).[377] During the COVID-19 pandemic, both tariff and non-tariff barriers were established by some states across the world to maintain their internal stability, avoid civil unrest and ensure sufficient food supplies for their population. For example, Russia restricted exports of wheat and Vietnam of rice.[378] In contrast, 'excess' buying of raw commodities by some importers, that is hoarding behaviours, occurred, for example, with the Philippines purchasing excess rice and Egypt and Saudi Arabia acquiring excess wheat to feed their populations.[379] This is despite trade restrictions being deemed to often provide the 'worst possible response to safeguard food security'.[380] Furthermore, due to 90% of UK flights being temporarily grounded, neither agri-food imports nor exports could be transported[381] – which is devastating in the context of perishable goods and contractual commitments.

Yet, generally, supply chains and markets are only addressed to a limited extent within the policies. As discussed in Chapter 3, Section 29 of the Agriculture Act addresses the issue of fair dealing between actors in the supply chain[382] – now looking beyond the producer and primary purchaser. Recognising disparities in bargaining power and the existence of long supply chains is essential, but more is needed. The Scottish stakeholder group (Farming and Food Production – Future Policy Group) notes the significance of all stages of the supply chain and the potential for private actors to also assist with improving the chain,[383] but little

377 Petetin (n172).

378 International Food Policy Research Institute, 'COVID-19 Food Trade Policy Tracker' (IFPRI) www.ifpri.org/project/covid-19-food-trade-policy-tracker accessed 1 May 2021.

379 World Bank, 'Commodity Markets Outlook: Implications of COVID-19 on Commodity Markets' (April 2020) https://openknowledge.worldbank.org/bitstream/handle/10986/33624/CMO-April-2020.pdf accessed 1 May 2021, 10.

380 J. Glauber, D. Laborde, W. Martin and R. Vos, 'COVID-19: Trade Restrictions Are Worst Possible Response to Safeguard Food Security' (IFPRI Blog 27 March 2020) www.ifpri.org/blog/covid-19-trade-restrictions-are-worst-possible-response-safeguard-food-security accessed 1 May 2021.

381 D. Wainwright and A. Homer, 'Coronavirus: Airports "at Risk" of Closure as Flights Drop 90%' (BBC News 21 April 2020) www.bbc.co.uk/news/uk-england-52323416 accessed 1 May 2021.

382 This is also supplemented by Sections 30 to 32 of the Agriculture Act on producer organisations. See also Chapter 3, Section 3.1.1.3.

383 Farming and Food Production – Future Policy Group (n59).

detail is available yet and it remains to be seen whether this is a substantive aspect of their report or taken up by the Scottish Government. Further detail is available in the Welsh and Northern Irish policies.

Wales makes an attempt to improve the resilience of agriculture and the rural economies via its supply chain with its 'Industry & Supply Chain' scheme.[384] In the *Sustainable Farming and Our Land* consultation, the Welsh Government highlighted the existence of a 'good case for supporting the development of the Welsh brand, encouraging collaboration among producers and shortening supply chains'.[385] Issues highlighted include the need locally for more abattoirs and enhanced storage and processing facilities, with proposals to fund capital investments to help address these issues and thereby shorten supply chains and develop resilience.[386] At this stage, the Welsh Government indicated that some of the supply chain measures would fall within the main Sustainable Farming Scheme and some might be funded separately. However, many of the measures proposed were also focused on the provision of information, networking and facilitating others in their efforts to improve the supply chain.[387] In the subsequent *White Paper*, the Welsh Government noted how Wales might be able to 'shorten the supply chain, improve security and retain the value of food produced within Wales based on its local and sustainable credentials'.[388] It expressly links 'enabling wider agri-food industry supports and supply chain; development beyond the farm gate' with the resilience of rural economies and sectors,[389] but then does not expand further on the matter – whether and how it is built upon remains to be seen.

Northern Ireland focuses further on supply chains, with one of its four objectives being 'an integrated, efficient, sustainable, competitive and responsive supply chain, with clear transmission of market signals and an overriding focus on high quality food and the end consumer'.[390] Whilst it states that the supply chain is mainly the responsibility of industry, the *Draft Agricultural Strategy* outlines a couple of measures whereby Northern Ireland could assist – including the provision of information, provision of incentives to 'foster greater cooperation and collaboration within the agri-food supply chain' and regulating against unfair practices.[391] Interestingly, a study on pork in Scotland demonstrated the substantial contribution that collaboration amongst producers and other actors in the supply chain could make towards risk management and thereby to supply

384 *White Paper* (n58) 32 and 35.
385 *Sustainable Farming and Our Land* (n221) 65.
386 Ibid 65 and 68–69.
387 Ibid 69.
388 *White Paper* (n58) 7.
389 Ibid 35.
390 *Draft Agricultural Strategy* (n193) 43.
391 Ibid.

chain resilience.[392] Utilising tools such as fostering collaboration as an attempt to disclaim responsibility, but, if done well, then this could be highly beneficial.

Notably, the more detailed Northern Ireland *Draft Agricultural Strategy* makes no comment about either short supply chains or diversification, even though both would help develop resilience on several fronts, e.g. potentially reducing environmental harms, facilitating food security, buffering from disruptions and helping local communities.[393] However, Minister Poots in Northern Ireland parliamentary debates in November 2020 highlighted the impact of COVID-19 on consumer behaviour, their turn to purchasing local (high quality) food and the significance of trust and confidence in produce – linked to high standards in agricultural production.[394]

One noticeable gap across the policies is that of cross-border issues – within the UK or beyond. This is despite the Northern Ireland *Draft Agricultural Strategy* noting the 'increasing volatility and uncertainty of the trading landscape', including the border on the Island of Ireland and access to EU and other markets.[395] Whilst it is possible to shorten or divert supply chains, cross-border challenges need to be identified and addressed as best possible – there is simply too great a reliance on imported inputs and external markets to ignore.[396] As discussed in Chapter 2, Section 2.3, regarding Northern Ireland and in Chapter 5, Section 5.2, more generally, the impacts of Brexit are already being felt on supply chains and access to markets. While the devolved administrations cannot resolve cross-border matters entirely, as either it relates to a UK internal market matter (raising the issue of common frameworks) or external relationships (largely a reserved matter), some mention of the issues and an outline of their own stance and potential mechanisms within their control might be expected and useful.[397]

Despite rhetoric within the policies about the importance of supply chains, they have yet to deliver on these aspects – perhaps because they do not fit as obviously with the narrative of public money for public goods, or because they are not easily addressed by the individual policies. Nonetheless, if agriculture is to be

392 P. Leat and C. Revoredo-Giha, 'Risk and Resilience in Agri-Food Supply Chains: The Case of the ASDA PorkLink Supply Chain in Scotland' (2013) 18(2) *Supply Chain Management* 219.

393 Petetin (n172). The EU also notes the significance of short supply chains for the resilience of regional and local food systems and reducing dependence on long-haul transportation. European Commission, 'A Farm to Fork Strategy for a Fair, Healthy and Environmentally-Friendly Food System' COM(2020) 381 final, 12–13.

394 Response by Minister Poots in Northern Ireland Assembly (n217).

395 *Draft Agricultural Strategy* (n193) 44.

396 M. Allen, 'Northern Ireland's Agri-Food Sector – Background and Possible "Brexit" Considerations' (Northern Ireland Assembly, Research and Information Service 345-16 Paper 66/16, 22 September 2016) www.niassembly.gov.uk/assembly-business/committees/2016-2017/agriculture-environment-and-rural-affairs/research-papers-2016/northern-irelands-agri-food-sector--background-and-possible-brexit-considerations/ accessed 1 May 2021; and DAERA and NISRA (n186) 57.

397 Trade agreements and the UK internal market are discussed in Chapter 5.

resilient, then the issue of supply chains must be addressed. Short supply chains could help promote environmental and economic resilience and social cohesion; they could also help address concerns regarding borders and trade disruption.

One final related point deserves highlighting, which is the issue of the workforce. Whilst this might not appear to fall within considerations of interconnectedness or multilevel issues, agriculture and related industries rely heavily on international labourers and in particular migrant workers – as noted in Chapter 1. COVID-19 amply highlighted this issue; in many countries around the world, lockdowns, the closing of borders and the grounding of aircraft meant that seasonal agricultural workers could not travel to their usual workplaces.[398] The UK struggled to recruit the 80,000 seasonal workers it needs annually to pick fruit and vegetables and the 'Pick for Britain' campaign only had mixed success.[399] This issue is not addressed directly in the policies, perhaps unsurprisingly as it raises questions over visas and international agreements – that are reserved matters. Yet, it is a matter of fundamental importance to the four nations[400] and there is scope to address elements within the policies, e.g. discussions of incentive schemes or working conditions. Mention is made of the need for training or informed and skilled workforces,[401] but not their availability.[402]

4.5.2 Path dependency

Despite intentions of creating tailored, world-leading policies, the four policies are not entirely independent or original in their content. Elements of path dependency are reflected in the policies and will also likely manifest in future. These are related to the substantial influence of the CAP and the devolved administrations' dependence on financing from Westminster. As with the blunter legal parameters outlined in Chapter 2, these can effectively constrain the four nations in the design and implementation of their policies, potentially undermining the fulfilment of their objectives. Whilst it is not always possible to avoid path dependency, it is essential at least to identify instances of it, understand its significance and reflect on how this can be taken into account within broader strategies. This may eventually enable the four nations to break away from elements of

398 S. Lakner, 'Effects of Coronavirus on Agricultural Production – A First Approximation (part 2)' (Arc 2020, 6 April 2020) www.arc2020.eu/effects-of-coronavirus-on-agricultural-production-a-first-approximation-part-2/ accessed 1 May 2021.

399 Petetin (n172).

400 Petetin and Gravey (n121).

401 *Draft Agricultural Strategy* (n193) 44.

402 Petetin and Gravey (n121). The UK Government extended the pilot scheme for seasonal workers (up to 30,000 persons). However, it still falls short of the 80,000 agricultural workers needed. DEFRA, 'Notice – Seasonal Workers Pilot Request for Information' (5 May 2021) www.gov.uk/government/publications/seasonal-workers-pilot-request-for-information/seasonal-workers-pilot-request-for-information accessed 1 May 2021.

path dependency and beat their own path more effectively – including to achieve resilience.

4.5.2.1 The CAP's shadow of the future

As highlighted in Chapter 1, recent agricultural policies within the UK were developed in the shadow of the CAP – with the overarching frameworks provided by the EU and then flexibility left to the devolved administrations and Westminster to develop and implement these within their own territories. With Brexit, in principle, there is freedom to move away from the CAP and indeed this has been a key ambition within the Leave discourse. However, the CAP was not created by the 27 other EU Member States, with no input from the UK. For instance, the UK played a crucial role in past reforms to green the CAP. It was the first Member State to support environmentally sensitive areas and was keen to embrace cross-compliance to protect habitats and ecosystems from intensive agricultural practices by reducing fertilisers, pesticides and herbicides use.[403] Further, in particular where matters are complex, inertia can set in at least temporarily – without clear, distinct ambitions and pathways to achieve these, it is easy to fall back into well-worn paths instead.

The combined result of these push and pull factors is reflected in the two prongs of the four policies. Thus, a key element within the Agriculture Act or in Wales (and to a lesser extent in Northern Ireland and Scotland) is the public money for public (environmental) goods approach and a move away from direct payments that support farmers' income, which is a central plank of the CAP. However, the public money for public goods approach should not be considered an entirely ground-breaking initiative. It, first, builds upon the AES within Pillar 2 of the CAP and, second, the UK had promoted the concept of public goods within the EU previously,[404] whilst third, future schemes emphasise actions (rather than purely outcomes). Whilst it no doubt brings significant innovations (including regarding governance), it nonetheless does not represent the absolute rejection of the CAP or a fundamental overhaul of policy. The direction of policy appears to have simply switched the two pillars of the CAP,[405] with the renewed focus on actions rather than solely outcomes aiming to provide a guaranteed income to farmers. Even the positive switch under the Agriculture Act to

403 Council Regulation (EEC) 797/85 on Improving the Efficiency of Agricultural Structures [1985] OJ L93/1. It was the first provision to allow support in ecologically vulnerable areas, called environmentally sensitive areas (ESAs). ESAs were actively supported in the UK and authorised under the Agriculture Act 1986.

404 HM Treasury and DEFRA (n70). UK environmental non-governmental organisations have been particularly effective in campaigning for a more sustainable CAP and have long called for the CAP to effectively reflect a 'public money for public goods' model. See E. Fouilleux and M. Ansaloni, 'The Common Agricultural Policy' in M. Cini and N. Pérez-Solórzano Borragán (eds), *European Union Politics* (OUP 2016) 308.

405 Chapter 1.

a multi-annual funding system of five years in order to provide certainty for farmers reflects the multi-annual financial framework of the CAP. Consequently, the path dependency between the UK and the CAP is blatant here and the policies replicate many of the CAP's attributes; these could be both strengths but also weaknesses for farmers, agri-food supply chains and environmental protection. It is essential that policy-makers across the UK do not simply fall back into these paths, but acknowledge continuing similarities and consider and learn from the experiences under the CAP.

However, the CAP is not static and it is under another round of reform (as is the EU more generally with the establishment of a newish EU Commission) and casts a shadow over UK developments.[406] As in the UK, a greater emphasis is placed on the delivery of results or outcomes in relation to environmental and climate action.[407] Thus, under the new CAP Strategic Plans,[408] Member States would link the receipt of financial support to 'tangible results' in line with the Green Deal.[409]

Within Pillar 1, the Basic Payment Scheme under current proposals would take the form of the Basic Income Support for Sustainability.[410] The aim of this income support is to merge cross-compliance and greening requirements into a new instrument called conditionality, where direct payments are given to farmers if SMRs and GAECs in the three areas of 'climate and the environment', 'public health, animal health and plant health' and 'animal welfare' are fulfilled.[411] Ceilings for direct payments under Pillar 1 may also be lower. To protect further the environment, Member States must design and implement eco-schemes (which replace greening requirements) but these will be voluntary for farmers.[412] Pillar 2 remains dedicated to rural development but changes could enable up to 30% of Pillar 1 payments (against 15% at the moment) to be re-allocated for environmental and climate measures. Yet again, environmental obligations are

406 For more on CAP trilogue, see S. Meredith and E. Kollenda, 'CAP Trilogue Negotiations Briefing' (Institute for European Environmental Policy 2021) https://ieep.eu/uploads/articles/attachments/6b0cc89c-8dd0-4efc-a32c-4a23dd9cf078/Briefing%20note%20on%20the%20Common%20Agricultural%20Policy%20trilogue%20negotiations%20(IEEP%202021).pdf?v=63783304864 accessed 1 May 2021.

407 European Commission, 'The Future of Food and Farming' COM(2017) 713, 18.

408 Proposal for a Regulation of the European Parliament and of the Council Establishing Rules on Support for Strategic Plans (n230) 129.

409 European Commission, 'CAP Strategic Plans Recommendations', https://ec.europa.eu/info/food-farming-fisheries/key-policies/common-agricultural-policy/cap-strategic-plans_en#recommendations accessed 1 May 2021. For critique, see A. Matthews, 'Can the Next CAP Help to Achieve Green Deal Targets?' (CAP Reform 18 May 2021) http://capreform.eu/can-the-next-cap-help-to-achieve-green-deal-targets/ accessed 31 May 2021.

410 Proposal for a Regulation of the European Parliament and of the Council Establishing Rules on Support for Strategic Plans (n230) Articles 17–25.

411 Ibid Article 11.

412 Ibid. For more on eco-schemes, see N. Röder and A. Matthews, 'Eco-Schemes a Work in Progress' (CAP Reform 6 January 2021) http://capreform.eu/eco-schemes-a-work-in-progress/ accessed 1 May 2021.

present under both pillars. It is to be hoped that what is proposed is more effective than the current system.[413]

This CAP reform enables further subsidiarity by giving greater powers to the Member States and their regions. Indeed, the CAP may even be at risk of losing its horizontal nature with the current proposals possibly giving too much autonomy to the Member States. This could potentially lead to divergences across the Member States and the CAP losing its 'commonality'. Also concerns of 'greenwashing'[414] have been raised especially since environmental ambitions would be more dependent on the appetite of Member States and their regions.

More generally, the EU aims to tackle climate change and handle other linked environmental challenges such as biodiversity loss, water and air pollution with its ambitious European Green Deal[415] and Farm to Fork Strategy.[416] The latter focuses on a holistic approach towards the sustainability of food systems with an emphasis on sustainable food consumption, food loss and waste prevention as well as sustainable food processing and distribution.[417] This radical approach towards increased policy coherence is much welcome and needed. In contrast, UK policies have not demonstrated the same appetite for joined-up or integrated approaches, which is leading to disjointed agricultural, food, environmental health and trade policies, especially when designing such policies. Arguably, one

413 European Court of Auditors, 'Greening: A More Complex Income Support Scheme, Not Yet Environmentally Effective' (Special Rapport n. 21/2017); and L. Cole et al., 'A Critical Analysis of the Potential for EU Common Agricultural Policy Measures to Support Wild Pollinators on Farmland' (2020) 57 *Journal of Applied Ecology* 681. Current CAP proposals are also subject to criticism. See European Court of Auditors, 'Opinion No 7/2018 (Pursuant to Article 322(1)(a) TFEU) Concerning Commission Proposals for Regulations Relating to the Common Agricultural Policy for the Post-2020 Period (COM(2018) 392, 393 and 394 final)'.

414 C. Nyssens and B. Dupeux, 'The European Commission Must Not Greenwash the Common Agricultural Policy' (CAP Reform 2020) http://capreform.eu/the-european-commission-must-not-greenwash-the-common-agricultural-policy/ accessed 1 May 2021; and A. Brogan and O. Moore, 'Eco-Scheming – Council Adopts a Position of No Ecological Substance' (Arc 2020, 21 October 2020) www.arc2020.eu/eco-scheming-council-adopts-a-cap-position-of-no-ecological-substance/ accessed 1 May 2021.

415 European Commission, 'The European Green Deal' COM(2019) 640 final.

416 For more on the relationship between the CAP reform and the Green Deal, see European Commission, 'Analysis of Links between CAP Reform and Green Deal' SWD(2020) 93 final.

417 Some key aspects of the Strategy (n394) include the reduction by 2030 of the use and risk of chemical and of more hazardous pesticides by 50%; nutrient losses by 50%; the use of fertilisers 20%; the overall EU sales of antimicrobials for farmed animals and aquaculture of 50%; and to reach 25% of agricultural land under organic farming by the same date. For critique of the Strategy, see H. Schebesta and J.J.L. Candel, 'Game-Changing Potential of the EU's Farm to Fork Strategy' (2020) 1 *Nature Food* 586; and H. Tertsch, 'Farm to Fork Strategy: A Partial Response to Our Farmers' Needs' (Euractiv 27 July 2020) www.euractiv.com/section/politics/opinion/farm-to-fork-strategy-a-partial-response-to-our-farmers-needs/ accessed 1 May 2021.

exception is that the Agriculture Act addresses WTO obligations, however, this is rather limited.

Consequently, post-Brexit, the opportunity arises to learn and build upon both past experiences and parallel reforms – whilst guarding against continued path dependency. In developing more ambitious and more tailored policies, the four nations have the potential to consider, adopt and adapt aspects of the current and future CAP. These should neither be adopted automatically nor rejected out of hand but considered carefully – including how they would operate in the new post-Brexit context. Key elements include the impact of reductions in direct payments and rural development funds (in light of both COVID-19 and Brexit) and how subsidiarity might function to respect devolution and the variations (e.g. in culture, farming types, geographical conditions) across the UK. Similarly, the EU will have the potential to reflect on and learn from the developments across the UK.

4.5.2.2 Financing

The second aspect where path dependency is visible relates to funding from Westminster – including for financial schemes within agricultural policies.[418] Chapter 5 considers how this funding might be determined, e.g. under the Barnett formula or linked to justified needs.[419] However, irrespective of which approach applies, funding from Westminster will either be linked to English payments on a *pro rata* basis or else Westminster/the UK Government will need to deem that the demand for funds is objectively justified (and therefore perhaps that they approve of the policies/schemes). The influence of this reality is already visible in the approaches to financial support within the Agriculture Act and the devolved policies.

Westminster has paved the way in its Agriculture Act, through the policy for England and the Schedules for Wales and Northern Ireland. The question of financial support is integral to any agricultural policy and is reflected in each of the proposals developed across the UK to date. As noted in Chapter 3, whilst not identical, there are considerable similarities visible in the two-pronged approaches[420] – with all of the policies so far looking to environmental outcomes and productivity. The public money for public goods approach is clearly visible across the UK, even if not expressly stated as such. There are also similarities in the treatment of direct payments and of rural development payments, as well as the rhetoric surrounding economic resilience, outcome-based payments, and productivity more generally. This is despite the considerable differences between

418 Chapter 2, Section 2.5.3.
419 Chapter 5, Section 5.2.1.
420 Section 3.2.1. See also Petetin, Gravey and Moore (n109).

farming in England and in the devolved administrations – indeed despite Wales, for instance, noting the significance of their small, family farms.[421]

This is not to say that the policies are identical, for instance, with variations regarding direct payments and changes to agricultural tenancies. Further, to what extent the eventual schemes mirror English approaches remain to be seen, but some seemingly minor yet significant differences are beginning to appear, e.g. the lack of a minimum claim size in Wales (so far)[422] compared to in England[423] (and possibly Northern Ireland).[424] Although the variations remain relatively limited to date, they demonstrate the capacity to move away from the English approach – including more fundamentally. Indeed, Scotland's transitional policy is understandably relatively banal, but there is a stated desire for a 'bespoke' policy, addressing the particular nature of crofts and that may entail 'radical' transformations in their future agricultural policy. How that will manifest remains to be determined.

The devolved administrations need to reflect on their own visions and what will work effectively within their own territories rather than toeing the line so closely – including engaging proactively with the UK Government to ensure their policies are facilitated. This is even more important in light of the controls granted to the Secretary of State under Sections 43 to 45 of the Agriculture Act in ensuring compliance with the Agreement on Agriculture, discussed in Chapter 3.[425] In particular, Section 44 provides for the Secretary of State to impose limits on Amber Box payments (on a UK level and for the four nations), whilst Section 45 grants the Secretary of State powers regarding the classification of payments.[426] It is also exacerbated by further centralising developments regarding complementary funding, such as the Levelling Up Fund,[427] and finance-related provisions in the Internal Market Act discussed in Chapter 5.[428] Whilst some influence by the UK level is inevitable, development of resilient policies mandates the devolved administrations taking greater ownership and tailoring their policies accordingly – including through challenging centralising measures.

421 *White Paper* (n58) 8.

422 *Sustainable Farming and Our Land* (n221) 56–57. It notes that the eligibility criteria were not being determined yet but that one option would be to focus on minimum levels of environmental outcomes, whereby any size of farm would be eligible provided that it could deliver such outcomes.

423 *SFI Paper* (n78). The *Paper* notes that the Sustainable Farming Incentive scheme will only initially be open to those farmers who currently receive support under the Basic Payment Scheme – the latter is limited to farms with a minimum of five hectares.

424 *Draft Agricultural Strategy* (n193) 30.

425 Chapter 3, Section 3.2.1. See also Petetin and Gravey (n121).

426 This is a major simplification of the provisions.

427 Chapter 5, Section 5.2.1.2.

428 Chapter 5, Section 5.2.3.1.2.

4.6 Conclusion

A clear overarching, ambitious objective is required for agricultural policies – one that addresses the very nature of agriculture in today's world and for the future. Resilience has the capacity to act as that objective, providing a holistic lens that reflects the multifunctional nature of farming and its complex interconnections within the ecosystem and society. It crucially also addresses the vulnerabilities posed to and by agriculture, enabling it to withstand future shocks. Consequently, resilience provides the path for transformation towards better (social-ecological services) functioning. A 21st-century, resilient agriculture goes beyond sustainability, beyond the act of farming and also beyond a narrow concept of public goods, to include components such as social-ecological services, net zero, agroecology and agri-food democracy. To achieve this, not only must there be resilience of agricultural systems (very broadly understood), but also the law, policies and governance approaches themselves must both promote resilience and be resilient. However, such forward-looking strategies require a major transformation of farming practices, societal values and approaches to governance.

Brexit provides a chance for such transformation, but such a focus on resilience (or similar concepts) remains largely lacking from the policies to date. The proposed policies demonstrate limited ambitions and largely appear to be framed around an economic approach facilitating a certain laissez-faire attitude, rather than adopting a holistic approach towards agriculture and the agri-food supply chain. Even Wales' resilience is relatively narrow and does not adequately address the social elements, in particular. This narrowness is reflected in the lack of consideration of contextual elements including the variations in the nature of farms or farmers in each nation. A more tailored approach that ensures the resilience of a diversity of farms and farmers is essential to the resilience of agriculture more generally. Further, the practicalities of developing and implementing transformational agricultural policies are proving more difficult than originally thought. The four nations appear to have lost their initial appetite for change, with a watering down of the initial approach to public money for public goods so that farmers will now be paid for actions at times instead of outcomes.

When it comes to governance, numerous facets bear examination, including the role of actors, approaches to land ownership, the existence of baselines and approaches to enforcement. With somewhat differing approaches across the policies, there are opportunities to learn from each other. The most positive aspects are seen in the collaborations on scale and landscape approaches within individual territories, which need to be drawn upon across all policies – this would assist with environmental and social objectives as well as the resilience of actors through, for instance, cooperatives or shortening and improving supply chains. On the other hand, changes in monitoring and enforcement may seem more efficient and proportionate, yet may undermine the system's effectiveness (for example, self-monitoring and loss of cross-compliance) and also impose new burdens on farmers (including self-monitoring). Finally, the policies raise flags regarding interconnectedness – at times ignoring this issue and yet, for instance, reflecting a high dependence between the UK and the CAP and between the UK and the devolved administrations, affecting the potential to adequately tailor policies and their ambition.

Overall, whilst the current four policies have positive elements, they have much greater potential than is currently being realised – both in achieving their own existing aims and also in fulfilling more ambitious visions such as resilience. They are still at an embryonic stage, even in the case of England, due to the dependence on the development of schemes and the potential to amend the legislation. A resilient agriculture demands not merely regular reviews of farming and its context, but also of the policies and subsequent schemes and agreements – it must be an iterative process throughout. Advantage should be taken of the pilot studies, in particular, to reflect on the limitations of the existing policies and how to further develop tailored policies for each of the four nations. However, it is also important to bear in mind that the parameters may shift in the future due to changes in the context of the ratification of new international agreements (including both trade and environmental ones), as is considered in Chapter 5.

5 Shaping governance

Changing contexts for future policies

The four nations have made varied progress to date in developing agricultural policies, as outlined in Chapters 3 and 4. They will continue to evolve and may be overhauled in future, especially if they are to address concerns highlighted in Chapter 4 and, furthermore, achieve resilience. However, in doing so, not only must the four nations reflect on the implications of multilevel governance outlined in Chapter 2, but they must also consider a range of other relevant internal and external parameters, including those that have developed since the United Kingdom (UK) left the European Union (EU).[1]

Crucially, there have been and will continue to be significant developments both in the UK's attempts to negotiate and navigate trade agreements (especially the twists and turns of the new UK/EU Trade and Cooperation Agreement (TCA)[2]) and in its evolving relationships with the devolved administrations where some considerable recentralisation of powers has occurred. Of particular relevance in international agreements is the question of the level of environmental, food and animal welfare standards, as well as labelling, that are and will be required for products to enter the UK and the extent to which such issues and decision-making involve and impact the devolved administrations. It is essential to highlight the implications of these developments to date and how they might continue to evolve to facilitate (or impede) resilient agricultural policies within the UK.

These legal and political developments create new parameters for the policies and can also impact more directly on agricultural policies and practices and their potential for resilience. It is worth recalling that resilience in this context would not merely demand high standards with suitable buffers across a range of areas, but simultaneously access to diverse (and valuable) markets and supply chains, meaningful stakeholder engagement (including by relevant political bodies),

1 And some that were already in place.

2 Trade and Cooperation Agreement between the European Union and the European Atomic Energy Community, of the One Part, and the United Kingdom of Great Britain and Northern Ireland, of the Other Part [2020] OJ L 444/14.

DOI: 10.4324/9780429503719-5

political accountability and integrated and coherent multilevel decision-making – numerous big, but important, asks.

5.1 The UK's altered trading relationships

The UK is not self-sufficient and relies on agri-food imports to ensure its food security. It also exports to countries around the world to ensure other countries' food security.[3] The UK faces increased challenges within the international community due to changes to its now weaker (and more isolated) economic position, its relationships with existing and future trading partners and increased volatility in agricultural markets. World Trade Organization (WTO) law and existing and future trade agreements also place constraints on UK agri-food policies and law. There are three main axes to the UK setting up its own trade policy – its own tariff schedule, its relationship with the EU and its relationship with the rest of the world. However, when setting such policy, recurrent issues around the level of environmental, food or animal welfare standards and labelling requirements have arisen, which could lead to the UK facing legal challenges in the WTO.[4]

5.1.1 The UK trade policy, its impact on agriculture and the role of the devolved administrations

On 1 January 2021, the UK Global Tariff or most favoured nation (MFN) tariff regime[5] and schedule of concessions replaced the EU Common External Tariff (CET). These tariffs apply to goods imported from countries with which the UK has not concluded a free trade agreement (FTA). The UK Global Tariff is specifically tailored to the UK economy and aims to facilitate international trade, ease administrative burdens, simplify the process for exporters and overall reduce red tape by removing some tariff variations, rounding tariffs down to standardised percentages, removing all tariffs below 2% and eliminating tariffs on products not (or scarcely) produced in the UK such as olives.[6]

New tariffs on agricultural products align reasonably closely with EU tariffs and provide a relative certainty and protection to the UK agri-food industry and

3 See Chapter 1.

4 Challenges may of course also be possible under individual trade agreements, but the WTO regime is the main one of relevance.

5 This MFN schedule published in early 2020 assumed that a trade agreement would be reached with the EU when this appeared very uncertain considering the stalemate in negotiations at the time. Generally, MFN tariffs are imposed on imports from other WTO Members, unless the Member is part of a customs union or free trade area. Consequently, MFN tariffs are the highest (most restrictive) that WTO Members can impose on one another.

6 Department for International Trade and HM Treasury, 'The Government Has Announced the UK's New MFN Tariff Regime, the UK Global Tariff (UKGT)' (19 May 2020) www.gov.uk/government/news/uk-global-tariff-backs-uk-businesses-and-consumers accessed 1 May 2021.

some relief in comparison to the 2019 draft tariffs, which would have liberalised trade in agri-food products in the UK.[7] These latest tariffs ensure a certain protection for UK farmers from world markets and cheaper imports. However, the UK Government has removed the variable EU tariff that can be applied on certain feed grains when world prices are low. At the height of the COVID-19 pandemic, the EU used this tool to increase its tariff on maize, sorghum and rye from €0 to €5.27/tonne to protect EU farmers from cheaper imports.[8] Removing variable tariffs could therefore increase pressures on arable farmers already badly affected by COVID-19 and highly variable, often extreme climatic events.[9]

Countries that trade with the UK without any preferential market access saw some changes to the applicable tariffs – generally positive. The average tariff for agricultural products is slightly reduced from 18.3% under the CET to 16% under the UK Global Tariff, whilst the tariff-free lines for such products increased from 16% to 23% – liberalising further UK imports in agri-food products.[10] Similarly, tariffs for processed agricultural products have dropped from 15.9% to 10.6%, whilst tariff-free lines rose from 29% to 41%.[11]

Crashing out without a trade agreement between the UK and the EU would have been disastrous to the EU but especially for agri-food supply chains in Great Britain since the EU is such an important trade partner for the UK in this field. Trade between Great Britain and the EU would have reverted back to trading on WTO terms and exiting tariffs (Northern Ireland being treated differently under the Protocol, as discussed in Chapter 2, Section 2.3). Therefore, the UK would have applied its MFN tariffs to EU products entering Great Britain. This would have meant that all the agri-food products originating from the EU would have been subject to these tariffs when exported to Great Britain, leading to increased prices for consumers and could have threatened food security in Great Britain (and arguably the UK) due to changes in the agri-food supply chain. Indeed, the British Retail Consortium indicated that the application of these tariffs to imports

7 HM Revenue & Customs (2019), 'Tax Information and Impact Note for the UK Tariff 2019' (13 March 2019) www.gov.uk/government/publications/tax-information-and-impact-note-for-the-uk-tariff-2019/tax-information-and-impact-note-for-the-uk-tariff-2019--2 accessed 1 May 2021.

8 European Commission, 'Maize, Sorghum and Rye Import Duties Updated by the European Commission' (27 April 2020) https://ec.europa.eu/info/news/maize-sorghum-and-rye-import-duties-updated-european-commission-2020-apr-27_en accessed 1 May 2021.

9 National Farmers' Union, 'NFU Insight: The UK's Global Tariff Schedule' (2020) www.nfuonline.com/news/eu-exit/eu-exit-news/nfu-insight-the-uks-global-tariff-schedule/ accessed 1 May 2021.

10 Department for International Trade, 'Public Consultation: MFN Tariff Policy – The UK Global Tariff (Government Response and Policy)' (May 2020) https://assets.publishing.service.gov.uk/government/uploads/system/uploads/attachment_data/file/885943/Public_consultation_on_the_UK_Global_Tariff_government_response.pdf accessed 1 May 2021, 10.

11 Ibid. Tariff and tariff-free lines for industrial goods follow the same pattern.

from the EU would raise costs by £3.1 billion a year unless a trade agreement was reached.[12]

The corollary is that the EU would have imposed its CET on products from Great Britain – likely reducing the attractiveness of these products for consumers due to their higher prices and making Great Britain producers less competitive and the implementation of the Northern Ireland Protocol[13] even more complicated.

EU levels of tariffs under WTO rules vary widely, but they are particularly high for meat and dairy. On average, a tariff of 12.8% plus €1,713 per tonne for British lamb exports to the EU would be imposed – almost tripling the price of lamb for EU consumers. This would have particularly affected Wales which exports 40% of its lamb, with 90% of those exports going to the EU;[14] and would have exacerbated the situation of sheep farmers, especially in Wales.

Overall, British products would have been less competitive on the EU markets and imports of EU products would have been more expensive for British consumers. Whilst the MFN schedule would have facilitated trade beyond the EU (slight decrease in tariffs relative to the EU CET), it would have thereby hindered trade with the EU (introduction of tariffs).[15]

As observed in Chapter 2, Section 2.4, tariff-rate quotas (TRQs) for agricultural products were introduced when the tariffication process occurred. The apportionment of the EU TRQs has proven problematic. In 2019, the EU and the UK agreed to a division of TRQs[16] but multiple WTO Members expressed their concerns because it had the possibility to change the balance of concessions between Members.[17] In early 2021, progress was made on such apportionment

12 F. Islam, 'Shoppers Could Pay More after No-Deal Brexit' (BBC News 25 September 2020) https://www.bbc.co.uk/news/business-54287283 accessed 1 May 2021.

13 Protocol on Ireland/Northern Ireland to the Agreement on the withdrawal of the United Kingdom of Great Britain and Northern Ireland from the European Union and the European Atomic Energy Community [2019] OJ C384I /1.

14 D. James, 'No-Deal Brexit Would "Kill" Welsh Lamb Trade' (Farmers Weekly 20 July 2020) www.fwi.co.uk/news/why-no-deal-brexit-would-be-disastrous-for-welsh-lamb accessed 1 May 2021.

15 This remains a possibility if issues around implementation and compliance with the TCA intensify.

16 Regulation (EU) No 2019/216 of the European Parliament and of the Council of 30 January 2019 on the Apportionment of Tariff Rate Quotas Included in the WTO Schedule of the Union Following the Withdrawal of the United Kingdom from the Union and Amending Council Regulation (EC) No 32/2000 [2019] OJ L38/1; Commission Implementing Regulation (EU) No 2019/386 of 11 March 2019 Laying Down Rules with Regard to the Apportionment of Tariff Rate Quotas for Certain Agricultural Products Included in the WTO Schedule of the Union Following the Withdrawal of the United Kingdom from the Union and with Regard to Import Licences Issued and Import Rights Allocated under those Tariff Rate Quotas [2019] OJ L70/4; Commission Implementing Regulation (EU) 2019/653 of 24 April 2019 Amending Regulation (EC) No 847/2006 as Regards the Union Tariff Quotas for Certain Prepared or Preserved Fish [2019] OJ L110/34.

17 WTO Council for Trade in Goods, 'Members Call on EU and UK to Use Brexit Extension to Resolve Market Access Concerns' (12 April 2019) www.wto.org/english/news_e/news19_e/good_12apr19_e.htm accessed 1 May 2021.

between the EU and the UK on trade flows with 22 WTO Members.[18] A turning point in the discussions was the signature of the TCA. Crucially the Agreement enables EU and UK TRQs to only be counted once (and not twice) when foreign products are traded between the two parties.[19] This is likely to have diminished the discontent of some Members.

Trade policy and trade agreements increasingly address several areas that fall within devolved competences. This is certainly the case for the farming and agri-food sector. The setting of tariffs and trade policy by the UK Government directly impacts farmers and the rest of the agri-food supply chain across the four nations, whilst the input of the devolved administrations into their design has been rather limited. Further, rules negotiated on issues such as agricultural support and agri-food standards, for example, have to be implemented at a devolved level. This is why copper-fastening the UK internal market, via the UK Internal Market Act 2020 and common frameworks, has been a key priority of the UK Government. Some level of cooperation is needed to avoid conflicts between the central government and devolved administrations as regards the implementation of international obligations resulting from trade agreements and tariff setting.[20] Without this, not only is the implementation of individual FTAs threatened and the UK opened up to litigation, but potential trading partners may be hesitant to conclude agreements. But involvement with the devolved administrations has so far been sporadic. There is a lack of formal mechanisms for the devolved administrations to feed into the formulation of trade policy (including tariffs) and future trade negotiations.

5.1.2 An overhauled relationship with the EU: the TCA and beyond

Whilst the UK/EU Withdrawal Agreement primarily provides only a guide to the future relationship,[21] the Northern Ireland Protocol remains post-transition and continues to govern aspects of the relationships on the Island of Ireland and thereby with the rest of the EU.[22] There is significant interdependence between the UK and the EU and access to the EU market is extremely valuable – especially

18 European Commission, 'The European Union and the United States Conclude Negotiations on Agricultural Quotas Agreement' (8 March 2021) https://ec.europa.eu/commission/presscorner/detail/en/IP_21_987 accessed 1 May 2021.

19 TCA, Article 54.

20 For more, see B. Melo Araujo, 'UK Post-Brexit Trade Agreements and Devolution' (2019) 39(4) *Legal Studies* 555; and S. Switzer and J.A. McMahon, 'Devolution and Post-Brexit Trade Agreements: Towards a Joint Trade Policy Committee?' (2019) 23 *Edinburgh Law Review* 266.

21 As noted in Chapter 2, one exception is the protection of geographical indications after the end of the transition period. See Agreement on the Withdrawal of the United Kingdom of Great Britain and Northern Ireland from the European Union and the European Atomic Energy Community [2019] OJ C384I /1, Article 54.2.

22 For more, see M. Thimont Jack and J. Rutter, 'Managing the UK's Relationship with the European Union' (Institute for Government February 2021) www.instituteforgovernment.org.uk/publications/managing-uk-eu-relationship accessed 1 May 2021.

for agri-food products. Maintaining preferential access to the EU market is vital for the agri-food supply chain and vice versa to maintain food security in the UK and promote resilience. The ratification of the TCA alleviates some but not all of these concerns and attention is now paid to the role of tariff and non-tariff barriers, the level playing field provisions as well as the long-term impact of the Agreement.

5.1.2.1 The importance of the TCA

As noted in Chapter 1, the TCA is the first FTA in the world that re-erects barriers to trade between parties rather than creating greater trade liberalisation between them. This point yet again highlights the sui-generis nature of Brexit. The major shift from the single market and customs union to free trade has deeply impacted trade between the parties. UK exports plummeted in January 2021 but by February 2021 exports has started to pick up albeit still being much lower than previous years – despite an increase in exports from Northern Ireland to the Republic of Ireland.[23] The UK remains, nonetheless, the largest and closest trading partner of the EU. The reorganisation of supply chains across both parties, especially in the agri-food sectors, has been immense.

More generally, the TCA is an Agreement that will evolve over time due to its governance architecture, its horizontal institutional framework and the key role of the Partnership Council in particular.[24] Many aspects of the TCA are left in the hands of the Partnership Council, the various Committees and working groups established.[25] Numerous provisions call for continuous discussions and negotiations between the two parties, for example, in relation to the management of fish stocks, security or governance. The TCA is meant to evolve as time passes; it is not an Agreement stuck in time.

23 Office for National Statistics, 'UK Trade: February 2021' (13 April 2021) www.ons.gov.uk/economy/nationalaccounts/balanceofpayments/bulletins/uktrade/february2021 accessed 1 May 2021.

24 TCA, Part One, Title III. For more, see F. Fabbrini (eds), *The Law & Politics of Brexit: Volume III – The Framework of New EU-UK Relationships* (OUP 2021); S. Fella et al., 'The UK-EU Trade and Cooperation Agreement: Summary and Implementation' (House of Commons Library, CBP-92106, 30 December 2020) https://commonslibrary.parliament.uk/research-briefings/cbp-9106-2/ accessed 1 May 2021; and, more generally, see S. Gstöhl and D. Phinnemore, 'The Future EU-UK Partnership: A Historical Institutionalist Perspective' (2021) 43(1) *Journal of European Integration* 99.

25 Article 8 of the TCA creates six committees related to the trade in goods: the Trade Specialised Committee on Goods; the Trade Specialised Committee on Customs Cooperation and Rules of Origin; the Trade Specialised Committee on Sanitary and Phytosanitary Measures; the Trade Specialised Committee on Technical Barriers to Trade; the Trade Specialised Committee on Level Playing Field for Open and Fair Competition and Sustainable Development; and the Trade Specialised Committee on Administrative Cooperation in VAT and Recovery of Taxes and Duties.

It is often claimed that with the European Union (Withdrawal) Act 2018,[26] the UK has incorporated the EU regulatory acquis, so trade could have remained the same from 1 January 2021 due to a lack of regulatory differences at that point. However, this was simply not possible because the legal basis of the relationship between the UK and the EU has fundamentally been altered from being underpinned by EU law and its single market and customs union to a free trade area with the TCA. It is that dramatic overhaul in the legal basis for the new relationship that creates 'red tape', modifies governance structures and increases the costs for supply chains within both parties despite the existence of the same regulatory standards at least initially.

It is also critical to bear in mind the relationship between the Northern Ireland Protocol and the TCA, where Northern Ireland is *de facto* remaining in the EU single market but part of the UK customs union.[27] Consequently, Northern Ireland applies two customs regimes with a border effectively created in the Irish Sea.

5.1.2.2 Tariffs and rules of origin requirements

Importantly for the agri-food supply chain, the TCA prohibits tariffs[28] and quantitative restrictions (quotas) for UK and EU goods that meet rules of origin requirements.[29] If rules of origin requirements are not met, products cannot be considered as originating and tariffs apply. To this extent, the TCA is an Agreement that is more wide-ranging than any other EU FTA. However, rules of origin requirements are particularly difficult to fulfil for composite and processed foods such as sandwiches or pizzas, which may contain ingredients from all around the globe.[30] In contrast, wholly obtained goods such as live animals or whole vegetables and fruits automatically qualify for preferential treatment if originating in the EU and/or the UK. Crucially, these rules generate 'an incentive to use locally produced inputs in the production of food and drink for export

26 European Union (Withdrawal) Act 2018, Sections 2 and 3.

27 For more on the impact of the Northern Ireland Protocol, see Chapter 2, Section 2.3.

28 TCA, Article 21. However, tariffs can be reinstated as a sanction for the non-respect of the level playing field provisions.

29 The rules of origin help identify goods eligible for preferential market access. For whole agricultural products, for example, the test of product origin will be whether they are unprocessed and harvested in the country. To determine product origin in the case of processed and manufactured goods, the principle of a 'last substantial transformation' applies. This means that the country where the 'last substantial transformation' occurs can claim the tariff preference. See Kyoto Convention of the Customs Cooperation Council (1973) (now known as the WCO). For more on rules of origin, see J. Basquill, 'Rules of Origin: A Brexit Headache for UK Exporters' (*Global Trade Review* 18 September 2020) www.gtreview.com/supplements/gtr-europe-2020/rules-origin-brexit-headache-uk-exporters/ accessed 1 May 2021.

30 TCA, Part Two, Title I, Chapter 2. The value added required to claim origin is different for each product.

to ensure eligibility for the zero-tariff preference'.[31] In the long term, this could positively lead to the strengthening of domestic agri-food industries and overall UK food security.[32] It could also lead to increased short supply chains, which could help promote resilience as discussed in Chapter 4.

To help reach the 'value-added' or 'originating' threshold under rules of origin requirements, bilateral cumulation applies under the TCA.[33] This allows goods from one party to be treated as if originating in the other party when determining whether the goods are 'originating' and qualify for preferential trade terms under the Agreement.[34] EU content (both material and processing) is counted as UK content in UK products exported to the EU, and vice versa. For example, Italian olives, which are processed into oil in the UK, could be considered as originating in the UK and be exported to the EU tariff-free. Content from third countries does not count as originating.

Due to the interconnectedness of the UK–EU agri-food supply chains, it is important to note that EU agri-food products, which are exported to the UK with no tariff, that are subsequently sold again into the EU, would face tariffs unless they have been substantially transformed. According to Melo Araujo, '[f]or many UK-EU traders, accepting tariffs may be easier than trying to comply'.[35] If this were to happen, both UK and EU agri-food products would face high MFN tariffs, impacting the prices paid by consumers and the competitiveness of products.

A major consequence of having rules of origin in place for UK–EU trade is that goods are now being checked on their origin – whilst under EU membership this was not the case – exacerbating trade flows and agri-food supply chains in particular due to their intricacies. As noted, these rules are complex and so are the checks to verify the origins of products.

31 A. Matthews, 'The EU-UK Trade and Cooperation Agreement' (13 January 2021) http://capreform.eu/the-eu-uk-trade-and-cooperation-agreement/ accessed 1 May 2021.

32 Institute of Welsh Affairs, 'Brexit and Trade: It's Even More Complicated than We Thought' (1 April 2019) www.iwa.wales/agenda/2019/04/brexit-and-trade-its-even-more-complicated-than-we-thought/ accessed 1 May 2021.

33 TCA, Article 40.

34 Basic rules of origin establish that only products either produced entirely or substantially transformed in a specific country may be considered as originating in that country. Cumulation constitutes a departure from these basic rules due to the extent of the interweave of existing supply chains, including for agri-food products. It is common for a product to be the result of inputs from multiple countries. The main aim of cumulation is to allow the components or processes contributed by different countries to be combined to meet the threshold for the product to be considered as originating in the final country of production.

35 B. Melo Araujo, 'Brexit Trade Problems: What's Gone Wrong and Can it Be Fixed? (The Conversation 14 January 2021) https://theconversation.com/brexit-trade-problems-whats-gone-wrong-and-can-it-be-fixed-153270 accessed 1 May 2021.

5.1.2.3 The incoming tide of non-tariff barriers

Challengingly, the Agreement reinstates customs formalities (including entry and exit summary declarations) and multiple administrative burdens at the border. These include security declarations, permits and licenses, conformity assessments, changes to value-added tax (VAT) treatment and biosecurity checks and inspections on agri-food products (including live animals, plants, food and feed), such as veterinary certifications, to comply with sanitary and phytosanitary (SPS) measures intended to prevent the spread of diseases and pests,[36] on top of the rules of origin procedures mentioned above. This effectively means that non-tariff barriers were re-erected between Great Britain and the EU.[37] The UK Government, farmers, food producers and processors, hauliers and commercial drivers face an Agreement with the EU that is not as financially and economically advantageous as when the UK was an EU member.[38]

As noted in Chapter 2, it is important to bear in mind that the TCA is complemented by the Northern Ireland Protocol and the EU-UK Joint Committee's progress on the implementation of the Protocol, especially in applying grace periods for specific (mostly agri-food) products and in providing flexibility in determining whether goods are 'at risk' or not of being transported from Great Britain via Northern Ireland into the EU. As such, the ongoing obstacles along the Irish Sea border are currently neither as restrictive as they might have been (if the Joint Committee had not made the progress it did) nor as they will be in the future (after the grace periods end).[39] All of these elements add to the complexities of the supply chains and puts the viability of businesses at risk.

The regulatory autonomy, that is the freedom to regulate wanted by the UK Government, means there is no longer mutual recognition of goods between the two parties or equivalence of standards (beyond the Sanitary and Phytosanitary (SPS Agreement) and the Technical Barriers to Trade (TBT) Agreements[40]). As a consequence and problematically, the TCA builds minimally upon the TBT Agreement (including conformity assessment, labelling and packaging requirements, certification and inspection procedures and product specifications) and

36 M. Dobbs and L. Petetin, 'Agriculture: Environmental, Food and Animal Health Standards' in H. Kassin, A. Jordan A and S. Ennis (eds), 'UK Regulation after Brexit' (The UK in a Changing Europe 25 February 2021) https://ukandeu.ac.uk/wp-content/uploads/2021/02/UK-regulation-after-Brexit.pdf accessed 1 May 2021, 51.

37 Because trade between Northern Ireland and the EU and vice versa falls under the scope of the Northern Ireland Protocol. Barriers between Great Britain and Northern Ireland are discussed in Chapter 2, Section 2.3.

38 European Commission, 'EU-UK Relations: Big Changes Compared to Benefits of EU Membership (Checklist)' (December 2020).

39 T. Edgington and C. Morris, 'Brexit: What is the Northern Ireland Protocol and Why Are There Checks?' (BBC News 15 March 2021) www.bbc.co.uk/news/explainers-53724381 accessed 1 May 2021.

40 Respectively, Uruguay Round Agreement on the Application of Sanitary and Phytosanitary Measures (1994); and Uruguay Round Agreement on Technical Barriers to Trade (1994).

the SPS Agreement only to the extent that annexes on the chemical, organic produce and wine sectors create closer relationships.[41] Further, in relation to technical barriers to trade, many goods have to undergo two sets of conformity assessments (in the UK and in the EU). Trade facilitation provisions, nonetheless, alleviate some of the procedures by enabling low-risk products to be self-certified and encouraging both parties to comply with standards set by international standardisation bodies.[42]

In comparison to what existed under EU law, there is now a lack of agri-food *equivalence* for SPS measures between the two parties; consequently, border controls are more regular and intense.[43] This sharply contrasts with the SPS provisions that include some equivalence in the EU New Zealand FTA Proposal,[44] the EU-Canada Comprehensive Economic and Trade Agreement (CETA)[45] or the Comprehensive and Progressive Agreement for Trans-Pacific Partnership (CPTPP).[46] In the TCA, there is no recognition by the importing party of the equivalence of the exporting party's SPS measures as meeting a similar level of protection as the importing party's level of protection. This means that, for instance, meat and poultry processing standards to reduce pathogens or residue limits for pesticides in foods originating from either the UK or the EU must be checked when products cross the border – leading to increased trade obstacles and unpredictability of trade. As noted, such a situation is at odds with the fact that, in early 2021, both the UK and EU had the same standards due to EU law and the single market.

Due to these increased procedures and formalities, early on many hauliers in Great Britain paused the transport of goods to both the EU and Northern Ireland as lorries were turned away at ports due to not having the necessary documents.[47] Hauliers now rely on direct journeys from Ireland to France to bypass Great Britain as a 'landbridge' and its bureaucracy and delays at the border and

41 TCA, Part Two, Title I, Chapter 3.

42 If both comply with the same international standard, then the approval of conformity is smoother. See TCA, Part Two, Title I, Chapter 4.

43 Ibid Chapter 3. See also Ministère de l'Agriculture et de l'Alimentation (France), 'Goods Imported from the United Kingdom into the European Union and Entering the EU via France' (November 2020).

44 European Commission, 'European Union's (EU) Proposal for the EU-New Zealand FTA – Chapter XX Sanitary and Phytosanitary Measures' (10 August 2018) https://trade.ec.europa.eu/doclib/docs/2018/december/tradoc_157577.pdf, especially Article X.11 on Equivalence.

45 Comprehensive Economic and Trade Agreement (CETA) between Canada, of the one Part, and the European Union and its Member States, of the other Part (2017), Chapter 5.

46 Comprehensive and Progressive Agreement for Trans-Pacific Partnership (2018), Chapter 7.

47 D. Staunton, 'Brexit: British Hauliers Pause Transport of Goods to EU and NI' (Irish Times 11 January 2021) www.irishtimes.com/news/world/uk/brexit-british-hauliers-pause-transport-of-goods-to-eu-and-ni-1.4455762?mode=amp accessed 1 May 2021.

consequently avoiding Welsh ports such as Holyhead, Fishguard or Pembroke Dock,[48] which negatively impacts the Welsh economy.[49]

All products exported from Great Britain to the EU have to comply with both UK *and* EU technical regulations, as well as regulatory compliance checks and controls and pre-notification requirements, including health certificates.[50] And vice versa. For example, products from Great Britain exported to Northern Ireland and the EU must comply with the Trade Control and Expert System (TRACES),[51] whereas EU products exported to Great Britain have to comply with the import of products, animals, food and feed system (IPAFFS) requirements as well as their respective home systems.[52] Simultaneous compliance with two different systems and rules is likely to increase difficulties and costs for agri-food businesses.[53] Positively, Northern Irish businesses have almost unfettered access to Great Britain and the EU, which could result in increased economic activity for the nation and long-term prosperity.

Designated border check-posts (BCPs) carry out checks and inspections for live animals and animal products between Great Britain and Northern Ireland and between Great Britain and the EU (and vice versa). Despite the UK Government and Northern Ireland's civil service building resources and infrastructure, bottlenecks have occurred, are occurring and will occur – especially at peak times of the year. Further, whilst capacity at BCPs along the Great Britain/EU border has increased, there is still no BCP at ports or airports in Wales.[54] Checks undertaken

48 See R. Lough and P. Halpin, 'After Brexit, Ireland and France Cut out the Middleman – Britain' (Reuters 22 January 2021) https://mobile.reuters.com/article/amp/idUSKBN-29R1ME accessed 1 May 2021.

49 See J. Campbell, 'Brexit: Welsh Ports under Threat from Post-Brexit Trade' (BBC News 25 March 2021) www.bbc.co.uk/news/uk-northern-ireland-56521780 accessed 1 May 2021; and G. Rao, 'How Brexit Has Changed Trade between Britain and Ireland' (Sky News 18 March 2021) https://news.sky.com/story/how-brexit-has-changed-trade-between-britain-and-ireland-12247998 accessed 1 May 2021.

50 DEFRA and Animal and Plant Health Agency, 'Guidance: Importing Animals, Animal Products and High-Risk Food and Feed not of Animal Origin' (31 December 2020) www.gov.uk/guidance/importing-or-moving-live-animals-animal-products-and-high-risk-food-and-feed-not-of-animal-origin accessed 1 May 2021.

51 This is the European Commission's online system that requires sanitary and phytosanitary certification, pre-notification and tracking (importation, exportation and intra-EU trade) of most agri-food products. See European Commission, 'TRACES' https://ec.europa.eu/food/animals/traces_en accessed 1 May 2021.

52 DEFRA and Animal and Plant Health Agency (n50).

53 Dobbs and Petetin (n36).

54 L. Petetin, 'Cloud Nine or Down to Earth? The Implications of a No Deal Brexit on Agriculture' (The UK in a Changing Europe 15 August 2019) https://ukandeu.ac.uk/cloud-nine-or-down-to-earth-the-implications-of-a-no-deal-brexit-on-agriculture/ accessed 1 May 2021. Some progress has been made in relation to the creation of a BCP in Holyhead but discussions are slower in relation to BCPs in Fishguard or Pembroke. See L. Griffiths, 'Written Statement: Announcement of Border Control Post Site Locations' (Welsh Government 12 March 2021) https://gov.wales/written-statement-announcement-border-control-post-site-locations accessed 1 May 2021.

at these posts are crucial to UK biosecurity to manage risks to human, animal and plant life and health and associated risks for the environment. Unless the capacity and infrastructure improve, trade is going to be re-directed via other entry points around the country over the long term (whilst bearing in mind the long-term effects of not being able to recruit EU veterinarians) – putting into question the ability of other ports and BCPs to cope and the consequences on the Welsh economy in particular. This is another reason why, for instance, Irish hauliers want to avoid Wales (and Great Britain), which negatively impacts Irish beef imports into Great Britain.[55]

All these non-tariff barriers lead to long delays for EU products coming into Great Britain and products from Great Britain exported to the EU.[56] The UK Government's slow preparation for the change in the trading relationship is indicated in the phasing in of checks on imports from the EU (especially in BCPs) with (extended) deadlines to late 2021 and 2022[57] – potentially putting UK biosecurity at risk. Similar issues also exist for trade between Northern Ireland and Great Britain due to the Northern Ireland Protocol. Higher costs of products ensue because of longer periods of time needed to transport products across borders (driver and lead time), the heightened likelihood of perishable products being spoiled and livestock becoming more distressed. Changes to logistics and transport have a major domino effect on supply chains. Indeed, after years of proclaiming that there would be frictionless trade between the two systems post-Brexit, the UK Government finally retracted this position in early 2020, acknowledging that there would be increased bureaucracy and costs at the borders with the EU's mainland (even with an agreement with the EU) due to the UK Government's red lines.[58] For example, some areas around Holyhead (with ferries coming and going to Ireland) and in Kent (both regarding ports and the Eurotunnel) are now identified areas for parking lorries to avoid queues of trucks on the roads. At the end of 2020 and until April 2021 a 'Kent Access Permit'[59] was required for lorry drivers to enter Kent. The permit was obligatory for heavy goods vehicles when crossing the Channel border between Great Britain and the

55 S. Carswell, 'Irish Food Trade Could Slide by One-Third if EU and UK Fail to Cut Deal' (Irish Times 1 October 2020) www.irishtimes.com/business/agribusiness-and-food/irish-food-trade-could-slide-by-one-third-if-eu-and-uk-fail-to-cut-deal-1.4368738 accessed 1 May 2021.

56 Institute of Welsh Affairs (n32).

57 See J. Marshall, 'Delaying Brexit Border Checks Solves Some Problems but Creates Others' (Institute for Government 12 March 2021) www.instituteforgovernment.org.uk/blog/delaying-brexit-border-checks accessed 1 May 2021. For an early recognition of the problem see M. Gove, 'Michael Gove Statement on EU Exit Preparations: 13 July 2020' (Cabinet Office 13 July 2020) www.gov.uk/government/speeches/michael-gove-statement-on-eu-exit-preparations-13-july-2020 accessed 1 May 2021.

58 G. Parker, 'Prepare for Brexit Trade Costs and Red Tape, Says Michael Gove' (Financial Times 10 February 2020) www.ft.com/content/37379a1e-4c28-11ea-95a0-43d18ec715f5 accessed 1 May 2021.

59 HC Deb 23 September 2020, voluntary 680, col 966.

EU;[60] it effectively created an(other) internal border within the UK.[61] In April 2021, the Kent Access Permit was abandoned as new rules are better understood and trade flows are positively smoother, despite still taking longer and involving more bureaucracy than in the past.

5.1.2.4 The level playing field provisions: regulatory divergence or a sensitive, dynamic alignment?

The TCA does not compel UK alignment with EU standards *per se* and this delivers on the regulatory autonomy the UK wanted. Broadly speaking, the UK is only bound to comply with international obligations under the WTO or other international (including environmental) agreements. This could have led to a lowering of the regulatory baseline and provided a competitive advantage to UK producers.[62] To ensure the maintenance of fair competition, the EU required the innovative (but also controversial) mechanism of the level playing field to avoid being undercut by the UK. This was really an EU 'red line' due to the large integration of the supply chains, the intertwined trade flows and the geographical proximity of the two parties.[63]

5.1.2.4.1 REGULATORY DIVERGENCE

The scope of Title XI of the TCA on 'level playing field for open and fair competition and sustainable development' includes competition (especially state aid), labour and social standards, and finally environment and climate.[64] Each area includes slightly different provisions and mechanisms to resolve disputes. The level playing field provisions within the TCA are innovative and depart from existing FTAs, especially the establishment of an alternative, autonomous, swift dispute settlement mechanism (more on this below).[65] The provisions represent the agreed compromise between the EU wanting regulatory alignment and the

60 UK Government, 'Check an HGV is Ready to Cross the Border (Kent Access Permit)' (20 April 2021) www.gov.uk/check-hgv-border accessed 1 May 2021.

61 As well as the internal border that effectively exists in the Irish Sea. The delays in implementing the Northern Ireland Protocol also contributed to these barriers. See Chapter 2.

62 P. Mariani and G. Sacerdoti, 'Trade in Goods and Level Playing Field' (Brexit Institute Working Paper *No 7/2021*) https://papers.ssrn.com/sol3/papers.cfm?abstract_id=3797021 accessed 1 May 2021, 7.

63 The EU may have wanted to avoid issues of environmental and social dumping.

64 TCA, Article 355(1). For more on the level playing field, see European Parliament, 'Briefing – The Level Playing Field for Labour and Environment in EU-UK Relations' (April 2021) www.europarl.europa.eu/RegData/etudes/BRIE/2021/690576/EPRS_BRI(2021)690576_EN.pdf accessed 1 May 2021. For an earlier account, see A. Jordan, V. Gravey, B. Moore and C. Reid, 'EU-UK Trade Relations: Why Environmental Policy Regression Will Undermine the Level Playing Field and What the UK Can Do to Limit it' (Brexit and Environment Network Research Paper on the Level Playing Field 2020).

65 TCA, Part Two, Title XI, Chapter 9.

UK wanting to diverge from EU regulations.[66] Within the environmental realm, Article 391 creates a non-regression obligation in environmental matters not to lower the *overall* level of environmental protection (including climate policy).[67] A similar obligation exists for levels of labour and social protection.[68] A common objective to achieve net zero by 2050[69] and agreed cooperation on animal welfare, antimicrobial resistance and sustainable food systems are included in the SPS Chapter.[70]

Under the level playing field and non-regression provisions, the UK (and the devolved administrations) can effectively diverge from EU standards (and vice versa), so long as such divergence does not negatively impact trade or investment. More specifically, UK and EU environmental and climate standards existing at the end of the transition period cannot be 'weaken[ed] or reduc[ed], in a manner affecting trade or investment between the Parties, its environmental levels of protection or its climate level of protection'.[71] Again, there are mirroring provisions for labour and social standards.[72] They constitute the baseline for the purpose of the TCA's level playing field provisions. Three aspects regarding non-regression and the level playing field bear highlighting: (i) the UK is not locked into EU legislation and, as noted, it can diverge from it; (ii) it is only when lower standards impact trade and investment that they could be struck down; and consequently (iii) regulatory divergence and thus regression are therefore possible if not affecting trade or investment.

Interestingly, the Agreement does not refer to the precautionary principle but to a precautionary approach due to what appears to be a refusal on the part of the UK to call it a principle, since footnote 52 to Article 356 states that 'in relation to the implementation of this Agreement in the territory of the Union, the precautionary approach refers to the precautionary principle'.[73] This shift in terminology could alarmingly indicate a downgrading of the role of precaution in policy-making for the UK Government from the role of a principle to the weaker one of an approach.[74] Here the UK position on precaution is closer to that of the United States of America (US) than that of the EU. This could indicate the beginning of a U-turn in the approach towards precaution more generally – departing from EU and devolved practices generally based on precaution,[75] with

66 This also provides an opportunity for the UK to further liberalise its economy.
67 TCA, Article 391.
68 Ibid Article 387.
69 Ibid Article 355(3).
70 Ibid Article 70(2).
71 Ibid Article 391(2).
72 Ibid Article 387(2).
73 Ibid Article 356.
74 For more, see J. Peel, 'Precaution – A Matter of Principle, Approach or Process' (2004) 5(2) *Melbourne Journal of International Law* 483.
75 See M. Dobbs, 'Attaining Subsidiarity-Based Multilevel Governance of Genetically Modified Cultivation?' (2016) 28(2) *Journal of Environmental Law* 245; and L. Petetin, 'Managing Novel Food Technologies and Member States' Interests: Shifting More Powers towards the

a stronger reliance on scientific evidence and risk analysis for SPS measures. A possible easing of regulatory frameworks could be on its way, for example, with gene editing in England[76] or the authorisation of a neonicotinoid (an insecticide) to treat sugar beet seed, although on an emergency basis.[77]

This approach towards precaution reflects the UK Government's general approach to environmental principles in the Environment Bill, entailing a weakening of the role and application of the environmental principles in EU law. Whilst the Environment Bill proposes to introduce domestic provisions on these, the obligation would be far weaker as it would be for Ministers of the Crown to 'have due regard to the policy statement on environmental principles'[78] – a statement which could be amended by the Environment Secretary of State and without adequate parliamentary scrutiny or control. As discussed by Reid in particular, these clauses lead to a considerable weakening of the role of these principles relative to their role under EU law.[79]

5.1.2.4.2 SPECIFIC PROVISIONS RELATING TO AGRICULTURE

In relation to agricultural subsidies, state aid provisions do 'not apply to subsidies that are subject to the provisions of Part IV or Annex 2 of the Agreement on Agriculture'.[80] As noted in Chapter 2, Section 2.4.2.3, Part IV of the WTO Agreement on Agriculture refers to Amber and Blue Box measures, whilst Annex 2 refers to Green Box measures. This means that the TCA does not place supplementary restrictions on financial support given to farmers and levels of support

Member States?' in M. Varju (ed.), *Between Compliance and Particularism: Member State Interests and European Union Law* (Springer 2019) 233.

76 DEFRA, 'Consultation: The Regulation of Genetic Technologies' (8 January 2021) https://consult.defra.gov.uk/agri-food-chain-directorate/the-regulation-of-genetic-technologies/ accessed 1 May 2021.

77 DEFRA, 'Statement on the Decision to Issue – With Strict Conditions – Emergency Authorisation to Use a Product Containing a Neonicotinoid to Treat Sugar Beet Seed in 2021' (8 January 2021) www.gov.uk/government/publications/neonicotinoid-product-as-seed-treatment-for-sugar-beet-emergency-authorisation-application/statement-on-the-decision-to-issue-with-strict-conditions-emergency-authorisation-to-use-a-product-containing-a-neonicotinoid-to-treat-sugar-beet accessed 1 May 2021.

78 Environment Bill 2019–2021, Clause 18. Clause 16 provides further detail on the policy statement.

79 C. Reid, 'Environmental Principles Take Root: Post-Brexit Environmental Governance across the UK (Parts 1 and 2)' (Brexit and Environment Network 14 and 16 July 2020) www.brexitenvironment.co.uk/2020/07/14/environmental-principles-take-root-post-brexit-environmental-governance/ accessed 1 May 2021; and www.brexitenvironment.co.uk/2020/07/16/watchdogs-compared-and-reviewed-post-brexit-environmental-governance-uk/accessed 1 May 2021. For concerns regarding an earlier version of the Bill, see M. Lee, 'The Environment Bill: A Framework for Progressive Environmental Law?' (Brexit and Environment Network 18 October 2019) www.brexitenvironment.co.uk/2019/10/18/framework-progressive-environmental-law/ accessed 1 May 2021.

80 TCA, Article 364(5).

can be maintained (or even increased) by the UK. These provisions sit outside the level playing field obligations and rebalancing mechanisms (discussed below). Consequently, the UK cannot complain about EU agricultural support levels if the EU remains within its WTO commitments and vice versa.[81]

Further in relation to agricultural products, the special agriculture safeguard mechanism (discussed in Chapter 2, Section 2.4.2.2) to protect farmers against surges in imports or price declines below a certain level under Article 5 of the WTO Agreement on Agriculture is reaffirmed in the TCA.[82] The UK (as well as the EU) could protect itself against situations where the quantity or value of agricultural imports suddenly surpasses a specific level. But the issue remains that it is unclear whether the UK can rely on the provision since it is the EU who tariffied the products on behalf of the UK, not the UK *per se*, when the Agreement on Agriculture was ratified.[83]

5.1.2.4.3 RESOLVING DISPUTES

Due to the novelty of the provisions on the level playing field and the potential changes to the basis for environmental, social and laboratory standards, disputes are likely to occur. There are two main mechanisms to resolve disputes relating to the level playing field: a sectoral mechanism linked to non-regression and a rebalancing mechanism.

As noted above in relation to environmental, labour and social protection, non-regression obligations exist. If one party believes that the other has lowered such protection in a way that affects trade or investment, then consultations start. If consultations do not resolve the issue, an expert panel (on the environment or labour and social matters) is established. The decision of the panel is not binding; but if it confirms a breach, the complaining party can adopt swift remedial measures (including the imposition of tariffs and quotas) and can suspend part of the Agreement, which would be crucial to the trade and economic interests of the complaining party.[84]

The rebalancing mechanism results from a more systematic undermining of the level playing field.[85] Over time one party might increase its protection levels, whilst the other does not and be negatively affected by this difference in levels of protection. If there is 'significant divergence' that is 'impacting on trade and investment', the rebalancing procedure may be triggered with consultation and an arbitration tribunal potentially created. After a consultation stage, an arbitration tribunal has 30 days to deliver its ruling.[86]

81 Matthews (n92).
82 TCA, Article 32(7)(a).
83 See Chapter 2, Section 2.4.2.
84 TCA, Articles 408 to 411.
85 Ibid Article 411.
86 Ibid Article 411(2).

The complaining party may proceed *unilaterally* to adopt necessary and proportionate rebalancing measures (including the unilateral imposition of tariffs or quantitative restrictions)[87] in two instances: if the consultation period expires without resolution (and if no arbitration tribunal is created) or if after 30 days there is no decision.[88] The other party may adopt countermeasures until the ruling is delivered. The rebalancing measures and countermeasures are to be adjusted once the decision of the arbitration tribunal is known. If after four years there are too many persistent breaches, a review of the Agreement is possible, which could result in an entire part being suspended.[89]

The thresholds set under the level playing field and the rebalancing mechanisms may be quite high to reach for two reasons. First, it may be particularly difficult to establish that there has effectively been a lowering of environmental, labour or social protection requirements, including the role of environmental principles in the decision-making process, or significant divergence.[90] Second, demonstrating the effect on trade or investment may also prove burdensome and difficult to measure. As a consequence, enforcing such provisions may prove problematic. Another point to make here is that within Title XI, the focus is on proving divergence rather than fostering convergence. This creates uncertainty for businesses. Ultimately, the rebalancing mechanism could create some regulatory alignment by the back door but it may be highly challenging to establish.

5.1.2.4.4 A SENSITIVE, DYNAMIC ALIGNMENT

How much differentiation there may be between the two systems and where the regulatory baseline would lie for each party remains to be seen; a sensitive, dynamic alignment appears a sensible choice[91] and quite likely due to the combination of mechanisms available. The level playing field obligations constitute innovative provisions that 'may help to give a push to raise standards in the Party that is seen as lagging behind'.[92]

Under the level playing field provisions, there is an obligation to 'strive to increase'[93] the parties' levels of environmental, social and labour protection.

87 Ibid Article 411(3)(c).
88 This is a very tight time to consider all the facts of the dispute and ensure a fair judicial process. Consequently, it may be challenging for a tribunal to meet the 30-day deadline, therefore facilitating the imposition of rebalancing measures by the complaining party.
89 TCA, Article 411(4).
90 V. Gravey, 'The Brexit Deal and the Environment: Pretty Ambitious yet Pretty Irrelevant?' (Brexit Institute, DCU 16 February 2021) http://dcubrexitinstitute.eu/2021/02/the-brexit-deal-and-the-environment/ accessed 1 May 2021.
91 A. Engel and L. Petetin, 'International Obligations and Devolved Powers – Ploughing through Competences and GM Crops' (2018) 20(1) *Environmental Law Review* 16, 29.
92 A. Matthews, 'Level Playing Field Provisions in the EU-UK TCA' (CAP Reform 14 January 2021) http://capreform.eu/level-playing-field-provisions-in-the-eu-uk-tca/ accessed 1 May 2021.
93 TCA, Article 387(4) and Article 391(5).

For example, the UK has historically promoted high animal welfare and has consistently pressed for more protection of EU standards in this area.[94] If the UK were to keep this momentum (which has been ongoing for centuries, so this would not come as a surprise) and raise its standards to promote resilience, this could have knock-on effects on the EU. If the UK's increased standards led to significant regulatory divergence and if as a result the UK trade would be negatively impacted, then the UK could rely on rebalancing measures. This would incentivise the EU to stay in line with the UK and thereby ensure a sensitive, dynamic alignment.

Further, the TCA is similar to a Canada-style agreement in its design but broader in scope and includes more ambitious provisions on state aid, the environment and climate standards, tied to conditionality. Through the level playing field mechanism, the EU seeks compliance with its rules and expectations as conditions, which can have legal consequences if such conditions are not fulfilled. Conditionality is thus being utilised by the EU as a tool of governance during EU membership, prior to accession[95] and now also when losing a member. The mechanism further indicates the importance of EU soft powers to export its (environmental, labour and social) standards and its model of good economic governance.

Even without the TCA, a sensitive, dynamic regulatory alignment to EU standards may occur. Many non-EU countries tend to align their standards to those of the EU to facilitate their trade with the EU. This process is called the 'Brussels effect'[96] or 'extraterritoriality of EU law'.[97] Both Bradford and Scott explain the global reach of EU law due to its power to regulate markets and influence regulation beyond the EU. This 'Brussels effect' may ultimately impact the UK's behaviour when wanting to deviate (or not) from EU standards, indicating

94 L. Petetin, 'The Role of the UK in Advocating for Higher Animal Welfare Standards' (Food, Farming & Countryside Commission, Trade Unwrapped 1 December 2020) https://trade-unwrapped.uk/read/the-role-of-the-uk-in-advocating-for-higher-animal-welfare-standards accessed 1 May 2021. See also the recent DEFRA consultation on transportation of live animals, DEFRA, 'Consultation: Improvements to Animal Welfare in Transport' (3 December 2020) https://consult.defra.gov.uk/transforming-farm-animal-health-and-welfare-team/improvements-to-animal-welfare-in-transport/ accessed 1 May 2021. Further, an Animal Welfare (Sentience) Bill was mentioned in the 2021 Queen's Speech. See Prime Minister's Office, 'The Queen's Speech 2021' (11 May 2021) https://assets.publishing.service.gov.uk/government/uploads/system/uploads/attachment_data/file/985029/Queen_s_Speech_2021_-_Background_Briefing_Notes.pdf accessed 1 May 2021, 132.

95 See F. Schimmelfennig and U. Sedelmeier, *The Europeanization of Central and Eastern Europe* (Cornell University Press 2005); and J. Bachtler and C. Mendez, *EU Cohesion Policy and European Integration: The Dynamics of EU Budget and Regional Policy Reform* (Routledge 2013).

96 A. Bradford, *The Brussels Effect: How the European Union Rules the World* (OUP 2020); and A. Bradford, 'The Brussels Effect' (2012) 107 *Northwestern University Law Review* 1.

97 J. Scott, 'The New EU "Extraterritoriality"' (2014) 51(5) *Common Market Law Review* 1343.

the 'EU's influence and market power on a global scale'[98] – possibly leading to a certain UK/EU convergence. It further signifies that the consequences of the 'Brussels effect' are akin to soft-law or act as a soft-law instrument beyond the jurisdiction of the EU by generating legal effects despite having no legal force.

5.1.2.5 *What about the shelf life of the TCA?*

Beyond the non-regression and the level playing field provisions, the Agreement provides for a horizontal, robust mechanism to resolve disputes that may arise between the UK and the EU on the interpretation or implementation of their commitments. Crucially, it creates disincentives for regulatory divergence resulting in disputes. If one party thinks there is a breach of an obligation, a consultation within the Partnership Council starts. If the issue is not solved, an *ad hoc* arbitration tribunal comprising of three arbitrators is set up and its decision is binding.[99] Cross-sector suspension of obligations (or retaliatory tariffs) can be applied in case of violations of the Agreement, as well as a partial suspension of the Agreement.

The Agreement creates a framework agreement that can either be built upon, i.e. supplemented by further agreements between the two parties, or taken apart every five years for trade provisions to be reviewed.[100] A 12-month termination clause can also be triggered by either side.[101] These provisions also add to the possible reviews under the rebalancing mechanism. As such, it is up to the politicians to make it or break it. Negotiations between the two parties are not over and the TCA will keep on evolving over time, creating little stability for businesses. However, this does also open up the possibility of introducing important changes to the TCA if the political will exists – including to facilitate more resilient agriculture, through, for instance, enhancing standards or reducing non-tariff barriers for trade.

The TCA indicates how regaining sovereignty was more important to the UK Government than ensuring a 'frictionless' trade. 'Taking back control' of laws and regulations, including achieving regulatory independence, won over the economy despite the economic downturn due to COVID-19. The ability for the UK to pass its own laws and negotiate trade agreements prevailed over maintaining the *status quo* and certainty for businesses. The Agreement ultimately delivers a somewhat *hard* Brexit, especially from an agricultural and food perspective.[102] In contrast and for the EU, the integrity of the single market is maintained with

98 Engel and Petetin (n91) 29.
99 TCA, Part Six, Title I.
100 Ibid Article 776.
101 Ibid Article 779.
102 This is also the case from an environmental perspective. See M. Dobbs and L. Petetin, "Written Evidence on the Future UK-EU Relations: Energy, Environment and Health' (House of Lords, EU Environment Sub-Committee, EEH0038, February 2021) https://committees.parliament.uk/writtenevidence/22500/pdf/ accessed 1 May 2021.

obligations on the level playing field and fair competition around environmental protection, climate, subsidies, state aid requiring British businesses not to undercut the EU. Yet, the constitutional integrity of the United Kingdom is in jeopardy.[103]

It is likely that the Agreement will lead to multiple disputes either under the horizontal dispute settlement provisions or the level playing field and rebalancing mechanisms. One interesting characteristic (or lack thereof) of the dispute settlement mechanism under the TCA is that natural or legal persons cannot be parties to a dispute (in contrast with investor-state dispute settlement (ISDS) provisions under FTAs).[104] This gap restricts opportunities for UK companies to start or be part of such proceedings when impacted – a key aspect of the Agreement to bear in mind when a dispute arises.

Overall, this new trading regime will have long-lasting, significant ramifications for UK agriculture and its food systems. Naturally, changes to agri-food supply chains created by the TCA, especially in relation to the reinstatement of non-tariff barriers and their economic consequences, remain to be fully seen. Negotiations between the two parties have not stopped with the signature of the TCA. Yet, EU trust has been seriously eroded due to the inconsistencies of the decisions of the UK Government – with the Internal Market Act (discussed below) and the unilateral extensions of the 'grace periods' in Northern Ireland exemplifying this – whilst trust is needed to ensure the good functioning and perennity of the Agreement, including when starting consultations. The damage has been done and it is unclear how it will be fixed. One aspect is certain – the UK will not remain at the top of the EU's agenda. The long-term, future relationship between the UK and the EU remains to be built but will it be acrimonious or pleasant? Time will tell.[105] However, the EU is not the UK's only market and Brexit is opening up other opportunities and challenges.

5.1.3 *Essential relationships with the rest of the world*

As noted in Chapter 2, international law creates obligations for the UK mostly through the WTO, the SPS and TBT Agreements and other FTAs to liberalise trade. In particular, FTAs can facilitate trade significantly, by reducing or eliminating tariff and non-tariff barriers, and therefore are very valuable to conclude. Some of these international obligations tend to be less specific, less onerous and without the same teeth as EU law regarding compliance and enforcement.

103 B. Pontin, 'Legal and Political Conceptions of Governance within the Environmental Act Debate' (2019) 31 *Environmental Law and Management* 85. See also Section 5.2 below.

104 For more, see N. Levrat, 'Governance: Managing Bilateral Relations' (Brexit Institute Working Paper No 10/2021) https://papers.ssrn.com/sol3/papers.cfm?abstract_id=3811236 accessed 1 May 2021.

105 There is a need for the considerations in Chapter 3 to be borne in mind in any future negotiations. In any case, compliance with WTO law would still be required. See Chapter 2, Section 2.4 and the discussion that follows.

Consequently, in some circumstances and under some agreements, access to non-EU markets may pose fewer extra burdens from the perspective of compliance with food, environmental and animal welfare standards when negotiating future trade agreements. However, FTAs also have the potential to raise standards.

5.1.3.1 Rolled-over or continuity FTAs

As an EU Member State, the UK benefitted from preferential market access granted in the context of EU FTAs with third countries. The EU has over 70 such FTAs.[106] Maintaining such agreements for the UK provides some continuity and certainty for UK businesses. If rolled-over or new FTAs were not agreed, the UK risked losing the benefit of preferential tariff treatment and facing MFN tariffs under WTO law applied by the signatories to these agreements, including for agricultural products. This would have meant the erection of often high tariff barriers between the UK and the relevant states, ultimately resulting in increased prices for UK exports and for foreign products entering the UK, thereby increasing costs for consumers. MFN tariffs on agricultural products can be quite significant. A United Nations Conference on Trade and Development (UNCTAD) study showed that the average applied tariff for agricultural products by developed, developing and least developed countries stood at 12%, 16% and 12%, respectively.[107]

The UK, surprisingly, had the capacity to undertake many bilateral negotiations and successfully negotiated multiple rolled-over FTAs (that is, signed new bilateral trade agreements with the EU's current FTA partners under the same terms) – whilst concomitantly negotiating its future trading relationship with the EU, the US and other countries.[108] The key rolled-over FTAs (in terms of UK trade with these respective countries) are with Canada, Switzerland, Iceland and Norway, South Africa and South Korea.

106 European Commission, 'Negotiations and Agreements' https://ec.europa.eu/trade/policy/countries-and-regions/negotiations-and-agreements/index_en.htm accessed 1 May 2021.

107 UNCTAD, 'Comparison of MFN Bound and Applied Tariffs Trade Weighted Averages on Agricultural Products of Developed, Developing and Least Developed Countries (LDCs): Current Status Reference' (UNCTAD Discussion Paper 22 September 2014) http://unctad.org/meetings/en/Contribution/tdb61_c03_UNCTAD.pdf accessed 1 May 2021.

108 Department for International Trade, 'Guidance: Existing UK Trade Agreements with Non-EU Countries' (29 January 2020) www.gov.uk/guidance/uk-trade-agreements-with-non-eu-countries accessed 1 May 2021.

5.1.3.2 Other FTAs

Other FTAs are to be completely renegotiated. In this instance, the *status quo* is not maintained for UK businesses, creating more uncertainty and possibly more barriers – making trading more difficult.[109]

Positively, the UK-Japan Comprehensive Economic Partnership Agreement 2020 (CEPA)[110] is the first new trade agreement that the UK has signed (since all the others were rolled-over agreements) in September 2020. It should, nonetheless, be noted that this Agreement only improves UK GDP by 0.07% (£1.5 billion) according to the UK Government's forecast.[111] The Agreement could lead to increased opportunities for UK agricultural exports and ensure their protection after entering Japan. UK pork and beef exports benefit from tariff reductions. Agri-food products receive increased protection under the Agreement with up to 70 geographical indications (compared to seven under the terms of the EU and Japan Economic Partnership Agreement) covering English sparkling wine, Stilton cheese, Yorkshire Wensleydale and Welsh lamb. Crucially, UK exports to Japan that contain EU components or ingredients count as goods originating from the UK – further facilitating UK exports to Japan under rules of origin and cumulation. Similar rules on Japanese products also apply to their products, facilitating Japanese exports to the UK.[112] However, it is worth noting that the direct and indirect costs (for instance, increased bureaucracy and traceability) of complying with the rules of origin under the UK-Japan agreement might be considerable and may affect business decisions on whether to export to Japan.[113] Further, in June 2021, the UK secured a new trade agreement with Norway, Iceland and Liechtenstein.[114]

109 It should be noted that both rolled-over and new free trade agreements only entered into force after the end of the transition period. Further, the consequences of ISDS provisions in (existing and future) agreements should be carefully considered. For more the relationship between sustainable agriculture and EU free trade agreements, see L. Ferraris, *The Pursuit of Sustainable Agriculture in EU Free Trade Agreements* (Wageningen Academic 2020). More generally on the EU trade policy, see B. Melo Araujo, *The EU Deep Trade Agenda: Law and Policy* (OUP 2016).

110 This Agreement, however, largely replicates the 2019 EU-Japan Economic Partnership Agreement, which explains the speed at which it was concluded.

111 HM Government, 'UK-Japan Free Trade Agreement: The UK's Strategic Approach' (4 January 2021) www.gov.uk/government/publications/uks-approach-to-negotiating-a-free-trade-agreement-with-japan/uk-japan-free-trade-agreement-the-uks-strategic-approach accessed 1 May 2021.

112 UK-Japan Comprehensive Economic Partnership Agreement 2020, Chapter 3 on Rules of Origin.

113 This is also a consideration for other trade agreements.

114 Department for International Trade, 'UK Secures New Deal with Norway, Iceland and Liechtenstein' (4 June 2021) www.gov.uk/government/news/uk-secures-new-deal-with-norway-iceland-and-liechtenstein accessed 7 June 2021.

In June 2021, the UK and Australia published a Trade Agreement in principle.[115] The Agreement will further liberalise trade in agricultural products between the two countries, with the elimination of tariffs (apart from long-grain rice) over a 15-year period and with tariff-rate quotas increasing over the same period to enable farmers to get used to the change in competitive conditions/trading environment.[116] Positively UK farmers will be able to export to Australia tariff-free over the medium- to long-term, but controversially issues around the levels of environmental, food and animal welfare standards arise, especially with the equivalence of certain SPS standards between the two countries.[117] It is also important to bear in mind that the Agreement is predicted to only boost the UK economy by a maximum of 0.02% over 15 years.[118] Crucially, trade negotiations with countries like the US could expect similar, tariff-free deals, liberalising UK agriculture even further.

The UK has started the formal procedure to request access to the Comprehensive and Progressive Agreement for Trans-Pacific Partnership 2018 (CPTPP).[119] The CPTPP is an FTA between eleven countries along the Pacific Rim: Canada, Mexico, Peru, Chile, New Zealand, Australia, Brunei, Singapore, Malaysia, Vietnam and Japan.[120] Joining the Agreement could be economically advantageous for the UK since it represents 13% of the world gross domestic product.[121] The Trade Agreement with Australia paves the way to joining the CPTPP. It should, nonetheless, be noted that the CPTPP is not 'simply' one agreement but also contains numerous bilateral agreements between each country party to the CPTPP and the CPTPP itself; it is rather an intricate affair. The Agreement includes market access commitments to reduce or eliminate tariffs, to not apply restrictions or prohibitions on the import or export of goods, and to treat imported products no less favourably than similar goods produced domestically (national treatment). Some agri-food products retain some protection; for instance, Japan keeps tariffs on rice and Canada on its dairy products. To this

115 At the time of writing, the precise content of the Agreement remains unknown.

116 Department for International Trade, 'UK-Australia FTA Negotiations: Agreement in Principle' (17 June 2021) www.gov.uk/government/publications/uk-australia-free-trade-agreement-negotiations-agreement-in-principle/uk-australia-fta-negotiations-agreement-in-principle accessed 18 June 2021.

117 Ibid.

118 Department for International Trade, 'UK-Australia Free Trade Agreement: The UK's Strategic Approach' (17 July 2020) www.gov.uk/government/publications/uks-approach-to-negotiating-a-free-trade-agreement-with-australia/uk-australia-free-trade-agreement-the-uks-strategic-approach accessed 1 May 2021.

119 Department for International Trade, 'Formal Request to Commence UK Accession Negotiations to CPTPP' (1 February 2021) www.gov.uk/government/news/formal-request-to-commence-uk-accession-negotiations-to-cptpp accessed 1 May 2021. The CPTPP developed after the US withdrew from the Trans-Pacific Partnership Agreement in 2017.

120 But there is no geographical limitation to membership. See CPTPP, Article 30.4.

121 J. Kane, 'Comprehensive and Progressive Agreement for Trans-Pacific Partnership (CPTPP)' (Institute for Government 2 February 2021) www.instituteforgovernment.org.uk/explainers/trade-cptpp accessed 1 May 2021.

extent, it contains provisions that are not as advantageous as the TCA. Crucially, however, when it comes to non-tariff barriers, the CPTPP includes some limited SPS equivalence which leads to reduced hurdles for agri-food products.[122] Further, some TCA and CPTPP obligations could clash and as such any potential issues should be ironed out beforehand.

The UK is also in discussions with countries such as the US,[123] India[124] and New Zealand to conclude other trade agreements. Much attention and discussion have revolved around the US agreement (although threatened at one point during the TCA negotiations when US Congressmen and President Joe Biden condemned an earlier vote on the Internal Market Bill 2019-2021 due to its inconsistency with the UK/EU Withdrawal Agreement and the Belfast Agreement/Good Friday Agreement 1998 – again eroding trust and faith in the UK Government). Ramifications of these future agreements for UK agriculture could be wide and varied, especially if imports with different or lower standards such as chlorine-washed chicken, genetically modified organisms (GMOs) and growth hormones in milk and beef[125] would be allowed in the UK, thereby putting farmers at a disadvantage.

5.1.3.3 Risks to levels of standards

Various DEFRA Secretaries of State and other ministers have persistently asserted that the negotiations of trade agreements after Brexit would not result in a reduction of environmental, food and animal welfare standards. However, there are ongoing inconsistencies between governmental statements ('achieving a higher level of environmental protection')[126] and the lack of guarantees to maintain standards in the Agriculture Act 2020 and in the Trade Act 2021 – despite

122 CPTPP, Article 7.8. This equivalence is subject to detailed rules.

123 For more on the UK approach, see Department for International Trade, 'The UK's Approach to Trade Negotiations with the US' (2 March 2020) www.gov.uk/government/publications/the-uks-approach-to-trade-negotiations-with-the-us accessed 1 May 2021. The US negotiating objectives (albeit under a different administration) can be found here, Office of the United States Trade Representative, 'United States-United Kingdom Negotiations: Summary of Specific Negotiating Objectives (February 2019) https://ustr.gov/sites/default/files/Summary_of_U.S.-UK_Negotiating_Objectives.pdf accessed 1 May 2021.

124 Discussions with India on a free trade agreement should start in autumn 2021. A UK-India trade and investment was already announced in May 2021. See Prime Minister's Office, 'Prime Minister Announces £1 Billion of New UK-India Trade' (4 May 2021) www.gov.uk/government/news/prime-minister-announces-1-billion-of-new-uk-india-trade accessed 1 May 2021.

125 See T.J. Centner and L. Petetin, 'Divergent Approaches Regulating Beta Agonists and Cloning of Food Animals: United States and European Union' (2020) 28(5–6) *Society and Animals* 613.

126 M. Gove, 'Farming for the Next Generation' (Oxford Farming Conference 2018) www.gov.uk/government/speeches/farming-for-the-next-generation accessed 1 May 2021.

numerous proposals to include amendments to this effect,[127] all were mostly rejected by the House of Commons. Lower standards could be achieved through, for instance, utilising less environmentally-friendly practices, using more chemicals in agri-food production to achieve higher yields or kill pests, reducing testing or tracing, importing chicken washed with chlorine[128] or GM-feed that is not EU authorised.[129] Other practices such as gene editing, animal cloning, growth hormones (e.g. recombinant bovine somatotropin (rBST) injected into cattle), antibiotic use in livestock and pesticides could also become more widespread.[130]

Farmers and other stakeholders have had recurring concerns and uneasiness as to the future level of standards across the UK[131] and the competition that may be faced by farmers relating to allowing imports with lower environmental, food and animal welfare standards with future trade agreements, for example, with Brazil, Argentina or the US – countries that are well-known for being pro-GMOs and trade talks with these countries have reinvigorated the controversy over GMOs.[132]

Late in the day, the UK Government tabled an amendment to the Agriculture Act to strengthen parliamentary scrutiny of free trade agreements. Before the conclusion of any FTAs, the Secretary of State has a duty to report to Parliament on their impacts on the UK level of standards in relation to human, animal and plant life and health, animal welfare and environmental protection.[133] The Trade and Agriculture Commission (TAC) provides scrutiny of future trade agreements and can voice its support or concerns in writing to Government with its reports.[134] The TAC possesses statutory footing under the Trade Act 2021.[135] It is mostly industry-led. Interestingly, there are no representatives from academia, despite academics being involved at length in parliamentary inquiries and pro-

127 For example, the House of Lords Amendment 93 to the Agriculture Bill was passed by the House of Lords on 22 September 2020. The amendment aimed to guarantee British standards in future trade agreements by preventing the import of agri-food products produced abroad at different, often lower standards. See FarmingUK Team, 'MPs Urged to Back Ag Bill Amendments or Risk Inferior Imports' (24 September 2020) www.farminguk.com/news/mps-urged-to-back-ag-bill-amendments-or-risk-inferior-imports_56605.html accessed 1 May 2021.

128 V. Gravey and C. Burns, 'Chlorinated Chicken Cluck Again' (The UK in a Changing Europe 10 June 2020) https://ukandeu.ac.uk/chlorinated-chickens-cluck-again/ accessed 1 May 2021.

129 European Parliament, 'Imports of GM Food and Feed: Right of Member States to Opt Out' (19 October 2015) www.europarl.europa.eu/thinktank/en/document.html?reference=EPRS_BRI(2015)569030 accessed 1 May 2021.

130 See Centner and Petetin (n125).

131 L. Petetin, V. Gravey and B. Moore, 'Setting the Bar for a Green Brexit in Food and Farming' (Soil Association 2019) www.soilassociation.org/green-brexit/ accessed 1 May 2021.

132 L. Petetin, 'GMO Cultivation in the UK: Brexit, the Devolved Administrations and International Trade' (Brexit and Environment Network 11 January 2018) www.brexitenvironment.co.uk/2018/01/11/gmos-devolution-trade/ accessed 1 May 2021.

133 Agriculture Act 2020, Section 42.

134 Ibid.

135 Trade Act 2021, Sections 8 to 11.

viding expertise to various governmental departments, or charities such as the RSPB or the National Trust who also could have brought other interests to the table. More positively, Caroline Drummond from the Linking Environment And Farming (LEAF) organisation is a member.[136] Further, the industry representatives on the TAC may want the *status quo* to remain, to help maintain certainty and avoid being placed at a competitive disadvantage.

The TAC only has an advisory function,[137] its reports are not binding on the UK Government and it can be repealed by the Secretary of State for International Trade – placing it in a precarious position.[138] In its Final Report, the TAC made 22 recommendations including developing a bold, ambitious agri-food trade strategy; having a minister leading on agri-food trade; being a leader in animal welfare and combatting antimicrobial resistance (AMR); increasing transparency by early stakeholder engagement on future FTAs; and improving country of origin information for consumers.[139]

Recommendation 8 calls for the liberalisation of tariffs on agri-food products with 'countries that can meet the high standards of food production expected from UK producers', including the possibility of 'lower[ing] tariffs and quotas to zero where equivalence is demonstrated for these standards'. It has particularly attracted the interest of stakeholders[140] and replicated the approach suggested in the first part of the National Food Strategy for England.[141] This would help reduce prices for consumers, whilst maintaining standards and not placing UK producers at a competitive disadvantage. It would also help open up markets to UK producers. However, this only addresses situations where the trade partners have equivalent high standards. The following position from Dalmeny, Chief Executive of Sustain summarises well the issues in the short- and long-term:

> in many cases global standards are lower than the UK's. […] We have been clear that tariffs are no substitute for clear blanket bans and that tariffs could be easily reduced or phased out over time, thus breaking the government's promise of "no compromise" on food standards.[142]

136 For more on Linking Environment and Farming (LEAF), see https://leafuk.org/ accessed 1 May 2021.
137 Trade Act 2021, Section 9.
138 Trade Act 2021, Section 11. See in contrast the obligations under the Climate Change Act 2008, Section 9.
139 Trade and Agriculture Commission, 'Final Report' (March 2021) https://assets.publishing.service.gov.uk/government/uploads/system/uploads/attachment_data/file/969045/Trade-and-Agriculture-Commission-final-report.pdf accessed 1 May 2021.
140 O. Delargy, 'Digging in to the Trade and Agriculture Commission Report' (Sustain 12 March 2021) www.sustainweb.org/blogs/mar21-trade-and-agriculture-commission-response/ accessed 1 May 2021.
141 National Food Strategy, 'Read Part One' www.nationalfoodstrategy.org/partone/ accessed 1 May 2021.
142 Delargy (n140). For more on tariffs, see P. Ungphakorn, 'A Real Beginners' Guide to Tariffs and the WTO' (Trade β Blog 8 July 2019) https://tradebetablog.wordpress.com/2018/07/28/a-real-beginners-guide-to-tariffs-and-the-wto/ accessed 1 May 2021.

Further, the effectiveness of labelling as a method of informing the consumer could be put into question; would it not be best to not have the products at all in the first place?

To conclude certain FTAs, the UK might have to agree to the sale of imported products of different (and possibly of lower) quality or by mechanisms not maintaining current UK environmental, animal welfare, food and consumer protection standards – something now possible without being constrained by EU membership and technically possible under the TCA provided that the limited non-regression obligations are not breached.[143] Besides potential issues for consumer protection and undermining national policy objectives, this would also risk UK producers being at a competitive disadvantage in the UK market and in markets abroad (as lower standards may entail lower costs). This may then lead to a downward spiral in standards for UK production. In contrast, such lower standards in the UK could facilitate trade with countries adopting similar standards, reduce costs for UK producers (and consumers) and maintain retailers in continued profitable enterprises but creating issues with trading with the EU due to standards of inferior quality and potentially safety.

Despite such possibilities, many UK producers are likely to maintain standards, if not by government, then by retailers and consumers wanting high-quality products.[144] Indeed, most of the large retailers are often responsive to consumer demands and have already indicated that they would not sell chlorine-washed chicken or rBST beef on their shelves thereby bolstering resilience. For example, Waitrose, Co-op, Aldi, Marks & Spencer and Sainsbury's have all pledged not to sell chlorine-washed chicken.[145] This situation recalls the removal of genetically modified (GM) ingredients by UK retailers (especially Waitrose, Tesco, Iceland, Marks & Spencer and Sainsbury's) in the late 1990s.[146] The debates around the level of standards reflects a wider issue around trust in the agri-food supply chain. Maintaining trust in food is not only important for retailers, the food industry, and the agricultural sector, it is also important for government, because trust is

143 As noted earlier in this chapter, if such obligations are breached, they are more challenging to enforce than obligations under EU law.

144 S. Loth, 'As a Crucial Vote Approaches, Will MPs Protect the UK's Food Standards? (Which 7 October 2020) www.which.co.uk/news/2020/10/will-mps-protect-the-uks-food-standards/ accessed 1 May 2021.

145 A. Payne, 'UK Supermarkets Promise to Never Sell Chlorinated Chicken in Blow to a Brexit Trade Deal with Trump' (Business Insider 9 July 2020) www.businessinsider.com/brexit-supermarkets-promise-never-sell-chlorinated-chicken-trump-trade-deal-2020-7?r=US&IR=T accessed 1 May 2021. Such concerns are still ongoing despite the UK Government asserting that chlorine-washed chicken or rBST beef would not be allowed on food shelves. See L. O'Carroll, 'UK Will Not Import Chlorinated Chicken from US, Ministers Say' (The Guardian 1 November 2020) www.theguardian.com/world/2020/nov/01/uk-will-not-import-chlorinated-chicken-from-us-ministers-brexit accessed 1 May 2021.

146 See P. Waugh, 'Tesco and Unilever Ban GM Products Banned' (The Independent 28 April 1999) www.independent.co.uk/news/tesco-and-unilever-ban-gm-products-banned-1090100.html accessed 1 May 2021; and J.L. Parcell and N.G. Kalaitzandonakes, 'Do Agricultural Commodity Prices Respond to GMO Bans?' in R.E. Evenson and V. Santaniello (eds), *Consumer Acceptance of Genetically Modified Foods* (CABI Publishing 2004) 1.

of importance for society as a whole. Trust in food 'exemplifies the issues of basic trust in modern society'.[147]

Furthermore, the knock-on impacts of any FTAs and lowering of standards need to be considered. Access to the EU market could be restricted under the level playing field and non-regression obligations if similar standards are not used. Consequently, two supply chains could be established with different standards: one that complies with EU standards and one for the rest of the world. This would prove very challenging and costly to implement, as it would require regular inspections to ensure both supply chains maintain the applicable standards and remain separate. The UK Government and the industry would need to reflect on whether the reduced costs and increased income from non-EU markets would be sufficient to compensate for the loss of the EU market, potential harm to the environment and society and the difficulties in justifying domestic financial support for a less environmentally-friendly or healthy agriculture. Naturally, market access obligations under the Internal Market Act (discussed below) also play a role in setting new standards within the UK.

More positively, markets for higher value-added and quality agri-food products are expanding worldwide to accommodate specific demands by consumers. The UK has embraced this trend towards voluntary labelling, such as those covered by EU quality labels (organic production, geographical indications, designation of origins) and more functional labelling (GM-free products). The UK possesses various protected geographical indications (PGI) and protected designation of origins (PDO) such as Cornish pasty, Welsh lamb, Welsh beef, Ayrshire New Potatoes/Ayrshire Earlies and Irish whiskey. However, the protection offered to these products may be in jeopardy in any future trade agreement. For example, when negotiating the Transatlantic Trade and Investment Partnership (TTIP) between the US and the EU, the EU wanted its geographical indications to receive protection in the US,[148] whilst congressmen expressed their concerns that 'the EU's abuse of [geographical indications] threatens U.S. sales and exports of a number of U.S. agricultural products'.[149] This is why it is crucial for trade and agricultural policies not to develop in isolation from each other. Similar hurdles could arise in a future UK/US trade agreement as well as with other countries. More generally, levels of standards and requirement requirements could be put into question by WTO Members.

147 F.W.A. Brom, 'Food, Consumer Concerns, and Trust: Food Ethics for a Globalizing Market' (2000) 12 *Journal of Agricultural and Environmental Ethics* 127, 131.

148 European Commission, 'Agriculture and Geographic Indications (GIs) In TTIP – A Guide to the EU's Proposal' (2016) http://trade.ec.europa.eu/doclib/docs/2016/march/tradoc_154372.pdf accessed 1 May 2021.

149 R.J. Ribble et al., 'Letter to Thomas J Vilsack, Secretary of Agriculture and Michael Forman, US Trade Representative' (2014) www.commonfoodnames.com/wp-content/uploads/House-Dairy-TTIP-Letter.pdf accessed 1 May 2021.

5.1.4 Possible WTO challenges

Under WTO law, if the UK maintains or, more problematically, increases environmental, food or animal welfare requirements or standards to protect and promote social and societal values and interests and overall resilience, this could constitute barriers to trade and lead to WTO challenges.[150] If a dispute arises, the dispute could be brought under the General Agreement on Tariffs and Trade (GATT),[151] SPS Agreement (but not on animal welfare grounds) and the TBT Agreement.[152]

5.1.4.1 Likeness, PPMs and the GATT

Under the General Agreement on Tariffs and Trade,[153] the UK could be accused of restricting trade under Article XI (on quantitative restrictions) but most importantly under Articles I (on the MFN) and III (on national treatment). The obligation not to discriminate under Articles I and III mostly applies to 'like products', since for products to benefit from the same preferential treatment and not be discriminated against, products must be 'like'. Article III, in particular paragraph 4, on national treatment is of particular relevance for agriculture, since it covers issues around the domestic regulatory treatment of agri-food products.[154] The Article has for purpose to ensure equality of 'competitive conditions between imported and like domestic products' in the internal market of each Member with regards to internal regulations (as well as taxes under paragraph 2 of Article

150 For a general overview of WTO law, see P. Van den Bossche and D. Prévost, *Essentials of WTO Law* (2nd edn, CUP 2021). For a more detailed account, see P. Van den Bossche and W. Zdouc, *The Law and Policy of the World Trade Organization Text, Cases, and Materials* (5th edn, CUP 2021). For more on the WTO and governance matters, see R. Howse, 'The World Trade Organization 20 Years On: Global Governance by Judiciary' 27(1) *European Journal of International Law* (2016) 9.

151 Uruguay Round General Agreement on Tariffs and Trade (1994).

152 This section is not meant to be exhaustive and covers the main issues likely to arise. Further, despite the SPS Agreement and TBT Agreement being *lex specialis*, this section commences with the GATT to enable to map out the overall framework more effectively.

153 Uruguay Round General Agreement on Tariffs and Trade (1994).

154 The issues around likeness and PPMs are also relevant and approached similarly in the SPS Agreement and TBT Agreement but the main focus here is on the GATT. Indeed, the scope of likeness in both the TBT and SPS Agreements is arguably 'remotely similar' to be in line with the scope of likeness in Article III-4. See W.M. Choi, *'Like Products' in International Trade Law: Towards a Consistent GATT/WTO Jurisprudence* (OUP 2003) 117. Therefore, generally, content on like products under the GATT is also applicable under the SPS Agreement as well as the TBT Agreement.

III).[155] It, therefore, aims to avoid protectionism.[156] Indeed, both the language of Article III and its function indicate that Article III is aimed at measures motivated by protectionist purpose.[157] Article III constitutes one of the most fundamental principles safeguarding the interests of foreign competitors against discriminatory domestic policy measures.[158]

5.1.4.1.1 LIKENESS MATTERS

The determination of the 'likeness' of two products is examined on a case-by-case basis to allow for a fair assessment with three key criteria under the border tax adjustment (BTA) criteria: the product's end-uses in a given market; consumers' tastes and habits, which change from country to country and the product's properties, nature and quality.[159] Determining 'likeness' is thus an 'exercise of market definition'.[160] Products with the same physical characteristics may not be considered 'like' if consumer preferences change the competitive relationship of the products.[161] In this event, two end-products which seem 'like' could justify different regulations. It is also important to note here that the decisive criterion in a likeness assessment is the competitive relationship between products, thus

155 *Canada – Certain Measures Concerning Periodicals*, WT/DS31/AB/R, 30 June 1997, 15. See also R. Read, 'Like Products, Health & Environmental Exceptions: The Interpretation of PPMs in Recent WTO Trade Dispute Cases' (2004) 5 *Estey Centre Journal of International Law and Trade Policy* 123, 126. For more on Article III-2, see R. Howse and D. Regan, 'The Product/Process Distinction – An Illusory Basis for Disciplining "Unilateralism" in Trade Policy' (2000) 11 *European Journal of International Law* 264; J.B. Goco, 'Non-Discrimination, "Likeness", and Market Definition in World Trade Organization Jurisprudence' (2006) 40 *Journal of World Trade* 315, 319; D.H. Regan, 'Regulatory Purpose and "Like Products" in Article III:4 of the GATT (With Additional Remarks on Article III:2)' (2002) 36 *Journal of World Trade* 443, 471; and A. Kumar and A. Chatterjee, 'Reflections on the Bubble of Likeness' (2010) 16 *International Trade Law and Regulation* 51.

156 *Japan – Taxes on Alcoholic Beverages (Japan-Alcoholic Beverages)*, WT/DS8/AB/R, WT/DS10/AB/R and WT/DS11/AB/R, 4 October 1996, paragraph 111; and *Korea – Taxes on Alcoholic Beverages*, WT/DS75/AB/R and WT/DS84/AB/R, 18 January 1999, paragraph 120.

157 Regan (n155) 451. See also, D.H. Regan, 'Further Thoughts on the Role of Regulatory Purpose under Article III of the General Agreement on Tariffs and Trade' (2003) 37 *Journal of World Trade* 738; and R. Hudec, '"Like Product": The Differences in Meaning in GATT Articles I and III' in T. Cottier and P. Mavroidis (eds), *Regulatory Barriers and the Principle of Non-Discrimination in World Trade Law* (University of Michigan Press 2000) 101, 105.

158 M.G. Desta, *The Law of International Trade in Agricultural Products: From GATT 1947 to the WTO Agreement on Agriculture* (Kluwer Law International 2002) 339.

159 Working Party Report, 'Border Tax Adjustments', BISD 18S/97 (2 December 1970).

160 Goco (n155) 315.

161 G. Marceau, 'Do PPM Concerns Have A Future?' in D. Prévost, I. Alexovicova and J. Hillebrand Pohl (eds), *Restoring Trust in Trade: Liber Amicorum in Honour of Peter Van den Bossche* (Hart Publishing 2018) 175, 184.

adopting an economic approach. For instance, in a future WTO dispute regarding UK market access, the exporting Member could argue that its product is 'like' a UK product which is obtaining better treatment, whereas the importing Member, here the UK, would deny that such 'likeness' exists. Grass-fed beef constitutes a good example here. Another typical example is whether GM and non-GM products would be considered 'like products'.

Article III-4 does 'not provide for equal treatment of all "like" products, but rather for equality as between domestic and imported "like" products'.[162] Like domestic and foreign products must be compared. Here the *EC-Biotech* case, which related to the suspension of GMO (biotech) approvals by (some Member States of) the EU, is of particular relevance. In this case, there were a range of aspects at stake but the emphasis was on procedure. The EU treated conventional and biotech foods differently (the latter facing a *de facto* moratorium); the same treatment was given to domestic and imported biotech foods. Argentina, in relation to the product-specific measures adopted by some EU countries, claimed a violation of Article III-4 that accorded less favourable treatment to the biotech products compared with like non-biotech products.[163] The panel in the case did not address specifically the question of whether biotech and conventional products were like products, but it rejected Argentina's claim by stating that:

> Argentina is not alleging that the treatment of products has differed depending on their origin. In these circumstances, it is not self-evident that the alleged less favourable treatment of imported biotech products is explained by the foreign origin of these products rather than, for instance, a perceived difference between biotech products and non-biotech products in terms of their safety, etc. Argentina has not adduced argument and evidence sufficient to raise a presumption that the alleged less favourable treatment is explained by the foreign origin of the relevant biotech products.[164]

The panel arguably implies that Argentina had not been comparing the right like products and therefore that biotech and conventional products were not like products. If this tendency is confirmed in WTO jurisprudence, different processes such as genetic modification or animal cloning[165] could be enough for biotech foods and conventional foods to be unlike.

As consumers separate conventional and biotech foods in their buying habits, it creates *de facto* segmented markets and this should be relevant to the panel. Thus,

162 Howse and Regan (n(n155) 259.

163 *European Communities – Approval and Marketing of Biotech Products (EC-Biotech)*, WT/DS291/R, WT/DS292/R and WT/DS293/R, 29 September 2006, paragraph 7.2512.

164 Ibid paragraph 7.2514.

165 See L. Petetin, 'Clone Wars? The Challenges of Cloned Food in EU, US and WTO Law' (2009) 11 *Environmental Law Review* 246.

the 'consumers' tastes and habits' criterion emerges as the underpinning of any competitive relationship in particular with biotech foods as they raise various concerns (especially ethical, moral or environmental).[166] In that sense, Choi's market-based economic analysis of a like product determination would restore likeness to 'the genuine power of the self-determination rule of democracy' by offering the simple proposition that 'what the people see as being "like" ought to be "like"; and what the people believe will be "like in the near future" ought to be considered "like in the near future."'[167]

This appears to be in line with an agri-food democracy approach to food provisioning.

The main issue, however, remains that the consumer tastes and habits prong is determined by a competitive relationship, instead of looking into the aims and effects of a measure or its regulatory purpose. Porges and Trachtman confirm this issue by stating that the Appellate Body in the *EC-Asbestos* case recognised that 'the defence of legitimate regulation in national treatment cases requires attention to a challenged regulation's purpose, not just a formalistic analysis based on the BTA Adjustments factors' as the BTA criteria 'generally ignore regulatory concerns and focus on competitive likeness'.[168] Adopting a purely economic approach to the BTA criteria is not sufficiently forward-looking enough.

There is genuine debate as to how far it is possible to look beyond the BTA criteria. For some, such as Regan and Hudec, the BTA criteria and their 'canonical status' should be reconsidered as 'the BTA list was never put forward as more than a representative list of possible criteria that had been suggested to or in the Working Party'.[169] Choi admits the unsuitability of the BTA criteria by stating that 'despite its handiness, the traditional Border Tax Adjustment Report approach lacks the precision and flexibility that are necessary to face changes in specific social contexts not contemplated in the original GATT'.[170] This is a key point: the criteria should be able to adapt as time passes and different morals, ethics and values are involved depending on the situation at stake. Because of all these hurdles, an 'aim and effects' approach was developed by commentators following key decisions by the Dispute Settlement Body, which subsequently evolved into a 'regulatory purpose' approach.

Following an 'aim and effects' approach, products would not be considered 'like' if the regulatory distinction between them is made on legitimate, non-protectionist policy grounds and if it does not have a protectionist effect.[171] The

166 Regan (n155) 465.
167 Choi (n154) 155.
168 A. Porges and J.P. Trachtman, 'Hudec and Domestic Regulation: The Resurrection of Aim and Effects' (2003) 37 *Journal of World Trade* 783, 785.
169 Respectively, Regan (n155) 465 and Hudec (n157) 112.
170 Choi (n154) 155.
171 C. Button, *The Power to Protect: Trade, Health and Uncertainty in the WTO* (Hart 2004) 16.

great advantage of the 'aim and effects' test is that 'it protects Members pursuing legitimate social policies from facing the burden of justifying their measures under Article XX because no breach of Article III would be found'.[172] This is a crucial point. Under this approach, there are two conditions for 'likeness' under Article III-4: a competitive relationship between products and the regulatory purpose of the measure under review, which should be based on a non-protectionist policy.[173] Under such a test, and following the example of biotech foods, UK higher regulations could find substantiation in the moral, ethical or environmental grounds on which they could rely to justify different treatment between biotech and conventional foods.

In contrast, for Button, the 'aim and effects' test generates concerns about regulatory autonomy and its status is doubtful.[174] Importantly, for Du, Marceau, Charnovitz and Choi, the Appellate Body in the *Japan-Alcoholic Beverages* case expressly rejected the GATT 'aim and effects' test by asserting that the 'legislative or regulatory intent' of a measure was irrelevant in a likeness determination.[175] However, for Howse and Regan, the case 'may or may not have rejected "the aim and effects test", but it clearly did not reject consideration of aim and effects' and therefore suggests that regulatory purpose could be relevant to the determination of likeness.[176] Indeed, the Appellate Body stated that panels are free to use their 'best judgment' in making a determination of 'likeness'.[177] This 'best judgment' approach could give the possibility for the panels to look beyond the BTA criteria and develop their own analysis. For these last commentators, the *Japan-Alcoholic Beverages* case shows the evolution of the 'aim and effects' test into an evaluation of the regulatory purpose of the measure in question. Assessing the regulatory purpose of a measure would allow any panel to analyse, for example, *why* the UK adopted certain regulatory requirements for biotech foods[178] or grass-fed beef

172 Ibid.
173 Regan (n155) 464.
174 Button (n171) 16.
175 See *Japan-Alcoholic Beverages*, paragraphs 99 to 101 (specifically referring to Article III-2). See also M. Du, *The Regulation of Product Standards in World Trade Law* (Hart Publishing 2020) 50; Choi (n154) 154; Marceau (n161) 185; and S. Charnovitz, 'Book Review: "Like Products" in International Trade Law: Towards a Consistent GATT/WTO Jurisprudence' (2004) 98 *American Journal of International Law* 610, 614.
176 Howse and Regan (n155) 266 and 268. See also, Regan (n157) 739.
177 *Japan-Alcoholic Beverages* paragraph 21.
178 As shown in the preambles and objectives of the Regulation (EU) 2015/2283 of the European Parliament and of the Council of 25 November 2015 on Novel Foods, Amending Regulation (EU) No 1169/2011 of the European Parliament and of the Council and repealing Regulation (EC) No 258/97 of the European Parliament and of the Council and Commission Regulation (EC) No 1852/2001 OJ L327/1; Regulation (EC) No 1829/2003 of the European Parliament and of the Council of 22 September 2003 on Genetically Modified Food and Feed [2003] OJ L268/1; Regulation (EC) 1830/2003 of the European Parliament and of the Council of 22 September 2003 concerning the Traceability and Labelling of Genetically Modified Organisms and the Traceability of Food and Feed Products produced from Genetically Modified Organisms and amending Directive

(in contrast with feed-lot beef[179]) and thereby enable regulatory approaches that promote resilience.

5.1.4.1.2 PPMS MATTERS

The issue of 'likeness' is closely connected with the debate as to the validity of measures conditioned upon process and production methods (PPMs). It is important to note that the WTO Agreements do not formally prohibit regulation upon the basis of PPMs. Two types of PPMs should be distinguished. First, 'product-related PPMs' find their way into the end-product; for instance, pesticides residues present in agri-food products. Second, 'non-product-related PPMs' are not linked to the nature of the end-product itself, but to its method of production, manufacturing or harvest; for example, high animal welfare standards, grass-fed beef or the amount of greenhouse gases that were generated during the manufacturing process, as these are processes that leave no trace in the final product, often to enhance specific societal values, ethics or interests in particular linked to environmental protection. Genetic modification can fall under either of these categories depending on the presence of residues or other physical changes in the end-product.

It is the latter category that is particularly problematic since products are physically 'like' but some Members may wish to adopt measures that distinguish between products due to the other (non-economic) dimensions they embed. In particular, the difficulty is to know whether physically identical end-products manufactured with different processes are like products. Such PPMs embed credence characteristics or attributes[180] into consumer products and certain consumers wish to differentiate between products on the basis of such credence characteristics.[181] Indeed, Members are increasingly regulating goods on the basis of non-product related PPMs, creating further market segmentation for products that would appear to be 'like' as end-products (and retailers increasingly develop their 'niche' markets attracting premium prices based upon such credence characteristics).

For many, a basic tenet of the GATT/WTO legal system is that non-product-related PPMs 'are not relevant criteria on which trading partners can differentiate

---

2001/18/EC [2003] OJ L268/24; and the Regulation (EC) No 178/2002 of the European Parliament and of the Council of 28 January 2002 Laying Down the General Principles and Requirements of Food Law, Establishing the European Food Safety Authority and Laying Down Procedures in Matters of Food Safety [2002] OJ L 31/1, more generally.

179 For more on concentrated animal feeding operations and their regulation, see T.J. Centner and L. Petetin, 'Permitting Program with Best Management Practices for Shale Gas Wells to Safeguard Public Health' (2015) 163 *Journal of Environmental Management* 174.

180 Such as grass-fed, organic, carbon-neutral, animal welfare, local, fair trade or sustainable.

181 A. Swinbank, 'Like Products, Animal Welfare and the World Trade Organization' *(2006) 40 Journal of World Trade* 687, 707.

between goods',[182] because it is widely thought that 'qualitative criteria for trade regulation are generally inconsistent with the product-based customs methodology enshrined in Article III'.[183] However, the *US-Shrimp I and 21.5* cases would indicate otherwise.[184] In these cases, US measures banned the importation of shrimp harvested in a manner that may harm sea turtles (by incidentally capturing them), unless the technology was certified for exporters by the US as avoiding killing endangered sea turtles. These fishing methods are not reflected in the end-product, yet, according to Marceau, the Appellate Body 'opened the door to the idea that in principle PPM-based regulatory distinctions (whether product or non-product based) can be justified under Article XX and thus be WTO consistent'.[185] For Charnovitz, PPMs can be an 'appropriate instrument of environmental policy';[186] it all depends on the rationale of the measure and its implementation,[187] that is whether the measure creates discrimination or disguised restrictions.

Non-product-related PPM-based measures crucially offer valid means for Members to protect their consumers or listen to their ethics, values or interests, including protecting the environment, and bolster resilience. Importing Members, such as the UK, are not demanding the use of a particular PPM in the exporting country; they simply regulate what products and standards are permitted within their own territory, whether imported or produced domestically. Thus, the position on non-product related PPMs is more nuanced than it appears and the UK could be successful when raising regulatory standards and its baseline. To sum up and for example, if the UK wanted to raise its animal welfare standards for lamb and resulting products for UK and foreign products, this could negatively impact lamb exporters to the UK such as New Zealand. New Zealand could seek to advance that the likeness of products, wherever produced, cannot be affected by animal welfare standards which do not show through into the end-product (here lamb and derived products). The question is the following: despite their similar physical characteristics, is a leg of lamb resulting from high animal welfare standards 'unlike' a leg of lamb that is produced with lower animal welfare standards, so that different domestic regulatory treatment would not breach GATT provisions? Such a measure would be non-product-related PPM-based because there would not be any difference in the end-product. If these products which seem 'like' can be rendered

182 Ibid 687.
183 Read (n155) 127.
184 *United States – Import Prohibition of Certain Shrimp and Shrimp Products (US-Shrimp I)*, WT/DS58/AB/R, 12 October 1998 and *United States – Import Prohibition of Certain Shrimp and Shrimp Products (US-Shrimp 21.5)*, WT/DS58/AB/R/RW, 22 October 2001.
185 Marceau (n161) 186 and S. Charnovitz, 'The Law of Environmental "PPMs" in the WTO: Debunking the Myth of Illegality' (2002) 27 *Yale Journal of International Law* 59, 97.
186 Ibid 61.
187 Ibid 110.

'unlike' due to different non-product-related PPMs, then different regulatory treatments could ensue and therefore there would not be a breach of GATT provisions (and therefore there would be no need for the UK to involve Article XX to justify the measure). If the PPM criteria, here animal welfare standards for lamb, change the competitive relationship of the products then the two products may be more swiftly considered 'unlike' following the BTA criteria. If the competitive relationship remains unchanged, the difference in treatment would be more difficult to substantiate but the 'aims and effects' or regulatory purpose test could play a role in such a determination. As noted above, due to the ongoing debates, there is a lack of certainty regarding which test would apply. This adds to the ambiguity of what the final determination from a panel would be.

An important point to note again is that any such measure adopted by the UK would need not to create discrimination between domestic and foreign products as per Article III-4 GATT. As will be seen in the following section, it is often on this aspect that measures restricting trade are found inconsistent with GATT provisions.

As noted, PPM-based measures are often based on environmental, ethical or moral grounds that may 'coerce' exporting Members into changing their policies and resulting standards and therefore affecting the sovereignty of exporting Members and putting into question the extra-jurisdictional or extra-territoriality of such measures.[188] This is particularly problematic for developing countries, which have to comply with such (often costly) measures if they wish to export. As a result, it is often argued that these measures constitute disguised protectionist practices.[189] In contrast, supporters of PPMs argue that, for example, the environment and biodiversity – the global commons – ought to be protected and PPM-based measures are a good mechanism to do so. This point remains unresolved in WTO jurisprudence. But the WTO should not ask consumers to accept foreign products made through processes that they do not want just in the interest of promoting greater trade.[190] With the ongoing climate and biodiversity crises, whilst bearing in mind the ambition of overall resilience, it is more important than ever for Members to think about the consequences of the measures they adopt and, when designing measures based on PPMs, to make sure that these measures are applied in a non-discriminatory manner.

188 Ibid 70; M. Du, 'Permitting Moral Imperialism? The Public Morals Exception to Free Trade at the Bar of the World Trade Organization' (2016) 50(4) *Journal of World Trade* 675, 676.

189 Marceau (n161) 187; and C. Glinski, 'CSR and the Law of the WTO – The Impact of Tuna Dolphin II and EC – Seal Products' (2017) 1 *Nordic Journal of Commercial Law* 120, 125.

190 Charnovitz (n185) 68.

5.1.4.2 *Article XX GATT*

In the event that a UK measure was declared inconsistent with GATT provisions (especially Article I, III or XI), it could potentially be justified by one of the general exceptions to the GATT system under Article XX. If the measure fulfils the conditions of the Article, compatibility with GATT law would ensue. These exceptions are, nonetheless, limited.[191] The role of Article XX is to find an equilibrium between trade liberalisation with the general provisions of the GATT and non-trade interests, including the protection and promotion of moral, ethical and societal values.[192] Article XX and its exceptions provide the UK with a crucial pathway to justify a measure restricting trade, such as raising the regulatory baseline for animal welfare or grass-fed beef, for example.

The regulatory purpose of a measure that restricts trade would be assessed here. Article XX imposes a two-tiered balancing test: first, there is a provisional justification of the measure under an exception listed in paragraphs (a)–(j) (exhaustive list); second, a further appraisal of the same measure must be made under the introductory clauses (the chapeau) of Article XX.[193] This means that traditionally there is a determination first as to whether a measure is 'provisionally justified' under one of the specific exceptions of Article XX GATT and, if so, whether the measure is applied in a non-discriminatory way under the chapeau. Article XX's chapeau states that a measure must not create 'a means of arbitrary or unjustifiable discrimination between countries where the same conditions prevail, or a disguised restriction on international trade'. The chapeau entails a balancing act, between the right of one Member to invoke an exception under Article XX and the rights of other Members.[194]

However, this approach has been put in question in the *Indonesia – Importation of Horticultural Products, Animals and Animal Products* case. The Appellate Body rejected the argument put forward by Indonesia that it was an error of law for the panel to look at the chapeau first and only afterwards to consider a specific exception.[195] This could indicate that WTO jurisprudence is moving towards

191 *United States – Wool Shirts*, WT/DS33/AB/R, 25 April 1997, paragraph 335.

192 For more, see P. Delimatsis and L. Reins (eds), *Trade and Environmental Law* (Edward Elgar Publishing 2021); and G. Marceau and J. Wyatt, 'The WTO's Efforts to Balance Economic Development and Environmental Protection: A Short Review of Appellate Body Jurisprudence' (2013) 1(1) *Latin American Journal of International Trade Law* 291.

193 *United States – Standards for Reformulated and Conventional Gasoline (US-Gasoline)*, WT/DS2/AB/R, 29 April 1996, 18. For more on Article XX GATT, see D.M. McRae, 'GATT Article XX and the WTO Appellate Body' in M. Bronckers and R. Quick (eds), *New Directions in International Economic Law: Essays in Honour of John H. Jackson* (Kluwer Law International 2000) 219.

194 *US-Shrimp I* paragraph 159. See also Charnovitz (n185) 81.

195 *Indonesia – Importation of Horticultural Products, Animals and Animal Products*, WT/DS478/AB/R and WT/DS478/AB/R, 9 November 2017, paragraph 5.100.

interpreting the chapeau as the main safeguard against abusive application of the exceptions.

Article XX (g), (b) and (a) are of specific interest here since they can broadly cover agri-environmental matters[196] and strengthen resilience. Under Article XX, a measure can be saved by exception (g) if it 'relat[es] to the conservation of exhaustible natural resources if such measures are made effective in conjunction with restrictions on domestic production or consumption'; under exception (b) if it is 'necessary to protect human, animal or plant life or health'; or under exception (a) if it is 'necessary to protect public morals'. This would mean that the trade-restrictive measure would be consistent with the GATT.

Each exception or ground of justification under Article XX relies on different terms: (a) and (b) utilise the term 'necessary' whilst (g) uses 'relating to'.[197] Consequently, each ground of justification does not call for 'the same kind or degree of connection or relationship between the measure under appraisal and the state of interest or policy sought to be promoted or realized'.[198] This is confirmed in the *EC-Seal Products* case where the Appellate Body asserted that there must be 'a sufficient nexus between the [challenged] measure and interest protected'.[199] As a result, different standards have to be met under every single paragraph regarding the relationship between the measure at issue and the value or objective pursued.[200]

Article XX (g) has been nicknamed the 'environment exception' of the GATT.[201] Although the word 'environment' has not been included in the text of Article XX (g) (it refers to the 'conservation of exhaustible natural resources'), this exception has been used to justify unilateral environmental measures taken by

196 H. Andersen, 'Protection of Non-Trade Values in WTO Appellate Body Jurisprudence: Exceptions, Economic Arguments, and Eluding Questions' (2015) 18(2) *Journal of International Economic Law* 383.

197 In *US-Gasoline*, the Appellate Body stated that '[i]t does not seem reasonable to suppose that the WTO Members intended to require, in respect of each and every category, the same kind or degree of connection or relationship between the measure under appraisal and the state interest or policy sought to be promoted or realized'. See *US-Gasoline*, 18.

198 Ibid 16–17.

199 *European Communities – Measures Prohibiting the Importation and Marketing of Seal Products (EC-Seal Products)*, WT/DS400/AB/R and WT/DS401/AB/R, 22 May 2014, paragraph 5.169.

200 The remainder of this section will focus on the interests protected under each exception.

201 Article XX (g) contains three different requirements: first, that the measure for which the provision is invoked concerns 'exhaustible natural resources'; second; that the measure is 'related to' the conservation of those resources; finally, that the measure is 'made effective in conjunction with restrictions on domestic production or consumption'.

countries that might impact trade.[202] For example, exception (g) could be used to protect against environmental degradation.[203]

In the *US-Shrimp I* case, the Appellate Body asserted that the protection of turtles fell under this exception as '[l]iving resources are just as "finite" as petroleum, iron ore and other non-living resources'.[204] The import ban at issue was provisionally justified under Article XX (g) but the measure failed to meet the requirements of the chapeau of Article XX since it created arbitrary and unjustifiable discrimination.[205] The measure was therefore inconsistent with GATT provisions, here Article XI. The US had to go back to the drawing board and amend the measure. More positively from an environmental standpoint, in the *US-Shrimp 21.5* case, which deals with the implementation phase of the *US-Shrimp I* case, the amended US measures are now consistent with GATT provisions. The Appellate Body rejected the reasoning of the panel that Article XX could not justify measures conditioning access to domestic markets on whether the exporting Member complies with or adopts a policy unilaterally prescribed by the importing country.[206] The new US measures meet the conditions of the chapeau for two reasons: first, the serious, good faith efforts made by the US to negotiate an international agreement (even if the agreement has not been concluded);[207] second, the new measures allow 'sufficient flexibility' by requiring that other Members' programmes simply be 'comparable in effectiveness' to the US programme, as opposed to the previous standard that they are 'essentially the same'.[208] This confirms that WTO jurisprudence can protect the environment for as long as the measures erected do not create arbitrary and unjustifiable discrimination or disguised restriction to trade.

Further, Article XX (b) enables Members to adopt a trade-restrictive measure taken 'to protect human, animal or plant life or health' if it is 'necessary'. In the *EC-Asbestos* case, the Appellate Body for the first time upheld a health measure in favour of the protection of health and consumers under Article XX (b). It

202 Under the regime of the GATT, see *United States – Prohibition of Imports of Tuna and Tuna Products from Canada*, BISD 29S/91, 22 February 1982. Under the regime of the WTO, see *United States – Restrictions on Imports of Tuna (US-Tuna I)*, WT/DS29/R, 16 June 1994; and *US-Shrimp I*. For previous accounts on the 'trade and environment' relationship, see A. Fijalkowski and J. Cameron, *Trade and the Environment: Bridging the Gap* (Cameron May 1998); and N. Bernasconi-Osterwalder et al., *Environment and Trade: A Guide to WTO Jurisprudence* (Earthscan 2005).

203 More controversially, it could also be used to argue against the patenting of GM crops. See M. Dobbs, 'Genetically Modified Crops, Agricultural Sustainability and National Opt-Outs: Enclosure as the Loophole?' (2017) 54(4) *Common Market Law Review* 1093.

204 *US-Shrimp I*, paragraph 128.

205 Ibid paragraphs 125 to 145.

206 *US-Shrimp 21.5*, paragraph 121.

207 Ibid paragraph 123.

208 Ibid paragraph 144.

reaffirmed that 'a Member was free to choose its own level of protection'.[209] Indeed, Members can decide to raise their regulatory baseline. Nothing in the GATT (and other WTO Agreements) prevents them from doing so 'in principle'. As such, the UK could increase its life or health regulatory standards and, if this leads to a breach of GATT disciplines, they could be saved under the exception.[210]

Exception (a) of Article XX is of real interest here. The exception can be invoked by Members if the measures are 'necessary to protect public morals'. It could be used by the UK, for instance, to defend measures on net-zero targets that would maintain important values to UK society.[211] Crucially, the *EC-Seal Products* case indicates that this exception can be relied on to justify a measure restricting trade based on higher animal welfare requirements.[212] In this case, although the EU regime's restriction on trade in seal products was consistent with WTO law under the exception, it failed to fulfil the non-discrimination criteria of the chapeau.

In its interpretation of 'public morality', the panel and Appellate Body in the *EC-Seal Products* case relied on the *US-Gambling* case and Article XIV (a) GATS (the equivalent of Article XX (a) GATT). In *US-Gambling*, the panel stated that 'public morals' denote (i) 'standards of right and wrong conduct maintained by or on behalf of a community or nation',[213] of which (ii) 'the content of these concepts for Members can vary in time and space, depending upon a range of factors, including prevailing social, cultural, ethical and religious values'[214] and (iii) 'Members should be given some scope to define and apply for themselves the concepts of "public morals" and "public order" in their respective territories, according to their own systems and scales of values'.[215] Overall, it was reasserted that 'Members, in applying similar societal concepts, have the right to determine the level of protection that they consider appropriate'.[216] Nielsen contends that there appears to be 'no manner in which a moral policy can be second guessed by

209 *European Communities – Measures Affecting Asbestos and Products Containing Asbestos (EC-Asbestos)*, WT/DS135/AB/R, 12 March 2001, paragraph 174. See also *Brazil – Measures Affecting Imports of Retreaded Tyres*, WT/DS332/R, 12 June 2007, paragraph 7.46.

210 Although raising standards would require strong justification by the UK. In the *EC-Asbestos* case, the Dispute Settlement Body was influenced by scientific certainty of asbestos being carcinogenic. See *EC-Asbestos*, paragraph 174.

211 More controversially, the exception could even be used in principle to restrict the cultivation of GM crops (although the moral outrage towards GM crops would have to be high). See M. Dobbs, 'Legalising General Prohibitions on Cultivation of Genetically Modified Organisms' (2012) 11(12) *German Law Journal* 1347.

212 *EC-Seal Products*, paragraphs 5.145–5.146.

213 *United States – Measures Affecting the Cross-Border Supply of Gambling and Betting Services (US-Gambling)*, WT/DS285/R, 10 November 2004, paragraph 6.465. See L. Bartels, 'The Chapeau of the General Exceptions in the WTO GATT and GATS Agreements' (2015) 109 *American Journal of International Law* 95.

214 *US-Gambling*, paragraph 6. 461.

215 Ibid.

216 Ibid.

the panels or the Appellate Body, because the policy in most cases is a community- or region-specific policy'.[217] For Davies, the solution to rendering a measure legitimate under Article XX (a) is 'not to ask the trade court whether a moral view is right or wrong or sensible, but whether it is genuine and consistent' and 'in fact an authentic reflection of moral views within that jurisdiction'.[218] Naturally, evidence is also key to any such determination.[219]

Animal welfare, as a matter of public policy, could be relied upon by the UK to increase standards. The UK has been at the forefront of animal welfare since the 18th and 19th centuries, with philosophers such as John Locke and Jeremy Bentham who highlighted that unnecessary cruelty toward animals is morally wrong. The UK was also the first country in the world to put in place legislation designed to protect animals with the Cruelty to Animals Act 1835 and the Cruelty to Animals Act 1876. The Animal Welfare Act 2006 places a duty of care on owners and keepers to take reasonable steps to meet the welfare needs of animals (inclusive of farmed animals).[220] More recently, the 2021 Queen's Speech mentions an Animal Welfare (Sentience) Bill.[221] Such a strong, historical UK attachment to animal welfare embedded in higher standards could be the basis to invoke Article XX (a) if these standards were found inconsistent with a GATT provision. Overall, Article XX thereby enables Members to follow specific policy objectives (inclusive of resilience) and creates policy space for Members – bearing in mind that such standards would still need to pass muster under the chapeau and its non-discrimination requirements.

217 L. Nielsen, *The WTO, Animals and PPMs* (Martinus Nijhoff Publishers 2007) 233.

218 G. Davies, 'Morality Clauses and Decision Making in Situations of Scientific Uncertainty: The Case of GMOs' (2007) 6 *World Trade Review* 249, 262.

219 For more on animal welfare and public morality, see R. Cunningham and S. Vindedzis, 'Four Legs Good, Two Legs Bad? Animal Welfare vs the World Trade Organisation (Featuring Article XX of the General Agreement on Tariffs and Trade and Article 2 of the Technical Barriers to Trade)' (2017) 38 *Adelaide Law Review* 311; A. Herwig, 'Too Much Zeal on Seals? Animal Welfare, Public Morals, and Consumer Ethics at the Bar of the WTO' (2016) 15(1) *World Trade Review* 109; P. Conconi and T. Voon, 'EC-Seal Products: The Tension between Public Morals and International Trade Agreements' (2016) 15(2) *World Trade Review* 211; K. Sykes, 'Sealing Animal Welfare into the GATT Exceptions: The International Dimension of Animal Welfare in WTO Disputes' (2014) 13(3) *World Trade Review* 471; and R. O'Gorman, 'Of Eggs, and Seals, and Leghold Traps: Internal and External Public Morality as a Factor in European Union Animal Welfare Legislation' in J.A. McMahon and M.N. Cardwell (eds), *Research Handbook on EU Agriculture Law* (Research Handbook in European Law, Edward Elgar Publishing 2015) 323.

220 Petetin (n94).

221 See Prime Minister's Office, 'The Queen's Speech 2021' (11 May 2021) https://assets.publishing.service.gov.uk/government/uploads/system/uploads/attachment_data/file/985029/Queen_s_Speech_2021_-_Background_Briefing_Notes.pdf accessed 11 May 2021, 132.

5.1.4.3 *The SPS Agreement and the turn to science*

As noted in Chapter 2, Section 2.4.3, under the SPS Agreement, relying on scientific evidence is the main way to raise standards to protect human, animal or plant life or health. The SPS Agreement elaborates on Article XX b) GATT and SPS measures ensure, for example, that consumers are supplied with food that is safe to eat according to specific standards. It plays a crucial role in the debate around trade and non-trade values under WTO law and provides an attempt to balance the protection of life and health against SPS risks and the liberalisation of trade.[222]

The scope of application of the SPS Agreement is defined under Article 1.1 and the Agreement 'applies to all sanitary and phytosanitary measures which may, directly or indirectly, affect international trade'.[223] This is an important provision that assesses both the type of measure at stake, that is its text, but also its objective, application and implementation.[224]

This means that if the UK adopts a measure to improve its level of protection, for instance, by raising standards or banning certain pesticides residues in food, the measure should be based on scientific justification or the precautionary principle (Article 5.7) for temporary measures;[225] these aspects will be addressed in turn.

5.1.4.3.1 A CENTRAL ROLE FOR SCIENTIFIC JUSTIFICATION

The emphasis on science and scientific evidence in the text of the SPS Agreement indicates a 'scientization of risk' or 'turn to science'.[226] Under the SPS Agreement, science was embraced to manage the trade-health relationship. With science as the organising principle, trade no longer has to give way to health assertions that have no scientific justification.[227] The Agreement transforms the premises of international trade law, as it is predominantly based on science and not discrimination

222 SPS Agreement, Article 2.1.

223 SPS Agreement, Article 1.1. This Article was broadly interpreted in the *EC-Biotech* case.

224 See *European Communities – Measures Concerning Meat and Meat Products (EC-Hormones)*, WT/DS26/AB/R, 16 January 1998, paragraphs 184–186; *Australia – Measures Affecting Importation of Salmon (Australia-Salmon)*, WT/DS18/AB/R, 20 October 1998, paragraph 124; *Japan – Measures Affecting Agricultural Products (Japan-Agricultural Products II)*, WT/DS76/AB/R, 22 February 1999; *Japan – Measures Affecting the Importation of Apples (Japan-Apples)*, WT/DS245/AB/R, 26 November 2003.

225 See *EC-Biotech* case.

226 For Scott, a turn to science has indeed occurred. See J. Scott, *Commentary on the Sanitary and Phytosanitary Measures Agreement* (OUP 2007). For Mavroidis, the SPS Agreement stop shorts of going beyond non-discrimination, even if there are necessity and scientific evidence requirements. See P.C. Mavroidis, 'Come Together? Producer Welfare, Consumers Welfare, and WTO Rules' in E.U. Petersmann and J. Harrison (eds), *Reforming the World Trading System: Legitimacy, Efficiency, and Democratic Governance* (OUP 2005) 285.

227 Button (n171) 228.

as the basis for adjudication.[228] The establishment of the SPS Agreement has been a milestone in the emergence of the WTO as a binding authority able to decide science-based disputes. Of course, non-discrimination is still present in the Agreement. The text of Articles 2.3 and 5.5 on non-discrimination is drawn from the chapeau of Article XX GATT and creates a standard for dealing with claims of de facto discrimination and mirrors the old form of non-discrimination under the GATT.[229]

There is an obligation of a risk assessment as the basis to an SPS measure under Article 5.1.[230] This risk assessment must be based on 'sufficient scientific evidence' under Article 2.2 and determined on a case-by-case basis.[231] The SPS Agreement provides for an exception to this rule under Article 5.7 by allowing members to adopt 'provisional measures' where 'relevant scientific evidence is insufficient'.[232]

By setting science as the main basis for a food safety measure, the SPS Agreement largely 'eliminates from a government's consideration these personal notions of risk' which could lead to a 'disjunction between the people and governmental action, as well as between law and culture, in an attempt to avoid disguised protectionism'.[233] This obligation to base an SPS measure on scientific justification leaves limited leeway to Member to base their regulations and standards on non-scientific grounds. With the 'turn to science', the WTO has, nonetheless, been charged with 'ignoring the cultural dimension of risk, and the democratic underpinnings of regulation'.[234] Thus, scientific evidence requirements can create hurdles for regulators who sincerely pursue objectives other than protectionism.[235]

A WTO Member first chooses its own, appropriate level of protection in Article 3.3,[236] and then chooses the means to achieve the level of protection sought. The Appellate Body, in the *Australia-Salmon* case, found that the 'determination of

228 Scott (n226) 3.

229 See R.E. Hudec, 'GATT/WTO Constraints on National Regulation: Requiem for an "Aim and Effects" Test' (1998) 32 *International Lawyer* 619, 645; and Scott (n226) 141.

230 *EC-Hormones*, paragraph 177.

231 *Japan-Agricultural Products II*, paragraph 84.

232 Article 5.7 SPS Agreement. This will be developed in the next section.

233 M.A. Echols, *Food Safety and the WTO: The Interplay of Culture, Science and Technology* (Kluwer Law International 2001) 28.

234 Scott (n226) 3.

235 A. Sykes, 'Domestic Regulation, Sovereignty and Scientific Evidence Requirements: A Pessimistic View' in G.A. Bermann and P.C. Mavroidis (eds), *Trade and Human Health and Safety* (CUP 2006) 257, 258.

236 Article 3.3 establishes an autonomous right to attain a higher level of protection and not just an exception from the general obligation to 'base' its level of protection on international standards under Article 3.1. International standards are used as benchmarks against which Members must base their SPS measures. If Members do not base their measures on international standards, under the footnote to Article 3.3, there must be a scientific justification that the standards are not sufficient to achieve the level of protection desired.

the appropriate level of protection was a prerogative of the Member concerned and not of a panel or of the Appellate Body'.[237] The panel cannot choose the level of protection of the Member; it must respect it. Therefore, in the *EC-Hormones* case, where the EU decided to ban the use of rBST, the panel had to respect that choice. The same would be applicable to a ban on pesticides or GM foods by the UK and the panel would not be able to question and review such a choice. Therefore, if the UK aims at achieving a high level of food and animal safety (by banning a pesticide such as neonicotinoids that can harm bees[238]), then it is entitled to do so. The panel or Appellate Body could, nonetheless, in the appropriate circumstances find that the level of protection breaches WTO rules and unlawfully restricts trade as occurred in the *EC-Hormones* case.

In the *EC-Hormones* case, the EU argued that the main motivation for the ban was the protection of the health and safety of its population and that consumer anxiety over the safety of beef treated with hormones were legitimate factors supporting its ban on growth hormones.[239] For the Appellate Body, the documentation accompanying the enactment of the prohibition made clear the depth and extent of the anxieties experienced within the EU concerning the results of the general scientific studies (showing the carcinogenicity of hormones), the dangers of abuse (highlighted by scandals relating to black-marketing and smuggling of prohibited veterinary drugs in the EU) of hormones and other substances used for growth promotion and the intense concern of consumers within the EU over the quality and drug-free character of the meat available in its internal market.[240] The Appellate Body concluded that it was unable to share the inference made by the panel that the ban was not really designed to protect its population from the risk of cancer, but rather to keep out US and Canadian hormone-treated beef and thereby to protect the domestic beef producers in the European Communities.[241] Thus, the Appellate Body reversed the conclusion of the panel that the EU had acted inconsistently with the requirements set out in Article 5.5 of the SPS Agreement on risk assessment.[242] Therefore, there is potential for the Appellate Body to take into account other factors under Article 5.5.[243] Ultimately, however, the Appellate Body fell short of approving the EU ban, asserting the inclination towards science, risk assessment and scientific justification as a basis for SPS meas-

237 *Australia-Salmon*, paragraph 199. For more on *Australia-Salmon*, see F.J. Garcia, 'The Salmon Case: Evolution of Balancing Mechanisms for Non-Trade Values in WTO' in G.A. Bermann and P.C. Mavroidis (eds), *Trade and Human Health and Safety* (CUP 2006) 133. See also, *EC-Hormones*, paragraphs 157 to 160.

238 European Commission: 'Bee Health: EU Takes Additional Measures on Pesticides to Better Protect Europe's Bees' (16 July 2013) https://ec.europa.eu/commission/presscorner/detail/en/IP_13_708 accessed 1 May 2021.

239 *EC-Hormones*, paragraph 83.

240 Ibid paragraph 245.

241 Ibid.

242 Ibid paragraph 246.

243 For more please see Hudec (n229) 647; and Regan (n155) 460.

ures. In particular, the EU measure was found to be inconsistent with Articles 5.1 and 5.2 (as well as Article 3.3) because the EU did not proceed to a risk assessment.[244]

An additional issue relates to the UK/EU ban on the use of rBST, and so-called growth hormones, injected into cows and on any meat or milk derived from animals that have been injected with growth hormones. The US won its case under Articles 3.3, 5.1 and 5.2 (on risk assessment) against the EU, since the EU ban was considered to be based on consumer anxiety towards such foods rather than scientific evidence (as required under the SPS Agreement). Ever since the US has suspended trade concessions with the EU by imposing higher import tariffs on specific EU products. However, a Memorandum of Understanding has now been agreed to allow the US to export non-hormone treated beef to the EU, especially Hilton beef, which appears to have alleviated some of the US concerns.[245] If the ban is maintained in the UK, a WTO dispute against the UK could be looming. Conversely, the US could put pressure on the UK to remove the ban, which would raise consumer and farming concerns domestically.

5.1.4.3.2 THE PRECAUTIONARY PRINCIPLE

In the case where there is 'insufficient scientific evidence', Article 5.7 can be used to base an SPS measure upon 'available pertinent information' instead of a comprehensive risk assessment for provisional measures only. Article 5.7 is a 'qualified exemption', not an exception to Article 2.2.[246] Article 5.7 establishes four cumulative requirements which must be met by a Member to adopt and maintain a provisional SPS measure. The measure must: (i) be imposed in respect of a situation where 'relevant scientific information is insufficient'; (ii) be adopted 'on the basis of available pertinent information'; (iii) 'seek to obtain the additional information necessary for a more objective assessment of risk'; and (iv) 'review the [...] measure accordingly within a reasonable period of time'.[247] What is meant by 'sufficiency' and 'scientific evidence' is central.

The SPS Agreement does not posit a defined line between circumstances in which there is a scientific justification and circumstances in which there is not. For the Appellate Body, 'insufficient scientific evidence' is different from 'scientific uncertainty': the two concepts are 'not interchangeable'.[248] However, arguably, there is not much difference between the two, in particular, as Article

244 *EC-Hormones*, paragraphs 208–209.

245 For more, see European Commission, 'The European Union and the United States Sign an Agreement on Imports of Hormone-Free Beef' (2 August 2019) https://ec.europa.eu/commission/presscorner/detail/en/IP_19_5010 accessed 1 May 2021.

246 *Japan-Agricultural Products II*, paragraph 80.

247 Ibid paragraph 89. See also, for instance, E. Stokes, 'The Role of Risk Assessment in Precautionary Intervention: A Comparison of Judicial Trends in the EC and WTO' (2007) 4 *Journal for European Environmental Planning Law* 455, 458.

248 *Japan-Apples*, paragraph 184.

5.7 has been interpreted as reflecting the precautionary principle within the SPS Agreement and the principle applies in the case of scientific uncertainty.[249]

In the *EC-Hormones* case, the Appellate Body dealt with the relevance of the precautionary principle in the interpretation of the SPS Agreement. The Appellate Body declared that the principle had not been written into the SPS Agreement as a ground for justifying SPS measures that are otherwise inconsistent with the obligations of members set out in particular provisions of that Agreement.[250] It also added that the precautionary principle found reflection in Article 5.7 and that there was 'no need to assume that Article 5.7 exhausted the relevance of a precautionary principle', which is reflected in the sixth paragraph of the preamble and in Article 3.3.[251] It concluded that the precautionary principle did not override the provisions of Article 5.1 of the SPS Agreement, whereby an SPS measure must be based on a risk assessment.[252] If the precautionary principle were introduced to a greater extent, it would remove the linchpin of the SPS Agreement which is the scientific justification principle.[253]

Overall, the UK would need to rely on scientific evidence based on a risk assessment or on the precautionary principle (but only for a provisional period) to create a measure that would, for example, ban the use of pesticides (as well as being non-discriminatory in its implementation).

5.1.4.4 The TBT Agreement and labelling requirements

As noted in Chapter 2, Section 2.4.3, the TBT Agreement allows technical regulations,[254] including labelling requirements, designed to meet legitimate national objectives under Article 2.2. The TBT Agreement aims to minimise the impact of technical regulations and standards on international trade and to ensure

249 See, for instance, Button (n171) 131; and N. Salmon, 'A European Perspective on the Precautionary Principle, Food Safety and the Free Trade Imperative of the WTO' (2002) 27 *European Law Review* 138, 146. More generally, see Stokes (n247) 455.

250 *EC-Hormones*, paragraph 124.

251 Ibid.

252 Ibid paragraph 125. A similar approach was adopted in the *EC-Biotech* case where the panel did not recognise the precautionary principle as a general principle of international law and interpreted the SPS Agreement largely in isolation from international law. For more on the role of precautionary principle see D. French, 'The Regulation of Genetically Modified Organisms and International Law: A Call for Generality' in L. Bodiguel and M.N. Cardwell (eds), *The Regulation of Genetically Modified Organisms: Comparative Approaches* (OUP 2010) 355; and J.A. McMahon, 'The *EC-Biotech* Decision: Another Missed Opportunity?' in L. Bodiguel and M.N. Cardwell (eds), *The Regulation of Genetically Modified Organisms: Comparative Approaches* (OUP 2010) 337.

253 Button (n171) 162. For more, see I. Cheyne, 'Gateways to the Precautionary Principle in WTO Law' (2007) 19 *Journal of Environmental Law* 155; and D.A. Kysar, 'Preferences for Processes: The Process/Product Distinction and the Regulation of Consumer Choice' (2004) 118 *Harvard Law Review* 525.

254 These are mandatory under Annex 1.1. Whilst compliance with technical standards is not mandatory under Annex 1.2.

that they are genuinely useful, and not arbitrary or an excuse for protectionism to achieve harmonisation.[255] If the UK were to increase its labelling requirements, for example, to impose the mandatory labelling of chlorine-washed chicken or milk or meat containing growth hormones (if the current ban would be removed), to avoid consumer deception or enhance the protection of human health or safety together with animal health or the environment,[256] then they could fall under the scope of the legitimate objectives of the TBT Agreement. Generally, labelling is perceived as 'trade friendly'[257] and is preferred to other restrictive measures such as bans.

Article 2.1 states that

> Members shall ensure that in respect of technical regulations, products imported from the territory of any Member shall be accorded treatment no less favourable than that accorded to like products of national origin and to like products originating in any other country.

It is complemented by Article 2.2 to provide comprehensive coverage of non-discrimination.[258] Members should seek to avoid unnecessary obstacles to trade and must elaborate technical requirements in a way that is not more trade-restrictive than necessary to fulfil a legitimate objective.[259] A Member could argue that the UK is restricting trade in an unnecessary manner and, second, that such requirements do not fulfil the legitimate objectives enunciated in Article 2.2. The Article creates a 'not more trade-restrictive than necessary' obligation.[260]

255 For more on the TBT Agreement, see A. Barrios Villarreal, 'International Standardization and the Agreement on Technical Barriers to Trade' (CUP 2018); and A. Davies, 'Technical Regulations and Standards under the WTO Agreement on Technical Barriers to Trade' (2014) 41(1) *Legal Issues of Economic Integration* 37.

256 TBT Agreement, Article 2.2. As observed in Chapter 2, the list is not exhaustive and additional social priorities may be included. See Chapter 2, Section 2.4.3 and also *United States – Measures Concerning the Importation, Marketing and Sale of Tuna and Tuna Products (US-Tuna II (Mexico))*, WT/DS381/AB/R, 16 May 2012, paragraph 313; and Button (n171) 86.

257 Du (n175) 232. For more on eco-labelling (so voluntary labelling) see ibid 231.

258 For more on the role of Articles 2.1. and 2.2 of the TBT Agreement, see S. Lester and W. Stemberg, 'The GATT Origins of TBT Agreement Articles 2.1 and 2.2' (2014) 17(1) *Journal of International Economic Law* 215. After the *EC-Seal Products* case, the relationship between Article XX and Article 2.1 TBT Agreement has been blurred. See G. Marceau G and T.P. Trachtman, 'A Map of the World Trade Organization Law of Domestic Regulation of Goods: The Technical Barriers to Trade Agreement, the Sanitary and Phytosanitary Measures Agreement, and the General Agreement on Tariffs and Trade' (2014) 48(2) *Journal of World Trade* 351–432; and G. Marín Durán, 'Measures with Multiple Competing Purposes after *EC – Seal Products*: Avoiding a Conflict between GATT Article XX-Chapeau and Article 2.1 TBT Agreement' (2016) 19(2) *Journal of International Economic Law* 467.

259 TBT Agreement, Article 2.2.

260 *US-Tuna II (Mexico)*, paragraph 318.

The proper use of labels for agricultural and food products to signal (quality) attributes has been one of the most contentious issues in the implementation of the TBT Agreement.[261] In the *EC-Asbestos* case, the Appellate Body declared that technical regulations had to meet three criteria: first, the technical regulation must apply to an identifiable product or group of products; second, it must lay down one or more characteristics of the product and, third, compliance with the product characteristics is made mandatory.[262] Any labelling requirements would have to meet these conditions.

Labelling requirements were also at the heart of the 2009 *US-Tuna II (Mexico)* case. In this case, the US considered tuna fishing as particularly harmful to dolphins and developed a 'dolphin-safe' labelling scheme for tuna products sold in the US that would enable consumers to know if tuna was harvested using methods that would not endanger dolphins.[263] As the Appellate Body considered that the two key objectives (the consumer information objective and the dolphin protection objective) of the scheme were to inform consumers and to protect dolphins, they both fell within the scope of legitimate objectives in Article 2.2 TBT Agreement.

Despite the 'dolphin-safe' labelling requirements being based on non-product related PPMs,[264] the Appellate Body confirmed that the scheme fell under the scope of the TBT Agreement, and more specifically Annex 1.1 as a technical regulation.[265] Article 2.1 on technical regulations consists of three elements: first, the measure constitutes a technical regulation within the meaning of Annex 1.1; second, the imported products must be 'like' the domestic product; and, third, the treatment accorded to imported products must be less favourable than that given to like domestic products and like products from other Members.[266] The label was, nonetheless, struck down by the Appellate Body because tuna captured with or without endangering dolphins were deemed like products; consequently the scheme discriminated among like products by creating 'less favourable

261 Swinbank (n181) 703.

262 See *EC-Asbestos*, paragraphs 66 to 70. For more on the *EC-Asbestos*, see R. Howse and E. Türk, 'The WTO Impact on Internal Regulations: A Case Study of the *Canada–EC Asbestos* Dispute' in G.A. Bermann and P.C. Mavroidis (eds), *Trade and Human Health and Safety* (CUP 2006) 77. See also *European Communities – Trade Description of Sardines*, WT/DS231/AB/R, 26 September 2002, paragraph 176.

263 For more on the case, see G. Shaffer, 'United States – Measures Concerning the Importation, Marketing and Sale of Tuna and Tuna Products' (2013) 107(1) *American Journal of International Law* 192; E. Baroncini and C. Brunel, 'A WTO Safe Harbour for the Dolphins: The Second Compliance Proceedings in the US – Tuna II (Mexico) Case' (2020) 19(2) *World Trade Review* 196.

264 Du (n175) 18. Indeed, the TBT Agreement explicitly refers to product-related PPMs in Annex 1.1 See above Section.

265 *US-Tuna II (Mexico)*, paragraph 199.

266 *United States – Measures Affecting the Production and Sale of Clove Cigarettes*, WT/DS231/AB/R, 4 April 2012, paragraph 87.

treatment' for Mexican tuna products under Article 2.1.[267] For the Appellate Body, the difference in treatment did not originate solely from 'legitimate regulatory distinctions'.[268]

Assessing the extraterritoriality of the labelling scheme, the Appellate Body asserted that the mere fact that a WTO Member adopts a measure requiring the exporting Member to comply with its domestic policy requirements is an integral part of any technical regulation and may negatively impact trade and is allowed under the provisions of the TBT Agreement.[269] Here, it is acknowledged that, by nature, such measures impact exporting Members.

Similarly to the Shrimp saga, the US amended its labelling scheme after the Appellate Body found the measure inconsistent with the TBT Agreement for creating discrimination. In the 2015 *US-Tuna II 21.5 (Mexico)* case (the implementation phase case), the Appellate Body reached the conclusion that the US scheme enabled better consumer information and dolphin protection through the improved administrative mechanism of certification and monitoring of dolphin safety and therefore the revised measure was no longer more trade-restrictive than necessary.[270] The new US regime is now consistent with the provisions under the TBT Agreement and enables the protection of dolphins.

Under this Agreement, the UK would not have to necessarily rely on science but rather create a measure that is non-discriminatory to fulfil a legitimate objective such as carbon labelling or growth hormones or chlorine-washed chicken labelling. If such foods are labelled in order to inform consumers, it could be perceived as an aim of avoiding consumer deception under Article 2.2. Such labelling requirements could be consistent with the TBT Agreement for as long as these requirements are not more trade-restrictive than necessary, that is they do not create means for protectionism.

Consequently, the UK could be successful in introducing and/or maintaining high regulatory standards if challenged (bearing in mind the obligations under the TCA and other FTAs). Amending the agricultural or related policies to strengthen regulatory baselines is feasible, but care would need to be taken to ensure that they either do not breach provisions of the WTO Agreements in the first instance or that they fall within a relevant justification and are not simply protectionist or discriminatory to create disguised restrictions to trade. Once again, this could be used to bolster the resilience of agricultural policies as they are developed in the future. However, whilst the potential to label is valuable, it is generally not as effective a restriction as a ban.

267 *US-Tuna II (Mexico)*, paragraph 297. However and interestingly, the Appellate Body identified the scheme as 'not more trade-restrictive than necessary' under Article 2.2 to fulfil the objectives of the scheme.

268 *United States – Measures Concerning the Importation, Marketing and Sale of Tuna and Tuna Products (US-Tuna II 21.5 (Mexico))*, WT/DS381/AB/R/US and WT/DS381/Appellate Body/RW2, 14 December 2018, paragraph 6.263.

269 *US-Tuna II (Mexico)*, paragraph 338.

270 *US-Tuna II 21.5 (Mexico)* case.

Overall, WTO law and trade agreements can have considerable sway over UK and devolved agricultural policies and practices – with the TCA as a central, but not sole example. They can help facilitate (or hinder) market access, in relation to tariffs and non-tariff barriers. They can also impact standards and regulatory baselines, pushing them alternatively upwards or downwards. Market access, environmental, food or animal welfare standards, ethics and more are all at stake here. Consequently, there is considerable scope still to use trade to help promote resilient agricultural policies for the future, but the UK and devolved administrations must reflect carefully on the relationships between external trade and internal policies and law and how they can be developed in a symbiotic fashion – including through dispute mechanisms if necessary. Naturally, the devolved administrations should have a say in any changes to the levels of such standards in devolved matters and should not only be simply required to implement changes to comply with international obligations.

5.2 A recentralisation of powers

Alongside changes on an international level, there have been three key areas of development within the UK, directly and indirectly impacting on devolved agricultural policies (beyond the path dependency observed in Chapter 4, Section 4.5.2). Reflecting the constitutional limitations of devolution and, to an extent, the sense of urgency due to the Brexit timeline (and the impact of issues such as COVID-19), all three relate to the recentralisation of powers despite agriculture being devolved in principle: financing, common frameworks and crucially the UK internal market. It should not, however, be thought that it has all gone the way of the centralised government, with no compromise or willingness to cooperate from the UK level or indeed no push-back from the devolved administrations.

5.2.1 Financing concerns

The question of financing is raised repeatedly across this book on two fronts: first, the financial support of farmers and others involved in agri-industry or land use and second, the funding provided to the devolved administrations from Westminster – whether under the block grant or otherwise.[271] They are clearly linked in practice, as the latter is necessary to help develop, implement and enforce agricultural policies – including via the financial support schemes.

271 As noted below, the Levelling Up fund followed by the UK Shared Prosperity Fund will replace the EU Structural Funds.

5.2.1.1 *Financial schemes*

The four nations' agricultural policies all entail some version of financial support schemes – predominately focused on the two-pronged approach, but with some variations as discussed in Chapters 3 and 4. The UK Government has in principle respected devolution and the right of the devolved administrations to determine their own policies and financial schemes; although the Agriculture Act 2020 does address some aspects regarding financing for Northern Ireland and Wales, it does not directly impose any restrictions on the devolved administrations on the nature of their potential financial support schemes.[272] However, its provisions that aim to ensure compliance with the Agreement on Agriculture could have a profound effect on the devolved administrations' policies.

As outlined in Chapters 2 and 3, the Agreement on Agriculture imposes some limits on financial support given to those in the agri-food industry. For instance, support aimed at incentivising increased production would fall within the Amber Box and be subjected to the strictest controls. This makes the classification of financial support significant, as there is some flexibility regarding support that falls within the Blue and Green Boxes – remembering that the Green Box can include support that promotes environmental objectives. Further, due to the limits as to the amount available for Amber Box support applying to the nation state as a whole, here the UK rather than the devolved administrations, it means that any financial support granted by one devolved may limit the ability of other devolved administrations to provide their own financial support – as the overall limit is reduced.[273] Finally, the ultimate responsibility for compliance with the Agreement on Agriculture rests with the UK.

Consequently, Sections 43 to 45 of the Agriculture Act 2020 are intended to ensure that the UK complies with its international obligations under the Agreement on Agriculture, by allowing ultimately the Secretary of State to determine the classification of individual forms of financial support (which Box they fall within) and the maximum support permitted under the Amber Box. Crucially, as discussed in Chapter 3, this is a less centralised version than that found in the Agriculture Bill 2017–2019 due to considerable pushback from the devolved administrations following intense debates.[274] Here, at least, the UK is not seeking to impose upper limits on the use of support within the Blue and Green Boxes

272 It is worth noting, however, that the Internal Market Act's new provisions on financial assistance and subsidies noted below appear to impinge on the devolved administrations and their funding of policies.

273 Financing in one devolved administration is also relevant to the others as it may impact upon competitiveness and a level playing field within the UK – see below regarding common frameworks and the internal market.

274 This is explained in detail in Chapter 3, Section 3.2.2. See, for example, Climate Change, Environment and Rural Affairs (CCERA) Committee of the Senedd Cymru, 'Report on the Supplementary Legislative Consent Memorandum for the Agriculture Bill' (June 2019) https://senedd.wales/laid%20documents/cr-ld12551/cr-ld12551-e.pdf accessed 1 May 2021.

(not required by the Agreement on Agriculture). Further, the devolved administrations are to be involved in the initial decision-making regarding classification and the maximum support available under the Amber Box, but the Secretary of State can at the end of the day act as the judge in their own court.[275]

How such provisions are implemented and enforced will be crucial to devolved agricultural policies – potentially pushing them away from direct payments and more towards environmental schemes. As noted in Chapter 2, the EU has moved direct payments away from the Amber and Blue Boxes towards the Green Box.[276] It is essential that the devolved administrations utilise the opportunity in these provisions to engage wholeheartedly in their implementation (including the classification of payments), whilst still ensuring all payments are within the letter and spirit of the Agreement on Agriculture. This will help to counter the centralisation to an extent and facilitate the development of policies tailored to the particular contexts of each devolved administration. To do otherwise risks increasing the level of path dependency already demonstrated when it comes to the financial schemes, as discussed in Chapter 4, Section 4.5.2. However, the controls via the WTO Sections of the Agriculture Act are not the only ones that exist in practice.

5.2.1.2 Funding the nations: agriculture and beyond

As discussed in Chapter 2, Section 2.5, the devolved administrations are highly dependent on funding received from Westminster. This is typically via the block grant using the Barnett formula, which could impact negatively on the funding for the devolved administrations.[277] As the UK Government has stated that this approach will not be taken to providing funding for agriculture post-Brexit,[278] this begs the question as to how such funding will be determined – with no clear answer to date.

Whilst there was a review undertaken by Lord Bew in 2019 regarding a related funding issue in agriculture,[279] it did not specifically address wider agricultural funding and also was focused on the 2020–2022 period. Nonetheless, it provides

275 See Chapter 3, Section 3.2.2.

276 This point is developed in Chapter 2, Section 2.4.2.3.

277 As noted in Chapter 3, Section 3.1.1, the President of the Farmers' Union of Wales considered that the UK Government's current allocation for England results in a 35% cut for Wales. See Farmers' Union of Wales, 'FUW Stresses Need for Clarity on Funding for Wales at Roundtable Meeting with Secretary of State for Environment, Food and Rural Affairs' (19 March 2021) https://fuw.org.uk/en/news/14441-fuw-stresses-need-for-clarity-on-funding-for-wales-at-roundtable-meeting-with-secretary-of-state-for-environment-food-and-rural-affairs accessed 1 May 2021.

278 FarmingUK Team, 'Gove Guarantees Agri Funding Will Not Be 'Barnettised' Post-Brexit' (FarmingUK 12 October 2018) www.farminguk.com/news/gove-guarantees-agri-funding-will-not-be-barnettised-post-brexit_50455.html accessed 1 May 2021.

279 Lord P. Bew, 'Intra-UK Allocations Review' (UK Government, September 2019) https://assets.publishing.service.gov.uk/government/uploads/system/uploads/attachment_data/file/829757/intra-allocation-uk-review.pdf accessed 1 May 2021.

some valuable insights. It highlighted that the Barnett formula was inappropriate for agriculture – and considered so by stakeholders across the UK.[280] The Bew report also outlines a range of potential factors that could be considered in determining the basis for funding, including simply respect for the Devolution Settlements and maintaining stability, including current allocations.[281]

One alternative not highlighted there expressly, but overlapping to an extent with various factors, is that of 'needs' – bearing in mind, for instance, policy objectives, the nature of the land and the economic viability of the farms.[282] If applied objectively (and in light of the policy ambitions), such an approach would ensure enough funding to support resilient agricultural policies tailored appropriately to the context of each nation. The Bew report recommended that a 'needs-based approach' be taken regarding convergence funding, in light of the nature of the quality of the land across the four administrations[283] – but this specific recommendation was only as a 'one-off solution'.[284] A needs-based approach also reflects a floor for the funding Wales receives under the block grant, which could be extended to the rest of the UK and would provide much greater flexibility[285] – although with caveats. The two main caveats would remain that (i) the funding might still be part of the block grant and therefore not ringfenced and (ii) the UK might seek to exercise some control over the definition of needs and whether they are reasonable or not, including therefore over set policy objectives and how these are achieved. Clearly it would be essential for the devolved administrations to resist any such efforts and maintain control over their own policies and therefore needs.

Nothing has yet been determined regarding future intra-UK allocation of agriculture funding, but as acknowledged in the Bew Report, it will be essential for the devolved administrations to work closely with Westminster to ensure that the basis for determining funding is appropriate for agriculture[286] and that the UK Government does not end up curtailing their powers to set agricultural policies.

280 Ibid 68.
281 Ibid section 6.
282 This 'needs-based' approach has been proposed in relation to the UK Shared Prosperity Fund. See P. Brien, 'The UK Shared Prosperity Fund' (House of Commons Library, CBP-8527, 29 January 2021) 16. In October 2020, the Welsh Affairs Select Committee identified that such funds be allocated on a needs-based formula. See House of Commons, Welsh Affairs Select Committee, 'Wales and the Shared Prosperity Fund: Priorities for the Replacement of EU Structural Funding' (2 October 2020).
283 Bew (n279) 70–72.
284 Ibid 72.
285 M. Keep, 'The Barnett Formula' (House of Commons Library, CBP 7386, 23 January 2020) http://researchbriefings.files.parliament.uk/documents/CBP-7386/CBP-7386.pdf accessed 1 May 2021, section 1.4. As noted by Keep in Section 2.1, this extension has previously been suggested.
286 This was also recognised in the UK Government's response to the Bew Review. See DEFRA et al., 'UK Government Response to the Independent Intra-UK Allocations Review (Bew Review)' (6 September 2019) www.gov.uk/government/publications/domestic-farm-support-funding-bew-review-government-response/uk-government-response-to-the-independent-intra-uk-allocations-review-bew-review accessed 1 May 2021.

On this front, the proposals noted below regarding financial assistance more generally in the context of the Internal Market Act are also relevant.

However, the block grant or a potential ring-fenced agricultural fund are not the sole considerations when it comes to funding for the four nations that could be used to promote a resilient agriculture. There have been significant developments regarding complementary funding programmes. For instance, to replace EU Structural Funds, the Levelling Up Fund was announced in March 2021.[287] This is the foundation to the UK Shared Prosperity Fund, the details of which are not yet confirmed but it will start in 2022.[288] The £4.8 billion Levelling Up Fund includes £800 million to be shared between Wales, Scotland and Northern Ireland over the next four years. However, in Wales, counties such as Gwynedd and Anglesey that are usually recipients of EU Structural Funds are not included in the priority list.[289] Despite the clear impacts on devolution, such decisions have been taken with no input from the Welsh Government (facilitated by the Internal Market Act provisions discussed below).[290]

As outlined in Chapters 3 and 4, the four nations have made varying progress in developing their own agricultural policies. However, whilst there are some significant variations and Scotland has pronounced that it is creating a 'bespoke' policy, nonetheless there has been considerable influence to date by the English approach over the devolved policies – reflecting path dependency as flagged in Chapter 4.[291] In particular, the two-pronged approach is seen in the Welsh and Northern Irish proposals, as well as Scotland's transitional policy. Focus points on environmental goods and productivity are reflected throughout. The developments in approaches to the Agreement on Agriculture, as well as funding for the devolved administrations, highlight the importance for the devolved administrations of identifying and challenging centralising steps, especially where there

287 See HM Treasury, Ministry to House, Communities and Local Government and Development for Transport, 'Levelling Up Fund: Prospectus' (March 2021) https://assets.publishing.service.gov.uk/government/uploads/system/uploads/attachment_data/file/966138/Levelling_Up_prospectus.pdf accessed 1 May 2021.

288 The design and management of the Shared Prosperity Fund remain uncertain at the time of writing. In particular, the limited engagement with the devolved administrations and questions over the allocation system and amount of funding available have led to concerns from the devolved administrations. See House of Commons, Welsh Affairs Select Committee, 'Correspondence: Wales and the Shared Prosperity Fund' https://committees.parliament.uk/work/41/wales-and-the-shared-prosperity-fund/publications/3/correspondence/ accessed 1 May 2021.

289 See BBC News, 'Row after Gwynedd Placed in Lowest Priority Group for Levelling Up Fund' (4 March 2021) www.bbc.co.uk/news/uk-wales-politics-56279405 accessed 1 May 2021.

290 See House of Commons, Welsh Affairs Select Committee (n288). For these reasons, the organisation the Good Law Project considered a legal challenge of the Fund. See A. Bounds and J. Pickard, 'Levelling Up Fund Design is Unlawful, Says UK Campaign Group' (Financial Times 5 April 2021) www.ft.com/content/9757ad6d-45b8-4db5-95f8-2d236a670af7accessed 1 May 2021.

291 See Chapter 4, Section 4.5.2.

may already be path dependency or where it may arise in future. Otherwise, the centralised bodies and their policies may gain greater traction in the devolved administrations, despite not being tailored suitably to the localities.

5.2.2 Common frameworks and their insufficient advances

Some progress has been made on common frameworks – with more work completed than might at first be apparent.[292] It is the implementation of the Joint Ministerial Committee's (JMC) principles,[293] through the initial determination of what frameworks might be required and their subsequent development, that is of particular interest here for future agricultural policy. The significance is in part through already shaping governance, whether in imposing fresh restrictions or enabling specific measures, and in part through providing insight into what the UK Government in particular deems essential to centralise and their approach to operationalising this. It should be remembered when considering the development of common frameworks that there is commonality currently – even if technically there are not UK common frameworks and some divergence does exist currently, the regimes across the UK are based on EU common frameworks and therefore there are varying degrees of existing regulatory harmonisation. But at the heart of EU common frameworks is the principle of subsidiarity reflected in EU mechanisms of multilevel governance,[294] whilst UK common frameworks are based on the principle of commonality that recentres policy formulation.[295]

As noted by Brennan, Dobbs and Gravey, the choice of frameworks reflects a 'clear prioritisation in protecting a UK single market and facilitating trade',[296] whereas objectives such as environmental protection are effectively cast-aside – despite the obvious status of water, for instance, as a 'common resource'[297] and

292 The latest official report provides only limited information on progress. See Cabinet Office, 'The European Union (Withdrawal) Act and Common Frameworks: 26 June to 25 September 2020' (9th Statutory Report December 2020) https://assets.publishing.service.gov.uk/government/uploads/system/uploads/attachment_data/file/941711/The_European_Union__Withdrawal__Act_and_Common_Frameworks.pdf accessed 1 May 2021. However, there has been considerable work undertaken, as reflected in evidence given to the House of Lords Scrutiny Committee. See House of Lords, Common Frameworks Scrutiny Committee, 'Common Frameworks: Building a Cooperative Union' (1st Report of Session 2019–21, HL Paper 259, 31 March 2021). This does of course highlight issues over transparency, as noted by the Committee at 16–23.

293 See Chapter 2, Section 2.5 for further details.

294 For more on multilevel governance see Chapter 2.

295 L. Petetin, 'Setting the Path for UK and Devolved Agriculture' in I. Antonopoulos, M. Bell, A. Cavoski and L. Petetin (eds), *The Governance of Agriculture in Post-Brexit UK* (Routledge forthcoming 2022).

296 C. Brennan, M. Dobbs and V. Gravey, 'Out of the Frying Pan, into the Fire? Environmental Governance Vulnerabilities in Post-Brexit Northern Ireland' (2019) 21(2) *Environmental Law Review* 84, 94.

297 This is one of the JMC's key factors for considering whether a common framework might be needed.

the UK's supposed aim of a 'Green Brexit'. No frameworks are considered necessary for land use, environmental impact assessments, water quality or water flooding and only political frameworks for areas such as air and marine quality – despite the potential for serious transboundary effects in each of these. This is also reflected, for instance, in efforts to develop individual environmental policies across the UK and the Environment Bill 2019–2021 being proposed predominately for England, with some elements for Wales and Northern Ireland – but crucially not applying uniformly across the UK. This will lead to not merely divergence between the UK and the EU, but also between different parts of the UK, and risk downward spirals in environmental governance as discussed in Chapter 3. This exclusion of environmental issues from common frameworks for the main part conflicts directly with the JMC's own principles and criteria, as well as the ideas of subsidiarity outlined in Chapter 2.

In contrast, not only did the JMC prioritise certain areas for the development of common frameworks, but greater progress has been made in these areas since. A range of areas directly relevant to agriculture was deemed to potentially require legislative frameworks, including plant health, animal health and welfare, organic farming, GMO marketing and cultivation,[298] pesticides, fertilisers, agricultural support and food labelling and compositional standards.[299] Indeed, over half of the listed areas directly relate to agricultural production across the length of the supply chain. From a practical perspective, having common frameworks for these areas makes sense – for instance, they should facilitate shared food and production standards that would enable human and animal health, as well as consumer protection, all whilst levelling internal playing fields and facilitating internal trade and broad compliance with international obligations.

Progress on some of the areas within the common framework process has been limited, impacted by the general pressures posed by Brexit and also the added challenges of COVID-19.[300] In an updated 2020 analysis, of all 154 areas identified, only 18 were considered to require legislative frameworks[301] and this has been further reduced since[302] – thereby arguably easing the burden for those tasked with replacing them. At the time of writing, whilst efforts were ongoing across the board and considerable foundational work had been completed, only seven frameworks (including on nutrition labelling, composition and standards; on hazardous substances (planning); on food and feed safety and hygiene; and on food compositional standards and labelling) had been provisionally approved by

298 Note however that GMOs have been removed since – without any reasons or announcements to this effect, as noted in Chapter 2, Section 2.3.2.

299 UK Government, 'Frameworks Analysis 2020: Breakdown of Areas of EU Law that Intersect with Devolved Competence in Scotland, Wales and Northern Ireland' (2020) https://assets.publishing.service.gov.uk/government/uploads/system/uploads/attachment_data/file/919729/Frameworks-Analysis-2020.pdf accessed 1 May 2021.

300 Cabinet Office (n292).

301 UK Government (n299).

302 House of Lords, Common Frameworks Scrutiny Committee (n292) 16–21.

the JMC and then prepared for parliamentary scrutiny.[303] Other significant frameworks were still formally in the offing. For instance, the eventual framework for UK agricultural support is intended to cover agricultural and rural support spending, enforcement and marketing standards; crisis measures, public intervention and private storage aid; cross-border holdings (within the UK); data collection and sharing.[304] However, the House of Lords Scrutiny Committee reported that 'almost all common frameworks [were] operational since the end of the transition period' – despite them not being published prior to the end of the transition period or during the three month period between then and the publication of the Scrutiny Committee's Report.[305]

This discrepancy highlights a serious concern in the implementation of the common framework process (as with the identification of areas noted in Chapter 2, Section 2.5). Whilst the process remains somewhat collaborative vis-à-vis the devolved administrations, there is insufficient transparency or engagement with stakeholders to date. Although this is understandable to an extent due to the time pressures and limited resources, it weakens the quality, legitimacy and accountability of the process and resulting frameworks. As noted by the House of Lords Scrutiny Committee, whilst the process also needs to be sped up, there is simultaneously a need for much greater transparency and engagement throughout the process,[306] as well as continued scrutiny in future.[307] These considerations will be essential in reviewing the common frameworks in future.

Whilst the Agriculture Act 2020 initially made slow progress too, it has since been passed and with considerable significance to areas supposedly to be addressed by common frameworks at most, including regarding the use of fertilisers, labelling and classification of financial support. The difficulty that ensues is that whilst the Agriculture Act 2020 does facilitate a UK-wide (or Great Britain) approach in some areas, it (i) does not actually guarantee high standards in doing so; (ii) provides for the UK Government to develop the content at a later stage, which essentially entails a centralisation power; (iii) does so by bypassing the common framework approach despite covering devolved matters; and (iv) enables the UK Government to act unilaterally and impose an English approach on the devolved administrations – especially since Scotland was not involved in the drafting of the Act.

303 Cabinet Office, 'UK Common Frameworks' (22 December 2020) www.gov.uk/government/collections/uk-common-frameworks#uk-common-frameworks---2021-provisional-frameworks accessed 1 May 2021.
304 DEFRA, 'Farming for the Future: Policy and Progress Update' (February 2020) https://assets.publishing.service.gov.uk/government/uploads/system/uploads/attachment_data/file/868041/future-farming-policy-update1.pdf accessed 1 May 2021, 41; and UK Government (n299) 46.
305 House of Lords, Common Frameworks Scrutiny Committee (n292) 3, 23 and 49.
306 Ibid 16–23 and 47–49.
307 Ibid 45.

Thus, in seeking the maintenance of some UK-wide frameworks, the UK Government has prioritised their existence and content over *how* they are and will be designed – with some kickback by the devolved administrations and in particular Scotland.[308] A shift from the common framework process based on cooperation, collaboration and even consensus to a unilaterally developed framework in the Agriculture Act 2020 is clearly visible; this recentralisation to the detriment of the devolved administrations and without providing any guarantees regarding standards is highly concerning. It is also exemplified by the more recent Internal Market Act.

5.2.3 *The UK internal market, its underpinnings and consequences*

Whilst the eventual Internal Market Act 2020 has been toned down to an extent, the original Internal Market Bill 2019–2021 sent shockwaves around the legal and political world – not just within the UK but also beyond. Whilst the Act's core aim of furthering the UK internal market was expected and legitimate in principle, the Bill proposed to achieve this through some considerable centralisation of powers[309] and through being willing to conflict outright with international law – including the very UK/EU Withdrawal Agreement and Northern Ireland Protocol that this same UK Government co-authored, signed and campaigned on. Whilst the Act stepped back on the international law elements in particular (discussed in Section 5.2.3.2), it largely maintains its recentralisation of powers. Indeed, it is worth noting that, like the Agriculture Act 2020, although the Internal Market Act creates some significant UK-wide and Great Britain-wide rules, it is once more outside the common framework process.[310] Further, Scotland recently passed the UK Withdrawal from the European Union (Legal Continuity) (Scotland) Act which provides for continued Scottish alignment with EU law in devolved matters including on animal health and welfare, plant health and environmental protection.[311] The extent to which divergence will play out remains to be seen but is likely to create issues within the UK internal market.

308 See Chapter 3 and how Scotland has consistently refused to engage with the Agriculture Act 2020.

309 This was also flagged at the White Paper stage, see D. Torrance, 'Reserved Matters in the United Kingdom' (House of Commons Library, CBP-8544, 5 April 2019) https://researchbriefings.files.parliament.uk/documents/CBP-8544/CBP-8544.pdf accessed 1 May 2021.

310 The Bill's impact assessment expressly states that the Bill is being evaluated in comparison with a 'do nothing' option 'because [...] Common Frameworks have not been agreed'. See BEIS, 'Impact Assessment on the Internal Market Bill' (9 September 2020) https://publications.parliament.uk/pa/bills/cbill/58-01/0177/UK%20Internal%20Market%20Bill%20Impact%20Assessment%2008092020.pdf accessed 1 May 2021, 16. It should be noted that even if a unilaterally imposed UK-wide framework were deemed necessary, it would not need to be in the form currently proposed.

311 UK Withdrawal from the European Union (Continuity) (Scotland) Act 2021, Sections 1 and 2.

Both the initial Bill and subsequent Act provide some interesting insights into UK Government thinking and will have significant ramifications – including for domestic agricultural policy.

5.2.3.1 Centralising powers yet again

Centralisation of powers occurring under the Act is visible in key elements that will be addressed in turn and in particular with the use of the principle of mutual recognition. The legality of the Act as to its impact on devolved legislative competences has, nonetheless, been challenged by the Welsh Government.

5.2.3.1.1 THE IMPACT OF THE PRINCIPLE OF MUTUAL RECOGNITION

The Act introduces two key 'market access' principles[312] that are to apply across Great Britain but not fully to Northern Ireland[313] (due to the Northern Ireland Protocol). They are familiar at first glance, as they are the principles of mutual recognition and non-discrimination[314] and EU versions have applied in the UK for decades. The discussion herein examines the principle of mutual recognition as it directly affects agri-food.

The Act's principle of mutual recognition focuses on the role of 'relevant requirements', interpreted very broadly to include, for instance, production methods, environmental standards, identification or tracing procedures and food characteristics.[315] The Act distinguishes between requirements that exist prior to the passing of the Act (excluded from the mutual recognition principle)[316] and new[317] requirements introduced after that date (subject to mutual recognition).

312 Regarding the original Bill, see M. Dougan, 'United Kingdom Internal Market Bill: Implications for Devolution' (15 September 2020) www.liverpool.ac.uk/media/livacuk/law/2-research/eull/UKIM,Briefing,Paper,-,Prof,Michael,Dougan,15,September,2020.pdf accessed 1 May 2021.

313 Internal Market Act, Section 11.

314 Internal Market Act, Sections 2 and 5 respectively. Although not discussed here, the non-discrimination principle complements mutual recognition, as it is intended to stop one part of the UK from discriminating against goods that originate from another part of the UK – including via indirect discrimination. Further, similar approaches can be seen in the context of services, which are also relevant to the agri-food industry but they are outside the scope of this book.

315 Internal Market Act, Section 3.

316 Ibid Section 4. Such requirements must also *not* have been common across the rest of the UK at the time.

317 New requirements need not be those introduced as brand new for the first time. They may also include ones where existing requirements are substantially amended. See Dougan (n312). For example, if there were an existing requirement (in place before the Internal Market Act was passed) that seaweed products could only be produced from three specific types of seaweed, this would be excluded from the mutual recognition principle. However, if this were later amended to limit it to two specific types of seaweed, then the requirement could now be deemed new and fall within the scope of the provision.

Thus, the Act provides that any product produced or *imported* into one part of Great Britain[318] and permitted to be used or sold there would be permitted to be used or sold anywhere across Great Britain – without being bound by new relevant requirements. Whilst any part of the UK may introduce new requirements, these can no longer apply to such goods coming from elsewhere in Great Britain. So far, this mirrors to a great extent the EU's approach to mutual recognition.

However, the exceptions to the mutual recognition principle provide a significant departure from EU law with profound ramifications for devolution – something which is not adequately addressed in the Government's Impact Assessment.[319] Via Section 10, Schedule 1 provides for limited exclusions to mutual recognition, for instance, based on preventing the spread of pests or diseases that pose threats to human, animal or plant health such as vCJD (variant Creutzfeldt-Jakob disease), ash dieback disease or foot and mouth disease. However, these justifications are far narrower than under EU law[320] and can only be amended by the Secretary of State[321] – entailing further centralisation since the devolved administrations (individually or collectively) cannot modify these exclusions – away from the principle of subsidiarity[322] towards, yet again, the principle of commonality.[323]

During the parliamentary process, the House of Lords proposed two key changes relevant to these aspects. Firstly, it proposed protecting common frameworks, whereby mutual recognition would not apply where harmonised measures had already been developed or even where they were under consideration with the common frameworks process. Secondly, it proposed broader exemptions in the

318 Under Section 11 of the Internal Market Act, the principle also applies to Northern Irish 'qualifying goods', but not to goods from Great Britain entering Northern Ireland.

319 BEIS (n310). This document focuses primarily on economic or monetary impacts, briefly noting on pages 3 and 25, that local policy effectiveness may be curtailed, with societal benefits 'not fully realised' or 'foregone'.

320 Under Article 36 of the Consolidated Version of the Treaty on the Functioning of the European Union (TFEU) [2008] OJ C115/47, exceptions to the EU principle of mutual recognition include public health, consumer protection, the protection of health and life of humans, animals or plants and environmental protection. Where EU harmonisation exists, there are varied criteria in place facilitating variations by Member States (and territories within them) depending on the basis and level of the harmonisation measures, see Articles 114 and 193 TFEU.

321 Internal Market Act, Section 10 (2).

322 For more, see V. Gravey and A. Jordan, 'Towards an Ever Closer Union?' (Brexit and Environment Network 21 July 2020) www.brexitenvironment.co.uk/2020/07/21/towards-an-ever-closer-union/ accessed 1 May 2021; V. Gravey, A. Jordan and L. Petetin, 'United against Diversity? The UK Internal Market and Environmental Ambition' (Brexit and Environment Network 22 July 2020) www.brexitenvironment.co.uk/2020/07/22/united-against-diversity-uk-internal-market-environmental-ambition/ accessed 1 May 2021; and V. Gravey, 'The Internal Market Bill: Why Negative Integration is Causing such Negative Feelings' (Brexit and Environment Network 16 October 2020) www.brexitenvironment.co.uk/2020/10/16/internal-market-bill-why-negative-integration-is-causing-such-negative-feelings/ accessed 1 May 2021.

323 Petetin (n295).

form of 'public interest derogations', which would have provided the devolved administrations with considerable flexibility. The House of Commons rejected both of these proposals[324] in order to protect the UK internal market, although a weaker version of protection of common frameworks via Section 10 and Schedule 1 is then included in the final Act as a quasi-compromise.[325] Section 10(2) provides for the Secretary of State to regulate to amend Schedule 1 (exclusions from application of the market access principles), including now under Section 10(3) 'to give effect to an agreement that (a) forms part of a common framework agreement, and (b) provides that certain cases, matters, requirements or provision should be expressly excluded from the application of market access principles'. It is therefore only *agreed* upon common frameworks that can be excluded from the scope of the Act and where the framework has indicated that such matters should be excluded. Some flexibility is achieved through Section 10(4)'s definition of common frameworks to include those between a Minister of the Crown and even one devolved administration (so bilateral or trilateral frameworks are possible), but the exception still remains quite limited and dependent on the UK Government.

The approach adopted in the Act undermines the devolved administrations' ability to set new (or substantially revise) policies and legislate in a range of key areas or indeed to achieve their desired objectives. This is a clear interference with devolution and will most likely entail Westminster playing a key role in the determining of relevant policies, since trade agreements set by Westminster may, for instance, permit goods of a lower standard to be introduced across Great Britain and devolved administrations are required to implement international obligations. Furthermore, without the ability for a reasonably wide range of justifications as currently exists under EU law, there is the legal scope for a regulatory race to the bottom as the lowest common denominator becomes the one standard across Great Britain.[326] It would still be possible for one part of Great Britain to impose higher standards on produce originating in that part, but it would immediately place those local producers at a competitive disadvantage and potentially without any material benefits for the intended objectives. For instance, when raising standards relating to product characteristics or labelling information in one part of the UK, this would not prevent products with lower standards coming from other parts of the UK from being available on the shelves.

324 House of Lords, 'Amendments to the UK Internal Market Bill – Commons Reasons and Amendments to Words Restored to the Bill' (2020) https://publications.parliament.uk/pa/bills/lbill/58-01/156/5801156.pdf accessed 1 May 2021; and House of Commons, 'Proceedings on Consideration of Lords Amendments to the United Kingdom Internal Market Bill – Supplement to the Votes and Proceedings' (7 December 2020) https://publications.parliament.uk/pa/bills/cbill/58-01/0224/amend/UKIM_pro_ccla_1207.pdf accessed 1 May 2021.

325 House of Lords (n324).

326 Gravey, Jordan and Petetin (n322).

It may be difficult for a devolved administration to maintain higher standards against the economically dominant nation that is England (and its sheer size). Dougan, for instance, highlights two examples for Scotland where the principle of mutual recognition might apply: changes to minimum alcohol pricing, and the introduction of prohibitions on single use, non-recyclable plastic packaging. He notes that the application of mutual recognition – or even its potential application – 'would be a powerful disincentive' in acting in devolved matters and would 'effectively render the entire regulatory objective and scheme inoperable'.[327] England might also permit the import and sale of chlorine-washed chicken without any restrictions, which could then be sold similarly in Wales and Scotland even if they were to introduce and impose prohibitions or have labelling requirements on such chickens for their own producers.[328] Whilst Northern Ireland is excluded from having to apply mutual recognition, it is still impacted due to exporting to the market in Great Britain – where Northern Irish products may find themselves at a competitive disadvantage and this may have knock-on effects on both Northern Ireland's industry and policy.

Nonetheless, it should not be thought that a race to the bottom or decline in standards is the automatic outcome of the mutual recognition principle. No government will wish to be seen as the one pushing a decline in agri-food standards (with the UK Government pointing out that there was no need for guarantees in the Agriculture Bill because the level of food standards would be maintained).[329] The UK also has a positive position regarding animal welfare, as discussed above, and has been proclaiming its intent to have a 'Green Brexit'.[330] The Trade and Agriculture Commission could also play a valuable role here, through helping provide some input in trade developments[331] as discussed above. Furthermore, stakeholders – including consumers, farmers and retailers – can have their say through their decisions and choices[332] as well as lobbying.[333] This is also reflected

327 Dougan (n312) 7–8.

328 As observed earlier in this chapter, consumer preferences and decisions taken by actors such as retailers might prevent this from occurring. See T. Pilgrim, 'Aldi Rules Out Selling Chlorinated Chicken or Hormone-Injected Beef in UK' (Independent 8 July 2020) www.independent.ie/business/farming/agri-business/agri-food/aldi-rules-out-selling-chlorinated-chicken-or-hormone-injected-beef-in-uk-39347921.html accessed 1 May 2021.

329 BBC News, 'Agriculture Bill: Bid to Protect Post-Brexit Food Standards Rejected' (12 October 2020) www.bbc.com/news/uk-politics-54506185 accessed 1 May 2021.

330 See C. Baynes, 'Government to Set Up Environmental Watchdog to Deliver "Green Brexit", Says Michael Gove' (Independent 12 November 2017) www.independent.co.uk/news/uk/politics/michael-gove-environment-secretary-green-brexitandrew-marr-show-european-union-a8050626.html accessed 1 May 2021.

331 J. Evans, 'UK Trade Body to Push for Tough Standards on Imported Food' (Financial Times 10 January 2021) www.ft.com/content/62b1e447-c328-4026-b791-4e8306643f5a accessed 1 May 2021.

332 See Pilgrim (n328).

333 Although unsuccessful in pressuring the UK Government to insert provisions protecting high standards in the Trade Bill 2019–2021, a wide range of stakeholders came together to voice their concerns over potential decreases in standards. See S. Laville, 'Farmers Urge

in the nature of high-quality goods and the importance of reputation, for example, Welsh lamb, which can demand a premium. Not to mind that the TCA's level playing field provisions, including the non-regression principle, will impact to an extent on domestic policies and practices for the foreseeable future. All of these can put a brake on the potential decline in standards.

Finally, it is worth noting that the mutual recognition principle might (i) have incentivised the devolved administrations to legislate immediately (before the Internal Market Act was passed), so that any requirements were not 'new';[334] and/or (ii) continue to incentivise closer cooperation between the administrations and a push for common frameworks to raise standards – especially now in light of the amendments to Section 10. Crucially, a shared higher standard developed within a common framework would avoid the mutual recognition principle and lessen the likelihood of the subsequent race to the bottom. However, on the latter, the difficulty is that the Act is eroding trust further and, according to Section 10(4), there would need to be an agreement between a Minister of the Crown and at least one devolved administration in creating such frameworks – something that seems unlikely on issues such as GMOs, gene editing or potentially chlorine-washed chickens.

5.2.3.1.2 OTHER KEY ELEMENTS

Beyond the principles of market access, three main aspects bolster centralisation. First, the Internal Market Act addresses subsidies and their control (Section 52) and financial assistance (Section 50) across the UK (including beyond agriculture). For instance, Section 50 grants Ministers of the Crown considerable flexibility to provide financial assistance, including to individuals and devolved territories, for instance, via the UK Shared Prosperity Fund noted above – this is for a wide range of purposes, essentially as a Minister may deem appropriate.[335] Section 52 goes a step further, reserving powers over subsidies to the UK level with minimum consultations with the devolved administrations. On this front, Section 53 is also of interest as it addresses engagement of devolved authorities in the UK Government's consultation on subsidy control – with an obligation on the Government to share the consultation with the devolved administrations prior to publication. However, prior consultation or not, the UK Government creates a regime for Great Britain for state aid, whilst it arguably is

---

UK Government to Protect Food Standards in Post-Brexit Trade Bill' (The Guardian 21 May 2020) www.theguardian.com/environment/2020/may/21/farmers-urge-government-protect-food-standards-trade-bill accessed 1 May 2021. The cumulative pressures did however lead to developments with the creation of the Trade and Agriculture Commission. They also demonstrate the widespread concerns across varied types of stakeholders.

334 This option was highly restricted due to little parliamentary time being available before the Act was passed.

335 The lack of consultation with the devolved administrations is already exemplified in the Shared Prosperity Fund. See House of Commons, Welsh Affairs Select Committee (n288).

a devolved matter.[336] Although funding is provided to devolved administrations by Westminster and is currently calculated under the Barnett formula, nonetheless, it is up to the devolved administrations how they will allocate funding within their own territories – unless ring-fenced or permitted to meet specific objectives. If UK Ministers provide funding, this may conflict with devolved policies[337] – the UK could provide financial assistance to individuals or bodies for specific purposes that would undermine devolved policies, for instance, to intensify farming in a nature reserve or prevent subsidies approved by the devolved administrations in furtherance of central policies. Further, there is no clarity as to the relationship between Sections 50 and 52 on the one hand and the general funding or block grant provided to the devolved administrations – will monies received via these provisions eat away from the block grant or any other potential financial support the devolved administrations might receive? It appears from the Bill's Impact Assessment that this might be the case.[338] These provisions may create extra challenges for the devolved administrations seeking to design and implement tailored agricultural policies effectively.

Second, the Act ensures it cannot be legislated against by devolved administrations. As with other key Brexit legislation, it provides for it to be a protected Act.[339] In this way, once passed, the devolved administrations would effectively find their competence and actions limited – exemplified by the market access principles. Further, originally, Clause 45 provided for Clauses 42 and 43 (regarding the Northern Ireland Protocol) and corresponding implementing measures to be immune from legal challenges based on both international and domestic law – including therefore any of the Devolution Settlements or any primary legislation by devolved administrations. However, following continued negotiations with the EU on the implementation of the Northern Ireland Protocol, both Clauses 42 and 43 were amended substantially and Clause 45 was removed (see Section 5.2.3.2 below).

Third, whilst the UK Government purportedly seeks legislative consent from the devolved administrations, the EU (Withdrawal) Act 2018 and EU (Withdrawal Agreement) Act 2020 show a willingness to legislate without obtaining such consent. Prior to the placing of the Internal Market Bill before Parliament, there was no significant opportunity for the devolved administrations to contribute in a meaningful way, with no consensus achieved.[340] It instead

336 K. Hayward, 'The Internal Market Bill and Northern Ireland: Where it Comes from and What it Might Mean' (The UK in a Changing Europe 25 September 2020) https://ukandeu.ac.uk/explainers/the-internal-market-bill-and-northern-ireland-where-it-comes-from-and-what-it-might-mean/ accessed 1 May 2021.

337 See J. Bradbury, 'Welsh Devolution and the Union: Reform Debates after Brexit' (2021) 92(1) *Political Quarterly* 125, 127.

338 BEIS (n310) 43.

339 Internal Market Act, Section 54.

340 See Scottish Government, 'UK Internal Market White Paper: Initial Assessment by the Scottish Government' (12 August 2020) www.gov.scot/publications/uk-internal-market/

appears to be an English/UK Government approach being imposed unilaterally upon the devolved administrations. The devolved administrations have expressed their frustration, especially in light of the extensive and broad-sweeping powers outlined in the Bill, which resulted in Wales and Scotland withdrawing their legislative consent.[341] Whilst the Act was modified to address concerns regarding international law and tweaked in relation to common frameworks, it largely retains its significant centralising components. This also raises a significant concern for the UK Government regarding implementation and enforcement, as although the Act does provide for an enforcement body, it nonetheless is reliant upon the devolved administrations on a day-to-day basis to implement. That is of increasing importance since this is linked to existing and future trade agreements, as the UK could be held in breach if the devolved administrations did not fully comply with any ensuing international obligations to implement trade agreements.[342] Although the UK Government constitutionally[343] can revoke any devolved legislation that is incompatible with international obligations,[344] including under FTAs, it is still possible for the devolved administrations to impede the implementation of FTAs through acting in breach or simply not proactively acting to implement the FTAs. Without the devolved administrations' support, the UK risks trade disputes or potential partners refusing to conclude FTAs – with further knock-on effects for the devolved administrations and stakeholders.

In January 2021, the Counsel General for Wales sought permission for a judicial review[345] of the Internal Market Act 2020 to 'protect the Senedd from

---

accessed 1 May 2021. The Scottish Government notes that 'The UK Government published its White Paper on the "UK Internal Market" on 16 July with a four-week consultation period. No detail or copy had been shared with the Scottish Government in advance of publication. No draft Bill has been published'. For more on the position of Scotland regarding the Internal Market Act, see Scottish Government, 'After Brexit: The UK Internal Market Act and Devolution' (8 March 2021) www.gov.scot/publications/brexit-uk-internal-market-act-devolution/ accessed 1 May 2021. More generally on the impact of Brexit on EU regions, see G. Lagana, 'Has the European Union Empowered the Regions? A Pre- and Post-Brexit Preliminary Investigation of the United Kingdom' (2021) 28(1) *European Urban and Regional Studies* 34.

341 See L. Brooks and S. Morris, 'Plan for Post-Brexit UK Internal Market Bill "Is an Abomination"' (The Guardian 9 September 2020) www.theguardian.com/politics/2020/sep/09/plans-post-brexit-uk-internal-market-assault-devolution-scotland-wales accessed 1 May 2021. This is a continuation of the 'Sewel strike' by Scotland mentioned in Chapter 2, Section 2.5.2. See J. Sargeant, 'The Sewel Convention Has Been Broken by Brexit – Reform Is Now Urgent' (Institute for Government 21 January 2020) www.institutefor government.org.uk/blog/sewel-convention-has-been-broken-brexit-reform-now-urgent accessed 1 May 2021.

342 Ibid.

343 As discussed in Chapter 2, Section 2.5, the powers under the Devolution Settlements are limited.

344 S. Switzer and J.A. McMahon, 'Devolution and Post-Brexit Trade Agreements: Towards a Joint Trade Policy Committee?' (2019) 23 *Edinburgh Law Review* 266, 270.

345 Welsh Government, 'The Counsel General for Wales v the Secretary of State for Business, Energy and Industrial Strategy – Grounds for Judicial Review' (19 January 2021)

the attack on its competence made' by the Act.[346] The permission discusses the evolution of the model of devolution away from the 'conferred powers' given originally towards 'reserved powers' under the Government of Wales Act 2006 (as amended by the Wales Act 2017), where now 'the Senedd can legislate in any field unless and to the extent that the matter in question is expressly reserved to the Westminster Parliament'.[347] In the challenge, the Counsel General argues that the Internal Market Act implicitly repealed two areas previously devolved under the Government of Wales Act 2006, that is food standards and environmental protection. In April 2021, the Counsel General's application was rejected as 'premature',[348] because the 'relevant legal events ha[d] not yet arisen';[349] that is there was no legislation that could potentially conflict with the Internal Market Act and the challenge was deemed 'abstract'.[350] In the likely event that the legal or factual context changes, such as a piece of legislation proposed by the Senedd that introduces 'new requirements', the decision could be modified. When this occurs, the issue of whether or not the Internal Market Act restricts devolved legislative competence may be answered.

5.2.3.2 The international dimension

Despite last-minute amendments to the Internal Market Act addressing potential breaches of international law, the Bill nonetheless needs to be considered as it raised significant issues with potential ongoing ramifications. Simply put, placing the original Bill before Parliament breached the UK/EU Withdrawal Agreement and its provisions would have enabled repeated substantial breaches of the UK/EU Withdrawal Agreement, Northern Ireland Protocol and international law more generally[351] – including, trade law, human rights law, environmental law

---

https://gov.wales/sites/default/files/inline-documents/2021-01/210119%20Counsel%20General%20for%20Wales%20v%20Secretary%20of%20State%20for%20Business%20-%20grounds%20for%20judicial%20review.pdf accessed 1 May 2021.

346 J. Miles, 'Written Statement: Legal Challenge to the UK Internal Market Act 2020' (Welsh Government 19 January 2021) https://gov.wales/written-statement-legal-challenge-uk-internal-market-act-2020 accessed 1 May 2021.

347 Welsh Government Grounds for Judicial Review (n345) paragraph 27.

348 *R (On the Application of the Counsel General for Wales) v the Secretary of State for Business, Energy and Industrial Strategy* [2021] EWHC 950 (Admin) paragraph 38.

349 Ibid paragraph 30. The intention to legislate on single-use plastics, in particular, may have been key in the Welsh Government's decision to challenge the Internal Market Act. For more, see R. Caddell, 'What's SUP? Single-Use Plastics, the Internal Market Act and the Marine Environment of Wales' (Francis Taylor Building 7 May 2021) www.ftbchambers.co.uk/blogs/what%E2%80%99s-sup-single-use-plastics-internal-market-act-and-marine-environment-wales accessed 1 May 2021.

350 *R (On the Application of the Counsel General for Wales) v the Secretary of State for Business, Energy and Industrial Strategy*, paragraphs 32–33.

351 F. Fabbrini, 'From the Withdrawal Agreement to the Trade and Cooperation Agreement: Reshaping EU-UK Relations' (Brexit Institute Working Paper No 10/2020) https://papers.ssrn.com/sol3/papers.cfm?abstract_id=3756331 accessed 1 May 2021, 7–9.

and public international law as a whole.[352] Article 5 of the UK/EU Withdrawal Agreement is crucial to the initial analysis. It entails the principle of good faith[353] and imposes both a positive and negative obligation. Article 5 requires both the EU and the UK to 'take all appropriate measures [...] to ensure fulfilment of the obligations' and 'refrain from any measures which could jeopardise the attainment of the objectives of this Agreement'. Creating and placing the Bill before Parliament appears to be a measure that jeopardised the Agreement's objectives, in light of the Bill's provisions. The discussion that follows uses the numbering in the original text placed before Parliament.

Part 5 of the Bill on the Northern Ireland Protocol was on the face of it about ensuring the continued place of Northern Ireland within the UK internal market. Indeed, Clauses 40 and 41 used language that reflected both the Northern Ireland Protocol and Prime Minister Boris Johnson's repeated statements affirming Northern Ireland's place within the UK market.[354] However, first, despite claims by the UK Government to the contrary, it did not do much to directly address imports from Great Britain into Northern Ireland. Clause 40 required that all competent authorities across the UK have 'special regard' for Northern Ireland's 'integral place' in the UK's internal market and the 'free flow of goods between Great Britain and Northern Ireland' amongst other things, but the nature of the access would have remained largely dependent on the Joint Committee's assessment of which goods are 'at risk' and the ongoing negotiations between the UK and the EU. This survives in Section 46 of the Act, which remains vague and is largely innocuous from the perspective of international law.[355]

Three Clauses within Part 5 flew in the face of several substantive provisions within the Agreement and Northern Ireland Protocol from a legal perspective. Clause 42 provided significant flexibility to Ministers of the Crown to regulate the exit procedures or descriptions for goods going from Northern Ireland to Great Britain – even where this involved setting aside both international and domestic law.[356] This conflicted directly with some relatively limited, but nonetheless binding, requirements under the UK/EU Withdrawal Agreement and Northern Ireland Protocol – it is questionable as to why the UK would try legislating to avoid such minor hurdles where it involves breaking international law. However, Clause 43 was arguably where the UK's real interests laid.

352 See the discussion of the original Clause 45 that follows.
353 This is a general principle of international law.
354 See H. Stewart, J. Rankin and L. O'Carroll, 'Johnson Accused of Misleading Public over Brexit Deal after NI Remarks' (The Guardian 8 November 2019) www.theguardian.com/politics/2019/nov/08/boris-johnson-goods-from-northern-ireland-to-gb-wont-be-checked-brexit accessed 1 May 2021.
355 Hayward (n336). Hayward does note, however, that the provision might raise issues of whether the government maintains a position of 'rigorous impartiality' as required by the Belfast Agreement/Good Friday Agreement.
356 Internal Market Bill, Clause 47(8).

Clause 43 addressed the matter of state aid. As discussed in Chapter 2, Section 2.3.2.3, Article 10 of the Northern Ireland Protocol provides for EU state aid law (listed in Annex 5) to continue to apply to Northern Ireland[357] and also to any other state aid within the UK that might impact trade in Northern Ireland. Consequently, Article 10 could impact significantly on Great Britain and UK-wide state aid. Apparently, despite early warnings over the ramifications, this was not fully understood by the UK Government and Clause 45 was an attempt to cast aside Article 10. Clause 45 provided for the Secretary of State to regulate on state aid, irrespective of any domestic or international law – including the Protocol.

Furthermore, as noted Clause 45 expressly challenged both devolution and international law – as certain provisions and subsequent regulations under them were to have effect 'notwithstanding' any incompatibility or inconsistency with any relevant international or domestic law. Indeed, such laws were to 'ceas[e] to have effect so far and for as long as [they were] incompatible or inconsistent with' such provisions. Paragraph 4(c) of Clause 45 clarified that this would have extended beyond EU law to all international law – including therefore international environmental law, human rights law and trade law, such as the 1992 Convention on Biological Biodiversity, the 1950 European Convention on Human Rights, the 1998 Belfast Agreement/Good Friday Agreement, WTO Law and any FTAs. However, the EU element was clearly emphasised in Clause 45. This was further intensified by the combined treatment by Clauses 43 and 45 of the Court of Justice of the European Union (CJEU). Clause 43 regarding Article 10 (state aid) of the Protocol stated that regulations could be made to evade interpretations by the CJEU and Clause 45(4)(g) stated that international law encompassed judgments of the CJEU – despite the Protocol mandating that the CJEU is the ultimate authority for the interpretation of all EU law, including EU state aid law.

Yet, international law is binding – including the UK/EU Withdrawal Agreement and the Northern Ireland Protocol.[358] This is reflected in the 1969 Vienna Convention on the Law of Treaties, which the UK is a signatory to and which outlines that a treaty or another international agreement signed by a state (by someone with the requisite authority for the State) is binding upon that state.[359] Despite some suggestions that the UK Government could rely on Article 62 of the Vienna Convention to claim a fundamental change of circumstances, this simply was irrelevant as there were no circumstances that were

357 A limited exception is provided for Northern Ireland's agriculture. See Chapter 2, Section 2.3.2.3.

358 On the international law dimensions of the Withdrawal Agreement and specifically the questions raised here regarding its binding nature, dispute resolution and unilateral action, see F. Fabbrini (eds), *The Law & Politics of Brexit: Volume II – The Withdrawal Agreement* (OUP 2020); and S. Peers, 'The End – Or a New Beginning? The EU/UK Withdrawal Agreement' (2020) 39(1) *Yearbook of European Law* 122, 136–142.

359 1969 Vienna Conventional on the Law of Treaties, Article 26 and *pacta sunt servanda*.

'not foreseen'.[360] There is also a specific (binding) dispute resolution mechanism within the UK/EU Withdrawal Agreement[361] and Article 16 provides for either the UK or the EU to take unilateral safeguard measures where necessary and specific criteria are met. The UK Government bypassed all of these mechanisms with the Bill. Accordingly, in October 2020, the European Commission began taking legal action against the UK and sent a letter of formal notice to the UK for breaching its obligations under the UK/EU Withdrawal Agreement.[362]

The Bill was described by the UK Government as entailing a breach of international law in a 'very specific and limited way'.[363] This is inaccurate and irrelevant. It was a blatant breach of international law[364] – an international agreement that the UK government had recently voluntarily signed up to. It was not outdated or unilaterally imposed. But the UK's actions here led to 'international outcry'[365] and broader ramifications beyond EU legal action are also visible: a substantial grouping from the European Parliament indicated that they would not approve any trade agreement between the EU and the UK if the matter were not resolved;[366] President Biden and other politicians in the US stated that a trade agreement between the UK and the US would not be possible if the UK breached the Northern Ireland Protocol and endangered the Belfast Agreement/Good Friday Agreement;[367] and the reputation of the UK as one that follows international law risks being in smithereens.[368] Who will enter into a contract with someone known to repudiate a contract shortly after writing and concluding it, even if presented as a negotiating tactic?

Consequently, the House of Lords once more proposed changes to address these issues, through substantial revisions to the Bill. The House of Commons initially rejected these amendments. However, following progress in EU negotiations – in the form of the Joint Committee Decisions and Declarations regarding

360 Even if the provision were applicable, this would lead to the repudiation of the entire UK/EU Withdrawal Agreement and not simply individual provisions.
361 Peers (n358) 138.
362 European Commission, 'Withdrawal Agreement: European Commission Sends Letter of Formal Notice to the United Kingdom for Breach of its Obligations' (1 October 2020) https://ec.europa.eu/commission/presscorner/detail/en/ip_20_1798 accessed 1 May 2021.
363 See comment made by the Secretary of State for Northern Ireland, Brandon Lewis in HC Deb 8 September 2020, vol 679, col 509.
364 Fabbrini (n351).
365 Ibid 8.
366 B. Fox, 'MEPs Vow to Veto UK Trade Pact if it Breaks Withdrawal Agreement' (Euractiv 12 September 2020) www.euractiv.com/section/uk-europe/news/meps-vow-to-veto-uk-trade-pact-if-its-breaks-withdrawal-agreement/ accessed 1 May 2021.
367 The Newsroom, 'No Trade Deal if Good Friday Agreement Broken' (Newsletter 16 September 2020) www.newsletter.co.uk/news/politics/no-trade-deal-if-good-friday-agreement-broken-2972886 accessed 1 May 2021.
368 J. Borger, 'Brexit Bill Hugely Damaging to UK's Reputation, Says Ex-Ambassador' (The Guardian 15 September 2020) www.theguardian.com/politics/2020/sep/15/kim-darroch-new-brexit-bill-damaging-to-uks-international-reputation accessed 1 May 2021.

the implementation of the Northern Ireland Protocol[369] and more generally regarding a Brexit deal – the UK Government agreed to make significant amendments to the Bill in order to address concerns over international law.[370] The result has been amendments to the content of Clause 43 (now Section 48) and the effective removal of Clauses 42[371] and 45 – with the result that the Act no longer breaches international law in any obvious or indeed 'specific and limited' way. Whether the UK's international reputation can be similarly salvaged is another matter.

5.3 Conclusion

Overall, there have been significant developments within the UK and also between the UK and other States that will impact considerably on UK governance and the continued development of domestic agricultural policy and the resilience of agriculture. The landscape is not the same as prior to the Brexit referendum, nor even as when the UK/EU Withdrawal Agreement was concluded or even in the aftermath of the signature of the TCA.

On the international plane, the UK needs to reinvent itself as a sole trader, shape new relationships based on existing EU FTAs and form new alliances by forging new trade agreements. In particular, the TCA establishes much-impeded access to the EU market for products from Great Britain (and vice versa) in comparison to EU membership, but provides much greater access than a 'no deal'. How the provisions on the level playing field and non-regression will work in practice and how they will be adjudicated upon will directly impact the political, legal and economic relationships between the UK and the EU. One essential aspect to bear in mind in relation to these provisions is that if the UK decides to raise standards and promote resilience, the EU might have to follow suit (if trade or investment were negatively impacted), thereby not infringing upon any aspirations for the UK to become an environmental world leader.[372] How this Agreement fluctuates through time will directly affect the agri-food supply chain. Crucially, removing some SPS barriers in the not-too-distant future could positively benefit the industry.

In any case, compliance with WTO agreements (including the GATT, Agreement on Agriculture and SPS and TBT Agreements) cannot be avoided. Agri-food is clearly affected by changes to the UK's new position within the international community and WTO challenges could be on the horizon, especially

369 This is discussed in Chapter 2, Section 2.3.

370 Although not stated, it is quite possible that the statements from US politicians regarding the importance of the Northern Ireland Protocol and the Belfast Agreement/Good Friday Agreement also impacted the row-back.

371 Issues relevant to Clause 42 are addressed to an extent in Section 47 of the Act, but mainly already existed in the original Bill and do not raise the same concerns.

372 DEFRA, 'Health and Harmony: The Future for Food, Farming and the Environment in a Green Brexit' (Cm 9577, February 2018) 5.

in relation to food, environmental and animal welfare standards. Further, the question around the level of UK standards and competition could appear as a deal-breaker with multiple countries especially the EU and the US. However, WTO law does not prevent the UK from introducing or maintaining high standards or baselines regarding the environment, health, consumer choice or morality – care is simply needed in designing and justifying the provisions. Since FTAs may impact positively or negatively regarding both standards and market access, the UK Government and devolved administrations must consider carefully what future they see for agricultural policy and how FTAs can help in achieving their aims – this applies equally to the existing aims as to if the policies were adapted to achieve resilience. In particular, coherence between trade and agricultural policies are needed to achieve such resilience.

Within the UK, the issues around agricultural financing, common frameworks and the Internal Market Act all appear to lead to a recentralisation of powers towards Westminster – yet again affecting agri-food. The tensions between the Devolution Settlements and the Internal Market Act are clearly visible and they are likely to reshape the constitutional underpinnings of the UK. Specifically, the problems around the lowest common denominator and only very muted support of common frameworks in the Internal Market Act and the lack of coverage of wider agri-environmental issues in common frameworks could result in a lack of agricultural (and environmental) policy innovation across the four nations, especially in the devolved administrations – as reflected in the limited amendments in the Agriculture Act or the Trade Act to preserve the existing level of environmental, agricultural, food and animal welfare standards. Further, the identification of the suitability (or not) of common frameworks and the UK internal market indicates that it is the central *executive* 'taking back control' rather than the (central or devolved) legislatures – as also indicated in the Agriculture Act 2020 (and the European Union (Withdrawal) Act 2018[373]).[374] This is further amplified by the limited stakeholder engagement, lack of transparency and lack of accountability demonstrated in the common framework process to date and highlighted by the House of Lords' Scrutiny Committee.[375]

These developments create new legal and political parameters for the policies that can directly affect their content and functions, e.g. the impact of the TCA's level playing field provisions and the mutual recognition principle in the Internal Market Act. The developments simultaneously impact agriculture, through affecting standards, market access, competition – key considerations for any agriculture policy. It is essential that the four nations bear in mind these developments when reviewing and creating or revising their agricultural policies, including developing resilience. This may be easier to do currently than normal, as the policies are at a relatively early stage and not yet embedded into the systems.

373 See Chapter 2, Section 2.5.
374 Petetin (n295).
375 House of Lords, Common Frameworks Scrutiny Committee (n292), 16–23, 45 and 47–49.

However, this is not a one-way street and some of these parameters may be open to challenge and adaptation; if there is good reason for the nations to seek to develop their policies in a specific direction and this would conflict with any of the parameters either existing or currently evolving, then it is essential to reflect, engage and push for change of the parameters instead – or indeed push to protect the existing parameters, if preferred. As a starting point for this, it is necessary to enhance the role of the devolved administrations and stakeholders across the range of issues discussed in this chapter, as well as improving collaborative relationships between the wide range of actors – reflecting both the multilevel nature of agriculture and the interdependence of the policy actors and stakeholders.

6 Treading new, resilient paths?

Brexit poses numerous challenges and opportunities for the United Kingdom (UK), the devolved administrations and their populations, including in the context of agriculture. New policies are needed *in lieu* of the Common Agricultural Policy (CAP), creating an opportunity for policy-makers to reflect and decide: simply tweak the CAP or undertake substantial overhauls, including of the very values underpinning the policies. However, the policies cannot be created in a vacuum, but must be tailored appropriately to the political, legal and practical contexts to ensure their legality, legitimacy and effectiveness, including fundamentally the resilience of agriculture.

This book has sought to explore these issues, by delineating the evolving parameters, sketching out the four agricultural policies as developed to date, and providing an analysis of those policies. Overall, it demonstrates that the four policies remain insufficiently ambitious, even within the existing parameters, and highlights the key lessons that can be learnt for UK and devolved agriculture and beyond. However, crucially, it is possible to improve both the agricultural policies and the surrounding parameters in a synergistic manner, thereby truly leading to the foundations for a resilient agriculture.

This chapter draws together the strands of discussions from across the earlier chapters, teasing out and synopsising the main points.

It focuses on three aspects: the main traits of the policies; a pathway to a more futuristic, ambitious agricultural policy based on resilience; and the new context and governance system within which UK agricultural policies are developing.

6.1 New agricultural policies by design?

The four agricultural policies in Wales, Northern Ireland, England and Scotland remain at early stages in their development – including even within the Agriculture Act, as it needs further development, and much will depend on its implementation (including environmental land management schemes (ELMS)). The seeds have been sown, enabling an overview and evaluation as highlighted in Chapters 3 and 4. However, there still remains considerable scope to shape and design these policies, or even to overhaul them entirely if appropriate. Furthermore, lessons can

DOI: 10.4324/9780429503719-6

be drawn from both their overarching approaches and the mechanisms used to achieve these – including for beyond the UK.

Despite calls for de-regulation, more sovereignty and slogans of 'taking back control', practicalities and pressures mean that agricultural policies across the four nations are not as revolutionary as they could be. This is not unusual for either the central government or the devolved administrations. When part of the European Union (EU), agricultural policies across the four nations already lacked a certain edge in comparison to practices heavily used across the rest of the EU. Practices such as social agriculture, agroecology, agroforestry or organic food procurement[1] or ensuring the perennity of 'very small' farms (England and Wales had a minimum claim size of five hectares to receive direct payments, while Northern Ireland and Scotland chose three hectares during the 2014–2020 CAP), generally, were not considered worthy of government/CAP support.[2] Such a lack of aspiration in post-Brexit policy is, therefore, not a total surprise but is still rather disappointing.

Despite the partial eradication of direct payments and the rhetoric over the years regarding the CAP, the two-pronged approach of public (environmental) goods and productivity in the Agriculture Act largely reflects the two pillars of the CAP, with a switch in emphasis. As noted, this path dependency is not limited to the EU, but also exists between England and the devolved administrations. The fact that England has been quicker out of the starting blocks has impacted devolved aspirations – something that will only be accentuated by other elements of the UK internal relationships, including funding of the devolved administrations. While some variations exist across the policies, with an emphasis in Wales on cultural identity or language and Scotland's stakeholder group indicating that other considerations such as social contributions may be recognised in their eventual report, the focus remains largely limited to these two prongs and even a narrow, economic understanding thereof, as reflected in the centrality of the concept of natural capital. The result is that so far the policies are insufficiently tailored to the four nations and the weaknesses of England's approach, e.g. regarding the impacts on small farms and rural communities, could be replicated and even exacerbated in the devolved administrations. The picture becomes more interesting again when one turns to the development and implementation of the two prongs.

The first prong raises numerous issues, starting with the progressive taming of the approach to public goods, due to the difficulties of creating schemes based on payments for *outcomes* (rather than *actions*).[3] Initially, outcomes would

1 L. Petetin, V. Gravey and B. Moore, 'Setting the Bar for a Green Brexit in Food and Farming' (Soil Association 2019) www.soilassociation.org/green-brexit/ accessed 1 May 2021.

2 Similarly, the four nations have been resistant to the capping of direct payments under the CAP and have traditionally allocated a small budget for rural development programmes.

3 Furthermore, economic or competitive considerations may have come into play: whereas EU farmers still receive direct payments so long as they effectively meet cross-compliance requirements, a purely outcome-based system would have required domestic farmers to go beyond cross-compliance to unlock payments (thereby placing them at a competitive disadvantage).

have had to be achieved to receive financing, but now there are clear indications that actions or stepping-stones are acceptable. There are strong benefits of a combined approach on this front, but this needs to be carefully designed[4] and not developed in a haphazard manner. The schemes then need further development, in considering the more specific targets and mechanisms that could be used (typically indicative rather than prescriptive or exhaustive) to deliver public goods – with clear underpinning values to achieve these.[5] Key strengths of the policies include the focus on co-design, especially of the schemes; the consideration of collaboration and landscape approaches; and the (partial) willingness to re-evaluate land ownership regimes to promote public goods – although each of these also raises new challenges in their implementation, e.g. enforcement, the potential for regulatory capture, complexities of coordination, and interference with private ownership rights.

In part, regarding compliance with scheme criteria and, in part, as a distinct issue, concerns must be flagged regarding standards. The policies should not risk the four nations' administrations disavowing responsibility as seems to be the case at times – ultimate responsibility for delivering the objectives and enforcing the policies lies with the administrations, including through monitoring, enforcing and applying sanctions where necessary and upholding complementary regulatory regimes. Cross-compliance and the regulatory burdens under the CAP were not perfect, but the shift away from cross-compliance towards risk-based monitoring, self-monitoring and the reliance on information provided by farmers opens up the potential for abuse of the system and breach of regulatory standards. Further, whilst Scotland and Wales have guaranteed the maintenance of standards – alongside or within their agricultural policies – the same is not entirely the case for England or Northern Ireland, and there may be negative shifts in future.

The focus of the second prong is on increased productivity and prosperity – a narrow view of agri-food and of economics surrounding farming, which does not adequately reflect the value and role of farming and especially of small, family farms. The approaches vary to some extent across the policies, with some acknowledgement of the limited economic viability of farms (especially in less favoured areas) or their sensitivity to environmental or market conditions. But the core message remains: become profitable, or else. Again, there is a lack of clarity as to how this is to be achieved, especially considering that UK farmers will be competing with EU, US and other foreign farmers who may continue to receive high levels of support and often rely on economies of scale. As highlighted in Chapter 4, some farms and farmers will simply not be able to continue, especially without current levels of guaranteed payments. Linked to this, there is typically

4 M.S. Reed et al., 'Improving the Link between Payments and the Provision of Ecosystem Services in Agri-Environment Schemes' (2014) 9 *Ecosystem Services* 44.

5 The extensive piloting of the different schemes, especially ELMS to date, indicates that the four nations might be trying to achieve this, but this is at the risk of creating uncertainties for farmers.

limited focus on supply chains, the role of cooperatives or improving the quality of the produce, which might have knock-on effects on the economic viability and profitability of industry – including the farms.

Generally, much more is and was possible. The rhetoric surrounding Brexit has been one of sovereignty and ambition – focused on reclaiming power and designing world-leading systems and policies, as stated in the 2018 *Health and Harmony* Consultation:

> Now we are leaving the EU we can design a more rational, and sensitive agriculture policy which promotes environmental enhancement, supports profitable food production and contributes to a healthier society.[6]

But assessing the actual policies and their practicalities indicates a rather different story – the substance simply does not match the rhetoric, with a degree of 'greenwashing' also present.

Shocks like Brexit, COVID-19 and the climate and biodiversity crises (and repeated calls for net-zero ambitions) have seemingly failed to provide the necessary impetus to foster a 21st-century agriculture that is truly resilient, despite the scope within devolved, UK and international frameworks to develop such policies away from the CAP. Worse, the opposite may arise instead: these shocks could intensify the weaknesses identified in the policies. Thus, the neglect of small farms and focus on productivity, in conjunction with these pressures, could lead to a restructure and consolidation of the industry and an overhaul of the countryside as we know it with the expansion of larger units of production through land consolidation and amalgamation.[7] Further, competing demands on rural land use in the UK will be exacerbated in the future due to the numerous societal pressures and demands, including housing (expansion of cities), transport, infrastructure, recreational activities and the 'food versus feed' and 'food versus fuel' debates. All of these have knock-on effects, e.g. on the rural community, biodiversity and supply chains. Together with the heightened political tensions within the UK and with the EU, they simultaneously heighten the need for ambitious, resilient policies whilst making them more challenging to establish. To become resilient, a much greater overhaul of agriculture, agricultural policy and, indeed, the approach to designing agricultural policy is needed.

6 DEFRA, 'Health and Harmony: The Future for Food, Farming and the Environment in a Green Brexit' (*Health and Harmony Consultation*) (Cm 9577, February 2018) 5.

7 As well as the ability to make lump-sum payments under the Agriculture Act 2020 and for farmers to retire. See Agriculture Act, Section 13.

6.2 Towards a 21st-century, resilient UK and devolved agriculture

Something beyond these two prongs is needed – even if they were to be undertaken in the most effective manner possible. At the heart of this is the need for a clear, forward-looking ambition – ensuring that agricultural policies are founded on appropriate values. This does not need to be restricted to either a single value or to traditional or historical approaches. Interpreting sustainability as an approach to agriculture has been central to motivate change and given rise to some reforms, but existing reforms are no longer sufficient to tackle the challenges facing agriculture and the agri-food system. To this end, this book proposes to focus on the concept of resilience.

Agricultural resilience not only includes the social, economic and environmental aspects of sustainability, but also the health of the farmers and the public. Indeed, it entails the resilience of every complementary component necessary to ensure the continued survival of agriculture and the agri-food system. In this respect, it also encompasses the resilience of agricultural policies, i.e. the policies must promote resilience of agriculture and also be resilient themselves. Further, the legal and political systems within which they operate must be resilient. This is a highly demanding and complex, but holistic, approach. It also goes beyond maintaining stability, to ensure that there is a margin of safety built-in that ensures protection from shocks. Resilience, therefore, is linked with notions of adaptive capacity – the ability to adapt as necessary to survive and thrive in turbulent conditions – and adaptive law, governance and management.

Operationalising this brings to the fore the importance of flexibility, the role of stakeholders, and polycentric (but integrated) approaches, thresholds, tailored approaches, iterative processes and much more. No exact rulebook exists precisely because of the need for flexibility, adaptive capacity and tailored approaches, but the complexity reflects the real-life challenges of agriculture in the 21st century.

6.2.1 Complementary pathways towards a resilient agriculture

To be more than simple rhetoric and achieve resilience in practice, more specific pathways could be adopted to work in tandem with each other to further resilience in agriculture. The key pathways (social-ecological services, net zero, agroecology and agri-food democracy) address both the current threats to agriculture (and its components) and the multiple facets of resilience.

6.2.1.1 Socio-ecological services

Socio-ecological services turn the focus to agriculture's links with the farmers themselves, consumers and broader society – reflecting another core facet of resilience. Returning to the existing policy proposals and their focus on public goods, it should not be thought that there is an inherent conflict between public goods and other mechanisms such as agroecology or socio–ecological services.

Reframing the UK and devolved administrations' interpretations of public goods to include socio-ecological services (including regenerative and agroecological systems) would enable financial support for other services delivered by farmers and the wider countryside. It could provide the much-needed glue for rural communities and contribute to the wider economy via their produce, tourism, culture and environment (biodiversity, genetic diversity of crops and livestock), as well as the Welsh, Irish and Scottish languages. Further, food is the archetypal example of a private/market good resulting from the provisioning of ecosystem services. However, the policies' current approach of largely limiting food as an economic good is reductive. A wider interpretation of public goods in light of the social-ecological services approach would enable the broader contribution of food to society to be recognised and valued accordingly.

6.2.1.2 Net-zero agriculture

Since agriculture is simultaneously a substantial source of greenhouse gases, generally and also in the UK, and also impacted by climate change with extreme weather events, influencing human migration, affecting imports of inputs or pollinators and leading to future sea level rises, ensuring net zero is crucial. Climate change must be addressed and agriculture must play its role in this.

Multiple pathways, practices and actions exist to achieve a resilient, net-zero agriculture that rest both within and beyond farming. Within farming, the level of emissions could be reduced with the use of new technologies (including the reduction of food loss across the supply chain and not only food waste, and the use of GPS technology for precision agriculture), alternative land use (including no-till agriculture) and the actual delivery of public goods (rather than simply payments for purely actions). The diversification of farms, for instance, with the generation of renewable energy through anaerobic digestion or the increase in the number of (suitable) trees on the land (including the take-up of agroforestry), is also an option to explore.

6.2.1.3 Agroecology

Agroecology offers itself as a potential holistic tool, through recognising the symbiotic connections between agriculture, the environment, nature and humans. The application of agroecological processes and principles could optimise, restore and enhance the productive capacities of UK farms – including their overall resilience.[8] Agroecology is increasingly supported by the scientific community as a

8 T. Greenham, D. McCann and L. Macfarlane, 'Farming Smarter: Investing in Our Future' (Food Farming & Countryside Commission, March 2021) https://ffcc.co.uk/assets/downloads/FINAL-Farming-Smarter-Investing-in-our-Future-1.pdf accessed 1 May 2021.

pathway to improve the resilience (and sustainability) of agri-food systems.[9] It supports local food systems and farmers through three main techniques: exploring on-farm synergies, such as linking fertiliser subsidies directly to agroecological investments on the farm ('subsidy to sustainability'); supporting decentralised participatory research and the dissemination of knowledge by relying on existing farmers' organisations and networks; and increasing the budget for agroecological research at field, farm and community levels, and national and sub-national levels.[10] In light of the new IPBES, IPCC, CCC and IDDRI reports,[11] agroecology appears as a strong contender to solve some of the climatic and biodiversity challenges but also social issues lying ahead.

Arguing that moving towards regenerative methods of farming such as agroecology, agroforestry or organic farming is not profitable and would not feed the world is simply weak.[12] Agroecology and similar practices do not necessitate a decline in production outputs or of nutritional quality – indeed, through, for instance, reducing the quantity of beef and dairy production, it may be possible to diversify and improve the quality and variety of food so that imports could be reduced, especially through decreasing the reliance on imports of feed. Consumer awareness and behaviour has shifted in recent years, but a much greater change would be needed to help in this development.

6.2.1.4 Agri-food democracy

An agri-food democracy pathway enables farmers and citizens to participate actively, provide different perspectives on how agri-food is produced and consumed, and co-design the resilience of agri-food systems. This recognises that production and consumption, and therefore sustainable production and sustainable consumption, are two sides of the same coin – if the goal is to improve the agri-food system and make it more sustainable and resilient, then both sides must be simultaneously tackled. For instance, greater support for agroecological practices, including horticulture, across the UK would bring broader environmental and societal benefits where managed well, because it encourages other

9 A. Wezel and V. Soldat, 'A Quantitative and Qualitative Historical Analysis of the Scientific Discipline of Agroecology' (2009) 7(1) *International Journal of Agricultural Sustainability* 3. See also Office of the United Nations High Commissioner for Human Rights, 'Final Report: The Transformative Potential of the Right to Food – Report of the Special Rapporteur on the Right to Food, Olivier De Schutter' (2014) A/HRC/25/57, 8.

10 Ibid 23.

11 Respectively, see Intergovernmental Science-Policy Platform on Biodiversity and Ecosystem Services, 'Global Assessment Report on Biodiversity and Ecosystem Services' (2019); Intergovernmental Panel on Climate Change, 'Special Report: Global Warming of 1.5°C' (2019); Committee on Climate Change, 'Net Zero – The UK's Contribution to Stopping Global Warming' (May 2019); and X. Poux and P.M. Aubert, 'An Agroecological Europe in 2050: Multifunctional Agriculture for Healthy Eating – Findings from the Ten Years For Agroecology (TYFA) Modelling Exercise' (IDDRI 2018).

12 Ibid.

forms of food consumption (beyond animal products) combined potentially with shorter supply chains (resulting in reduced carbon footprints) and also promotes a greater diversity of land use.

Democratic agri-food systems necessitate changes throughout the entire system encompassing a combined 'hayfork to the table fork' and 'nose-to-tail eating' approach, with shorter, more resilient and democratic agri-food supply chains, supporting local retailers and a reduction of food surplus and food waste. Agri-food democracy thereby helps ensure fair and sufficient income for farmers, and more broadly can promote equitable and just approaches to ensure decency and social justice in the agri-food system. Further, by rooting the system in agri-food democracy, the system can be appropriately tailored and also promote buy-in and encourage behavioural change across the supply chains. Modifying citizen behaviour and generating social and societal change to achieve net zero includes altering purchasing practices and asking questions about sustainability, food miles and overconsumption of meat. Indeed, food can be used as a pathway to connect citizens, to pass on culture, heritage, family cooking traditions, and provide access to local products – embedding (local) food culture is an example of a socio-ecological service. However, this entails first giving meaningful voice to farmers and stakeholders more generally in co-designing democratic agri-food systems.

6.2.2 Co-designing resilience

A combination of the above pathways (social-ecological services, net zero, agro-ecology and agri-food democracy) would help ensure a resilient agriculture – recognising the multifunctionality, interconnectedness and vulnerabilities of agriculture. These pathways are complementary, but may at times conflict with each other or even with themselves. They also may function differently in different contexts. Consequently, the question still arises as to how to design and integrate these pathways. The significance is heightened by how substantial the changes these pathways may call for.

For instance, net-zero targets will not be achievable unless adequate policies support these ambitions and incentivise these changes (financially or otherwise), including rewarding farmers who truly deliver transformational land uses to achieve climate mitigation and adaptation objectives. Farmers and agricultural workers must be paid a fair price for their produce, make a living wage and have decent working conditions.[13] UK and devolved policies that include long-term ambitions need to properly rise to these ambitions and set clear targets. Similarly, a trade policy that would support agri-food and favour low-carbon products is

13 L. Petetin, 'The COVID-19 Crisis: An Opportunity to Integrate Food Democracy into Post-Pandemic Food Systems' (2020) 11(S2) *European Journal of Risk Regulation* 326. As indicated, a fair standard of living for farmers is a goal of the CAP but ultimately it is not reached due to flawed implementation.

essential.[14] In line with an agri-food democracy approach, all actors throughout the supply chain and beyond need to be involved in the decision-making process in designing and implementing domestic policies and feeding into relevant trade policies – this would also reduce the risks of regulatory capture by any one interest group.

As part of a social-ecological services frame and reflecting agri-food democracy, co-producing knowledge in the design and implementation of schemes becomes a central plank of policies. Diversified and differentiated duties and responsibilities amongst stakeholders linked to the interconnectedness and complexity of ecosystems, the social specifics and the context of rural areas could become key characteristics of governmental agricultural policies.

6.3 A new landscape?

However, the UK and devolved administrations are not operating in a vacuum or with a *carte blanche* when considering how to develop or re-design their agricultural policies. Farming faces a wide range of complexities ranging from the impact of COVID-19 to the lack of access to agricultural workers. International trade also affects the UK on multiple fronts: (i) the UK as a whole is not self-sufficient and relies on foreign imports of up to 36% of its agri-food products;[15] (ii) international obligations arise from World Trade Organization (WTO) membership and trade agreements (existing and future ones); and (iii) the UK has to reinvent its position on the international scene as a single actor (rather than being part of a big trading block) whilst bearing in mind competition issues and international market volatility.

Despite British farming remaining intrinsically unchanged to date, the context within which it operates has been completely overhauled, e.g. in terms of the significance of retained EU law,[16] the UK/EU Withdrawal Agreement and the Northern Ireland Protocol,[17] the Trade and Cooperation Agreement (TCA),[18]

14 L. Petetin and M. Dobbs, 'Collaborating for Agricultural Sustainability' (Centre for Environmental Justice, 13 June 2018) https://blogs.cardiff.ac.uk/environmental-justice-research-unit/2018/06/13/collaborating-agricultural-sustainability/ accessed 1 May 2021.

15 DEFRA, DAERA, Welsh Government Knowledge and Analytical Services and the Scottish Government, Rural and Environment Science and Analytical Services, 'Agriculture in the United Kingdom 2019' (2020) https://assets.publishing.service.gov.uk/government/uploads/system/uploads/attachment_data/file/950618/AUK-2019-07jan21.pdf accessed 1 May 2021, Table 14.1.

16 Via the European Union (Withdrawal) Act 2018 and to a lesser extent the European Union (Withdrawal Agreement) Act 2020.

17 Protocol on Ireland/Northern Ireland to the Agreement on the withdrawal of the United Kingdom of Great Britain and Northern Ireland from the European Union and the European Atomic Energy Community [2019] OJ C384I /1.

18 Trade and Cooperation Agreement between the European Union and the European Atomic Energy Community, of the One Part, and the United Kingdom of Great Britain and Northern Ireland, of the Other Part [2020] OJ L 444/14.

and the UK Internal Market Act 2020. Chapters 2 and 5 delineated new legal and political parameters emerging from both within and beyond the UK; these parameters directly and indirectly impact the UK and its agriculture, and are shaking farming to its core. However, it should be borne in mind that the UK and devolved administrations will have varying capacity to shape and affect these parameters – they are not irreversibly fixed in stone.

6.3.1 Evolving international relationships

The UK's position on the international scene is in flux, with profound implications for agriculture. Central to agriculture, the CAP has, is and will keep casting a shadow over British farming due to its policies and regulatory frameworks, trade relationships with the EU and the EU's physical vicinity. In particular, ongoing area-based income support in the current and upcoming CAP may disadvantage UK farmers. Also, the CAP's two-pillar, dichotomic approach when it comes to financial support appears difficult to evade and it creeps its way back into UK and devolved farming policies (and each CAP reform).

Furthermore, both new (the TCA, Northern Ireland Protocol and free trade agreements (FTAs)) and existing international agreements (WTO agreements and their obligations) affect the functioning of the UK vis-à-vis policy and legal content, the UK internal market and devolution. Seven key points are highlighted here. First, in relation to setting its own schedule of tariffs, this will remain a proposed schedule until it receives certification – that is, approval from all WTO Members. When Russia joined the WTO it was forced to reduce its tariffs on agricultural products from around 13% on average to around 10%.[19] Similarly, political pressure could be placed on the UK to further liberalise its agriculture and diminish its tariffs.

Second, the Agreement on Agriculture of the WTO comes into sharper focus. The UK's obligation to comply with the Agreement on Agriculture previously was filtered via the EU and the CAP – including through looking to the allowances granted to the EU for expenditure, especially under the Amber Box, and through the EU's interpretation of the financial schemes and which Box they fall within. Now, that filter has been removed and the obligations to comply and justify approaches fall directly on the UK. Without the advantage of being a member of a major trading block anymore, the UK may be more easily pressured. This has knock-on, recentralising effects on the domestic regime and the relationships with the devolved administrations.

Third, the trade relationship with the EU is fundamentally changed. Central to this are the Northern Ireland Protocol, the TCA and more general international law – including WTO law. The Northern Ireland Protocol largely

19 WTO, 'Working Party Seals the Deal on Russia's Membership Negotiation' (10 November 2011) www.wto.org/english/news_e/news11_e/acc_rus_10nov11_e.htm accessed 1 May 2021.

minimises impacts on the trade relationship between Northern Ireland and the EU. However, the same is not true for the relationship between Great Britain and the EU or even between Great Britain and Northern Ireland. New hurdles (especially non-tariff barriers) arise for those in the agri-food industry that will make continued viability challenging. Both administrative burdens (such as customs declarations, security declarations, appropriate permits and licenses) and biosecurity checks and inspections on agri-food products (including live animal, plants, food and feed), erected to comply mainly with international obligations, especially sanitary and phytosanitary (SPS) measures have sharply increased.[20] This has caused a reduction in the level, flow and speed of trade between Great Britain and the EU and also between Great Britain and Northern Ireland, due to the efforts to ensure no hard border on the Island of Ireland.

Even the TCA's provisions and instruments cannot fully offset many of these hurdles. Non-tariff barriers are simply too numerous and too burdensome, especially when sovereignty is prioritised and there is a persistent refusal by the UK Government to agree to regulatory alignment and ensuring level playing fields beyond the limited provisions in the TCA. As observed, multiple disruptions to the agri-food supply chains have arisen since the end of the transition period and are still ongoing both in terms of imports and exports. Further, the sheer scale of the demands on the four nations, but especially the devolved administrations, is reflected in the UK deciding not to impose SPS checks on imports to Great Britain until January 2022 due to lack of readiness.[21]

Fourth, the shift in UK-EU trade relations has substantial knock-on effects. Obstacles such as the 'Kent Access Permit' hindered free trade *within* the UK and the remaining administrative hurdles and physical checks have repercussions on international trade passing *through* the UK. Trade flows across the UK and between the UK and the EU are being re-routed. For example, direct shipping has increased from the Republic of Ireland to France (thereby avoiding using the UK as a 'landbridge'), including via a new sea route between Rosslare and Dunkerque. Other complications also appear where plant nurseries in Wales see their exports travelling through Wales, England, the Netherlands, Belgium, France and ultimately the Republic of Ireland.[22] Further, the creation of a sea border between Great Britain and Northern Ireland raises concerns over the unity and union of the UK.

Fifth, individual FTAs can impact SPS and TBT (technical barriers to trade) standards relating to environmental, food and animal welfare domestically and

20 M. Dobbs and L. Petetin, 'Agriculture: Environmental, Food and Animal Health Standards' in H. Kassin, A. Jordan and S. Ennis (eds), 'UK Regulation after Brexit' (The UK in a Changing Europe 25 February 2021) https://ukandeu.ac.uk/wp-content/uploads/2021/02/UK-regulation-after-Brexit.pdf accessed 1 May 2021, 51.

21 J. Partridge, 'Eight Major Government U-Turns on Post-Brexit Controls' (The Guardian 13 March 2021) www.theguardian.com/politics/2021/mar/13/eight-major-government-u-turns-on-post-brexit-controls accessed 1 May 2021.

22 HC Deb 10 March 2021, vol 690, col 875.

also on other FTAs. For instance, if standards are lowered as a result of one FTA, it might create inconsistencies with agreed FTAs (for example, the FTA with Australia could lead to inconsistencies with the TCA's level playing field provisions) or put the conclusion of other FTAs beyond reach. Whilst rolled-over FTAs do not impact existing internal standards *per se*, flexibility in setting such standards could be reduced in the future and legal challenges could be brought (against standards hindering access to the UK) under specific FTAs as well as more generally under WTO law, in particular the Sanitary and Phytosanitary (SPS Agreement) and Technical Barriers to Trade (TBT) Agreements[23] and the General Agreement on Tariffs and Trade (GATT)[24] (including issues around likeness and process and production methods (PPMs)). However, Article XX GATT could also enable the UK to justify higher standards, for instance, to reflect the British public morals towards high animal welfare.[25] It is essential for the UK to consider whether to prioritise ease of access and the completion of swift deals or the maintenance (or even improvement) of standards – and the scope they have to achieve either or both of these. For these reasons, changes to UK trade policy call for careful assessments and monitoring to indicate which sectors and/or UK regions would benefit from trade agreements and which ones would bear economic losses or otherwise be impacted upon negatively. It also calls for coherence across policies (trade, agriculture, health, food and environment) to ensure a holistic approach to the setting of these standards. As always, the devil is in the detail.

Sixth, relating to the level of standards, the UK Government and the House of Commons have consistently refused to address adequately the concerns over potential imports of agri-food products of lower standards and allow greater scrutiny of trade agreements within the Trade Act 2021.[26] The TCA could have helped guarantee standards within the UK, but the shallow nature of the Agreement means that regulatory convergence is not required under the TCA and a spiral to the bottom is indeed possible. Recent UK governmental developments around neonicotinoids and gene editing indicate that this existing regulatory baseline could be already changing. However, although not equivalent to EU membership, some controls do exist; level playing field and non-regressions obligations (i) require that neither the EU nor the UK regress below the 2020 baseline in a manner that impacts trade or investment; and (ii) can enable the party willing to increase its levels of protection to utilise the rebalancing mechanisms if negatively

23 Respectively, Uruguay Round Agreement on the Application of Sanitary and Phytosanitary Measures (1994); and Uruguay Round Agreement on Technical Barriers to Trade (1994).

24 Uruguay Round General Agreement on Tariffs and Trade (1994).

25 Whilst ensuring non-discrimination or disguised restrictions on trade when setting the detailed provisions of the measure. See Chapter 5.

26 Section 42 of the Agriculture Act 2020 on the reporting of FTAs is rather limited and lacks teeth.

impacted.[27] Consequently, a sensitive, dynamic alignment in practice could be a positive possibility.

Last, most FTAs impact devolved matters, yet engagement by the Department of International Trade (DIT) with the devolved administrations has been limited. The overlap with devolved matters enhances the need for the UK to be able to adjust policy or law across the UK, as FTAs might require access at lower standards to the entirety of the UK market such as chlorine-washed chicken or new types of agri-food technologies such as gene editing. As the corollary to this, the devolved administrations need a voice in the formulation of trade policy based on collaboration and cooperation – rather than simply being on the receiving end of unilateral, centrally adopted decisions. Options could include increased consultations between the devolved administrations and the DIT to keep the information flowing between the different levels of government.[28] However, engagement would need to be meaningful, including via formal input into the decision-making process. Such changes would need to address questions of both a political and constitutional nature regarding devolution, parliamentary sovereignty and the (constitutional) future of the Union – questions which have been on the back burner for the UK Government. Internal issues must be ironed out before introducing new international legal obligations.

6.3.2 Shifting internal dynamics

Internally, the UK is facing a constitutional crisis, which could result in a fragmentation of the Union (with Scottish independence increasingly important and the aspirations towards Welsh independence soaring since the Brexit referendum vote).[29] This is exacerbated by the UK's policy and legal responses to Brexit, in particular through the decision to prioritise 'taking back control' *vis-à-vis* the EU, the UK internal market and the creation of new FTAs. A clear and obvious recentralisation of powers is well underway for the sake of ensuring a smooth transition, but with profound implications for other objectives, such as environmental, human health and animal welfare protection, as well as devolution and internal relationships within the Union. This is exemplified by the approach to the development of common frameworks, the passage of the Internal Market Act 2020 and elements of the Agriculture Act.

27 Some degree of regulatory convergence may also be maintained based on the Brussels effect.

28 This should be matched by enhanced stakeholder engagement at all levels and not just via the Trade and Agriculture Commission.

29 For Scotland, see A. McDonnell, 'SNP Maintain Strong Lead in Holyrood Voting Intention' (YouGov 12 November 2020) https://yougov.co.uk/topics/politics/articles-reports/2020/11/12/scottish-independence-yes-51-49-no accessed 1 May 2021; and for Wales, see ITV, 'Poll Reveals Highest Support for Welsh Independence Ever Recorded' (4 March 2021) www.itv.com/news/wales/2021-03-04/poll-reveals-highest-support-for-welsh-independence-ever-recorded accessed 1 May 2021.

The common frameworks are ambiguous on the issue of centralisation. They are clearly a centralising mechanism, but they are collaborative in nature and intended to respect devolution in contrast with unilaterally imposed UK Government measures. Further, they do not necessarily guarantee a high level of protection of their objectives, but the criteria underpinning common frameworks encompass that they enable the management of the UK internal market and 'common resources' (including nature). They, therefore, have significant potential to help develop a resilient agriculture across the UK, whilst respecting variations across the four nations and devolution. However, this is not accurately mirrored in either the identification of areas that might require common frameworks or in their subsequent development. Instead, what is seen is a considerable effort to create a UK-wide approach in matters that tie into the internal market and potential future trade agreements (but not trade itself, as a reserved matter). This has included areas where devolved administrations have very strong and diverse opinions, including organic produce. Yet, broader agri-environmental issues (including biodiversity protection or cross-border environmental harm) are largely left to the devolved administrations, even though they raise concerns over shared natural resources. Further, there has been very limited transparency or stakeholder engagement.

The choice of the UK Government to focus on elements central to the internal market and trade agreements, without ensuring high levels of environmental protection, agri-food standards or consumer protection, denotes that internal and external trade are their core policy objectives – something that is only emphasised by (i) the reluctance of the Government to accept key amendments to the Agriculture Act or the Trade Act 2021 that would guarantee not to lower standards; (ii) the pursuit of the governmental preference for a unitary, Kingdom exit;[30] (iii) the choice of a centrally imposed statute for the Internal Market Act (rather than a more collaborative common framework), created without substantial input from the devolved administrations and contrary to their preferences; and (iv) the very narrow limitations on the proposed role of mutual recognition in the Internal Market Act. The approach to the Internal Market Act in particular will have profound impacts, legally (especially constitutionally) and politically, across the UK – with knock-on effects for future policy, but also cooperation and collaboration.

On the financing side, further recentralisation arises from the Internal Market Act's provisions on state aid and the Agriculture Act's provisions on the classification of financial support (although some retreat on the WTO aspects can be observed between the Agriculture Bill 2017–2019 and the Agriculture Act 2020). This last point, combined with the lack of clarity regarding funding for the devolved administrations, makes designing long-term policies highly challenging and dependent on the political goodwill of Westminster.

30 B. Pontin, 'Legal and Political Conceptions of Governance within the Environmental Act Debate' (2019) 31 *Environmental Law and Management* 85.

It is also worth highlighting the tensions surrounding the implementation of the Northern Ireland Protocol and the sea border between Northern Ireland and Great Britain. As noted above and in Chapter 2, considerable hurdles arise for trade between Northern Ireland and Great Britain due to a combination of general international trade law, Brexit and the Northern Ireland Protocol. These have been ameliorated, but not resolved, by the Joint Committee and the TCA. In this instance, Brexit sacrificed Northern Ireland's position within the UK, despite the rhetoric about respecting Northern Ireland's place in the Union. Brexit, in conjunction with the Northern Ireland Protocol (and surrounding legal and political debates), has increased tensions within Northern Ireland and between Northern Ireland and Westminster.

6.3.3 Multilevel relationships and parameters

The multilevel considerations, outlined in greater detail in Chapters 2 and 5, are essential in determining the parameters for the four nations' agricultural policies. They determine what is legally and politically possible within the current and evolving governance context. They also affect the wider context within which the policies will operate, e.g. determining market access, and thereby impacting upon the broader resilience of agriculture. For instance, the UK's progress with FTAs has been impressive, but does not fully compensate for the loss of EU membership and subsequent restrictions on access to the EU market – with further implications for standards (highlighted by the limited role of the TCA and the new FTA with Australia[31]) and the UK internal market (due to the position of Northern Ireland). These will have profound impacts for agriculture and more broadly. While nothing has been set in stone yet that prevents modifying standards or maintaining or overhauling approaches, the wheels have started turning, with a need to reflect closely and swiftly on how they are changing and the implications thereof.

Addressing existing and future multilevel relationships and legal parameters is not simply a matter of legality, but also is an important issue for resilience – social–ecological resilience depends on the resilience of the legal and social systems as much as the ecological system.[32] If agriculture is to be resilient, the legal and political relationships must also be resilient. To achieve that, at a minimum there needs to be the clear recognition and respect of such relationships and parameters – and any adjustments must be undertaken in an appropriate manner. Future developments internationally and internally are not simply a matter

31 Department for International Trade, 'UK-Australia FTA Negotiations: Agreement in Principle' (17 June 2021) www.gov.uk/government/publications/uk-australia-free-trade-agreement-negotiations-agreement-in-principle/uk-australia-fta-negotiations-agreement-in-principle accessed 18 June 2021.

32 C.A. Arnold and L.H. Gunderson, 'Adaptive Law' in A.S. Garmestani and C.R. Allen (eds), *Social-Ecological Resilience and Law* (Columbia University Press 2014) 317, 321. They refer to the need for 'poly-resilience'.

of interest for the UK Government, but for the devolved administrations also (and all stakeholders). Yet, the approach of the UK Government has been to act unilaterally, with seeming disregard at times for both internal and external relationships.

As discussed in Chapter 3, the Agriculture Act acknowledges implicitly the rights of the devolved administrations to develop their own policies,[33] whilst concomitantly imposing controls unilaterally to ensure compliance with obligations under the Agreement on Agriculture regarding financial support.[34] The complicated nature of devolution is further reflected in the revisions undertaken during the Parliamentary process, and ultimately in the promulgation of the Act without obtaining Scottish legislative consent. Yet, the UK Government risks pushing the devolved administrations too far by bypassing legislative consent, undermining the UK's constitutional underpinnings, the smooth implementation of trade deals and the effective operation of the internal market. Developing these provisions in a more collaborative manner and even through common frameworks would have been more respectful of devolution and the internal political and legal relationships.

Whilst the existing internal and external parameters do not impose excessive restrictions on the four nations, they also affect the context and the potential is there for the parameters to become increasingly burdensome. Whilst the UK Government has a more substantial say over their development, they are a matter of concern for all affected and the four nations must engage in a more collaborative manner to help shape their evolution if agriculture is to have a positive, resilient future – through ensuring high standards, access to markets, mutually beneficial relationships between the nations and the space and flexibility to develop appropriate, tailored policies.

6.4 Final food for thought

Overall, what precisely constitutes a resilient agriculture fit for the 21st century remains elusive due to its multidimensional facets and its temporal, spatial and normative dimensions. However, these very facets and dimensions provide us with clues as to the starting point, as they highlight the need for flexibility, longevity and a holistic approach. First, a suitable overarching objective is needed to address these issues and to provide coherency and ensure societal values are respected – something that is missing to varying degrees across all the policies. The two prongs hint at economic and environmental values, but they are incomplete, imbalanced and insufficient by themselves; economic and especially environmental and social considerations are pivotal, but not exclusively. Resilience can play the requisite role. It entails a more holistic approach and looks to the future – including through preparing for the inevitable shocks and leading to a

33 This was expressly noted in *Health and Harmony Consultation* (n6) 7.
34 Agriculture Act 2020, Sections 43 to 45.

green recovery. Second, social-ecological services can underpin such a unified and integrated framework – especially in the context of a 21st-century agriculture, where it keeps farmers on the land, generates generational renewal, seeks net-zero emissions and adopts agroecological farming systems.

However, achieving such a type of resilient agriculture sooner rather than later will require a core transformation of the UK and devolved agri-food and surrounding policies – something going far beyond the existing proposals. For the UK and the devolved administrations, this implies the development of ambitious polices that are truly co-designed, respectful of the Devolved Settlements and with the support in particular of trade policy. Despite potential concerns over legal constraints, if the political will exists then neither international nor domestic law prevents such approaches – reflected in the varying treatment of the Boxes under the Agreement on Agriculture and even in the creation of FTAs. Care is needed to ensure that the UK does not create extra burdens or challenges for itself (and the devolved administrations) – with key roles for the devolved administrations in also helping shape international relations and policies. However, a sense of urgency is also present, both to provide industry with certainty in terms of financial and trade support (facilitating them in delivering social-ecological services) and to improve resilience before the context becomes more challenging (e.g. due to environmental degradation or fresh international obligations).

Overall, opportunities arise to deliver resilient agricultural policies at the UK and devolved levels, based on social-ecological services and ensuring adaptive capacity – including by adapting and strengthening the proposed systems of public goods. If the political will exists, several steps could be taken to help achieve this:

- Place farmers and other stakeholders (where relevant) at the heart of the decision-making process for agricultural policies and relevant schemes to produce optimal goods and services in line with agri-food democracy;
- Ensure the coherence of policies holistically across a variety of sectors and in particular agricultural, food, environmental, health and trade policies to create and improve policy formulation and ultimately outcomes;
- Integrate ambitious environmental and social objectives (including the multifaceted elements of rural development) at the centre of the policies, rebalancing the equilibrium in favour of these objectives where agroecological processes and principles play a decisive role;
- Increase considerations around public health especially in relation to nutritional and dietary aspects in light of 'food in the Anthropocene';
- Establish appropriate targets towards a net-zero agriculture to mitigate climate change and for all social-ecological services that policy measures intend to deliver;
- Focus on the adaptive capacity of each interrelated component necessary for agriculture's survival;
- Develop indicative criteria and thresholds for each desired outcome, with incentives linked to actions, milestones and final outcomes;

- Improve effective implementation by identifying synergic measures including training, advice and capacity building for farmers (and thereby fostering social capital);
- Secure monitoring, compliance and enforcement by creating effective mechanisms and avoiding regulatory capture;
- Provide space for innovative approaches, supported by co-design, experiential learning, education etc;
- Guarantee actions are taken at the appropriate scale, with corresponding incentives, coordination and support;
- Ensure positive, collaborative relationships/engagements between the devolved administrations and the UK Government to guarantee coherency and complementarity between devolved and reserved policies (especially trade); and
- Identify and adapt international and domestic parameters to the extent appropriate.

Finally, whilst the focus of the book's discussion is on the evolution of agricultural policies within the UK, the lessons are largely applicable for developing agricultural policies beyond the UK, bearing in mind the regional, national and international policy and legal context, landscape, and parameters within which they evolve. Thus, the adopted overarching ambition of resilience and the identified complementary pathways are capable of being transferred beyond the UK. Further, successful implementation of the policy across the UK would be facilitated if other countries adopted similar, high priorities (as opposed to just seeking to obtain competitive advantage).

Similarly, whether for agricultural policies beyond the UK or for the development of other policies within the UK, broader lessons can be learned. In particular, considerations such as contextualising, holistic thinking, policy coherence, ambition and resilience are clearly relevant beyond this specific instance of UK and devolved agriculture. The issue around where and at what level decisions are taken and who can participate cannot be ignored either. There are numerous legal and practical factors that create parameters for decision-making – parameters that are not always obvious, are continuously evolving and are not entirely within the UK or devolved administrations' control. Yet, when the complexities are unpacked and the parameters mapped out, it is apparent that pathways exist to achieve the design and implementation of resilient agricultural policies, if the actors are willing to be innovative and take the necessary steps.

Brexit consequently has posed numerous challenges, but the opportunity to re-think agricultural policies and their governance within the UK should be seized with both hands and used also as a learning experience and tool. There is the real potential to develop ambitious, resilient agricultural policies if the political will exists.

Bibliography

Academic & secondary sources

Articles

Altieri MA, Nicholls CI, Henao A and Lana MA, 'Agroecology and the Design of Climate Change-Resilient Farming Systems' (2015) 35 *Agronomy for Sustainable Development* 869–890.

Andersen H, 'Protection of Non-Trade Values in WTO Appellate Body Jurisprudence: Exceptions, Economic Arguments, and Eluding Questions' (2015) 18(2) *Journal of International Economic Law* 383–405.

Andersson A, Höjgård S and Rabinowicz E, 'Evaluation of Results and Adaptation of EU Rural Development Programmes' (2017) 67 *Land Use Policy* 298–314.

Ansell CK, Sørensen E and Torfing J, 'The COVID-19 Pandemic as a Game Changer for Public Administration and Leadership? The Need for Robust Governance Responses to Turbulent Problems' (2021) 23(7) *Public Management Review* 1–12.

Ansell CK and Trondal J, 'Governing Turbulence: An Organizational-Institutional Agenda' (2018) 1(1) *Perspectives on Public Management and Governance* 43–57.

Ballet J, 'Propriété, Biens Publics Mondiaux, Bien(s) Commun(s): Une Lecture des Concepts Economiques' (2008) *Développement Durable et Territoires* (Dossier 10: Biens Communs et Propriété). Also available online http://developpementdurable.revues.org/5553.

Baroncini E and Brunel C, 'A WTO Safe Harbour for the Dolphins: The Second Compliance Proceedings in the US – Tuna II (Mexico) Case' (2020) 19(2) *World Trade Review* 196–215.

Bartels L, 'The Chapeau of the General Exceptions in the WTO GATT and GATS Agreements' (2015) 109 *American Journal of International Law* 95–125.

Bateman IJ and Balmford B, 'Public Funding for Public Goods: A Post-Brexit Perspective on Principles for Agricultural Policy' (2018) 79 *Land Use Policy* 293–300.

Bennett E et al., 'Toward a More Resilient Agriculture' (2014) 5 *The Solutions Journal* 65–75.

Bidwell OW, 'Where Do We Stand on Sustainable Agriculture?' (1986) 41 *Journal of Soil and Water Conservation* 317–320.

Blake MK, 'More than Just Food: Food Insecurity and Resilient Place Making through Community Self-Organising' (2019) 11(10) *Sustainability* 2942–2964.

Blake MK, 'The Multiple Ontologies of Surplus Food' (2019) 27 *Europe Now* – available online https://www.europenowjournal.org/2019/05/06/the-multiple-ontologies-of-surplus-food/.

Blank Y, 'Federalism, Subsidiarity, and the Role of Local Governments in an Age of Global Multilevel Governance' (2009) 37 *Fordham Urban Law Journal* 509–558.

Bowers JK, 'British Agricultural Policy Since the Second World War' (1985) 33(1) *The Agricultural History Review* 66–76.

Bradbury J, 'Welsh Devolution and the Union: Reform Debates after Brexit' (2021) 92(1) *Political Quarterly* 125–131.

Bradford A, 'The Brussels Effect' (2012) 107 *Northwestern University Law Review* 1–67.

Bradshaw C, 'England's Fresh Approach to Food Waste: Problem Frames in the Resources and Waste Strategy' (2020) 40(2) *Legal Studies* 321–343.

Bradshaw C, 'Waste Law and the Value of Food' (2018) 30(2) *Journal of Environmental Law* 311–331.

Brennan C, Dobbs M and Gravey V, 'Out of the Frying Pan, into the Fire? Environmental Governance Vulnerabilities in Post-Brexit Northern Ireland' (2019) 21(2) *Environmental Law Review* 84–110.

Brom FWA, 'Food, Consumer Concerns, and Trust: Food Ethics for a Globalizing Market' (2000) 12 *Journal of Agricultural and Environmental Ethics* 127–139.

Brown TC, Bergstrom JC and Loomis JB, 'Defining, Valuing, and Providing Ecosystem Goods and Services' (2007) 47(2) *Natural Resources Journal* 329–376.

Burns C, 'Will Brexit Degrade UK Environmental Policy?' (2020) 119(815) *Current History* 101–106.

Burns C, Moore B, Gravey V and Jordan A, 'Green Brexit: Rhetoric or Reality?' (2019) 10(2) *Political Insight* 37–39.

Burton RJF and Schwarz G, 'Result-Oriented Agri-Environment Schemes in Europe and Their Potential for Promoting Behavioural Change' (2013) 30(1) *Land Use Policy* 628–641.

Cardwell MN, 'Brexit and Agriculture: Implementing a New Legal Framework for Agricultural Support' (2017) 19 *The Cambridge Yearbook of European Legal Studies* 311–335.

Cardwell MN, 'The Polluter Pays Principle in European Community Law and Its Impact on UK Farmers' (2006) 59 *Oklahoma Law Review* 89–113.

Cardwell MN and Smith F, 'Renegotiation of the WTO Agreement on Agriculture: Accommodating the New Big Issues' (2013) *International and Comparative Law Quarterly* 865–898.

Carter HO, 'Agricultural Sustainability: An Overview and Research Assessment' (1989) 43(3) *California Agriculture* 16–18 and 37.

Ceccarelli S et al., 'Plant Genetic Resources and Plant Improvement as Tools to Develop Sustainable Agriculture' (1992) 28(1) *Experimental Agriculture* 89–98.

Centner TJ and Petetin L, 'Divergent Approaches Regulating Beta Agonists and Cloning of Food Animals: United States and European Union' (2020) 28(5–6) *Society and Animals* 613–632.

Centner TJ and Petetin L, 'Permitting Program with Best Management Practices for Shale Gas Wells to Safeguard Public Health' (2015) 163 *Journal of Environmental Management* 174–183.

Chan KMA, 'Payments for Ecosystem Services: Rife with Problems and Potential – For Transformation towards Sustainability' (2017) 140 *Ecological Economics* 110–122.

Charnovitz S, 'The Law of Environmental "PPMs" in the WTO: Debunking the Myth of Illegality' (2002) 27 *Yale Journal of International Law* 59–110.

Charnovitz S, 'Book Review: "Like Products" in International Trade Law: Towards a Consistent GATT/WTO Jurisprudence' (2004) 98 *American Journal of International Law* 610–614.

Cheyne I, 'Gateways to the Precautionary Principle in WTO Law' (2007) 19 *Journal of Environmental Law* 155–172.

Chowdhury N and Wessel R, 'Conceptualising Multilevel Regulation in the EU: A Legal Translation of Multilevel Governance?' (2012) 18 *European Law Journal* 335–357.

Cole L et al., 'A Critical Analysis of the Potential for EU Common Agricultural Policy Measures to Support Wild Pollinators on Farmland' (2020) 57 *Journal of Applied Ecology* 681–694.

Conconi P and Voon T, '*EC-Seal Products*: The Tension between Public Morals and International Trade Agreements' (2016) 15(2) *World Trade Review* 211–234.

Cunningham R and Vindedzis S, 'Four Legs Good, Two Legs Bad? Animal Welfare vs the World Trade Organisation (Featuring Article XX of the General Agreement on Tariffs and Trade and Article 2 of the Technical Barriers to Trade)' (2017) 38 *Adelaide Law Review* 311–349.

Davies A, 'Technical Regulations and Standards under the WTO Agreement on Technical Barriers to Trade' (2014) 41(1) *Legal Issues of Economic Integration* 37–63.

Davies G, 'Morality Clauses and Decision Making in Situations of Scientific Uncertainty: The Case of GMOs' (2007) 6 *World Trade Review* 249–263.

DeClerck FAJ et al., 'Ecological Approaches to Human Nutrition' (2011) 32 supp 1 *Food and Nutrition Bulletin* 41S–50S.

Delcros F, 'The Legal Status of Agriculture in the World Trade Organization' (2002) 36 *Journal of World Trade* 219–253.

Dobbs M, 'Attaining Subsidiarity-Based Multilevel Governance of Genetically Modified Cultivation?' (2016) 28(2) *Journal of Environmental Law* 245–273.

Dobbs M, 'Genetically Modified Crops, Agricultural Sustainability and National Opt-Outs: Enclosure as the Loophole?' (2017) 54(4) *Common Market Law Review* 1093–1122.

Dobbs M, 'Legalising General Prohibitions on Cultivation of Genetically Modified Organisms' (2012) 11(12) *German Law Journal* 1347–1372.

Dobbs M, 'National Governance of Public Health Responses in a Pandemic?' (2020) 11(2) *European Journal of Risk Regulation* 240–248.

Dobbs M, Gravey V and Petetin L, 'Driving the European Green Deal in Turbulent Times' (2021) 9(3) *Politics and Governance* 316–326.

Donald PF, Sanderson FJ, Burfield IJ and van Bommel FPJ, 'Further Evidence of Continent-Wide Impacts of Agricultural Intensification on European Farmland Birds, 1990–2000' (2006) 116(3–4) *Agriculture, Ecosystems & Environment* 189–196.

Douglas-Scott S, 'The Future of the United Kingdom' (2019) SI *European Journal of Legal Studies* 245–274.

Du M, 'Permitting Moral Imperialism? The Public Morals Exception to Free Trade at the Bar of the World Trade Organization' (2016) 50(4) *Journal of World Trade* 675–704.

Engel A and Petetin L, 'International Obligations and Devolved Powers – Ploughing through Competences and GM Crops' (2018) 20(1) *Environmental Law Review* 16–31.

England RW, 'Natural Capital and the Theory of Economic Growth' (2000) 34 *Ecological Economics* 425–431.

Fisher B, Turner RK and Morling P, 'Defining and Classifying Ecosystem Services for Decision Making' (2009) 68 *Ecological Economics* 643–653.

Forman RTT and Baudry J, 'Hedgerows and Hedgerow Networks in Landscape Ecology' (1984) 8 *Environmental Management* 495–510.

Francis C et al., 'Agroecology: The Ecology of Food Systems' (2003) 22 *Journal of Sustainable Agriculture* 99–118.

Franks JR, 'An Assessment of the Landscape-Scale Dimensions of Land Based Environmental Management Schemes Offered to Farmers in England' (2019) 83(2) *Land Use Policy* 147–159.

Gallopín GC, 'Linkages between Vulnerability, Resilience, and Adaptive Capacity' (2006) 16(3) *Global Environmental Change* 293–303.

Glinski C, 'CSR and the Law of the WTO – The Impact of Tuna Dolphin II and EC – Seal Products' (2017) 1 *Nordic Journal of Commercial Law* 120–148.

Goco JB, 'Non-Discrimination, "Likeness", and Market Definition in World Trade Organization Jurisprudence' (2006) 40 *Journal of World Trade* 315–340.

Gravey V, 'Finally Free to Green Agriculture Policy? UK Post-Brexit Policy Developments in the Shadow of the CAP and Devolution' 18(2) (2019) *EuroChoices* 11–16.

Gravey V, Petetin L and Dobbs M, 'Quitter la PAC, Comment et Pour Quoi Faire ? La (Re)Construction des Politiques Agricoles Britanniques au Coeur des Turbulences du Brexit' (2021) 73(3) *Politique Européenne* 150–178.

Gstöhl S and Phinnemore D, 'The Future EU-UK Partnership: A Historical Institutionalist Perspective' (2021) 43(1) *Journal of European Integration* 99–115.

Gunderson L, 'Ecological Resilience – In Theory and Application' (2000) 31 *Annual Review of Ecological Systems* 425–439.

Hamilton ND, 'Moving toward Food Democracy: Better Food, New Farmers, and the Myth of Feeding the World' (2011) 16 *Drake Journal of Agricultural Law* 117–145.

Hanon LE and Sisk TD, 'Hedgerows in an Agri-Natural Landscape: Potential Habitat Value for Native Bees' (2009) 142(10) *Biological Conservation* 2140–2154.

Hansen JW, 'Is Agricultural Sustainability a Useful Concept' (1996) 50 *Agricultural Systems* 117–143.

Hardin G, 'The Tragedy of the Commons' (1968) 162 *Science* 1243–1248.

Hasund KP and Johansson M, 'Paying for Environmental Results is WTO Compliant' (2016) 15 *EuroChoices* 33–38.

Helm D, 'Agriculture after Brexit' (2017) 33 suppl 1 *Oxford Review of Economic Policy* S124–S133.

Herwig A, 'Too Much Zeal on Seals? Animal Welfare, Public Morals, and Consumer Ethics at the Bar of the WTO' (2016) 15(1) *World Trade Review* 109–137.

Herzon I et al., 'Time to Look for Evidence: Results-Based Approach to Biodiversity Conservation on Farmland in Europe' (2018) 71 *Land Use Policy* 347–354.

Hodge I, 'Agri-Environment Policy in an Era of Lower Government Expenditure: CAP Reform and Conservation Payments' (2013) 56(2) *Journal of Environmental Planning and Management* 254–270.

Holling CS, 'Resilience and Stability of Ecological Systems' (1973) 4(1) *Annual Review of Ecology and Systematics* 1–23.

Hooghe L and Marks G, 'Unraveling the Central State, but How? Types of Multi-Level Governance' (2003) 97(2) *American Political Science Review* 233–243.

Howe HR and Ross M, 'Brexit's Shades of Green – (Missing) the Opportunity to Transform Farming in England?' (2019) 31(3) *Journal of Environmental Law* 413–441.

Howse R, 'The World Trade Organization 20 Years On: Global Governance by Judiciary' (2016) 27(1) *European Journal of International Law* 9–77.

Howse R and Regan D, 'The Product/Process Distinction – An Illusory Basis for Disciplining "Unilateralism" in Trade Policy' (2000) 11 *European Journal of International Law* 249–289.

Hudec RE, 'GATT/WTO Constraints on National Regulation: Requiem for an "Aim and Effects" Test' (1998) 32 *International Lawyer* 619–649.

Ishihara H, Pascual U and Hodge I, 'Dancing with Storks: The Role of Power Relations in Payments for Ecosystem Services' (2017) 139 *Ecological Economics* 45–54.

Jack B, 'Implementing European Agricultural Law in Northern Ireland and the Republic of Ireland: A Common Policy?' (2003) 54(4) *Northern Ireland Legal Quarterly* 377–411.

Jarosz L, 'Comparing Food Security and Food Sovereignty Discourses' (2014) 4(2) *Dialogues in Human Geography* 168–181.

Jenkins V, 'Sustainable Management of Natural Resources: Lessons from Wales' (2018) 30(3) *Journal of Environmental Law* 399–423.

Jenkins V, 'Welsh Devolution and the Protection of the Environment: The Story so Far and the Future Challenges' (2016) 96 *E-law* (now *Murdoch University Law Review*) 23–24.

Keeney DR, 'Toward a Sustainable Agriculture: Need for Clarification of Concepts and Terminology' (1989) 4(3–4) *American Journal of Alternative Agriculture* 101–105.

Kerner DA and Thomas JS, 'Resilience Attributes of Social-Ecological Systems: Framing Metrics for Management' (2014) 3 *Resources* 672–702.

Kis K, Gal J and Veha A, 'Effectiveness, Efficiency and Sustainability in Local Rural Development Partnerships' (2015) 6(3–4) *Applied Studies in Agribusiness and Commerce* 31–38.

Kumar A and Chatterjee A, 'Reflections on the Bubble of Likeness' (2010) 16 *International Trade Law and Regulation* 51–61.

Kysar DA, 'Preferences for Processes: The Process/Product Distinction and the Regulation of Consumer Choice' (2004) 118 *Harvard Law Review* 525–642.

Lagana G, 'Has the European Union Empowered the Regions? A Pre- and Post-Brexit Preliminary Investigation of the United Kingdom' (2021) 28(1) *European Urban and Regional Studies* 34–39.

Leat P and Revoredo-Giha C, 'Risk and Resilience in Agri-Food Supply Chains: The Case of the ASDA PorkLink Supply Chain in Scotland' (2013) 18(2) *Supply Chain Management* 219–231.

Lee M, 'Accountability for Environmental Standards after Brexit' (2017) 19(2) *Environmental Law Review* 89–92.

Lee M, 'Brexit and Environmental Protection in the United Kingdom: Governance, Accountability and Law Making' (2018) 36(3) *Journal of Energy & Natural Resources Law* 351–359.
Lefebvre M et al., 'Agricultural Landscapes as Multi-Scale Public Good and the Role of the Common Agricultural Policy' (2015) 58(12) *Journal of Environmental Planning and Management* 2088–2112.
Lester S and Stemberg W, 'The GATT Origins of TBT Agreement Articles 2.1 and 2.2' (2014) 17(1) *Journal of International Economic Law* 215–232.
Lin BB, 'Resilience in Agriculture through Crop Diversification: Adaptive Management for Environmental Change' (2011) 61(3) *BioScience* 183–193.
Lopolito A, Nardone G and Sisto R, 'Towards a Comprehensive Evaluation of Local Action Groups in LEADER Programmes' (2011) 10(1) *Mediterranean Journal of Economics, Agriculture and Environment* 43–49.
Maccaferri M, 'Splendid Isolation Again? Brexit and the Role of the Press and Online Media in Re-Narrating the European Discourse' (2019) 16(4) *Critical Discourse Studies* 389–402.
MacRae RJ, Hill SB, Henning J and Mehuys GR, 'Agricultural Science and Sustainable Agriculture: A Review of the Existing Scientific Barriers to Sustainable Food Production and Potential Solutions' (1989) 6(3) *Biological Agriculture and Horticulture* 173–219.
MacRae RJ, Hill SB, Mehuys GR and Henning J, 'Farm-Scale Agronomic and Economic Conversion from Conventional to Sustainable Agriculture' (1990) 43 *Advances in Agronomy* 155–198.
Marceau G and Trachtman JP, 'A Map of the World Trade Organization Law of Domestic Regulation of Goods: The Technical Barriers to Trade Agreement, the Sanitary and Phytosanitary Measures Agreement, and the General Agreement on Tariffs and Trade' (2014) 48(2) *Journal of World Trade* 351–432.
Marceau G and Wyatt J, 'The WTO's Efforts to Balance Economic Development and Environmental Protection: A Short Review of Appellate Body Jurisprudence' (2013) 1(1) *Latin American Journal of International Trade Law* 291–314.
Marchese D et al., 'Resilience and Sustainability: Similarities and Differences in Environmental Management Applications' (2018) 613 *Science of the Total Environment* 1275–1283.
Marín Durán G, 'Measures with Multiple Competing Purposes after *EC – Seal Products*: Avoiding a Conflict between GATT Article XX-Chapeau and Article 2.1 TBT Agreement' (2016) 19(2) *Journal of International Economic Law* 467–495.
Matzdorf B and Lorenz J, 'How Cost-Effective Are Result-Oriented Agri-Environmental Measures? – An Empirical Analysis in Germany' (2010) 27(2) *Land Use Policy* 535–544.
Maye D, Ilbery B and Watts D, 'Farm Diversification, Tenancy and CAP Reform: Results from a Survey of Tenant Farmers in England' (2009) 25 *Journal of Rural Studies* 333–342.
McMahon J, 'Brexit, Trade and Agriculture: Waiting for Answers' (2018) 17(1/2) *Journal of International Trade Law and Policy* 19–33.
McNeill B, 'Is the Grass Always Greener? Understanding Grazing and Cropping Rights in Northern Ireland' (2021, forthcoming) 11 *Modern Studies in Property Law* 3–23.
Mechlem K, 'Food Security and the Right to Food in the Discourse of the United Nations' (2004) 10 *European Law Journal* 631–648.

Melo Araujo B, 'UK Post-Brexit Trade Agreements and Devolution' (2019) 39(4) *Legal Studies* 555–578.
Michalek J, Ciaian P and Di Marcantonio F, 'Regional Impacts of the EU Rural Development Programme: Poland's Food Processing Sector' (2020) 54(10) *Regional Studies* 1389–1401.
Moxey A and White B, 'Result-Oriented Agri-Environment Schemes in Europe: A Comment' (2014) 39 *Land Use Policy* 397–399.
Ojo OM et al., 'Brexit: Potential Impacts on the Economic Welfare of UK Farm Households' (2021) 55(9) *Regional Studies* 1583–1595.
Ostrom E, 'A General Framework for Analyzing Sustainability of Social-Ecological Systems' (2009) 325(5939) *Science* 419–422.
Ostrom E, 'Collective Action and the Evolution of Social Norms' (2000) 14(3) *Journal of Economic Perspectives* 137–158.
Ostrom E, Janssen MA and Anderies JM, 'Going beyond Panaceas' (2007) 104(39) *Proceedings of the National Academy of Sciences* 15176–15178.
Patton M, Kostov P, McErlean S and Moss J, 'Assessing the Influence of Direct Payments on the Rental Value of Agricultural Land' (2008) 33(5) *Food Policy* 397–405.
Peel J, 'Precaution – A Matter of Principle, Approach or Process' (2004) 5(2) *Melbourne Journal of International Law* 483–501.
Peers S, 'The End – Or a New Beginning? The EU/UK Withdrawal Agreement' (2020) 39(1) *Yearbook of European Law* 122–198.
Peters BG, 'What is So Wicked about Wicked Problems? A Conceptual Analysis and a Research Program' (2017) 36(3) *Policy and Society* 385–396.
Petetin L, 'Clone Wars? The Challenges of Cloned Food in EU, US and WTO Law' (2009) 11 *Environmental Law Review* 246–263.
Petetin L, 'Frankenburgers, Risks and Approval' (2014) 5(2) *European Journal of Risk Regulation* 168–186.
Petetin L, 'The COVID-19 Crisis: An Opportunity to Integrate Food Democracy into Post-Pandemic Food Systems' (2020) 11(S2) *European Journal of Risk Regulation* 326–336.
Pieraccini M, 'Towards Just Resilience: Representing and Including New Constituencies in Adaptive Governance and Law' (2019) 31(2) *Journal of Environmental Law* 213–234.
Prager K, 'Agri-Environmental Collaboratives for Landscape Management in Europe' (2015) 12 *Current Opinion in Environmental Sustainability* 59–66.
Prager K, Reed M and Scott A, 'Encouraging Collaboration for the Provision of Ecosystem Services at a Landscape Scale – Rethinking Agri-Environmental Payments' (2012) 29(1) *Land Use Policy* 244–249.
Pretty J, 'The Sustainable Intensification of Agriculture' (1997) 21 *Natural Resources Forum* 249–274.
Pontin B, 'Legal and Political Conceptions of Governance within the Environmental Act Debate' (2019) 31 *Environmental Law and Management* 85–95.
Porges A and Trachtman JP, 'Hudec and Domestic Regulation: The Resurrection of Aim and Effects' (2003) 37 *Journal of World Trade* 783–799.
Râmniceanu I and Ackrill R, 'EU Rural Development Policy in the New Member States: Promoting Multifunctionality?' (2007) 23(4) *Journal of Rural Studies* 416–429.
Ravenscroft N, '"Post-Feudalism" and the Changing Structure of Agricultural Leasing' (1999) 16 *Land Use Policy* 247–257.

Read R, 'Like Products, Health & Environmental Exceptions: The Interpretation of PPMs in Recent WTO Trade Dispute Cases' (2004) 5 *Estey Centre Journal of International Law and Trade Policy* 123–146.

Reed MS et al., 'A Place-Based Approach to Payments for Ecosystem Services' (2017) 43 *Global Environmental Change* 92–106.

Reed MS et al., 'Improving the Link between Payments and the Provision of Ecosystem Services in Agri-Environment Schemes' (2014) 9 *Ecosystem Services* 44–53.

Regan DH, 'Regulatory Purpose and "Like Products" in Article III:4 of the GATT (With Additional Remarks on Article III:2)' (2002) 36 *Journal of World Trade* 443–478.

Rittel HWJ and Webber MM, 'Dilemmas in a General Theory of Planning' (1973) 4 *Policy Sciences* 155–169.

Rockström J et al., 'Planetary Boundaries: Exploring the Safe Operating Space for Humanity' (2009) 14(2) *Ecology and Society* 32. Also available online http://www.ecologyandsociety.org/vol14/iss2/art32/.

Rodgers CP, 'Delivering a Better Natural Environment? The Agriculture Bill and Future Agri-Environment Policy' (2019) 21(1) *Environment Law Review* 31–48.

Ruhl JB, 'General Design Principles for Resilience and Adaptive Capacity in Legal Systems – With Applications to Climate Change Adaptation' (2011) 89(5) *North Carolina Law Review* 1373–1404.

Russi D, Margue H, Oppermann R and Keenleyside C, 'Result-Based Agri-Environment Measures: Market-Based Instruments, Incentives or Rewards? The Case of Baden-Württemberg' (2016) 54 *Land Use Policy* 69–77.

Ruzza C and Pejovic M, 'Populism at Work: The Language of the Brexiteers and the European Union' (2019) 16(4) *Critical Discourse Studies* 432–448.

Salmon N, 'A European Perspective on the Precautionary Principle, Food Safety and the Free Trade Imperative of the WTO' (2002) 27 *European Law Review* 138–155.

Samuelson PA, 'The Pure Theory of Public Expenditure' (1954) 36 *The Review of Economics and Statistics* 387–389.

Schebesta H and Candel JLL, 'Game-Changing Potential of the EU's Farm to Fork Strategy' (2020) 1 *Nature Food* 586–588.

Schumacher R, 'Deconstructing the Theory of Comparative Advantage' (2013) 2 *World Economic Review* 83–105.

Scott A, 'The Role of Concordats in the New Governance of Britain: Taking Subsidiarity Seriously?' (2001) 5(1) *Edinburgh Law Review* 21–48.

Scott J, 'The New EU "Extraterritoriality"' (2014) 51(5) *Common Market Law Review* 1343–1380.

Shaffer G, 'United States – Measures Concerning the Importation, Marketing and Sale of Tuna and Tuna Products' (2013) 107(1) *American Journal of International Law* 192–199.

Shucksmith M and Rønningen K, 'The Uplands after Neoliberalism? The Role of the Small Farm in Rural Sustainability' (2011) 27(3) *Journal of Rural Studies* 275–287.

Steffen W et al., 'Planetary Boundaries: Guiding Human Development on a Changing Planet' (2015) 347(6223) *Science* 1259855.

Stoeckl N et al., 'The Crowding Out of Complex Social Goods' (2018) 144 *Ecological Economics* 65–72.

Stokes E, 'The Role of Risk Assessment in Precautionary Intervention: A Comparison of Judicial Trends in the EC and WTO' (2007) 4 *Journal for European Environmental Planning Law* 455–467.

Sutherland L et al., 'Adaptation, Resilience and CAP Reform: A Comparison of Crofts and Livestock Farms in Scotland' (2017) 133(3–4) *Scottish Geographical Journal* 192–213.

Swinbank A, 'Like Products, Animal Welfare and the World Trade Organization' (2006) 40 *Journal of World Trade* 687–712.

Swinbank A and Tranter R, 'Decoupling EU Farm Support: Does the New Single Payment Scheme Fit within the Green Box?' (2005) 6(1) *Etsey Centre Journal of International Law and Trade Policy* 47–61.

Switzer S and McMahon JA, 'Devolution and Post-Brexit Trade Agreements: Towards a Joint Trade Policy Committee?' (2019) 23 *Edinburgh Law Review* 266–272.

Sykes K, 'Sealing Animal Welfare into the GATT Exceptions: The International Dimension of Animal Welfare in WTO Disputes' (2014) 13(3) *World Trade Review* 471–498.

Tonge J, 'The Impact of Withdrawal from the European Union upon Northern Ireland' (2016) 87(3) *Political Quarterly* 338–342.

Tuomisti H et al., 'Does Organic Farming Reduce Environmental Impacts? – A Meta-Analysis of European Research' (2012) 112 *Journal of Environmental Management* 309–320.

Van Huylenbroeck G, Vandermeulen V, Mettepenningen E and Verspecht A, 'Multifunctionality of Agriculture: A Review of Definitions, Evidence and Instruments' (2007) 1 *Living Reviews in Landscape Research* 3–43.

Vischer R, 'Subsidiarity as a Principle of Governance: Beyond Devolution' (2001–2002) 35 *Indiana Law Review* 103–142.

Walker B, Holling CS, Carpenter SR and Kinzig AP, 'Resilience, Adaptability and Transformability in Social-Ecological Systems' (2004) 9(2) *Ecology and Society* 5.

Walker BH et al., 'A Handful of Heuristics and Some Propositions for Understanding Resilience in Social-Ecological Systems' (2006) 11(1) *Ecology and Society*, Article 13. Available on http://www.ecologyandsociety.org/vol11/iss1/art13/.

Waylen K et al., 'The Need to Disentangle Key Concepts from Ecosystem-Approach Jargon' (2014) 28(5) *Conservation Biology* 1215–1224.

Wehling S and Diekmann M, 'Importance of Hedgerows as Habitat Corridors for Forest Plants in Agricultural Landscapes' (2009) 142(11) *Biological Conservation* 2522–2530.

Wezel A and Soldat V, 'A Quantitative and Qualitative Historical Analysis of the Scientific Discipline of Agroecology' (2009) 7(1) *International Journal of Agricultural Sustainability* 3–18.

Willett W et al., 'Food in the Anthropocene: The EAT–Lancet Commission on Healthy Diets from Sustainable Food Systems' (2019) 393(10170) *The Lancet* 447–492.

Books

Abbot C and Lee M, *Environmental Groups and Legal Expertise: Shaping the Brexit Process* (UCL Press 2021).

Alabrese M, *Il Regime della Food Security nel Commercio Agricolo Internazionale. Dall'Havana Charter al Processo di Riforma dell'Accordo Agricolo WTO* (Giappichelli 2018).
Ayres I and Braithwaite J, *Responsive Regulation* (OUP 1992).
Bachtler J and Mendez C, *EU Cohesion Policy and European Integration: The Dynamics of EU Budget and Regional Policy Reform* (Routledge 2013).
Barrios Villarreal A, *International Standardization and the Agreement on Technical Barriers to Trade* (CUP 2018).
Bernasconi-Osterwalder N et al., *Environment and Trade: A Guide to WTO Jurisprudence* (Earthscan 2005).
Bohman B, *Legal Design for Social-Ecological Resilience* (CUP 2021).
Bradford A, *The Brussels Effect: How the European Union Rules the World* (OUP 2020).
Button C, *The Power to Protect: Trade, Health and Uncertainty in the WTO* (Hart 2004).
Cardwell M, *The European Model of Agriculture* (OUP 2004).
Choi WM, *'Like Products' in International Trade Law: Towards a Consistent GATT/WTO Jurisprudence* (OUP 2003).
Daly HE and Cobb JB jr, *For the Common Good: Redirecting the Economy towards Community, the Environment and a Sustainable Future* (Beacon Press 1994).
Desta MG, *The Law of International Trade in Agricultural Products: From GATT 1947 to the WTO Agreement on Agriculture* (Kluwer Law International 2002).
Du M, *The Regulation of Product Standards in World Trade Law* (Hart Publishing 2020).
Echols MA, *Food Safety and the WTO: The Interplay of Culture, Science and Technology* (Kluwer Law International 2001).
Elliott M and Thomas R, *Public Law* (OUP 2011).
Estella A, *The EU Principle of Subsidiarity and Its Critique* (OUP 2002).
Ferraris L, *The Pursuit of Sustainable Agriculture in EU Free Trade Agreements* (Wageningen Academic 2020).
Fijalkowski A and Cameron J, *Trade and the Environment: Bridging the Gap* (Cameron May 1998).
Gliessman SR, *Agroecology: The Ecology of Sustainable Food Systems* (CRC Press 2015).
Harris JM and Roach B, *Environmental and Natural Resource Economics: A Contemporary Approach* (Routledge 2017).
Jack B, *Agriculture and EU Environmental Law* (Ashgate Publishing 2009).
Lagana G, *The European Union and the Northern Ireland Peace Process* (Palgrave 2021).
Macrory R, *Regulation, Enforcement and Governance in Environmental Law* (2nd edn, Hart Publishing 2014).
Melo Araujo B, *The EU Deep Trade Agenda: Law and Policy* (OUP 2016).
McMahon JA, *EU Agricultural Law and Policy* (Edwar Elgar 2019).
McMahon JA, *The WTO Agreement on Agriculture: A Commentary* (Oxford Commentaries in International Law, OUP 2007).
Millard J-B and Bosse-Platière H, *Les Biens Communs en Agriculture, Tragédie ou Apologie?* (AFDR, Agridées and LexisNexis 2020).
Nielsen L, *The WTO, Animals and PPMs* (Martinus Nijhoff Publishers 2007).
Ostrom E, *Governing the Commons: The Evolution of Institutions for Collective Action* (CUP 1990).

Pontin B, *The Environmental Case for Brexit: A Socio-legal Perspective* (Hart Publishing 2019).
Ricardo D, *On the Principles of Political Economy and Taxation* (John Murray 1817).
Rodgers CP, *Agricultural Law* (Bloomsbury Professional Ltd 2016).
Rodgers CP, *The Law of Nature Conservation* (OUP 2013).
Schimmelfennig F and Sedelmeier U, *The Europeanization of Central and Eastern Europe* (Cornell University Press 2005).
Scott J, *Commentary on the Sanitary and Phytosanitary Measures Agreement* (OUP 2007).
Smith F, *Agriculture and the WTO: Towards a New Theory of International Agricultural Trade Regulation* (Edward Elgar 2009).
Snyder FG, *Law of the Common Agricultural Policy* (Sweet and Maxwell 1985).
Szajkowska A, *Regulating Food Law* (Wageningen Academic Publishers 2012).
Van den Bossche P and Prévost D, *Essentials of WTO Law* (2nd edn, CUP 2021).
Van den Bossche P and Zdouc W, *The Law and Policy of the World Trade Organization Text, Cases, and Materials* (5th edn, CUP 2021).
Vellvé R, *Saving the Seed: Genetic Diversity and European Agriculture* (Earthscan 1992).
@BorderIrish, *I Am the Border, so I Am* (HarperCollins 2019).

Edited chapter

Ansell CK, Trondal J and Øgård M, 'Turbulent Governance' in Ansell CK, Trondal J and Øgård M (eds) *Governance in Turbulent Times* (OUP 2016) 1–33.
Anthony G, 'Devolution Issues, Legislative Power, and Legal Sovereignty' in Antoine A (eds) *Le Droit Public Britannique: État des Lieux et Perspectives* (Société de Législation Comparée 2015) 95, 98.
Arnold CA and Gunderson LH, 'Adaptive Law' in Garmestani AS and Allen CR (eds) *Social-Ecological Resilience and Law* (Columbia University Press 2014) 317–364.
Baldock D, 'Twisted Together: European Agriculture, Environment and the Common Agricultural Policy' in McMahon JA and Cardwell MN (eds) *Research Handbook on EU Agriculture Law* (Research Handbook in European Law, Edward Elgar Publishing 2015) 125–149.
Blackstock KL, Brown K, Davies B and Shannon P, 'Individualism, Cooperation and Conservation in Scottish Farming Communities' in Cheshire L, Higgins V and Lawrence G (eds) *Rural Governance* (Routledge 2007) 191–207.
Brownsword R, 'Regulatory Coherence-A European Challenge' in Purnhagen K and Rott P (eds) *Varieties of European Economic Law and Regulation* (Springer 2014) 235–258.
Cardwell MN, 'The Direct Payments Regime: Delivering "A Fair Standard of Living for the Agricultural Community"?' in McMahon JA and Cardwell MN (eds) *Research Handbook on EU Agriculture Law* (Research Handbook in European Law, Edward Elgar Publishing 2015) 41–61.
Dobbs M, 'Northern Ireland's Agricultural Quagmire: How to Develop a Sustainable Agricultural Policy?' in Antonopoulos I, Bell M, Cavoski A and Petetin L (eds) *The Governance of Agriculture in Post-Brexit UK* (Routledge, forthcoming 2022).
French D, 'The Regulation of Genetically Modified Organisms and International Law: A Call for Generality' in Bodiguel L and Cardwell MN (eds) *The Regulation of Genetically Modified Organisms: Comparative Approaches* (OUP 2010) 355–374.

Fouilleux E and Ansaloni M, 'The Common Agricultural Policy' in Cini M and Pérez-Solórzano Borragán N (eds) *European Union Politics* (OUP 2016) 308–322.
Garcia FJ, 'The Salmon Case: Evolution of Balancing Mechanisms for Non-Trade Values in WTO' in Bermann GA and Mavroidis PC (eds) *Trade and Human Health and Safety* (CUP 2006) 133–152.
Garmestani AS, Allen CR, Ruhl JB and Holling CS, 'The Integration of Social-Ecological Resilience and Law' in Garmestani AS and Allen CR (eds) *Social-Ecological Resilience and Law* (Columbia University Press 2014) 368–382.
Geelhoed M, 'Agroecology, GMOs and Post-Brexit Regulations' in Antonopoulos I, Bell M, Cavoski A and Petetin L (eds) *The Governance of Agriculture in Post-Brexit UK* (Routledge, forthcoming 2022) 1–8.
Gravey V, 'Brexit and the Common Agricultural Policy: There and Back Again' in Antonopoulos I, Bell M, Cavoski A and Petetin L (eds) *The Governance of Agriculture in Post-Brexit UK* (Routledge, forthcoming 2022).
Grossman MR, 'The Uruguay Round Agreement on Agriculture and Domestic Support' in Cardwell MN, Grossman MR and Rodgers CP (eds) *Agriculture and International Trade: Law, Policy, and the WTO* (CABI Publishing 2003) 27–47.
Hecht SB, 'The Evolution of Agroecological Thought' in Altieri MA (eds) *Agroecology – The Science of Sustainable Agriculture* (2nd edn, CRC Press 2018) 1–20.
Holling CS and Gunderson LH, 'Resilience and Adaptive Cycles' in Holling CS and Gunderson LH (eds) *Panarchy: Understanding Transformations in Human and Natural Systems* (Island Press 2002) 25–62.
Howse R and Türk E, 'The WTO Impact on Internal Regulations: A Case Study of the *Canada–EC Asbestos* Dispute' in Bermann GA and Mavroidis PC (eds) *Trade and Human Health and Safety* (CUP 2006) 77–117.
Hudec RE, '"Like Product": The Differences in Meaning in GATT Articles I and III' in Cottier T and Mavroidis P (eds) *Regulatory Barriers and the Principle of Non-Discrimination in World Trade Law* (University of Michigan Press 2000) 101–123.
Hunt J, 'Devolution' in Dougan M (eds) *The UK after Brexit: Legal and Policy Challenges* (Intersentia 2017) 35–52.
Marceau G, 'Do PPM Concerns Have a Future?' in Prévost D, Alexovicova I and Hillebrand Pohl J (eds) *Restoring Trust in Trade: Liber Amicorum in Honour of Peter Van den Bossche* (Hart Publishing 2018) 175–197.
Mavroidis PC, 'Come Together? Producer Welfare, Consumers Welfare, and WTO Rules' in Petersmann EU and Harrison J (eds) *Reforming the World Trading System: Legitimacy, Efficiency, and Democratic Governance* (OUP 2005) 285–303.
McMahon JA, 'The *EC-Biotech* Decision: Another Missed Opportunity?' in Bodiguel L and Cardwell M (eds) *The Regulation of Genetically Modified Organisms: Comparative Approaches* (OUP 2010) 337–354.
McMahon JA and Desta MG, 'The Agreement on Agriculture: Setting the Scene' in McMahon JA and Desta MG (eds) *Research Handbook on the WTO Agriculture Agreement: New and Emerging Issues in International Agricultural Trade Law* (Research Handbooks on the WTO Series, Edward Elgar 2013) 1–44.
McRae D, 'GATT Article XX and the WTO Appellate Body' in Bronckers M and Quick R (eds) *New directions in International Economic Law: Essays in Honour of John H. Jackson* (Kluwer Law International 2000) 219–236.
O'Connor B, 'The Impact of the Doha Round on the European Union's Common Agricultural Policy' in McMahon JA and Cardwell MN (eds) *Research Handbook*

on EU Agriculture Law (Research Handbook in European Law, Edward Elgar Publishing 2015) 387–411.

O'Gorman R, 'Of Eggs, and Seals, and Leghold Traps: Internal and External Public Morality as a Factor in European Union Animal Welfare Legislation' in McMahon JA and Cardwell MN (eds) *Research Handbook on EU Agriculture Law* (Research Handbook in European Law, Edward Elgar Publishing 2015) 323–341.

Parcell JL and Kalaitzandonakes NG, 'Do Agricultural Commodity Prices Respond to GMO Bans?' in Evenson RE and Santaniello V (eds) *Consumer Acceptance of Genetically Modified Foods* (CABI Publishing 2004) 1–8.

Petetin L, 'Food Democracy in Food Systems' in Thompson PB and Kaplan DM (eds) *Encyclopedia of Food and Agricultural Ethics* (2nd edn, Springer 2016) 1–7.

Petetin L, 'La Dimension Agricole du Brexit' in Abis S and Brun M (eds) *Le Déméter 2020* (Iris éditions 2020) 119–128.

Petetin L, 'Managing Novel Food Technologies and Member States' Interests: Shifting More Powers towards the Member States?' in Varju M (eds) *Between Compliance and Particularism: Member State Interests and European Union Law* (Springer 2019) 233–253.

Petetin L, 'Setting the Path for UK and Devolved Agriculture' in Antonopoulos I, Bell M, Cavoski A and Petetin L (eds) *The Governance of Agriculture in Post-Brexit UK* (Routledge, forthcoming 2022).

Petetin L, 'The EU Common Agricultural Policy: Towards a More Sustainable Agriculture?' in Ako R and Olawuyi D (eds) *Food and Agricultural Law: Readings on Sustainable Agriculture and the Law in Nigeria* (Afe Babalola University Press 2015) 201–224.

Rodgers CP, 'Legal Models for Implementing Agri-Environment Policy after Brexit' in Antonopoulos I, Bell M, Cavoski A and Petetin L (eds) *The Governance of Agriculture in Post-Brexit UK* (Routledge, forthcoming 2022).

Saba A, 'Results-Based Agri-Environmental Schemes for Delivering Ecosystem Services in the EU: Established and Emerging Trends' in Alabrese M, Brunori M, Rolandi S and Saba A (eds) *Agricultural Law* (Springer 2017) 83–122.

Smith F, 'Mind the Gap: "Greening" Direct Payments and the World Trade Organization' in McMahon JA and Cardwell MN (eds) *Research Handbook on EU Agriculture Law* (Research Handbook in European Law, Edward Elgar Publishing 2015) 412–436.

Subedi S, 'The Challenge of Managing the "Second Agricultural Revolution" through International Law: Liberalization of Trade in Agriculture and Sustainable Development' in Schrijver NJ, Weiss F (eds) *International Law and Sustainable Development: Principles and Practice* (Martinus Nijhoff 2004) 161–184.

Sykes A, 'Domestic Regulation, Sovereignty and Scientific Evidence Requirements: A Pessimistic View' in Bermann GA and Mavroidis PC (eds), *Trade and Human Health and Safety* (CUP 2006) 257–270.

Edited collections

Antonopoulos I, Bell M, Cavoski A and Petetin L (eds) *The Governance of Agriculture in Post-Brexit UK* (Routledge, forthcoming 2022).

Cardwell MN, Grossman MR and Rodgers CP (eds) *Agriculture and International Trade: Law, Policy, and the WTO* (CABI Publishing 2003).

De Schutter O and Cordes KY (eds) *Accounting for Hunger: The Right to Food in the Era of Globalisation* (Hart Publishing 2011).

Delimatsis P and Reins L (eds) *Trade and Environmental Law* (Edward Elgar Publishing 2021).

Fabbrini F (eds) *The Law & Politics of Brexit: Volume II – The Withdrawal Agreement* (OUP 2020).

Fabbrini F (eds) *The Law & Politics of Brexit: Volume III – The Framework of New EU-UK Relationships* (OUP 2021).

Grossman MR (eds) *Agriculture and the Polluter Pays Principle* (British Institute of International and Comparative Law 2009).

Hazell R and Rawling R (eds) *Devolution, Law Making and the Constitution* (Inprint Academic 2005).

Hendriks SL (eds) *Food Security Policy, Evaluation and Impact Assessment* (Routledge 2019).

Jasanoff S (eds) *States of Knowledge: The Co-production of Science and Social Order* (Routledge 2004).

Ladha JK and Peoples MB (eds) *Management of Biological Nitrogen Fixation for the Development of More Productive and Sustainable Agricultural Systems* (Springer 1995).

McMahon JA and Cardwell MN (eds) *Research Handbook on EU Agriculture Law* (Research Handbook in European Law, Edward Elgar Publishing 2015).

McMahon JA and Desta MG (eds) *Research Handbook on the WTO Agriculture Agreement: New and Emerging Issues in International Agricultural Trade Law* (Research Handbooks on the WTO Series, Edward Elgar 2013).

Meléndez-Ortiz R, Bellmann C and Hepburn J (eds) *Agricultural Subsidies in the WTO Green Box: Ensuring Coherence with Sustainable Development Goals* (CUP 2009).

Monteduro M, Buongiorno P, Di Benedetto S and Isoni A (eds), *Law and Agroecology – A Transdisciplinary Dialogue* (Springer 2015).

Plieninger T and Bieling C (eds) *Resilience and the Cultural Landscape: Understanding and Managing Change in Human-Shaped Environments* (CUP 2012).

Shattuck A, Schiavoni C and VanGelder Z (eds) *The Politics of Food Sovereignty: Concept, Practice and Social Movements* (Routledge 2017).

Research papers, blogs and similar online resources

Baldwin R and Black J, 'Really Responsive Regulation' (LSE Law, Society and Economy Working Papers 15/2007) https://www.lse.ac.uk/law/working-paper-series/2007-08/WPS15-2007BlackandBaldwin.pdf.

Barnard C, 'Northern Ireland in the Negotiations and the Withdrawal Agreement' in Menon A (eds) *Brexit and the Island of Ireland* (The UK in a Changing Europe 2018) https://ukandeu.ac.uk/wp-content/uploads/2018/05/Brexit-and-Island-of-Ireland.pdf, 12–14.

Barnett A, 'Nature-Based Solutions in the Green Recovery' (RSPB 2020) https://www.rspb.org.uk/globalassets/downloads/policy-briefings/policy-briefing_nature-based-solutions-in-the-green-recovery_the-rspb.pdf.

Brink L, 'UK Brexit and WTO Farm Support Limits' (CAP Reform 13 July 2016) http://capreform.eu/uk-brexit-and-wto-farm-support-limits/.

Brink L and Orden D, 'Taking Stock and Looking Forward on Domestic Support under the WTO Agreement on Agriculture' (International Agricultural Trade Research Consortium Commissioned Paper No. 23, 2020).

British Veterinary Association, 'New Immigration Rules Risk No Vets in Abattoirs, Warns BVA' (19 December 2018) https://www.bva.co.uk/news-and-blog/news-article/new-immigration-rules-risk-no-vets-in-abattoirs-warns-bva/.

Brogan A and Moore O, 'Eco-Scheming – Council Adopts a Position of No Ecological Substance' (Arc 2020 21 October 2020) https://www.arc2020.eu/eco-scheming-council-adopts-a-cap-position-of-no-ecological-substance/.

Caddell R, 'What's SUP? Single-Use Plastics, the Internal Market Act and the Marine Environment of Wales' (Francis Taylor Building 7 May 2021) https://www.ftbchambers.co.uk/blogs/what%E2%80%99s-sup-single-use-plastics-internal-market-act-and-marine-environment-wales.

Cardwell M, 'Farming Policy' in Kassin H, Jordan A and Ennis S (eds) *UK Regulation after Brexit* (The UK in a Changing Europe 25 February 2021) https://ukandeu.ac.uk/wp-content/uploads/2021/02/UK-regulation-after-Brexit.pdf, 48–50.

Cardwell M, 'Results-Based Agri-Environmental Scheme Design: Regulatory Implications' – draft paper (2021).

Charnovitz S, 'The WTO Appellate Body Crisis: A Critique of the EU's Article 25 Proposal' (International Economic Law and Policy Blog 2 June 2019) https://ielp.worldtradelaw.net/2019/06/the-wto-appellate-body-crisis-a-critique-of-the-eus-article-25-proposal.html.

ClientEarth, 'Environmental Groups Launch Brexit Regulation Court Challenge Over Wildlife Risk' (21 June 2019) https://www.clientearth.org/latest/latest-updates/news/environmental-groups-launch-brexit-regulation-court-challenge-over-wildlife-risk/.

Connolly A, 'What the Brexit Deal Means for Northern Ireland' (The UK in a Changing Europe 31 December 2020) https://ukandeu.ac.uk/what-the-brexit-deal-means-for-northern-ireland/.

Davis J, Feng S, Patton M and Binfield J, 'Impacts of Alternative Post-Brexit Trade Agreements on UK Agriculture: Sector Analyses Using the FAPRI-UK Model' (FAPRI-UK Project, Agri-Food and Biosciences Institute, August 2017) https://content17.green17creative.com/media/99/files/FAPRI_UK_Brexit_Report.pdf.

Delargy O, 'Digging in to the Trade and Agriculture Commission Report' (Sustain 12 March 2021) https://www.sustainweb.org/blogs/mar21-trade-and-agriculture-commission-response/.

De Schutter O et al., 'Towards a Common Food Policy for the European Union: The Policy Reform and Realignment that is Required to Build Sustainable Food Systems in Europe' (IPES Food 2019).

Dobbs M and Petetin L, 'Agriculture: Environmental, Food and Animal Health Standards' in Kassin H, Jordan A and Ennis S (eds) *UK Regulation after Brexit* (The UK in a Changing Europe 25 February 2021) https://ukandeu.ac.uk/wp-content/uploads/2021/02/UK-regulation-after-Brexit.pdf, 51–53.

Dougan M, 'United Kingdom Internal Market Bill: Implications for Devolution' (15 September 2020) https://www.liverpool.ac.uk/media/livacuk/law/2-research/eull/UKIM,Briefing,Paper,-,Prof,Michael,Dougan,15,September,2020.pdf.

Driessen B, 'Why Small Farms Must Be Included in New Land Use Schemes' (Food Research Collaboration 18 March 2021) https://foodresearch.org.uk/foodvoices/small-farmers-must-be-included-in-new-land-use-schemes/.

Ecological Land Cooperative, 'Small Farm Profits' (2018) https://ecologicalland.coop/small-farm-profits.

Fabbrini F, 'From the Withdrawal Agreement to the Trade and Cooperation Agreement: Reshaping EU-UK Relations' (Brexit Institute Working Paper No. 10/2020) https://papers.ssrn.com/sol3/papers.cfm?abstract_id=3756331.

Farmers' Union of Wales, 'FUW Stresses Need for Clarity on Funding for Wales at Roundtable Meeting with Secretary of State for Environment, Food and Rural Affairs' (19 March 2021) https://fuw.org.uk/en/news/14441-fuw-stresses-need-for-clarity-on-funding-for-wales-at-roundtable-meeting-with-secretary-of-state-for-environment-food-and-rural-affairs.

Farmers' Union of Wales, 'Farmers' Union of Wales Response to the Welsh Government's Agriculture (Wales) White Paper' (25 March 2021) https://www.fuw.org.uk/images/Consultation_Responses/Agriculture_Wales_White_Paper_FUW_Response-FINAL.pdf.

Farmers' Union of Wales, 'FUW Reacts to Agriculture (Wales) White Paper' (16 December 2020) https://fuw.org.uk/en/news/14273-fuw-reacts-to-agriculture-wales-white-paper.

Forshaw T, 'The Devolved Nations and Agricultural Policy: Scotland' (Agriculture and Horticultural Development Board 4 December 2020) https://ahdb.org.uk/news/the-devolved-nations-and-agricultural-policy-scotland.

Game and Wildlife Conservation Trust, 'March 2018: Balancing Environmental Payments and Trade' (March 2018) https://www.gwct.org.uk/policy/appg/march-2018/.

Garnett T et al., 'Grazed and Confused' (Food Climate Research Network, Oxford Martin Programme on the Future of Food, Environmental Change Institute, University of Oxford 2017) https://www.oxfordmartin.ox.ac.uk/publications/grazed-and-confused/.

Garnett T and Godfray C, 'Sustainable Intensification in Agriculture: Navigating a Course through Competing Food System Priorities' (Food Climate Research Network, Oxford Martin Programme on the Future of Food 2012).

Glauber J, Laborde D, Martin W and Vos R, 'COVID-19: Trade Restrictions Are Worst Possible Response to Safeguard Food Security' (IFPRI Blog 27 March 2020) https://www.ifpri.org/blog/covid-19-trade-restrictions-are-worst-possible-response-safeguard-food-security.

Graham T, 'ELMS – The UK's Environmental Land Management Scheme' (Stephens Scown 6 April 2021) https://www.stephens-scown.co.uk/specialist-sectors/rural/elms-the-uks-environmental-land-management-scheme/.

Gravey V, 'Agricultural Policy' in Burns C, Jordan A and Gravey V (eds) *The EU Referendum and the UK Environment: An Expert Review* (The UK in a Changing Europe 2016) 36–45.

Gravey V, 'Balancing Positive and Negative Integration in the EU's Internal Market' (Brexit and Environment Network 16 October 2020) https://www.brexitenvironment.co.uk/2020/10/16/internal-market-bill-why-negative-integration-is-causing-such-negative-feelings/.

Gravey V, 'Northern Ireland Agriculture after Brexit: Policy Development in the Absence of Government' (Sustainable Food Trust 11 October 2019) https://sustainablefoodtrust.org/articles/northern-ireland-agriculture-after-brexit-policy-development-in-the-absence-of-government/.

Gravey V, 'The Brexit Deal and the Environment: Pretty Ambitious yet Pretty Irrelevant? (Brexit Institute, DCU 16 February 2021) http://dcubrexitinstitute.eu/2021/02/the-brexit-deal-and-the-environment/.
Gravey V, 'The Internal Market Bill: Why Negative Integration is Causing such Negative Feelings' (Brexit and Environment Network 16 October 2020) https://www.brexitenvironment.co.uk/2020/10/16/internal-market-bill-why-negative-integration-is-causing-such-negative-feelings/.
Gravey V and Burns C, 'Chlorinated Chicken Cluck Again' (The UK in a Changing Europe 10 June 2020) https://ukandeu.ac.uk/chlorinated-chickens-cluck-again/.
Gravey V and Jordan A, 'Towards an Ever Closer Union?' (Brexit and Environment Network 21 July 2020) https://www.brexitenvironment.co.uk/2020/07/21/towards-an-ever-closer-union/.
Gravey V, Jordan A and Burns C, 'Environmental Policy after Brexit: Mind the Governance Gap' (The UK in a Changing Europe 10 August 2016) https://www.brexitenvironment.co.uk/2016/08/10/environmental-policy-after-brexit-mind-the-governance-gap/.
Gravey V, Jordan A and Petetin L, 'United against Diversity? The UK Internal Market and Environmental Ambition' (Brexit and Environment Network 22 July 2020) https://www.brexitenvironment.co.uk/2020/07/22/united-against-diversity-uk-internal-market-environmental-ambition/.
Gravey V and Reid C, 'Taking Back and Sharing Control? Brexit and the Common Environmental Frameworks' (Brexit and Environment Network 12 March 2018) www.brexitenvironment.co.uk/2018/03/12/common-environmental-frameworks.
Gravey V and Whitten L, 'The NI Protocol and the Environment: The Implications for Northern Ireland, Ireland and the UK' (Brexit and Environment, Environmental Governance Island of Ireland Network Policy Briefs 1/2021) https://www.brexitenvironment.co.uk/research-projects/egii/.
Hayward K, 'The Internal Market Bill and Northern Ireland: Where it Comes from and What it Might Mean' (The UK in a Changing Europe 25 September 2020) https://ukandeu.ac.uk/explainers/the-internal-market-bill-and-northern-ireland-where-it-comes-from-and-what-it-might-mean/.
Hayward K and Smith T, 'Making the Irish Sea Border Work Will Require Partnership, Cross-Border Cooperation, and Preparation' (LSE Blog 15 May 2020) https://blogs.lse.ac.uk/brexit/2020/05/15/making-the-irish-sea-border-work-will-require-partnership-cross-border-cooperation-and-preparation/.
Hejnowicz A and Hartley S, 'New Directions: A Public Goods Approach to Agricultural Policy Post-Brexit' (Brexit and Environment Network 2018).
Hird V, 'Farmers Need Power and Money; It's Time for Ambitious Thinking on Trading Systems and Investment' (18 February 2021) https://www.sustainweb.org/blogs/feb21-farmers-need-power-money/.
Hurley P et al., 'Co-Designing the Environmental Land Management Scheme in England: The Why, Who, and How of Engaging "Harder to Reach" Stakeholders' (University of Sheffield 2020) https://osf.io/preprints/socarxiv/k2ahd/.
Institute for Government, 'Irish Backstop' (24 February 2020) https://www.instituteforgovernment.org.uk/explainers/irish-backstop.
Institute for Government, 'UK-EU Future Relationship: The Deal' (2020) https://www.instituteforgovernment.org.uk/publication/future-relationship-trade-deal.

Institute of Welsh Affairs, 'Brexit and Trade: It's Even More Complicated than We Thought' (1 April 2019) https://www.iwa.wales/agenda/2019/04/brexit-and-trade-its-even-more-complicated-than-we-thought/.

Jordan A, Burns C, and Gravey G, 'Three Brexit Governance Gaps No One is Talking about' (Green Alliance Blog 6 December 2017) https://greenallianceblog.org.uk/2017/12/06/three-brexit-governance-gaps-no-one-is-talking-about/.

Jordan A, Gravey V, Moore B and Reid C, 'EU-UK Trade Relations: Why Environmental Policy Regression Will Undermine the Level Playing Field and What the UK Can Do to Limit it' (Brexit and Environment Network, Research Paper on the Level Playing Field 2020).

Kane J, 'Comprehensive and Progressive Agreement for Trans-Pacific Partnership (CPTPP)' (Institute for Government 2 February 2021).

KPMG, 'VAT and Customs Changes – December 2020: The Key Changes for Businesses Operating on the Island of Ireland' (22 December 2020) https://home.kpmg/ie/en/home/insights/2020/12/brexit-vat-and-customs.html.

Lakner S, 'Effects of Coronavirus on Agricultural Production – A First Approximation (part 2)' (Arc 2020 6 April 2020) https://www.arc2020.eu/effects-of-coronavirus-on-agricultural-production-a-first-approximation-part-2/.

Lancaster T, 'Twitter Post' (10 March 2021) https://twitter.com/tommlancaster/status/1369705217789472768.

Landworkers' Alliance, 'Feeding the Future' (November 2014) http://www.campaignforrealfarming.org/wp-content/uploads/2014/11/Feeding-the-Future-Landworkers-Alliance-A4-low-res.pdf.

Laughton R, 'A Matter of Scale: A Study of the Productivity, Financial Viability and Multifunctional Benefits of Small Farms (20 Ha and Less)' (The Landworkers' Alliance and the Centre for Agroecology, Water and Resilience 2017) https://www.scholacampesina.org/wp-content/uploads/2018/10/A-Matter-of-Scale-Report-LWA-2017.pdf.

Lee M, 'The Environment Bill: A Framework for Progressive Environmental Law?' (Brexit and Environment Network 18 October 2019) https://www.brexitenvironment.co.uk/2019/10/18/framework-progressive-environmental-law/.

Levrat N, 'Governance: Managing Bilateral Relations' (Brexit Institute Working Paper No. 10/2021) https://papers.ssrn.com/sol3/papers.cfm?abstract_id=3811236.

Lewis J, 'To Meat or Not to Meat' (Soil Association 2019) https://www.soilassociation.org/blogs/2019/november/25/eating-meat-good-or-bad-for-the-environment/.

Lopez Marco L, 'Social Agriculture as Multiculturalism and Symbol of a Generative Welfare' (29 June 2018) http://www.simra-h2020.eu/index.php/2018/06/29/social-agriculture-as-multiculturalism-and-symbol-of-a-generative-welfare/.

Loth S, 'As a Crucial Vote Approaches, Will MPs Protect the UK's Food Standards? (Which 7 October 2020) https://www.which.co.uk/news/2020/10/will-mps-protect-the-uks-food-standards/.

Lyon J et al., 'Inclusive Design of Post-Brexit Agri-Environmental Policy: Identifying and Engaging the "Harder to Reach" Stakeholders. A Quick Scoping Review' (Universities of Sheffield and Reading 2020) https://figshare.shef.ac.uk/articles/report/Inclusive_design_of_post-Brexit_Agri-Environmental_Policy_Identifying_and_engaging_the_Harder_to_Reach_stakeholders_A_Quick_Scoping_Review/12506582.

Mariani P and Sacerdoti G, 'Trade in Goods and Level Playing Field' (Brexit Institute Working Paper No. 7/2021) https://papers.ssrn.com/sol3/papers.cfm?abstract_id=3797021.

Marshall J, 'Delaying Brexit Border Checks Solves some Problems but Creates Others' (Institute for Government 12 March 2021) https://www.instituteforgovernment.org.uk/blog/delaying-brexit-border-checks.

Matthews A, 'Can the Next CAP Help to Achieve Green Deal Targets?' (CAP Reform 18 May 2021) http://capreform.eu/can-the-next-cap-help-to-achieve-green-deal-targets/.

Matthews A, 'Establishing the UK's Non-Exempt Limit on Agricultural Support after Brexit' (CAP Reform 29 January 2017) http://capreform.eu/establishing-the-uks-non-exempt-limit-on-agricultural-support-after-brexit/.

Matthews A, 'Level Playing Field Provisions in the EU-UK TCA' (CAP Reform 14 January 2021) http://capreform.eu/level-playing-field-provisions-in-the-eu-uk-tca/.

Matthews A, 'Recent Trends in EU WTO Domestic Support Notifications'(CAP Reform 5 October 2018) http://capreform.eu/recent-trends-in-eu-wto-domestic-support-notifications/.

Matthews A, 'The Protective Effect of EU Agricultural Tariffs' (CAP Reform 24 February 2020) http://capreform.eu/the-protective-effect-of-eu-agricultural-tariffs/.

McIlroy J, 'Tackling Agricultural Ammonia Emissions in Northern Ireland' (Agri-Food and Biosciences Institute 4 February 2021) https://www.afbini.gov.uk/news/tackling-agricultural-ammonia-emissions-northern-ireland-first-article-series-seven-being.

Melo Araujo B, 'Brexit Trade Problems: What's Gone Wrong and Can it Be Fixed? (The Conversation 14 January 2021) https://theconversation.com/brexit-trade-problems-whats-gone-wrong-and-can-it-be-fixed-153270.

Moore B, 'Loosening the Constraints: The Environment in the Revised Brexit Deal' (Brexit and Environment Network 17 October 2019) https://www.brexitenvironment.co.uk/2019/10/17/revised-brexit-deal/.

Nature Friendly Farming Network, 'NI Agri-Environment Scheme Update' https://www.nffn.org.uk/ni-agri-environment-scheme-update/.

National Farmers' Union, 'Achieving Net Zero: Farming's 2040 Goal' (2019).

National Farmers' Union, 'NFU Insight: The UK's Global Tariff Schedule' (2020) https://www.nfuonline.com/news/eu-exit/eu-exit-news/nfu-insight-the-uks-global-tariff-schedule/.

National Farmers' Union Cymru, 'White Paper Policy Proposals Do Not Match Industry's Ambition, Says NFU Cymru' (28 March 2021) https://www.nfu-cymru.org.uk/news/latest-news/white-paper-policy-proposals-do-not-match-industry/.

N8 AgriFood, 'Key Challenges for Agrifood Supply Chains Post-Brexit' (2019).

N8 AgriFood, 'N8 AgriFood Academics Give Evidence to House of Commons International Trade Committee on COVID-19 and the Impacts on the Food System' (4 May 2020) https://www.n8agrifood.ac.uk/international-trade-committee-covid19-evidence/.

Nyssens C and Dupeux B, 'The European Commission Must Not Greenwash the Common Agricultural Policy' (CAP Reform 2020) http://capreform.eu/the-european-commission-must-not-greenwash-the-common-agricultural-policy/.

Owen J, 'Brexit Deal: The Withdrawal Agreement' (Institute for Government 2 July 2020) https://www.instituteforgovernment.org.uk/explainers/brexit-deal-withdrawal-agreement.
Paun A, Sargeant J and Nicholson E, 'Sewel Convention' (Institute for Government 8 December 2020) https://www.instituteforgovernment.org.uk/explainers/sewel-convention.
Petetin L, 'A Road to a Green Recovery' (Green Recovery Wales Festival, RSPB Cymru 21 July 2020) https://community.rspb.org.uk/getinvolved/wales/b/wales-blog/posts/a-road-to-a-green-recovery.
Petetin L, 'Building Democratic Food Systems Following COVID-19' (Food Manifesto Wales 1 June 2020) https://foodmanifesto.wales/2020/06/01/building-democratic-food-systems-following-covid-19/.
Petetin L, 'Cloud Nine or Down to Earth? The Implications of a No Deal Brexit on Agriculture' (The UK in a Changing Europe 15 August 2019) https://ukandeu.ac.uk/cloud-nine-or-down-to-earth-the-implications-of-a-no-deal-brexit-on-agriculture/.
Petetin L, 'GMO Cultivation in the UK: Brexit, the Devolved Administrations and International Trade' (Brexit and Environment Network 11 January 2018) https://www.brexitenvironment.co.uk/2018/01/11/gmos-devolution-trade/.
Petetin L, 'Post-Brexit Agricultural Support and the WTO: Using Both the Amber and Green Boxes?' (Brexit and Environment Network 21 June 2018) https://www.brexitenvironment.co.uk/2018/06/21/post-brexit-agricultural-support-wto-using-amber-green-boxes/.
Petetin L, 'The Role of the UK in Advocating for Higher Animal Welfare Standards' (Food, Farming & Countryside Commission, Trade Unwrapped 1 December 2020) https://tradeunwrapped.uk/read/the-role-of-the-uk-in-advocating-for-higher-animal-welfare-standards.
Petetin L and Dobbs M, 'Collaborating for Agricultural Sustainability' (Centre for Environmental Justice 13 June 2018) https://blogs.cardiff.ac.uk/environmental-justice-research-unit/2018/06/13/collaborating-agricultural-sustainability/.
Petetin L and Gravey V, 'The Agriculture Bill: 8 Key Provisions and Recommendations' (Brexit and Environment Network 24 January 2020) https://www.brexitenvironment.co.uk/2020/01/24/agriculture-bill-8-key-provisions/.
Petetin L, Gravey V and Moore B, 'Setting the Bar for a Green Brexit in Food and Farming' (Soil Association 2019) https://www.soilassociation.org/green-brexit/.
Poux X and Aubert PM, 'An Agroecological Europe in 2050: Multifunctional Agriculture for Healthy Eating – Findings from the Ten Years for Agroecology (TYFA) Modelling Exercise' (IDDRI 2018).
Reid C, 'Environmental Principles Take Root: Post-Brexit Environmental Governance across the UK (Parts 1 and 2)' (Brexit and Environment Network 14 and 16 July 2020) https://www.brexitenvironment.co.uk/2020/07/14/environmental-principles-take-root-post-brexit-environmental-governance/ and https://www.brexitenvironment.co.uk/2020/07/16/watchdogs-compared-and-reviewed-post-brexit-environmental-governance-uk/.
Ribble RJ et al., 'Letter to Thomas J Vilsack, Secretary of Agriculture and Michael Forman, US Trade Representative' (2014) http://www.commonfoodnames.com/wp-content/uploads/House-Dairy-TTIP-Letter.pdf.

Röder N, 'Payments for the Environment – New Turmoil Around an Old Issue' (CAP Reform 2 March 2021) http://capreform.eu/payments-for-the-environment-new-turmoil-around-an-old-issue/.

Röder N and Matthews A, 'Eco-Schemes a Work in Progress' (CAP Reform 6 January 2021) http://capreform.eu/eco-schemes-a-work-in-progress/.

Royal Society for the Protection of Birds, 'State of Nature 2019' (2019).

Royal Society for the Protection of Birds Cymru, 'Wales' Annual Report 2019–2020' (2020).

Royal Society of Arts, 'Food Farming and Countryside Commission, Our Future in the Land' (July 2019).

Russell M, 'Keynote Speech – Scotland, Brexit and Devolution' (Institute for Government 25 March 2019) https://www.instituteforgovernment.org.uk/events/keynote-speech-michael-russell-msp-scotland-brexit-and-devolution.

Sanderson Bellamy A and Marsden T, 'A Welsh Food System Fit for Future Generations' (WWF Cymru 2020).

Sargeant J, 'The Article 16 Vaccine Row is Over – But the Damage Has Been Done' (Institute for Government 30 January 2021) https://www.instituteforgovernment.org.uk/blog/article-16-vaccine-row.

Sargeant J, 'The Sewel Convention Has Been Broken by Brexit – Reform is Now Urgent' (Institute for Government 21 January 2020) https://www.instituteforgovernment.org.uk/blog/sewel-convention-has-been-broken-brexit-reform-now-urgent.

Scotland's Rural College, 'Voluntary Coupled Support' (2020) https://www.sruc.ac.uk/info/120560/cap_reform/1397/voluntary_coupled_support.

Sheldon J and Phylip H, 'Devolution Arrangements within the UK during the Next Phase of Brexit' (The UK in a Changing Europe 30 March 2020) https://ukandeu.ac.uk/brexit-and-intergovernmental-coordination-within-the-uk/.

Sinibaldi A, 'Sustainability, Biodiversity and Territory: The Social Agriculture Role' (Interreg Europe 2018) https://www.interregeurope.eu/fileadmin/user_upload/tx_tevprojects/library/Forum%20social%20Agriculture.pdf.

Smail J, 'Third Country Status for UK in Trade Deal with EU' (Food Manufacture 24 December 2020) https://www.foodmanufacture.co.uk/Article/2020/12/24/Brexit-third-country-status-for-UK-in-trade-deal-with-EU.

Stafford R et al., 'Nature-Based Solutions for Climate Change in the UK: A Report by the British Ecological Society' (British Ecological Society 2021) www.britishecologicalsociety.org/nature-basedsolutions.

Stojanovic A, 'Brexit Deal: The Northern Ireland Protocol' (Institute for Government 5 February 2020) https://www.instituteforgovernment.org.uk/explainers/brexit-deal-northern-ireland-protocol.

Sustain, 'Delivering Synergies and Multiple Public Goods: Why Whole Farm Systems Must be Central to Environmental Land Management and the Agricultural Transition Plan' (February 2021) https://www.sustainweb.org/publications/delivering-synergies-and-multiple-public-goods/.

Sustainable Food Trust, 'Grazed and Confused – An Initial Response from the Sustainable Food Trust' (3 October 2017) https://sustainablefoodtrust.org/articles/grazed-and-confused-an-initial-response-from-the-sustainable-food-trust/.

The Irish Border, 'Twitter Post' (8 February 2018) https://twitter.com/BorderIrish/status/961582201363148801.

Thimont Jack M, 'Common Agricultural Policy' (Institute for Government 17 March 2020) https://www.instituteforgovernment.org.uk/explainers/common-agricultural-policy.

Thimont Jack M, 'Withdrawal Agreement Act' (Institute for Government 2 July 2020) https://www.instituteforgovernment.org.uk/explainers/withdrawal-agreement-act.

Thimont Jack M and Rutter J, 'Managing the UK's Relationship with the European Union' (Institute for Government February 2021) https://www.instituteforgovernment.org.uk/publications/managing-uk-eu-relationship.

Tsouvalis-Gerber J and Little R, 'Co-Design, Co-Production and Participatory Policy Making – Insights from the Social Sciences' (University of Sheffield 2020) https://figshare.shef.ac.uk/articles/report/Co-Design_Co-production_and_Participatory_Policy_Making_-_Insights_From_the_Social_Sciences/11569620/2.

Ungphakorn P, 'A Real Beginners' Guide to Tariffs and the WTO' (Trade β Blog 8 July 2019) https://tradebetablog.wordpress.com/2018/07/28/a-real-beginners-guide-to-tariffs-and-the-wto/.

Whitfield K, 'Agriculture (Wales) White Paper' (Wales Environment Link 21 April 2021) https://waleslink.org/agriculture-wales-white-paper/.

Wildlife and Countryside Link, 'A Future Sustainable Farming and Land Management Policy for England' (discussion paper September 2017) https://www.wcl.org.uk/docs/Link%20farming%20and%20land%20use%20policy%20paper%20FINAL%20Sep%202017.pdf.

Zappettini F, 'From Euroscepticism to Outright Populism: The Evolution of British Tabloids' (LSE Blog 4 January 2019) https://blogs.lse.ac.uk/brexit/2019/01/04/from-euroscepticism-to-outright-populism-the-evolution-of-british-tabloids/.

Newspaper articles

Andrews C, 'Brexit: Why Are the Shelves Empty in Some Supermarkets?' (BBC News 7 January 2021) https://www.bbc.co.uk/news/uk-northern-ireland-55575988.

Basquill J, 'Rules of Origin: A Brexit Headache for UK Exporters' (Global Trade Review 18 September 2020) https://www.gtreview.com/supplements/gtr-europe-2020/rules-origin-brexit-headache-uk-exporters/.

Baynes C, 'Government to Set Up Environmental Watchdog to Deliver "Green Brexit", Says Michael Gove' (Independent 12 November 2017) www.independent.co.uk/news/uk/politics/michael-gove-environment-secretary-green-brexitandrew-marr-show-european-union-a8050626.html.

BBC News, 'Agriculture Bill: Bid to Protect Post-Brexit Food Standards Rejected' (12 October 2020) https://www.bbc.com/news/uk-politics-54506185.

BBC News, 'Row after Gwynedd Placed in Lowest Priority Group for Levelling Up Fund' (4 March 2021) https://www.bbc.co.uk/news/uk-wales-politics-56279405.

Borger J, 'Brexit Bill Hugely Damaging to UK's Reputation, Says Ex-Ambassador' (The Guardian 15 September 2020) https://www.theguardian.com/politics

/2020/sep/15/kim-darroch-new-brexit-bill-damaging-to-uks-international-reputation.

Bounds A and Pickard J, 'Levelling Up Fund Design is Unlawful, Says UK Campaign Group' (Financial Times 5 April 2021) https://www.ft.com/content/9757ad6d-45b8-4db5-95f8-2d236a670af7.

Brooks L and Morris S, 'Plan for Post-Brexit UK Internal Market Bill "Is an Abomination"' (The Guardian 9 September 2020) https://www.theguardian.com/politics/2020/sep/09/plans-post-brexit-uk-internal-market-assault-devolution-scotland-wales.

Calcea N, 'How Much Has Brexit Cost the UK?' (New Statesman 18 March 2021) https://www.newstatesman.com/politics/economy/2021/03/how-much-has-brexit-cost-uk.

Campbell J, 'Brexit: EU Says UK Grace Period Extension Breaches International Law' (BBC News 3 March 2021) https://www.bbc.com/news/uk-northern-ireland-56262527.

Campbell J, 'Brexit: Welsh Ports under Threat from Post-Brexit Trade' (BBC News 25 March 2021) https://www.bbc.co.uk/news/uk-northern-ireland-56521780.

Campbell J, 'Brexit: EU to Begin Legal Action Over Alleged NI Protocol Breach' (BBC News 15 March 2021) https://www.bbc.com/news/uk-northern-ireland-56381046.

Campbell J, 'Brexit: What Are the Backstop Options?' (BBC News 16 October 2019) https://www.bbc.com/news/uk-northern-ireland-politics-44615404.

Campbell J, 'Cross-Border Trade in Ireland "Has Increased Dramatically" in 2021' (BBC 15 April 2021) https://www.bbc.com/news/uk-northern-ireland-56760634.

Carswell S, 'Irish Food Trade Could Slide by One-Third if EU and UK Fail to Cut Deal' (Irish Times 1 October 2020) https://www.irishtimes.com/business/agribusiness-and-food/irish-food-trade-could-slide-by-one-third-if-eu-and-uk-fail-to-cut-deal-1.4368738.

Colson T, 'Why 25% of English Farms Could Go Bankrupt after Brexit' (UK Business Insider 16 April 2018) https://www.businessinsider.com/quarter-english-farms-bankrupt-after-brexit-2018-4?r=US&IR=T.

Edgington T and Morris C, 'Brexit: What is the Northern Ireland Protocol and Why Are There Checks?' (BBC News 15 March 2021) https://www.bbc.com/news/explainers-53724381.

Evans J, 'UK Trade Body to Push for Tough Standards on Imported Food' (Financial Times 10 January 2021) https://www.ft.com/content/62b1e447-c328-4026-b791-4e8306643f5a.

FarmingUK Team, 'Farmers "Will Be Frustrated" Over Defra Dual Use Announcement' (Farming UK 22 September 2015) https://www.farminguk.com/news/farmers-will-be-frustrated-over-defra-dual-use-announcement_37134.html.

FarmingUK Team, 'Gove Guarantees Agri Funding Will Not Be "Barnettised" Post-Brexit' (Farming UK 12 October 2018) https://www.farminguk.com/news/gove-guarantees-agri-funding-will-not-be-barnettised-post-brexit_50455.html.

FarmingUK Team, 'MPs Urged to Back Ag Bill Amendments or Risk Inferior Imports' (24 September 2020) https://www.farminguk.com/news/mps-urged-to-back-ag-bill-amendments-or-risk-inferior-imports_56605.html.

Foote N, 'Expert: UK Risks Farm Consolidation, Fragmentation Post-Brexit' (Euractiv 29 April 2021) https://www.euractiv.com/section/agriculture-food/news/expert-uk-risks-farm-consolidation-fragmentation-post-brexit/.
Fox B, 'MEPs Vow to Veto UK Trade Pact if it Breaks Withdrawal Agreement' (Euractiv 12 September 2020) https://www.euractiv.com/section/uk-europe/news/meps-vow-to-veto-uk-trade-pact-if-its-breaks-withdrawal-agreement/.
Hayward K, 'When it Comes to the Irish Border, The Government's Reheated Customs Proposals Are Nothing Less than Magical Thinking' (Prospect Magazine 14 May 2018) https://www.prospectmagazine.co.uk/politics/when-it-comes-to-the-irish-border-the-governments-reheated-customs-proposals-are-nothing-less-than-magical-thinking.
Hipwell D and Mayes J, 'Northern Ireland Faces Brexit Food Time Bomb on New Paperwork' (Bloomberg 4 August 2020) https://www.bloomberg.com/news/articles/2020-08-04/northern-ireland-faces-brexit-food-time-bomb-on-new-paperwork?sref=yMmXm5Iy.
Inman P, 'Number of Europe's Poorest Regions in UK "More than Doubles"' (The Guardian 10 December 2019) https://www.theguardian.com/business/2019/dec/10/number-of-europes-poorest-regions-in-uk-more-than-doubles.
Islam F, 'Shoppers Could Pay More after No-Deal Brexit' (BBC News 25 September 2020) https://www.bbc.co.uk/news/business-54287283.
ITV, 'Poll Reveals Highest Support for Welsh Independence Ever Recorded' (4 March 2021) https://www.itv.com/news/wales/2021-03-04/poll-reveals-highest-support-for-welsh-independence-ever-recorded.
James D, 'No-Deal Brexit Would "Kill" Welsh Lamb Trade' (Farmers Weekly 20 July 2020) https://www.fwi.co.uk/news/why-no-deal-brexit-would-be-disastrous-for-welsh-lamb.
Kay A, 'Defra Makes Decision to Let Quarter of UK Farms 'Disappear' (Farmers Guardian 29 March 2018) https://www.fginsight.com/news/news/defra-makes-decision-to-let-quarter-of-uk-farms-disappear-57116.
Kay A, 'Scottish Direct Payments Will Not Distort UK Market after Brexit, Says Eustice' (Farmers Guardian 23 November 2020) https://www.fginsight.com/news/news/scottish-direct-payments-will-not-distort-uk-market-after-brexit-says-eustice-114714.
Laville S, 'Farmers Urge UK Government to Protect Food Standards in Post-Brexit Trade Bill' (The Guardian 21 May 2020) https://www.theguardian.com/environment/2020/may/21/farmers-urge-government-protect-food-standards-trade-bill.
Lough R and Halpin P, 'After Brexit, Ireland and France Cut out the Middleman – Britain' (Reuters 22 January 2021) https://mobile.reuters.com/article/amp/idUSKBN29R1ME.
Lowe Y, 'Explainer: What is Article 16 of the Northern Ireland Protocol?' (The Guardian 29 January 2021) https://www.theguardian.com/uk-news/2021/jan/29/explainer-what-is-article-16-of-the-northern-ireland-protocol.
Martin R, 'Independent Strategic Review' to Examine Future of NI's Agri-Food Sector' (Agriland 9 February 2021) https://www.agriland.co.uk/farming-news/independent-strategic-review-to-examine-future-of-nis-agri-food-sector/.
McBride S, 'DUP Minister Edwin Poots Halted Work on Irish Sea Border Posts after Party Meeting' (NewsLetter 15 September 2020) https://www.newsletter.co.uk

/news/politics/dup-minister-edwin-poots-halted-work-irish-sea-border-posts-after-party-meeting-2971287.

McBride S, 'System for Getting Supplies to Northern Ireland May Be Five Days from Collapse Due to Irish Sea Border, Hauliers Warn Michael Gove' (NewsLetter 9 January 2021) https://www.newsletter.co.uk/news/politics/system-getting-supplies-northern-ireland-may-be-five-days-collapse-due-irish-sea-border-hauliers-warn-michael-gove-3090602.

McCann P, 'Agri Environment Scheme Area Down by 30%' (Irish Farmers Journal 3 June 2020) https://www.farmersjournal.ie/agri-environment-scheme-area-down-by-30-548992.

McClements F, 'DUP Minister Orders Halt to Construction of Inspection Facilities for Post-Brexit Checks' (Irish Times 26 February 2021) https://www.irishtimes.com/news/politics/dup-minister-orders-halt-to-construction-of-inspection-facilities-for-post-brexit-checks-1.4496277.

Meredith A, 'Dyson Farming Empire Now Worth More than £500m' (Farmers Weekly 2 October 2019) https://www.fwi.co.uk/business/dyson-farming-empire-now-worth-more-than-500m.

Morris S and Carrell S, 'Tories Using Brexit to Grab Back Devolved Powers, Say Ministers' (The Guardian 26 February 2018) https://www.theguardian.com/politics/2018/feb/26/tories-using-brexit-to-grab-back-devolved-powers-say-ministers.

Ní Aodha G, 'How Has Trade between Ireland and Great Britain Been Affected in the First Two Weeks of Brexit?' (The Journal 17 January 2021) https://www.thejournal.ie/brexit-trade-changes-5324709-Jan2021/.

O'Carroll L, 'UK Will Not Import Chlorinated Chicken from US, Ministers Say' (The Guardian 1 November 2020) https://www.theguardian.com/world/2020/nov/01/uk-will-not-import-chlorinated-chicken-from-us-ministers-brexit.

Partridge J, 'Eight Major Government U-Turns on Post-Brexit Controls' (The Guardian 13 March 2021) https://www.theguardian.com/politics/2021/mar/13/eight-major-government-u-turns-on-post-brexit-controls.

Payne A, 'UK Supermarkets Promise to Never Sell Chlorinated Chicken in Blow to a Brexit Trade Deal with Trump' (Business Insider 9 July 2020) https://www.businessinsider.com/brexit-supermarkets-promise-never-sell-chlorinated-chicken-trump-trade-deal-2020-7?r=US&IR=T.

Pilgrim T, 'Aldi Rules Out Selling Chlorinated Chicken or Hormone-Injected Beef in UK' (Independent.ie 8 July 2020) https://www.independent.ie/business/farming/agri-business/agri-food/aldi-rules-out-selling-chlorinated-chicken-or-hormone-injected-beef-in-uk-39347921.html.

Rao G, 'How Brexit Has Changed Trade between Britain and Ireland' (Sky News 18 March 2021) https://news.sky.com/story/how-brexit-has-changed-trade-between-britain-and-ireland-12247998.

Raphael TL, 'County Farms: Public Land for Public Good' (Farming the Future 26 June 2020) https://www.farmingthefuture.uk/post/county-farms-public-land-for-public-good.

Staunton D, 'Brexit: British Hauliers Pause Transport of Goods to EU and NI' (Irish Times 11 January 2021) https://www.irishtimes.com/news/world/uk/brexit-british-hauliers-pause-transport-of-goods-to-eu-and-ni-1.4455762?mode=amp.

Stewart H, Rankin J and O'Carroll L, 'Johnson Accused of Misleading Public Over Brexit Deal after NI Remarks' (The Guardian 8 November 2019) https://www.theguardian.com/politics/2019/nov/08/boris-johnson-goods-from-northern-ireland-to-gb-wont-be-checked-brexit.

Tertsch H, 'Farm to Fork Strategy: A Partial Response to Our Farmers' Needs' (Euractiv 27 July 2020) https://www.euractiv.com/section/politics/opinion/farm-to-fork-strategy-a-partial-response-to-our-farmers-needs/.

The Newsroom, 'No Trade Deal if Good Friday Agreement Broken' (Newsletter 16 September 2020) https://www.newsletter.co.uk/news/politics/no-trade-deal-if-good-friday-agreement-broken-2972886.

Wainwright D and Homer A, 'Coronavirus: Airports "at Risk" of Closure as Flights Drop 90%' (BBC News 21 April 2020) https://www.bbc.co.uk/news/uk-england-52323416.

Waugh P, 'Tesco and Unilever Ban GM Products Banned' (The Independent 28 April 1999) https://www.independent.co.uk/news/tesco-and-unilever-ban-gm-products-banned-1090100.html.

Young D, 'Permanent Facilities for Brexit Checks at NI Ports Will Not Be Ready "Until 2023"' (Irish Examiner 15 April 2021) https://www.irishexaminer.com/news/arid-40266926.html.

Webpages

Agri-Food and Biosciences Institute, 'Agri-Environment Scheme Monitoring' https://www.afbini.gov.uk/articles/agri-environment-scheme-monitoring.

ALA Dispute Resolution, https://aladisputeresolution.co.uk/.

APPG Agroecology, 'Inquiry – Agroecology as a Nature Based Solution' (2021) https://agroecology-appg.org/inquiry-agroecology-as-a-nature-based-solution/

Commission on Ecosystem Management, 'Nature-Based Solutions' (IUCN 2020) https://www.iucn.org/commissions/commission-ecosystem-management/our-work/nature-based-solutions.

Farm Safety Foundation, https://www.yellowwellies.org/.

Farming Community Network, https://fcn.org.uk/.

Farming Connect, https://businesswales.gov.wales/farmingconnect/.

Food Ethics Council, 'Food Citizenship' https://www.foodethicscouncil.org/programme/food-citizenship/.

International Food Policy Research Institute, 'COVID-19 Food Trade Policy Tracker' (IFPRI) https://www.ifpri.org/project/covid-19-food-trade-policy-tracker.

Linking Environment And Farming (LEAF), https://leafuk.org/.

Vote Leave Campaign, 'Briefing – Taking Back Control from Brussels' (2016) http://www.voteleavetakecontrol.org/briefing_control.html.

Official sources

Official documents

BEIS, 'Impact Assessment on the Internal Market Bill' (9 September 2020) https://publications.parliament.uk/pa/bills/cbill/58-01/0177/UK%20Internal%20Market%20Bill%20Impact%20Assessment%2008092020.pdf.

BEIS, '2017 UK Greenhouse Gas Emissions' (2017) https://assets.publishing.service.gov.uk/government/uploads/system/uploads/attachment_data/file/776083/2017_Final_emissions_statistics_one_page_summary.pdf.

BEIS, '2019 UK Greenhouse Gas Emissions, Final Figures. Statistical Release: National Statistics' (2 February 2021) https://assets.publishing.service.gov.uk/government/uploads/system/uploads/attachment_data/file/957887/2019_Final_greenhouse_gas_emissions_statistical_release.pdf.

Cabinet Office, 'The European Union (Withdrawal) Act and Common Frameworks: 26 June to 25 September 2020' (9th Statutory Report December 2020) https://assets.publishing.service.gov.uk/government/uploads/system/uploads/attachment_data/file/941711/The_European_Union__Withdrawal__Act_and_Common_Frameworks.pdf.

Committee on Climate Change, 'Net Zero – The UK's Contribution to Stopping Global Warming' (May 2019).

DAERA, 'Independent Strategic Review of NI Agri-Food' (2021) https://www.daera-ni.gov.uk/articles/independent-strategic-review-ni-agri-food.

DAERA, 'Letter from the Permanent Secretary for Northern Ireland to the Northern Ireland Affairs Committee' (20 June 2018) https://www.parliament.uk/globalassets/documents/commons-committees/northern-ireland-affairs/2017-19/Correspondence-2017-19/Correspondence-from-DAERA-relating-Brexit-and-Northern-Ireland-Agriculture-20-June-18.pdf.

DAERA, 'Northern Ireland Future Agricultural Policy Framework: Stakeholder Engagement' (1 August 2018) https://www.daera-ni.gov.uk/sites/default/files/consultations/daera/NI%20Future%20Agricultural%20Policy%20Framework%20-%20Stakeholder%20Engagement%20-%20FINAL_0.pdfv.

DAERA and NISRA, 'Statistical Review of Northern Ireland Agriculture 2019' (2020) https://www.daera-ni.gov.uk/sites/default/files/publications/daera/Stats%20Review%202019%20final.pdf.

DEFRA, 'A Green Future: Our 25 Year Plant to Improve the Environment' (2018) https://assets.publishing.service.gov.uk/government/uploads/system/uploads/attachment_data/file/693158/25-year-environment-plan.pdf.

DEFRA, 'Consultation: Direct Payments to Farmers: Lump Sum Exit Scheme and Delinked Payments in England' (May 2021) https://consult.defra.gov.uk/agricultural-policy/lump-sum-and-delinked-payments-england/supporting_documents/lumpsumexitschemedelinkedpaymentsconsultation.pdf.

DEFRA, 'Consultation: Improvements to Animal Welfare in Transport' (3 December 2020) https://consult.defra.gov.uk/transforming-farm-animal-health-and-welfare-team/improvements-to-animal-welfare-in-transport/.

DEFRA, 'Consultation: The Regulation of Genetic Technologies' (8 January 2021) https://consult.defra.gov.uk/agri-food-chain-directorate/the-regulation-of-genetic-technologies/.

DEFRA, 'Environmental Land Management: Policy Discussion Document' (February 2020) https://consult.defra.gov.uk/elm/elmpolicyconsultation/supporting_documents/ELM%20Policy%20Discussion%20Document%20230620.pdf.

DEFRA, 'Farming for the Future: Policy and Progress Update' (February 2020) https://assets.publishing.service.gov.uk/government/uploads/system/uploads/attachment_data/file/868041/future-farming-policy-update1.pdf.

DEFRA, 'Farming Statistics: Final Crop Areas, Yields, Livestock Populations and Agricultural Workforce at June 2019 – United Kingdom' (19 December 2019) https://www.gov.uk/government/statistics/farming-statistics-final-crop-areas-yields-livestock-populations-and-agricultural-workforce-at-1-june-2019-uk.

DEFRA, 'Farming Statistics: Land Use, Livestock Populations and Agricultural Workforce at 1 June 2019 – England' (2019) https://assets.publishing.service.gov.uk/government/uploads/system/uploads/attachment_data/file/868945/structure-jun19-eng-28feb20.pdf.

DEFRA, 'Health and Harmony: The Future for Food, Farming and the Environment in a Green Brexit' (Cm 9577, February 2018).

DEFRA, 'Structure of the Agricultural Industry in England and the UK at June' (Farm Type Breakdown for Commercial Holdings) (26 April 2021) https://www.gov.uk/government/statistical-data-sets/structure-of-the-agricultural-industry-in-england-and-the-uk-at-june.

DEFRA, 'Statement on the Decision to Issue – With Strict Conditions – Emergency Authorisation to Use a Product Containing a Neonicotinoid to Treat Sugar Beet Seed in 2021' (8 January 2021) https://www.gov.uk/government/publications/neonicotinoid-product-as-seed-treatment-for-sugar-beet-emergency-authorisation-application/statement-on-the-decision-to-issue-with-strict-conditions-emergency-authorisation-to-use-a-product-containing-a-neonicotinoid-to-treat-sugar-beet.

DEFRA, 'Sustainable Farming Incentive: Defra's Plans for Piloting and Launching the Scheme' (16 March 2021) https://www.gov.uk/government/publications/sustainable-farming-incentive-scheme-pilot-launch-overview/sustainable-farming-incentive-defras-plans-for-piloting-and-launching-the-scheme.

DEFRA, 'The Path to Sustainable Farming: An Agricultural Transition Plan 2021 to 2024' (November 2020) https://assets.publishing.service.gov.uk/government/uploads/system/uploads/attachment_data/file/954283/agricultural-transition-plan.pdf.

DEFRA, 'Total Income from Farming in the United Kingdom, First Estimate for 2019' (7 May 2020) https://assets.publishing.service.gov.uk/government/uploads/system/uploads/attachment_data/file/884101/agricaccounts-tiffstatsnotice-07may20i.pdf.

DEFRA and Animal and Plant Health Agency, 'Guidance: Importing Animals, Animal Products and High-Risk Food and Feed not of Animal Origin' (31 December 2020) https://www.gov.uk/guidance/importing-or-moving-live-animals-animal-products-and-high-risk-food-and-feed-not-of-animal-origin.

DEFRA, DAERA, Welsh Government Knowledge and Analytical Services and the Scottish Government, Rural and Environment Science and Analytical Services, 'Agriculture in the United Kingdom 2019' (2020) https://assets.publishing.service.gov.uk/government/uploads/system/uploads/attachment_data/file/950618/AUK-2019-07jan21.pdf.

DEFRA and Environment Agency, 'Reduce Pollution Risks When You Use Manure or Fertiliser' (2 April 2018) https://www.gov.uk/guidance/rules-for-farmers-and-land-managers-to-prevent-water-pollution#reduce-pollution-risks-when-you-use-manure-or-fertiliser.

DEFRA and Government Statistical Service, 'The Future Farming and Environment Evidence Compendium' (September 2019) https://assets.publishing.service.gov.uk/government/uploads/system/uploads/attachment_data/file/834432/evidence-compendium-26sep19.pdf.

DEFRA and Welsh Government, 'UK and Welsh Government Bilateral Agreement on WTO Provisions within the Agriculture Bill' (21 March 2019) https://www.gov.uk/government/publications/agriculture-bill-progress-with-devolved-administrations/uk-and-welsh-government-bilateral-agreement-on-wto-provisions-within-the-agriculture-bill.
DEFRA et al., 'UK Government Response to the Independent Intra-UK Allocations Review (Bew Review)' (6 September 2019) https://www.gov.uk/government/publications/domestic-farm-support-funding-bew-review-government-response/uk-government-response-to-the-independent-intra-uk-allocations-review-bew-review.
Department for International Trade, 'Guidance: Existing UK Trade Agreements with Non-EU Countries' (29 January 2020) https://www.gov.uk/guidance/uk-trade-agreements-with-non-eu-countries.
Department for International Trade, 'Public Consultation: MFN Tariff Policy – The UK Global Tariff (Government Response and Policy)' (May 2020) https://assets.publishing.service.gov.uk/government/uploads/system/uploads/attachment_data/file/885943/Public_consultation_on_the_UK_Global_Tariff_government_response.pdf.
European Commission, 'Factsheet on 2014–2020 Rural Development Programme for England (United Kingdom)' (2020) https://ec.europa.eu/info/sites/info/files/food-farming-fisheries/key_policies/documents/rdp-factsheet-england_en.pdf.
European Commission, 'Factsheet on 2014–2020 Rural Development Programme for Northern Ireland (United Kingdom)' (2020) https://ec.europa.eu/info/sites/default/files/food-farming-fisheries/key_policies/documents/rdp-factsheet-northern-ireland_en.pdf.
European Commission, 'Factsheet on 2014–2020 Rural Development Programme for Scotland (United Kingdom)' (2020) https://ec.europa.eu/info/sites/info/files/food-farming-fisheries/key_policies/documents/rdp-factsheet-scotland_en.pdf.
European Commission, 'Factsheet on 2014–2020 Rural Development Programme for Wales (United Kingdom)' (2020) https://ec.europa.eu/info/sites/info/files/food-farming-fisheries/key_policies/documents/rdp-factsheet-wales_en.pdf.
FAO, 'Livestock's Long Shadow? Environmental Issues and Options' (2006) http://www.fao.org/3/a0701e/a0701e00.htm.
FAO, 'Price Volatility in Agricultural Markets: Evidence, Impact on Food Security and Policy Responses' (December 2010) http://www.fao.org/economic/es-policybriefs/briefs-detail/en/?no_cache=1&uid=48900.
FAO, 'The State of Food and Agriculture: Migration, Agriculture and Rural Development' (2018) http://www.fao.org/state-of-food-agriculture/2018/en/.
FAO, 'The 10 Elements of Agroecology: Guiding the Transition to Sustainable Food and Agricultural Systems' (2018).
HM Government, 'The Ten Point Plan for a Green Industrial Revolution' (2020) https://www.gov.uk/government/publications/the-ten-point-plan-for-a-green-industrial-revolution.
HMRC, 'UK Regional Trade in Goods Statistics – Quarter 2 2020' (2020) https://assets.publishing.service.gov.uk/government/uploads/system/uploads/attachment_data/file/917852/RTS_Q2_2020.pdf).
HM Treasury and DEFRA, 'A Vision for the Common Agricultural Policy' (December 2005).

HM Treasury, Ministry to House, Communities and Local Government and Development for Transport, 'Levelling Up Fund: Prospectus' (March 2021) https://assets.publishing.service.gov.uk/government/uploads/system/uploads/attachment_data/file/966138/Levelling_Up_prospectus.pdf.

House of Commons, Welsh Affairs Select Committee, 'Correspondence: Wales and the Shared Prosperity Fund' https://committees.parliament.uk/work/41/wales-and-the-shared-prosperity-fund/publications/3/correspondence/.

Intergovernmental Panel on Climate Change, 'Special Report: Global Warming of 1.5°C' (2019).

Intergovernmental Science-Policy Platform on Biodiversity and Ecosystem Services, 'Global Assessment Report on Biodiversity and Ecosystem Services' (2019).

Joint Ministerial Committee (EU Negotiations), 'Communique – Common Frameworks: Definition and Principles' (16 October 2017) www.gov.uk/government/uploads/system/uploads/attachment_data/file/652285/Joint_Ministerial_Committee_communique.pdf.

Lawton J et al., 'Making Space for Nature: A Review of England's Wildlife Sites and Ecological Network' (DEFRA 2010) https://webarchive.nationalarchives.gov.uk/20130402170324/http:/archive.defra.gov.uk/environment/biodiversity/documents/201009space-for-nature.pdf.

Miles J, 'Written Statement: Legal Challenge to the UK Internal Market Act 2020' (Welsh Government 19 January 2021) https://gov.wales/written-statement-legal-challenge-uk-internal-market-act-2020.

National Food Strategy, 'Read Part One' (20 July 2020) https://www.nationalfoodstrategy.org/partone/.

Office of the United Nations High Commissioner for Human Rights, 'Agroecology and the Right to Food – Report Submitted by the Special Rapporteur on the Right to Food, Olivier De Schutter' (2010) A/HRC/16/49.

Office of the United Nations High Commissioner for Human Rights, 'Final Report: The Transformative Potential of the Right to Food – Report of the Special Rapporteur on the Right to Food, Olivier De Schutter' (2014) A/HRC/25/57.

Prime Minister's Office, 'The Queen's Speech 2021' (11 May 2021) https://assets.publishing.service.gov.uk/government/uploads/system/uploads/attachment_data/file/985029/Queen_s_Speech_2021_-_Background_Briefing_Notes.pdf.

Protocol on Ireland/Northern Ireland in the Draft 'Agreement on the Withdrawal of the United Kingdom of Great Britain and Northern Ireland from the European Union and the European Atomic Energy Community, as Endorsed by Leaders at a Special Meeting of the European Council on 25 November 2018' (2018) https://assets.publishing.service.gov.uk/government/uploads/system/uploads/attachment_data/file/759019/25_November_Agreement_on_the_withdrawal_of_the_United_Kingdom_of_Great_Britain_and_Northern_Ireland_from_the_European_Union_and_the_European_Atomic_Energy_Community.pdf.

RESAS (Scottish Government), 'Agricultural Facts and Figures: 2019' (2020) https://www.gov.scot/binaries/content/documents/govscot/publications/statistics/2019/06/agriculture-facts-figures-2019/documents/agriculture-facts-figures-2019/agriculture-facts-figures-2019/govscot%3Adocument/agriculture-facts-figures-2019.pdf.

Rural Payments Agency, 'Guide to Cross Compliance in England: 2016' (6 January 2016) https://www.gov.uk/guidance/guide-to-cross-compliance-in-england-2016/gaec-4-providing-minimum-soil-cover.

Scottish Government, 'A Future Strategy for Scottish Agriculture, Final Report by the Scottish Government's Agriculture Champions' (May 2018) https://www.gov.scot/binaries/content/documents/govscot/publications/progress-report/2018/05/future-strategy-scottish-agriculture-final-report-scottish-governments-agriculture-champions/documents/00536005-pdf/00536005-pdf/govscot%3Adocument/00536005.pdf.

Scottish Government, 'A Healthier Future: Scotland's Diet and Healthy Weight Delivery Plan' (July 2018) https://www.gov.scot/binaries/content/documents/govscot/publications/strategy-plan/2018/07/healthier-future-scotlands-diet-healthy-weight-delivery-plan/documents/00537708-pdf/00537708-pdf/govscot%3Adocument/00537708.pdf.

Scottish Government, 'An Interim Discussion Document from the Scottish Government's Agriculture Champions' (17 November 2017) https://www.gov.scot/publications/interim-discussion-document-scottish-governments-agriculture-champions/.

Scottish Government, 'After Brexit: The UK Internal Market Act and Devolution' (8 March 2021) https://www.gov.scot/publications/brexit-uk-internal-market-act-devolution/.

Scottish Government, 'Food and Drink' https://www.gov.scot/policies/food-and-drink/good-food-nation/.

Scottish Government, 'Joint statement on the EU (Withdrawal) Bill' (13 July 2017) https://news.gov.scot/news/eu-withdrawal-bill.

Scottish Government, 'Legislative Consent Memorandum: Agriculture Bill' (October 2018) https://archive2021.parliament.scot/S5ChamberOffice/SPLCM-S05-19.pdf.

Scottish Government, 'Protecting Scotland's Future: The Government's Programme for Scotland 2019–2020' (3 September 2019) https://www.gov.scot/publications/protecting-scotlands-future-governments-programme-scotland-2019-20/pages/5/.

Scottish Government, 'Recipe for Success: Scotland's National Food and Drink Policy' (2009) https://www.gov.scot/binaries/content/documents/govscot/publications/strategy-plan/2009/06/recipe-success-scotlands-national-food-drink-policy/documents/0083283-pdf/0083283-pdf/govscot%3Adocument/0083283.pdf?forceDownload=true.

Scottish Government, 'Scottish Agriculture: Economic Reports' (2021) https://www.gov.scot/collections/economic-report-on-scottish-agriculture/.

Scottish Government, 'Stability and Simplicity: Proposals for a Rural Funding Transition Period' (June 2018) https://www.gov.scot/publications/stability-simplicity-proposals-rural-funding-transition-period/.

Scottish Government, 'UK Internal Market White Paper: Initial Assessment by the Scottish Government' (12 August 2020) https://www.gov.scot/publications/uk-internal-market/.

Scottish Parliament, 'Interparliamentary Forum on Brexit' https://www.parliament.scot/parliamentarybusiness/CurrentCommittees/106398.aspx.

Stennett A, 'Northern Ireland Trade in Goods, 2018' (Northern Ireland Assembly Research Matters 8 April 2019) https://www.assemblyresearchmatters.org/2019/04/08/northern-ireland-trade-in-goods-2018/.

UK Government, 'Decision of the Withdrawal Agreement Joint Committee on Agricultural Subsidies' (17 December 2020) https://assets.publishing.service.gov.uk/government/uploads/system/uploads/attachment_data/file/949845/Decision_of_the_Withdrawal_Agreement_Joint_Committee_on_agricultural_subsidies.pdf.

UK Government, 'Decision of the Withdrawal Agreement Joint Committee on the Determination of Goods Not at Risk' (17 December 2020) https://assets.publishing.service.gov.uk/government/uploads/system/uploads/attachment_data/file/949846/Decision_of_the_Withdrawal_Agreement_Joint_Committee_on_the_determination_of_goods_not_at_risk.pdf.

UK Government, 'Frameworks Analysis' (2018) www.gov.uk/government/uploads/system/uploads/attachment_data/file/686991/20180307_FINAL__Frameworks_analysis_for_publication_on_9_March_2018.pdf.

UK Government, 'Frameworks Analysis 2020: Breakdown of Areas of EU Law that Intersect With Devolved Competence in Scotland, Wales and Northern Ireland' (2020) https://assets.publishing.service.gov.uk/government/uploads/system/uploads/attachment_data/file/919729/Frameworks-Analysis-2020.pdf.

UK Government 'Revised Frameworks Analysis: Breakdown of Areas of EU Law that Intersect with Devolved Competence in Scotland, Wales and Northern Ireland' (2019) https://assets.publishing.service.gov.uk/government/uploads/system/uploads/attachment_data/file/792738/20190404-FrameworksAnalysis.pdf.

UK Government, 'The Northern Ireland Protocol' (Cm 346, December 2020) https://assets.publishing.service.gov.uk/government/uploads/system/uploads/attachment_data/file/950601/Northern_Ireland_Protocol_-_Command_Paper.pdf.

UK Government, 'Unilateral Declarations by the European Union and the United Kingdom of Great Britain and Northern Ireland in the Withdrawal Agreement Joint Committee on Article 10(1) of the Protocol' (17 December 2020) https://assets.publishing.service.gov.uk/government/uploads/system/uploads/attachment_data/file/946286/Unilateral_declarations_by_the_European_Union_and_the_United_Kingdom_of_Great_Britain_and_Northern_Ireland_in_the_Withdrawal_Agreement_Joint_Committee_on_Article_10_1__of_the_Protocol.pdf.

UK Government, 'Unilateral Declarations by the European Union and the United Kingdom of Great Britain and Northern Ireland in the Withdrawal Agreement Joint Committee on Human and Veterinary Medicines' (17 December 2020) https://assets.publishing.service.gov.uk/government/uploads/system/uploads/attachment_data/file/946659/Unilateral_declarations_by_the_European_Union_and_the_United_Kingdom_of_Great_Britain_and_Northern_Ireland_in_the_Withdrawal_Agreement_Joint_Committee_on_human_and_veterinary_medicines.pdf.

UK Government, 'Unilateral Declarations by the United Kingdom of Great Britain and Northern Ireland and the European Union in the Withdrawal Agreement Joint Committee on Meat Products' (17 December 2020) https://assets.publishing.service.gov.uk/government/uploads/system/uploads/attachment_data/file/946283/Unilateral_declarations_by_the_United_Kingdom_of_Great

_Britain_and_Northern_Ireland_and_the_European_Union_in_the_Withdrawal_Agreement_Joint_Committee_on_meat_products.pdf.

UK Government, 'Unilateral Declarations by the United Kingdom of Great Britain and Northern Ireland and the European Union in the Withdrawal Agreement Joint Committee on Official Certifications' (17 December 2020) https://assets.publishing.service.gov.uk/government/uploads/system/uploads/attachment_data/file/946284/Unilateral_declarations_by_the_United_Kingdom_of_Great_Britain_and_Northern_Ireland_and_the_European_Union_in_the_Withdrawal_Agreement_Joint_Committee_on_official_certification.pdf.

United Nations General Assembly, 'Visit to the United Kingdom of Great Britain and Northern Ireland, Report of the Special Rapporteur on Extreme Poverty and Human Rights' (April 2019) https://undocs.org/A/HRC/41/39/Add.1.

Welsh Government, 'Agriculture in Wales' (2019) https://gov.wales/sites/default/files/publications/2019-06/agriculture-in-wales-evidence.pdf.

Welsh Government, 'Animal Health and Welfare Framework: Implementation Plan 2019 to 2020' (19 July 2019) https://gov.wales/animal-health-and-welfare-framework-implementation-plan-2019-2020.

Welsh Government, 'Antimicrobial Resistance in Animals and the Environment: Implementation Plan' (15 July 2019) https://gov.wales/antimicrobial-resistance-animals-and-environment-implementation-plan.

Welsh Government, 'Consultation Document: Agricultural Tenancy Reform' (9 April 2019) https://gov.wales/sites/default/files/consultations/2019-04/agricultural-tenancy-reform-consultation-document.pdf.

Welsh Government, 'Consultation Document: Agriculture (Wales) White Paper' (16 December 2020).

Welsh Government, 'Consultation Document: Brexit and Our Land – Securing the Future of Welsh Farming' (2018).

Welsh Government, 'Consultation Document: Our Ambition to Further Develop Wales' Food and Drink Sector' (2019).

Welsh Government, 'Consultation Document: Sustainable Farming and Our Land' (2019).

Welsh Government, 'Farming Facts and Figures, Wales 2019' (2019) https://gov.wales/sites/default/files/statistics-and-research/2019-07/farming-facts-and-figures-2019-492.pdf.

Welsh Government, 'Food for Wales, Food from Wales 2010/2020 – Food Strategy for Wales' (2010).

Welsh Government, 'Summary of Responses Prepared by Wavehill Ltd: Sustainable Farming and Our Land' (2020) https://gov.wales/sites/default/files/consultations/2020-05/sustainable-farms-summary-of-responses_1.pdf.

Welsh Government, 'The Counsel General for Wales v the Secretary of State for Business, Energy and Industrial Strategy – Grounds for Judicial Review' (19 January 2021) https://gov.wales/sites/default/files/inline-documents/2021-01/210119%20Counsel%20General%20for%20Wales%20v%20Secretary%20of%20State%20for%20Business%20-%20grounds%20for%20judicial%20review.pdf.

Welsh Government, 'Welsh Agricultural Statistics: 2016' (2016) https://gov.wales/welsh-agricultural-statistics-2016.

WTO, 'Export Competition Ministerial Decision' (WT/MIN(15)/45 – WT/L/980, 19 December 2015).

WTO Notification, 'Domestic Support: European Union – Reporting Period: Marketing Year from 1 July 2016 to 30 June 2017' (G/AG/N/EU/55, 28 March 2019).

Parliamentary reports

Climate Change, Environment and Rural Affairs (CCERA) Committee of the Senedd Cymru, 'Report on the Supplementary Legislative Consent Memorandum for the Agriculture Bill' (June 2019) https://senedd.wales/laid%20documents/cr-ld12551/cr-ld12551-e.pdf.

House of Commons, Environment, Food and Rural Affairs Committee, 'Scrutiny of the Agriculture Bill, Tenth Report of Session 2017–19' (HC 1591, 27 November 2018).

House of Commons, Northern Ireland Affairs Committee, 'Brexit and Agriculture in Northern Ireland' (5th Report of Session 2017–29, HC Paper 939, October 2018) https://publications.parliament.uk/pa/cm201719/cmselect/cmniaf/939/939.pdf.

House of Commons, Welsh Affairs Select Committee, 'Wales and the Shared Prosperity Fund: Priorities for the Replacement of EU Structural Funding' (2 October 2020).

House of Lords, Common Frameworks Scrutiny Committee, 'Common Frameworks: Building a Cooperative Union' (1st Report of Session 2019-21, HL Paper 259, 31 March 2021).

House of Lords, European Union Committee, 'Brexit: Agriculture' (20th Report of Session 2016-17, HL Paper 169, May 2017).

House of Lords, European Union Committee, 'Brexit: Devolution' (4th Report of Session 2017-19, HL Paper 9, July 2017).

House of Lords, Food, Poverty, Health and the Environment Committee, 'Hungry for Change: Fixing the Failures in Food' (Report of Session 2019-20, HL Paper 85, July 2020).

Briefing papers, reports and reviews

Allen M, 'Northern Ireland's Agri-Food Sector – Background and Possible "Brexit" Considerations' (Northern Ireland Assembly, Research and Information Service 345-16 Paper 66/16, 22 September 2016) http://www.niassembly.gov.uk/assembly-business/committees/2016-2017/agriculture-environment-and-rural-affairs/research-papers-2016/northern-irelands-agri-food-sector--background-and-possible-brexit-considerations/.

Baker C, 'Obesity Statistics' (House of Commons Library, CBP-3336, 21 January 2021) https://commonslibrary.parliament.uk/research-briefings/sn03336/.

Bew A, 'Intra-UK Allocations Review' (UK Government, September 2019) https://assets.publishing.service.gov.uk/government/uploads/system/uploads/attachment_data/file/829757/intra-allocation-uk-review.pdf.

Brien P, 'The UK Shared Prosperity Fund' (House of Commons Library, CBP-8527, 29 January 2021) https://commonslibrary.parliament.uk/research-briefings/cbp-8527/.

Buckwell A et al., 'Towards a Common Agricultural and Rural Policy for Europe' (European Economy, Reports and Studies, No. 5, European Commission Directorate General for Economic and Financial Affairs 1997).

Chaplin S et al., 'Pilot Results-Based Payment Approaches for Agri-Environment Schemes in Arable and Upland Grassland Systems in England: Final Report' (Natural England and Yorkshire Dales National Park Authority 2019).

Cymru CLA, Cymru FWAG and Cymru GWCT, 'Final Report of the Berwyn, Migneint, Black Mountains & Radnor Upland Recovery Project' https://www.gwct.org.uk/wales/research/berwyn,-migneint,-black-mountains-radnor-upland-recovery-project/.

Coe S and Downing E, 'The Agriculture Bill (2017–19)' (House of Commons Library, CBP-8405, 25 October 2018) https://researchbriefings.files.parliament.uk/documents/CBP-8405/CBP-8405.pdf.

Committee on Agriculture of the WTO, 'Special Session: Special Agricultural Safeguard' (Background Paper by the Secretariat, G/AG/NG/S/9/Rev.1, 19 February 2002).

Cooper T, Hart K and Baldock D, 'Provision of Public Goods through Agriculture in the European Union' (Institute for European Environmental Policy, Report Prepared for DG Agriculture and Rural Development, Contract No 30-CE-0233091/00-28, 2009).

Curtis J, 'Joint Committee Decisions on the Northern Ireland Protocol' (House of Commons Library, CBP-9102, 23 December 2020) https://researchbriefings.files.parliament.uk/documents/CBP-9102/CBP-9102.pdf.

Curtis J, 'Northern Ireland Protocol: Article 16 and EU Vaccine Export Controls' (House of Commons Library, Insight 2 February 2021) https://commonslibrary.parliament.uk/northern-ireland-protocol-article-16-and-eu-vaccine-export-controls/.

De Gorter H, Ingco M, Ignacio L and Hranaiova J, 'Market Access: Agricultural Policy Reform and Developing Countries' (The World Bank Group, Trade Note, 10 September 2003) documents1.worldbank.org/curated/en/544511468761421468/pdf/269240TradeNote06.pdf.

Díaz S et al., 'Summary for Policymakers of the Global Assessment Report on Biodiversity and Ecosystem Services' (IPBES Secretariat 2019).

Downing E and Coe S, 'Brexit: Future UK Agriculture Policy' (House of Commons Library, CBP-8218, 11 September 2018) https://researchbriefings.files.parliament.uk/documents/CBP-8218/CBP-8218.pdf.

Dwyer J et al., 'Public Goods and Ecosystem Services from Agriculture and Forestry – A Conceptual Approach' (Institute for European Environmental Policy, Project Report Pegasus, 2015).

European Court of Auditors, 'Greening: A More Complex Income Support Scheme, Not Yet Environmentally Effective' (Special Rapport No. 21/2017).

European Court of Auditors, 'Opinion No 7/2018 (Pursuant to Article 322(1)(a) TFEU) Concerning Commission Proposals for Regulations Relating to the Common Agricultural Policy for the Post-2020 Period (COM(2018) 392, 393 and 394 final)'.

European Environment Agency, 'The European Environment – State and Outlook 2020: Knowledge for Transition to a Sustainable Europe' (2019).

Expert Working Group on Sustainable Land Management, 'Delivering Our Future, Valuing Our Soils: A Sustainable Agricultural Land Management Strategy for Northern Ireland' (21 October 2016) https://www.daera-ni.gov.uk/sites/default

/files/publications/daera/16.17.079%20Sustainable%20Land%20Management%20Strategy%20final%20amended.PDF.
FAO, 'Report of the Expert Consultation on a Good Agricultural Practices (GAP) Approach' (2003) http://www.fao.org/tempref/GI/Reserved/FTP_FaoRlc/old/foro/bpa/pdf/good.pdf.
FAO, 'State of Food and Agriculture 2012' (2012) www.fao.org/docrep/017/i3028e/i3028e.pdf.
Fella S et al., 'The UK-EU Trade and Cooperation Agreement: Summary and Implementation' (House of Commons Library, CBP-92106, 30 December 2020) https://commonslibrary.parliament.uk/research-briefings/cbp-9106-2/.
Food Farming & Countryside Commission, 'Growing a Mandate for Change' (RSA 2017) https://www.thersa.org/globalassets/pdfs/reports/rsa-ffc-commission-prospectus.pdf.
Food Farming & Countryside Commission, 'Lay of the Land: Report of the Northern Ireland Inquiry' (RSA 19 September 2019) https://www.thersa.org/globalassets/pdfs/reports/rsa-ffcc-northern-ireland---lay-of-the-land-final_september19.pdf.
Gerritsen E et al., 'Using Nature-Based Solutions to Foster Synergies between Biodiversity and Climate: Missed Chances and New Opportunities for a Sustainable Future' (Institute for European Environmental Policy and Ecologic Institute 2020) https://think2030.eu/wp-content/uploads/2021/04/Using-nature-based-solutions-to-foster-synergies-between-biodiversity-and-climate-23.04.21.pdf.
Gocht A et al., 'Economic and Environmental Impacts of CAP Greening: CAPRI Simulation Results' (Joint Research Centre, European Commission 2016).
Greenham T, McCann D and Macfarlane L, 'Farming Smarter: Investing in Our Future' (Food Farming & Countryside Commission March 2021) https://ffcc.co.uk/assets/downloads/FINAL-Farming-Smarter-Investing-in-our-Future-1.pdf.
Greig A, Spowage M and Roy G, 'UK Interregional Trade Estimation: Estimates of Trade between Northern Ireland, Scotland, Wales and England' (Economic Statistics Centre of Excellence, Discussion Paper June 2020) https://www.escoe.ac.uk/publications/uk-interregional-trade-estimation-estimates-of-trade-between-northern-ireland-scotland-wales-and-england/.
IPCC, 'Climate Change and Land: An IPCC Special Report on Climate Change, Desertification, Land Degradation, Sustainable Land Management, Food Security, and Greenhouse Gas Fluxes in Terrestrial Ecosystems' (August 2019).
Keenleyside C et al., 'Results-Based Payments for Biodiversity Guidance Handbook: Designing and Implementing Results-Based Agri-Environment Schemes 2014–20' (Report prepared for the European Commission, Institute for European Environmental Policy, 2014) https://ec.europa.eu/environment/nature/rbaps/handbook/docs/rbaps-handbook.pdf.
Keep M, 'The Barnett Formula' (House of Commons Library, CBP-7386, 23 January 2020) http://researchbriefings.files.parliament.uk/documents/CBP-7386/CBP-7386.pdf.
Kenyon W, 'SPICe Briefing – The UK Agriculture Bill' (The Scottish Parliament, SB18-69, October 2018) https://sp-bpr-en-prod-cdnep.azureedge.net/published/2018/10/29/The-UK-Agriculture-Bill/SB18-69.pdf.
Lóránt A and Allen B, 'Net-Zero Agriculture in 2050: How to Get There?' (Institute for European Environmental Policy 2019).

Meredith S and Kollenda E, 'CAP Trilogue Negotiations Briefing' (Institute for European Environmental Policy 2021) https://ieep.eu/uploads/articles/attachments/6b0cc89c-8dd0-4efc-a32c-4a23dd9cf078/Briefing%20note%20on%20the%20Common%20Agricultural%20Policy%20trilogue%20negotiations%20(IEEP%202021).pdf?v=63783304864.

National Council of Rural Advisers, 'A New Blueprint for Scotland's Rural Economy: Recommendations to Scottish Ministers' (September 2018) https://www.gov.scot/binaries/content/documents/govscot/publications/research-and-analysis/2018/09/new-blueprint-scotlands-rural-economy-recommendations-scottish-ministers/documents/00540988-pdf/00540988-pdf/govscot%3Adocument/00540988.pdf.

National Trust, 'Public Money for Public Benefit: The Basis for a Post-Brexit Farm System' (19 June 2017) https://ntplanning.files.wordpress.com/2017/06/paper-2-national-trust-post-cap-series-public-benefits-june-20171.pdf.

Natural Capital Committee, 'The State of Natural Capital: Restoring Our Natural Assets' (2nd report to the Economic Affairs Committee March 2014).

OECD, 'Environmental Cross Compliance in Agriculture' (2010) https://www.oecd.org/agriculture/topics/agriculture-and-the-environment/documents/environmental-cross-compliance-in-agriculture.pdf.

OECD, 'Policy Instruments to Support Green Growth in Agriculture' (OECD Green Growth Studies 2012).

OECD, 'Water Governance in OECD Countries: A Multi-Level Approach' (OECD Studies on Water 2011).

OECD and FAO, 'The OECD-FAO Agricultural Outlook 2013–2022' (2013) www.oecd.org/site/oecd-faoagriculturaloutlook.

Paun A, 'SPICe Briefing – Common UK Frameworks after Brexit'(SB18-09 February 2019) https://sp-bpr-en-prod-cdnep.azureedge.net/published/2018/2/2/Common-UK-Frameworks-after-Brexit/SB%2018-09.pdf.

Stacey DG, 'Farm Inspection and Regulation Review' (December 2018) https://assets.publishing.service.gov.uk/government/uploads/system/uploads/attachment_data/file/764286/farm-inspection-regulatio-review-final-report-2018.pdf.

Sustain, 'Defra Launch the New Farm Support Scheme Pilot and Invite Farmers to Get Involved' (10 March 2021) https://www.sustainweb.org/news/mar21-details-sustainable-farm-incentive-pilot/

Torrance D, 'EU Powers after Brexit: "Power Grab" or "Power Surge"?' (House of Commons Library, Insight 29 July 2020) https://commonslibrary.parliament.uk/eu-powers-after-brexit-power-grab-or-power-surge/.

Torrance D, 'Reserved Matters in the United Kingdom' (House of Commons Library, CBP-8544, 5 April 2019) https://researchbriefings.files.parliament.uk/documents/CBP-8544/CBP-8544.pdf.

Trade and Agriculture Commission, 'Final Report' (March 2021) https://assets.publishing.service.gov.uk/government/uploads/system/uploads/attachment_data/file/969045/Trade-and-Agriculture-Commission-final-report.pdf.

UNCTAD, 'Comparison of MFN Bound and Applied Tariffs Trade Weighted Averages on Agricultural Products of Developed, Developing and Least Developed Countries (LDCs): Current Status Reference' (UNCTAD Discussion Paper 22 September 2014) http://unctad.org/meetings/en/Contribution/tdb61_c03_UNCTAD.pdf.

Underwood E, 'Result Indicators Used in Europe: Results-Based Payments for Biodiversity – Supplement to Guidance Handbook' (Supplement to the Report Prepared for the European Commission, Institute for European Environmental Policy 2014) https://ec.europa.eu/environment/nature/rbaps/handbook/docs/result-indicators.pdf.

Vojtech V, 'Policy Measures Addressing Agri-Environmental Issues' (OECD Food, Agriculture and Fisheries Papers, No. 24/2010).

Watson R et al., 'UK National Ecosystem Assessment: Understanding Nature's Value to Society' (UNEP-WCMC 2011).

Welsh Government, 'Securing Wales' Future: Transition from the European Union to a New Relationship with Europe' (2017) https://gov.wales/sites/default/files/2017-01/30683%20Securing%20Wales%C2%B9%20Future_ENGLISH_WEB.pdf.

Working Party Report, 'Border Tax Adjustments', BISD 18S/97 (2 December 1970).

World Bank, 'Commodity Markets Outlook: Implications of COVID-19 on Commodity Markets' (April 2020) https://openknowledge.worldbank.org/bitstream/handle/10986/33624/CMO-April-2020.pdf.

WWF and RSPB, 'Nature-Based Solutions' (2020) https://www.rspb.org.uk/globalassets/downloads/Nature_Based_Solutions_NDC_ReportV2.pdf.

Webpages

Cabinet Office, 'UK Common Frameworks' (22 December 2020) https://www.gov.uk/government/collections/uk-common-frameworks#uk-common-frameworks---2021-provisional-frameworks.

DEFRA, 'Dame Glenys Stacey Review Proposes Farm Regulation Shake-Up' (13 December 2018) https://www.gov.uk/government/news/dame-glenys-stacey-review-proposes-farm-regulation-shake-up.

DEFRA, 'Environmental Land Management Tests and Trials: 23 Burns Farmer Group' (14 October 2020) https://www.gov.uk/government/case-studies/environmental-land-management-tests-and-trials-23-burns-farmer-group.

DEFRA, 'Notice – Seasonal Workers Pilot Request for Information' (5 May 2021) https://www.gov.uk/government/publications/seasonal-workers-pilot-request-for-information/seasonal-workers-pilot-request-for-information.

DEFRA, 'Test and Trials – Phase 3 "Landscape Recovery"' https://www.contractsfinder.service.gov.uk/Notice/cf1dcfa5-34af-4cee-819c-dd327e8cf2d5.

Department for International Trade, 'Formal Request to Commence UK Accession Negotiations to CPTPP' (1 February 2021) https://www.gov.uk/government/news/formal-request-to-commence-uk-accession-negotiations-to-cptpp.

Department for International Trade, 'The UK's Approach to Trade Negotiations with the US' (2 March 2020) https://www.gov.uk/government/publications/the-uks-approach-to-trade-negotiations-with-the-us.

Department for International Trade, 'UK-Australia Free Trade Agreement: The UK's Strategic Approach' (17 July 2020) https://www.gov.uk/government/publications/uks-approach-to-negotiating-a-free-trade-agreement-with-australia/uk-australia-free-trade-agreement-the-uks-strategic-approach.

Department for International Trade, 'UK Secures New Deal with Norway, Iceland and Liechtenstein' (4 June 2021) https://www.gov.uk/government/news/uk-secures-new-deal-with-norway-iceland-and-liechtenstein.

Department for International Trade and HM Treasury, 'The Government Has Announced the UK's New MFN Tariff Regime, the UK Global Tariff (UKGT)' (19 May 2020) https://www.gov.uk/government/news/uk-global-tariff-backs-uk-businesses-and-consumers.

European Commission, 'Agriculture and Geographic Indications (GIs) In TTIP – A Guide to the EU's Proposal' (2016) http://trade.ec.europa.eu/doclib/docs/2016/march/tradoc_154372.pdf.

European Commission: 'Bee Health: EU Takes Additional Measures on Pesticides to Better Protect Europe's Bees' (16 July 2013) https://ec.europa.eu/commission/presscorner/detail/en/IP_13_708.

European Commission, 'CAP Strategic Plans Recommendations', https://ec.europa.eu/info/food-farming-fisheries/key-policies/common-agricultural-policy/cap-strategic-plans_en#recommendations.

European Commission, 'Commission Consults on New EU Soil Strategy' (2 February 2021) https://ec.europa.eu/environment/news/commission-consults-new-eu-soil-strategy-2021-02-02_en.

European Commission, 'Farming for Biodiversity: The Results-Based Agri-Environment Schemes' https://ec.europa.eu/environment/nature/rbaps/index_en.htm.

European Commission, 'Maize, Sorghum and Rye Import Duties Updated by the European Commission' (27 April 2020) https://ec.europa.eu/info/news/maize-sorghum-and-rye-import-duties-updated-european-commission-2020-apr-27_en.

European Commission, 'LEADER' https://ec.europa.eu/info/food-farming-fisheries/key-policies/common-agricultural-policy/rural-development_en#leader.

European Commission, 'Negotiations and Agreements' https://ec.europa.eu/trade/policy/countries-and-regions/negotiations-and-agreements/index_en.htm.

European Commission, 'Questions & Answers: EU-UK Trade and Cooperation Agreement' (24 December 2020) https://ec.europa.eu/commission/presscorner/detail/en/qanda_20_2532.

European Commission, 'The European Union and the United States Conclude Negotiations on Agricultural Quotas Agreement' (8 March 2021) https://ec.europa.eu/commission/presscorner/detail/en/IP_21_987.

European Commission, 'The European Union and the United States Sign an Agreement on Imports of Hormone-Free Beef' (2 August 2019) https://ec.europa.eu/commission/presscorner/detail/en/IP_19_5010.

European Commission, 'TRACES' https://ec.europa.eu/food/animals/traces_en.

European Commission, 'United Kingdom – Country Files' https://ec.europa.eu/info/food-farming-fisheries/key-policies/common-agricultural-policy/rural-development/country/uk_en.

European Network for Rural Development, 'LAG Database' https://enrd.ec.europa.eu/leader-clld/lag-database_en.

European Parliament, 'Briefing – The Benefits of EU Membership Are Not Measured by Net Operating Balances' (February 2020) https://www.europarl.europa.eu/RegData/etudes/BRIE/2020/648145/IPOL_BRI(2020)648145_EN.pdf.

European Parliament, 'Briefing – The Level Playing Field for Labour and Environment in EU-UK Relations' (April 2021) https://www.europarl.europa.eu/RegData/etudes/BRIE/2021/690576/EPRS_BRI(2021)690576_EN.pdf.

European Parliament, 'Imports of GM Food and Feed: Right of Member States to Opt Out' (19 October 2015) https://www.europarl.europa.eu/thinktank/en/document.html?reference=EPRS_BRI(2015)569030.

European Parliament, 'The Common Agricultural Policy – Instruments and Reforms' (Fact Sheets on the European Union November 2020) https://www.europarl.europa.eu/factsheets/en/sheet/107/the-common-agricultural-policy-instruments-and-reforms.

Farming and Food Production – Future Policy Group, 'Minutes from 27 October 2020' (27 October 2020) https://www.gov.scot/binaries/content/documents/govscot/publications/minutes/2020/11/farming-and-food-production-future-policy-group-update-october-2020/documents/farming-and-food-production-future-policy-group-update-october-2020/farming-and-food-production-future-policy-group-update-october-2020/govscot%3Adocument/FFP-FPG%2B-%2B27%2BOctober%2B2020%2B-%2BSummary%2BMinutes.pdf.

GATT Newsletter, 'Mid-Term Review: Final Agreement at Geneva' (Uruguay Round Special Issue May 1989) https://docs.wto.org/gattdocs/q/GG/GATTFOCUS/61.pdf.

Gove M, 'Farming for the Next Generation' (Oxford Farming Conference 2018) https://www.gov.uk/government/speeches/farming-for-the-next-generation.

Gove M, 'Michael Gove Statement on EU Exit Preparations: 13 July 2020' (Cabinet Office 13 July 2020) https://www.gov.uk/government/speeches/michael-gove-statement-on-eu-exit-preparations-13-july-2020.

Griffiths L, 'Written Statement: Announcement of Border Control Post Site Locations' (Welsh Government 12 March 2021) https://gov.wales/written-statement-announcement-border-control-post-site-locations.

Griffiths L, 'Written Statement – Publication of the Agriculture (Wales) White Paper' (Welsh Government 16 December 2020) https://gov.wales/written-statement-publication-agriculture-wales-white-paper.

HM Government, 'UK Enshrines New Target in Law to Slash Emissions by 78% by 2035' (20 April 2021) https://www.gov.uk/government/news/uk-enshrines-new-target-in-law-to-slash-emissions-by-78-by-2035.

HM Government, 'UK-Japan Free Trade Agreement: The UK's Strategic Approach' (4 January 2021) https://www.gov.uk/government/publications/uks-approach-to-negotiating-a-free-trade-agreement-with-japan/uk-japan-free-trade-agreement-the-uks-strategic-approach.

HM Revenue & Customs (2019), 'Tax Information and Impact Note for the UK Tariff 2019' (13 March 2019) https://www.gov.uk/government/publications/tax-information-and-impact-note-for-the-uk-tariff-2019/tax-information-and-impact-note-for-the-uk-tariff-2019--2.

Hughes J, 'What We Mean by "Co-Design"' (DEFRA Blog 11 December 2020) https://defrafarming.blog.gov.uk/2020/12/11/what-we-mean-by-co-design/.

James G, 'The Farming Investment Fund: An Overview' (DEFRA Blog 30 March 2021) https://defrafarming.blog.gov.uk/2021/03/30/the-farming-investment-fund-an-overview/.

McDonnell A, 'SNP Maintain Strong Lead in Holyrood Voting Intention' (YouGov 12 November 2020) https://yougov.co.uk/topics/politics/articles-reports/2020/11/12/scottish-independence-yes-51-49-no.

Ministère de l'Agriculture et de l'Alimentation (France), 'Goods Imported from the United Kingdom into the European Union and Entering the EU via France' (November 2020).

Nègre F, 'WTO Agreement on Agriculture, Fact Sheets on the European Union' (European Parliament 2020) https://www.europarl.europa.eu/factsheets/en/sheet/111/wto-agreement-on-agriculture.

Office for National Statistics, 'UK Trade: February 2021' (13 April 2021) https://www.ons.gov.uk/economy/nationalaccounts/balanceofpayments/bulletins/uktrade/february2021.

Office for National Statistics, 'UK Trade: January 2021' (12 March 2021) https://www.ons.gov.uk/economy/nationalaccounts/balanceofpayments/bulletins/uktrade/january2021.

Office of the United States Trade Representative, 'United States-United Kingdom Negotiations: Summary of Specific Negotiating Objectives (February 2019) https://ustr.gov/sites/default/files/Summary_of_U.S.-UK_Negotiating_Objectives.pdf.

Powley A, 'The Future Farming Resilience Fund: Supporting Farmers through Transition' (DEFRA Blog 25 March 2021) https://defrafarming.blog.gov.uk/2021/03/25/the-future-farming-resilience-fund-supporting-farmers-through-transition/.

Prime Minister's Office, 'Prime Minister Announces £1 Billion of New UK-India Trade' (4 May 2021) https://www.gov.uk/government/news/prime-minister-announces-1-billion-of-new-uk-india-trade.

Scottish Government, 'Moving to Low Carbon Farming' (7 February 2020) https://www.gov.scot/news/moving-to-low-carbon-farming/.

The Team, 'Shaping the New Landscape Recovery Scheme' (DEFRA Blog 1 April 2021) https://defrafarming.blog.gov.uk/2021/04/01/shaping-the-new-landscape-recovery-scheme/.

UK Government, 'Check an HGV is Ready to Cross the Border (Kent Access Permit)' (20 April 2021) https://www.gov.uk/check-hgv-border.

UNEP, 'The UN Environment Programme and Nature-Based Solutions' (2021) https://www.unep.org/unga/our-position/unep-and-nature-based-solutions.

United Nations, Department of Economic and Social Affairs, 'The 17 Goals' https://sdgs.un.org/goals.

United Nations, Human Rights, Office of the High Commissioner, 'Special Rapporteur on the Right to Food' https://www.ohchr.org/en/issues/food/pages/foodindex.aspx

World Customs Organization, 'The New 2022 Edition of the Harmonized System Has Been Accepted' (8 January 2020) http://www.wcoomd.org/en/media/newsroom/2020/january/the-new-2022-edition-of-the-harmonized-system-has-been-accepted.aspx.

WTO, 'Agriculture: Fairer Markets for Farmers' (2021) https://www.wto.org/english/thewto_e/whatis_e/tif_e/agrm3_e.htm.

WTO, 'Trade Dialogues on Food' Series, Webinar on 'International Trade and Food Security in the Era of COVID-19' (30 April 2020) https://www.youtube.com/watch?v=g0J9IfP0TGY.

WTO, 'Working Party Seals the Deal on Russia's Membership Negotiation' (10 November 2011) https://www.wto.org/english/news_e/news11_e/acc_rus_10nov11_e.htm.

WTO Council for Trade in Goods, 'Members Call on EU and UK to Use Brexit Extension to Resolve Market Access Concerns' (12 April 2019) https://www.wto.org/english/news_e/news19_e/good_12apr19_e.htm.

EU documents

Communication from the Commission to the Council, the European Parliament, the European Economic and Social Committee and the Committee of the Regions – Thematic Strategy for Soil Protection, COM/2006/0231 final.
Declaration of the Council of the European Communities and of the Representatives of the Governments of the Member States Meeting in the Council of 22 November 1973 on the Programme of Action of the European Communities on the Environment (1973) OJ C112/1 ('First Environmental Action Plan' 1973–1977).
European Commission, 'A Farm to Fork Strategy for a Fair, Healthy and Environmentally-Friendly Food System' COM(2020) 381 final.
European Commission, 'Analysis of Links between CAP Reform and Green Deal' SWD(2020) 93 final.
European Commission, 'CAP Reform – An Explanation of the Main Elements' (European Commission Memo 25 October 2013).
European Commission, 'EU Biodiversity Strategy for 2030: Bringing Nature Back into Our Lives' COM(2020) 380 final.
European Commission, 'EU-UK Relations: Big Changes Compared to Benefits of EU Membership (Checklist)' (December 2020).
European Commission, 'European Governance – A White Paper' COM(2001)428, [2001] OJ C287/1.
European Commission, 'European Union's (EU) Proposal for the EU-New Zealand FTA – Chapter XX Sanitary and Phytosanitary Measures' (10 August 2018) https://trade.ec.europa.eu/doclib/docs/2018/december/tradoc_157577.pdf.
European Commission, 'The European Green Deal' COM(2019) 640 final.
European Commission, 'The Future of Food and Farming' COM(2017) 713.
European Commission, 'Withdrawal Agreement: European Commission Sends Letter of Formal Notice to the United Kingdom for Breach of Its Obligations' (1 October 2020) https://ec.europa.eu/commission/presscorner/detail/en/ip_20_1798.

Hansard, parliamentary proceedings and debates

HL Deb 21 July 1998, vol 592, col 791.
HC Deb 8 September 2020, vol 679, col 509.
HC Deb 10 March 2021, vol 690, col 875.
HC Deb 23 September 2020, vol 680, col 966.
Northern Ireland Assembly, 'Agriculture Bill: Legislative Consent Motion' (Debates 31 March 2020) https://www.theyworkforyou.com/ni/?id=2020-03-31.5.4&p=13867.
Northern Ireland Assembly, 'Basic Payment Scheme Simplifications and the Direction of Travel for Future Agricultural Policy in Northern Ireland, including Support Payments' (Debates 17 November 2020) https://www.theyworkforyou.com/ni/?id=2020-11-17.1.90.
Scottish Parliament, 'Future Rural Policy and Support' (Debates 10 January 2019) https://archive2021.parliament.scot/parliamentarybusiness/report.aspx?r=11875&mode=html.

Scottish Parliament, 'Meeting of the Parliament: Session 5' (Debates 6 March 2019) https://www.parliament.scot/api/sitecore/CustomMedia/OfficialReport?meetingId=11979, Motion on 'Supporting Scottish Agriculture'.

Written evidence to parliamentary and departmental inquiries

Burns C, Gravey V and Dobbs M, 'Written Evidence on the UK Environment Bill for the Committee on Environment, Agriculture and Rural Affairs of the Northern Ireland Assembly' (March 2020) http://www.niassembly.gov.uk/globalassets/committee-blocks/agriculture-environment-and-rural-affairs/2017---2022/brexit-and-environment-group-briefing-paper.pdf.

Cardwell MN, 'Evidence on Brexit and Agriculture' (House of Lords, European Union Committee, ABR0049, 2017) http://data.parliament.uk/writtenevidence/committeeevidence.svc/evidencedocument/eu-energy-and-environment-subcommittee/brexit-agriculture/written/48863.html.

Dobbs M, Gravey V, and Petetin L, 'Written Evidence on the NI Future Agricultural Policy Framework' (October 2018) https://pureadmin.qub.ac.uk/ws/portalfiles/portal/159763464/DAERA_Engagement_on_NI_Future_Agricultural_Policy_Framework_Dobbs_Gravey_Petetin.pdf.

Dobbs M and Petetin L, 'Written Evidence on the Future UK-EU Relations: Energy, Environment and Health' (House of Lords, EU Environment Sub-Committee, EEH0038, February 2021) https://committees.parliament.uk/writtenevidence/22500/pdf/.

Dobbs M, Petetin L and Gravey V, 'Written Evidence on the Scrutiny of Agriculture Bill' (House of Commons, EFRA Committee, SAB0044, October 2018) http://data.parliament.uk/writtenevidence/committeeevidence.svc/evidencedocument/environment-food-and-rural-affairs-committee/scrutiny-of-the-agriculturebill/written/91290.html.

Mullen T and Hunt J, 'Review of Implications of Brexit-Related UK Legislation for Devolved Competence' (27 August 2019) https://archive2021.parliament.scot/S5_Finance/General%20Documents/201908_Paper_by_Prof_Tom_Mullen_and_Prof_Jo_Hunt.pdf.

Nature Matters NI, 'Northern Ireland Future Agricultural Framework: A Response from Nature Matters Northern Ireland' (October 2018) https://www.nienvironmentlink.org/cmsfiles/Northern-Ireland-Future-Agricultural-Framework---Nature-Matters-NI-response.pdf.

National Farmers' Union Cymru, 'NFU Cymru Response: Welsh Government Consultation Agriculture (Wales) White Paper' (28 March 2021) https://www.nfu-cymru.org.uk/nfu-cymru/documents/consultation-response-white-paper-final/.

Petetin L, 'Written Evidence on Support for Agriculture and the Rural Economy – Post Brexit Transition' (Scottish Government 14 August 2018) https://consult.gov.scot/agriculture-and-rural-communities/economy-post-brexit-transition/consultation/view_respondent?sort=submitted&order=descending&uuId=46918591.

Petetin L and Dobbs M, 'Written Evidence on the UK Agriculture Bill' (Climate Change, Environment and Rural Affairs Committee of the Senedd Cymru,

November 2018) http://www.senedd.assembly.wales/documents/s80616/Paper%20-%20Dr%20Petetin%20and%20Dr%20Dobbs.pdf.

Petetin L, Dobbs M and Gravey V, 'Written Evidence Brexit and Our Land Consultation – Welsh Government' (2018) http://orca.cf.ac.uk/117590/.

Petetin L, Dobbs M, Hunt J, Pontin B and Pritchard H, 'Written Evidence on the LCM in Relation to the UK Agriculture Bill' (Climate Change, Environment and Rural Affairs Committee of the Senedd Cymru, CCERA(5) AB09, 2021) https://business.senedd.wales/documents/s99656/Paper%20-%20Dr%20Ludivine%20Petetin%20Dr%20Mary%20Dobbs%20Prof%20Jo%20Hunt%20Prof%20Ben%20Pontin%20and%20Dr%20Huw%20Pritchard.html?CT=2.

Index

Note: References in **bold** refer to tables.

For Product Safety Concerns and Information please contact our EU representative GPSR@taylorandfrancis.com
Taylor & Francis Verlag GmbH, Kaufingerstraße 24, 80331 München, Germany

www.ingramcontent.com/pod-product-compliance
Ingram Content Group UK Ltd.
Pitfield, Milton Keynes, MK11 3LW, UK
UKHW020021200926
475702UK00014B/2004
9781032190730